Time Out

Tokyo

timeout.com/tokyo

Guides

Published by Time Out Guides Ltd, a wholly owned subsidiary of Time Out Group Ltd.
Time Out and the Time Out logo are trademarks of Time Out Group Ltd.

© Time Out Group Ltd 2005
Previous editions 1999, 2001, 2003

10 9 8 7 6 5 4 3 2 1

This edition first published in Great Britain in 2005 by Ebury Publishing
Ebury Publishing is a division of The Random House Group Ltd, 20 Vauxhall Bridge Road, London SW1V 2SA

Random House Australia Pty Limited, 20 Alfred Street, Milsons Point, Sydney, New South Wales 2061, Australia
Random House New Zealand Limited, 18 Poland Road, Glenfield, Auckland 10, New Zealand
Random House South Africa (Pty) Limited Isle of Houghton, Corner Boundary
Road & Carse O'Gowrie, Houghton 2198, South Africa

Random House UK Limited Reg. No. 954009

Distributed in USA by Publishers Group West
1700 Fourth Street, Berkeley, California 94710

Distributed in Canada by Penguin Canada Ltd
10 Alcorn Avenue, Toronto, Ontario, Canada M4V 3B2

For further distribution details, see www.timeout.com

T0 31 December 2006: 1-904978-37-1
From 1 January 2007: 9781904978374

A CIP catalogue record for this book is available from the British Library

Colour reprographics by Wyndeham Icon, 3 & 4 Maverton Road, London E3 2JE

Printed and bound in Germany by Appl

Papers used by Ebury Publishing are natural, recyclable products made from wood grown in sustainable forests

Time Out Guides Limited
Universal House
251 Tottenham Court Road
London W1T 7AB
Tel + 44 (0)20 7813 3000
Fax + 44 (0)20 7813 6001
Email guides@timeout.com
www.timeout.com

Editorial

Editor Cath Phillips
Consultant Editor Nicholas Coldicott
Deputy Editor Adam Barnes
Listings Checkers Takata Mai, Hiromi Paterson, James Catchpole
Proofreader Tamsin Shelton
Indexer Jonathan Cox

Editorial/Managing Director Peter Fiennes
Series Editor Ruth Jarvis
Deputy Series Editor Lesley McCave
Business Manager Gareth Garner
Guides Co-ordinator Holly Pick
Accountant Kemi Olufuwa

Design

Art Director Scott Moore
Art Editor Tracey Ridgewell
Senior Designer Oliver Knight
Designer Chrissy Mouncey
Digital Imaging Dan Conway
Ad Make-up Charlotte Blythe

Picture Desk

Picture Editor Jael Marschner
Deputy Picture Editor Tracey Kerrigan
Picture Researcher Helen McFarland

Advertising

Sales Director Mark Phillips
International Sales Manager Ross Canadé
International Sales Executive Simon Davies
Advertising Assistant Lucy Butler

Marketing

Marketing Director Mandy Martinez
Marketing & Publicity Manager, US Rosella Albanese

Production

Production Director Mark Lamond
Production Controller Samantha Furniss

Time Out Group

Chairman Tony Elliott
Managing Director Mike Hardwick
Group Financial Director Richard Waterlow
Group Commercial Director Lesley Gill
Group General Manager Nichola Coulthard
Group Circulation Director Jim Heinemann
Group Art Director John Oakey
Online Managing Director David Pepper
Group Production Director Steve Proctor
Group IT Director Simon Chappell

Contributors

History Steve Walsh. **Tokyo Today** Tama Miyake Lung (*Girl talk* Anna Kunnecke). **Architecture** Steve Walsh. **Sex & the City** Rob Schwartz. **Where to Stay** Tama Miyake Lung. **Introduction** Cath Phillips. **Ginza** Nicholas Coldicott (*Something fishy* Yukari Pratt; Tsukiji facts and figures courtesy of Theodore C Bestor). **Marunouchi** Nicholas Coldicott. **Shinjuku** Rob Schwartz (*How to play pachinko* Clive France). **Shibuya** Nicholas Coldicott (*Manga mania* Paul Gravett). **Harajuku & Aoyama** Rob Schwartz (*Points of faith* Stephen Forster). **Ebisu & Daikanyama** Nicholas Coldicott (*Etiquette* Nicholas Coldicott). **Asakusa** Stephen Forster (*Take me to the river* Clive France). **Ueno** Stephen Forster. **Yanaka** Stephen Forster. **Roppongi** Nicholas Coldicott. **Odaiba** John Paul Catton (*Getting into hot water* Stephen Forster). **Ikebukuro** Tom Baker. **Further Afield: Naka-Meguro** Martin Webb; **Shimo-Kitazawa** John Paul Catton; **The Chuo line** James Barrett. **Restaurants** Robbie Swinnerton (*Menu Reader* Hosose Masami). **Bars** Nicholas Coldicott. **Coffee Shops** Steve Walsh. **Festivals & Events** Rab Paterson. **Children** Obe Mitsuru, Obe Rie. **Clubs** Rob Schwartz. **Film** Rob Schwartz. **Galleries** Jeff Hammond. **Gay & Lesbian** Ken Panadero. **Music: Classical** Dan Grunebaum; **Jazz** James Catchpole; **Rock & pop** Rob Schwartz. **Performing Arts** Dan Grunebaum. **Sport & Fitness** Fred Varcoe. **Yokohama** Robbie Swinnerton. **Hakone** Nigel Kendall. **Kamakura** Robbie Swinnerton. **Nikko** Robbie Swinnerton. **Other Trips** Clive France (*Climbing Mt Fuji* Nicholas Coldicott). **Directory: Getting Around, Resources A-Z** Anna Kunnecke. **Getting by in Japanese** Hosose Masami, Adam Barnes.

The Editor would like to thank: all contributors to the previous editions; Kylie Clark and Takahashi Ayumi of the Japan National Tourist Organisation; Mizuno Yoshimi of the Tokyo Convention & Visitors Bureau; Nina Gopal of ANA; Martin and Michiyo Meldrum; Traci Consoli; and especially Nick, Nigel Kendall, Paul Davies, Yamane Miki and Mike Harrison. **Maps** JS Graphics (john@jsgraphics.co.uk).

Photography by Karl Blackwell, except: pages 10, 15, 16, 201, 253 Corbis; pages 197, 270, 277, 281 Japan National Tourist Organisation; page 198 Rex Features; page 215 Disney Enterprises/Album/AKG; page 241 Rob Schwartz; page 248 Watanabe Fumio; page 250 Miyamoto Akira; page 251 Sakurai Takehiko; page 256 Empics Ltd; page 282 Clive France.

Contents

Introduction

Is Tokyo finally going to take its place on the global traveller's map? Despite being the world's largest metropolis, Japan's capital has remained a remarkably undiscovered destination for years. But this may be about to change: the latest available figures (for January to August 2004) show an increase in tourist numbers to the country of an impressive 34 per cent. This is partly thanks to the Japanese government's active encouragement of foreign visitors (after years of not doing so), while recent Hollywood hits such as *Lost in Translation* and *The Last Samurai* have also raised Japan's profile on the world stage.

And about time too. Tokyo is a fantastic place. If you're expecting historical sightseeing, think again: earthquakes, wartime bombing and the Japanese passion for the new means that little of the past remains. Tokyo may not have the individual icons to match the must-see sights of some other world cities, but if you're after the excitement and dynamism of a truly modern metropolis, you can do no better. Tokyo is a city – or rather a collection of mini cities – that renews itself at a speed unimaginable in the West. And the fact that's it's so vast means that there's always more to explore.

Don't be deterred by fears of expense. Years of recession may not please banks and economists, but visitors should rejoice. Tokyo is surprisingly affordable, and prices have changed little in a decade, during which time cities such as London and New York have caught up.

Similarly, the language barrier is not necessarily the problem you might anticipate. Although many signs in shops and on the streets remain in Japanese only, things are getting easier all the time for first-time visitors. English signage in stations is very good, and a recent redesign of the city's subway map – colour-coding the subway lines and numbering all the stations – makes getting around the capital a blast. If you have time, you will find that learning *katakana*, the syllabary used to spell out foreign words, will boost your enjoyment of Toyko significantly, enabling you to read menus and shop names.

Our advice? Get here quick, before the rest of the world catches up.

ABOUT THE TIME OUT CITY GUIDES

The *Time Out Tokyo Guide* is one of an expanding series of Time Out City Guides produced by the people behind London and New York's successful listings magazines. Our guides are all written and updated by resident experts who have striven to provide you with all the most up-to-date information you'll need to explore the city, whether you're a local or first-time visitor.

THE LOWDOWN ON THE LISTINGS

Above all, we've tried to make this book as useful as possible. Addresses, telephone numbers, websites, transport information, opening times, admission prices and credit card details are all included in our listings. And, as far as possible, we've given details of facilities, services and events, all checked and correct at the time we went to press. However, in Tokyo, businesses open and close with lightning speed. Furthermore, many restaurants and bars can close unexpectedly for the day at the whim of the owner. Before you go out of your way, we would advise you whenever possible to phone and check opening times.

While every effort has been made to ensure the accuracy of the information contained here, the publishers cannot accept responsibility for any errors it may contain.

PRICES AND PAYMENT

Prices throughout this guide are given in Japanese yen (¥). The prices we've supplied should be treated as guidelines, not gospel. If they vary wildly from those we've quoted, please write and let us know. We aim to give the best and most up-to-date advice, so we always want to know if you've been badly treated or overcharged, or if (as we hope) you've been pleasantly surprised.

We have noted whether venues take credit cards, but have only listed the major cards – American Express (**AmEx**), Diners Club (**DC**), **JCB**, MasterCard (**MC**) and Visa (**V**). Note that most small businesses and tourist sights in Japan do not accept credit cards.

THE LIE OF THE LAND

We have divided the main city area of Tokyo's 23 wards by district. The Sightseeing section, starting on p54, contains street maps of the key areas, with all local recommendations clearly

marked. The map on p56 provides an overview of the 23 wards of Tokyo, while the map on p57 shows how the individual maps fit into the city. All listings contain the name of the nearest station(s), the train and subway lines that serve that station, and the most convenient station exit(s). Map references are provided if possible.

TELEPHONE NUMBERS

The area code for central Tokyo is 03. This is always followed by an eight-digit number. All central telephone numbers given in this guide omit the 03 prefix. The outlying areas of Tokyo have different codes. For such places, the full number is provided. Numbers starting with the prefix 0120 are freephone numbers, while most mobile phone numbers in Japan begin with the prefix 090. The international dialling code for Japan is 81. For more details on using telephones in Tokyo, see p295.

Advertisers

We would like to stress that no establishment has been included in this guide because it has advertised in any of our publications and no payment of any kind has influenced any review. The opinions given in this book are those of Time Out writers and entirely independent.

NAMES

Japanese names throughout the guide are written in Japanese-style: family name followed by given name.

ESSENTIAL INFORMATION

For all the practical information you'll need for visiting the city – including visa and customs information, advice on facilities for the disabled, emergency telephone numbers and medical services, plus a list of useful websites and the full lowdown on Tokyo's vast, amazingly efficient rail and subway networks – turn to the Directory chapter. You'll find it at the back of the guide, starting on p284.

A full map of all rail and subway services in Greater Tokyo is on pp316-7, and a map of the subway system only on pp318-9. There is also a map of areas of interest near Tokyo on p315.

LET US KNOW WHAT YOU THINK

We hope you enjoy the *Time Out Tokyo Guide*, and we'd like to know what you think of it. We welcome tips for places that you believe we should include in future editions and take notice of your criticism of our choices. You can email us at guides@timeout.com.

There is an online version of this book, along with guides to over 45 other international cities, at **www.timeout.com**.

YO! Sushi...
experience
the taste
of Toyko,

right here
right now

早い

楽しい 新しい

Yo! Sushi is the world's
No.1 conveyor belt
restaurant with over 130
freshly prepared hot
and cold dishes for you
to enjoy.

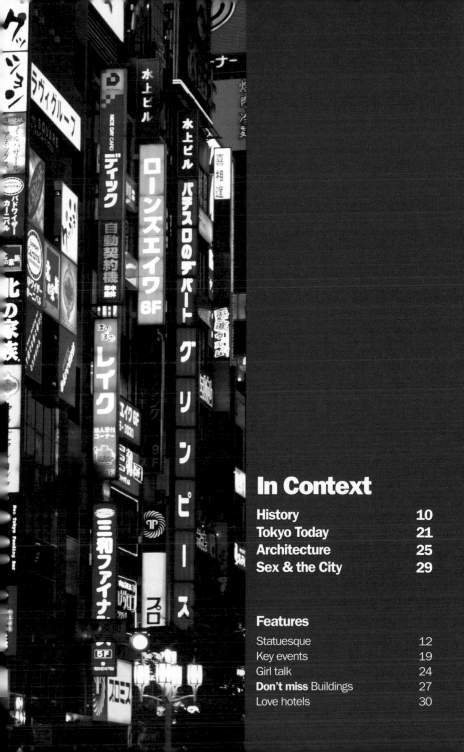

In Context

Mt Fuji seen from Nihonbashi, by Hiroshige Utagawa, 1840.

History

From fishing village to economic superpower and beyond.

Archaeological evidence suggests that the Tokyo metropolitan area was inhabited as long ago as the late Paleolithic period, and stone tools belonging to hunter-gatherers of pre-ceramic culture have been discovered at sites such as Nogawa in western Tokyo prefecture.

Pottery featuring rope-cord patterns developed in Japan during the so-called Jomon period (10,000-300 BC). Around 6,000 years ago, Tokyo Bay rose as far as the edge of the high ground that makes up the central *yamanote* area of the modern city; its retreat left behind a marshy shoreline that provided a rich food source. The late Jomon shell mounds at Omori, identified in 1877 by US zoologist ES Morse as he gazed from the window of a Shinbashi-Yokohama train, were the site of Japan's first modern archaeological dig and forerunner to a long line of similar excavations.

The Yayoi period (300 BC-AD 300) is named after the Yayoi-cho district near Tokyo University in Hongo, where in 1884 the Mukogaoka shell mound yielded the first evidence of a more sophisticated form of pottery. Along with other advances such

as wet-rice cultivation and the use of iron, this seems to have been introduced from the Asian mainland. Only after arriving on the southern island of Kyushu did new techniques spread through to the main island of Honshu.

KYOTO: THE FIRST IMPERIAL CAPITAL

Kanto (the region in which Tokyo sits) remained a distant outpost as the early Japanese state started to form around the Yamato court, which emerged in the fourth century as a loose confederation of chieftains in what is now Nara prefecture before slowly extending to other parts of the country. Chinese ideographs and Buddhism both arrived via the Korean peninsula.

Senso-ji Temple (*see p97*) in Asakusa supposedly dates from 628, when two fishermen are said to have discovered a gold statue of the *bodhisattva* Kannon in their nets. Under Taika Reform from 645, the land on which Tokyo now stands became part of Musashi province, governed from Kokufu (modern-day Fuchu City). State administration was centralised in emulation of the Tang imperial model and China's advanced civilisation exerted a strong influence.

After the imperial capital was moved to Heian (now Kyoto) in 794, a Japanese court culture flourished. Emperors became largely figureheads, manipulated by a series of powerful regents from the dominant Fujiwara family. The invention of the *kana* syllabary helped the writing of classics such as Sei Shonagon's *Pillow Book* and Lady Murasaki's *Tale of Genji*. The emperors were largely figureheads, manipulated by powerful regents from the dominant Fujiwara family. But the political power of the Kyoto court nobles went into slow decline as control of the regions fell into the hands of the local military aristocracy.

An early revolt against Kyoto rule was staged by Taira no Masakado, a tenth-century rebel. According to one version of the story, a quarrel over a woman among different members of the 'Eight Bands of Taira from the East' in 931 escalated into full-scale military conflict, during which Masakado won control of all eight provinces of Kanto. He then declared himself emperor of a new autonomous state.

After defeat by central government forces in 940, grisly evidence of Masakado's demise was dispatched to Kyoto. Legend has it that his severed head took to the skies and flew back to be reunited with his other remains in the fishing village of Shibasaki. The site is now in the Otemachi financial district, but has remained untouched by generations of city builders, perhaps fearful of Masakado's vengeful spirit.

Tokyo's original name, Edo ('Rivergate'), is thought to derive from a settlement near where the Sumida river enters Tokyo Bay. Its first known use goes back to a minor member of the Taira clan, Edo Shigenaga, who is thought to have adopted it after making his home in the area. In August 1180 Shigenaga attacked the forces of Miura Yoshizumi, an ally of the rival Minamoto clan. He switched sides three months later, though, just as shogun-to-be Minamoto no Yoritomo entered Musashi province.

By the late 12th century the rise of provincial warrior clans had developed into the struggle between the Taira and Minamoto families, later chronicled in *The Tale of Heike*. After Minamoto no Yoritomo wiped out the last of the Tairas in 1185, the emperor dubbed him Seii Tai Shogun ('Barbarian-Subduing Generalissimo'). Yoritomo shunned Kyoto, setting up his government in Kamakura (*see pp272-5*).

THE WAY OF THE WARRIOR

This inaugurated a period of military rule that was to last till the 19th century. *Bushido*, 'the way of the warrior', emphasised martial virtues, while the samurai class emerged as a powerful force in feudal society. Nevertheless, attempted

Mongol invasions in 1274 and 1281 were only driven back by stormy seas off Kyushu, something attributed to the *kamikaze*, or 'wind of the gods'. Dissatisfaction grew with the Kamakura government, and in 1333 Ashikaga Takauji established a new shogunate in the Muromachi district of Kyoto.

The first castle at Edo was erected in 1457 by Ota Dokan, a *waka* poet known as Ota Sekenaga before taking a monk's tonsure in 1478, and now celebrated as Tokyo's founder. Above the Hibiya inlet, he constructed fortifications overlooking the entrance to the Kanto plain for northbound travellers along the Pacific sea road. To improve navigation, he also diverted the Hira river east at Kandabashi to form the Nihonbashi river.

In 1486, during a military clash between branches of the locally powerful Uesugi family, Ota was falsely accused of betraying his lord, and met his end at the home of Uesugi Sadamasa in Sagami (modern-day Kanagawa).

> **'The layout of Edo reflected the social order. Less than one-fifth of the land held half the population.'**

Central government authority largely disappeared following the Onin War (1467-77), as regional lords, or *daimyo*, fought for dominance. Only after a century of on-off civil strife did the country begin to regain unity under Oda Nobunaga, although his assassination in 1582 meant that final reunification was left to Toyotomi Hideyoshi. In 1590 Hideyoshi established control of the Kanto region after successfully besieging Odawara Castle, stronghold of the powerful Go-Hojo family.

Hideyoshi ordered his ally Tokugawa Ieyasu to exchange his lands in Shizuoka and Aichi for the former Go-Hojo domains in Kanto. Rather than Odawara (which lies in present-day Kanagawa prefecture), Ieyasu chose Edo as his headquarters. A new castle was built on the site of Ota Dokan's crumbling fortifications. After Hideyoshi's death, Ieyasu was victorious in the struggle for national power at the Battle of Sekigahara in 1600, and three years later was named shogun. The emperor remained in Kyoto, but Edo became the government capital of Japan.

EDO ERA (1600-1868)

When Ieyasu arrived in 1590, Edo was little more than a few houses at the edge of Hibiya inlet. This changed quickly. Equally divided between military and townspeople, the population grew dramatically before levelling off in the early 18th century at around 1.2 million. In an age when London still had under one million people, Edo was probably the world's biggest metropolis. Fifteen successive Tokugawa shoguns ruled for more than 250 years. All roads led to Edo: five highways radiated from the city, communications aided by regular post stations, including Shinagawa, Shinjuku, Itabashi and Senju.

The regional feudal lords retained local autonomy, but a system of alternate annual residence forced them to divide their time between their own lands and the capital. *Daimyo* finances were drained by the regular

journeys with retinues and the need to maintain large residences in Edo. There was little chance to foment trouble in the provinces and, as a further inducement to loyalty, family members were kept in Edo as permanent hostages.

Although Tokugawa Ieyasu's advisers had included Englishman Will Adams (whose story is fictionalised in the novel *Shogun*), a policy of national seclusion was introduced in 1639. Contact with Western countries was restricted to a small Dutch trade mission on the island of Dejima, near Nagasaki in Kyushu, far from Edo. This policy didn't change for more than 200 years, resulting in Japan's culture remaining remarkably self-contained and untouched.

Statuesque

Everyone knows the Hachiko dog memorial outside Shibuya station and the big Buddha out in Kamakura. Where, though, are the statues commemorating the heroes of Tokyo's history and culture?

Basho Matsuo (1644-1694)
Garden of Basho Memorial Museum, 1-6-3 Tokiwa, Koto-ku (3631 1448). Morishita station (Oedo, Shinjuku lines), exit A1. **Open** 9.15am-4.30pm Tue-Sun.
The *haiku* master lived in the Edo districts of Nihonbashi and Fukugawa before setting out on the journey immortalised in *The Narrow Road to the Deep North*. His statue stares thoughtfully across Sumida river from a waterfront spot.

Danjuro IX (1838-1903)
Behind Asakusa Kannon (Senso-ji) Temple; see p97. **Map** p93.
Many credited the original statue of the beloved *kabuki* star with turning back the flames that swept the city after the 1923 earthquake. Wartime authorities requisitioned the figure, and many of historic Senso-ji's older buildings subsequently burned down in US bombing raids. The current statue dates from 1985, when Danjuro XII assumed the illustrious name.

Godzilla (created 1954)
Square near Hibiya Chanter, Ginza. Hibiya station (Chiyoda, Hibiya, Mita lines), exit A4. **Map** p60.
The giant of Japanese monster movies is interpreted by some as an allegory for earthquakes and other forms of mass destruction. The statue, happily not life-size, was erected in 1995 close to the Yurakucho

railway bridge smashed in the original 1954 movie and again in *Godzilla 1985*.

Hearn, Lafcadio (1850-1904)
Koizumi Yakumo Memorial Park, 1-7 Okubo, Shinjuku-ku. Shin-Okubo station (Yamanote line).
The celebrated Irish-Greek writer was among the first to introduce traditional Japanese folktales to the West in the Meiji era, with works such as *In Ghostly Japan* and *Kwaidan*. A bust of the great man adorns the memorial park close to the site of his former residence.

Kusunoki Masashige (died 1336)
South-east corner of Imperial Palace Plaza. Hibiya station (Chiyoda, Hibiya, Mita lines), exit B6. **Map** p66.

The layout of Edo reflected the social order, with the high ground of central Tokyo (known as *yamanote*) the preserve of the military classes, and the townspeople occupying the *shitamachi* ('low city') areas outside the castle walls to the east. There was also an attempt to conform to Chinese principles of geomancy by having the two temples that would hold the Tokugawa family tombs, Kanei-ji (*see p99*) and Zojo-ji (*see p111*), in the auspicious north-east and south-west of the city. More problematically, since Mt Fuji lay west rather than north (the traditionally favoured direction for a mountain), Edo Castle's main gate (Otemon) was placed on its east side, instead of the usual south.

A previously obscure warrior who sacrificed his life in support of a 14th-century emperor, but found himself promoted to national hero status five centuries later, following the Meiji Restoration. Mounted on horseback, his statue still occupies pride of place outside the Imperial Palace.

Oishi Kuranosuke (1659-1703)
Sengaku-ji Temple; see p128.
A statue of the samurai leader of the successful 47 *ronin* attack greets vistors to Sengaku-ji Temple, which holds the graves of the loyal retainers and their avenged master.

Ota Dokan (1432-86)
Inside Glass Building, Tokyo International Forum; see p235. **Map** p60.
The founder of the first Edo Castle, a keen hunter, stands bow and arrow in hand, just inside the post-modernist splendour of Tokyo International Forum. The statue was left behind on the site, previously occupied by the old Tokyo Metropolitan Government building, when the city rulers decamped to Shinjuku in 1991.

Saigo Takamori (1827-77)
Southern end of Ueno Park; see p100.
Map p103.
The leader of the doomed Satsuma rebellion against the Meiji government was posthumously pardoned in 1891, opening the way for the popular warrior to be immortalised in bronze (pictured). However, he is presented in deliberately unheroic fashion: dressed in civvies and walking his dog.

Completed in 1638, Edo Castle was the world's largest. Its outer defences extended 16 kilometres (ten miles). The most important of the four sets of fortifications, the *hon-maru* or principal fortress, contained the shogun's residence, the inner chambers for his wife and concubines, and the halls of state. The keep stood on an adjacent hill, overlooking the city. Between the double set of moats, regional *daimyo* had their mansions arranged in a strict hierarchy of 'dependent' and 'outside' lords.

East of the castle walls, the low-lying *shitamachi* districts were home to merchants, craftsmen, labourers and others attracted to Edo's wealth and power. Less than one-fifth of the land, much of it reclaimed, held around half the population. The curving wooden bridge, Nihonbashi, was the hub of the nation's highways and the spot from which all distances were measured.

Nearby were wealthy merchants' residences and grand shops such as Echigoya (forerunner of today's Mitsukoshi department store), the city's prison and the fish market. Behind grand thoroughfares, the crowded backstreet tenements of Nihonbashi and Kanda were a breeding ground for disease and were in constant danger of flooding. Fires were common in the largely wooden city.

The worst conflagration was the 'Long Sleeves Fire' of 1657, in which the original castle buildings were destroyed and more than 100,000 people died, around a quarter of Edo's total population. The flames began at a temple, Hommyo-ji in Hongo, where monks had been burning two long-sleeved kimono belonging to young women who had recently died. The fire raged for three days; by the morning of the fourth day, three-quarters of Edo had gone up in smoke.

Reconstruction work was soon under way. Roads were widened and new fire breaks introduced. Many had perished because they couldn't escape across the Sumida river, which, for military reasons, had no bridges: opening up Fukagawa and Honjo for development, a bridge was now erected at Ryogoku. There was also a general dispersal of temples and shrines to outlying areas such as Yanaka and reclaimed land in Tsukiji. The Yoshiwara 'pleasure quarters' (licensed prostitution area) were moved out too – from Ningyocho to beyond Asakusa and the newly extended city limits.

New residences for *daimyo* were established outside the castle walls, leading to a more patchwork mix of nobles' estates and townspeoples' districts, although the basic pattern of *shitamachi* areas in the east was retained. *Daimyo* mansions inside the castle were rebuilt in a more restrained style. The innermost section of the reconstructed castle was more subdued, lacking the high tower of its predecessor.

One byproduct of the stability of the Tokugawa regime was that the large number of military personnel stationed in Edo found themselves with relatively little to do. A complex bureaucracy developed and there were ceremonial duties, but members of the top strata of the feudal system found themselves outstripped economically by the city's wealthy merchants. In these circumstances, a daring vendetta attack staged by the band of masterless samurai known later as the 47 *ronin* caused a sensation.

In 1701, provoked by Kira Yoshinaka, the shogun's chief of protocol, Lord Ako, had drawn his sword inside Edo Castle, an illegal act for which he was forced to commit ritual suicide. Two years later, 46 of his former retainers (one dropped out at the last moment) attacked the Edo mansion of Kira, the man they blamed for their master's death. Emerging with Kira's head, they marched through the city to offer it to Lord Ako's grave at Sengaku-ji Temple (*see p128*). Despite public acclaim for their righteous actions, the 46 were themselves now sentenced to ritual suicide.

The incident forms the basis of one of *kabuki*'s most popular plays, *Kanadehon Chushinjura* (*The Treasury of the Loyal Retainers*), written originally for *bunraku* puppet theatre and first staged in 1748. The story was diplomatically relocated to 14th-century Kamakura.

A vibrant new urban culture grew up in Edo's *shitamachi* districts. During the long years of peace and relative prosperity, the pursuit of pleasure provided the populace, particularly the city's wealthy merchants, with welcome relief from the feudal system's stifling social confines. Landscape artists such as Hiroshige (1797-1868) depicted a city of theatres, temples, scenic bridges, festivals and fairs. There were numerous seasonal celebrations, including big firework displays (still held) to celebrate the summer opening of the Sumida river, as well as cherry blossom viewing along its banks in spring.

Kabuki, an Edo favourite, didn't always have the approval of the high city. In 1842 a government edict banished theatres up the Sumida river to Asakusa, where they stayed until the fall of the shogunate. As the district already boasted the temple of Senso-ji, with its fairs and festivals, and the Yoshiwara pleasure quarters lay only a short distance away, the act merely cemented Asakusa's position as Edo's favoured relaxation centre.

THE AMERICANS ARRIVE

Notice that Japan could no longer isolate itself from the outside world arrived in Edo Bay in 1853 in the shape of four US 'black ships' under the command of Commodore Matthew Perry. Hastily prepared defences were helpless, and the Treaty of Kanagawa signed with Perry the following year proved to be the thin end of the wedge, as Western powers forced further concessions. In 1855 Edo suffered a major quake that killed over 7,000 and destroyed large parts of the lower city. In 1859 Townsend Harris, the first US consul-general, arrived to set up a mission at Zenpuku-ji Temple in Azabu.

Voices of discontent had already been raised against the government: there were increasingly frequent famines, and proponents of 'National Learning' called for a return to some purer form of Shinto (the native religion). The foreign threat now polarised opinion. In 1860 the senior councillor of the shogunate government, Ii Naosuke, was assassinated outside Edo Castle. Under the slogan 'expel the barbarian, revere the emperor', a series of incidents took place against foreigners. Power drained from Edo as the government looked to build a unified national policy by securing imperial backing in Kyoto. *Daimyo* residences in Edo were abandoned after the old alternate residence requirement was abolished in 1862.

The Tokugawa regime was finally overthrown early in 1868, when a coalition of forces from the south declared an imperial 'restoration' in Kyoto in the name of the 15-year-old emperor Meiji, and then won a military victory at Toba-Fushimi. Edo's population fell to around half its former level as remaining residents of the *yamanote* areas departed. A last stand by shogunate loyalists at the Battle of Ueno was hopeless, and left in ruins large parts of the Kanei-ji temple complex, which housed the tombs of several Tokugawa shoguns.

MEIJI ERA (1868-1912)

Following the restoration of imperial rule, the emperor's residence was swiftly transferred from Kyoto to Edo, which was renamed Tokyo ('Eastern Capital'). The city now became both the political and imperial capital, with the inner section of Edo Castle serving as the new Imperial Palace. By the mid 1880s the population had reverted to its earlier level, but the *shitamachi* area lost much of its cultural distinctiveness as wealthier residents moved to smarter locations. Industrialisation continued to bring newcomers from the countryside. By the end of the Meiji era in 1912, Tokyo housed nearly two million people.

To the south-west of the palace, the districts of Nagatacho and Kasumigaseki became the

The aftermath of the Allied bombing of Tokyo in 1945. *See p17.*

heart of the nation's new government and bureaucratic establishment. 'Rich country, strong army' was the rallying cry, but learning from abroad was recognised to be essential: government missions were dispatched overseas, foreign experts brought in, and radical reforms initiated in everything from education to land ownership.

> **'Marunouchi became the site of a business district called "London Town" because of its Victorian-style office buildings.'**

Laying the foundations of a modern state meant sweeping away much of the old feudal structure. Government was centralised, the *daimyo* pensioned off. The introduction of conscription in 1873 ended the exclusive role of the warrior class. Disaffected elements led by Saigo Takamori (*see p12* **Statuesque**) rebelled in Satsuma in 1877, but were defeated by government forces. The following year, six former samurai from Satsuma staged a revenge attack and murdered Meiji government leader Okubo Toshimichi.

Ending old social restrictions fuelled economic development. The Bank of Japan was established in 1882, bringing greater fiscal and monetary stability. Industrialisation proceeded apace and factories sprang up near the Sumida river and in areas overlooking Tokyo Bay.

After 1894 Marunouchi became the site of a business district called 'London Town' because of its blocks of Victorian-style office buildings. In 1889 a written constitution declared the emperor 'sacred and inviolable'. Real power remained with existing government leaders, but there was a nod to greater popular representation. Elections were held among the top 1.5 per cent of taxpayers, and the first session of the Imperial Diet (parliament) took place in 1890.

By the early 1890s the government was making progress on ending the much-hated 'unequal treaties' earlier conceded to the West. Taking a leaf from the imperialists' book, Japan seized Taiwan in 1895 after a war with China. Ten years later its forces defeated the Russians in Manchuria and Korea, during the Russo-Japanese War. This was the first victory over a Western power by an Asian country, but there were riots in Hibiya Park at the peace treaty's perceived leniency towards Russia. In 1910 Japan annexed Korea.

New goods and ideas from overseas started to pour into Tokyo, especially after Japan's first train line started services between Yokohama and Shinbashi station in 1872. Men abandoned their traditional topknots; married women followed the lead of the empress and stopped blackening their teeth. There were gas lights, beer halls, the first department stores and public parks, and even ballroom dancing at Hibiya's glittering Rokumeikan reception hall (designed by British architect Josiah Conder), where the elite gathered in their best foreign finery to display their mastery of the advanced new ways.

After a major fire in 1872 the former artisan district of Ginza was redeveloped with around 900 brick buildings; newspaper offices were the first to flock to what would become Tokyo's most fashionable area. Asakusa kept in touch with popular tastes through attractions such as the Ryounkaku brick tower: at 12 storeys, it was Tokyo's tallest building and contained the city's first elevator. Asakusa was also home to Japan's first permanent cinema, which opened in 1903, and the cinemas, theatres and music halls of the Rokku district remained popular throughout the early decades of the 20th century.

TAISHO ERA (1912-26)

The funeral of Emperor Meiji in 1912 was accompanied by the ritual suicide of General Nogi, a hero of the Russo-Japanese War (the house where he killed himself can be seen at Nogi Jinja; *see p110*). The new emperor Taisho was in constant poor health and his son, Hirohito, became regent in 1921.

There was a brief flowering of 'Taisho Democracy': in 1918 Hara Takashi became the first prime minister from a political party, an appointment that came after a sudden rise in rice prices prompted national disturbances, including five days of rioting in the capital. Hara was assassinated in 1921 by a right-wing extremist, but universal male suffrage was finally introduced in 1925.

Tokyo was beginning to spill over its boundaries and part of Shinjuku was brought inside the city limits in 1920, an early indication of the capital's tendency to drift further westwards following the expansion of suburban train lines. Ginza was enjoying its heyday as a strolling spot for fashionable youth. In nearby Hibiya, a new Imperial Hotel, designed by world-famous American architect Frank Lloyd Wright, opened in 1923.

Such modernisation could not quell the forces of nature, however. Shortly before noon on 1 September 1923, the Kanto region was hit by a devastating earthquake. High winds fanned the flames of cooking fires and two days of terrible conflagrations swept through Tokyo and the surrounding area, including Yokohama, leaving more than 140,000 dead and large areas devastated. Around 63 per cent of Tokyo homes were destroyed in the Great Kanto Earthquake, with the traditional wooden buildings of the old *shitamachi* areas hardest hit. Rumours of well-poisoning and other misdeeds led vigilante groups to massacre several thousand Koreans before martial law was imposed.

Temporary structures were quickly in place and there was a short building boom. The destruction in eastern areas accelerated the population movement to the western suburbs, but plans to remodel the city were largely laid aside because of cost.

Frank Lloyd Wright's **Imperial Hotel**, demolished in the 1960s.

In Context

SHOWA ERA (1926-89)

Hirohito became emperor in 1926, ushering in the Showa era. His 63-year reign – the longest of any Japanese emperor – coincided with a period of extraordinary change and turbulence. Tokyo recovered gradually from the effects of the 1923 earthquake and continued growing. Post-quake reconstruction was declared officially over in 1930. In 1932 Tokyo's boundaries underwent major revision to take account of changing population patterns, with growing western districts such as Shibuya and Ikebukuro, and the remaining parts of Shinjuku, coming within the city limits. The total number of wards jumped from 15 to 35 (later simplified to the 23 of today) and the city's land area increased sevenfold. At a stroke, the population doubled to over five million, making Tokyo the world's second most populous city after New York.

The early 20th-century era of parliamentary government was not to last. Political stability fell victim to the economic depression that followed a domestic banking collapse in 1927 and the Wall Street crash two years later. Extremist nationalist groups saw expansion overseas as the answer to the nation's problems. In November 1930, after signing a naval disarmament treaty, prime minister Hamaguchi Osachi was killed by a right-wing extremist in Tokyo station.

In 1931 dissident army officers staged a Japanese military takeover of Manchuria, bringing conflict with world opinion. Pre-war party government ended after a shortlived rebellion of younger officers on 15 May 1932; prime minister Inukai Tsuyoshi and other cabinet members were assassinated and a series of national unity governments took over, dependent on military support. A puppet state, Manchukuo, was declared in Manchuria and Japan left the League of Nations. On 26 February 1936 the army's First Division mutinied and attempted a coup in the name of 'Showa Restoration'. Strategic points were seized in central Tokyo, but the rebellion was put down.

In an atmosphere of increasing nationalist fervour and militarism, Japan became involved in widening international conflict. Full-scale hostilities with China broke out in July 1937 (imperial troops killed 300,000 in the Chinese capital in the infamous Rape of Nanking), but Japanese forces got bogged down after early advances. In 1940 Japan signed a tripartite park with Germany and Italy. Western powers, led by the US, declared a total embargo of Japan in summer 1941. Negotiations between the two sides reached an impasse, and on 7 December 1941 Japan attacked the US Pacific fleet at Pearl Harbor.

After a series of quick successes in the Pacific and South-east Asia, Japanese forces began to be pushed back after the Battle of Midway in June 1942. By late 1944 Tokyo lay within the range of American bombers. A series of incendiary attacks devastated the capital; the pre-dawn raid by 300 bombers on 10 March 1945 is estimated to have left 100,000 dead, a million people homeless and a quarter of the city obliterated. On 6 August an atomic bomb was dropped on Hiroshima, followed by another on Nagasaki three days later. Cabinet deadlock left the casting vote to the emperor, whose radio broadcast to the nation on 15 August announced Japan's surrender.

Much of Tokyo lay in ruins; food and shelter posed immediate problems. As many as one in ten slept in temporary shelters during the first post-war winter.

POST-WAR PROSPERITY

Following surrender, Japan was occupied by Allied forces under the leadership of General Douglas MacArthur, who set about demilitarising the country and promoting democratic reform. The emperor kept his throne, but renounced his divine status. Article nine of the new constitution of 1946 included strict pacifist provisions, and the armed forces were disbanded. In 1948 seven 'Class A' war criminals, including wartime prime minister Tojo Hideki, were executed.

'The Tokyo Olympics were held in 1964, the same year bullet trains started running between the capital and Osaka.'

The outbreak of the Korean War in 1950 provided a tremendous boost to the Japanese economy, with large contracts to supply US forces. Under MacArthur's orders, a limited rearmament took place, leading to the eventual founding of the Self-Defence Forces (as Japan's military is called). A new security treaty with the US was signed in 1951, and the occupation ended in 1952.

With national defence left largely in US hands, economic growth was the priority under the long rule of the pro-business Liberal Democratic Party (LDP), formed in 1955. Prosperity started to manifest itself in the shape of large new office buildings in central Tokyo. In 1960 prime minister Ikeda Hayato announced a plan to double national income over a decade – a target achieved with ease in the economic miracle years that followed.

The Olympics were held in Tokyo in 1964, the same year *shinkansen* (bullet trains) started running between the capital and Osaka. Improvements to Tokyo's infrastructure were made in preparation for the Olymics; after the Games were over, redevelopment continued apace. Frank Lloyd Wright's Imperial Hotel, amazingly a survivor of both the 1923 earthquake and the war, was demolished in 1967, the year the city's inner 23 wards achieved their peak population of almost nine million. To the west of Shinjuku station, Tokyo's first concentration of skyscrapers started to take shape during the early 1970s.

Despite the economic progress, there was an undercurrent of social discontent. Hundreds of thousands demonstrated against renewal of the US-Japan Security Treaty in 1960 (which allowed American military bases on Japanese soil), and the end of the decade saw students in violent revolt. In 1970 novelist Mishima Yukio dramatically ended his life after failing to spark a nationalist uprising at the city's Ichigaya barracks. In Chiba, radical groups from the other end of the political spectrum joined local farmers to battle with riot police, delaying completion of Tokyo's new international airport at Narita from 1971 to 1975 and its opening until 1978.

The post-war fixed exchange rate ended in 1971 and growth came to a temporary halt with the oil crisis of 1974, but the Japanese economy continued to outperform its Western competitors. Trade friction developed, particularly with the US. After the Plaza Accord financial agreement of 1985, the yen jumped to new highs, inflating the value of Japanese financial assets. Shoppers switched to designer labels as a building frenzy gripped Tokyo, which was deemed the world's most expensive city. Land values soared and feverish speculation fuelled a 'Bubble economy'.

HEISEI ERA (1989-)

The death of Hirohito in 1989 at the age of 87 came at the beginning of the sweeping global changes marking the end of the Cold War. Hirhito's son, Akihito, took over, becoming Japan's 125th emperor and introducing the Heisei period.

As the 1990s wore on, the system that had served Japan so well in the post-war era stumbled. A collapse in land and stock market prices brought the Bubble economy to an end in 1990 and left Japanese banks with a mountain of bad debt. An economy that had been the envy of the world became mired in its deepest recession since the end of World War II.

Tokyo ushered in a new era in 1991, when the metropolitan government moved to a thrusting new skyscraper in Shinjuku (Kanze Tengo's twin-towered Tokyo Metropolitan Government Building; *see p76*), symbolising the capital's shift away from its traditional centre. In January 1995 the Kobe earthquake reminded Tokyo residents of their vulnerability to natural disaster. In March a sarin gas attack on city subways by members of the Aum Shinrikyo doomsday cult provoked more horror and much agonised debate. Discussions about moving the national government to a less quake-prone location continued. Special events to mark the opening of the Odaiba waterfront development were cancelled on cost grounds.

Longstanding demands for an end to 'money politics' finally proved irresistible in 1993, when the LDP lost power for the first time in 38 years. A shortlived nine-party coalition enacted a programme of political reform, but the LDP clawed its way back to power in 1994 through an unlikely partnership with its erstwhile foe, the rapidly declining Japan Socialist Party, and remained at the heart of subsequent coalitions.

In a new climate of job insecurity and fragile consumer confidence, the 'Heisei recession' proved resilient to the traditional stimulus of public works programmes. In April 1999, attracted by the promise of strong leadership, Tokyo voted hawkish former-LDP independent, Ishihara Shintaro, as their new governor. Two years later, LDP outsider Koizumi Junichiro took over as prime minister from Mori Yoshiro, boasting record popularity ratings and promising reform with 'no sacred cows'. Nevertheless, the slow pace of political and economic change in Japan continued to frustrate observers.

Tokyo sat out Japan's co-hosting of the 2002 football World Cup, with the final held in nearby Yokohama, but the event improved the nation's ties with neighbouring South Korea. Relations with China, however, stayed in the deep freeze, bedevilled by Koizumi's controversial annual visits to Yasukuni Shrine (*see p68* **Ghosts of war**), which honours Japan's war dead, including convicted war criminals. At the same time, revelations about North Korea's nuclear arms programme and its abduction of Japanese citizens in the 1970s and 1980s worsened relations between the two countries.

In 2003 the 400th anniversary of the government's move to Edo coincided with the opening of a string of new skyscraper development projects in the capital, notably Roppong Hills and Shiodome City. As a digital electronics boom raised hopes of a sustainable economic recovery, Japanese authorities worked hard to keep a lid on the yen's renewed strength.

Key events

c10,000-300 BC Jomon period.
c300 BC-AD 300 Yayoi period; introduction of wet-rice cultivation, bronze and ironware into Japan from continental Asia.
1st century Japan ('land of Wa') first mentioned in Chinese chronicles.
4th century Yamato court exists in Nara area.
6th century Buddhism introduced from Korea.
710 Nara becomes imperial capital.
794 Capital moves to Heian (Kyoto).
1019 Murasaki Shikibu writes *Tale of Genji*.
1180 First recorded use of the name Edo.
1185-1333 Kamakura is site of military government.
1274, 1281 Attempted Mongol invasions.
1457 Ota Dokan builds first castle at Edo.
1590 Edo becomes headquarters of Tokugawa Ieyasu. Construction of Edo Castle.
1592 Toyotomi Hideyoshi invades Korea.
1598 Withdrawal from Korea.
1603 Ieyasu named shogun; Edo becomes seat of national government.
1635 Edicts formalise system of alternate residence in Edo for feudal lords.
1639 National seclusion policy established.
1657 'Long Sleeves Fire' decimates Edo.
1688-1704 *Genroku* period of cultural flowering.
1703 47 *ronin* vendetta carried out.
1707 Mt Fuji erupts, ash falls on Edo.
1720 Ban on import of foreign books lifted.
1742 Floods and storms kill 4,000 in Edo.
1787-93 Kansei reforms; rice granaries set up in Edo after famine and riots.
1804-29 Bunka-Bunsei period; peak of Edo merchant culture.
1825 Government issues 'Order for Repelling of Foreign Ships'.
1841-3 Reforms to strengthen economy.
1853 Arrival of US 'black ships' at Uraga.
1854 Treaty of Kanagawa signed with US Commodore Perry.
1855 Earthquake kills over 7,000 in Edo.
1860 Ii Naosuke assassinated.
1862 End of alternate residence system.
1868 Tokugawa shogunate overthrown in Meiji Restoration. Imperial residence moved from Kyoto; Edo renamed Tokyo.
1869 Yasukuni Shrine established to Japan's war dead. Rickshaws appear in Tokyo.
1871-3 Meiji leaders tour US and Europe.
1872 Shinbashi to Yokohama train service.
1874 Tokyo's first gas lights appear in Ginza.
1877 Satsuma rebellion.
1889 New Meiji constitution promulgated.

1894-5 Sino-Japanese War.
1902 Anglo-Japanese alliance signed.
1904-5 Russo-Japanese war.
1910 Korea brought into Japanese Empire.
1912 Emperor Meiji dies; Taisho era begins.
1923 Great Kanto Earthquake; 140,000 died and Tokyo devastated.
1925 Universal male suffrage introduced.
1926 Hirohito becomes emperor.
1927 Asia's first subway line opens between Asakusa and Ueno.
1930 Post-earthquake reconstruction declared officially complete.
1931 Military takeover of Manchuria.
1932 Prime minister Inukai Tsuyoshi assassinated. Extension of Tokyo boundaries means city's population is doubled.
1933 Japan leaves League of Nations.
1936 Army rebellion in central Tokyo.
1937 Hostilities in China; Rape of Nanking.
1940 Tripartite pact with Germany and Italy.
1941 Pearl Harbor attack begins Pacific War.
1945 Incendiary bombing of Tokyo. Atomic bombs dropped on Hiroshima and Nagasaki. Japan surrenders; occupation begins.
1946 Emperor renounces divinity. New constitution promulgated.
1951 Security Treaty signed with US.
1952 Occupation ends.
1954 Release of first *Godzilla* film.
1955 Liberal Democratic Party (LDP) formed, along with Japan Socialist Party.
1960 Demonstrations against renewal of US-Japan security treaty.
1964 Tokyo Olympic Games. First *shinkansen* bullet train runs between Tokyo and Osaka.
1968-9 Student unrest.
1971 Yen revalued from US$360 to $308.
1989 Death of Hirohito; Heisei era begins.
1990 End of 'Bubble economy'.
1993 LDP loses power after 38 years.
1994 Socialist Party's Murayama Tomiichi becomes prime minister in coalition with LDP.
1995 Kobe earthquake. Sarin gas attack on Tokyo subway.
1998 Asian economic crisis spreads.
2000 Mori Yoshiro replaces Obuchi Keizo as LDP leader and prime minister.
2001 Koizumi Junichiro replaces Mori Yoshiro.
2002 Japan co-hosts football World Cup; Koizumi visits North Korea.
2003 400th anniversary of government move to Edo.
2004 Japanese troops deployed in Iraq.

Tokyo Today

Problems natural and man-made confront Japan's capital.

To hear Hollywood and the rest of the outside world tell it, Tokyo is a city of sword-slinging samurai and fun-loving cartoon characters who live on the cutting edge of all that is cool. Japan's capital unquestionably remains a world leader in wealth, creativity and innovation, but beneath its neon-lit surface is a society grappling with the inevitable effects of outgrowing its own traditions.

The most visible shifts have come in the form of big-name developments encompassing hotels, office towers, luxury apartments and shopping complexes designed to lure suburbanites back to the city. Decades of unbridled construction have culminated in old-time business quarters being reinvented as shopping and dining destinations. Even the infamous red-light district of Roppongi will soon be home to a Ritz Carlton hotel in a new luxury complex, the Mid-Town Project, which is set to rival the Mori family's wildly popular Roppongi Hills site.

But as the few remnants of Tokyo's *shitamachi* ('low city') districts get swallowed up by skyscrapers, the environmental costs are set to soar. The heat island effect has already led temperatures in the city to climb three degrees in the past century, creating a climate that is more tropical than temperate. Diesel fumes are also fuelling a rise in respiratory problems, while incinerators and office buildings endlessly pump out harmful greenhouse gases.

Meanwhile, the threat of natural disasters looms ever larger after the strongest earthquake to hit Japan in ten years triggered landslides and, for the first time ever, the derailment of a *shinkansen* train in the western prefecture of Niigata in late 2004. Japan is located on the notoriously unstable Pacific 'rim of fire' and that quake was about 240 kilometres (150 miles) from Tokyo, so the likelihood of the 'Big One' hitting the capital itself only increases as the years progress. The year 2004 also saw a record number of typhoons sweep across the Kanto plain, as well as the hottest summer in Tokyo since the meteorological agency began keeping records in 1923.

OLD AND YOUNG

The metropolitan and national governments are enacting measures to combat the nation's environmental problems, but perhaps more difficult to solve will be its population dilemma. The combination of a rapidly ageing society and a record-low birth rate suggests Japan's population could shrink 20 per cent by 2050, with more than 35 per cent of those remaining aged 65 or older.

In Tokyo alone, the net population increase has declined steadily since 1968. And with Japanese youth increasingly shunning traditional roles, the number of newborns could nosedive further. Princess Sayako, the only daughter of Emperor Akihito and Empress Michiko, became an unwitting role model for a new generation of Japanese women putting career and independence ahead of marriage and parenthood when she announced her engagement in 2004 at the ripe age of 35. This new breed of woman is also being celebrated in books and pop culture with nicknames like *make inu* ('underdog').

'Cracks are appearing in Tokyo's traditionally mild-mannered society.'

But it's not just women taking themselves off the baby track. Recent surveys show that young Japanese in general are becoming more reluctant to have children, forcing lawmakers to create incentive plans for all potential mothers and fathers. If efforts fail, the country could face substantial economic and social crises in caring for its elderly while striving to maintain its place in the global order. The baby bust already has corporations envisioning factories staffed by robots and experts predicting an abandoned capital that slowly returns to nature.

For the time being, however, Tokyo remains a city that lives well. The finest in international fashion and food are represented in its department stores and shopping districts, including the world's largest Louis Vuitton, Christian Dior and Chanel stores. Even Japan Inc appears to be emerging from a long slump. Nearly 20 years after the infamous Bubble, finance minister Takenaka Heizo has declared the country ready to take aggressive steps to reform its economy. Consumer spending and corporate profits have edged up while banks chip away at a mountain of bad debt.

But while the economy strengthens, cracks are appearing in Tokyo's traditionally mild-mannered society. The intense pressure placed on academic success is being partially blamed for the growing number of cases of *hikokimori*,

or young men and women who seclude themselves in their rooms for years at a time. Homelessness remains a fact of city life, with tented communities lining the edges of most parks and rivers. Arranged through internet chat rooms, group suicides are also becoming more frequent. This is helping fuel Japan's already high suicide rate, with a record 34,000 such deaths in 2003.

Even Princess Masako, once a noted diplomat and now wife of the heir, Prince Naruhito, took the unusual step of withdrawing from public life for one year due to the strain of adjusting to royal life and the pressure to produce a male heir. The couple have a three-year-old daughter, but the law does not allow for female ascension – although a commission was set up in 2005 to discuss whether to change the succession rules.

Although Tokyo remains one of the world's safest cities, violent crime is edging up along with disturbing accounts of child abuse and what authorities say is a rise in organised crime among the foreign community. In an effort to combat these new social ills, Tokyo Governor Ishihara Shintaro has taken a page from former New York Mayor Rudolph Giuliani's book by launching a clean-up campaign complete with youth curfews and surveillance cameras.

Efforts are also being made to sanitise the nightlife districts of Shinjuku, Shibuya, Ikebukuro and Roppongi by raiding illegal clubs, cracking down on *yakuza* and bringing in more family-friendly entertainment. Special attention is also being given to rounding up foreigners who have overstayed or violated their visas.

FOREIGN RELATIONS

The targeting of Chinese and African immigrants in particular is evidence that Japan remains a relatively closed society wary of widespread overseas influences. Despite a burgeoning foreign community and the rise of non-Japanese among the ranks of business, sport and entertainment, officials have yet to embrace calls to throw open its borders to combat depopulation and increase the workforce. Racism towards *gaijin* is widely accepted, in fact, with many establishments in outlying areas, from bars to hostess clubs, having signs outside in English saying 'Japanese only'.

The two nationalities that comprise more than half of the country's nearly two million foreign residents are, in fact, the source of its greatest political friction. China and Korea have repeatedly denounced Prime Minister Koizumi Junichiro for visiting Tokyo's Yasukuni Shrine, which honours Class A war criminals among the nation's military dead.

Tensions remain strained since North Korea admitted kidnapping a least a dozen Japanese in the 1970s and '80s for a spy programme, eight of whom have reportedly died. Five survivors have since returned to Japan amid much fanfare – particularly surrounding Soga Hitomi, her husband Charles Jenkins, a former US Army sergeant who defected to North Korea in 1965, and their two daughters – but questions abound over the fates and remains of the other victims. Anti-Japanese sentiment also flared at an Asia Cup soccer match in Beijing, and Japan has for the first time since World War II officially declared China a threat in its defence policies after a Chinese submarine entered Japanese waters unannounced in 2004.

But as much as the former adversaries dislike each other, they are inextricably joined. China already supplies an ever-growing percentage of Japan's foodstuffs and has lured a number of Japanese companies looking for low-cost manufacturing. On top of that, in 2004 the Middle Kingdom usurped the United States as Japan's largest trading partner. Meanwhile, more and more Japanese youth are studying Chinese and seeking jobs in the bustling cities of Shanghai and Beijing – and vice versa.

Korea is also enjoying a boom in Japan, largely set off by the popular TV drama *Winter Sonata* and its star Bae Yong Joon. Thousands of female fans flocked to see 'Yong-sama' on his first visit to Tokyo, and thousands more have reportedly booked tours to visit locations from the show in Korea. With its most popular actor a Korean and its top sumo wrestler, Asashoryu, a Mongolian, Japan may well go global after all.

> **'The threat of terror in the post-9/11 world has many calling for a stronger military – which would require a revision of Japan's pacifist constitution.'**

The prime minister, for one, hopes so. Koizumi is leading efforts to gain a permanent seat on the UN Security Council, and has taken the unprecedented step of sending troops to a war zone, in Iraq. While peace marches are still a common sight in Tokyo, the government was able to push through the extension of the Self-Defence Force mission in Iraq and thereby set the stage for further international involvement. In fact, the threat of terror in the post-9/11 world has many calling for a stronger military, a move that would require a revision of Japan's pacifist constitution.

As Koizumi and company strive to make their mark internationally, so do Japan's pop culture leaders. Whereas the Land of the Rising Sun was once known for churning out one space-age electronic star after another, these days Tokyo is gaining a reputation as the Capital of Cool. Hollywood has lauded Japan-inspired films such as *The Last Samurai*, *Kill Bill*, *The Ring* and *Memoirs of a Geisha*. Sports fans worldwide have rallied around European soccer superstar Nakata Hidetoshi, and Major League baseball players Suzuki Ichiro and Matsui Hideki. Meanwhile, at home, Japanese media and the public alike have cheered the achievements of their Oscar-winning animators and record-breaking Olympic athletes.

Like the city itself, Tokyoites have learned to thrive in a state of flux. Trends, fashions, restaurants and celebrities come and go as quickly as the cherry blossoms of spring. But with each passing year, the Japanese people enjoy greater opportunity and freedom to follow their own path. Where exactly it will take them remains to be seen, but no doubt it will begin in Tokyo.

Girl talk

Tokyo is a safe, easy and fascinating place for Western women, but their experience of the city is very different from Western men's – especially if they're white-skinned and blonde-haired. Here's a brief guide to the things that women will notice that men won't.

The paparazzi effect
Unless you are already a celebrity, you won't be prepared for what it feels like to be gazed at constantly – and not always furtively. If you can, try to feel complimented, not paranoid.

Porn
Some men read porn comics (sometimes violent, paedophiliac rape fantasies) on trains and in public places, without even being self-conscious. The violent overtones to sexuality in Japan can be very disturbing: for example, pubic hair cannot be depicted, but blood-soaked minors can.

How safe it is
Ironically, women walk around Tokyo freely, alone, without feeling frightened. It is a very safe city – although sexual assault in particular is under-reported, partly because of a lingering belief that rape between acquaintances isn't rape, but sex. Don't abandon your common sense, of course, but enjoy the freedom.

Except on trains
Where you may find yourself groped by roving hands. Crying *chikan* (pervert) while holding the offending hand aloft is remarkably effective, as is a loud stream of English invective. Public opinion is changing, and making a fuss may actually bring help from fellow passengers. Then again, be prepared to have everyone ignore you in an embarrassed fashion.

The hulk factor
Even petite women feel huge here. Clothing sizes are tiny, and many shops don't sell shoes larger than a European 39 (US size 7). Don't despair. Many Japanese women wish they had more curves, and butt pads and padded bras are hotsellers. Seriously, butt pads.

The dating wasteland
While there are exceptions, most Japanese men are not interested in dating Western women (or just too scared), while Japanese women just *adore* Western men. (This is called the Charisma Man effect, after the popular comic strip.) This means even nice Western men go through an unavailable/annoying period that can last for weeks to years. Don't worry: it's not you, it's Tokyo.

The Caucasian phenomenon
Your appearance will sometimes grant you preferential treatment. It will also sometimes slam doors in your pretty pale face. Either way, you'll be conspicuous, so try to handle both gracefully. Men experience this too.

Clothes matter
Tokyo is a fashion mecca – if you're into that sort of thing. If you're not, dress up anyway. Grooming counts here like nowhere else. Outside Tokyo, stockings are still considered good manners. In the city, anything – *anything* – goes. You will develop an urge to destroy all things Louis Vuitton, but this will pass.

The babe community
Pick up a copy of *Being A Broad in Japan* (¥3,000 plus p&p) by Caroline Pover, or visit the website: www.being-a-broad.com. It's the essential girl's manual to living in Tokyo.

Aoyama Technical College. *See p27.*

Architecture

Nature and fashion have created a city that is constantly regenerating itself.

Architecturally, the jumbled cityscape of Tokyo isn't as immediately striking as those of New York, Paris or London. It lacks grand boulevards, historic monuments and a sense of ordered urban planning. Instead, the visitor's initial impression is one of a very contemporary kind of confusion – nondescript high-rises jostling gleaming space-age designs, one-storey dwellings beneath looming skyscrapers, giant video screens and banks of neon, throngs of pedestrians below webs of tangled overhead cables.

Without the ancient temples of Kyoto and Nara, historic or traditional-style buildings are relatively few and far between in the present-day Japanese capital. This is partly a result of nature: a history of fires and terrible earthquakes has stripped the city of much of its architectural heritage. And partly the result of man-made forces: heavy wartime bombing, compounded by breakneck post-war economic development and an unsentimental lack of attachment to the old. The metropolis, as a result, is in a constant state of reinvention.

Tokyo has been a laboratory for the meeting and synthesis of local and Western styles ever since it first flung its doors open to the wider world back in 1868. This drive to embrace the future continues to inform the development of the city's architecture today.

TRADITIONAL STYLES
Japanese architecture has traditionally been based on the use of wooden materials. Very few original structures remain from the city's former incarnation as Edo, capital of the Tokugawa shoguns, although parts of the imposing pre-modern fortifications of the 17th-century Edo Castle can still be seen when walking around the moat and gardens of the Imperial Palace, built on part of the castle site.

The original wooden houses and shops of Edo-era *shitamachi* districts ('low city') have now almost completely disappeared. Outside the very heart of the city, some recognisably traditional features, such as eaves and tiled roofs, are still widely used on modern suburban housing, while tatami mats and

Fuji TV headquarters in Odaiba. *See p28.*

sliding doors are common inside even more Western-style apartment blocks.

The city's shrines and temples are overwhelmingly traditional in form, though not often old. The **Meiji Shrine** is an impressive example of the austere style and restrained colours typical of Shinto architecture, which is quite distinctive from that of Buddhist temples, where the greater influence of Chinese and Korean styles is usually apparent. Many present-day buildings of older religious institutions are reconstructions of earlier incarnations; the well-known temples of **Senso-ji** and **Zojo-ji** are both examples, although in these cases some remnants of earlier structures also survive. The Sanmon Gate of Zojo-ji, which dates from 1605, and **Gokoku-ji**, which dates from 1681, are rare, unreconstructed survivors.

In contrast, when the wooden building of **Hongan-ji** temple in Tsukiji burned down for the ninth time in the temple's long history after the 1923 earthquake, it was rebuilt in sturdier stone. The design by architect Ito Chuta, also responsible for the earlier Meiji Shrine, was also quite different: an eye-catching affair recalling Buddhism's roots in ancient India.

WESTERNISATION & REACTION

After the Meiji Restoration of 1868, the twin influences of Westernisation and modernisation quickly made themselves felt in Tokyo, the new national capital. Early attempts to combine Western and traditional elements by local architects resulted in extraordinary hybrids featuring Japanese-style sloping roofs rising above wooden constructions with ornate front façades of a distinctly Western style. Kisuke Shimizu's Hoterukan (1868) at the Foreign Settlement in Tsukiji and his First National Bank (1872) in Nihonbashi were two notable Tokyo examples. Neither survives today.

Tokyo's earliest buildings of a purely Western design were chiefly the work of overseas architects brought to Japan by the new Meiji government. Englishman Thomas Waters oversaw the post-1872 redevelopment of Ginza with around 900 red-brick buildings, thought to be more resilient than wooden Japanese houses. Ironically, none of them made it through the 1923 earthquake.

Waters's fellow countryman Josiah Conder, who taught at Tokyo Imperial University, was the most influential Western architect of the early Meiji period, with important projects in the capital including ministry buildings, the original Imperial Museum (1881) at Ueno and Hibiya's Rokumeikan reception hall (1883). His **Furukawa mansion** (1914) in Komagome and **Nikolai Cathedral** (1891) in Ochanomizu still exist, although the latter was badly damaged in the 1923 earthquake.

Later Meiji official architecture was often a close reflection of Western styles, although it was Japanese architects who increasingly handled the prestige projects. Remaining red-brick structures of the period include the **Ministry of Justice** (1895), constructed in Kasumigaseki by the German firm of Ende and Bockman, and the **Crafts Gallery** of the National Museum of Modern Art (1910), which once housed the administrative headquarters of the Imperial Guard. The imposing **Bank of Japan** building (1896) was built by one of Conder's former students, Tatsuno Kingo, who was also responsible for the Marunouchi wing of **Tokyo Station** (1914), modelled on Centraal Station in Amsterdam. A far more grandiose overseas inspiration, that of Versailles, is said to have been used for **Akasaka Detached Palace** (1909), created by Katayama Tokuma, whose other work includes the **Hyokeikan** building (1909) of the renowned Tokyo National Museum in Ueno Park.

The era after World War I saw the completion of Frank Lloyd Wright's highly distinctive Imperial Hotel (1922), which famously survived the Tokyo earthquake shortly after its opening, but was demolished in the 1960s. The period after the earthquake saw the spread of social housing, and a prominent example, finally knocked down only in 2003, was the Dojunkai Aoyama tenement apartment blocks (1926) on Omotesando. Another post-quake innovation was the *kanban* (signboard) style, designed to protect buildings against fire by a cloaking of sheet copper, and often still seen today in the heavily oxidised green mantles of pre-war shops.

The influence of overseas trends can be discerned in the modernism of Yoshida Tetsuro's **Tokyo Central Post Office** (1931) and the art deco of **Tokyo Metropolitan Teien Art Museum** (1933), built originally as a mansion for Prince Asaka and planned mainly by French designer Henri Rapin. The present-day **Diet Building** (1936) also shows a strong art deco influence, but its design became a source of heated debate in the increasingly nationalist climate of the period when it was completed.

Don't miss ▶ Buildings

In the jumbled cityscape of a capital blessed with more than its fair share of dramatic buildings, which ones shouldn't be missed?

Museum
Edo-Tokyo Museum
The alien-spacecraft look of Kikutake Kiyonori's 1992 creation is made up of traditional elements recalling the city's past. Its height, 62m (203ft), exactly matches that of the old Edo Castle. *See p98.*

Religious
Tsukiji Hongan-ji
3-15-1 Tsukiji, Chuo-ku (3541 11.31/ www.tsukijihongwanji.jp). Tsukiji station (Hibiya line), exit 1.
A stunning, 1935 Indian-style stand-out in a city of generally disappointing temples.

Shop
Prada
5-2-6 Minami-Aoyama, Minato-ku (www.prada.com/6418 0400). Omotesando station (Chiyoda, Ginza, Hanzomon lines), exit A5. **Map** p85.
Resembling a huge green crystal, this 2003 fashion store (pictured) looks stunning at dusk, when the bubble-glass is lit from within. Herzog & de Meuron (creators of London's Tate Modern) were responsible.

Skyscraper
Tokyo Metropolitan Building
The twin-towered Gotham City epic from Tange Kenzo, built in 1991, remains the capital's tallest skyscraper at 243m (797ft), despite recent competition. *See p76.*

Traditional style
Kabuki-za
Grandly meets preconceptions of what a *kabuki* theatre should look like. The original 1925 design harked back to the medieval Momoyama era, a style that was retained when it was rebuilt in 1951. *See p246.*

Just plain weird
Aoyama Technical College
7-9 Uguisudanicho, Shibuya-ku. Shibuya station (Yamanote, Ginza, Hanzomon lines), south exit.
Outlandish 1991 postmodernism from Watanabe Sei that throws together strangely haphazard angles, insect-like protrusions and blocks of spectacular red on metal. It is also widely known as Gundam, after the popular sci-fi *anime*. Pictured p25.

A reaction against Westernisation had already been apparent in the work of Ito Chuta, who had looked toward Asian models. Demands for a distinctive national look led to the so-called 'Imperial Crown' style, usually represented by the main building of the **Tokyo National Museum** (1938) in Ueno. This was the design of Watanabe Hitoshi, an architect of unusual versatility whose other works include the **Hattori Building** (1932) of Wako department store at Ginza 4-chome crossing, and the **Daiichi Insurance Building** (1938). The latter was used by General MacArthur as his Tokyo headquarters after the war, and is now the shorter, older part of the DN Tower 21 complex in Hibiya.

POST-WAR TOKYO

The priority in the early post-war period was often to provide either extra office space for companies trying to cope with the demands of an economy hurtling along at double-digit growth rates, or a rapid answer to the housing needs of the city's growing population. Seismic instability meant that tall buildings were not initially an option, and anonymous, box-like structures proliferated.

Even as architects gained confidence in new construction techniques designed to provide greater protection against earthquakes, many of the initial results were strangely undistinguished. The city's first cluster of skyscrapers, built in west Shinjuku from the early 1970s, has been described as resembling a set of urban tombstones. Even so, a later addition, the imposing, twin-towered **Tokyo Metropolitan Government Building** (1991) by Tange Kenzo, is now among the capital's best-known landmarks.

The dominant figure of post-war Japanese architecture, Tange has managed to embrace both Western and traditional Japanese elements in an astonishing variety of high-profile Tokyo projects, which stretch right back to the now-demolished metropolitan offices in Yurakucho (1957). Well-known works include **St Mary's Cathedral** (1963) in Edogawabashi, **Yoyogi National Stadium** (1964), the **Hanae Mori Building** (1978) on Omotesando, **Akasaka Prince Hotel** (1983) and the **UN University** (1992) in Aoyama.

Tange's long career also connects completely different generations of Japanese architects. One collaborator was Maekawa Kunio, a pre-war student of Le Corbusier in Europe, who became one of Japan's foremost modern architects with works such as **Tokyo Metropolitan Festival Hall** (1961) and the **Tokyo Metropolitan Art Museum** (1975). Another was acclaimed postmodernist Isozaki Arata, the man responsible for the **Ochanomizu Square Building** (1987), as well as the Museum of Contemporary Art (1986) in Los Angeles.

Tokyo ordered itself something of a postmodernist makeover as the Bubble economy took hold during the 1980s, and the resultant splurge of 'trophy architecture' left the city with a string of new and enjoyably arresting landmarks. The **Spiral Building** (1985) in Aoyama is one contribution to the new city look by Maki Fumihiko; another is the strange, low-level **Tokyo Metropolitan Gymnasium** (1990) in Sendagaya. Also difficult to ignore is the **Super Dry Hall** in Asakusa by Philippe Starck, one of an increasing number of foreign architects to have worked on projects in Tokyo in recent years. These include Rafael Vinoly, creator of the stunning **Tokyo International Forum** (1996) on the site of the old Tokyo government building in Yurakucho, and Norman Foster, whose **Century Tower** (1991) is located near Ochanomizu.

The reclamation of Tokyo Bay also opened up land for a wide range of projects. On Odaiba, designated as a futuristic showcase back in the Bubble era, Tange's **Fuji TV** headquarters (1996), Watanabe Sei's **K-Museum** (1996) and Sato Sogokeikau's extraordinary **Tokyo Big Sight** (1994) all vie for attention, while the interior of the **Venus Fort** shopping mall (1999) offers a bizarre Vegas-style take on Ancient Rome. Nearby, on the city side of Rainbow Bridge, an imposing new generation of high-rise offices in Odaiba thrusts upwards on the waterfront skyline, defying gloomy talk of economic recession.

Skyscrapers, such as the **Mori Tower** (2003) of Roppongi Hills, seemed to dominate major urban renewal schemes in the early years of the new century, although Ando Tadao's low-level redevelopment of the old Dojunkai Aoyama block on Omotesando, set to open in 2005, is an exception. Looming over the Imperial Palace, the new **Marunouchi Building** (2002), on the site of the city's first modern office block, cheerfully cast aside an old taboo prohibiting buildings that look down on the emperor's residence. A slew of striking designer fashion stores includes buildings for **Maison Hermès** (Renzo Piano, 2001) and **Chanel** (Peter Marino, 2004) in Ginza, and for **Prada** (Herzog & de Meuron, 2003) and **Tod's** (Ito Toyo, 2005) in Aoyama.

As for the future, one thing is certain: Tokyo will continue to rebuild itself, as it has for hundreds of years. If the buildings today aren't to your taste, come back in 20 years and there will be a whole new set for you to enjoy.

The gateway to **Kabuki-cho**.

Sex & the City

There's a lot of it about.

Whether drenched in the neon glow of Tokyo's red-light districts or bathed in images of kimono-clad geisha serving sake to honoured customers, the concept of sexuality and the sex industry in Japan has continued to cast a spell over foreign visitors to the country. From early in the 20th century to the heyday of the 1950s, the image of Japanese women as 'exotic' and catering to a man's every need has continued to inform Western media. Such ideas were no doubt bolstered by American GIs' 'playground' approach to Japan, during both the US occupation after World War II and the Vietnam War. The advent of the Bubble economy in the 1980s, aided by novelist/filmmaker Murakami Ryu's cult film *Tokyo Decadence* (1992), updated the impression to twisted and slinky S&M babes servicing men. The atmosphere may have changed some, but the themes remained.

What are behind these perceptions? Do they have any basis in reality? What is the sex scene in Tokyo really like?

PUBLIC AND PRIVATE

The cultural approach to sexuality in Japan, and by extension the sex industry, differs from that of the West. To start with, there is a lack of both Judaeo-Christian concepts of guilt associated with sex, and any appreciable feminist movement to assert that sex is a way in which men wield power over women. The irrelevance of these models can be seen to have both positive and negative effects. The sexual atmosphere in Japan may be thought of as freer and less guilt-ridden, and at the same time less self-reflective and considered, than in the West.

To start a basic discussion of the topic one must be familiar with the important Japanese concept of *honne* (real value) versus *tatemae* (face value). The clear distinction between the two allows people to follow their desires freely in private, but respect the taboos in public.

Thus, public openness about sex in Japan is rather inhibited. Teenage boys may talk raunchily about sex (and they do), but the rest of society is reluctant to. For example, a foreign film may mention genitalia explicitly in its dialogue, but the Japanese subtitles usually employ less graphic wording, such as 'down there' – though every adult native Japanese speaker would know exactly what was being referred to. In fact, in modern Japanese there is no regularly used indigenous word for the sexual act. One can use *sekusu*, clearly borrowed from English, or the more popular *echi*, which is thought by many to also derive from a foreign root. In any case, *echi* can mean horny, sex or simply naughty. It does not have to mean the sexual act.

Such attitudes also extend to the media. In September 2001 there was a fatal fire in an unsafe club building in Shinjuku's Kabuki-cho. Here's how the *Daily Mainichi* reported the incident: 'Investigators believe that the Kabuki-cho fire started in front of the elevator near the mah jong parlour on the third floor of the four-storey building. All of the victims were either in the mah jong parlour or in the establishment on the fourth floor.'

The 'establishment on the fourth floor' was a highly dubious hostess club called Superloose, where 27 of the fire's 44 victims perished. Superloose's speciality was providing customers with young women dressed as schoolgirls. State broadcaster NHK went to great pains to get just the right angle to make sure the Superloose sign was invisible on TV, even as it filmed the fight to put the fire out.

'In modern Japanese there is no regularly used indigenous word for the sexual act.'

With such public reticence to talk about sex it may surprise some that, by all estimations, Japan is an extremely active society sexually. Pre-marital and teenage sex is a usual (if unacknowledged) occurrence, stretching down into middle school (under-16s)

Love hotels

Japan's chronic lack of privacy – and the thinness of its rice-paper walls – has helped create a thriving tradition of 'love hotels'. These short-stay establishments (usually rented in two-hour blocks) are ubiquitous, with entire sections of the capital's neighbourhoods devoted to them. And while slightly risqué, the use of such places has much in common with sex in general in Japan – not talked about openly, but widely indulged. They offer such a quintessentially Japanese experience that any couple travelling to Tokyo should try one out, if only for the afternoon.

The system for using a love hotel varies from place to place, but the basics are simple enough. Open all day and (mostly) all night, they offer rates for different blocks of time. Overnight rates are relatively cheap compared to other hotels (so they can be used as emergency accommodation), but most will not admit overnight guests until after midnight at the earliest so as to maximise profit from the day trade.

On entering a hotel, you are typically faced with pictures of each room with their prices listed beneath – the cheaper is for a short 'break', the higher for an overnight 'stay'. Only the illuminated rooms are unoccupied. Push the button on the room of your choice, then go to the front desk to collect the key. In cheaper love hotels all rooms may be the same and you simply go to the service window (you are often unable to see the clerk and vice versa) and pay for the required time. Some hotels are totally automatic, with machines printing out room numbers so that guests can avoid the potential embarrassment of seeing another human face. Go up to your room, lock the door and the rest is up to you.

As with any hotel, the more you pay, the more you're likely to get. Prices for a two-hour visit range from around ¥3,500 for a room with a bed, TV, bathroom and nothing more, to ¥15,000-plus for a room with its own swimming pool, swings or bondage paraphernalia. All love hotels have immaculate bathrooms, some with jacuzzi or sauna, since the Japanese like to wash before jumping in the sack. When you leave, pay the person on the desk; in automatic hotels, simply feed your money into the talking machine by the door.

The highest concentrations of love hotels in Tokyo are to be found in the Kabuki-cho district in Shinjuku, Dogenzaka in Shibuya and by the railway tracks near Ikebukuro station, although there are clusters in many other areas too. You'll even find a sprinkling in swankier neighbourhoods, such as Ebisu.

The big scandal a few years ago concerned *enjo kosai* ('assisted dating'), where girls as young as 15 were regularly prostituting themselves with no pressure from pimps or economics. The practice was simply employed by those just past puberty in order to buy trendier gear (this speaks to the importance attached to consumerism in Japan, but that's another issue). A law was enacted to enhance punishment of the men involved – it says something that the standing regulations weren't sufficient – and the first man caught was a Buddhist priest. The scandal died down, but assisted dating still continues.

Not only does Japanese society have a roaring, behind-closed-doors sexuality and an active sex industry, it also has a clear fascination with *rorikon* (Lolita complex) – Japan's expression for its sexual obsession with young, supposedly innocent girls. Many have noted that Japan's gigantic manga (comic book) culture often depicts wide-eyed pubescent girls being thrust into sexual situations (significantly, while these scenarios are explicit, the penis cannot be shown, even in comic book form). Leaflets in public phone booths for all manner of sexual services often depict young girls in suggestive poses.

This fascination with teenage girls also hints at another facet of sexual activity in Japan. The Western concept that one should pursue sexual partners near one's own age holds little sway in Japan. A stroll through any love hotel district in Tokyo will reveal elderly gentlemen with their much younger companions, or sometimes vice versa. In addition, upper-middle-class and upper-class men and women often take mistresses/lovers, a custom that is accepted on an unspoken level. This practice is greatly divided by class as it takes money in Tokyo to maintain these relationships, even if one is not dealing with sex-for-money per se.

In major sex industry hotspots such as Shibuya and Shinjuku's Kabuki-cho, services on offer range from hostess clubs, where women simply pour men's drinks and

Bron Mode

2-29-7 Kabuki-cho, Shinjuku-ku (3208 6211/ www.hotel-guide.jp). Shinjuku station (Yamanote, Chuo, Sobu lines), east exit; (Marunouchi line), exit B7; (Shinjuku line), exit 1 or Shinjuku-Nishiguchi station (Oedo line), exit D3. **Rates** ¥7,140-¥10,290 break; ¥11,490-¥20,000 stay. **Credit** AmEx, MC, V.

Flashy and futuristic looking, the Bron Mode fancies itself as a little bit upmarket. Rooms have karaoke, jet bath/jacuzzi and sauna, and gay and lesbian couples are welcome.

Hotel Listo

2-36-1 Kabuki-cho, Shinjuku-ku (5155 9255). Shinjuku station (Yamanote, Chuo, Sobu lines), east exit; (Marunouchi line), exit B7; (Shinjuku line), exit 1 or Shinjuku-Nishiguchi station (Oedo line), exit D3. **Rates** ¥5,500- ¥14,700 break; ¥10,000-¥28,000 stay. **Credit** AmEx, DC, MC, V.

A newer love hotel in Kabuki-cho, surrounded by fir trees so discretion is assured.

Meguro Club Sekitei

2-1-6 Shimo-Meguro, Meguro-ku (3494 1211). Meguro station (Yamanote, Mita, Nanboku lines), west exit. **Rates** ¥9,000- ¥13,000 break; ¥13,000-¥19,000 stay. **Credit** AmEx, MC, V.

A famous Tokyo love hotel, standing on its own like a fairytale palace. Check in and pay via a machine in the foyer. Rooms are huge and well furnished. Karaoke, jet bath/ sauna and free drinks are standard, as are microwave ovens. Don't ask.

P&A Plaza

1-17-9 Dogenzaka, Shibuya-ku (3780 5211/www.p-aplaza.com). Shibuya station (Yamanote, Ginza lines), south exit; (Hanzomon line), exit 5. **Rates** ¥5,500- ¥15,800 break; ¥9,8000-¥29,3000 stay. **Credit** AmEx, MC, V. **Map** p79.

One of the most famous love hotels in the capital, located in Doganzaka near Shibuya station. The P&A's top-priced suite contains a swimming pool. Jet bath or jacuzzi come as standard in all rooms.

Villa Giulia

2-27-8 Dogenzaka, Shibuya-ku (3770 7781). Shibuya station (Yamanote, Ginza lines), Hachiko exit; (Hanzomon line), exit 1. **Rates** ¥5,500-¥9,500 break; ¥9,500-¥18,000 stay. **Credit** AmEx, DC, MC, V. **Map** p79.

From the outside Villa Giulia looks rather like an Italian restaurant. Inside, it's clean and fully automatic. Push a button, take a slip for your room, then follow the spoken (Japanese) instructions for payment.

ALTERNATE WORLDS

To see this state of affairs as purely perversion or a patriarchy run riot would be a mistake. Japan has numerous and energetic sexual subcultures, and the straight, male-oriented sex industry is merely one aspect of a multifaceted world. Expressions of these erotic dimensions extend to the gay and committed straight couples' worlds too, and these realms, which find less exposure in the media, are perhaps more important.

Homosexuality has long been an accepted private pursuit in Japan. Old samurai tales are rife with affirmative descriptions of gay love. No one batted an eyelash when (now) conservative TV commentator and filmmaker Oshima Nagisa enthusiastically portrayed exactly this in his 1999 movie *Gohatto*. Some of Japan's earliest personal literature includes references to lesbianism, and the virulent condemnation of this conduct so prevalent in the West has rarely surfaced in Japan.

Tokyo has a thriving gay and lesbian community, which is only somewhat observant of the Japanese strictures of *tatamae* – witness the lively, annual Tokyo International Lesbian & Gay Film Festival, now more than a decade old. There is also a relatively visible gay sex industry, mostly centered around 'host' services. In a stunning reversal of common sense, but in keeping with a prostitute's separation of professional and private, many suppliers insist their boys actually be straight. The services are provided simply as business. (For more information on Tokyo's homosexual scene, see the **Gay & Lesbian** chapter, starting on p226.)

The straight couples' universe has an interesting sexual expression in Japan as well. The couples' *kissaten* (literally, coffee shop) is a scene that straddles the line between swinging and exhibitionism. Couples visit dimly lit clubs that resemble a low-slung living room and engage in sex with their partner, or if consensual, other members of the club. These clubs, and their newer incarnation, the 'happening bar', are surprisingly numerous and inexpensive. In general, admittance is limited to couples and some engage in sex only with their own partner, but many make friendships with others or simply enjoy watching them. Foursomes are not unusual either.

Ultimately, sexuality and its spin-offs in Japan are far more diverse than often portrayed in the Western media. Lolita-centred sensationalism may sell magazines, but such a narrow focus is more a reflection of the West's value system than an accurate portrayal of Japanese culture. Be prepared for a new sexual universe.

contribute conversation, to straightforward brothels, with a whole spectrum of lewd entertainment in between.

This is where Japan's taste for euphemism is brought to the fore. The term 'fashion massage' is code for manual stimulation, while a 'fashion health' massage means oral sex. Such services are provided by the basic in-house sex shops, but to spice up these categories, many go by such names as *gakuen tengoku* ('schoolgirl heaven'). Additionally, there are places called 'soapland', which offer a hot Japanese bath followed by sex. Formerly called Turkish baths, their current name is rumoured to derive from a diplomatic incident in which the Turkish ambassador to Tokyo asked a taxi driver to take him to a Turkish bath, where he was offered more than he bargained for. Following an official complaint, all such establishments were renamed soaplands.

Where to Stay

Where to Stay

Bed or futon, hostel or palace, traditional or ultra-modern? The choice is yours.

Tokyo's accommodation scene is everything you would expect from one of the world's major cities. Choices range from some of the most exclusive hotels on the planet to tiny rooms with straw mats and communal baths; from the sublime – Grand Hyatt, anyone? – to the ridiculous – we love those love hotels. And despite the city's reputation, budget travellers should be able to find somewhere to sleep and still have money left over for sake and noodles.

Tokyo's sheer size means that the location of your accommodation will have a major impact on the nature of your stay. Before booking, you should think about the sort of experience you're after. If nightlife rocks your boat, then think about Shibuya or Roppongi. Culture? Asakusa or Ueno. Something in between? Shinjuku or Ebisu. Do you want all the trappings of a Western hotel room, such as a bed, or are you happy to go native (and perhaps save some cash) and sleep on a futon?

Most of the top hotels in Tokyo offer Western-style accommodation, although some also give you the option of a slightly pricier Japanese-style room. As you would expect, all these hotels offer every possible comfort and convenience. Business hotels are designed with commercial travellers primarily in mind. They are a step down in quality and service from the top-end spots, and rooms are often on the small side, but they also offer decent value for money. Mid-range and budget hotels have the standard trappings of such enterprises the world over.

A traditional Japanese-style inn (*see p45* **Fancy a futon?**) provides one of the best ways to enhance your enjoyment of the city. If you want to meet some locals in a domestic environment, *minshuku* are the equivalent of a Western B&B. For a less salubrious, but ultra-Japanese accommodation experience, consider a night (or less) at a love hotel (*see p30* **Love hotels**). Capsule hotels are the last resort of the drunk, desperate and male (most are men-only). They offer cheap accommodation in a small tube that's barely big enough to sleep in. You might want to try one for the experience, but extended stays are unheard of.

We've also provided information on various agencies that can help foreigners seeking longer-term accommodation.

SALES TAX

All room rates are subject to Japan's usual five per cent sales tax, but if your bill climbs to the equivalent of over ¥15,000 per night (including service charges), you will be liable to an additional three per cent tax. Then there's a flat-rate surcharge of ¥100 per night for rooms costing ¥10,000-¥14,999, rising to ¥200 for rooms costing ¥15,000 or over. This money goes to help the metropolitan government promote Tokyo as a tourist destination.

No tipping is expected in any Tokyo hotel, although most high-end places include a standard service charge of 10-15 per cent in their room rates. Ask when booking.

Ginza Mercure. *See p36.*

Ginza & around

Deluxe

Conrad Tokyo

Tokyo Shiodome Bldg, 1-9-1 Higashi-Shinbashi,
Minato-ku (6388 8000/fax 6388 8001/
www.conradtokyo.co.jp). Shiodome station
(Oedo, Yurikamome lines), exit 9; Shinbashi station
(Yamanote, Asakusa lines), exit 1; (Ginza line),
exit 2. **Rooms** 290. **Rates** ¥52,000-¥62,000 single;
¥57,000-¥67,000 double; ¥79,000-¥500,000 suite.
Credit AmEx, DC, JCB, MC, V.

One of several luxury hoteliers to set up shop in
Tokyo in recent years, the Conrad opened in July
2005 high above the glimmering Shiodome complex.
Its 290 rooms – said to be the largest in Tokyo at
48sq m (517sq ft) – feature modern Japanese design
and occupy the top ten floors of the 37-storey Tokyo
Shiodome Building. No expense has been spared;
extras include a 25m swimming pool, ten-room spa,
floor-to-ceiling windows, plasma-screen TVs and
wireless internet. The Conrad is also home to
provocative British chef Gordon Ramsay's first
restaurant in Japan. The Grand Hyatt may be in for
some competition among the VIP crowd.
Bar. Business centre. Concierge. Gym. Internet
(high-speed/wireless). No-smoking rooms. Parking.
Pool (indoor). Restaurants (3). Room service (24hr).
Spa. TV (satellite/video on demand/DVD).

Dai-ichi Hotel Tokyo

1-2-6 Shinbashi, Minato-ku (3501 4411/
fax 3595 2634/www.daiichihotels.com/hotel/tokyo).
Shinbashi station (Yamanote, Asakusa, Ginza
lines), exits Hibiya, 7. **Rooms** 277. **Rates** ¥27,000-
¥34,000 single; ¥31,000-¥48,000 double; ¥80,000-
¥350,000 suite. **Credit** AmEx, DC, JCB, MC, V.
Map p60.

This 1993 tower, a ten-minute walk from Ginza,
appears to be losing out to the increasing number
of new hotels in nearby mini metropolis Shiodome
City. The interior is a strange mix of styles: the
entrance hall is a self-conscious echo of the
grandeur of old European luxury hotels; the restaurants are a tribute to the designers' ability to cram
many different styles of interior decor into one
building. Rooms, however, are immaculate, of a
good size and beautifully furnished and decorated.
A sleek swimming pool and fitness centre are available in the annex.
Bars (2). Business centre. Concierge. Gym.
Internet (high-speed). No-smoking rooms. Parking
(¥1,000/night). Pool (indoor). Restaurants (10).
Room service (24hr). Spa. TV (cable/satellite/
pay movies).

Hotel Seiyo Ginza

1-11-2 Ginza, Chuo-ku (3535 1111/fax 3535
1110/www.seiyo-ginza.com). Ginza-Itchome station
(Yurakucho line), exits 7, 10. **Rooms** 77. **Rates**
¥45,000-¥60,000 single/double; ¥60,000-¥200,000
suite. **Credit** AmEx, DC, MC, V. **Map** p60.

Calling itself an 'ultra-luxury hotel management
company', Rosewood Hotels & Resorts took over the
Seiyo in 2000 and has since elevated the already
upscale boutique property to unrivalled heights of
fancy. The 77 rooms have all been refurbished, each
in its own distinct style, to recreate a 'personal
residence' away from home. Winner of *Travel &*
Leisure magazine's award for the best hotel in Asia
in 2004, the Seiyo offers around-the-clock butler and
concierge services, and twice-daily housekeeping. It
also enjoyed the distinction of hosting the world's
most expensive dinner, created by chef Joel

Booking outfits

Hotel Finder

www.japanhotelfinder.com.
An internet-only booking service that offers
substantial discounts on stays at many of
Tokyo's top hotels.

Japan City Hotel Association

www.jcha.or.jp/english.
Like the Japan Inn Group, this is a
collective of owners of mid-priced hotels.
The website offers direct links to each
member hotel.

Japan Inn Group

www.jpinn.com.
An umbrella organisation founded and
run by *ryokan* owners across Japan, it
offers direct links to members' premises
via its website.

Japan Youth Hostels

www.jyh.or.jp/english/index.html.
Comprehensive listing and booking
service for all youth hostels in Japan.

Japanese Guest Houses

www.japaneseguesthouses.com.
Online listing and booking service for
ryokan and *minshuku* around the country.

Welcome Inn Reservation Centre

www.itcj.or.jp/indexwel.html.
Run by the International Tourism Centre of
Japan (ITCJ) and aimed at non-Japanese-
speaking visitors, this very useful service
offers budget accommodation (up to
¥8,000 single, ¥13,000 double) at some
250 hotels around Japan. You can book
online or in person at JNTO's TIC offices
(*see p297*) at Narita Airport and in central
Tokyo, where you can also pick up a
directory of participating inns in English.

Robuchon and wine expert Robert Parker, at $13,000 per person, including a three-night stay.
Bars (2). Business centre. Concierge. Gym. Internet (high-speed). No-smoking floors (2). Parking (free). Restaurants (3). Room service (24hr). TV (cable/video on command).

Imperial Hotel

1-1-1 Uchisaiwaicho, Chiyoda-ku (3504 1111/ fax 3581 9146/www.imperialhotel.co.jp). Hibiya station (Chiyoda, Hibiya, Mita lines), exits A5, A13 or Yurakucho station (Yamanote, Yurakucho lines), Hibiya exit. **Rooms** 1,052. **Rates** ¥30,000-¥60,000 single; ¥35,000-¥90,000 double; ¥60,000-¥1,000,000 suite. **Credit** AmEx, DC, JCB, MC, V. **Map** p60.

There has been an Imperial Hotel on this site overlooking Hibiya Park since 1890. This 1970 tower block-style building replaced the glorious 1923 Frank Lloyd Wright creation that famously survived the Great Kanto Earthquake on its opening day. It's currently in the midst of a five-year renovation plan that began with new decor for the Imperial's penthouse bar and restaurant and will conclude with the overhaul of the lobby and all guest rooms by 2008. For a sneak peek at the changes, check into the already completed Imperial Floors, featuring plush new beds, high-tech bathrooms and a range of personalised services.
Bars (3). Business centre. Concierge. Disabled-adapted room. Gym. Internet (high-speed). No-smoking rooms. Parking (free). Pool (indoor). Restaurants (14). Room service (24hr). TV (cable/satellite/pay movies).

Expensive

Other recently opened smart hotels in Shiodome are the **Park Hotel Tokyo** (Shiodome Media Tower, 1-7-1 Higashi-Shinbashi, Minato-ku, 6252 1111, fax 6252 1001, www.parkhotel tokyo.com) and the **Royal Park Shiodome Tower** (1-6-3 Higashi-Shinbashi, Minato-ku, 6253 1111, fax 6253 1111, www.rps-tower.co.jp).

Ginza Mercure

2-9-4 Ginza, Chuo-ku (4335 1111/fax 4335 1222/ www.mercureginza.com). Ginza-Itchome station (Yurakucho line), exit 11. **Rooms** 209. **Rates** ¥18,375 single; ¥24,150 double; ¥47,250 suite. **Credit** AmEx, DC, JCB, MC, V. **Map** p60.

This French-owned hotel opened in autumn 2004 in a great central location, just behind Matsuya department store. Niftily converted from an existing office building, it has the feel of a European boutique hotel, featuring smart cherrywood furniture, stylish wallpaper and black and white photos of old Paris. All the rooms vary in size (numbers 16 and 18 are the biggest), and there are 18 special 'ladies' rooms' on the eight, ninth and tenth floors. The breakfast room doubles as a French bistro, and staff speak English. A good choice for both business and independent travellers.

Bar. Business centre. Concierge. Disabled-adapted room. No-smoking rooms. Internet (high-speed). Parking (¥1,500/night). Restaurant. TV (cable/satellite/pay movies).
Other locations: Mercure Hotel Narita 818-1 Hanazaki-cho, Narita, Chiba-ken (0476 23 7000).

Mitsui Urban Hotel

8-6-15 Ginza, Chuo-ku (3572 4131/fax 3572 4254/ www.mitsuikanko.co.jp/urban/ginza). Shinbashi station (Yamanote, Asakusa, Ginza lines), Ginza exit. **Rooms** 265. **Rates** ¥14,500-¥20,500 single; ¥25,000-¥34,800 twin; ¥25,000-¥28,800 double. **Credit** AmEx, DC, JCB, MC, V. **Map** p60.

The Mitsui is an unassuming, practical choice on the edge of Ginza. Rooms are quite small and basically furnished, and the relative lack of facilities is reflected in the price. The lobby looks somewhat dated with its marble, gold and black decor, but the hotel's proximity to Ginza's nightlife quarter means it's often filled with Japanese businessmen and kimono-clad hostesses on their way to or from work.
Bar. Internet (high-speed). No-smoking floor. Parking (¥1,500/night). Restaurants (4). Room service (10pm-midnight). TV.

Moderate

Hotel Ginza Daiei

3-12-1 Ginza, Chuo-ku (3545 1111/fax 3545 1177). Higashi-Ginza station (Hibiya line), exit 3; (Asakusa line), exits A7, A8. **Rooms** 106. **Rates** ¥11,965-¥13,960 single; ¥16,000 double; ¥18,000-¥21,800 twin; ¥23,000 triple. **Credit** AmEx, DC, JCB, MC, V. **Map** p60.

Hotels

For traditional Japan
Homeikan Honkan. *See p43.*

For reliving *Lost in Translation*
Park Hyatt Tokyo. *See p39.*

For hanging with the hipsters
Claska. *See p51.*

For prices cheaper than chips
Hotel New Koyo. *See p51.*

For meeting fellow travellers
Kimi Ryokan. *See p49.*

For the charm of yesteryear
Hilltop Hotel. *See p37.*

For style at bargain prices
Hotel Villa Fontaine Shiodome. *See p37.*

For budget thrills in Shinjuku
Star Hotel Tokyo. *See p37.*

A well-situated, no-frills hotel that's well past its prime, the Ginza Daiei does offer decent-sized rooms with plain, functional pine furniture and inoffensive, light decor. Services are minimal, but high-speed internet has been installed in recent years. If you opt for the top-price 'Healthy Twin' room, you'll get the added bonus of a jet bath.

Internet (high-speed). No-smoking rooms. Parking (¥1,000/night). TV.

Hotel Villa Fontaine Shiodome

1-9-2 Higashi-Shinbashi, Minato-ku (3569 2220/ fax 3569 2111/www.villa-fontaine.co.jp). Shiodome station (Oedo line), exit 10; (Yurikamome line), Shiodome Sumitomo Bldg exit. **Rooms** 497. **Rates** ¥10,000-¥16,000 single; ¥14,000-¥18,000 double; ¥21,000 triple. **Credit** AmEx, DC, JCB, MC, V.

Prices are surprisingly low at this super-stylish hotel (opened 2004) in the gleaming Shiodome complex. A funky approach to interior design has resulted in, for example, a striking atrium/lobby area with cone-shaped lights and unusual artworks by the lifts. The well-designed rooms make the most of their small size, using discreetly patterned luxury fabrics and nifty shutter/blind combinations. Free, always-on broadband internet access is a bonus. A shame about the disappointing buffet breakfast. This is the smartest of the hotel's seven locations, which include Roppongi, Ueno and Nihonbashi.

Business centre. Disabled-adapted room. Internet (high-speed). No-smoking rooms. Parking (¥2,100/night). TV (cable/pay movies).

Other locations: seven other sites in Tokyo (central reservations 5339 1200).

Marunouchi & around

Deluxe

Four Seasons Hotel Tokyo at Marunouchi

Pacific Century Place, 1-11-1 Marunouchi, Chiyoda-ku (5222 7222/fax 5222 1255/ www.fourseasons.com/marunouchi). Tokyo station (Yamanote, Marunouchi lines), Yaesu south exit. **Rooms** 57. **Rates** ¥58,000-¥84,000 single/double; ¥98,000-¥400,000 suite. **Credit** AmEx, DC, JCB, MC, V. **Map** p66.

The Four Seasons offers unparalleled luxury and style in the heart of the city's business district. It's decorated in cool, modern timber, beautifully lit to create a suitably serene atmosphere. The rooms are among the biggest in any Tokyo hotel, and some boast great views across the railway tracks to Tokyo International Forum. Service is multilingual and utterly impeccable, as you're entitled to expect for the price. Each room comes with high-speed internet access, a 42in plasma TV screen with sur-round-sound and a DVD player.

Bar. Business centre. Concierge. Gym. Internet (high-speed). No-smoking rooms. Parking (¥5,000/night). Restaurant. Room service (24hr). Spa. TV (cable/satellite/CD/DVD player).

Expensive

Hilltop Hotel

1-1 Kanda-Surugadai, Chiyoda-ku (3293 2311/fax 3233 4567/www.yamanoue-hotel.co.jp). Ochanomizu station (Chuo, Marunouchi lines), Ochanomizubashi exit. **Rooms** 74. **Rates** ¥15,750-¥21,000 single; ¥23,100-¥33,600 double/twin; ¥42,000-¥52,500 suite. **Credit** AmEx, DC, JCB, MC, V. **Map** p66.

Not many hotels in Tokyo can be said to exude gen-uine charm, so the Hilltop deserves some credit for retaining its old-fashioned traditions, with antique writing desks and small private gardens for the more expensive suites. That said, it recently remod-elled its seventh storey, now called the Art Septo Floor, with funky new furniture and decor, plus large-screen TVs and enhanced stereos. Known throughout Tokyo as a literary hangout, the Hilltop tries to boost the concentration of blocked writers by pumping ionised air into every room.

Bars (3). Internet (high-speed). Japanese & Western rooms. Parking (¥1,000/day). Restaurants (7). Room service (7am-2am). TV (cable/satellite).

Marunouchi Hotel

1-6-3 Marunouchi, Chiyoda-ku (3217 1111/ fax 3217 1115/www.marunouchi-hotel.co.jp). Tokyo station (Yamanote line), Marunouchi north exit; (Marunouchi line), exit 12. **Rooms** 205. **Rates** ¥23,300 single; ¥26,765-¥44,290 double/ twin; ¥46,500 triple; ¥115,700-¥115,900 suite. **Credit** AmEx, DC, JCB, MC, V. **Map** p66.

There's been a Marunouchi Hotel since 1924; it's latest incarnation opened in the new Oazo building (*see p176*) in autumn 2004. The lobby is on the sev-enth floor, from where a truly spectacular atrium soars through the centre of the hotel. Rooms (which vary considerably in size) are on the ninth to 17th floors – hence some fantastic views over the train tracks of neighbouring Tokyo station – and major in sumptuous materials in a palate of browns and golds. Restaurants include Japanese and French ones, and business facilities are good. A classy joint.

Bar. Disabled-adapted rooms. Internet (high-speed). No-smoking rooms. Parking (¥1,500/night). Restaurants (5). Room service (7am-10pm). TV (cable/satellite).

Moderate

Hotel Kazusaya

4-7-15 Nihonbashi-Honcho, Chuo-ku (3241 1045/ fax 3241 1077/www.h-kazusaya.co.jp). Shin-Nihonbashi station (Sobu Kaisoku line), exit 8 or Kanda station (Yamanote, Ginza lines), east exit or Mitsukoshimae station (Ginza, Hanzomon lines), exit A10. **Rooms** 71. **Rates** ¥8,925-¥9,975 single; ¥10,500-¥12,600 double; ¥14,700 twin; ¥18,900 triple. *Japanese (3-4 people)* ¥22,050-¥25,200. **Credit** AmEx, DC, JCB, MC, V. **Map** p66.

There has been a Hotel Kazusaya in Nihonbashi since 1891, but you'd be hard pushed to know it from the modern exterior of the current building, in one of the last *shitamachi* areas in the heart of Tokyo's business district. Inside, you'll find good-sized, functionally furnished rooms, including one Japanese-style tatami room for three to four guests. Service is obliging, although only minimal English is spoken. *Internet (high-speed). Japanese & Western rooms. No-smoking rooms. Parking (¥2,100/day). Restaurant. TV (cable/satellite/pay movies).*

Kayabacho Pearl Hotel

1-2-5 Shinkawa, Chuo-ku (3553 8080/ fax 3555 1849/www.pearlhotel.co.jp/kayabacho). Kayabacho station (Hibiya, Tozai lines), exit 4B. **Rooms** 268. **Rates** ¥8,295-¥9,345 single; ¥15,960-¥21,000 twin; ¥18,585-¥23,625 triple. **Credit** AmEx, DC, JCB, MC, V. **Map** p66.
An upmarket business hotel in the heart of the business district, the Pearl has good-sized, well-furnished rooms and reasonable service. Staff speak some English. An unexpected plus is the canalside location. *Business centre. No-smoking rooms. Parking (¥1,500/night). Restaurant. TV (cable/pay movies).*

Ryokan Ryumeikan Honten

3-4 Kanda-Surugadai, Chiyoda-ku (3251 1135/ fax 3251 0270/www.ryumeikan.co.jp/honten.html). Ochanomizu station (Chuo, Marunouchi lines), Hijiribashi exit. **Rooms** 12. **Rates** ¥10,000-¥13,100 single; ¥17,000-¥18,000 double; ¥22,500-¥24,000 triple. **Credit** AmEx, DC, JCB, MC, V. **Map** p66.
Just south of Ochanomizu's Russian Nikolai Cathedral, this *ryokan* is modern and clean, with helpful staff and good-sized Japanese rooms. Architecturally, though, it's a nightmare, occupying part of a modern office block that blends completely into the surrounding skyscrapers. The interior is a testament to how ingeniously the Japanese can disguise the shortcomings of a building to produce a pleasant atmosphere, but you still might find yourself wishing you'd stayed somewhere a little more traditional. The branch in Nihonbashi is slightly cheaper and more imposing. *Internet (high-speed). Japanese rooms only. Parking (free). Restaurant. Room service (7.30am-10pm). TV (cable/satellite).*
Other locations: Hotel Yaesu Ryumeikan 1-3-22 Yaesu, Chuo-ku (3271 0971/fax 3271 0977).

Sumisho Hotel

9-14 Nihonbashi-Kobunacho, Chuo-ku (3661 4603/ fax 3661 4639/www.sumisho-hotel.co.jp). Ningyocho station (Asakusa, Hibiya lines), exit A5. **Rooms** 86. **Rates** ¥7,000 single; ¥10,500-¥19,500 twin; ¥11,000 double. *Japanese* ¥13,500-¥19,500. **Credit** AmEx, DC, JCB, MC, V. **Map** p66.
A little tricky to find, this charming Japanese-style hotel manages to take an ugly modern Tokyo building and imbue it with something quintessentially Japanese; in this case a small pond, which you need to cross to get to the foyer. It's a pleasant enough place to stay, with good facilities and a high level of service, although non-Japanese speakers may find it hard to make themselves understood. The

first floor contains a communal bath, although all rooms are equipped with their own bathrooms. *Internet (high-speed). Japanese & Western rooms. Restaurant. TV (cable/satellite).*

Budget

Hotel Nihonbashi Saibo

3-3-16 Nihonbashi-Ningyocho, Chuo-ku (3668 2323/ fax 3668 1669/www.hotel-saibo.co.jp). Ningyocho station (Asakusa, Hibiya lines), exit A4. **Rooms** 126. **Rates** ¥7,600-¥9,900 single; ¥10,000 double; ¥12,000 twin. **Credit** AmEx, DC, JCB, V. **Map** p66.
The good news for anyone looking to stay in this quiet area not far from Tokyo station is that while the Saibo has remodelled its interior and guest rooms – rooms are still small and services sparse, however – the bargain rates have been retained. A good bet for solo travellers looking for functional and relatively modern accommodation. *Internet (high-speed/shared terminal). Restaurants (2). TV (satellite/pay movies).*

Sakura Hotel

2-21-4 Kanda-Jinbocho, Chiyoda-ku (3261 3939/ fax 3264 2777/www.sakura-hotel.co.jp). Jinbocho station (Hanzomon, Mita, Shinjuku lines), exits A1, A6. **Rooms** 43. **Rates** ¥3,780 dorm; ¥6,090-¥7,140 single; ¥7,875 double; ¥8,400 twin. **Credit** AmEx, DC, JCB, MC, V. **Map** p66.
Of all the budget hotels and *ryokan* in Tokyo, this is the most central, located in the Jinbocho district just a mile or so north of the Imperial Palace. Small groups can use the dorm rooms, which sleep six. Rooms are tiny but clean, and all are no-smoking. Staff are on duty 24 hours a day and speak good English. Book well in advance. *Internet (shared). No smoking. Restaurant. TV.*

YMCA Asia Youth Centre

2-5-5 Sarugakucho, Chiyoda-ku (3233 0611/fax 3233 0633/www.ymcajapan.org/ayc). Suidobashi station (Chuo line), east exit; (Mita line), exit A1. **Rooms** 55. **Rates** ¥5,040-¥6,300 single; ¥9,240-¥11,550 twin; ¥11,592-¥14,490 triple. **Credit** JCB, MC, V.
Part of the Korean YMCA in Japan, this centre offers many of the same facilities and services you'd expect at a regular hotel, a fact reflected in its relatively high prices. In terms of location, it shares many advantages with the nearby Hilltop Hotel (*see above*). The smallish rooms are Western in style, with their own bathrooms. *Internet (shared terminals). Restaurant. TV.*

Shinjuku

Deluxe

Hilton Tokyo

6-6-2 Nishi-Shinjuku, Shinjuku-ku (3344 5111/ fax 3342 6094/www.hilton.com/hotels/TYOHITW). Nishi-Shinjuku station (Marunouchi line), exit C8

or Tochomae station (Oedo line), exit C8. Free bus
from Keio department store (bus stop 21), Shinjuku
station, west exit. **Rooms** 806. **Rates** ¥34,000 single;
¥37,000 double; ¥45,000-¥120,000 suite. **Credit**
AmEx, DC, JCB, MC, V. **Map** p73.

A luxury hotel in west Shinjuku, the Hilton opened
in 1984 after vacating its previous premises in
Akasaka (now the Capitol Tokyu; see p46). Rooms
are of a good size, although the views, often blocked
by other towers in the area, can be disappointing.
As you'd expect, the standard of service is high. For
business travellers, the hotel offers five executive
floors, with separate check-in, a fax in each room and
their own guest relations officers on hand to help out
and advise. The Hilton is also one of few Tokyo
hotels to have its own tennis courts.
*Bar. Business centre. Concierge. Disabled-adapted
rooms. Gym. No-smoking rooms. Internet
(high-speed). Japanese & Western rooms. Parking
(¥1,500/night). Pool (indoor). Restaurants (6).
Room service (24hr). TV (cable/satellite/pay movies).*
Other locations: Hilton Tokyo Bay 1-8
Maihama, Urayasu-shi, Chiba-ken (047 355 5000).

Keio Plaza Hotel

*2-2-1 Nishi-Shinjuku, Shinjuku-ku (3344 0111/
fax 3345 8269/www.keioplaza.com). Shinjuku
station (Yamanote line), west exit; (Marunouchi line),
exit A17; (Shinjuku line), exit B1 or Tochomae
station (Oedo line), exits A1, B1.* **Rooms** 1,450.
Rates ¥21,567 single; ¥30,230 double/twin;
¥41,880 triple. **Credit** AmEx, DC, JCB, MC, V.
Map p73.

The lavish decor that once made this Tokyo's most
prestigious hotel now looks seriously dated compared to the likes of the two Hyatts. The location,
however, is still tough to beat: a stone's throw from
the world's busiest train station, with upper floors
offering superlative views of the metropolis. In
spring 2005 the hotel opened three floors of 'Plaza
Premier' rooms: spacious, elegant spaces with all the
electronics and business support expected of a luxury hotel. The Plaza plans to continue renovations
until all floors have been updated, a venture likely
to take a decade.
*Bars (4). Business centre. Disabled-adapted rooms.
Gym. No-smoking rooms. Internet (high-speed).
Parking (¥1,000/night). Pool (outdoor). Restaurants
(13). Room service (24hr). TV (cable/satellite).*

Park Hyatt Tokyo

*3-7-1-2 Nishi-Shinjuku, Shinjuku-ku (5322 1234/
fax 5322 1288/http://tokyo.park.hyatt.com).
Shinjuku station (Yamanote, Marunouchi lines),
west exit; (Shinjuku line), exit 6 or Tochomae station
(Oedo line), exit A4. Free shuttle bus from in front
of Shinjuku L Tower, Shinjuku station, west exit.*
Rooms 178. **Rates** ¥53,000-¥65,000 double/twin;
¥120,000-¥300,000 suite. **Credit** AmEx, DC, JCB,
MC, V. **Map** p73.

Despite being Tokyo's most decorated hotel, the
Park Hyatt is perhaps best known for its starring
role in Sofia Coppola's 2003 hit *Lost in Translation*.
The director (a frequent guest) described it as a
'floating island' above the city. By Tokyo standards, it's a small, intimate establishment, a feeling

The stylish lobby/breakfast area at the **Hotel Villa Fontaine Shiodome**. *See p37.*

emphasised by the well-lit decor and artworks on display. The reception is on the glass-walled 41st floor, with stunning views over the whole of the city. Service is attentive but not overly fussy, and the immaculately equipped rooms are among the largest in any Tokyo hotel. Recent years have also seen enhancement to the already celebrated Club on The Park aesthetic and fitness centre.

Bars (2). Business centre. Concierge. Disabled-adapted rooms. Gym. Internet (high-speed). No-smoking rooms. Parking (free). Pool (indoor). Restaurants (4). Room service (24hr). Spa. TV (cable/satellite/DVD).

Moderate

Shinjuku Washington Hotel

3-2-9 Nishi-Shinjuku, Shinjuku-ku (3343 3111/ fax 3342 2575/www.wh-rsv.com/english/shinjuku). Shinjuku station (Yamanote, Marunouchi lines), south exit; (Oedo, Shinjuku lines), exits 6, 7. **Rooms** 1,296. **Rates** ¥10,000-¥12,500 single; ¥11,100-¥19,200 double/twin. **Credit** AmEx, DC, JCB, MC, V. **Map** p73.

A step down in price and luxury from other west Shinjuku hotels, the Washington nonetheless offers a high standard of accommodation and service. Its main target market is business travellers, so rooms tend to be small and blandly furnished (though some have been redecorated recently). Also, there is now a women-only floor, and a business floor with upgraded amenities. The newer annex (containing 337 rooms) offers roughly the same level of service, with more modern decor.

Bar. Disabled-adapted rooms. Internet (high-speed). No-smoking rooms. Parking (¥100-¥250/30mins). Restaurants (4). Room service (main bldg 6-11pm; annex 6-10pm). TV (cable/VCR).

Other locations: Akihabara Washington Hotel 1-8-3 Sakuma-machi, Kanda, Chiyoda-ku (3255 3311/fax 3255 7343); **Tokyo Bay Ariake Washington Hotel** 3-1-28 Ariake, Koto-ku (5564 0111/fax 5564 0525).

Star Hotel Tokyo

7-10-5 Nishi-Shinjuku, Shinjuku-ku (3361 1111/ fax 3369 4216/www.starhotel.co.jp/city/tokyo.html). Shinjuku station (Yamanote line), west exit; (Marunouchi, Shinjuku lines), exit D4 or Shinjuku-Nishiguchi station (Oedo line), exit D4. **Rooms** 214. **Rates** ¥9,450-¥12,100 single; ¥17,850-¥18,900 double; ¥17,850-¥27,300 twin. **Credit** AmEx, JCB, MC, V. **Map** p73.

In terms of position, the Star offers everything its more expensive west Shinjuku rivals do. Tucked among all-night restaurants on a noisy main road, it's a great location from which to base your Tokyo explorations, with the red-light district of Kabuki-cho on one side and access to the rest of the city via Shinjuku station on the other. Rooms are tiny and frill-free, but the Star has made some cosmetic upgrades in recent years and remains one of the best options on its side of Shinjuku.

Bar. Internet (high-speed). No-smoking rooms. Parking (¥1,500/night). Restaurants (3). Room service (5-10pm). TV (cable).

Budget

Shinjuku Palace Hotel

2-8-12 Kabuki-cho, Shinjuku-ku (3209 1231). Shinjuku station (Yamanote line), east exit; Shinjuku-Sanchome station (Marunouchi, Shinjuku lines), exit C7. **Rooms** 34. **Rates** ¥6,700-¥6,800 single; ¥9,800 double; ¥10,500 twin. *Japanese* ¥9,800. **No credit cards.**

A palace in name only, this hotel in the heart of Kabuki-cho offers basic, no-frills accommodation aimed primarily at local businessmen or salarymen who've stayed one drink too long and missed the last train home. Surrounded by late-night noodle joints and love hotels, the Palace is clean and friendly; just don't expect to be able to make much meaningful communication in English. Rooms are small, but how much time are you going to spend here?

Japanese & Western rooms. TV.

Shibuya

Deluxe

Cerulean Tower Tokyu Hotel

26-1 Sakuragaokacho, Shibuya-ku (3476 3000/ fax 3476 3001/www.ceruleantower-hotel.com). Shibuya station (Yamanote line), south exit; (Ginza, Hanzomon lines), Hachiko exit. **Rooms** 414. **Rates** ¥27,720-¥39,270 single; ¥36,960-¥66,990 double/twin; ¥93,400-¥438,900 suite. *Japanese* ¥75,075-¥77,385. **Credit** AmEx, MC, V. **Map** p79.

Shibuya was bereft of top-class accommodation until this hotel opened in late 2001. Housed on the 19th to 37th floors of the area's tallest building, the Cerulean offers grandstand views. In addition to the usual restaurants and bars, it also has a *noh* theatre (see p246) and a jazz club, JZ Brat (see p237). Room furnishings may be a step down from the likes of the Grand Hyatt, but so is the price. Except, that is, for the 35th to 37th Executive Floors, which offer free access to the gym, daily newspapers, web TV and refreshments in the salon.

Bars (2). Business centre. Concierge. Disabled-adapted rooms. Gym. Internet (high-speed). Japanese & Western rooms. No-smoking rooms. Parking (free). Pool (indoor). Restaurants (6). Room service (24hr). Spa. TV (cable/satellite).

Expensive

Arimax Hotel Shibuya

11-15 Kamiyamacho, Shibuya-ku (5454 1122/ fax 3460 6513/www.arimaxhotelshibuya.co.jp). Shibuya station (Yamanote, Ginza, Hanzomon lines), Hachiko exit. **Rooms** 23. **Rates** ¥22,145-¥33,695 single; ¥27,920-¥39,670 double; ¥75,475 suite. **Credit** AmEx, DC, JCB, MC, V. **Map** p79.

Hilltop Hotel. *See p37.*

Modelled on European boutique hotels, the Arimax offers a choice of English or neo-classical room styles and exudes the atmosphere of a long-established gentlemen's club, with warm, dim lighting and dark wood panelling the dominant decorative themes. All guest rooms include business amenities. The only drawback may be the location, about 15 minutes' walk from the buzzing centre of Shibuya. *Bar. Internet (high-speed). Parking (free). Restaurant. Room service (drinks 5pm-midnight Mon-Fri, 5-11pm Sat, Sun; food 5-9.30pm daily). TV (cable).*

Excel Hotel Tokyu

Shibuya Mark City, 1-12-2 Dogenzaka, Shibuya-ku (5457 0109/fax 5457 0309/www.tokyuhotels.co.jp/ en/TE/TE_SHIBU). Inside Shibuya station (Yamanote, Ginza, Hanzomon lines). **Rooms** 408. **Rates** ¥20,790-¥27,720 single; ¥26,565-¥41,580 twin; ¥24,255-¥28,875 double; ¥34,650 triple; ¥41,580 quadruple; ¥115,500 suite. **Credit** AmEx, DC, JCB, MC, V. **Map** p79.

Situated in the Mark City complex attached to Shibuya station, the Excel is very popular with domestic visitors wanting to be in the heart of Shibuya. Pleasant, clean, with spacious rooms and nice views, it's one of few good-quality hotels in this part of town. There are six special floors: two for women only with added security, three for business travellers, and a 'Healing Floor' with aromatherapy, soothing music and relaxation programmes. *Bar. Concierge. Disabled-adapted rooms. Internet. No-smoking floors. Parking (¥1,500/night). Restaurants (2). Room service (7am-10am; 9pm-midnight). Spa. TV (satellite).*

Ebisu

Deluxe

The Westin Tokyo

1-4-1 Mita, Meguro-ku (5423 7000/fax 5423 7600/ www.westin-tokyo.co.jp). Ebisu station (Yamanote, Hibiya lines), east exit. **Rooms** 445. **Rates** ¥53,200-¥68,200 single; ¥58,400-¥74,400 double/twin; ¥120,200-¥465,500 suite. **Credit** AmEx, DC, JCB, MC, V.

The Westin, at the far end of Ebisu's giant Garden Place development, opened in 1994. Its spacious lobby attempts to recreate the feeling of a European palace, while all guest rooms are palatial in size and feature soft lighting and antique-style furniture. A good view is pretty much guaranteed. *Bars (3). Business centre. Concierge. Disabled-adapted rooms. Internet (high-speed). No-smoking rooms. Parking (¥1,000/night). Restaurants (6). Room service (24hr). TV (cable/satellite/pay movies).*

Moderate

Hotel Excellent

1-9-5 Ebisu-Nishi, Shibuya-ku (5458 0087/ fax 5458 8787/www.soeikikaku.co.jp). Ebisu station (Yamanote line), west exit; (Hibiya line), exit 3. **Rooms** 127. **Rates** ¥9,150 single; ¥11,550 double; ¥13,100 twin. **Credit** DC, MC, V.

A thoroughly basic but phenomenally popular business hotel offering no-frills accommodation in small, functional and bland rooms. The main reason for its success is its location, one stop away from Shibuya on the Yamanote line and in the heart of the lively Ebisu area. *Bar. Internet (high-speed). No-smoking rooms. Restaurants (2). TV (cable).*

Asakusa

Expensive

Asakusa View Hotel

3-17-1 Nishi-Asakusa, Taito-ku (3847 1111/ fax 3842 2117/www.viewhotels.co.jp/asakusa). Tawaramachi station (Ginza line), exit 3. **Rooms** 338. **Rates** ¥13,000-¥18,000 single; ¥19,000-¥34,000 double/twin; ¥50,000-¥300,000 suite. *Japanese* ¥40,000-¥63,000. **Credit** AmEx, DC, JCB, MC, V. **Map** p93.

EVERYTHING YOU NEED
FOR THE
PERFECT BREAK

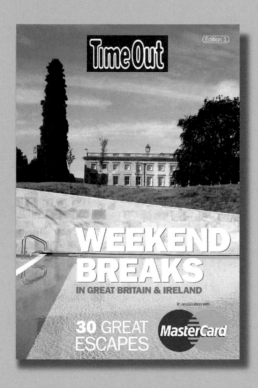

With its uniformed staff and marble lobby some-what incongruent with this downtown, working-class neighbourhood, the Asakusa View boasts a fairly high standard of accommodation, and its rates reflect its status as the only luxury hotel in the area. If you want to make the hotel live up to its name, go for a room as high up as you can: the view from the top over Asakusa and the Sumida river is worth catching. Non-visitors can also pop in for a drink to the Belvedere lounge on the 28th floor. A nice touch is that the sixth floor is given over to Japanese-style rooms, complete with their own garden.
Bars (3). Concierge. Disabled-adapted rooms. Japanese & Western rooms. No-smoking rooms. Parking (¥1,000/night). Pool (indoor). Restaurants (3). Room service (7am-11pm). TV (cable).

Moderate

Hotel Sunroute Asakusa

1-8-5 Kaminarimon, Taito-ku (3847 1511/ fax 3847 1509/www.sunroute-asakusa.co.jp). Tawaramachi station (Ginza line), exit 3. **Rooms** 120. **Rates** ¥8,925-¥11,025 single; ¥17,325-¥19,950 twin; ¥15,225 double; ¥13,860 disabled-adapted room. **Credit** AmEx, DC, MC, V. **Map** p93.
Small rooms and lack of facilities notwithstanding, this business hotel offers reasonable value for money for those determined to sleep in beds rather than on futons. The building is simple and clean with a vaguely European ambience. US diner-style chain restaurant Jonathan's is situated on the second floor. *Disabled-adapted room. Internet (shared terminal). No-smoking rooms. Parking (¥1,500/night). Restaurant. TV (cable/satellite/pay movies).*

Ryokan Shigetsu

1-31-11 Asakusa, Taito-ku (3843 2345/fax 3843 2348/www.shigetsu.com). Asakusa station (Ginza line), exits 1, 6; (Asakusa line), exit A4. **Rooms** 23. **Rates** ¥7,665 single; ¥14,700 twin. *Japanese* ¥9,450 single; ¥16,800-¥26,250 double. **Credit** AmEx, MC, V. **Map** p93.
Barely 30 seconds' walk from Asakusa's market and temple complex, yet surprisingly peaceful, the Shigetsu offers a choice of comfortable rooms in Japanese and Western styles in an elegant down-town setting. All rooms have their own bathrooms, although there is a Japanese-style communal bath on the top floor. Recent years have seen a shift back to Japanese-style rooms, with 15 of the 23 now fea-turing traditional tatami and futon furnishings. Booking is recommended and can be made through the Japan Inn Group (*see p35* **Booking outfits**). *Internet (shared terminal). Japanese & Western rooms. No-smoking rooms. Restaurant. TV.*

Sukeroku No Yado Sadachiyo

2-20-1 Asakusa, Taito-ku (3842 6431/fax 3842 6433/www.sadachiyo.co.jp). Asakusa station (Ginza line), exits 1, 6; (Asakusa line), exit A4 or Tawaramachi station (Ginza line), exit 3. **Rooms** 20. **Rates** ¥15,000 single; ¥19,000-¥28,000 double; ¥28,500-¥42,000 triple. **Credit** MC, V. **Map** p93.

This smart, modern *ryokan* is wonderfully situated five minutes' walk from Asakusa's temple. From the outside the building resembles a cross between a European chalet and a Japanese castle, but inside it's pure Japanese, with receptionists shuffling around the desk area dressed in kimono. Staff are obliging, but speak only minimal English. All rooms are Japanese-style and come in a variety of sizes, the smallest being just five mats. The communal Japanese baths should help make a stay here a memorable and incredibly relaxing experience. *Internet (shared terminal). Japanese rooms only. Room service (7.30am-10pm). TV.*

Budget

Sakura Ryokan

2-6-2 Iriya, Taito-ku (3876 8118/fax 3873 9456/ www.sakura-ryokan.com). Iriya station (Hibiya line), exit 1. **Rooms** 18. **Rates** ¥5,500-¥6,600 single; ¥10,000-¥11,000 double/twin. *Japanese* ¥5,500-¥6,600 single; ¥10,000-¥11,000 double; ¥13,200-¥13,800 triple. **Credit** AmEx, DC, JCB, MC, V.
Ten minutes' walk north from Asakusa's temple complex, in the traditional downtown area of Iriya, the Sakura is a friendly, traditional, family-run *ryokan*. Of the Japanese-style rooms, only two have their own bathrooms, while seven of the Western-style rooms have baths. There's also a communal bath on each floor. *Internet (shared terminal). Japanese & Western rooms. Parking (¥1,000/night). TV.*

Ueno & around

Expensive

Sofitel Tokyo

2-1-48 Ikenohata, Taito-ku (5685 7111/ fax 5685 6171/www.sofiteltokyo.com). Yushima station (Chiyoda line), exit 1. **Rooms** 83. **Rates** ¥30,000-¥34,000 single; ¥35,000 double; ¥41,000 twin; ¥58,000-¥105,000 suite. **Credit** AmEx, DC, JCB, MC, V. **Map** p103.
The Sofitel is, you might say, distinctive. Shaped like an enormous white Christmas tree, it towers over neighbouring Ueno Park. Inside, guest rooms are bigger than average, and the hotel's brilliant white colouring makes it lighter than most. *Bar. Business centre. Disabled-adapted room. Gym. Internet (high-speed). No-smoking rooms. Parking (¥1,500/day). Restaurant. Room service (24hr). Spa. TV (cable/satellite).*

Moderate

Homeikan Honkan/ Daimachibekkan

5-10-5 Hongo, Bunkyo-ku (Honkan 3811 1181/ Daimachibekkan 3811 1186/fax 3811 1764/ www1.odn.ne.jp/homeikan). Kasuga station (Mita line), exits A5, A6 or Hongo-Sanchome station (Oedo line), exit 2; (Marunouchi line), Hongo-Nichome exit. **Rooms** Honkan 24; Daimachibekkan 30; Morikawabekkan 33. **Rates** ¥6,500-¥7,500 single; ¥11,000-¥13,000 double; ¥13,500-¥16,500 triple; special long-stay rate available. **Credit** AmEx, DC, JCB, MC, V.

This wonderful old *ryokan* in the sleepy streets of Hongo looks just like a Japanese inn ought to: wooden, glass-fronted and with an ornamental garden at the front. And its owners plan to keep it that way following the *ryokan's* designation as an important cultural property by the Ministry of Education. Be sure to speak to Homeikan's cordial, English-speaking manager Koike Kunio when making a reservation – he can help you choose a room and, if need be, direct you away from the rowdy Japanese students who often lodge here. The inn is divided into two buildings, which face each other, with another branch a five-minute walk away. The only drawback is its location, around 20 minutes' walk from the nearest real action around Ueno or Ochanomizu stations.
Internet (shared terminal). Parking (free). Room service (7am-10pm). TV.
Other locations: Morikawabekkan 6-23-5 Hongo, Bunkyo-ku (3811 8171/fax 3811 1764).

Ueno First City Hotel

1-14-8 Ueno, Taito-ku (3831 8215/fax 3837 8469/ www.uenocity-hotel.com). Yushima station (Chiyoda line), exit 6. **Rooms** 77. **Rates** ¥8,000-¥8,500 single; ¥11,000-¥16,000 double/twin. *Japanese* (1-6 people) ¥8,400-¥24,000. **Credit** AmEx, DC, JCB, MC, V. **Map** p103.
A cut above the normal business hotel, this place offers comfortable Western- and Japanese-style accommodation in a modern, red-brick block not far from Ueno Park and its myriad attractions.
Bar. Internet (shared terminal). Japanese & Western rooms. No-smoking rooms. Restaurant. TV (satellite).

Budget

Hotel Edoya

3-20-3 Yushima, Bunkyo-ku (3833 8751/ fax 3833 8759/www.hoteledoya.com). Yushima station (Chiyoda line), exit 5. **Rooms** 49. **Rates** ¥4,960-¥7,850 single. *Japanese* ¥6,930-¥8,950 single; ¥7,960-¥12,930 double/twin; ¥11,550-¥17,670 triple/quadruple. **Credit** AmEx, DC, JCB, MC, V. **Map** p103.
This mainly Japanese-style *ryokan*, not far from Ueno Park, offers a good standard of accommodation at reasonable prices. There's a small Japanese tearoom and garden on the first floor, and the roof has an open-air hot bath for both men and women.
Japanese & Western rooms. Parking (free). Restaurant. TV.

Ryokan Katsutaro

4-16-8 Ikenohata, Taito-ku (3821 9808/ fax 3821 4789/www.katsutaro.com). Nezu station (Chiyoda line), exit 2. **Rooms** 7. **Rates** ¥5,200

single (no bath); ¥8,400-¥16,000 2-4 people (no bath); ¥9,600-¥17,200 2-4 people (with bath). **Credit** AmEx, MC, V. **Map** p103.
In a backstreet on the northern side of Ueno Park, Katsutaro is a small, friendly *ryokan* with good-sized rooms and the atmosphere of a real family home (which it is). Rooms can be occupied by up to four people, at an extra charge of roughly ¥4,000 per person. The owner speaks a little English, but have a phrasebook handy if you want the conversation to progress. Just a short walk away is the Annex (¥6,000 single, ¥10,000-¥12,000 double), which is more modern and has more facilities.
Internet (high-speed/shared terminal). Japanese rooms only. Parking (free). TV.
Other locations: **Annex** 3-8-4 Yanaka, Taito-ku (3828 2500/fax 3821 5400).

Ueno Tsukuba Hotel

2-7-8 Moto-Asakusa, Taito-ku (3834 2556/ fax 3839 1785/www.hotelink.co.jp). Inaricho station (Ginza line), exit 2. **Rooms** 111. **Rates** ¥5,000-¥5,500 single; ¥8,000 twin; ¥7,000 semi-double; ¥12,000 triple. *Japanese* ¥4,725 single; ¥4,200 per person 2-5 people. **No credit cards**. **Map** p103.
A basic business hotel in Ueno, the Tsukuba is clean and good value for money. Rooms are tiny, so opt for a Japanese-style room, where the futon is cleared away in the morning. Western-style rooms have baths, but if you stay in a Japanese room you'll be expected to bathe Japanese-style in the communal bath on the ground floor. The hotel is two minutes' walk from Inaricho station on the Ginza line.
Internet (high-speed/wireless). Japanese & Western rooms. Parking (¥2,100/night). TV.
Other locations: Iriya Station Hotel 1-25-1 Iriya, Taito-ku (3872 7111/fax 3872 7113).

Yanaka

Budget

Ryokan Sawanoya

2-3-11 Yanaka, Taito-ku (3822 2251/fax 3822 2252/www.tctv.ne.jp/members/sawanoya). Nezu station (Chiyoda line), exit 1. **Rooms** 12. **Rates** ¥4,700-¥5,000 single (no bath); ¥9,240 double (no bath); ¥9,870 double (with bath); ¥12,600 triple (no bath); ¥14,175 triple (with bath). **Credit** AmEx, MC, V. **Map** p103.
One of the few *ryokan* to cater almost exclusively for foreign visitors, Sawanoya has a small library of English-language guidebooks and provides its own map of the old-style Yanaka area. Rooms are small but comfortable, and there are signs in English reminding you how to behave and how to use the bath. More expensive rooms have their own bath; cheaper ones have access to the communal bath and shower. There's also a small coffee lounge. The couple who own the place will do everything possible to make your stay enjoyable.
Internet (high-speed/shared terminal). Japanese rooms only. TV.

Roppongi & Akasaka

Deluxe

Akasaka Prince Hotel

1-2 Kioi-cho, Chiyoda-ku (3234 1111/fax 3262 5163/ www.princehotelsjapan.com/akasakaprincehotel). Akasaka-Mitsuke station (Ginza, Marunouchi lines), exit D or Nagatacho station (Hanzomon, Nanboku, Yurakucho lines), exits 7, 9A, 9B. **Rooms** 761. **Rates** ¥28,900-¥42,800 single; ¥38,200-¥48,600 twin; ¥42,800-¥52,000 double; ¥42,800-¥150,200 suite/Japanese.* **Credit** AmEx, DC, JCB, MC, V.

Situated to the west of the Imperial Palace complex and designed by award-winning architect Tange Kenzo, the 40-storey Akasaka Prince is part of a complex that includes a convention centre, European-style guesthouse, banqueting building and numerous restaurants. Inside the main tower it's all glittering marble and bright lights. The building's clean lines extend to the furnishings in the rooms, which are elegantly simple.

Bars (3). Business centre. Concierge. Disabled-adapted room. Gym. Japanese & Western rooms. No-smoking rooms. Parking (free). Pool (outdoor). Restaurants (10). Room service (24hr). TV (cable/satellite/DVD rental).

Fancy a futon?

Homeikan Honkan. *See p43.*

If you can bear to forgo a few home comforts, such as a bed and feather pillow, then staying in a *ryokan* (traditional Japanese inn) is a great choice, particularly since they tend to be cheaper than Western-style hotels. *Ryokan* also make excellent lodgings for groups of more than two: you can have as many futon as you can fit on the tatami (straw mat) floor, for an extra charge that is significantly less than the price of another room.

There are a few matters of *ryokan* etiquette. First, remove your shoes when entering. Staff will show you to your room, and introduce you to the waiting flask of hot water and green tea. Decor will include a *shoji* (sliding paper screen) and a *tokonoma* (alcove), which is for decoration not for storing luggage. Inside the cupboard you will find a *yukata* (dressing gown) and *tanzen* (bed jacket), which can be worn inside the

inn and double as pyjamas. When putting on a *yukata*, put the left side over the right.

By day the futons are folded away in a cupboard, providing much more living space than a room with fixed beds. Staff will make up the futons at around 8pm. They'll be back the following morning at about 8am with breakfast. More expensive *ryokan* usually have private bathrooms, but at the cheaper end of the scale you will be expected to bathe Japanese-style in a communal bath. For tips on bathing etiquette, *see p114* **Getting into hot water**.

Most *ryokan* are family-run businesses, so many impose a curfew of 11pm. If you're going to be out later, tell your hosts. If a curfew doesn't suit you, check with the individual *ryokan* in advance. Many *ryokan* are in the older parts of town, such as Asakusa and Yanaka; we've listed nine of the best in this chapter.

ANA Hotel Tokyo

*1-12-33 Akasaka, Minato-ku (3505 1111/
fax 3505 1155/www.anahoteltokyo.jp/e). Tameike-
Sanno station (Ginza, Nanboku lines), exit 13.*
Rooms 901. **Rates** ¥31,185-¥34,650 single;
¥40,425-¥51,975 twin; ¥40,425-¥75,075 double;
¥48,510-¥51,975 triple; ¥80,850-¥323,400 suite.
Credit AmEx, DC, JCB, MC, V. **Map** p109.

This 29-storey hotel, owned by All Nippon Airways,
is leading the renovation charge among Tokyo's
Japanese-owned hotels. Its airy lobby has been
redone in gleaming marble and cherry, with the
modern space broken up by cascading waterfalls
and artworks. Spacious, well-equipped rooms are
being renovated in stages, with the higher floors fin-
ishing first and all work due for completion by 2006.
The hotel provides stunning views on a clear day –
you can see Mt Fuji from the open-air rooftop pool.
*Bars (3). Business centre. Concierge. Disabled-
adapted room. Gym. Internet (high-speed). No-
smoking rooms. Parking (¥1,000/night). Pool
(outdoor). Restaurants (8). Room service (6am-2am).
Spa. TV (satellite/pay movies).*

Capitol Tokyu Hotel

*2-10-3 Nagatacho, Chiyoda-ku (3581 4511/
fax 3581 5822/www.capitoltokyu.com). Tameike-
Sanno station (Ginza, Nanboku lines), exit 5 or
Kokkai-Gijidomae station (Chiyoda, Marunouchi
lines), exit 5.* **Rooms** 455. **Rates** ¥30,030-¥33,495
semi-double; ¥38,115-¥69,300 double/twin; ¥115,500-
¥438,900 suite. **Credit** AmEx, DC, JCB, MC, V.

For its first 20 years, until 1983, this was the Tokyo
Hilton. It hosted the Beatles in 1966, while more
recent guests have included Michael Jackson. The
hotel has capitalised on its celebrity clientele for
decades, but recent years have seen the interior finally catch up with the reputation. The lobby and
restaurant floors have been revamped in wood and
marble, while all Japanese-accented guest rooms
were renovated by 2003. The location is close
enough to the centre to be interesting, but isolated
enough, overlooking the Hie Shrine, to be peaceful.
*Bar. Business centre. Concierge. Disabled-adapted
rooms. Gym. Internet (high-speed). No-smoking
rooms. Parking (free). Pool (outdoor). Restaurants
(6). Room service (24hr). TV (cable/pay movies).*

Grand Hyatt Tokyo

*6-10-3 Roppongi, Minato-ku (4333 1234/fax 4333
8123/www.tokyo.grand.hyatt.com). Roppongi station
(Hibiya line), exit 1C; (Oedo line), exit 3.* **Rooms** 390.
Rates ¥43,000-¥58,000 single/double; ¥80,000-
¥500,000 suite. **Credit** AmEx, DC, MC, V. **Map** p109.

Until 2003 the Park Hyatt Tokyo reigned supreme
as Tokyo's icon of luxurious living. Then the Grand
Hyatt Tokyo opened up in a corner of Roppongi
Hills, and the celebs and jet set faced a dilemma. The
newcomer can't compete with the Park Hyatt's
views, but it edges its rival for stylish, modern
rooms and amenities that include two flat-screen
TVs. High-rollers can enjoy a presidential suite that
occupies the entire 21st floor and boasts its own Zen
garden and outdoor heated pool.

Marunouchi Hotel: smart choice. *See p37.*

*Bars (3). Business centre. Concierge. Gym. Internet
(high-speed). No-smoking rooms. Parking (¥2,000/
night). Pool (indoor). Restaurants (7). Room service
(24hr). Spa. TV (cable/satellite/DVD/CD player).*

Hotel New Otani Tokyo

*4-1 Kioi-cho, Chiyoda-ku (3265 1111/
fax 3221 2619/www1.newotani.co.jp/en/tokyo).
Akasaka-Mitsuke station (Ginza, Marunouchi lines),
exit D or Nagatacho station (Hanzomon, Nanboku,
Yurakucho lines), exit 7.* **Rooms** 1,600. **Rates**
¥29,000-¥52,000 single; ¥34,000-¥57,000 double;
¥80,000-¥850,000 suite. *Japanese* ¥55,000-¥74,000.
Credit AmEx, DC, JCB, MC, V.

The New Otani sprawls like a mini metropolis over
a vast area ten minutes' walk west of the Imperial
Palace. From the outside the building bears the unattractive hallmarks of its 1969 construction, but
inside the dim lighting and spacious foyers produce
the feeling of a luxury cruise ship. To the rear of the
hotel is a beautifully laid out and tended Japanese
garden. Within the garden stand several of the
hotel's numerous restaurants, which include the
only branch of the legendary Parisian eaterie La
Tour D'Argent. Capacity was increased in 1979 by
the addition of a 40-storey tower block.
*Bars (4). Business centre. Concierge. Disabled-
adapted rooms. Gym. Internet (high-speed). Japanese
& Western rooms. No-smoking rooms. Parking (free).
Pools (indoor/outdoor). Restaurants (26). Room
service (6am-1am). Spa. TV (cable/satellite/pay movies).*

Hotel Okura Tokyo

*2-10-4 Toranomon, Minato-ku (3582 0111/
fax 3582 3707/www.okura.com/tokyo). Roppongi-
Itchome station (Nanboku line), exit 3 or Tameike-
Sanno station (Ginza, Nanboku lines), exit 13.*
Rooms 858. **Rates** ¥30,450 single; ¥31,125-
¥126,000 double; ¥89,250-¥525,000 suite.
Credit AmEx, DC, JCB, MC, V. **Map** p109.

The Okura, next door to the US Embassy, doesn't appear to have changed much since its cameo appearance alongside James Bond in 1967's *You Only Live Twice*. The huge wooden lobby's gold and beige decor evokes that era's understated hipness, while the guest rooms offer an antiquated fusion of European and Japanese styles. But the Okura is taking steps to modernise itself, beginning with two 'Relaxation Floors' that feature jet baths, saunas and massage services in plush new rooms.
Bars (3). Business centre. Concierge. Disabled-adapted rooms. Gym. Internet (high-speed). No-smoking rooms. Parking (free). Pools (indoor/outdoor). Restaurants (9). Room service (24hr). Spa. TV (satellite/pay movies).

Tokyo Prince Hotel Park Tower

3-3-1 Shibakoen, Minato-ku (3432 1111/ fax 3434 5551/www.princehotels.co.jp/parktower-e). Akabanebashi station (Oedo line), Akabanebashi exit. **Rooms** 673. **Rates** ¥34,000-¥70,000 double/twin; ¥104,000-¥980,000 suite. *Japanese* ¥115,000-¥230,000 suite. **Credit** AmEx, DC, JCB, MC, V.
Occupying the corner of Shiba Park next to the Tokyo Tower, this 33-storey luxury hotel opened in spring 2005, offering everything from a jazz bar to a natural hot-spring spa. All rooms have internet service, jet baths and balconies with views across the park and as far as Mt Fuji, plus all the amenities you'd expect for the price. The Royal Suite even comes with a full-time butler.
Bars (2). Business centre. Concierge. Disabled-adapted rooms. Gym. Internet (high-speed). No-smoking rooms. Japanese & Western rooms. Parking (¥500/30mins). Pool (indoor). Restaurants (2). Room service (24hr). Spa. TV (cable/satellite/pay movies).

Expensive

Hotel Arca Torre Roppongi

6-1-23 Roppongi, Minato-ku (3404 5111/fax 3404 5115/www.arktower.co.jp). Roppongi station (Hibiya, Oedo lines), exit 3. **Rooms** 77. **Rates** ¥11,000-¥13,000 single; ¥14,000-¥17,000 double; ¥21,000 twin. **Credit** AmEx, DC, MC, V. **Map** p109.
Arca Torre is a smart, bright, high(ish)-rise business hotel sandwiched between the adults' playground of Roppongi and the Roppongi Hills complex. Rooms are small and functional; if you want a bigger room, go for a twin. The vibe is vaguely Italian, with lots of marble flourishes and a first-floor café. For nightlife lovers, the hotel's location is hard to beat, but light sleepers will bemoan the noisy streets.
Disabled-adapted room. No-smoking rooms. Restaurants (2). TV (satellite/pay movies).

Hotel Avanshell

2-14-4 Akasaka, Minato-ku (3568 3456/ fax 3568 3599/www.avanshell.com). Akasaka station (Chiyoda line), exit 2 or Tameike-Sanno station (Ginza, Nanboku lines), exit 10. **Rooms** 71. **Rates** ¥15,750-¥23,625 single; ¥19,950-¥31,500 double; ¥34,650 triple; ¥25,988-¥40,952 suite. **Credit** AmEx, DC, JCB, MC, V.

The Avanshell is the latest incarnation of a one-time serviced apartment building on a side street in Akasaka, a fact that's reflected in the mini kitchens and other apartment-style touches. Long-term stays are encouraged, with a range of electronics and other items available to rent. Rooms are designed around five themes, with names like Zen, Primo and Ultimo, and are pleasingly spacious, with large living and work areas in addition to separate bedrooms.
Internet (high-speed). Japanese & Western rooms. No-smoking floors. Parking (¥1,575/night). Restaurant. Room service (5.30-10pm). TV (cable/satellite).

Roppongi Prince Hotel

3-2-7 Roppongi, Minato-ku (3587 1111/fax 3587 0770/www.princehotelsjapan.com/roppongiprincehote l). Roppongi-Itchome station (Nanboku line), exit 1. **Rooms** 216. **Rates** ¥21,367 single; ¥24,832-¥28,297 twin; ¥26,565-¥28,297 double; ¥46,200-¥60,060 suite. **Credit** AmEx, DC, JCB, MC, V. **Map** p109.
The best way to view the Roppongi Prince Hotel is to stand on the roof and look down. The hotel was designed by architect Kurokawa Kisho around a perspex-sided, open-air pool heated to 30°C all year round. It's handily located in a quiet backstreet five minutes from the nightlife of Roppongi. The (small-ish) rooms are up for renovation at the end of 2005.
Bar. Internet (high-speed). No-smoking rooms. Parking (¥2,000/night). Pool (outdoor). Restaurants (4). Room service (11am-11pm). TV (cable/pay movies).

Moderate

Hotel Ibis

7-14-4 Roppongi, Minato-ku (3403 4411/fax 3479 0609/www.ibis-hotel.com). Roppongi station (Hibiya, Oedo lines), exit 4A. **Rooms** 182. **Rates** ¥13,382-¥15,461 single; ¥16,285-¥26,765 double; ¥22,145-¥26,675 twin; ¥27,720 triple; ¥41,980 suite. **Credit** AmEx, DC, JCB, MC. **Map** p109.
It seems hard to believe, given the recent burst of building activity in the area, but just three years ago, this was the closest hotel to the centre of Roppongi. Now, with all the new competition, Hotel Ibis is looking a little worn, and customers may well be enticed elsewhere. That said, it's always clean, functional and good value. And perhaps no other can claim to embody Roppongi more effectively, with a gentle-men's club off the front desk, a karaoke lounge downstairs, plus Italian and Vietnamese restaurants thrown into the mix.
Bar. Disabled-adapted rooms. Internet (shared terminal). No-smoking rooms. Parking (¥2,100/night). Restaurants (3). TV (cable/satellite).

Budget

Asia Center of Japan

8-10-32 Akasaka, Minato-ku (3402 6111/ fax 3402 0738/www.asiacenter.or.jp). Nogizaka station (Chiyoda line), exit 3. **Rooms** 173. **Rates**

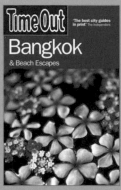

¥8,610 single; ¥10,290 semi-double; ¥12,390-¥14,490 double; ¥16,590 twin; ¥45,150 suite. **Credit** AmEx, JCB, MC, V.

Founded by the Ministry of Foreign Affairs in the 1950s as a cheap place for visiting students to stay, this has long since outgrown its origins and offers comfortable, no-frills accommodation to all visitors on a budget. A new building was added in 2003, offering a greater variety of Western-style rooms with clean if unexciting furnishings. The in-house dining hall offers a gathering place and breakfast buffet for a reasonable ¥945. Very convenient for the Aoyama area.

Disabled-adapted rooms. Internet (high-speed). No-smoking floor. Parking (¥1,500/night). Restaurant. TV (pay movies).

Odaiba

Deluxe

Le Meridien Grand Pacific Tokyo

2-6-1 Daiba, Minato-ku (5500 6711/fax 5500 4507/www.grandpacific.lemeridien.com). Daiba station (Yurikamome line). **Rooms** 884. **Rates** ¥26,000-¥37,000 single; ¥31,000-¥42,000 double/twin; ¥39,000-¥45,345 triple; ¥80,000-¥130,000 suite. **Credit** AmEx, DC, JCB, MC, V. **Map** p113.

Luxury hotels don't come much more luxurious than this. Le Meridien opened in 1998 on the island area of Odaiba and has spectacular views over Rainbow Bridge and the Tokyo skyline. The only real drawback is its location: Odaiba is great for a day out, but as a base for touring Tokyo it's inconvenient. Perhaps appreciating the lack of any real local character, the hotel supplies some of its own through a third-floor art gallery and, more bizarrely, a museum of music boxes one floor down. Even if you don't stay here, it's worth visiting the Sky Lounge on the 30th floor for one of Tokyo's best views.

Bars (3). Business centre. Concierge. Disabled-adapted rooms. Gym. No-smoking rooms. Parking (¥1,000/night). Pools (indoor/outdoor). Restaurants (7). Room service (6am-1am). Spa. TV (cable/satellite).

Ikebukuro

Budget

Kimi Ryokan

2-36-8 Ikebukuro, Toshima-ku (3971 3766/ www.kimi-ryokan.jp). Ikebukuro station (Yamanote, Marunouchi, Yurakucho lines), exits west, C6. **Rooms** 38. **Rates** ¥4,500 single; ¥6,500-¥7,500 double. **No credit cards. Map** p119.

A *ryokan* that caters almost exclusively to foreign visitors, Kimi offers simple, small, Japanese-style rooms. Bathing and toilet facilities are communal but very clean; there's even a Japanese bath for use at set times. Downstairs in the communal lounge,

backpackers and travellers exchange gossip. Kimi also runs an information and accommodation service for foreigners apartment-hunting in Tokyo (3986 1604), and a telephone answering service for businesspeople (3986 1895). Booking is advised. *Japanese rooms only. TV room (cable/satellite).*

Shinagawa

Deluxe

The Strings Hotel Tokyo

Shinagawa East One Tower 26F-32F, 2-16-1 Konan, Minato-ku (4562 1111/fax 4562 1112/ www.stringshotel.com). Shinagawa station (Yamanote line), Konan exit. **Rooms** 206. **Rates** ¥37,000-¥56,000 single; ¥45,000-¥62,000 double; ¥140,000-¥200,000 suite. **Credit** AmEx, DC, JCB, MC, V.

Opened in 2003, ANA's Strings Hotel brings a new level of class and service to the revitalised Shinagawa district. Its rooms occupy the top floors of a gleaming new skyscraper and are decked out in soothing earth tones. The 59 higher-end Club Rooms offer sparkling views over Tokyo Bay, as well as extra amenities including one complimentary meal per day. The hotel's convenient location just off the JR Tokaido *shinkansen* tracks also makes it a great base for travelling between cities.

Bar. Business centre. Concierge. Disabled-adapted rooms. Gym. Internet. No-smoking rooms. Parking (¥1,500/night). Restaurants (2). Room service (24hr). TV (cable/satellite/pay movies).

Expensive

Le Meridien Hotel Pacific Tokyo

3-13-3 Takanawa, Minato-ku (3445 6711/ fax 3445 5137/www.pacific-tokyo.com). Shinagawa station (Yamanote line), Takanawa exit. **Rooms** 954. **Rates** ¥25,610 single; ¥33,895-¥38,550 double/twin; ¥58,150-¥150,900 suite. **Credit** AmEx, DC, JCB, MC, V.

This 1971 monolith benefits from an extensive, pleasant garden that gives it a sense of space that many Tokyo hotels lack. It might look its age from the outside and the decor is a mix of bland and garish, but there's no faulting the facilities. Rooms are of a good size and kept bang up to date thanks to what appears to be a constant process of renovation and redecoration. The Shinagawa area hasn't got much to recommend it, though it's a short hop into the centre via the Yamanote line and the bullet train line makes it a popular choice for business travellers. This is another of the hotels frequently used by travel companies for package tours and stopovers.

Bars (3). Business centre. Concierge. Disabled-adapted rooms. Internet (high-speed). No-smoking rooms. Parking (free). Pool (outdoor). Restaurants (6). Room service (6am-midnight). Spa. TV (cable/satellite).

Sukeroku No Yado Sadachiyo: Japanese living in the heart of Asakusa. *See p43.*

Takanawa Prince Hotel, New Takanawa Prince Hotel & Sakuro Tower

3-13-1 Takanawa, Minato-ku (3442 1111/ fax 3444 1234/www.princehotels.co.jp/english). Shinagawa station (Yamanote line), Takanawa exit then free shuttle bus. **Rooms** New Takanawa Prince 946; Takanawa Prince 414; Sakura Tower 309. **Rates** ¥20,000 single; ¥24,200 double/twin; ¥75,000 suite. **Credit** AmEx, DC, JCB, MC, V.

The Takanawa Prince, the New Takanawa Prince and the Sakura Tower – all part of the same chain – operate as separate hotels, with separate tariffs, but they are linked by glorious landscaped grounds and guests can use the facilities of all three. The oldest, the Takanawa Prince, recently remodelled its rooms with new wallpaper, carpeting and furniture, as well as air-con units and liquid-crystal TVs. It has also added a number of rooms specially for women. The New Takanawa Prince is gaudy from the outside, but impressive within, while the Sakura Tower, a pink monster of a building, offers the most up-to-date facilities and priciest accommodation. Services listed below are for all three hotels combined.

Bars (5). Business centre. Concierge. Disabled-adapted rooms. Gym. Internet (high-speed). Japanese & Western rooms. No-smoking rooms. Parking (free). Pools (2, outdoor). Restaurants (18). Room service (24hr). Spa. TV (cable).

Elsewhere

Deluxe

Four Seasons Hotel Tokyo at Chinzan-so

2-10-8 Sekiguchi, Bunkyo-ku (3943 2222/ fax 3943 2300/www.fourseasons.com/tokyo). Mejiro station (Yamanote line), then 61 bus or
Edogawabashi station (Yurakucho line), exit 1A. **Rooms** 283. **Rates** ¥43,000-¥50,000 single; ¥48,000-¥55,000 double; ¥68,000-¥500,000 suite. **Credit** AmEx, DC, JCB, V.

Inconveniently located in the wilds of northern Tokyo, this is a breathtakingly opulent and beautiful hotel popular with locals on weekend escapes and celebrities seeking privacy away from the bright lights of the city. Take a stroll around the Japanese garden – with its own firefly population as well as ancient statues from Nara and Kamakura – then enjoy the wide open spaces of the lobby area. Everything is immaculate, from the service to the decor of the rooms, a mixture of old Japanese and European styles.

Bars (2). Business centre. Concierge. Disabled-adapted rooms. Gym. No-smoking rooms. Internet (high-speed). Parking (free). Pool (indoor). Restaurants (4). Room service (24hr). Spa. TV (satellite).

InterContinental Tokyo Bay

1-16-2 Kaigan, Minato-ku (5404 2222/fax 5404 2111/www.interconti-tokyo.com). Takeshiba (Tokyo monorail) station or Hamamatsucho station (Yamanote line), south exit. **Rooms** 339. **Rates** ¥36,000-¥62,000 double; ¥100,000-¥300,000 suite. **Credit** AmEx, DC, JCB, MC, V.

The InterContinental opened in the mid 1990s in the hitherto little-explored area that fronts Tokyo's Sumida river. Amid the grim industrial surroundings, the luxurious hotel and the adjoining New Pier Takeshiba shopping and dining complex stand out like a diamond in a cowpat. If its location is the hotel's main shortcoming, then its prime selling point is the view, over the river and spectacular Rainbow Bridge to the island of Odaiba. All rooms, and their bathrooms, have a river prospect.

Bars (2). Business centre. Concierge. Internet (high-speed). No-smoking rooms. Parking (¥1,500/night). Restaurants (6). Room service (24hr). Spa. TV (cable/satellite/pay per view).

Expensive

Claska

1-3-18 Chuo-cho, Meguro-ku (3719 8121/fax 3719 8122/www.claska.com). Gakugei-Daigaku station (Tokyu Toyoko line) then 10mins walk. **Rooms** 9. **Rates** ¥10,500-¥12,600 single; ¥18,900-¥84,000 double. **Credit** AmEx, DC, JCB, MC, V.

Nine rooms occupying two floors: hotels don't get any more exclusive than the Claska. Add the funky designer vibe and you have one of the most sought-after spots in the city. Having opened in 2003 in a refurbished business hotel, the Claska prides itself on offering a new style of living. Each room is set up and styled differently, with the most expensive boasting a 41sq m (441sq ft) terrace. The rest of the building is taken up by a hip bar/restaurant, gallery, dog-grooming salon, bookshop, open-plan work-space and residential hotel. It's a little far from the action, but manages to draw its share of bright young things with nightly DJ sets in the lobby. *Bar. Internet (high-speed). Parking (free). Restaurant. Room service. TV (cable/satellite).*

Moderate

Hotel Bellegrande

2-19-1 Ryogoku, Sumida-ku (3631 8111/fax 3631 8112/www.hotel-bellegrande.co.jp). Ryogoku station (Oedo line), west exit. **Rooms** 150. **Rates** ¥9,450 single; ¥12,700-¥16,800 double; ¥13,750-¥42,400 twin; ¥84,800 suite. **Credit** AmEx, DC, JCB, V.

A modern, business-style hotel barely a wrestler's stride from the sumo stadium in Ryogoku – a quiet, traditional area that comes alive during the city's three annual sumo tournaments. The unglamorous location is reflected in the prices of the rooms, which are small but comfortable. There are ten designated ladies' rooms with a few added amenities. Booking is recommended during the sumo tournaments. *Bar. No-smoking rooms. Parking (¥1,500/night). Restaurants (5). TV.*

Budget

Hotel New Koyo

2-26-13 Nihonzutumi, Taito-ku (3873 0343/ fax 3873 1358/www.newkoyo.jp). Minowa station (Hibiya line), exit 3. **Rooms** 75. **Rates** ¥2,500-¥2,700 single; ¥4,800 double. **Credit** AmEx, MC, V.

Clean and friendly, with facilities that put more expensive places to shame (kitchens on each floor, laundry machines, a Japanese-style bath), the New Koyo may offer the cheapest overnight stay in Tokyo. Rooms are tiny, however, and the place is slightly out of the way, although central Tokyo is easily accessible from the nearby Hibiya line station. The owners also run a more traditional and upmarket Japanese-style inn, the Andon (www.andon.co.jp), in the same area. *Internet (shared terminal). Japanese & Western rooms. TV.*

Juyoh Hotel

2-15-3 Kiyokawa, Taito-ku (3875 5362/ fax 5603 5775/www.juyoh.co.jp). Minami-Senju station (Hibiya line), south exit. **Rooms** 76. **Rates** ¥3,200 single; ¥6,400 double. **No credit cards.**

Another cheap option in Taito-ku, the Juyoh caters almost exclusively for foreigners. The rooms are miniscule, and since only three of them are doubles, early booking is essential, via the well-designed website. The second floor is reserved for female guests. Bath and shower facilities are shared. Doors close at 1am and reopen at 5am. *Internet (wireless/shared terminals). No-smoking rooms. TV.*

Tokyo International Youth Hostel

Central Plaza 18F, 1-1 Kaguragashi, Shinjuku-ku (3235 1107/fax 3267 4000/www.tokyo-yh.jp). Iidabashi station (Sobu line), west exit; (Nanboku, Oedo, Tozai, Yurakucho lines), exit 2B. **Rooms** 33. **Rates** ¥3,500 per person; ¥2,000 children. **No credit cards.**

Shared rooms (men and women sleep separately) are the order of the day at this hostel, which occupies the 18th and 19th floors of a skyscraper above Iidabashi station. All rooms are spotless, and the entire place is no-smoking. Guests are not allowed into the building between 10am and 3pm. The excellent website is regularly updated with room availability information; weekends tend to be booked up ages in advance. Watch out for the 11pm curfew. *Disabled-adapted rooms. Japanese & Western rooms. No smoking.*

Other options

Minshuku

Expect to pay around ¥5,000 per night. You should book at least two days in advance.

Japan Minshuku Centre

Kotsu Kaikan Bldg B1F, 2-10-1 Yurakucho, Chiyoda-ku (3216 6556/fax 3216 6557/ www.koyado.net). Yurakucho station (Yamanote line), Ginza exit; (Yurakucho line), exit A8. **Open** 10am-8pm Mon-Sat.

Minshuku Association of Japan

302 Shinjuku Eiko Bldg, 7-17-14 Nishi-Shinjuku, Shinjuku-ku (3364 1855/www.minshukukyokai.com). Shinjuku station (Yamanote line), west exit; (Marunouchi line), exit D5; (Shinjuku, Oedo lines), exit 3. **Open** 10am-5pm Mon-Fri.

Capsule hotels

Capsule Hotel Azuma

3-15-1 Higashi-Ueno, Taito-ku (3831 4047/ fax 3831 7103/www2.famille.ne.jp/~uenoyado/ azuma.html). Ueno station (Yamanote line), Asakusa or Hirokoji exits; (Ginza, Hibiya lines), exit 1. **Capsules** 144. **Rates** ¥3,500. **No credit cards. Map** p103.

Central Land Shibuya

1-19-14 Dogenzaka, Shibuya-ku (3464 1777/
3464 7771/www.shibuyadogenzaka.com/capsule).
Shibuya station (Yamanote, Ginza, Hanzomon lines),
Hachiko exit. **Capsules** 140. **Rates** ¥3,700.
Credit MC, V. **Map** p79.

Shinjuku Kuyakusyo-Mae Capsule Hotel

1-2-5 Kabuki-cho, Shinjuku-ku (3232 1110/
www.toyo-bldg.ne.jp/hotel). Shinjuku station
(Yamanote line), east exit; (Marunouchi line),
exit B7; (Shinjuku, Oedo lines), exit 1. **Capsules**
460. **Rates** from ¥4,200. **No credit cards.**
Map p73.

Long-term accommodation

Finding long-term accommodation in Tokyo
can be a nightmare for foreigners. Many
Japanese landlords refuse to deal with non-
Japanese, so specialist companies have stepped
into the breach to let to foreigners, sometimes
by the week. If you do find something suitable,
it probably won't be cheap. You will be required
to pay a damage deposit (*shikikin*), usually
equivalent to between one and three months'
rent, a brokerage fee (*chukairyo*) to the agent,
usually another month's rent, and finally key
money (*reikin*), usually one or two months'
rent – a non-refundable way of saying thank
you to the landlord for having you. You then
have to find a month's rent in advance.

Understandably deterred by the cost of
finding a place of their own, many foreigners
fall back on so-called *gaijin* houses – apartment
buildings full of foreigners sharing bathrooms,
cooking facilities and, in some cases, rooms.
All the operations listed below are used to
dealing with foreigners and offer a full range
of accommodation.

Asahi Homes

3-2-19 Roppongi, Minato-ku (3583 7544/fax 3583
7587/www.asahihomes.co.jp). Roppongi-Itchome
station (Nanboku line), exit 1. **Credit** AmEx, DC,
MC, V.
Upmarket agency offering fully serviced apartments
in well-chosen locations, with a minimum stay of one
week. Weekly rent starts from ¥66,150 for a studio,
rising to ¥310,800 for a three-bedroom apartment,
including internet and weekly maid service.

Bamboo House

Office Bamboo Nippori 1F, 2-5-4 Nishi-Nippori,
Ararkawa-ku (3645 4028/fax 4400 3008/
www.bamboo-house.com). Mikawashima station
(Joban line). **Credit** AmEx, MC, V.
A chain of serviced apartments and guesthouses
scattered across the less fashionable parts of Tokyo
and Chiba. Rooms are 9-12sq m (32-43sq ft), with
shared facilities. Daily rates start from ¥3,500;
monthly rates from ¥58,000.

Cozy House

3-15-11 Ichikawa, Ichikawa City, Chiba-ken
(047 379 1539/www.cozyhouse.net). *Konodai station*
(Keisei line) then 10mins walk. **Rooms** 7. **Rates**
¥2,940-¥4,725 daily shared; ¥4,725 daily private;
¥30,450-¥52,500 monthly shared; ¥77,700-¥80,850
monthly private. **Credit** (deposit only) MC, V .
Cozy House has two locations, a cheaper one in more
central Kita-ku, and this main branch, slightly out
of the way in Chiba. Its aim is to bring foreigners in
Japan together, to which end the incredibly friendly
owner lays on demos of Japanese crafts and traditions. A 15-minute train ride from Tokyo station.
Other locations: 15-1 Sakae-cho, Kita-ku
(090 8176 0764).

Hoyo Tokyo

4-19-7 Kita-Shinjuku, Shinjuku (3362 0658/
fax 3362 9438/www.hoyotokyo.jp). *Okubo station*
(Chuo, Sobu lines), north exit. **Open** 9.30am-6.30pm
Mon-Fri. **No credit cards.**
An agency with 1,000 units, Hoyo offers studio apartments from ¥42,000 per week (plus a deposit of
¥50,000) or ¥135,000 per month. Family apartments
cost from ¥300,000 a month (¥100,000 deposit).

Oak House

4-30-3 Takashimadaira, Itabashi-ku (3780 1660/fax
5784 3370/www.oakhouse.jp). *Shin-Takashimadaira*
station (Mita line). **No credit cards.**
This guesthouse agency offers private rooms for
¥53,000 per week in this location, as well as dorm-
style accommodation, shared rooms and private
apartments around the city.

Sakura House

K1 Bldg 2F, 7-2-6 Nishi-Shinjuku, Shinjuku-ku
(5330 5250/fax 5330 5251/www.sakura-house.com).
Shinjuku station (Yamanote line), west exit;
(Marunouchi line), exit D5; (Shinjuku, Oedo lines),
exit 3. **Open** 8.50am-5.50pm Mon-Sat. **Credit** DC,
MC, V.
Owned by the people who operate the Sakura Hotel
(*see p38*), which is in itself a guarantee of quality,
this agency offers guesthouses and apartments in
83 locations around the city.

Tokyo Apartment

3-2-24 Roppongi, Minato-ku (5575 7575/fax 5575
7117/www.tokyoapt.com). *Roppongi-Itchome station*
(Nanboku line), exit 2. **Open** 9am-6pm Mon-Fri.
Credit DC, MC, V.
An agency that deals exclusively with foreigners,
and offers everything from one-night backpacker
deals to fully fledged, long-term apartment contracts. Apartments start at ¥100,000 per month.

Weekly Center

Central reservations 5950 1111/www.weeklycenter.
co.jp. **Rates** ¥25,000-¥60,000/wk. **No credit cards.**
This budget chain has a dozen locations dotted
around Tokyo, offering weekly stays for around the
same price as top hotels charge for one night.
Monthly rates are also available. The cheapest central branch is in Ochanomizu.

Sightseeing

Features

Maps

Introduction

Grab your camera and a train ticket, and start exploring.

Sightseeing

Tokyo lies at one end of the highly developed Pacific belt that runs west along the coast of Japan's main Honshu island to Osaka and holds around half the national population of 127 million. In a country where up to two-thirds of the land is mountainous, the greater Tokyo metropolis sprawls relentlessly over much of the Kanto plain, Japan's largest plain and a natural population magnet.

Determining exactly how many people live in the Tokyo area depends on how you define it. The UN Department of Economic and Social Affairs Population Division ranks Tokyo as the world's largest urban agglomeration by far, with a population in 2003 of 35 million – that's 27 per cent of Japan's entire population, all living on less than two per cent of the nation's land. At the heart of the city lie the 23 inner wards, or *ku* (see map on p56), covering 616 square kilometres (238 square miles) and currently home to 8.28 million people. After a decline in the 1990s, the population of the 23 *ku* is on the rise again, indicating a definite move back towards the bright lights of the city.

GETTING AROUND

Despite Tokyo's size, it's a remarkably easy city to get around – thanks to one of the most comprehensive and efficient train and subway systems in the world.

Probably the best way to orientate yourself is by Japan Railways' Yamanote train line, which circles the central areas of the city, linking important districts such as Shinjuku, Shibuya, Ikebukuro, Ueno, Tokyo and Shinagawa. The growth of these huge transport hubs, connected to subways and suburban train lines, means Japan's capital lacks the focus of a single central area but instead possesses a whole series of multi-functional sub-centres, each one boasting its own unique flavour.

The name of the Yamanote line recalls an older division between the smarter *yamanote* areas on the higher ground to the west and south of the city and the lower-lying *shitamachi* downtown districts. The comparison is far from exact, however, since the present-day loop runs through both old *yamanote* and old *shitamachi* districts, as well as through western areas that lay outside the official city limits until as late as 1932. Even so, the broad sweep of the magic Yamanote circle is generally taken to define the central part of the city.

Criss-crossing the middle of the loop and extending beyond its borders is a network of 12 subway lines, all colour-coded with numbered stations (Meiji-Jingumae station, for example, is C03 on the green Chiyoda line). English signage is good, so, despite the plethora of tunnels and passageways in stations and between different lines, it's easier than you might expect to make your way about. There's a subway map, in English, on pp318-9, and a map showing all the stations on the Yamanote line on p320.

Tokyo is also a great walking city; distances between neighbourhoods make using public transport a necessity, but exploring on foot, along main thoroughfares and down tiny local streets, is the best way to get a feel for the distinctive character of each area. The city is also very safe. Crime is virtually unknown, and it's not only possible but very enjoyable to wander through the streets of the centre at the dead of night. In fact, it's the only time you'll ever be alone.

SIGHTSEEING AREAS

We've divided the Sightseeing section by area. In a city with no street names (see p290 **Understanding addresses**), finding a particular shop or building can be tricky. To help, we've provided detailed street maps within each chapter (with sights of interest marked on); but it's also a good idea to arm yourself with a bilingual atlas. The map on p57 shows how these individual maps fit into the city as a whole.

The tour starts with the upmarket shopping district of **Ginza**, which adjoins **Maranouchi**, site of the Imperial Palace and the geographical heart of Tokyo. We then head west to the nightlife, shopping and government zone of **Shinjuku** – Tokyo's biggest sub-centre, anchored by a huge and confusing station complex – and the nearby youthful playground of **Shibuya**. Between the two lie **Harajuku**, home of the imperial Meiji Shrine, and neighbouring, more upmarket **Aoyama**. Also on the west side but further south are the two small, suburban neighbourhoods of **Ebisu** and **Daikanyama**.

We then move north-east to the historic *shitamachi* districts: **Asakusa**, which hugs the east bank of the Sumida river and was the capital's entertainment area back in the Edo era; **Ueno**, focused on museum-packed Ueno Park; and, adjoining it to the north, the tight-knit communities of low-rise **Yanaka**. From there it's a jump south to noisy, buzzy **Roppongi** with its self-contained mini-city of Roppongi Hills, then a journey across the waters of Tokyo Bay to the futuristic cityscape of **Odaiba** island. Finally comes the bustling northern sub-centre of **Ikebukuro**.

In the **Further Afield** chapter, we've also included suggestions for worthwhile destinations outside the Yamanote line loop, such as **Shimo-Kitazawa**, **Naka-Meguro** and stations along the **Chuo line**. Out here, on the city's suburban commuter railway lines, life is lived at a more relaxed pace, and locals are friendlier and eager to chat. For excursions well beyond the city limits, see **Trips Out of Town**, starting on p262.

MUSEUM TIPS

The general rules for visiting museums and galleries are as follows: most are closed on Monday, entrance fees are paid in cash, ID is required for discount admission, admission ends 30 minutes before the museum closes, lockers are free (with a refundable key deposit of ¥100), photography is forbidden, there is little disabled access. Many museums offer little or no explanation in English, and places that hold temporary exhibitions are often open only sporadically. Some museums close on national holidays, while others are open; if so, they will usually shut the following day. Nearly all museums close over the New Year's holiday, from around 28 December to 3 January.

Museum-hoppers should get a **Grutt Pass**, which offers free or reduced admission to numerous facilities (44 for the 2004 season). Costing ¥2,000, it's valid for two months from first use and is available from participating museums and tourist offices (see p297).

Sightseeing

Don't miss Sights

Get an overview

Tokyo has no shortage of observation decks: the **Tokyo Metropolitan Government Building No.1** (see p76) and Roppongi Hills' **Tokyo City View** (see p110) are two of the best.

Visit Harajuku on Sunday

Two worlds in one: tranquil **Meiji Shrine** and costumed kids that hang about by its entrance. See p87.

Catch some culture

Experience drama and tradition at Ginza's **Kabuki-za**. See p246.

Take in a temple

There's a temple or shrine on almost every corner, but **Asakusa Kannon Temple** is unmissable. See p97.

Follow the night

Shinjuku (see pp70-6), **Shibuya** (see pp77-82) and **Roppongi** (see pp107-11) are the city's after-dark playgrounds.

Go fishing

Get up early to visit bustling **Tsukiji** fish market then eat sushi for breakfast. See p63 **Something fishy**.

Go shopping

Everyone else does, so you might as well.

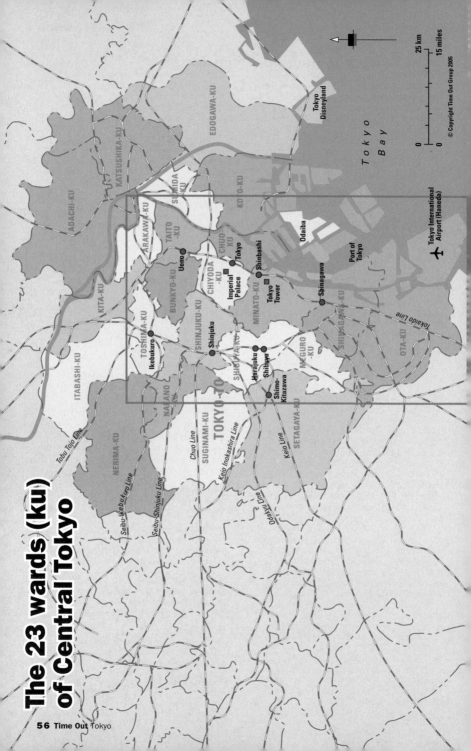

The 23 wards (ku) of Central Tokyo

Central Tokyo

ITABASHI-KU

TOSHIMA-KU

Sugamo

ARAKAWA-KU

Ikebukuro

See p119

Nippori

TAITO-KU

See p103

See p93

BUNKYO-KU

Ueno

Takadanobaba

Ueno Park

Asakusa

Sumida River

Yamanote Line

Chuo Line

NAKANO-KU

SHINJUKU-KU

Shin-Okubo

Akihabara

SUMIDA-KU

See p73

See p66

CHIYODA-KU

Kanda

Shinjuku

Shinjuku Gyoen

Yotsuya

Imperial Palace

KOTO-KU

Yoyogi

Tokyo

Yurakucho

See p85

Yoyogi Park

Harajuku

Shimbashi

CHUO-KU

SHIBUYA-KU

Tokyo Tower

See p60

Shibuya

Hamamatsucho

Shimo-Kitazawa

See p109

MINATO-KU

See p79

Daikanyama

Ebisu

Tamachi

Naka-Meguro

SETAGAYA-KU

Rainbow Bridge

MEGURO-KU

Meguro

Shinagawa

Gotanda

Yurikamome Line

Tokyu Toyoko Line

Osaki

See p112

SHINAGAWA-KU

Tokyo Bay

OTA-KU

Tokyo International Airport (Haneda)

Tokaido Line

N

0   3 km

0   1 mile

Ginza

Do as the locals do, and take a stroll around Tokyo's smartest shopping area.

Map p60

Japan's continuing economic woes have brought bargain shopping to Tokyo, caused real estate prices to dive and sent banks to the edge of bankruptcy. But it's business as usual in Ginza, Tokyo's smartest neighbourhood. Ladies saunter the wide streets dressed head to toe in luxury brands, shopping for more of the same. Politicians and businessmen on bottomless expense accounts quaff overpriced drinks in the company of kimono-clad bar staff. Less affluent types simply come to dream.

Crammed into Ginza's eight main *chome* are over 10,000 shops, many of them selling goods at Bubble-era prices. The area's reputation for exclusivity stretches right back to the 19th-century Meiji period, when Ginza became the first part of Tokyo to be rebuilt in red brick rather than wood. Red brick was thought to offer greater protection from natural disasters, a theory disproved in 1923, when the area was razed by the Great Kanto Earthquake. Unfortunately, not one single red brick from Ginza's first golden era survives today.

What does survive, though, is the Tokyo pastime of 'Ginbura', or Ginza strolling. For Tokyo, the area has unusually wide pavements, which lend themselves to window-shopping and aimless wandering. On weekends from noon, cars are banned from the main street, **Ginza Dori** (also called **Chuo Dori**), to create what is known as *hokousha tengoku* (pedestrian heaven), and cafés spill out on to the road, lending the area a European feel.

Tiny shops selling traditional items such as kimono, *wagashi* (Japanese sweets) and go-boards sit side by side with brand giants such as Hermès, Gucci and Louis Vuitton. Foreign retail chains choose to have their first Japanese outlets in prestigious Ginza before opening up elsewhere. The latest big names to be lured to the area include Apple Computer, Barneys New York and Chanel, whose building boasts top French chef Alain Ducasse's restaurant **Beige Tokyo** (5159 5500, www.beige-tokyo.com), on the tenth floor.

The reputation of the area for elegance and class is fiercely guarded by local shopkeepers. After the closure of the Sogo department store near Yurakucho station in 2001, they mounted strong resistance to the arrival of discount electronics superstore Bic Camera – which took

Ginza's **yon-chome crossing** includes...

over the Sogo building, giving the company its first presence in designer-label land.

While boutiques and restaurants with fearsome prices are the norm in Ginza, there are bargains to be had. As elsewhere in Tokyo, most restaurants offer special set-lunch deals, the difference here being that you have a chance to eat food for around ¥1,500 that might cost ten times as much in the evening. Most restaurants are off the main drag, many of them in basements, so take a walk around the backstreets and check out the prices, which are usually posted on boards outside. (If they're not, don't go in – unless you want to terrify your bank manager.) For fashion, **RagTag** (3-3-15 Ginza, 3535 4100, www.ragtag.jp/shop/ginza. html, open 11am-8pm daily) is a six-storey second-hand clothing shop that deals only in the biggest brands. Ginza's fickle fashionistas keep the store stocked with barely worn garments from the latest catwalk collections.

There are many ways to explore Ginza on foot, but setting off from Yurakucho station is a good one. The **Tokyo TIC** tourist office (see p297) is here too. Take the exit for Ginza and walk down a narrow street, then straight through the arcade running inside the Mullion complex – home to the Hankyu and Seibu department stores and several cinemas. You come out at the multi-directional zebra crossings of Sukiyabashi (Sukiya Bridge). Confusingly, there is no bridge. There used to be one going from the present-day Sukiyabashi Hankyu department store towards Hibiya, across the old outer moat of Edo Castle (now the Imperial Palace), but both bridge and waterway were casualties of 1960s road construction. Today a small monument marks the spot where the bridge stood.

Standing with Sukiyabashi Hankyu department store on your right, you will see a Sony sign on the other side of the crossing. The electronic giant's eight-storey showcase, the **Sony Building** (see p179), will appeal to technology and gaming fans alike. All the latest Sony models are on display, with staff eager to talk you through them. The sixth floor is a free PlayStation arcade where you can try the latest games; it's packed with kids at weekends, so visit during the week. The basement holds two floors of Sony Plaza, a chain that stocks import snacks, cosmetics and other colourful goodies. The narrow tower next door, made of semi-translucent gold glass bricks that seem to glow from within at night, is the **Hermès** flagship, designed by Renzo Piano.

Walk down Sotobori Dori (Outer Moat Avenue, once part of Edo Castle's waterway defences), towards Ginza 8-chome and Shinbashi. Ginza streets are named and laid out in a grid, so it's difficult to get lost. Stop off at some of the small art galleries, most of which are free to enter. When you reach the boundary of Ginza at Gomon Dori, turn left towards Ginza Dori and the narrower streets of Sony Dori, Namiki Dori, Nishi Gobangai Dori and Suzuran Dori. Whichever route you take back to **Harumi Dori** (the other major thoroughfare), the atmospheric streets between Ginza Dori and Sotobori Dori are the best pottering area in Ginza. Zigzag towards the main crossroads in the district: the intersection of Ginza Dori and Harumi Dori – known as yon-chome crossing because it's in on the edge of the Ginza-four sub-district (yon means four).

When you reach the crossing, you will see **Le Café Doutor Ginza** (see p167) at the base of the cylindrical **San-ai Building**. The large green frog on top of the police box is to provide good luck for drivers. On the other side of Harumi Dori is **Wako** (see p175), a venerable watch and jewellery department store famous for its dazzling window displays and clocktower. In Ozu's classic film Tokyo Story

(1953), two women are chauffeur-driven past Wako, the store representing the high-class, modern face of Tokyo. 'Outside Wako at yon-chome crossing' is a common meeting spot.

Facing Wako, on the other side of Ginza Dori, is upscale department store **Mitsukoshi** (see p173; the bronze lion at its entrance is another popular meeting point). And on the fourth corner is yet another rendezvous point, the **Nissan Gallery**, where the latest models are exhibited on the ground floor. Famous paper specialist **Kyukyodo** (see p189) is also here, next door to the San-ai Building.

From the yon-chome crossing, with your back to Wako, heading left along Ginza Dori will take you past more high-class stores – spectacular at night when the neon signs are switched on – and, eventually, into Kyobashi where you'll find the **Metropolitan Police Museum**, the **National Film Centre** and one of Tokyo's best Indian restaurants, **Dhaba India** (see p137).

Heading straight down Harumi Dori, meanwhile, will take you to the traditional-style **Kabuki-za** theatre (see p246), home of kabuki. Reserved seats are pricey, but a single act of the day-long programme can be enjoyed for around ¥1,000. You'll have to queue for tickets, and opera glasses are essential, but it's a good way to get a taste of Japan's traditional performing arts. Behind Kabuki-za is the **World Magazine Gallery** (3-13-10 Ginza, 3545 7227, open 11am-7pm Mon-Fri), a reference-only library where you can browse 800 titles for free.

Continue walking down Harumi Dori, turn right on to Shinohashi Dori, and you'll

...the **San-ai Building**.

Ginga

KYOBASHI

CHUO-KU

TSUKIJI

National Film Centre

Kyobashi Station

CHUO-DORI

TOKYO EXPRESSWAY

MARONNIER DORI

MATSUYA DORI

Tsukiji Station

HARUMI DORI

World Magazine Gallery

Kabuki-za

SHOWA DORI

Tiffany

Ginza-Itchome Station

Meidi-ya

Matsuya

Printemps Ginza

Mitsukoshi

Nissan Gallery

Higashi-Ginza Station

Tokyo TIC

Tokyo Kotsu Kaikan Bldg

Seibu

Wako

GINZA

HARUMI DORI

San-ai Building

Matsuzakaya

Sony Building

Ginza Station

Tokyo International Forum

Imperial Theatre

Idemitsu Museum of Art

Yurakucho Station

Yurakucho Hankyu

Sukiyabashi Hankyu

GINZA DORI / CHUO DORI

Yamaha Hall

NAMIKI DORI

Shiseido

Hakuhinkan

SOTOBORI DORI

Hibiya Station

Hibiya Chanter

Tokyo Takarazuka Theatre

Nissei Theatre

YURAKUCHO

CHIYODA-KU

Imperial Hotel

Mizuho Bank

Yamanote Line

Shinbashi Station

MARUNOUCHI-NAKA DORI

Moat

Hibiya Park

HIBIYA DORI

Kasumigaseki Station

Hibiya Public Hall

Uchisaiwaicho Station

Hibiya Hospital

UCHISAIWAICHO

SHINBASHI

To Tsukiji Fish Market

ATAGO DORI

150 m

150 yds

© Copyright Time Out Group 2005

eventually reach **Tsukiji Fish Market**, one of the world's largest wholesale markets and one of the city's unmissable sights (*see 63* **Something fishy**).

On the northern side of the Yamanote line tracks, opposite the famous **Imperial Hotel** (*see p36*), is the **Takarazuka** theatre (*see p249*), home to an all-female musical revue. *Takarazuka* is imbued with less tradition and history than *kabuki*, but it's an equally unique experience. Next door is a large park, **Hibiya Koen**. Once the parade ground for the Japanese army, it was turned into the country's first Western-style park in 1903, complete with rose gardens, bandstand and open-air theatre. It's a great spot for an impromptu picnic or romantic late-night stroll. At the northern end of the park is a moat, which surrounds the expansive grounds of the **Imperial Palace** (*see p64*).

Also in the vicinity are the **Sake Plaza**, for fans of Japan's national brew, and the **Tokyo Disneyland Ticket Centre** (Hibiya Mitsui Bldg, 1-1-2 Yurakucho, Chiyoda-ku, 3595 1777, open 10am-7pm daily). The theme park is out of town, but this is the best place to get tickets; staff speak English.

SHINBASHI AND SHIODOME

Away to the southern limits of Ginza, towards the area around Shinbashi station, you'll see a collection of skyscrapers gleaming in the distance. This complex, known as **Shiodome**, opened in mid 2003 on the site of a former Japan Railways goods yard. In clement weather the wide-open plazas often host buskers and performance artists. The commercial and cultural impact of Shiodome was muted somewhat by the almost simultaneous opening of Roppongi Hills, a larger, ritzier rival. Shiodome hasn't attracted the upmarket

restaurants or designer boutiques (though it's got some smart hotels), and thus isn't drawing the crowds enjoyed by its cross-town competitor, but it's worth a visit for a taste of ultra-modern Tokyo.

One of the skyscrapers is home to Dentsu, Japan's largest ad agency; in the basement lies the **ADMT Advertising Museum Tokyo**, a great, interactive look at over 300 years of ads in Japan. The museum is at the rear of **Caretta Shiodome** (*see p176*), a shopping and dining arcade that also houses **Shochu Authority** (Caretta Shiodome B2F, 1-8-2 Higashi-Shimbashi, 5537 2105, open 10am-9pm daily), a spacious shop with over 3,200 varieties of sake and knowledgeable staff on hand. Sitting quietly between the skyscrapers of Shiodome is a fascinating glimpse of the area's past. The **Old Shinbashi Station** is a reconstruction of one of Tokyo's first railway stations, the foundations of which are now visible through the glass floor.

After shopping and eating your way around the gleaming modernity of Shiodome, take a five-minute walk to **Hama-Rikyu Garden**, a one-time duck hunting ground and the most picturesque spot in the Ginza area. The juxtaposition of the green trees and lawns against the backdrop of Shiodome's looming glass monoliths is pretty astonishing.

ADMT Advertising Museum Tokyo

Caretta Shiodome B1F-B2F, 1-8-2 Higashi-Shimbashi, Minato-ku (6218 2500/www.admt.jp). Shinbashi station (Yamanote line), Shiodome exit; (Asakusa, Ginza lines), exit 6 or Shiodome station (Oedo, Yurikamome lines), exit 6. **Open** 11am-6.30pm Tue-Fri; 11am-4.30pm Sat. **Admission** free. This fab little museum is devoted to Japanese advertising, from 17th-century woodblock prints to modern product placement techniques. Although

Hermès (left) and **Sony Buildings**. *See p59.*

English explanations are limited, the images largely speak for themselves. Inspired technology allows touch-screen browsing of historic ads, and on-demand viewing of award-winning commercials from the past three decades. The museum also contains a library of over 100,000 digitised images.

Hama-Rikyu Detached Garden (Hama-Rikyu Onshi Teien)

1-1 Hama-Rikyu Teien, Chuo-ku (3541 0200). Shiodome station (Oedo, Yurikamome lines), exit 10 or Suijo water bus. **Open** *9am-5pm daily.* **Admission** ¥300; ¥150 concessions. **No credit cards.**

This tranquil garden, once a hunting ground for the Tokugawa shogunate, now cowers in the giant shadow of the new Shiodome development. The garden's main appeal lies in the abundance of water in and around it and the fact that it feels deceptively spacious, thanks to beautiful landscaping. Situated on an island, it is surrounded by an ancient walled moat with only one entrance, over the Nanmon Bridge (it's also possible to reach Hama-Rikyu by boat from Asakusa; *see p95* **Take me to the river**). The focal points are the huge pond, which contains two islands (one with a teahouse) connected to the shore by charming wooden bridges, and a photogenic 300-year-old pine tree. Access to the garden has been much improved since the opening of nearby Shiodome station.

Metropolitan Police Department Museum

Matsushita Denko Tokyo Honsha Bldg B2-2F, 3-5-1 Kyobashi, Chuo-ku (3581 4321/ www.keishicho.metro.tokyo.jp/index.htm). Kyobashi station (Ginza line), exit 2. **Open** *10am-6pm Tue-Sun.* **Admission** free. **Map** p60.

With a reputation lying somewhere between inept and corrupt, Japan's police force needs a little more than this drab collection of artefacts to turn things around. The absence of anything relating to modern crime-fighting might alarm more than reassure visitors, and the most exciting-looking exhibit is an arcade-style gaming machine that, disappointingly, turns out to be a safe-driving simulator. But if you've been dragging your kids around designer boutiques all day, you might redeem yourself here: diminutive visitors can dress as mini officers, sit on a Kawasaki police motorcycle with flashing lights, peer into a helicopter and meet force mascot Pipo-kun. Just be sure to keep your hands where they can see them.

National Film Centre

3-7-6 Kyobashi, Chuo-ku (3561 0823/www.momat. go.jp/english/index.html). Kyobashi station (Ginza line), exit 1. **Open** *11am-6pm Tue-Fri.* **Library** *10am-6pm Tue-Fri.* **Admission** ¥500; ¥100-¥300 concessions; free under-6s; additional charge for special exhibitions. **No credit cards. Map** p60.

Japanese and foreign films – 19,000 of them – star at the country's only national facility devoted to the preservation and study of cinema, an offshoot of the National Museum of Modern Art. Fans throng to its two cinemas for series focusing on, for example, DW Griffith or Korean films from the 1960s. Visitors can also check out the library of film books on the fourth floor or exhibitions of photos, graphic design and film-related items (often drawn from its own collection) in the gallery on the seventh floor.

Old Shinbashi Station

1-5-3 Higashi-Shinbashi, Minato-ku (3572 1872). Shinbashi station (Yamanote line), Shiodome exit; (Asakusa, Ginza lines), exits 3, 4 or Shiodome station (Oedo, Yurikamome lines), exits 3, 4. **Open** *11am-6pm Tue-Sun.* **Admission** free.

A painstaking reconstruction of the Shinbashi passenger terminus, part of the first railway in Japan, which opened in 1872 and ran from here to Yokohama. The current structure (opened in 2003) stands on the foundations of the original. These were uncovered during excavations, and can be viewed through a glass floor in the basement. Those of ironic bent may notice that Londoners still use stations every day that would be considered archaeological treasures in Tokyo, but such quibbles aside, this is a brilliant small-scale project, with a permanent railway history exhibition hall and full English labelling. There's a pleasant café on the ground floor.

Sake Plaza

Nihon Syuzo Centre Bldg 1F, 4F, 1-1-21 Nishi-Shinbashi, Minato-ku (3519 2019/www.japansake. or.jp). Toranomon station (Ginza line), exits 9, 10 or

Kasumigaseki station (Chiyoda, Hibiya, Marunouchi lines), exits A11, C3, C4. **Open** 10am-6pm Mon-Fri. **Admission** free. **Map** p60.

The recession, and too many freeloaders, seem to have struck Sake Plaza. The once free tasting now incurs a ¥550 charge for a five-cup sample. It's still a bargain, though, compared with bar prices, and you no longer have to try and identify your drinks by region, which is a relief.

Getting there

The Ginza area is well served by trains. There's Yurakucho station (JR Yamanote and Yurakucho subway lines); Hibiya station (Chiyoda, Hibiya and Mita subway lines); and Ginza station (Ginza, Hibiya and Marunouchi subway lines). Shinbashi is on the Yamanote, Asakusa and Ginza lines, while Shiodome is on the Oedo subway and Yurikamome monorail.

Something fishy

Take advantage of your jet lag and pay an early morning visit to one of Tokyo's most memorable sights, the wholesale fish market at Tsukiji. Colourful, cacophonous, chaotic – it's a fascinating spectacle. Some 50,000 workers and wholesalers and 14,000 retailers come daily to do business. Over 1,600 stalls sell 450 varieties of seafood – fresh, frozen, processed, smoked, dried, pickled – and much of it unfamiliar. If it lives in water, you'll probably find it here.

There's been a fish market in Tokyo since 1590, but Tsukiji's current location is much younger, established in 1935. It comprises an inner and an outer market. The inner section, strictly wholesale, is where the auction (and the action) happens. The tuna auction is the one to watch: it starts around 5am and is finished by 6.30am. Auctions of vegetables and fruit follow, and the bulk of the market's business is done by midday.

After the auction, visit the outer market, which has wider, quieter alleys and is far easier to navigate. It's open to all and offers a wide range of foodstuffs and kitchen goods. Don't miss breakfast at one of the numerous restaurants near the main gate – noodles, curry, tempura and *tonkatsu* are all available, but sushi is the thing: it's the freshest in Tokyo.

Well-behaved visitors are welcome, but note the following: dress in casual clothes and comfortable shoes that you don't mind getting dirty; flash photography is not permitted during the auction; watch out for (and give way to) the numerous moving vehicles and vendors.

Tsukiji is open six days a week. It's closed on Sundays, national holidays, two Wednesdays per month and also for an extended period around New Year and for Obon in August. Tsjukijishijo station (exit A2) on the Oedo subway line is on the doorstep; to find the auction area, walk straight through the market from the main gate to the end. You can pick up a useful map from the tourist offices (*see p297*) or visit the website www.tsukiji-market.or.jp/tukiji_e.htm.

The future of Tsukiji is under discussion, with plans to shift it to neighbouring Koto ward, although such a move wouldn't happen until at least 2012.

Sightseeing

Marunouchi

The imperial, financial and geographical heart of the city.

Map p66

Nothing of what is currently known as Marunouchi really lives up to its name, which means 'within the moat or castle walls'. But the world that was once within the walls was the most influential in Japan. Tokyo has been home to the Japanese royal family since 1868 and the Imperial Palace occupies a chunk of prime real estate in the geographical centre of the city, on part of the former site of Edo Castle, seat of the Tokugawa shogun.

Edo came to life in 1457 as Ota Dokan settled where the palace now stands. Once the shogun decided to rule from here too, his castle became the centre of the city. The Marunouchi area was created as he decreed that all *daimyo* (feudal lords) must live in Edo for half the year. This set in motion the reclaiming of land from the sea to make room for the compounds and residences of each *daimyo*. These were huge projects, built to house a population of anything from 500 to 5,000 people. The palace grew and the walls expanded to include more of the area around it. But, eventually, the process was reversed and the castle grounds shrank as the city took on a life of its own. Meanwhile, the palace became isolated, closing its doors to the outside world. But even today Marunouchi remains the centre of Tokyo in many senses – political, imperial, economic and geographical.

Although people do come to shop and play here, many visitors make a beeline for the **Imperial Palace**. It's directly in front of Tokyo station's central exit, across from Hibiya Dori, about 500 metres away. The moat and stone walls and outer gardens (planted with marvellously twisted pine trees) still divide it from the city, as they did long ago. The palace itself is out of bounds, except on 2 January and 23 December (the emperor's birthday), when the non-imperial masses are graciously allowed into some of the grounds. On the other 363 days, the closest visitors can get is to take photos of the scenic Nijubashi (Double Bridge), with a part of the palace buildings in the background. You can also stroll around the landscaped **Imperial Palace East Gardens**, which house a few historical remains and a Japanese-style garden.

At the top end of the East Gardens, across the main road, is another park, **Kitanomaru Koen**. This slightly unkempt section of the imperial grounds is home to the delights of the **Nippon Budokan** (*see p255*), **Japan Science Foundation Museum** and **National Museum of Modern Art**. The park's cherry trees make a popular, postcard-perfect sight at blossom time in April.

Marunouchi went through a second heyday in the Meiji era (1868-1912), when it became the economic centre of the country. The army sold the land to Mitsubishi after the emperor's restoration and the area became famous for its buildings, a showcase of foreign architecture then dubbed London Town. These were not only the pride of the city, but also a sign that the country had opened to the world. The main remaining example is **Tokyo station**, built to resemble Amsterdam's Centraal station. The station, the traditional starting point for a Marunouchi tour, contains a small **art gallery**. Other cultural outposts include the **Idemitsu Museum of Arts**, opposite the bottom corner of the Imperial Palace site; the **Bridgestone Museum of Art**, east of Tokyo station; and also the **Communications Museum,** just to the north of the station.

In a similar vein to Wall Street or the City of London, Tokyo's central business district has traditionally been a sedate area, especially at weekends, but the last few years have seen a major transformation. With heavyweight financing provided by Mitsubishi Real Estate, Marunouchi has been reinvented as a consumer hotspot. The focal point of the area's renewal is the 36-storey **Marunouchi Building** (*see p176*). Known locally as the 'Marubiru', it's an impeccably clean and modern-looking shopping, restaurant and office complex. It was the first construction that was ever allowed to overlook the grounds of the Imperial Palace, an indication that commercialism trumps tradition in 21st-century Japan. The restaurants on the top two floors offer superlative views over the palace grounds and, in the other direction, the neighbouring area of Ginza.

Marubiru's newest neighbour is another shopping, dining and office centre known as **Oazo** (*see p176*), which houses book retailer Maruzen's vast flagship store, as well as the smart **Marunouchi Hotel** (*see p37*).

The most dramatic transformation of all has occurred on **Naka Dori** (Centre Street), which runs from Marunouchi Building to Yurakucho station. Once a quiet street of office buildings,

Begin your tour at **Tokyo station**.

it has been repaved, lined with trees and now has the exclusive feel of a Bond Street or Fifth Avenue. Baccarat, Hermès and Emporio Armani are just some of the high-end retailers to have opened here. The street also boasts a listed building, **Meiji Seimeikan**, although you might have trouble spotting it now that it's been cocooned within **My Plaza**, yet another high-end shopping/dining/office complex. The very useful **TCVB tourist office** (*see p297*) is on the opposite corner from My Plaza, at the junction of Babasaki Dori and Hibiya Dori.

For fans of modern architecture, one of the most striking constructions is the **Tokyo International Forum** (*see p235*), close to Yurakucho station. Divided into two buildings, the most eye-catching is the ship-shaped Glass Hall Building designed by Rafael Vinoly, with a glass roof and 60-metre (197-foot) glass wall. The adjacent building is far less impressive, but hides an interior bustling with people attending conventions and other social events. The three main halls are increasingly used for concerts, film premières and festivals.

Going east under the train tracks leads to Pacific Century Place, opened in 2001, which contains Tokyo's second **Four Seasons** hotel (*see p37*), and plenty of restaurants and coffee bars. From here it's easy walking distance to Kyobashi and Nihonbashi, two areas that give a taste of an older Tokyo before the swank new consumer complexes hit town.

Nihonbashi has an important place in the history of Tokyo, as depicted by several *ukiyo-e* artists of the 19th century. There's not much

left now. The renowned Nihonbashi bridge (where all distances to and from Tokyo used to be calculated), a wooden structure in Edo days, was rebuilt in stone in the Meiji period and now lies in the shadow of an elevated highway, retaining none of the character it once had. For sightseers, there's the **Tokyo Stock Exchange**, **Kite Museum**, the **Bank of Japan** and its adjacent **Currency Museum**.

FURTHER AFIELD

Within easy reach of Marunouchi are a couple of worthwhile sights. In **Akihabara** – the best place in the city to buy new electronic goods (*see p181* **Electric Town**) – lies the **Transportation Museum**. The three floors of air, sea and land vehicles include Emperor Meiji's imperial carriage and Japan's first locomotive. Two stops from Tokyo station on the Chuo line is **Ochanomizu**, an area famous for sports shops and universities, which also boasts **Nikolai Cathedral** (4-1 Kanda-Surugadai, Chiyoda-ku, 3291 1885, open to visitors 1-3.30pm Tue-Fri, Japanese service 10am Sun). This cruciform Russian Orthodox church, complete with an onion dome, was designed by British architect Josiah Conder and completed in 1891. The original, larger dome was destroyed in the 1923 Great Kanto Earthquake. It occupies the site of a former Edo-period watchtower and offers visitors a commanding view of the area.

Bank of Japan

2-1-1 Nihonbashi-Hongokucho, Chuo-ku (English tours 3279 1111/www.boj.or.jp). Mitsukoshimae station (Ginza, Hanzomon lines), exits A8, B1. **Tours** (1hr; book 1wk ahead) 9.45am, 11am, 1.30pm, 3pm Mon-Fri. **Admission** free. **Map** p66.
The Bank of Japan consists of two buildings, descriptively named Old and New. The New Building is where all the banking activities take place, and the Old Building... well, it just looks nice. The first Western-style construction by Japanese builders is said to be modelled on London's Bank of England.

Bridgestone Museum of Art

1-10-1 Kyobashi, Chuo-ku (3563 0241/ www.bridgestone-museum.gr.jp). Tokyo station (Yamanote, Chuo, Marunouchi, Sobu lines), Yaesu (central) exit. **Open** 10am-8pm Tue-Sat; 10am-6pm Sun. **Admission** ¥800; ¥500-¥600 concessions; free under-12s. **Credit** AmEx, JCB, MC, V. **Map** p66.
Ishibashi Shojiro, founder of the giant Bridgestone Corporation, wheeled his private collection into this museum back in 1952. Impressionism, European modernism and Japanese Western-style paintings form the core holdings, but exhibitions can cover genres ranging from Ancient Greek to 20th-century abstraction. For a taste of what's inside, stroll past the artworks displayed in the street-level front windows. There's a tearoom on the first floor.

Marunouchi

CHUO-KU

NIHONBASHI-KAYABACHO

SHIN OHASHI DORI

NIHONBASHI

YAESU

KYOBASHI

UCHIKANDA

KANDA-NISHIKICHO

HONGO DORI

YASUKUNI DORI

CHUO DORI

OTEMACHI

MARUNOUCHI

HIBIYA DORI

SOTOBORI DORI

NAKA DORI

KOKYO-GAIEN

CHIYODA-KU

UCHIBORI DORI

KITANOMARU PARK

SANBANCHO

AOYAMA DORI

YASUKUNI DORI

Akihabara Station
Akihabara JR Station
Kanda Station
Kanda JR Station
Awajicho Station
Jimbocho Station
Kudanshita Station
Takebashi Station
Otemachi Station
Hanzomon Station
Nagatacho Station
Sakuradamon Station
Hibiya Station
Yurakucho Station
Tokyo Station
Otemachi Station
Nihonbashi Station
Mitsukoshimae Station
Kodenmacho Station
Ningyocho Station
Kayabacho Station
Hatchobori Station
Kyobashi Station

Mitsukoshi
Takashimaya
Maruzen Bookstore
Pokemon Center
Daimaru
Bridgestone Museum of Art
National Film Centre
Tokyo International Forum
Central Post Office
Marunouchi Building
TCVB Tourist Office
Imperial Theatre
Imperial Palace Plaza
Idemitsu Museum of Art
Hibiya Station
Imperial Palace
Otemon Gate
Chuo Police Station

Moat

300 m
300 yds

© Copyright Time Out Group 2005

Communications Museum

2-3-1 Otemachi, Chiyoda-ku (3244 6811). Otemachi station (Chiyoda, Hanzomon, Marunouchi, Mita, Tozai lines), exit A5. **Open** *9am-4.30pm Tue-Sun.* **Admission** ¥110; ¥50 concessions. **Credit** (shop, over ¥3,000 only) AmEx, JCB, MC, V. **Map** p66.

This massive museum relays the stories and technological histories of national public broadcasting company NHK, telecoms giant NTT and the now defunct Post & Telecommunications Ministry. Philatelists can peruse 280,000 old and new stamps from Afghanistan to Zimbabwe (including the world's first, an 1840 English penny black). Kids can race post office motor bikes in a video game, compare international post boxes and ogle a room-sized mail sorter. On the telecommunications floor, ample interactive displays teach how the phone works. A full range of historic public payphones – from pink to yellow to green – is sealed behind glass. The gift shop sells vintage postcards and collectable stamps.

Currency Museum

1-3-1 Nihonbashi-Hongokucho, Chuo-ku (3277 3037/ www.imes.boj.or.jp/cm/english_htmls/index.htm). Mitsukoshimae station (Ginza, Hanzomon lines), exits A5, B1. **Open** *9.30am-4.30pm Tue-Sun. Closed 5, 6 Mar.* **Tours** (1hr) 1.30pm Tue, Thur. **Admission** free. **Map** p66.

Run by the Bank of Japan, this museum traces the long history of money in the country, from the use of imported Chinese coins in the late Heian period (12th century) to the creation of the yen and the central bank in the second half of the 19th century. See beautiful, Edo-period, calligraphy-inscribed gold oblongs, occupation era notes from Indonesia and the Philippines, Siberian leather money and Thai leech coins. Or get the feel for some serious dosh by lifting ¥100 million yen (about the size of two phone books), safely stored inside a plexiglas box.

Idemitsu Museum of Arts

Tei Geki Bldg 9F, 3-1-1 Marunouchi, Chiyoda-ku (3213 9404/www.idemitsu.co.jp/museum). Hibiya station (Chiyoda, Hibiya, Mita lines), exit B3. **Open** *10am-5pm Tue-Thur, Sat, Sun; 10am-7pm Fri.*

Admission ¥800; free-¥500 concessions; free under-15s. **Credit** (shop only) MC, V. **Map** p66.

Idemitsu Sazo, founder of Idemitsu Kosan Co, collected traditional Chinese and Japanese art for more than 70 years. This museum (opened in 1966) features displays drawn from the respected permanent collection of ceramics, calligraphy and painting (for example, Rimpa-style irises painted by Sakai Hoitsu on a six-fold screen). There's also a good view of the Imperial Palace grounds.

Imperial Palace East Gardens (Kokyo Higashi Gyoen)

Chiyoda, Chiyoda-ku. Otemachi station (Chiyoda, Hanzomon, Marunouchi, Mita, Tozai lines), exits C10, C13B. **Open** *9am-4.30pm daily.* **Admission** free; token collected at gate to be submitted on leaving. **Map** p66.

This is the main park of the Imperial Palace, accessible through three old gates: Otemon (five minutes from Tokyo station), Hirakawamon (close to Takebashi bridge) and Kita-Hanebashimon (near Kitanomaru Park).There are few historical features in the manicured park, except for two old watchhouses, the remains of the old dungeon at the northern end (near Kitahanebashi-mon) and, at the exit into the next area, a wall of hand-carved stones dropping a great height into the water. There's also the small Museum of Imperial Collections.

Japan Science Foundation Science Museum (Kagaku Gijutsukan)

2-1 Kitanomaru Koen, Chiyoda-ku (3212 8544/ www.jsf.or.jp). Takebashi station (Tozai line), exit 1A or Kudanshita station (Hanzomon, Shinjuku, Tozai lines), exit 2. **Open** *9.30am-4.50pm daily.* **Admission** ¥600; ¥250/¥400 concessions. **No credit cards**. **Map** p66.

This museum takes to extremes the maxim 'learning by doing'. The unique five-spoke building, in a corner of Kitanomaru Park, consists of five floors of interactive exhibits. Its drab, dated entrance belies the fun displays inside. Children can learn the rudiments of scientific principles while standing inside a huge soap bubble, lifting a small car using pulleys and generating electricity by shouting. There's not a lot of English used, but much of the interaction does not need any translation.

Kite Museum

Taimeiken 5F, 1-12-10 Nihonbashi, Chuo-ku (3275 2704/www.tako.gr.jp). Nihonbashi station (Asakusa, Ginza, Tozai lines), exit A4, C5. **Open** 11am-5pm Mon-Sat. **Admission** ¥200; ¥100 concessions. **No credit cards. Map** p66.
This uplifting museum is a cornucopia of kites, including Indonesian dried leaves, giant woodblock-print samurai and a huge styrofoam iron. The former owner of the first-floor restaurant (one of Tokyo's earliest forays into Western-style dining) spent a lifetime collecting the 2,000 kites now layering the walls, packing display cases and crowding the ceiling. Don't expect detailed explanations of the exhibits; this is more of a space for putting a private hobby on public display – as often happens in Tokyo. The museum is not clearly marked, but look for the long white sign on the corner of the building.

National Museum of Modern Art

3-1 Kitanomaru Koen, Chiyoda-ku (5777 8600/ www.momat.go.jp/english/index.html). Takebashi station (Tozai line), exits 1A, 1B. **Open** *Art Museum* 10am-5pm Tue-Thur, Sat, Sun; 10am-8pm Fri. *Crafts Gallery* 10am-5pm Tue-Sun. **Admission** ¥420;

Ghosts of war

Japan's most controversial landmark is a Shinto shrine that serves as the national war memorial. Yasukuni Shrine houses the souls of almost 2.5 million war dead, from the Meiji Restoration through to World War II, but it is 14 spirits in particular that raise international ire. In 1979 Yasukuni leaders announced that they had secretly enshrined the wartime leaders executed as Class A war criminals by the Allies. So the shrine, already a focal point for nationalism and imperialist sentiment, honours, among others, Tojo Hideki, the prime minister who ordered the Pearl Harbor attack, and Matsui Iwane, the general who ordered the destruction of Nanking. The shrine's website decries the 'sham-like tribunal of the Allied forces' and argues that the category of Class A war criminal is a modern, Western construct and irrelevant to the Shinto religion.

Current Prime Minister Koizumi Junichiro is the first premier to make annual visits to the shrine, delighting his nationalist supporters but provoking anger from Japan's neighbours and wartime victims, most notably China and the Koreas. His assertions that the visits are private rather than official do little to pacify his critics. In 2004 the shrine appointed a new chief priest, Nanbu Toshiaki, a one-time Dentsu ad executive, no doubt hoping to boost the shrine's image and reverse a dwindling support base of war veterans and right-wingers.

The shrine itself is one of Tokyo's grandest, conceived in 1869 by Emperor Meiji to commemorate those who died defending him against the Shogun's army. An imposing 25-metre (82-foot) *torii* is the first of three gates that lead to the main hall. The spacious grounds boast a *noh* theatre, sumo ring, a courtyard full of ginkgo trees and the Yushukan, a museum dedicated to Japan's war dead.

The museum offers a wealth of fascinating artefacts from Japanese combat dating back to medieval times. Samurai armour, *kaiten* suicide torpedoes and photographs of kamikaze pilots with their families all evoke powerful scenes from Japanese history. But its approach is heavy-handed in places.

At its most extreme it teaches that the Russo-Japanese War (1904-5) inspired both Ho Chi Minh and Mahatma Gandhi, and suggests that the Pearl Harbor attack saved the US economy. The historical narratives, in Japanese and English, also largely disregard atrocities such as the Nanking Massacre, but they do spotlight aspects that are glossed over in most Western accounts, such as the effect of US-imposed trade embargos on the decision to attack Pearl Harbor. The not-so-subtle message is that the conflicts were induced first by anti-imperialists, then later by the manoeuvring of Western nations. If the message sinks in, visitors can stop by the gift shop for a 'Japan Number One!' headband or, less explicably, a furry penguin.

Yasukuni Shrine & Japanese War-Dead Memorial Museum

3-1-1 Kudankita, Chiyoda-ku (3261 8326/ www.yasukuni.or.jp). Kudanshita station (Hanzomon, Shinjuku, Tozai lines), exits 1, 3 or Ichigaya station (Chuo, Nanboku, Shinjuku, Sobu, Yurakucho lines), exits A3, A4. **Open** *Grounds* 6am-5pm daily. *Museum* 9am-5pm daily. **Admission** *Shrine* free. *Museum* ¥800; ¥300-¥500 concessions. **Admission** ¥800. **No credit cards. Map** p66.

¥70-¥130 concessions; free seniors, under-16s; additional charge for special exhibitions. Free 3 Nov, 1st Sun of mth. **Credit** (shop only) AmEx, JCB, MC, V. **Map** p66.

This is an alternative-history MOMA, one consisting mostly of Japanese art from the turn of the 20th century on. Noteworthy features of the permanent collection are portraits by early Japanese modernist Kishida Ryusei and grim wartime paintings by Fujita Tsuguharu. The 1969 building, designed by Taniguchi Yoshiro (father of architect Taniguchi Yoshio) was renovated to the tune of ¥7.8 billion in 2001. Its location next to the moat and walls of the Imperial Palace make it a prime stop for viewing spring cherry blossoms and autumn foliage. Nearby is the Crafts Gallery, an impressive 1910 European-style brick building, once the base for the legions of guards who patrolled the Imperial Palace. The exhibits are very different from those in the main building, comprising Japanese and foreign handicrafts from the Meiji era to the present (part of the 2,400-piece permanent collection).

Tokyo Station Gallery

Inside Tokyo station, 1-9-1 Marunouchi, Chiyoda-ku (3212 2485/www.ejrcf.or.jp). Tokyo station (Yamanote, Chuo, Marunouchi, Sobu lines). **Open** 10am-7pm Tue-Fri; 10am-6pm Sat, Sun. **Admission** ¥600; ¥400 concessions; free children Sat. **No credit cards. Map** p66.

Your JR train ticket helps to support this small museum; it's run by East Japan Railways and located inside sprawling Tokyo station, near the Marunouchi central entrance. Though the station's aged brick walls may not be the best background for paintings, they do give a look deep into the past. The museum has no permanent holdings, but brings in shows from around Japan and the world.

Tokyo Stock Exchange (Tokyo Shoken Torihiki Sho)

2-1 Nihonbashi-Kabutocho, Chuo-ku (3665 1881/www.tse.or.jp). Kayabacho station (Hibiya, Tozai lines), exit 11. **Open** 9am-4.30pm Mon-Fri. **Tour** (English) 1.30pm daily. **Admission** free. **Map** p66.

Come and watch the Japanese economy collapse for yourselves. Sadly, you won't be able to witness much wailing and gnashing of teeth, since the TSE, home to global giants such as Toyota and Sony, abolished its trading floor in 1999. The stock market of the world's second largest economy is now run almost entirely by sophisticated computers, which means the building is eerily quiet, the former trading floor taken over by a huge glass cylinder with the names and real-time stock prices of listed companies revolving at the top. Apart from the cylinder, there is very little movement. If you want to catch what little action is left, visit on a weekday during trading hours (9-11am, 12.30-3pm). The guided tour lasts approximately 40 minutes and includes a 20-minute video explaining the history and function of the TSE. On the way out, don't forget to invest in a souvenir T-shirt, mug or golf balls.

Imperial Palace: the classic shot. *See p64.*

Transportation Museum (Kotsu Hakubutsukan)

1-25 Kanda-Sudacho, Chiyoda-ku (3251 8481/www.kouhaku.or.jp). Akihabara station (Yamanote, Hibiya lines), Electric Town exit. **Open** 9.30am-5pm Tue-Sun. **Admission** ¥310; ¥150 concessions. **No credit cards. Map** p66.

From rickshaws to rockets, this large museum is a compendium of land, sea, air and space transport. It began life as a railway museum in 1921 and the exhaustive and exhausting train section is where you'll still find the kids. See how Tokyo's JR lines start their day in a massive model railway set-up. Virtually drive a Yamanote line train through Tokyo in a real conductor car or change antique switching lights from red to green. The museum has the first train used in Japan – an 1872 steam locomotive made in England that travelled between Shinbashi and Yokohama – and the latest, an experimental maglev system. The gift shop is stocked with every conceivable Japanese model train, unique transportation paraphernalia and unusual souvenirs.

Getting there

Tokyo station is the terminus of the JR Chuo line and is on the JR Yamanote and Keihin Tohoku lines, as well as the Marunouchi subway line. It is also the main terminus for *shinkansen* bullet trains. Other subways stations dot the area too.

Shinjuku

Shopping and sex on one side, skyscrapers and views on the other.

Map p73

Shinjuku is Tokyo's largest sub-centre and easily the most cosmopolitan area of the city, with luxurious department stores, sleazy strip-clubs, smoky jazz bars and gay porn shops all just a few blocks from each other. The area is divided into two distinct east and west sections by the JR Yamanote and Chuo train lines, with the entertainment and shopping districts to the east and the business and government districts to the west.

It is also a major transportation hub. In fact, Shinjuku station is the busiest in the world, with two million punters passing through daily. Those photos you've seen of thrashing commuters being pushed on to crowded trains by uniformed guards in the Tokyo rush hour? Shinjuku station, every morning of the week, from 7.30am onwards. Get up early and take a camera, but don't expect there to be much room to stand on the platform. One word of warning: like many of Tokyo's railway stations, Shinjuku has tunnels that stretch for miles underground on several basement and sub-basement levels and it is somewhat difficult to negotiate between the east, west and south sections of the area. Before you go anywhere, make sure you have a good idea of which station exit you need (there are around 50). You're bound to get lost at some point, though – everyone does.

EAST AND SOUTH SIDES

Head out of the east exit from the Yamanote line station and you'll see on the opposite side of the main street of Shinjuku Dori the large video screen of **Studio Alta** – a popular meeting spot. The east side is where all the action is. It houses the glitzy neon and dodgy hostess bars of **Kabuki-cho**, Japan's largest red-light area, as well the gay district of Ni-chome (2-chome) and the colourful bars of San-chome (3-chome). Numerous music venues and nightclubs are scattered throughout the area.

Kabuki-cho lies north of Yasukuni Dori and contains hundreds of restaurants, bars, sex clubs, *pachinko* parlours and love hotels – if you're male. you won't get five yards before some strip-club tout tries to lure you into their premises. It's not a particularly dangerous area, but explore with caution and don't flash your wallet too openly. Adjoining it is **Golden Gai**, a collection of tiny watering holes that are a throwback to earlier days. Not all welcome *gaijin*; *see p163* **Golden Gai** for those that do.

Occupying a substantial plot between Golden Gai and Meiji Dori is the large **Hanazono Shrine**. Erected in the 16th century, the shrine has been rebuilt many times but still retains the gripping presence of a historical monument that is very active. With striking orange pillars, railings and *torii* (gates), it holds numerous very lively festivals, notably a three-day event at the end of May and a pre-New Year's fest at the end of November.

Shinjuku is also one big shopping zone. Department store **My City** (*see p174*) perches above the east side of the station, notable mainly for the Shunkan restaurant area on the seventh and eighth floors. Modern art lines the walls, and restaurants include Wolfgang Puck, the Gumbo & Oyster Bar and Okinawan specialist Nabbie & Kamado. Numerous other department stores, including Mitsukoshi, Marui, My Lord, Keio and Lumine, line Shinjuku Dori and the surrounding streets. The granddaddy of them all, and the expat's fave for its larger-than-usual clothes, is **Isetan** (*see p172*).

Consumption is definitely the name of the game here. In fact, the city planners (although that's a vague notion in Japan) clearly thought there wasn't enough spending going on in Shinjuku, so in the early 1990s they built a huge shopping complex, **Takashimaya Times Square** (*see p174*), to the south of the station. At one end is the 240-metre (787-foot) shaft of the **NTT DoCoMo Yoyogi Building**, resembling a cross between the Empire State Building and a Venetian clocktower. The complex occupies old train switching grounds; now Shinjuku's revitalised south exit has taken its place as a destination for shoppers, restaurant-hunters and party-goers.

It may surprise some that for all Shinjuku's consumerist dazzle, it is also steeped in counter-culture. **Ni-chome** is the most active and open gay and lesbian district in the country, with queer literature, advertisements and goods openly displayed (something unusual for Japan) on airy side streets (*see chapter* **Gay & Lesbian**, starting on p226, for full details).

The bright lights of **Shinjuku Dori** (top) and low-key **Omoide Yokocho**.

The little alleyways between Kabuki-cho and Golden Gai house avant-garde performance houses as well as intellectual denizens set up as tiny bars. Indeed, Shinjuku was the explosive epicentre of Japan's active and demonstrative youth movement in the 1960s (something that can be viewed in director Oshima Nagisa's 1968 classic *Diary of a Shinjuku Thief*). This feeling has never left some of the smaller byways of the east side.

Further east and south of Shinjuku Dori is the vast green lung of **Shinjuku Gyoen**, one of Tokyo's largest parks. It's a spectacular sight at *hanami* (cherry blossom viewing), when its 1,500 trees paint the whole place pink. And to the north of Kabuki-cho, centred on Shin-Okubo station, is Tokyo's 'Koreatown', a district that has seen a resurgence in recent years as Korean culture becomes increasingly fashionable in Tokyo. For good restaurants in the area, *see p140* **Seoul survivors**.

WEST SIDE

The west side offers a clutch of skyscrapers (Tokyo's only such neighbourhood), a plethora of banking, insurance and other company headquarters and some smart hotels, including the celebrated **Park Hyatt Tokyo** (*see p39*). Among the corporate high-rises are the **Sompo Japan Museum**, worth a look for some of its famous (and famously expensive) paintings, and the **Toto Super Space**, where you can view the latest in Japan's celebrated toilet technology.

The Tokyo government's headquarters, known as Tocho and designed by Tange Kenzo, are also here. Completed in 1991, the twin-towered centrepiece of this impressive complex is the **Tokyo Metropolitan Government Building No.1**: a must-visit architecturally and for the great – and free – views from its two

observation decks. Directly behind the TMG site is **Shinjuku Central Park**, better known for its homeless community than its scenery.

In stark contrast to the gleaming high-rises is **Omoide Yokocho**, just outside the station's north-west exit. This narrow alleyway lined with ramshackle yakitori stalls and bars, each with seating for no more than a handful of customers, is the last remnant of a vanished world. It dates from the post-war years when Shinjuku was the site of a thriving black market; whatever you needed you could find it in the area's teeming and seamy side streets. Atmospheric, intimate and distinctly out of step with modern-day Tokyo, Omoide Yokocho may not exist for much longer if the developers have their way.

South of the main road of Koshu Kaido is women's fashion college Bunka Gakuen, which founded the small **Bunka Gakuen Costume Museum** on its 60th anniversary in 1979. Further west lies the **Tokyo Opera City** complex, containing halls for classical music (*see p234*), one of the city's best-funded private contemporary art galleries (*see p223*) and the **NTT Inter Communication Centre**, a museum of media arts. Adjacent is the **New National Theatre, Tokyo** (*see p233*).

ELSEWHERE

Shinjuku is also a good jumping-off point for other neighbourhoods. To the south, Yoyogi is a large area that abuts Yoyogi Park and the **Meiji Shrine** complex (*see p88*) and contains the **Sword Museum**.

Heading east, back towards Chiyoda-ku, is Yotsuya, home to one of Tokyo's more surprising buildings. The **Akasaka Detached Palace** (aka Geihinkan, 2-1-1 Moto-Akasaka, Minato-ku) is a hybrid of Versailles and

Buckingham Palace. Its construction, in the early years of the 20th century, was intended to prove that Japan could do anything the West could. The late Emperor Hirohito lived here when he was crown prince, but the only people allowed in these days are visiting dignitaries – a great pity. Nearby is the Tokyo Fire Department-owned **Fire Museum**, which offers an insight into the key role fire has played in the development of the city.

Bunka Gakuen Costume Museum

3-22-7 Yoyogi, Shibuya-ku (3299 2387/ www.bunka.ac.jp/museum/hakubutsu.htm). Shinjuku station (Yamanote, Chuo, Sobu lines), south exit; (Oedo, Shinjuku lines), exit 6. **Open** 10am-4.30pm Mon-Sat. **Admission** ¥500; ¥200-¥300 concessions. **No credit cards. Map** p73.

The small collection includes examples of historical Japanese clothing, such as an Edo-era fire-fighting coat and a brightly coloured, 12-layer *karaginumo*

outfit. Kamakura-period scrolls illustrate the types of dress worn by different classes of people. The displays change four or five times a year.

Fire Museum

3-10 Yotsuya, Shinjuku-ku (3353 9119/ www.tfd.metro.tokyo.jp/ts/museum.htm). Yotsuya-Sanchome station (Marunouchi line), exit 2. **Open** 9.30am-5pm Tue-Sun. **Admission** free.

This museum traces the cultural history of fire-fighting, from decorative uniforms to vintage ladder trucks to the elaborate pompoms used to identify neighbourhood brigades. Between 1603 and 1868 97 major conflagrations swept through Tokyo. Scale models, sound and lights recreate an Edo-period blaze in miniature. Video monitors show footage of the fires that destroyed the city after the 1923 Great Kanto Earthquake and World War II fire bombing. Elsewhere, cartoon stories (in Japanese) teach children what to do in case fire breaks out at home. Kids also love climbing into the rooftop helicopter.

How to play *pachinko*

Pachinko sets little alarm bells ringing in polite society. Nobody will admit to playing, but the sheer number of parlours proves that plenty of people are. And some people make a good living as a result: the 'pachi-pros', as the serial gamblers are known, can reap up to ¥300,000 on a good day; and right beside them are the wannabes who lose much more.

A *pachinko* machine resembles a cross between a pinball and slot machine, and uses zillions of mini steel balls. Gaudily decorated, ear-splittingly noisy parlours are to be found all over Tokyo, from the bustling shopping areas to the hushed suburbs.

If you stand in Shinjuku's Kabuki-cho, surrounded by palatial parlours blasting a cacophony of bleeps and whirrs, it will be hard to believe that *pachinko* is, technically, illegal. But it is. So there are a few hoops to jump through to circumvent the law. First you need to buy a prepaid card from a machine near the entrance (so you'll be gambling points rather than money). Slip your card into the slot, push the ball-eject button, turn the handle to flick the balls, and you're rolling.

Now comes the tricky part. The balls have to land in the centre hole to start the numbers on the screen revolving. This is done by inching the handle back and forth to find the optimum setting. Once you're satisfied the balls are going in (aim for at least ten hits every ¥500), wedge a coin into the handle to hold it in place and wait to win. In the meantime you're free to read a book, call a friend or write a short story. Any sudden ejaculation of steel balls means you're a winner: cash them in or continue playing.

In the unlikely event that your machine pays out, you'll have to carry your little balls to a desk where you can exchange them for a variety of gaudy prizes. The least enticing ones may look like taped-up lumps of rock,

NTT Inter Communication Centre

Tokyo Opera City Tower 4F, 3-20-2 Nishi-Shinjuku,
Shinjuku-ku (0120 144 199/www.ntticc.or.jp).
Hatsudai station (Keio New line), east exit. **Open**
10am-6pm Tue-Sun. Closed 2nd Sun Feb, 1st Sun
Aug. **Admission** ¥800; ¥400-¥600 concessions.
Credit (shop only) AmEx, DC, JCB, MC, V.
Opened by telecoms giant NTT in 1996, this museum
is at the leading edge of media design and arts. The
permanent collection includes a timeline of technology, art videos and interactive installations, and
sound pieces designed for its anechoic chamber.

Shinjuku Gyoen

11 Naito-cho, Shinjuku-ku (3350 0151/
www.shinjukugyoen.go.jp). Shinjuku-Gyoenmae
station (Marunouchi line), exit 1. **Open** *Park* 9am-
4.30pm Tue-Sun; daily during cherry blossom
(early Apr) and chrysanthemum (early Nov) seasons.
Greenhouse 11am-3pm Tue-Sun. **Admission** ¥200;
¥50 concessions. **No credit cards**. **Map** p73.

Shinjuku Gyoen opened as an imperial garden in
1906, during Japan's push for Westernisation, and
was the first place in the country that many non-
indigenous species were planted. The fascination
with the West is evident in the garden's layout: there
are both English- and French-style sections, as well
as a traditional Japanese garden.

Sompo Japan Museum

Sompo Japan Bldg 42F, 1-26-1 Nishi-Shinjuku,
Shinjuku-ku (3349 3081/www.sompo-japan.co.jp/
museum). Shinjuku station (Yamanote, Chuo,
Sobu lines), west exit; (Marunouchi line), exits A16,
A17; (Shinjuku line), exit 3 or Shinjuku-Nishiguchi
station (Oedo line), exit D1. **Open** 10am-6pm
Tue-Sun. **Admission** ¥500; ¥300 concessions;
free under-15s; additional charge for special
exhibitions. **No credit cards**. **Map** p73.
The views from this 42nd-floor museum are spectacular. Perhaps to compete, the owner, insurance
company Yasuda (as the firm was previously called),

or fake gold bars. Opt for these 'special
prizes' anyway, and take them to a small
window somewhere off-premises (look on
the counter for a map) where someone will
repurchase your bars for solid yen.
    Winning at pachinko is largely a matter of
luck, but there are some pointers. First, you
don't simply plonk yourself down at any old
machine. No, you reconnoitre, you suss out
the *pachinko* parlour; you see who's winning,
which machines haven't paid out. Once
you've picked a machine, throw a pack of

cigarettes into the trough to mark your
spot – smoking is compulsory.
    Most serious players believe the machines
are rigged, sometimes in the player's favour.
You'll notice that the people seated by
the entrance are on incredible winning
streaks. The battle for a door seat explains
why you'll see long lines of people waiting
up to two hours each morning for the
parlours to open. It also explains why
latecomers rarely win – they're subsidising
the door seats.

purchased Van Gogh's 1889 *Sunflowers* in 1987 for the then record-breaking price of over ¥5 billion (£24 million). There is now some concern that it may not be authentic, but no one is certain. This symbol of Japan's go-go Bubble years hangs alongside Cézanne's *Pommes et Serviette* (bought in 1990) in a dim glass box. The museum's core work is by Japanese artists, specifically Togo Seiji (1897-1978), who donated 200 of his own pieces and 250 items from his art collection. There are also temporary exhibitions.

Sword Museum

4-25-10 Yoyogi, Shibuya-ku (3379 1386).
Sangubashi station (Odakyu line). **Open** 10am-4.30pm Tue-Sun. **Admission** ¥525; free concessions.
No credit cards.
The confiscation of swords as offensive weapons during the American occupation after World War II threatened the traditional Japanese craft of sword-making. To safeguard it, the Society for the Preservation of Japanese Art Swords was established in 1948. Twenty years later, it opened this museum to display its collection of centuries-old swords and fittings. Even non-enthusiasts may find themselves mesmerised by their qualities: mysterious, wave-like patterns, sharkskin handles and sculptured guards.

Tokyo Metropolitan Government Building No.1

2-8-1 Nishi-Shinjuku, Shinjuku-ku (5321 1111/
observatory 5320 7890/www.yokoso.metro.tokyo.jp).
Tochomae station (Oedo line), exit 4. **Open** *North Observatory* 9.30am-11pm Tue-Sun. *South Observatory* 9.30am-5.30pm Mon, Wed-Sun.
Admission free. **Map** p73.
Two of the best views over Tokyo have the added bonus of being free (unlike the Mori Tower's City View; *see p110*). Each of the TMG twin towers (243m/797ft tall) has an observation deck on the 45th floor, affording a 360° panorama interrupted only by

the other tower – on a clear day you can see Mt Fuji. Admire the cityscape while sipping a coffee from the cafeteria in the centre of the vast floor. The south observatory is the best choice by day; after dark, the view from the north deck is preferable. There's a tourist office (*see p297*) in the base of the north tower. The easiest way to get to the TMG complex from Shinjuku station is by underground tunnel; it's well signed. Other buildings in west Shinjuku with free viewing areas include the Shinjuku Centre Building (53F) and the Nomura Building (49F), both of which are open late.

Toto Super Space

L-Tower Bldg 26F-27F, 1-6-1 Nishi-Shinjuku
(3345 1010). Shinjuku station (Yamanote, Chuo,
Sobu lines), west exit; (Marunouchi line), exits A16,
A17; (Shinjuku line), exit 3 or Shinjuku-Nishiguchi
station (Oedo line), exit D1. **Open** 10am-6pm daily.
Closed 1st & 3rd Wed of mth. **Admission** free.
Map p73.
It's hard to spend any time at all in Japan without building up an interest in toilets. This showroom, operated by the country's leading maker of bathroom hardware, has something to intrigue even the most jaded loo user. As well as the now standard bidet toilets, Toto also makes baths that fill themselves automatically and can be switched on via the internet. The latest thing is toilets that analyse what's deposited in there. No, really.

Getting there

Shinjuku is served by about a dozen railway lines, including the JR Yamanote Chuo, Saikyo and Sobu lines, and the Keio line, the Odakyu line and the Seibu Shinjuku line. It's also on the Marunouchi, Oedo and Shinjuku subway lines. Tochomae (on the Oedo line) is the closest station to the TMG headquarters, while Shinjuku-Sanchome (Marunouchi and Shinjuku lines) is convenient for Kabuki-cho and Ni-chome.

Tokyo Metropolitan Building.

Shibuya

Bright and brash, and teeming with teens.

Center Gai.

Map p79

'Shibuya' roughly translates as 'valley of refinement', which is a particularly inapt name for this hotbed of pop culture and lowbrow entertainment. From the music videos and commercials that roar from three giant liquid crystal display screens opposite the station, to the karaoke touts and sex industry scouts that roam the station exits, there's little that is refined about Shibuya.

But for a taste of teen Tokyo there's nowhere better. The city's youth have made Shibuya their playground, and the shops, cafés, clubs, bars and restaurants largely cater to their tastes, making the area fast, fun and affordable. During the day, shopping is Shibuya's raison d'être, with music and fashion dominating the area's stores. When darkness falls and the neon is switched on, myriad clubs, bars, cinemas, live venues and less salubrious establishments keep the area throbbing through the night.

Shibuya is one of Tokyo's major sub-centres and an important transport hub. All the action happens on the west side of the Yamanote line tracks; the JR station's Hachiko exit is the gateway to most of the area's attractions.

In the paved square outside the exit is a small bronze statue of the eponymous **Hachiko**, a dog of legendary loyalty who walked to Shibuya to meet his owner at the end of each day, then travelled vainly to the station for a further seven years after the old man's death. By the time of Hachiko's own demise in 1935, the dog had become a Tokyo legend and its obituary was carried in newspapers. The canine's statue is now Shibuya's most popular – and thus overcrowded – meeting spot.

Next to the square is the world's busiest pedestrian crossing, also named Hachiko, across which a scuttling horde pours in every direction every three minutes. To a backdrop of blaring video screens and neon-clad buildings, this is the Tokyo of popular imagination; watch it all from the second floor of Starbucks (just as Scarlett Johansson did in *Lost in Translation*).

On the far side of Hachiko crossing is the entrance to **Center Gai**, a pedestrian street lined predominantly with cheap chain restaurants, mobile phone vendors and trainer shops. It's also the see-and-be-seen strip for Tokyo's teen trendsetters, who mill around in the latest garish fashions. The likely source of their threads is **109** (*see p180*), a ten-storey collection of boutiques, a block to the left of Center Gai, that caters exclusively to flamboyantly attired teenage girls. Whether or not such clothing is to your taste, a visit to see the young shoppers in action is an essential Tokyo experience.

The street immediately to the right of 109 leads to **Bunkamura**, a massive arts centre owned by the same corporation (Tokyu) as the fashion superstore, but catering to a very different crowd. After navigating the noise and neon to get here, it's the perfect spot for a breather. It contains, among other things, **Le Cinema** (*see p217*), performance spaces **Theatre Cocoon** (*see p251*) and **Orchard Hall** (*see p233*) and a good museum.

A right turn at Bunkamura will lead you back to the bustle. The Shibuya BEAM building on the right-hand side is home to **Equus Plaza**, a must for horse racing fans, and a large basement branch of manga/*anime* specialist **Mandarake** (*see p193*). Catering to fans of all incomes, teens can browse old comics while high-rolling geeks can, at the time of writing, snap up a *Princess Mononoke* anime cel for a mere ¥472,000.

Continue to the next T-junction, head left and you'll find yet another Tokyu-run institution – **Tokyu Hands** (*see p192*). Often misleadingly termed a stationery or hardware store, it hawks everything from hi-fis to Halloween masks, and is the best place to find the latest, quirkiest, only-in-Japan novelties. Vinyl enthusiasts should explore the surrounding streets, where dozens of vinyl-only music stores, some little

larger than a cupboard, offer 'Shibuya taste' discs: mainly hip hop, house and reggae. DJing is an enduring craze among Tokyo's youth, and Shibuya supplies most of the vinyl.

Between Tokyu Hands and the next main street, Koen Dori, is another teen haven, **Parco** (*see p182*), the hip division of Seibu department store. It takes up three separate buildings (Part 1, Part 2 and Part 3); at the top of Part 3 is the **Parco Museum of Art & Beyond**, which hosts an eclectic mix of trendsetting shows.

The rest of Shibuya is a winding maze of streets and the best approach is simply to wander everywhere. It can be a disorientating experience – but that's part of the fun – and with each of the main roads leading downhill to the station, it's hard to become seriously lost.

If you tire of consumerism, Shibuya also houses some quirky museums, including the **Tobacco & Salt Museum**, the **TEPCO Electric Energy Museum** (both north of Parco) and the **Eyeglass Museum** (on Dogenzaka). Further west in the Shoto area, quiet contemplation is the order of the day at two small art museums: the **Toguri Museum** and the **Shoto Museum**. Nearby is the unusual **Gallery Tom** (2-11-1 Shoto, 3467 8102, open 10.30am-5.30pm Tue-Sun, admission ¥600), which has been catering for the visually impaired for two decades. It's the only gallery in town where visitors are encouraged to get touchy-feely with the sculptures and 3-D art. Further out, a couple of stops from Shibuya on the Keio Inokashira line, is the low-key **Japan Folk Crafts Museum**.

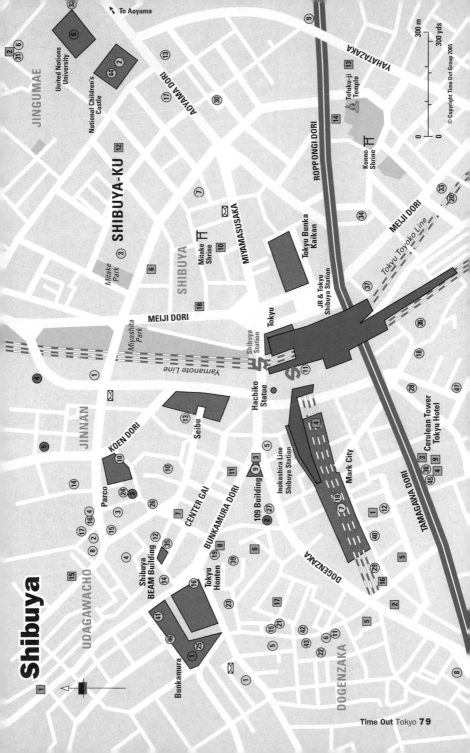

Hachiko crossing outside Shibuya station and the **109 Building** (below right). *See p77.*

When the shops close, head back towards Bunkamura and turn left. This takes you uphill to the hub of Shibuya's nightlife, home to several of Tokyo's best-known clubs (**Womb, Vuenos, Club Asia, Ruby Room, Neo**; *see p209-11* for details) as well as a great many of its love hotels. From around ¥3,000 you can 'rest' with a friend for a couple of hours, or you might choose to fork out ¥30,000 for a night at the luxurious **P&A Plaza** where the suite boasts a private swimming pool (*see p30* **Love hotels**).

Over the past few years Shibuya has been pushing its image upmarket. First, a trio of train operators joined forces to tack **Mark City** (*see p176*) on to the side of the existing station. This shopping and dining complex currently houses shops and restaurants designed to attract a (slightly) more moneyed crowd. Next came the grand **Cerulean Tower Tokyu Hotel** (*see p40*) on the south side of the station, followed by Zero Gate, the gleaming

home of French-owned club/restaurant **La Fabrique** (*see p210*). The newest arrival is Meiji Dori's curiously named Picasso 347 shopping tower, which houses spacious FCUK and Hilfiger stores as well as a cinema, sports complex and café terrace.

Some complain that these shiny additions detract from the area's downbeat charm. But the same protests have been heard since the original Tokyu department store rose up beside the station in 1934 (some of the original shops displaced by Tokyu still operate underneath Hachiko), and the army of luridly clad young ladies strolling the streets suggest the newcomers haven't made much difference yet.

Bunkamura The Museum

Bunkamura B1, 2-24-1 Dogenzaka, Shibuya-ku (3477 9111/www.bunkamura.co.jp). Shibuya station (Yamanote, Ginza lines), Hachiko exit; (Hanzomon line), exit 3A. **Open** 10am-7pm Mon-Thur, Sun; 10am-9pm Fri, Sat. **Admission** usually ¥1,000. **Credit** (shop only) AmEx, JCB, MC, V. **Map** p79.

Probably the best museum in Tokyo run by a department store chain (it's owned and operated by the Tokyu corporation, which also runs 109, Tokyu Hands and part of Mark City). It hosts international art blockbusters featuring subjects and artists ranging from Tintin to Picasso. Elsewhere in this major shopping and cultural centre are boutiques, an art-house cinema, two theatre/music spaces, an art bookshop and various restaurants.

Eyeglass Museum

Iris Optical 6F-7F, 2-29-18 Dogenzaka, Shibuya-ku (3496 3315). Shibuya station (Yamanote, Ginza lines), Hachiko exit; (Hanzomon line), exits 1, 3A. **Open** 11am-5pm Tue-Sun. **Admission** free. **Map** p79.

Not the flashiest of Tokyo's museums, this slightly dilapidated spot above an optician's is nevertheless an interesting diversion from shopping. Glasses galore sit quietly, with few annotations, for the viewing pleasure of spectacle fanatics. A 19th-century eyeglass workshop imported from France is complemented by a chipped mannequin.

Japan Folk Crafts Museum (Mingei-kan)

4-3-33 Komaba, Meguro-ku (3467 4527/ www.mingeikan.or.jp). Komaba-Todaimae station (Keio Inokashira line), west exit. **Open** 10am-5pm Tue-Sun. **Admission** ¥1,000; ¥200-¥500 concessions. **Credit** MC, V.

Kyoto University professor Yanagi Soetsu created this museum in 1936 to spotlight *mingei*, literally 'arts of the people'. The criteria for inclusion in the collection were that objects should be made anonymously, by hand, and in large quantities. Yanagi collected ceramics, metalwork, woodwork, textiles, paintings and other everyday items from Japan, China, Korea, Taiwan and Okinawa at a time when their beauty wasn't always recognised. Handwritten labels (in Japanese) and simple wooden display cases complement the rustic feel.

Parco Museum of Art & Beyond

Parco Part 3 7F, 15-1 Udagawacho, Shibuya-ku (3464 5111/www.parco-art.com). Shibuya station (Yamanote, Ginza lines), Hachiko exit; (Hanzomon line), exits 3A, 6, 7. **Open** 10am-8.30pm during exhibitions. **Admission** ¥700; ¥500 concessions. **Credit** AmEx, DC, JCB, MC, V. **Map** p79.

This top-floor gallery's programming policy perfectly fits the Shibuya demographic, with regularly changing exhibitions on pop culture themes, plus work by only the trendiest photographers and designers from Japan and overseas. Past shows have featured photos by the dog-loving William Wegman, and that enduring pop icon, Che Guevara.

Shoto Museum of Art

2-14-14 Shoto, Shibuya-ku (3465 9421). Shinsen station (Keio Inokashira line), north exit. **Open** 9am-5pm Tue-Sun. **Admission** ¥300; ¥100 concessions; free children Sat. **No credit cards.**

The Shoto's rough stone exterior gives way to curved walls encircling a central fountain. It's no Guggenheim, but this odd bit of ageing architecture (owned by Shibuya ward) sometimes hosts inspired shows. It's also inexpensive and quiet.

TEPCO Electric Energy Museum (Denryoku-kan)

1-12-10 Jinnan, Shibuya-ku (3477 1191/ www5.mediagalaxy.co.jp/Denryokukan). Shibuya station (Yamanote, Ginza lines), Hachiko exit; (Hanzomon line), exits 6, 7. **Open** 10am-6pm Mon, Tue, Thur-Sun. **Admission** free. **Map** p79.

'Let's make friends with electricity' is the slogan of this energy giant's six-storey homage to the joy of electrons and protons. Adults might tire quickly of the corporate message, but it's a great place to keep the kids busy. Teaching your offspring to play with electricity might not seem the sagest of lessons, but the innovative games and multimedia activities will keep them genuinely entertained.

Tobacco & Salt Museum

1-16-8 Jinnan, Shibuya-ku (3476 2041/ www.jti.co.jp/Culture/museum). Shibuya station (Yamanote, Ginza lines), Hachiko exit; (Hanzomon line), exits 6, 7. **Open** 10am-6pm Tue-Sun. **Admission** ¥100; ¥50 concessions. **No credit cards.** **Map** p79.

The tenuous rationale for this pairing of themes is that both were once nationalised commodities. Tobacco gets the most exposure, with two of the four floors devoted to the history, manufacture and culture of the killer leaf. Besides the gallery of packet designs, collection of pipes and videos of cigarette production, one of the most fascinating aspects of the museum is the number of families that bring their kids to learn about the marvel of smoking. On the third floor a 1.2-tonne block of Polish salt and a model *Cutty Sark* crafted from crystals are among the sodium-based exhibits. The top floor is often the best, with an ever-changing exhibition that has, in the past, ranged from matchbook designs to 19th-century prostitutes' wigs. If you're inspired to spark up, the gift shop sells a range of cigarettes.

Toguri Museum of Art

1-11-3 Shoto, Shibuya-ku (3465 0070/www.toguri-museum.or.jp). Shinsen station (Keio Inokashira line) or Shibuya station (Yamanote, Ginza lines), Hachiko exit; (Hanzomon line), exit 3A. **Open** 9.30am-5.30pm Tue-Sun. **Admission** ¥1,030; ¥420-¥730 concessions. **Credit** AmEx, DC, JCB, MC, V.

The art of porcelain is the focus of this quiet museum. Its 3,000 antique Chinese and Japanese pieces rotate through four shows a year. All displays are accompanied by captions in Japanese and English.

Getting there

Shibuya is on the Yamanote train line and the Ginza and Hanzomon subway lines, as well as various suburban rail lines including the JR Saikyo, Keio Inokashira, and Tokyu Toyoko and Denentoshi lines.

Sightseeing

Manga mania

The Japanese love – truly love – their comics. Known as manga (coined by Hokusai in 1814 and meaning 'crazy drawings'), they amount to almost 40 per cent of everything published in Japan. You can find manga magazines as thick as phone directories, and epic stories that take numerous volumes to complete. The 400-page *Shonen Jump* magazine, costing a mere ¥230, shifts three million copies a week (and has a record circulation of more than six million). Manga cover every subject under the sun, from child-raising to hardcore porn.

While manga have clearly been influenced by Western comics and animation, they also draw on Japan's long tradition of visual entertainments such as *ukiyo-e* ('floating world' prints), erotic *shunga* prints and the popular *kamishibai*, the travelling picture-story theatres.

The man principally responsible for starting this all-consuming love affair is Tezuka Osamu (1928-89), creator of Tetsuwan Atomu (aka Astro Boy) and founder of the post-war manga and *anime* (animated cartoons) industries. Since the war, manga have evolved into Japan's unique mass literary form with their own iconic vocabulary; they are the sources of many of the country's most successful films and TV series, both animated and live-action. Much of this success stems from the dizzying diversity of their stories, styles and subjects, and their appeal to both sexes and every age group and taste.

Traditionally, the biggest sellers have been the *shonen* titles for boys and the more adult *seinen* ranges for men, but there are some 40 *shojo* magazines for girls and, more recently, over 50 *redikomi* aimed at women. Written and drawn mainly by women, these cover everything from 'Office Lady' lifestyles, pregancy advice and sex therapy to raunchy erotica and the gloriously titled 'Truly Horrifying Mother-in-Law and Daughter-in-Law Comics', which tackle the trials of newly wed wives forced to live with their husbands' parents.

That's not counting niche titles covering such subjects as golf, *pachinko*, military history or the unique genre of *shonen ai* – stories about gay boys that are hugely popular with teenage girls. And don't forget *dojinshi* (self-published fanzines); Tokyo's twice-yearly Comiket fairs for *dojinshi* attract nearly half a million visitors.

Most manga are printed in black or one-colour ink on white or tinted newsprint, with perhaps a small full-colour section. They are read from what Westerners consider the 'back', and from right to left across the page. Most casual readers discard the magazines or leave them for others on trains or in cafés. What the Japanese prefer to buy and put on their shelves are the compact, usually paperback books that compile several episodes of a story in one volume.

Manga are widely available in most of Tokyo's bookshops, and department stores often dedicate large areas, sometimes entire floors, to them. Devoted readers may prefer specialist or second-hand outlets such as **Tora no Ana** (*see p179*) and **Mandarake** (*see p193*), while whole boutiques are dedicated to specific creators like Tezuka or characters like Doraemon. Myriad spin-off products range from figurines and games to clothes emblazoned with manga heroes and heroines. There are also numerous 24-hour manga cafés, such as **GeraGera** (*see p169*), where you can read from a vast quantity of manga books, both old and new, for a modest charge.

You will struggle to find English-language editions in Japan, but they are increasingly available in the West – manga has been the fastest growing book category in the US for a number of years.

Paul Gravett is the author of *Manga: Sixty Years of Japanese Comics* (Laurence King, 2004).

Harajuku & Aoyama

Mix with teenage hipsters en route to Tokyo's biggest Shinto shrine.

Map p85

The adjacent districts of Harajuku and Aoyama are the fashion centres of Tokyo – the former catering to a trend-driven, budget-conscious teen crowd, the latter to an upmarket, designer-clad older set.

The thoroughfare that connects the two areas is the wide, tree-lined boulevard of Omotesando. From the crossroads with Aoyama Dori and Omotesando subway station it stretches downhill to the junction with Meiji Dori, and on to Meiji-Jingumae subway station and nearby Harajuku JR station. Behind these is the green expanse of Yoyogi Park and the Meiji Jingu complex, Tokyo's largest and most important Shinto shrine.

Aoyama

People-watching among the designer goods and high-priced cups of coffee in Aoyama on any day of the week is always enjoyable. Every self-respecting fashion house has a flagship store here, from Hanae Mori to Christian Dior to Louis Vuitton, a brand that has become an indispensable accessory for young Japanese women. Striking newcomers to the designer scene include **Tod's**, which opened in early 2005 in a wraparound high-rise designed by Ito Toyo; and **Prada**, which occupies a standalone bubble-glass structure by Herzog & de Meuron (*see p27* **Don't miss: Buildings**).

A stroll along Omotesando is the perfect way to explore the area. Heading downhill from Omotesando station towards Harajuku you soon pass **Anniversaire** on the right, which features three floors of upscale shopping, a fancy French restaurant and a Parisian-style café. The café's outdoor seats are prime people-watching territory, but you'll pay through the nose for a cup of coffee. The basement gallery (5411 4288, www.anniversaire. co.jp, open noon-6pm Wed-Sun, admission ¥500) is worth checking out. More than 100 Chagall paintings are on permanent display, including *L'anniversaire* – hence the building's name.

Further down lies the former site of the government-subsidised apartment buildings (*danchi*) that occupied a hefty stretch of Omotesando since the 1920s. They are being replaced by a low-level commercial and

Trendy **Takeshita Dori**. *See p87.*

residential complex, designed by Ando Tadao; currently under construction, it is due for completion at the end of 2005. Still intact, however, is the neighbouring Meiji Jingu primary school.

On the opposite side of the road is the traditional façade of **Oriental Bazaar** (*see p190*). A godsend for souvenir hunters, the store's three floors are stuffed with all manner of Japanese goods. Best of all, everything is quite cheap, probably less than half the price you would pay at an average department store. Nearby is toy megastore **Kiddyland** (*see p193*). The epicentre of cute, cuddly, crazy and comical Japan, it offers every manner of toy, puzzle, game and doll imaginable – be prepared for sensory overload.

The side streets that lie in between Omotesando and Aoyama Dori are worth exploring; you'll come across narrow winding alleys, old-fashioned homes, tiny art galleries

Pass through the *torii* into the **Meiji Shrine** complex. *See p87*.

and foreigner-friendly **Las Chicas** (*see p143*), a complex of eating, drinking and art spaces set around a pretty courtyard.

Back at the Omotesando/Aoyama Dori crossing, there's much to explore along Aoyama Dori itself. Head south (towards Shibuya) and you'll soon pass, on the left, the white exterior of **Spiral Hall** (*see p224*), one of Tokyo's key art and design spaces. Just beyond is a turning into another key shopping street, **Kotto Dori**, which runs down to join Roppongi Dori. It has upmarket fashion houses next to effete French restaurants, plus some posh clubs and bars thrown in. A stroll along here at night should reveal a mix of well-to-do partiers, hardcore ravers and average folk out for a good time. For a healthy dose of whimsy, pop into the **Okamoto Taro Memorial Museum**, about halfway down Kotto Dori and one block to the left. Not far away is Aoyama's prime art oasis, the **Nezu Institute of Fine Arts**, set in tranquil woods, complete with ponds, stone trails and teahouses.

Further along Aoyama Dori is the massive **United Nations University Centre** and, next door, the **National Children's Castle** (*see p204*), a great resource for local parents. Among other attractions are a video library, fine arts studio, computer playroom and a very popular rooftop playport.

Heading in the opposite direction along Aoyama Dori (towards Akasaka) leads to the giant necropolis of **Aoyama Cemetery** (map p109), to the south of Gaienmae subway station. Occupying some of the most expensive land in Tokyo, it was once part of the local *daimyo*'s estate, and became a cemetery in 1872 after a brief stint as a silk farm. It contains more than 100,000 graves and is a good spot for cherry blossom viewing in April. On the other side of the main road is **Meiji Shrine Outer Garden** and various sports facilities built for the 1964 Olympics, including the **National Stadium** (*see p254*) and **Jingu Baseball Stadium** (*see p253*). Also in the vicinity is the **Watari-Um Museum of Contemporary Art**.

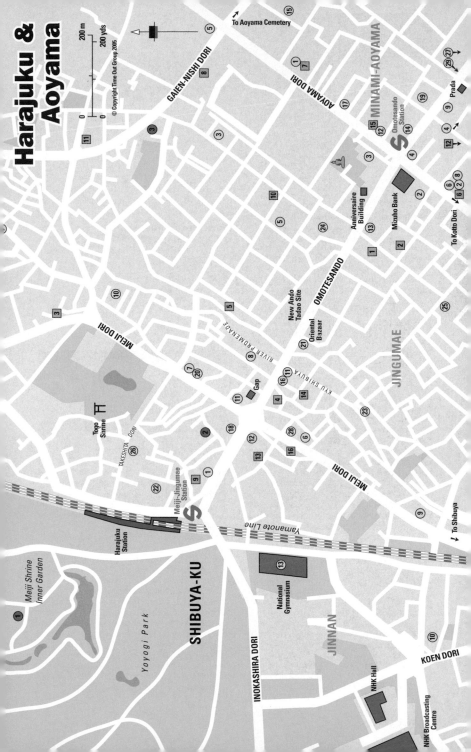

Nezu Institute of Fine Arts

6-5-1 Minami-Aoyama, Minato-ku (3400 2536/ www.nezu-muse.or.jp). Omotesando station (Chiyoda, Ginza, Hanzomon lines), exit A5. **Open** 9.30am-4.30pm Tue-Sun. **Admission** ¥1,000; ¥700 concessions. **No credit cards.**

Tobu Railway founder Kaichiro Nezu had a penchant for Chinese art and collected Shang and Zhou bronzes. Over the years, the museum's collection of over 7,000 objects has grown through donations of Korean ceramics and Japanese ink paintings from private collectors. Some of the most famous works are on permanent display, others rotate in temporary exhibitions.

Okamoto Taro Memorial Museum

6-1-19 Minami-Aoyama, Minato-ku (3406 0801/ http://taro-okamoto.or.jp). Omotesando station (Chiyoda, Ginza, Hanzomon lines), exit B1. **Open** 10am-6pm Mon, Wed-Sun. **Admission** ¥600; ¥300 concessions. **No credit cards.**

This two-storey museum just off Kotto Dori was once the studio of artist Taro Okamoto, who died in 1996. The adjoining café looks into a lovely tropical garden packed with his wacky sculptures.

United Nations University Centre

United Nations University Bldg, 5-53-70 Jingumae, Shibuya-ku (3499 2811/library 5467 1359/ www.unu.edu/ctr.html). Omotesando station (Chiyoda, Ginza, Hanzomon lines), exit B2. **Open** 10am-1pm, 2-5.30pm Mon-Fri. **Admission** free. **Map** p79.

The UNU Centre houses a permanent UN staff and hosts international conferences on global problems and offers classes. On the eighth floor is a good library for exploring human rights issues and global concerns. The galleries on the first and second floors are also worthy of a wander.

Watari-Um Museum of Contemporary Art

3-7-6 Jingumae, Shibuya-ku (3402 3001/ www.watarium.co.jp). Gaienmae station (Ginza line), exit 3. **Open** 11am-7pm Tue, Thur-Sun; 11am-9pm Wed. **Admission** ¥1,000; ¥800 concessions. **No credit cards. Map** p85.

Points of faith

Japanese adherents of Shinto number around 106 million, while those regarding themselves as Buddhists amount to 95 million. This tally of over 200 million is not bad for a country with a population of just 127 million. Clearly, when it comes to religion, the Japanese believe there's no harm in hedging one's bets. It is common for people to have their rites-of-passage ceremonies in a Shinto shrine, their marriage in a Christian chapel and their funeral in a Buddhist temple.

Though the great majority of Japanese happily embrace both native Shinto and imported Buddhism, these are about as different as two faiths could be. Shinto is unconcerned with matters of the afterlife, while this and individual salvation are high concerns of Buddhism.

Shinto is a primitive faith: it imparts no ethical doctrine and possesses no holy scriptures. It is at heart a system of animistic belief in natural spirits (*kami*) – the religious system of an ancient nation of rice farmers that has survived into the modern age. Many of Japan's numerous festivals, one of Shinto's most visible aspects, are fertility rites, supplicating the deities to bestow a good rice crop on to the community.

Purity has long been a major feature of Shinto, and this is evident at the place of worship (conventionally termed shrine in

English, to distinguish them from Buddhist temples). After passing through the shrine's distinctive *torii* (gate), worshippers often ritually wash their hands and mouth from a stone water basin before offering their prayers at the main hall.

Talismans play an important role too, so stalls at the shrine sell amulets for luck in driving, exams, health, love and so on. You'll also see collections of small wooden plaques (*ema* – pictured) on which people write wishes, white fortune-telling paper slips (*omikuji*) tied around trees in the grounds, and sometimes beautiful, colourful strings of 1,000 origami paper cranes (*senbazuru*).

By the time Buddhism arrived in Japan from Korea in the sixth century AD, it was already 1,000 years old, and in its long journey across Asia from India had picked up rituals, symbols and tenets that would have seemed utterly alien to its founders. Mahayana

Mario Botta designed this small art museum for the Watari family in 1990. It holds four exhibitions a year, some of which originate at the museum, while others are brought from abroad. There's a good art bookshop and a pleasant café in the basement.

Harajuku

Harajuku's emblematic shopping street is **Takeshita Dori** (see p177), a narrow pedestrianised thoroughfare of small clothes shops and crêpe stands patronised by the 11-20 set. The street, now a tourist attraction in itself, is a solid mass of humanity at weekends – a shuffle through this awe-inspiring sight is a must. It starts on the opposite side of the road from quaintly old-fashioned Harajuku station and winds its way to join Meiji Dori; halfway along are some steps leading up to **Togo Shrine**, the setting for a great flea market on the first and fourth Sundays of the month. The surrounding side streets are crammed with one-off clothing shops, quirky jewellery stores and eateries, and well worth a wander.

Key stores include **Laforet** (see p180) on the corner of Meiji Dori and Omotesando, opposite a huge branch of Gap. A popular meeting spot, it offers five floors of teenybopper shopping heaven with an art museum/event space as the cherry on top. Behind Laforet lies another world – the 'floating world' of ukiyo-e woodblock prints in the small, dimly lit and tatami-floored **Ukiyo-e Ota Memorial Museum of Art**. Leave your shoes in a locker at the entrance, and don't miss the basement gift shop. Fans of contemporary architecture should visit the **GA Gallery**, located north of Harajuku station, between the railway tracks and Meiji Dori.

The main nexus of teenybopper Tokyo extends from Takeshita Dori up towards the Meiji Shrine. On the bridge in front of the entrance to the shrine's Inner Garden, Tokyo's teen hipsters (mainly girls) hang out at weekends in outrageous cosu-purei (costume play) outfits. This expression of youthful exuberance has also become a major tourist attraction, and with some justification.

The costumes have gone from cool to inventive to bizarre, becoming one of the nation's major articulations of youth creativity. A favourite outfit over the past few years has been the 19th-century French maid's kit. Black and white, frilly and provocative, this get-up can be quite shocking on a 14-year-old Japanese girl – if it weren't for the innocent giggles and enthusiastic posing for the cameras. Another eye-catching offering is the nurse's uniform, with a twist. Not content to splatter their smocks with a bit of blood from supposed patients (in vogue a while back), the girls now complete the outfit with their own delicately arranged fake blood and bandages. Add to these a variety of sexy, goth, punk, school and superhero costumes, and Sundays in front of Meiji Shrine become pretty interesting.

The entrance to the **Meiji Shrine** is through an 11-metre (36-foot) torii (gate), the largest in the country, built from 1,600-year-old Japanese cypress trees imported from Taiwan. A wide gravel path winds through the thickly wooded Inner Garden, with various smaller paths leading off into the dense overhanging foliage, before reaching the shrine's buildings. As with the Imperial Palace and its grounds, this huge patch of green is instantly recognisable from observation decks across the city. The serene atmosphere, punctuated by birdsong, is a world away from the mayhem of Harajuku's shops.

Adjoining the Inner Garden are the lush expanses of **Yoyogi Park**, a favourite with couples and families, who spend warm afternoons lounging on the grass. Formerly

Buddhism, as practised in Japan, introduced the notion of bodhisattvas, who put off their own salvation in order to bring enlightenment to others. Kannon is a popular bodhisattva, as is Jizo, often seen by roadsides and in temples as a small stone figure wearing a red bib.

Temples are often very ornate and brightly coloured, while shrines tend to be more muted affairs. At both, people make offerings, often with a ¥5 coin, which is considered lucky. Temples also sell good luck charms, and commonly feature incense burners; you'll see people directing the smoke, which is deemed to have beneficial powers, over themselves.

You can't enter the main buildings at temples or shrines, but otherwise there are no off-limits areas and locals won't be offended by sightseers. Behave calmly and respectfully; if in doubt, copy other people's behaviour. Photography is widely permitted, but may be forbidden indoors at some temples – look for signs. You may be required to take off your shoes when entering temple buildings.

Must-see religious sites in Tokyo are the **Meiji Shrine** (see p88) and the **Asakusa Kannon (Senso-ji) Temple** (see p97); if you're really keen, head to the temple towns of **Kamakura** (see pp272-5) or **Nikko** (see pp276-8).

Sightseeing

a residential area for US military, then the site of the Olympic Village in 1964, it became a park in 1967. It's known for its autumn foliage, especially the golden gingko trees. At the southern end of the park, across Inokashira Dori, lie the headquarters of state broadcaster NHK and architect Tange Kenzo's **Yoyogi National Stadium** (*see p255*), also built for the Olympics and still one of Tokyo's most famous modern landmarks.

GA Gallery

3-12-14 Sendagaya, Shibuya-ku (3403 1581/ www.ga-ada.co.jp). Yoyogi station (Yamanote line), east exit; (Oedo line), exit A1. **Open** noon-6.30pm Tue-Sun. **Admission** ¥500; free concessions. **No credit cards**.

Global Architecture's annual 'GA Houses' and 'GA Japan' exhibitions make it one of Tokyo's best places for modern and contemporary Japanese and international architecture. The building also houses an excellent architecture bookshop.

Meiji Shrine & Inner Garden

1-1 Yoyogi-Kamizonocho, Shibuya-ku (3379 5511/ www.meijijingu.or.jp). Harajuku station (Yamanote line), Omotesando exit or Meiji-Jingumae station (Chiyoda line), exit 2. **Open** *Shrine & Inner Garden Spring, autumn* 5.40am-5.20pm daily. *Summer* 4am-5pm daily. *Winter* 6am-5pm daily. *Meiji Shrine Garden Mar-Oct* 9am-5pm daily. *Nov-Feb* 9am-4pm daily. **Admission** *Shrine & Inner Garden* free. *Meiji Shrine Garden* ¥500. *Treasure house* ¥200. **No credit cards**. **Map** p85.

Opened in 1920, the shrine is dedicated to Emperor Meiji – whose long reign (1868-1912) coincided with Japan's modernisation – and his consort, Empress Shoken. Exceedingly popular, especially at New Year, when it draws crowds of a million-plus, the shrine hosts numerous annual festivals, including two sumo dedicatory ceremonies in early January and at the end of September. Shinto weddings occur regularly. The current main building dates from 1958, a reconstruction after the original was destroyed during World War II. It is an impressive example of the austere style and restrained colours typical of Shinto architecture. A treasure house in the north of the complex holds imperial coaches and suchlike, but isn't that interesting. Just off the main path to the shrine, through the wooded Inner Garden, are two entrances to another garden, the little-visited Meiji Jingu Gyoen. It's neither large nor especially beautiful, but it is quiet – except in June when the iris field attracts admirers. Vegetation is dense, limiting access to the few trails, which lead to a pond and teahouse.

Ukiyo-e Ota Memorial Museum of Art (Ota Kinen Bijutsukan)

1-10-10 Jingumae, Shibuya-ku (3403 0880/ www.ukiyoe-ota-muse.jp). Harajuku station (Yamanote line), Omotesando exit or Meiji-Jingumae station (Chiyoda line), exit 5. **Open** 10.30am-5.30pm Tue-Sun. Closed 27-end of mth. **Admission** ¥1,000; ¥400 concessions. **No credit cards**. **Map** p85.

The late Seizo Ota, chairman of Toho Mutual Life Insurance, began collecting *ukiyo-e* prints after he saw that Japan was losing its traditional art to museums and collectors in the West. Temporary exhibitions drawn from the 12,000-strong collection often include works by popular masters such as Hiroshige and Hokusai.

Getting there

Omotesando station is on the Chiyoda, Ginza and Hanzomon subway lines. Harajuku station is on the Yamanote line and nearby Meiji-Jingumae is on the Chiyoda line.

Tokyo's teen hipsters. *See p87*.

Ebisu & Daikanyama

Head west for funky fashion and some unusual museums.

Dining destination **Ebisu** (also spelled Yebisu) and shopping haven **Daikanyama** form an upmarket patch of Tokyo within a stone's throw of Shibuya. Ebisu proper comes alive at night when hordes of young Tokyoites flock to drink and be merry at the area's myriad restaurants, while the self-contained plaza of Ebisu Garden Place is liveliest on weekends when shoppers and daytrippers crowd its stores, galleries and museums.

The weekend is also Daikanyama's appointed hour, as thousands of young, predominantly female, shoppers descend upon the scores of boutiques for serial wardrobe updates. A short walk from the west exit of Ebisu station, this prim neighbourhood is one of the few districts in Japan that has no McDonald's, Starbucks or Wendy's. One station down the tracks from Daikanyama is the increasingly hip neighbourhood of **Naka-Meguro** (see p122).

Just to the south of Ebisu and one stop further on the Yamanote line is **Meguro** station – the starting point for some unusual and entertaining diversions.

Ebisu

In 1887 Japanese Beer Brewing Ltd established a brewery for its first product: a beer named after endomorphic deity Ebisu, one of the seven gods of good fortune. The enormous success of the beverage – it is still one of the nation's best-selling lagers – led to the area taking its celestial name.

The connection with beer is appropriate – this area is renowned for its wealth of restaurants and is regarded as Tokyo's number one spot for rowdy *go-kon* (group blind dates). In fact, local ties with the liquid gold business are still strong – Ebisu's biggest attraction is **Ebisu Garden Place**, a mall development backed by Sapporo Beer, which serves as the location for its headquarters and a Sapporo Beer Hall and the **Beer Museum Yebisu**. A five-minute 'Skywalk' via a moving sidewalk from Ebisu station, the mall is a well-heeled mini city, housing dozens of shops including a small branch of Mitsukoshi department store, and a host of restaurants, foremost among which is chef extraordinaire Joel Robuchon's palatial **Taillevent Robuchon**

(5424 1338, www.taillevent.com/japon/), housed in a bright yellow, mock French château complete with wine shop and pâtisserie. Also figured into the development are the **Westin Tokyo** hotel (see p41), office towers, apartment buildings and the **Tokyo Metropolitan Museum of Photography**.

Venture out of the station through either the east or west exits and you are plunged into a buzzing mélange of restaurants, cafés, bars, pubs (including **What the Dickens**; see p162) and nightclubs (including **Milk**; see p213) and, underlining the area's suitability as a dating spot, even a couple of love hotels.

Beer Museum Yebisu

4-20-1 Ebisu Garden Place, Shibuya-ku (5423 7255/www.sapporobeer.jp/brewery/y_museum/). Ebisu station (Yamanote line), east exit; (Hibiya line), exit 1. **Open** 10am-6pm Tue-Sun. **Admission** free; beer additional ¥200. **No credit cards.**
Commemorating the brewery that stood on the space it now occupies, Sapporo built this museum along with the sprawling prim and proper mall in which it sits. Past the historical photographs, beer labels, old posters and video displays, there's a virtual reality tour of the brewing process and, at last, a lounge. Alas, the beer's not free.

Tokyo Metropolitan Museum of Photography

Ebisu Garden Place, 1-13-3 Mita, Meguro-ku (3280 0099/www.syabi.com/). Ebisu station (Yamanote line), east exit; (Hibiya line), exit 1. **Open** 10am-6pm Tue, Wed, Sat, Sun; 10am-8pm Thur, Fri. **Admission** from ¥300; from ¥150 concessions. **No credit cards.**
Occupying a four-floor building in one corner of Ebisu Garden Place, this is Tokyo's premier photography showcase. It boasts a large permanent collection and brings in the leading lights of the world of photography for regular star-studded shows. The small Images & Technology Gallery in the basement presents a multimedia history of optics, featuring tricks such as morphing and the occasional temporary media art exhibition.

Daikanyama

Daikanyama is one of Tokyo's busiest shopping districts with almost every available square metre devoted to clothing, mostly for girls in their late teens to early 20s. None of the big overseas brands has shops here – Daikanyama

Shopping and entertainment zone **Ebisu Garden Place**. *See p89*.

kids prefer cutesy home-grown designer labels to logo-laden branded merchandise. The area offers many opportunities for observing the often-risible outfits of Japan's most deeply afflicted fashion victims from the comfort of one of the numerous open-air cafés. Although the al fresco seats are limited, the area's hippest café, and a good place to check out Tokyo's beau monde, is **Frames** (Hikawa Bldg 1F, 2-11 Sarugacho, 5784 3384, www.frames-tokyo.info, open 11.30am-4.30pm/5pm daily), located above nightclub *Air* (*see p213*).

Although most of what's on offer at the shops has limited appeal, there are several good places for picking up souvenirs. Anyone who appreciates the Japanese aesthetic will find something of interest at **Okura** (20-11 Sarugacho, 3461 8511, open 11am/11.30am-8.30pm daily), where indigo-dyed T-shirts with traditional patterns are lined up alongside carefully crafted accessories in traditional materials like bamboo, hemp and silk.

Those who are keener on buying into the Japan of the future, rather than a retro look, should visit **Footsoldier** (Kinoshita Bldg 1F, 3-7 Sarugacho, 5784 1660, open 11am-7pm daily), the footwear outlet of Tokyo megabrand **A Bathing Ape** (*see p182*). A glass-encased conveyor belt carries the selection of phat sneakers around this minimalist store. Be prepared to pay big bucks – most of what is on display counts as highly desirable, limited-edition merchandise.

Daikanyama fashionistas also love to express themselves through headgear, and the area's number one hat emporium **CA4LA** (Daikanyama Address E-204, 17-5 Daikanyama-cho, 5459 0085, open noon-8pm daily) is

constantly packed with funky youngsters. The creations on display might be too extravagant for some tastes – but come on, live a little.

Meguro

The area around Meguro station has very little to offer visitors, but there are a couple of interesting museums in the area: the **Kume Art Museum**, next to the station's west exit, and the **Tokyo Metropolitan Teien Art Museum**, a short walk from the east exit. The latter is a 1930s French art deco house, once a prince's residence and now a beautiful blend of architectural showpiece, art museum and landscaped garden. Adjacent to the museum lie the botanical wonders of the **Nature Study Institute & Park**. Hungry folks who have made it to the museum should note that Tokyo's best doughnut shop, **Doughnut Plant** (La Residence de Shiroganedai 1F, 5-18-7 Shirokanedai, 5447 1095, www.doughnutplant.jp, open 9am-8pm daily), is just 100 metres further down the road.

Further away to the east of the station is the unmissable **Parasite Museum**, the world's only museum dedicated to parasites and, bizarrely enough, a popular dating spot.

Kume Art Museum

Kume Bldg 8F, 2-25-5 Kami-Osaki, Shinagawa-ku (3491 1510). Meguro station (Yamanote line), west exit. **Open** 10am-5pm Mon, Tue, Thur-Sun. **Admission** ¥500; ¥200-¥300 concessions. **No credit cards**.

Kume Kuchiro was one of the first Japanese artists to embrace the Impressionist style. This museum has changing displays of his paintings, with themes taken from his 1871-2 trek across the globe.

Nature Study Institute & Park

5-21-5 Shirokanedai, Minato-ku (3441 7176/ www.ins.kahaku.go.jp). Meguro station (Yamanote line), east exit or Shiroganedai station (Nanboku, Mita lines), exit 1. **Open** *May-Aug* 9am-5pm Tue-Sun. *Sept-Apr* 9am-4.30pm Tue-Sun. **Admission** ¥300; free concessions. **No credit cards.**

A primeval forest in central Tokyo? Yes, it's a remnant of the ancient Musashino plain. Established as a scientific study area in 1949, the park contains about 750 plants, 100 birds and 1,300 types of insect. Admission is limited to a few hundred people at a time, so that visitors can enjoy the turtle-filled ponds and forested hills in peace. The one-room museum at the entrance is hardly a destination in itself, but has a couple of interesting points, such as a map showing how the amount of greenery in Tokyo has decreased since 1677, largely as a result of dwindling temple grounds.

Parasite Museum

4-1-1 Shimo-Meguro, Meguro-ku (3716 1264). Meguro station (Yamanote line), west exit. **Open** 10am-5pm Tue-Sun. **Admission** free.

This unusual venture was opened in 1953 by Kamegai Satoru, a doctor whose practice was overwhelmed by patients afflicted with parasites caused by the poor sanitary conditions that were widespread in post-war Japan. The museum displays some 300 samples of 45,000 parasites he collected, 20 of which were discovered by his foundation. The second floor has a display of an 8.8m (29ft) tapeworm taken from the body of a 40-year-old man, with a ribbon next to it showing you just how long 8.8m really is. Ugh. The shop sells parasites preserved in plastic keyrings: the ideal gift for your nearest and dearest.

Tokyo Metropolitan Teien Art Museum

5-21-9 Shirokanedai, Minato-ku (3443 0201/ www.teien-art-museum.ne.jp). Meguro station (Yamanote line), east exit or Shiroganedai station (Nanboku, Mita lines), exit 1. **Open** 10am-6pm daily. Closed 2nd & 4th Wed of mth. **Admission** *Exhibitions* vary. *Garden* ¥200; free-¥100 concessions. **No credit cards.**

This 1933 art deco mansion, fronted by both a Western-style rose garden and a Japanese stroll garden with teahouse, was once the home of Prince Asaka Yasuhiko, the uncle of Emperor Hirohito, and his wife, Princess Nobuko, the eighth daughter of Emperor Meiji. The prince returned from a three-year stint in 1920s Paris enamoured of art deco and decided to build a modern residence. Henri Rapin designed most of the interior, while René Lalique added his touch to the crystal chandeliers and the doors. The actual house was completed by architects of the Imperial Household Department, foremost among them Yokichi Gondo. Regularly changing temporary shows – on such varied subjects as early Japanese jewellery and artist Emil Nolde – are spread through the museum and double as house tours.

Getting there

Ebisu station is on the Yamanote line and the Hibiya subway line; Meguro is also on the Yamanote line. Daikanyama is on the Tokyu Toyoko line.

Etiquette

First, the bad news: a guide to Japanese etiquette could fill volumes and still not capture all the intricacies of the social rules. Now the good news: few Japanese people understand these rules in any depth, and still fewer expect foreigners to follow them. That leaves just a few basic dos and don'ts to bear in mind.

DO

● Take your shoes off. Anytime you enter a home, sports club, public bath or Japanese-style restaurant or inn. If you see a raised step leading to wood or tatami mats, it's time to slip on the slippers.
● Refuse a compliment. Thanking someone for a flattering comment smacks of arrogance to Japanese ears.
● Use the money trays. Many shop staff prefer customers to place their money on small trays. Your change may come this way, or carefully balanced on a banknote.

DON'T

● Pour your own beer. Hold your glass while a fellow drinker pours, and be sure to keep their glass full too.
● Raise a toast with the phrase 'chin chin'. It refers to male genitalia in Japanese.
● Finish your food or drink. Forget what your parents told you about starving Africans; a clean plate or empty glass suggests you thought the serving meagre.
● Place your chopsticks vertically in your food. It signifies death.
● Blow your nose in public. Sniffle or snort if you need to, but keep the nasal juice in.

If you bear these rules in mind, your hosts should forgive your more subtle indiscretions. In return, you'll need to relax your own rules; bumping and barging are part of life in Tokyo and rarely elicit an apology, while spitting, public urination and noodle-slurping are all common behaviour. For how to behave in a bathhouse, *see p114* **Getting into hot water.** For business-related etiquette, *see p288.*

Sightseeing

Asakusa

The historic riverside quarter that's home to one of Tokyo's temple gems.

Map p93

Long before Roppongi and Shibuya figured on anybody's radar of interest, Asakusa (pronounced 'a-sak-sa') was *the* place for entertainment in Tokyo. For a couple of centuries up until around 1940, this area adjacent to the eastern bank of the Sumida river was far and away the most exciting and dynamic part of town. It's a fine example of *shitamachi*, the low-lying districts of the city where the commoners lived cheek by jowl until Tokyo's population began drifting westwards in the aftermath of the Great Earthquake of 1923 and fire bombing in World War II. With this westward shift, Asakusa became increasingly peripheral to mainstream city life.

Today a sense of faded grandeur still hangs over the area, but for the visitor the greatest appeal lies in the **Asakusa Kannon** temple. It is this temple complex and its environs that have helped make Asakusa into one of Tokyo's prime tourist attractions.

Also known as **Senso-ji**, Asakusa Kannon is Tokyo's oldest temple, with origins, so the remarkably precise story has it, dating to 18 March 628. That was when two brothers fishing on the Sumida river caught a five-centimetre (two-inch) golden statue in their net. Lacking wisdom in mysterious ways, they threw the statue back in the river twice, only for it to reappear both times. At this point they twigged that something out of the ordinary was happening, and took the statue to the village headman. He enshrined it in his house, and in 645 a hall was built for this image of Kannon, the Buddhist goddess of mercy, on the spot where today's temple stands. The complex also houses a Shinto shrine, **Asakusa Jinja**, which was established in 1649 to honour the two fishermen and the village headman.

In later years, Asakusa flourished because of its proximity to Yoshiwara, the biggest area of licensed prostitution in Edo (as Tokyo was known from 1600 to 1868). Seeking a little refreshment before the evening's main activities, Yoshiwara's clientele could find that and plenty of other diversions in Asakusa – from acrobats and magicians to comedians and performing monkeys. In particular, it flourished as the centre of *kabuki* theatre, a vastly popular form of entertainment whose leading actors were idolised like rock stars.

Nowadays, Asakusa is home to numerous festivals, both old and new. Tokyo's oldest and biggest festival, in May, is the **Sanja Matsuri** (*see p201*), a frenzied procession of more than a hundred *mikoshi* (portable shrines). The most modern is the **Asakusa Samba Carnival** (*see 198*) in late August, when hundreds of Brazilian and Japanese dancers parade through the streets. The **Sumida River Fireworks** (*see p198*), Japan's biggest annual summertime fireworks display, is held at the end of July and broadcast on national TV.

The Asakusa subway line station sits adjacent to the Sumida river at the end of Asakusa Dori; a few hundred metres north, next to Azumabashi (Azuma Bridge) is the Ginza line station, at the end of Kaminarimon Dori. Across the road, next to the Tobu Isesaki line station, stands Tokyo's oldest Western-style hostelry, **Kamiya Bar** (*see p165*). Built in 1880, it is renowned as the home of 'Denki-Bran' (Electric Brandy), an unusual alcoholic concoction that produces truly spectacular hangovers.

The alcoholic vein continues when you look over Azumabashi to the Bubble-era **Asahi Building**, home of one of Japan's four main brewing companies and the **Flamme d'Or** bar (*see p165*). Designed by Philippe Starck, this odd building is surmounted by a large golden sculpture that is supposed to be a poetical depiction of the foam on a glass of beer. The object's distinct shape causes many locals to refer to it more prosaically as the *unchi-biru* ('turd building'). In the face of such architectural extravagance, the local constabulary clearly didn't want to be left out, so the police box near the bridge sports a pagoda-style roof. North of the pier stretches **Sumida Koen**, a riverside park that is very popular during cherry blossom season.

The approach to Asakusa Kannon temple begins about 100 metres up Kaminarimon Dori from the bridge. It's impossible to miss the main gate to the temple, the **Kaminarimon** (Thunder Gate), with its gigantic red paper lantern. Even in Edo days, this lantern was one of the city's most distinctive sights. Between 1856 and 1858 the great *ukiyo-e* woodblock artist Hiroshige published a set of prints called 'One Hundred Views of Edo'. Among those evocative depictions of the old city, the

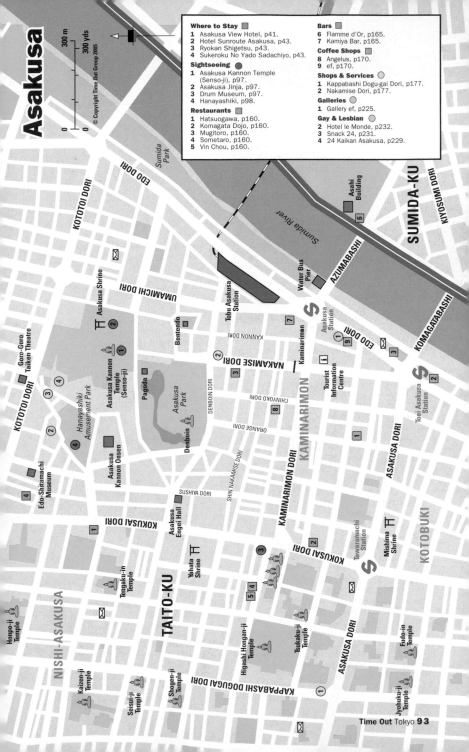

Asakusa

300 m

300 yds

0

© Copyright Time Out Group 2005

Where to Stay
1 Asakusa View Hotel, p41.
2 Hotel Sunroute Asakusa, p43.
3 Ryokan Shigetsu, p43.
4 Sukeroku No Yado Sadachiyo, p43.

Sightseeing
1 Asakusa Kannon Temple (Senso-ji), p97.
2 Asakusa Jinja, p97.
3 Drum Museum, p97.
4 Hanayashiki, p98.

Restaurants
1 Hatsuogawa, p160.
2 Komagata Dojo, p160.
3 Mugitoro, p160.
4 Sometaro, p160.
5 Vin Chou, p160.

Bars
6 Flamme d'Or, p165.
7 Kamiya Bar, p165.

Coffee Shops
8 Angelus, p170.
9 ef, p170.

Shops & Services
1 Kappabashi Dogu-gai Dori, p177.
2 Nakamise Dori, p177.

Galleries
1 Gallery ef, p225.

Gay & Lesbian
2 Hotel le Monde, p232.
3 Snack 24, p231.
4 24 Kaikan Asakusa, p229.

Snacks galore on Asakusa's streets.

Kaminarimon lantern is about the only one that could be identified by a modern-day Tokyoite. Black-garbed rickshaw drivers cruise the entrance looking for tourists to ferry around. Across the road is the **Asakusa Culture & Sightseeing Centre** (3842 5566, open 9.30am-8pm daily), which has maps, information and runs free one-hour tours of the area at 1.30pm and 3pm on Sundays.

From the gate stretches the lively thoroughfare of **Nakamise Dori** (*see p177*). For centuries this street was lined with stalls catering to the crowds on their way to and from the temple. Today there are about 150 stalls along its 300-metre (100-yard) length, selling such traditional goods as combs, fans, dolls, kimono, paper crafts, clothing, toys and snacks, many of which items would be instantly recognisable to any resident of old Edo. Absent from the scene are the former archery galleries. These were presided over by attractive young women, whose make-up and manner made it clear that when they escorted a male customer into their back room it wasn't with a view to stringing up his bow.

The temple is the main attraction in Asakusa, but there are plenty of other sights of interest. Heading north through the temple precincts will lead you to Kototoi Dori; turn left and you'll walk past the **Goro-Goro Taiken Theatre**, famous for displays of highly stylised swordsmanship. Turning left again at a small shopping street called Hisagao

Dori brings you to the entrance of Japan's oldest amusement park, **Hanayashiki**. Nearby is the small **Edo-Shitamachi Traditional Crafts Museum** (2-22-13 Asakusa, 3842 1990, open 10am-8pm daily, admission free), which displays traditional crafts made by local artists.

Just to the west beyond Hanayashiki is the small district of Rokku, centred on Rokku Eigagai. This was Edo and Tokyo's prime entertainment area, though, today, sadly, it's a pale imitation of its former self. Japanese folk music drifts from the open doorways of **Asakusa Engei Hall**, the home of *rakugoh* – traditional comic storytelling. Garish posters of 1960s yakuza gangster films are pasted outside the Shin-Gekijo, Meiga-za and Toho cinemas. Further south, on Kokusai Dori opposite the police box, is the delightful **Drum Museum**, located on the second floor of a shop selling musical instruments and Buddhist shrines.

Aside from the temple grounds and brash culture of Rokku, Asakusa's busy shopping streets are great places for an idle wander to see a slice of traditional life. You might chance upon a kimono shop owner kneeling at his counter in front of variegated bolts of cloth; or a half-dozen *sembei* (rice cracker) makers chatting as they toast crackers on a charcoal grill; or a tea merchant, with jade-green wares displayed in woven baskets and the delicious smell of roasting fresh tea wafting from his shop.

Shopping of a more specialised kind can be found by walking west (away from the river) to **Kappabashi Dogu-gai Dori** (*see p177*), Tokyo's main wholesale district for the restaurant industry. This is far more interesting than it sounds: it's where caterers come to buy all those (surprisingly expensive) plastic models of foodstuffs that you see displayed in restaurant windows. All manner of kitchen hardware is on sale, from ceramic bowls to small fish knives to cauldron-sized pots. Shops line either side of Kappabashi Dori; look for the 12-metre high (39-foot) chef's head atop the Niimi Building.

Further south and back towards the river are other wholesale districts, specialising in dolls, stationery and fashion accessories – the nearest stations are Kuramae and Asakusabashi. Near the latter is the **Japanese Stationery Museum**, where you can explore the history of writing and calculating implements.

ON THE RIVER

Asakusa can also be the starting point for a cruise on the Sumida river. One option is to take the water bus (*suijo* bus), which leaves every 20-45 minutes from the pier next to Azumabashi, heading south under 13 bridges

Take me to the river

Want to escape Tokyo's crowded streets? Then take to the water aboard one of the many *suijo* buses that ply five routes along the Sumida river and around Tokyo Bay. The water bus can't compete with the train, which is faster and cheaper, but in good weather it is difficult to think of a more pleasurable way to cross the city. Boats vary depending on which line you take, from the prosaic (a flat-topped wooden structure) to the fanciful (a paddlesteamer lookalike complete with pipe organ and fireplace) to the futuristic (the newest model, a green-glassed, super-sleek number that seems to have cruised out of the pages of the latest manga). All routes leave from Hinode Pier, a short walk from Hamamatsucho station on the Yamanote line.

The most popular route is the **Sumida River line**, whose boats grind their way for 40 minutes up the dark water to Asakusa, passing beneath 13 road and rail bridges. Many people do the trip in the other direction, having toured **Asakusa Kannon Temple** (*see p97*) and other sights, dropping in at the beautiful **Hama-Rikyu Detached Garden** (*see p62*).

Another popular destination, via the **Odaiba line**, is the artificial island of Odaiba, less than 30 minutes from Hinode Pier. Although Odaiba functions mainly as an industrial park, it does boast a number of attractions, including **Odaiba Seaside Park**, where Tokyoites get to frolic on a beach of shipped-in sand and sip cocktails year round in the many bars and restaurants stacked along the waterfront. Boats stop first at **Harumi**; once the mecca for Japan's convention-goers, this reclaimed area has been eclipsed by the new bureautropolis of Ariake, and now offers little of interest beside the Museum of Gas Science, a central cleaning factory and numerous redevelopment projects.

For a glimpse of the future, ride the **Tokyo Big Site/Palette Town line** to Ariake, 20 minutes from Hinode Pier. Afloat on Tokyo Bay, this area has been made famous by its monolithic convention centre, **Tokyo Big Sight**. Resembling a grain silo from Mars, the absurd structure towers over an asphalt grid of raised walkways, palm-lined avenues and office blocks. En route the boat makes a brief stop at the newly developed shopping and entertainment site of **Palette Town** on the north side of Odaiba. From the Big Sight Pier, some boats travel further on to **Kasai Seaside Park** (*see p128*), another half-hour away. In summer, the line extends to Edogawa, where there are a variety of entertainment spots.

Next is the **Museum of Maritime Science/ Shinagawa Aquarium line**. The first leg of this journey is a 25-minute cruise to Odaiba's Aomi, where three ships – two real, one concrete – comprise the **Museum of Maritime Science** (*see p116*). Continuing on to **Shinagawa Aquarium** (*see p203*) on the eastern side of the bay, the boat passes directly below Rainbow Bridge before careering suddenly toward the bank and disappearing down a tree-lined canal running parallel to the bay. Between is a thin strip of land that gradually widens into a remarkable example of man-made nature – the densely forested **Oi Seashore Park**. The aquarium is a short walk away.

Although the fifth and final excursion offers a simple shuttle to and from Odaiba Seaside Park, the **Harbor Cruise line** is best enjoyed as an evening round trip into the bay and back. The boat passes beneath Rainbow Bridge, whose illuminations compete with the surrounding shores in lighting up the bay.

Suijo Bus

Asakusa Pier office 3841 9178/Hinode Pier office 3457 7830/www.suijobus.co.jp. Typical one-way fares from Hinode Pier are ¥500 to Odaiba Seaside Park, ¥620 to Asakusa and ¥800 to Kasai Sealife Park.

Sightseeing

en route to beautiful **Hama-Rikyu Detached Garden** (*see p62*). There's a network of five water bus lines; for more details, *see p95* **Take me to the river**.

Or you could take a *yakata-bune* boat tour. These are leisurely cruises around Tokyo Bay on floating restaurants – and nicest at night. Several companies operate tours; try **Amisei** (3844 1869). Tickets are ¥10,000-¥20,000, but include as much food (tempura, sushi, yakitori) and drink (beer, sake, juice) as you can consume. Reservations are advisable.

RYOGOKU

Just across the Sumida river is Ryogoku, where sumo tournaments have been held for 300 years. You'll spot a few small statues of wrestlers outside the Ryogoku JR station and maybe a couple of souvenir stalls, but it's generally a nondescript area. It's home to the **Ryogoku Kokugikan** (*see p257*), the stadium where three of sumo's Grand Tournaments are held, in January, May and September, and various stables (*heya*), where the wrestlers live and train. Restaurants specialising in *chanko-nabe*, the stews the wrestlers eat, also cluster here; a good one to visit is **Yoshiba** (*see p150*).

If you're in town when no tournaments are in progress, it's possible to visit a stable to see the wrestlers in their daily morning practice sessions. There are over 40 stables in Tokyo, most situated close to the Kokugikan. Most allow visitors, on condition that they remain quiet – call ahead (in Japanese) to ask permission. The stables let you in for free, but take along a small gift, such as a bottle of sake, for the stablemaster, to show your appreciation. Photos are usually permitted, but don't point your feet towards the ring. Be warned: the day starts early. Junior wrestlers are up and about at 4am, and gruelling practice sessions start at around 5am. The higher ranked wrestlers start to appear at around 8am.

Recommended stables are **Azumazeki** (4-6-4 Higashi Komagata, Sumida-ku, 3625 0033), **Dewanoumi** (2-3-15 Ryogoku, Sumida-ku, 3633 4920), **Musashigawa** (4-27-1 Higashi-Nippori, Arakawa-ku, 3801 6343) and **Oshiogawa** (2-17-7 Kiba, Koto-ku, 3643 8156). There's also an up-to-date list of addresses at www.accesscom.com/~abe/03haruheya.html.

If you couldn't care less about sumo, the excellent **Edo-Tokyo Museum** is located next door to the Kokugikan. There's also the **Tokyo Metropolitan Memorial & Tokyo Reconstruction Museum**.

The stalls of **Nakamise Dori** (top) lead to the **Asakusa Kannon Temple** complex.

FURTHER AFIELD

Asakusa thrived in the Edo era because of its proximity to Yoshiwara, but little survives of the red-light district today. What was once a huge, walled pleasure area is now the home of massage parlours, 'soaplands' and love hotels. What does remain, though, is the sad structure of **Jokan-ji** temple, close to Minowa station (from Asakusa station, take the Ginza line to Ueno station, then the Hibiya line two stops to Minowa). The image of Yoshiwara may have a rakish, exotic appeal, but Jokan-ji presents the other side of the coin: this is where more than 11,000 prostitutes, mostly in their early 20s, were buried in a common grave.

From Minowa it is possible to get another experience of old Tokyo in the form of the **Arakawa Streetcar Line** (*see p120*). Old-fashioned green and cream trams trundle westwards along a 12-kilometre (eight-mile) route from Minowabashi station to Waseda, not far from Ikebukuro.

Asakusa Kannon Temple (Senso-ji) & Asakusa Jinja

2-3-1 Asakusa, Taito-ku (temple 3842 0181/shrine 3844 1575). Asakusa station (Asakusa, Ginza lines), exits 1, 3, 6, A4. **Open** *Temple* 6am-5pm daily. *Shrine* 6.30am-5pm daily. *Grounds* 24hrs daily. **Admission** free. **Map** p93.

The lively focus of traditional life in Tokyo, Asakusa Kannon is the city's most vivid reminder of the Edo era. Although the current buildings are constructed in a distinctly un-Edo-like ferro-concrete, they do offer an indication of the older city that lurks beneath the modern jacket of Tokyo. Most people enter from the south, through the main gate, Kaminarimon, past the stalls of Nakamise Dori and then through the two-storey Hozomon gate into the temple grounds proper. To the left stands a five-storey, 55m (180ft) pagoda, the second-highest in Japan; ahead are the magnificent sweeping roofs of the Main Hall with the gold-plated Gokuden shrine inside. Behind and to the right is Asakusa Jinja, the starting point of the Sanja Matsuri. A huge bronze incense burner stands in front of the Main Hall. The smoke is believed to have curative powers, and visitors usually stop to 'bathe' in it, often directing the smoke towards a troubled part of the body. You can make a wish, pick your fortune or buy good-luck charms from stalls. Other buildings and gardens occupy the extensive grounds.

Drum Museum (Taiko-kan)

Miyamoto Unosuke Shoten, Nishi-Asakusa Bldg 4F, 2-1-1 Nishi-Asakusa, Taito-ku (3842 5622/ www.tctv.ne.jp/members/taikokan). Tawaramachi station (Ginza line). **Open** 10am-5pm Wed-Sun. **Admission** ¥300; ¥150 concessions; free under-6s. **No credit cards. Map** p93.

With a clay drum from Mexico, an *udekki* from Sri Lanka and hundreds of other drums from around

Sightseeing

the world, this interactive museum is a fine place to visit. Find your own rhythm by banging on many of them (a blue dot means it's allowed, a red one means it's not).

Edo-Tokyo Museum

1-4-1 Yokoami, Sumida-ku (3626 9974/www.edo-tokyo-museum.or.jp). Ryogoku station (Sobu line), west exit; (Oedo line), exits A3, A4. **Open** 9.30am-5.30pm Tue, Wed, Sat, Sun; 9.30am-8pm Thur, Fri. **Admission** ¥600; free under-15s; additional fee for special exhibitions. **No credit cards**.

This large museum's outlandish architectural style may not appeal to everyone, but it houses the city's best and most comprehensive collection of displays dealing with the history of Tokyo and its earlier incarnation, Edo. Highlights include large-scale reconstructions of Nihonbashi bridge and a *kabuki* theatre, and incredibly detailed models of various quarters of the city at different eras. Exhibits outline lifestyles from those of Edo-period samurai to World War II families, and show how disasters both natural and man-made altered the city's landscape. The English labelling is good, and volunteer guides provide tours in English and other languages. You'll need a couple of hours to do it justice.

Hanayashiki

2-28-1 Asakusa, Taito-ku (3842 8780/ www.hanayashiki.net/first.html). Asakusa station (Asakusa, Ginza lines), exit 3. **Open** 10am-6pm Mon, Wed-Sun. **Admission** ¥900; ¥400 concessions. **No credit cards. Map** p93.

Hanayashiki has been in business since 1885 and still draws crowds. There are around 20 rides, more appealing for nostalgia than thrills – including Japan's oldest steel-track rollercoaster and a haunted house known as the Obake-yashiki. Most of the rides have been upgraded over the years, but their scope is limited due to the park's small size.

Japan Stationery Museum

1-1-15 Yanagibashi, Taito-ku (3861 4905). Asakusabashi station (Asakusa, Sobu lines), east exit. **Open** 10am-4pm Mon-Fri. **Admission** free.

Exhibits range from flints and a tablet from Mesopotamia through Egyptian papyrus to abacuses and typewriters with interchangeable *kanji* keys. One highlight is a 14kg (31lb) brush made from the hair of over 50 horses. Descriptions are in Japanese, but it is still possible to appreciate the objects just from their great age and character.

Tokyo Metropolitan Memorial & Tokyo Reconstruction Museum

2-3-25 Yokoami, Sumida-ku (3623 1200). Ryogoku station (Sobu line), west exit; (Oedo line), exits A3, A4. **Open** 9am-4.30pm daily. **Admission** free.

Following the Great Kanto Earthquake of 1923, some 40,000 people who had fled their homes perished on this site when sparks set clothing and bedding alight. The fire raged for nearly a day and a half, destroying three-quarters of the city and killing 140,000 people. Seven years later, a three-storey pagoda-topped memorial building was built; after World War II, the memorial's name was changed to include the 100,000 people who died in Tokyo's air raids. The Reconstruction Museum in a nearby building in the park contains wartime mementos. Both buildings are run-down and receive little attention, most of which is concentrated on the controversial Yasukuni Shrine (*see p68* **Ghosts of war**), which honours the war dead. Memorial services are held on 1 September and 10 March.

Getting there

Asakusa is on the Ginza and Asakusa subway lines and the Tobu Isesaki railway line. Water buses arrive at/depart from the pier next to Azumabashi.

Philippe Starck's **Flamme d'Or**.
See p92.

Ueno

Tokyo's first public park and an old-fashioned street market.

Map p103

Back in the days before feng shui was being taken up as rather a neat idea by some in the West, China's ancient rules of geomancy were being strictly applied in feudal Japan. And it is thanks to feng shui that Ueno, one of Tokyo's main sub-centres, came into being. Around the start of the 17th century, shogun Tokugawa Ieyasu began assiduously building a new administrative capital out of the fishing village in a swamp that Edo had been when he found it. His successor, Hidetada, was advised that he ought to build a great temple north-east of Edo Castle to guard against the evil spirits that were apt to enter from that inauspicious direction. So in 1625 he duly installed a massive complex of 36 temples in Ueno.

Only a hint remains today of this complex, but the land that those temples occupied holds the feature for which Ueno is now best known – its park. **Ueno Koen** was Tokyo's first public park when it opened in 1873, but just five years earlier it had been the site of the bloody Battle of Ueno between supporters of the new Meiji government and warriors still loyal to the Tokugawa shogun. The government won, but in the process **Kanei-ji**, the centre of the temple complex where six of Japan's 15 shoguns are buried, was destroyed. Today the site holds a temple and three cemeteries.

Ueno Park contains a whole slew of attractions – from museums to shrines and temples to a zoo. It lacks lawns and picnic areas, but it is famed for its collection of cherry trees. Enormous throngs of Tokyoites gather here every spring in blossom season, though these raucous affairs tend to focus more on portable karaoke machines than flowers. The groundsheets that the party-goers sometimes leave behind get reused for shelters by the homeless people who live in the park.

If you arrive at the JR station, head to the main (above-ground) hall, one of the few station buildings in Tokyo to have largely survived Japan's decades of redevelopment. The high ceilings and grandiose architectural style recall a time when this was one of the city's main transport hubs, ferrying people in from the north before the *shinkansen* dragged most passengers away to the main terminus at Tokyo station. That was when the east side of Tokyo was king, and Asakusa and Ueno

Busy **Ameyoko Market.** *See p101.*

were the city's playgrounds, before the action started to drift westwards, to Shibuya and Shinjuku. The first subway line in Asia opened in 1927 to link Asakusa to Ueno and is now part of the Ginza line.

There's more to Ueno than its park, though. Near the station there exists the area's other great attraction: a lively, exciting street market that offers a real flavour of the Tokyo of yesteryear. To the north of Ueno, across Kototoi Dori, is **Yanaka** (*see pp104-6*), another of Tokyo's *shitamachi* ('low city') districts; it's a short walk from the northern end of Ueno Park into Yanaka Cemetery and its environs.

INSIDE THE PARK

Take the park exit from the station, cross the road and pick up an English map from the information booth. Ueno Koen is home to some of Japan's greatest cultural assets and Tokyo's best collection of museums, which deal with Japanese history and culture, as well as science and the arts of other nations. The first you come to is the Le Corbusier-designed **National Museum of Western Art**. Next door is the **National Science Museum** (*see p204*) and, north of that, the **Tokyo National Museum**, the grandest museum in the park. All the other museums – the **Tokyo Metropolitan Art Museum**, the **University Art Museum** and **Ueno Royal Museum** – are within easy striking distance. For more information, see the individual entries below.

The park also contains **Ueno Zoo** (*see p203*), the most famous in the country with a diverse selection of critters, from a giant panda and Asian lions to wolf-like *dholes* and bison alongside more familiar animals. The zoo occupies the western section of the park. Near to its main entrance, just around from the kiddies' amusement park, is the approach to **Toshogu Shrine**, the finest of the park's historical monuments.

The most attractive part of Ueno Park is the southern area around **Shinobazu Pond** (Shinobazunoike). Given its present inland position, it may be difficult to imagine that this large pond was once part of an inlet of Tokyo Bay. Causeways divide the pond, which is now freshwater, into three: one section is part of Ueno Zoo and has a large colony of cormorants, one is a boating pond and the third is home to a great diversity of waterfowl and comes alive with pink lotus flowers in summer. At the centre of the three causeways is an island on which sits **Bentendo**, a strong contender for the title of most charming temple in Tokyo. It is dedicated to Benten (also called Benzaiten), the goddess of music and feminine beauty and the only female among the Seven Deities of Good Fortune (these auspicious figures are especially evident at New Year).

You can nourish more earthy parts at the food stalls which line the approach to the temple.

From Bentendo, cross over Dobutsuen Dori (the main path that bisects the park) to reach the red **Kiyomizu Kannondo** temple. It is dedicated to Kannon and is modelled on the famous Kiyomizu-dera temple in Kyoto. This was completed in 1631, and is one of the few temple buildings to have survived the destruction of the Battle of Ueno.

Nearby, in the south-east corner of this side of the park, stands the bronze statue of **Saigo Takamori**, a fascinating figure and the person on whom Katsumoto, the warrior played by Ken Watanabe in *The Last Samurai*, is based. Saigo played an instrumental role in the Meiji Restoration of 1868, which ended the reign of the shoguns and brought into power a new imperial government. Later, Saigo became disenchanted with the government he had done so much to create, and got mixed up with an ill-fated rebellion, which ended with Saigo and his supporters committing *hara-kiri*. It is this rebellion that formed the basis for the Tom Cruise film. Of course, Hollywood presents Katsumoto as a virile warrior, whereas by the time of his rebellion Saigo was so obese he had to be carried around in a chair. His statue in Ueno Park (unveiled in 1898) depicts him in deliberately unmilitary mode, in a kimono taking his dog for a walk.

Further south, at the corner of the pond next to the main road, stands the **Shitamachi Museum**. *Shitamachi* refers to the low-lying areas of Tokyo inhabited by the hoi polloi, and this small gem of a place recreates the city as it was in the 19th and early 20th century.

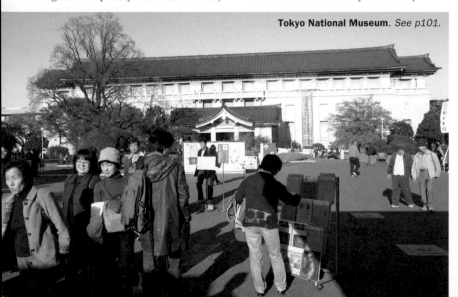

Tokyo National Museum. *See p101.*

OUTSIDE THE PARK

History of a very different kind is to be found in the area around **Ameyoko** (*see p177*), which begins close by Ueno station on the other side of the main road from the park. The name hints at the history of the place: the 'Ame' in Ameyoko originally referred to 'sweets' and the name meant 'confectioner's alley'. But during the occupation following World War II this became a major area for black-market goods, many of which came from the US military. Thus it was that the 'Ame-rican' aspect to the name took on significance.

Ameyoko is Tokyo's liveliest market, with more than 500 stalls shoehorned into a 400-metre (quarter-mile) stretch that leads south to Okachimachi station. The weekend crowds can be so thick that progress is at a snail's pace (watch your valuables; this a popular spot for pickpockets). As well as a myriad fishmongers and fruit and vegetable stalls, there are scores of small shops selling cheap jeans, T-shirts and goods 'inspired' by international designers. It is also, unusually for Tokyo, a reliable source of hard-to-find foods and spices. Families from South and South-east Asia stock up on chillies, basmati rice and coriander, while homesick Americans seek solace in Milky Way bars or Hershey's chocolate imported from the US, rather than Australia, as is the norm in Japan.

At a fork in the road about 90 metres (100 yards) into the market is a dubious-looking building with an amazing basement food hall selling whole frogs, durian fruit and other difficult-to-get delicacies from around the world. Meanwhile, under the railway tracks, cheap watches and electronic goods are the order of the day, along with bootleg CDs.

A couple of additional attractions are located across the western side of the park. Beyond the pond's boating area, on the other side of the main road, is **Yokoyama Taikan Memorial Hall**, dedicated to the life and work of one of Japan's greatest painters of the modern era. Following the road above the hall in a southerly direction will bring you to **Kyu Iwasaki-tei House & Gardens**, which was built by influential British architect Josiah Conder, one of many Westerners to bring Western learning to Japan in the nineteenth century.

Kyu Iwasaki-tei House & Gardens

1-3-45 Ikenohata, Taito-ku (3823 8033/www.tokyo-park.or.jp/english/jpgarden3.html#iwasaki). Yushima station (Chiyoda line), exit 1. **Open** 9am-5pm daily. **Admission** ¥150; free concessions. **No credit cards. Map** p103.
Built in 1896 for Iwasaki Hisaya, son of the founder of the Mitsubishi conglomerate, this compound reveals the fin-de-siècle sheen beneath Ueno's grimy surface. Conder designed the recently renovated main residence – a two-storey wooden structure with Jacobean and Pennsylvanian country house elements (and the first Western-style toilet in Japan) – and the adjacent billiards room in the form of a log cabin. In the large tatami rooms, visitors can sip green tea and admire *fusuma* (sliding doors) painted with seasonal motifs by Hashimoto Gaho.

National Museum of Western Art (Kokuritsu Seiyo Bijutsukan)

7-7 Ueno Koen, Taito-ku (3828 5131/ www.nmwa.go.jp). Ueno station (Yamanote line), park exit; (Ginza, Hibiya lines), Shinobazu exit. **Open** 9.30am-5pm Tue-Thur, Sat, Sun; 9.30am-8pm Fri. **Admission** ¥420; free-¥130 concessions; additional charge for special exhibitions. Free 2nd & 4th Sat of mth. **No credit cards. Map** p103.
The core collection housed in this 1959 Le Corbusier-designed building, Japan's only national museum devoted to Western art, was assembled by Kawasaki shipping magnate Matsukata Kojiro in the early 1900s. Considering that the collection was begun so recently, it is surprisingly good, ranging from 15th-century icons to Monet to Pollock.

Shitamachi Museum (Shitamachi Fuzoku Shiryokan)

2-1 Ueno Koen, Taito-ku (3823 7451/ www.taitocity.net/taito/shitamachi). Ueno station (Yamanote, Ginza, Hibiya lines), Shinobazu exit. **Open** 9.30am-4.30pm Tue-Sun. **Admission** ¥300; ¥100 concessions. **No credit cards. Map** p103.
This museum presents the living environment of ordinary Tokyoites between the pivotal Meiji Restoration of 1868 and the Great Earthquake of 1923. It's a small counterpart to the large-scale Edo-Tokyo Museum (*see p98*) in Ryogoku. Take off your shoes and step into re-creations of a merchant's shop, a coppersmith's workshop and a sweet shop. Everything has a hands-on intimacy: open up a drawer and you'll find a sewing kit or a children's colouring book. Upstairs are traditional toys that even today's sophisticated kids still delight in.

Tokyo Metropolitan Art Museum

8-36 Ueno Koen, Taito-ku (3823 6921/ www.tobikan.jp). Ueno station (Yamanote line), park exit; (Ginza, Hibiya lines), Shinobazu exit. **Open** *Main Gallery* 9am-5pm Tue-Sun. *Library* 9am-5pm daily (closed 3rd Mon of mth). **Admission** *Galleries* vary: free-¥1,500; free-¥500 concessions. *Library* free. **Credit** (gift shop only, over ¥3,000) JCB, MC, V. **Map** p103.
Designed by Maekawa Kunio, this brick-faced art museum was largely constructed underground to remain unobtrusive, with limited success. Temporary shows in the main hall feature everything from traditional Japanese art to art nouveau.

Tokyo National Museum (Tokyo Kokuritsu Hakubutsukan)

13-9 Ueno Koen, Taito-ku (3822 1111/ www.tnm.go.jp). Ueno station (Yamanote line), park exit; (Ginza, Hibya lines) Shinobazu exit.

Sightseeing

Open 9.30am-5pm Tue-Sun (until 8pm Fri during special exhibitions). **Admission** ¥420; free-¥130 concessions; additional charge for special exhibitions. **Credit** (gift shop only) JCB, MC, V. **Map** p103.

If you have just one day to devote to museum-going in Tokyo and are interested in Japanese art and arte-facts, this is the place to come. Japan's oldest and largest museum houses over 89,000 items in different buildings. Past the ornate gateway, there's a wide courtyard and fountain surrounded by three main buildings. Directly in front is the Honkan, or main gallery, dating from 1937, which displays the permanent collection of Japanese arts and antiquities. The 25 rooms regularly rotate their exhibitions of paintings, ceramics, swords, kimono, sculptures and the like. The Toyokan building to the right features three floors of artworks from other parts of Asia. The Hyokeikan, the 1909 European-style building to the left, is open only for special events. Behind the Hyokeikan is the Gallery of Horyu-ji Treasures, which houses some of Japanese Buddhism's most important and ancient artefacts, from the seventh-century Horyu-ji temple in Nara. The Heiseikan, behind the Honkan, holds month-long temporary blockbuster exhibitions of Japanese and Asian art. There are also plenty of places to eat around the complex, and a good gift shop.

Toshogu Shrine

9-88 Ueno Koen, Taito-ku (3822 3455). Ueno station (Yamanote line), park exit; (Ginza, Hibiya lines), Shinobazu exit. **Open** 9am-6pm daily. **Admission** ¥200; ¥100 concessions. **No credit cards. Map** p103.

Toshogu is dedicated to the first Tokugawa shogun, Ieyasu, and its style is similar to that of the shrine in Nikko (also called Toshogu; *see p276*) where he is buried. The Ueno Toshogu was built in 1627, then remodelled in 1651. It has withstood earthquakes and numerous fires as well as the Battle of Ueno, and is one of Tokyo's oldest buildings and a designated National Treasure. The huge lantern on the left before the first gate is one of the largest in Japan, and the approach to the shrine is lined with many smaller stone lanterns. Karamon, the front gate of the temple, is famous for its dragon carvings, which are said to be so lifelike that they sneak to Shinobazu Pond for a drink at night.

Ueno Royal Museum (Ueno no Mori Bijutsukan)

1-2 Ueno Koen, Taito-ku (3833 4195/www.ueno-mori.org). Ueno station (Yamanote line), park exit; (Ginza, Hibiya lines), Shinobazu exit. **Open** 10am-5pm daily. **Admission** varies; usually free. **No credit cards. Map** p103.

This medium-sized *kunsthalle* in the woods of Ueno Park holds the annual VOCA exhibition of emerging Japanese artists and touring shows from the likes of New York's MOMA and Barcelona's Picasso Museum. It has no permanent collection and its temporary exhibitions are sporadic.

University Art Museum

12-8 Ueno Koen (5685 7755/www.geidai.ac.jp/museum). Ueno station (Yamanote line), park exit; (Ginza, Hibiya lines), Shinobazu exit. **Open** 10am-5pm Tue-Sun. **Admission** ¥300; ¥100 concessions; additional charge for special exhibitions. **No credit cards. Map** p103.

The museum connected to Japan's most prestigious national art and music school has an impressive collection of over 40,000 objects, ranging from Japanese traditional art to Western paintings and photos. The large new building, opened in 1999, holds both permanent collections and some temporary exhibitions.

Yokoyama Taikan Memorial Hall

1-4-24 Ikenohata, Taito-ku (3821 1017/www.tctv.ne.jp/members/taikan). Yushima station (Chiyoda line), exit 1. **Open** 10am-4pm Thur-Sun. **Admission** ¥500; ¥200 concessions. **No credit cards. Map** p103.

Regarded as one of Japan's great modern painters, Yokoyama Taikan was born at the beginning of the Meiji Restoration and lived through 89 years of change. In his traditional Japanese house overlooking Shinobazu Pond, Yokoyama practised *nihonga* (traditional Japanese painting), taking Mt Fuji and other images from nature as his inspiration. If his paintings don't impress, his well-planned gardens will. The house closes in bad weather and occasionally during the summer.

Getting there

Ueno is on the Yamanote line and Ginza and Hibiya subway lines; if you're heading for the park, arriving via the Yamanote line is the best option. At the northern end of the park is Uguisudani station, also on the Yamanote line; and at the southern end, Keisei-Ueno station, on the Kesei line. Yushima and Nezu stations, on the Chiyoda line, are not far away.

Sightseeing

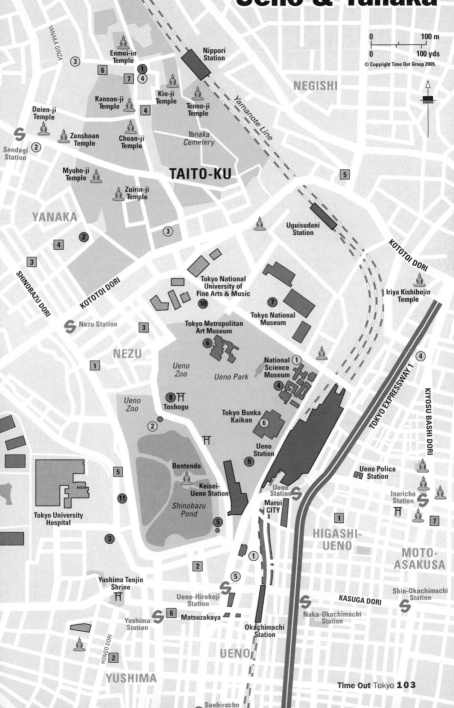

Ueno & Yanaka

NEGISHI

Nippori Station

Enmei-in Temple

Kio-ji Temple

Kannon-ji Temple

Tenno-ji Temple

Daien-ji Temple

Zenshoan Temple

Choan-ji Temple

Yanaka Cemetery

Sendagi Station

Myoho-ji Temple

TAITO-KU

Zuirin-ji Temple

YANAKA

Uguisudani Station

KOTOTOI DORI

Iriya Kishibojin Temple

SHINOBAZU DORI

KOTOTOI DORI

Tokyo National University of Fine Arts & Music

Tokyo National Museum

Nezu Station

Tokyo Metropolitan Art Museum

NEZU

Ueno Zoo

National Science Museum

TOKYO EXPRESSWAY 1

KIYOSU BASHI DORI

Ueno Zoo

Toshogu

Tokyo Bunka Kaikan

Ueno Police Station

Bentendo

Ueno Station

Inaricho Station

Keisei-Ueno Station

Shinobazu Pond

Tokyo University Hospital

Ueno Station

Marui CITY

HIGASHI-UENO

MOTO-ASAKUSA

Yushima Tenjin Shrine

Ueno-Hirokoji Station

KASUGA DORI

Shin-Okachimachi Station

Yushima Station

Matsuzakaya

Naka-Okachimachi Station

Okachimachi Station

UENO

YUSHIMA

HONGO DORI

Suehirocho

© Copyright Time Out Group 2005

Yanaka

Low, slow and bursting with temples.

Map p103

For many the familiar image of Tokyo is that of the neon glitz of *Lost in Translation* Shinjuku. But on the other side of town from the concrete canyons of the city's most frenetic sub-centre there exists a quiet world that has somehow managed to survive many of the upheavals of the past century. Welcome to Yanaka.

This low-key, low-rise area, together with the neighbouring districts of Nezu and Sendagi, is easily located since it forms a rough-shaped lozenge north-west of Ueno Park, between Nezu and Nishi-Nippori stations. But it's a world away from the grand museums and huge brash street market of Ueno. Yanaka survives as an endearing place where life seems to potter along more or less just as it did a century ago.

It is also home to Tokyo's highest concentration of temples, ranging from the grand to the decidedly humble. The temples were moved here from elsewhere in Tokyo following the 1657 Long Sleeves Fire, which destroyed much of the city. Yanaka has led something of a charmed life ever since. First it became a playground for the wealthy, and then almost a living museum of old Tokyo, escaping destruction in both the Kanto Earthquake of 1923 and air raids in World War II.

The best way to see Yanaka is on foot; the route described below takes in many of the area's most famous sights. If you're prepared to risk getting lost, there's a lot more to be discovered in its steep, winding backstreets.

A WALKING TOUR OF YANAKA

First, take the Yamanote line to Nippori station. Leave by the west exit, which will bring you to a narrow footpath at the foot of a flight of steps. In front of you at the top of the steps is the main street through Yanaka Cemetery, but before heading there take a look at **Tenno-ji** temple at the start of the road. Founded over 500 years ago and once covering a far larger area, its star attraction is the bronze Buddha, cast in 1690, that overlooks the temple gate. The temple gained notoriety in the early 19th century, when it was one of the few places where people could buy lottery tickets. Naturally, it became a very popular spot – until the government spoiled all the fun and closed the business down. Tenno-ji is also dedicated to Bishamonten, one of the Seven Deities of Good Fortune.

Leave the temple grounds and head down the central avenue of **Yanaka Cemetery** (opened 1874), one of Tokyo's largest graveyards and, along with Aoyama Cemetery, one of its most picturesque. These days the avenue is usually quiet, but over 150 years ago it was a den of iniquity, lined with tea shops that doubled as brothels and illegal gambling dens. However, the cemetery does become rather popular, during cherry blossom time. The Japanese are oddly fond of holding blossom-viewing parties in the grounds of the city's cemeteries, and Yanaka is noted for its blooming cherry trees.

The cemetery contains the remains of many prominent figures, including Natsume Soseki (1867-1916), usually regarded by the Japanese as their finest modern writer. Before new bank notes went into circulation in 2004, all the ¥1,000 notes bore his image. It is also the resting place of the last Tokugawa shogun, Yoshinobu (1837-1913), who surrendered power to the emperor in 1868.

Continue down the path until the *koban* (police box). To the left and slightly behind the *koban* is a small fenced-off area. The rubble inside is all that's left of Yanaka's five-storey pagoda, once the tallest building in Edo. Constructed in 1644, it burned down in 1772 and was rebuilt. It burned down for the last time in 1957, part of a macabre lovers' suicide pact. Turn right at the police box; the path you are on ends in a T-junction just past some modern houses. Facing you at the end of the street is **Choan-ji** temple, dedicated to Jurojin, a god of long life.

Turn right at the junction and on your left down a side street you will catch a glimpse of a traditional Japanese slate wall, part of the complex surrounding **Kannon-ji** temple. Kannon-ji is connected with the tale of the 47 *ronin,* two of whom were students here. Inside the grounds on the right is a small pagoda dedicated to their memory.

Turn left out of the temple and continue along the main road. Shortly afterwards, on a corner on the right, is **Saboh Hanahenro** (7-17-11 Yanaka, 3822 6387, open 11am-6pm Tue-Sun, map p103), a friendly corner restaurant/teahouse, and then **Sandara** (7-18-6 Yanaka, 5814 8618, open 10.30am-6pm Tue-Sun, map p103), a charming little shop that sells traditional Japanese pottery. On the

The tranquil garden at the heart of the **Asakura Choso Museum**.

other side of the road a little further on is **Ryusen-ji**, a minor temple, but picturesque with its bending trees and sloping roofs. An alternative refuelling stop is **Jinenjiyo** (5-9-25 Yanaka, 3824 3162, open 11.30am-4pm, 5.30-9pm Mon-Fri, 11am-9pm Sat, Sun, map p103), a quaint little coffee shop further up the road on your left. Its speciality is *'yakuzen* curry', which contains traditional Chinese medicines thought to be good for the circulation.

Further down, on the right, is **Asakura Choso Museum**, situated in the black concrete building that was at one point the house and studio of sculptor Asakura Fumio. Despite its unprepossessing façade, it's a fascinating dwelling well worth a visit. From the museum, turn right and continue along the street, passing on your right an alleyway lined with small drinking dens, or *nomiya*. This is **Hatsunei Komichi**, one of the last wooden-roofed covered arcades in Tokyo.

At the end of the street, turn left (to return to Nippori station, turn right) and follow the road to the right, down a flight of steps. On the way, on the left, you'll pass eccentric Persian/Turkish restaurant **Zakuro** (Nishi-Nippori Konishi Bldg B1F, Nishi-Nippori 3-14-13, 5685 5313, http://zakuro.oops.jp, open 11am-11pm daily, map p103). Turn right at the bottom of the steps, and 50 metres down the road stands **Midori-ya** (3-13-5 Nishi-Nippori, 3828 1746, open 10am-6.30pm daily, map p103), which is a traditional maker of hand-woven basketware.

Prices range from ¥500 for trinkets to over ¥30,000 for handbags. Return to the foot of the steps and turn right, into the incongruously named **Yanaka Ginza**, the area's main (pedestrianised) shopping street. A surprising number of traditional businesses still survive; notable among these is **Goto no Ame** (3-15-1 Nishi-Nippori, 3821 0880, open 10.30am-8pm Mon, Tue, Thur-Sat, 10.30am-7pm Sun), which sells traditional sweets, many made on the premises. Other shops offer such wares as *geta* (Japanese wooden shoes), green tea, *sembei* (rice crackers), pottery and tofu.

Turn left at the bottom of Yanaka Ginza, and walk straight on, past the **Annex Katsutaro Ryokan** (*see p44*), until you reach the traffic lights at the end of the street. Turn left at the lights and walk up the hill to **Daien-ji** temple, established in 1591. This is a highly unusual building in that it consists of two symmetrical halves. The left half was intended to serve as a Shinto shrine, the right as a Buddhist temple, but such plans were rejected by the shogunate, which enforced the separation of Buddhism and Shinto. The temple is famous for its colourful chrysanthemum festival in mid October.

Leave the temple, turn left, cross the road at the pedestrian crossing and turn right by the large white school building with a pagoda. Continue straight down this road, bearing left when it forks, to reach the **Daimyo Clock Museum**, which showcases the Japanese-style clocks made for Edo-era *daimyo* feudal lords.

Art paper at **Isetatsu** stationery shop.

Return to the main street from the museum, turn left and then next left, down a slope with a wonderful Japanese inn, **Ryokan Sawanoya** (*see p44*), close by a crossroads. Take the road to the right at this junction and follow the small street for about 500 metres. This brings you out to Sansaki-zaka, and just to the left is **Isetatsu** (2-18-9 Yanaka, 3823 1453, open 10am-6pm daily, map p103). This shop sells fine decorated papers, whose patterns are made from intricate carved wooden blocks.

Following Sansaki-zaka down brings you to Sendagi station (on the Chiyoda line). The walk can be ended here, or you can go on to **Nezu Shrine**, which at about 400 metres away: turn left on to the main road, Shinobazu Dori, and then right at the first main junction. Dating from 1706, the shrine is a colourful spot with a giant painted gate and landscaped gardens stretching up a hillside. For most of the year it's an attractive peaceful spot, but in April, when the hillside azalea bushes bloom, the whole place swarms with camera-toting visitors. An interesting time to visit throughout the year is 6.30am, when scores of locals gather to go through their daily communal exercises, all directed by a voice on a crackly radio.

Three art museums are also located nearby. Return to Shinobazu Dori, turn right and then continue as far as the big junction with Kototoi Dori. Turn right and walk for 300 metres until you reach a largeish junction; take the road to the left and you will soon see the **Tachihara**

Michizo Memorial Museum, followed by the **Takeshisa Yumeji Museum** and **Yayoi Museum**, located in the same building.

Asakura Choso Museum

7-18-10 Yanaka, Taito-ku (3821 4549/ www.taitocity.net/taito/asakura/). Nippori station (Yamanote line), west exit. **Open** 9.30am-4.30pm Tue-Thur, Sat, Sun. **Admission** ¥400; ¥150 concessions. **No credit cards. Map** p103.

This museum is the former house and atelier of Asakura Fumio (1883-1964), who was a leading figure in modern Japanese sculpture. The three-level building – designed by the artist in 1936 – melds modernism and traditional Japanese architecture. The centrepiece is a delightful rock and water garden, also designed by the artist. From the rooftop garden you can see how low-rise Yanaka still is compared with the rest of Tokyo.

Daimyo Clock Museum

2-1-27 Yanaka, Taito-ku (3821 6913). Nezu station (Chiyoda line), exit 1. **Open** 10am-4pm Tue-Sun. Closed July-Sept. **Admission** ¥300; ¥100-¥200 concessions. **No credit cards. Map** p103.

Daimyo feudal lords were the only people who could afford the clocks displayed here, which required adjusting twice a day. Before Japan adopted the solar calender in 1870, there was a set number of hours between sunrise and sunset, with the result that the length of an hour was longer in summer and shorter in winter. Times were named after the animals of the Chinese zodiac. This one-room museum displays dozens of other timepieces, from alarm clocks to watches worn with a kimono. There's a good English leaflet to guide you.

Tachihara Michizo Memorial Museum

2-4-5 Yayoi, Bunkyo-ku (5684 8780/ www.tachihara.jp). Nezu station (Chiyoda line), exit 1. **Open** 10am-5pm Tue-Sun. **Admission** ¥400; ¥200-¥300 concessions. **No credit cards**.

One of three small museums facing a historic gate of Tokyo University. This one is dedicated to Tachihara Michizo, an artist noted for his pastels. No English translations.

Takeshisa Yumeji Museum of Art & Yayoi Museum of Art

2-4-2 Yayoi, Bunkyo-ku (Takeshi Yumeji Museum 5689 0462/Yayoi Museum 3812 0012/www.yayoi-yumeji-museum.jp). Nezu station (Chiyoda line), exit 1. **Open** 10am-4.30pm Tue-Sun. **Admission** ¥800; ¥400-¥700 concessions. **No credit cards**.

Here are two museums under the same roof, both of them dedicated to the history of Japanese manga (comics) and illustrations.

Getting there

Nippori station is on the Yamanote line. Other stations in the area include Sendagi and Nezu, both on the Chiyoda line, and Nishi-Nippori, on both lines.

Roppongi

Sleazy or smart, all tastes are catered for in the expats' playground.

Map p109

For the expat party crowd there's only ever been one destination: Roppongi. Think deafening rock or trance music, strip clubs, hostess bars and tequila shots galore; ghostly quiet by day, rampant with hedonism each night. Not a subtle place.

So Tokyo's leading property magnate Mori Minoru raised a few eyebrows when, in 1995, he announced plans to build a huge, multi-billion-yen, upmarket urban development right next to the bedlam. **Roppongi Hills** opened to great fanfare in April 2003, and its popularity has yet to wane. Official figures claim 100,000 visitors each weekday, rising to 300,000 each weekend. The complex is designed as a 'city within a city', housing more than 200 cafés, restaurants and shops, hundreds of Conran-designed serviced apartments, a major art museum, the nine-screen **Virgin Toho Cinemas** (*see p219*), the Ashahi TV studio, several parks and the sumptuous **Grand Hyatt Tokyo** (*see p46*). With an emphasis on the luxury side of life, the only thing Roppongi Hills has in common with the rest of the area is the distinctly foreign feel; anyone looking for traditional Japan won't find it here.

Reaching Roppongi Hills is easy – the Hibiya and Oedo subway lines are on its doorstep – but navigating the complex is close to impossible, even with the official map. The layout swirls with corridors, escalators and floor plans so complex that the architects (who also designed Las Vegas's Bellagio casino-hotel) must have been instructed to disorientate visitors. In the middle is Mori's eponymous 54-storey tower – the top supposedly modelled on a samurai helmet – home to the world-class **Mori Art Museum** and an observation deck, **Tokyo City View** (both on the 52nd floor), and a wallet-busting private members club. Louise Bourgeois's huge spider sculpture, *Maman*, crouches benignly in front of the tower. For more details of what the complex contains, visit www.roppongihills.com.

The arrival of Mori's mini city has driven the area's image dramatically upmarket, with parents now bringing their offspring to Roppongi rather than ordering them to steer clear. Yet only a few blocks away the carnal pleasures continue unabated. To experience the flesh fest, head to the main crossing near

The iconic **Tokyo Tower**. *See p111.*

Roppongi station. Take exit 3 from the station, head right along Roppongi Dori, and you'll see a crowd milling in front of the **Almond** pastry shop (*see p170*), immediately recognisable by its pink and white striped awnings. This is the conventional meeting spot, where you'll meet the first of many strip-club or karaoke touts.

The road immediately next to Almond is a neglected street of crumbling buildings and the occasional restaurant, which leads down to the Roppongi Hills complex. But take the main street just beside it – with the illuminated spire of Tokyo Tower gleaming in the distance – and you're in the heart of the action. Street vendors, more strip-show touts and gaudy bar signs provide the ambience. At the weekend each of the bars and clubs will be rammed with party people in various states of intoxication.

The best known, and rowdiest, of the clubs is **Gas Panic** (*see p163*), a legendary meat market that likes its music loud and its customers drunk. But explore the side streets off this main strip and you'll find many similar establishments (*see pp162-5* for more bars in the area). Mega nightclubs include **Alife**, **Velfarre** and **Vanilla**, but there are plenty of other options (*see p213*).

Even if a night of debauchery doesn't appeal, Roppongi has plenty to offer on a culinary level. The area is short on Michelin stars, but the international crowd bring their international palates, and Roppongi boasts a greater variety of food than any other part of the city (*see pp146-50* for recommended restaurants).

Roppongi today betrays little of its roots. Until the 17th century the area was no more than a thoroughfare for Shibuya's residents. Things changed in 1626, however, when shogun Hidetaka chose Roppongi for his wife's burial ground. The four Buddhist priests who oversaw her funeral were each handed generous rewards by the grateful leader. All four spent their riches building new temples in the area, giving Roppongi its first image – as a centre of spirituality.

In the mid 18th century the area's official population stood at 454. It wasn't until the late 19th century that modern Roppongi began to take shape. The government decided to relocate a division of the Imperial Guard to the area, thus heralding the start of a long military association. Following World War II, the American occupiers also picked Roppongi as a base, and the area developed to serve the various visceral needs of military men.

Visiting GIs still populate the bars and clubs, but one significant change in recent years may give a clue to Roppongi's future. The former site of Japan's Defence Agency, located on the opposite side of the Roppongi intersection from Roppongi Hills, was sold to a property consortium in 2001. Construction is now under way on the **Mid-Town Project**, a massive luxury development from Skidmore, Owings & Merrill, the architects behind London's Canary Wharf and New York's forthcoming Freedom Tower. Scheduled to open in 2007, the plans borrow unashamedly from the Roppongi Hills model – promising luxury office space, smart apartments, trendy shopping and Tokyo's first Ritz-Carlton hotel. Whether Roppongi can sustain two 'cities within a city' remains to be seen, as does the impact on Old Roppongi of being sandwiched between two sparkling shrines to high-class consumerism. For now, the revelry continues.

Sights are few and far between, though contemporary art lovers will enjoy **Complex**, an old building on the slope leading to Roppongi Hills that contains a cluster of diminutive galleries, including **Ota Fine Arts** (*see p224*). Further afield are a couple of small private art museums, both housed in upmarket hotels – the **New Otani Museum** near Asakusa-Mitsuke station, and the **Okura Shukokan Museum of Fine Arts** near Roppongi-Itchome station.

South-east from the Roppongi intersection lies **Tokyo Tower**; it may have been trumped by taller buildings with better views, but it's still an iconic structure. The best spot for souvenir photos is adjoining **Shiba Koen**, with the Tower and **Zojo-ji Temple** next door framed in a classic Tokyo shot. In the summer several pools in the park are open to the public and there are playgrounds, a bowling alley and other attractions, all within walking distance. North of the tower is the **NHK Broadcast Museum**, which tunes you into the history of radio and TV in Japan.

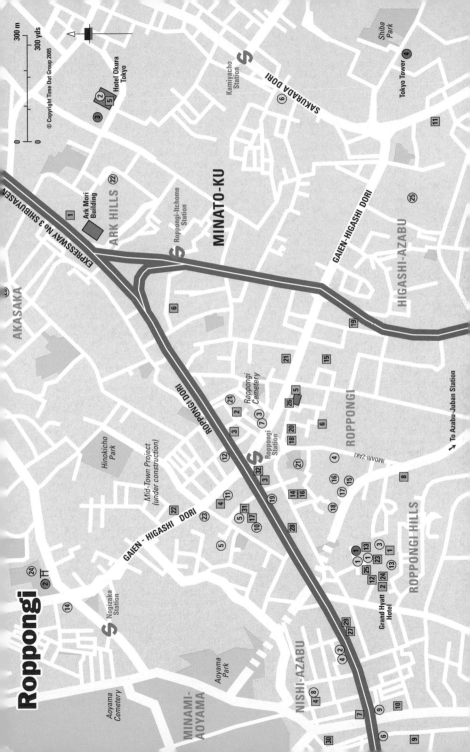

In the other direction from the Roppongi crossing, up Gaien-Higashi Dori, lies **Nogi Jinja**, dedicated to the memory of General Nogi Maresuke and an example of the key role that ritual suicide played in Japan's past.

NISHI-AZABU, AZABU-JUBAN AND HIROO

Before Roppongi Hills came along, **Nishi-Azabu** was the chalk to Roppongi's cheese. Loaded with stylish bars, restaurants and clubs, it pulls a sophisticated, dressed-up crowd. Like Roppongi, Nishi-Azabu lights up at sundown; unlike Roppongi, there's always an atmosphere of calm about the place. It's the perfect location for dates or client entertaining. Nishi-Azabu has no station, so access is via Roppongi station. Take exit 1 and walk down Roppongi Dori towards Shibuya. When you reach a crossroads with Hobson's ice-cream shop opposite you, that's the heart of Nishi-Azabu.

Further east is **Azabu-Juban**, another district rich in restaurants, though with a more traditional feel. This Azabu has a station on the Nanboku and Oedo subway lines, and comes alive each August for a festival featuring *taiko* drumming and traditional dancing. It's also home to an *onsen* (*see p114* **Getting into hot water**) and a large import food store, **Nissin** (*see p187*). Also in the area, although not within walking distance, is **Hiroo**, an expat haven thanks to the numerous embassies nearby. Its shops, cafés and restaurants betray strong Western influences, and most employ English-speaking staff.

Mori Art Museum & Tokyo City View

Mori Tower 52F-53F, 6-10-1 Roppongi, Minato-ku (6406 6100/www.mori.art.museum/html/eng/ index.html). Roppongi station (Hibiya, Oedo lines), exit 1. **Open** *10am-10pm Mon, Wed, Thur; 10am-5pm Tue; 10am-midnight Fri-Sun.* **Admission** ¥1,500. **Credit** AmEx, DC, JCB, MC, V. **Map** p109.

The exhibitions are world class, focused mainly on contemporary culture, but the secrets of the Mori Art Museum's success are location (part of the phenomenally popular Roppongi Hills), location (on the 52nd and 53rd floors of the Mori Tower, offering spectacular views) and location (within a two-floor 'experience' that includes a bar, café, shop and panoramic observation deck). One ticket allows access to all areas, so the museum draws plenty of guests who would never think to visit a contemporary art museum. The late opening hours are also an example of the museum's attempt to maximise accessibility. Exhibitions are deliberately varied – with past shows including Kusama Yayoi's polka dot visions and 'The Elegance of Silence' featuring East Asian art installed according to the principles of feng shui. The vista from Tokyo City View isn't quite 360° and it's expensive compared to the free Tokyo Metropolitan Government building observatory (*see p76*), but the views are arguably better, especially at night – and you can have a drink at the Museum Café (*see p164*).

New Otani Museum

Hotel New Otani, Garden Court 6F, 4-1 Kioicho, Chiyoda-ku (3221 4111/www.newotani.co.jp/ group/museum/index.html). Akasaka-Mitsuke station (Ginza, Marunouchi lines), exit D or Nagatacho station (Hanzomon, Nanboku, Yurakucho lines), exit 7. **Open** *10am-6pm Tue-Sun.* **Admission** ¥500; ¥200 concessions; free hotel guests. **No credit cards.**

The museum inside the New Otani, one of Tokyo's grande dame hotels, houses a collection of Japanese and Japanese-inspired woodblock prints, plus a selection of traditional Japanese and modern European paintings (including works by Vlaminck and School of Paris artists). The museum is small, consisting of two rooms near the hotel reception, but often has shows not seen elsewhere.

NHK Broadcast Museum

2-1-1 Atago, Minato-ku (5400 6900/ www.nhk.or.jp/museum/index-e.html). Kamiyacho station (Hibiya line), exit 3 or Onarimon station (Mita line), exit 2. **Open** *9.30am-4.30pm Tue-Sun.* **Admission** free.

This museum is run by the national public broadcasting company. The nation's first radio station began broadcasting in July 1925 from this location (NHK has since moved to bigger digs in Shibuya). There are two floors of early equipment, and vintage TV shows and news broadcasts play throughout the museum and can also be viewed in the video library.

Nogi Jinja

8-11-27 Akasaka, Minato-ku (3478 3001/house enquiries 3583 4151/www.nogijinja.or.jp). Nogizaka station (Chiyoda line), exit 1 or Roppongi station (Hibiya, Oedo lines), exit 7. **Open** *Walkway 8.30am-5pm daily. House 12, 13 Sept 9.30am-5pm.* **Admission** free. **Map** p109.

When Emperor Meiji died, on 13 September 1912, General Nogi Maresuke and his wife proved their loyalty by joining him in death; he killed himself by *seppuku* (disembowelment), she by slitting her throat with a knife. The house in which they died is adjacent to Nogi shrine, which is dedicated to his memory. The house is open only two days a year, on the eve and anniversary of their deaths, but an elevated walkway allows you to peek in through the windows, one of which provides a glimpse of Nogi's bloodstained shirt.

Okura Shukokan Museum of Fine Art

Hotel Okura, 2-10-3 Toranomon, Minato-ku (3583 0781/www.okura.com/tokyo/info/ shukokan.html). Roppongi-Itchome station (Nanboku line), exits 2, 3. **Open** *10am-4.30pm Tue-Sun.* **Admission** ¥700; ¥300-¥500 concessions; free hotel guests. **No credit cards. Map** p109.

The Mori Tower, centrepiece of the super-slick **Roppongi Hills** complex. *See p107.*

This two-storey Chinese-style building sits in front of the retro-modern Hotel Okura (*see p46*), one of Tokyo's finest. Inside there's a small mix of Asian antiquities: paintings, calligraphy, Buddhist sculpture, textiles, ceramics, swords, archaeological artefacts, lacquerware and metalwork. The exhibitions change five or six times a year.

Tokyo Tower

4-2-8 Shiba-Koen, Minato-ku (3433 5111/2/ www.tokyotower.co.jp). Kamiyacho station (Hibiya line), exit 1 or Onarimon station (Mita line), exit A1 or Akabanebashi station (Oedo line), Nakanobashiguchi exit. **Open** *Tower 9am-10pm daily. Other attractions 10am-9pm daily.* **Admission** *Main Observatory* ¥820; ¥310-¥460 concessions. *Special Observatory* ¥600; ¥350-¥400 concessions. *Waxwork Museum* ¥870; ¥460 concessions. *Trick Art Gallery* ¥400; ¥300 concessions. *Mysterious Walking Zone* ¥410; ¥300 concessions. *Admission to all attractions* ¥1,900; ¥950-¥1,100 concessions. **No credit cards**. **Map** p109.

The resemblance to the Eiffel Tower is deliberate, as is the superior height – 13m (43ft) taller than the Parisian structure. Back in 1958, when it was built, it must have been impressive. Nowadays, though, constructions such as the Mori Tower and Shinjuku's Tocho both offer more impressive views. The tower still functions as a radio and TV mast, but its days as the observation deck of choice are long gone. The attractions inside, including a wax museum and trick art gallery, only serve to highlight how dated the tower has become. But it remains Tokyo's most recognisable structure and, ironically, the most striking attraction when viewed at night from any of the other observation decks.

Zojo-ji Temple

4-7-35 Shiba Koen, Minato-ku (3432 1431/ www.zojoji.or.jp/en/). Shiba-Koen station (Mita line), exit A4 or Daimon station (Asakusa, Oedo lines), exit A6. **Open** *Temple 6am-5.30pm daily. Grounds 24hrs daily.* **Admission** free.

The main temple of the Buddhist Jodo sect in the Kanto area, Zojo-ji was built in 1393 and moved to its present location in 1598. In the 17th century 48 temples stood on this site. The main hall has been destroyed three times by fire in the last century, the current building being a 1970s reconstruction. The most historic element is the Sangedatsumon main gate, which dates back to 1605 and is the oldest wooden structure in Tokyo. Each of its three sections represents three of the stages that are necessary to attain nirvana. A mausoleum in the grounds contains tombs of six Tokugawa shoguns. There's also a cemetery, with row upon row of small statues of Jizo, guardian of (among other things) stillborn, aborted or miscarried babies. Each sports a red hat and bib and is adorned with plastic flowers.

Getting there

Roppongi station is on the Hibiya and Oedo subway lines. A concourse from exit 1C of the Hibiya line takes you direct to the heart of the complex, in front of the Mori Tower. Azabu-Juban is on the Oedo and Nanboku lines, and Hiroo on the Hibiya line.

Odaiba

On the waterfront: welcome to Tokyo's futuristic entertainment centre.

Map p113

Fans of Japanese film may well find the Tokyo Bay area familiar. It was the location of the highest grossing domestic live-action film to date, 2003's *Odoru Daisosasen 2* (aka *Bayside Shakedown 2*) – as is evident from the futuristic buildings that Detective Aoshima Shunsaku (Oda Yuji) runs past when chasing criminals.

Odaiba started out as a Bubble-era project to develop Tokyo Bay on reclaimed land, with the name being taken from the cannons placed offshore by the Tokugawa shogunate in the late Edo period to protect Japan from invasion. Over the past decade it's turned into something of a community apart from the rest of Tokyo, with nowhere else sharing its spacious atmosphere of wide avenues and cavernous modern architecture, with the water of Tokyo Bay just a couple of streets away. It's at its busiest on summer weekends; in winter it can be a windy and sparsely populated spot. It's also spectacular at night, when the buildings are transformed by multicoloured lighting effects.

A trip to Odaiba begins by taking the elevated, driverless Yurikamome monorail from Shinbashi or Shiodome stations and watching the view unfold. The gateway to Odaiba is **Rainbow Bridge**, named after the illuminations that light it up after dark. The bridge has become one of the most impressive additions to Tokyo's skyline – along with the ever-changing psychedelic patterns of the enormous Ferris wheel visible in the distance behind it. If you want to take things at a slower pace, you can also walk across the bridge – it takes about 30 minutes.

Coming over the bridge, the first sight that hits you is the extravagant 25-storey structure of the **Fuji TV headquarters**, designed by acclaimed Japanese architect Tange Kenzo and crowned by a 1,200-tonne glittering metal sphere. Inside the sphere is an observation deck that, on clear days, gives breathtaking views of Tokyo and its surroundings.

Get off at Odaiba Kaihin-Koen station if you want to visit the Fuji TV building, or to explore the nearby shopping and entertainment centre of **Decks** (www.odaiba-decks.com). The nautical theme for Decks is quickly evident – the wooden planks underfoot, portholes for windows, walkways and gantries overhead, palm trees in unlikely places. Inside, you'll

find the Island and Seaside Malls, the Joypolis Game Centre and several restaurants on the sixth floor. The Decks Tokyo Brewery, on the fifth floor, is notable for the Daiba brand micro-beer that is brewed on the premises.

Follow the signs to 'Daiba-Itchome Shotengai', on the fourth floor, and you'll find one of Odaiba's most intriguing attractions: a loving re-creation of 1960s Japan. Wander down corridors as dark and twisty as the streets of old Shanghai, and visit shops covered in old movie posters and selling food and toys from the hazily remembered post-war days. On the floor above is Little Hong Kong, a cluster of Chinese restaurants surrounded by mock-ups of 1940s railway stations, complete with sound effects – though it's not as impressive or entertaining as the Japanese *shotengai*.

Next to Decks is another mall, **Aqua City** (www.aquacity.co.jp). Here you'll find yet more shops, cafés and restaurants and the 13-screen Mediage cinema. In front of Aqua City, next to the water, is – oddly enough – a small-scale replica of the **Statue of Liberty**, built in France and erected in 2000.

From here you can walk (or jump back on the monorail to Aomi station) to **Palette Town**, home of the **Mega Web** amusement park, and the huge Stream of Starlight Ferris wheel. If you're thinking of taking a ride, however, be prepared for a wait – the queues can be massive, depending on the time of year. This area is also home to **Venus Fort** (*see p176*) – an unusual shopping mall aimed at women, with an Italianate interior and a fake sky that changes according to the time of day – and rock venue **Zepp Tokyo** (*see p240*).

There are also several museums worth seeing in Odaiba. The **Museum of Maritime Science** is built to look like an ocean liner and has the suit of a deep-sea diver guarding the entrance. The **National Museum of Emerging Science & Innovation**, located in a gleaming steel and glass precinct on the other side of Palette Town, is suitably space age in appearance; a huge sphere juts out from the side of the building and an ever-changing globe of planet Earth hangs high above its lobby. Compared with these, the exterior of the **Tokyo Metropolitan Waterworks Science Museum** is pretty unassuming, but there's plenty within to entertain and educate.

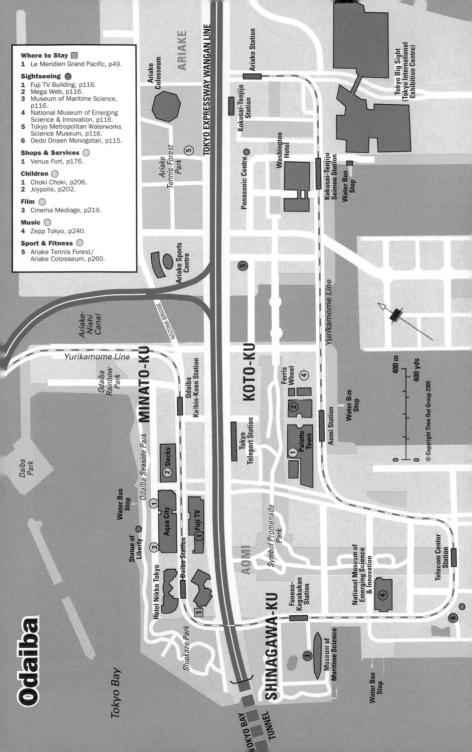

Getting into hot water

Godliness is next to cleanliness for the Japanese, and the country has a very long bathing tradition with its hot-spring baths (*onsen*) and public bathhouses (*sento*). To the foreigner, the two may seem similar – both involve stripping off and hopping into a communal tub with members of one's own sex – but there are distinct differences.

With very frequent earthquakes and volcanic eruptions, Japan is no quiet spot geologically. The upside of this is the great number of hot springs, rich in mineral content and endowed with therapeutic benefits, which have led to the building of myriad bathing facilities. Outdoor *onsen* (*rotenburo*) can be a wonderful experience: there is nothing like bathing outside in winter, surrounded by snow and drinking sake from a flask heated by the water. **Hakone** (*see p268-71*), an hour from Tokyo, is a famous hot-springs resort area, but you can also experience *onsen* life in the heart of the city.

Sento (literally, 'penny baths') generally use ordinary heated tap water and were far more plentiful in the days when most Japanese houses didn't have their own baths. A visit to a *sento* (identified by a sign depicting what looks like flames coming out of a handleless frying pan) is a fine way of experiencing a slice of traditional Japanese life. Older *onsen* and *sento* are often housed in delightful buildings that are a throwback to a more leisurely age.

Most *sento* are strictly segregated by gender, but some *onsen* allow mixed bathing. Below we list some of Tokyo's top bathing spots. Don't expect English to be spoken.

BATHING ETIQUETTE
Having paid and entered the relevant changing room – signs are written only in *kanji*, so make sure you know the difference between 'men' and 'women' – strip off completely and put your clothes in a locker. Japanese usually proceed into the bathing area with a small towel; most people bring their own, but these can usually be rented. The most important aspect of the code of behaviour is that you enter the bath completely clean. Pull up a stool and bucket, choose a 'scrubbing station' and wash yourself thoroughly, removing every trace of soap or shampoo. Then get into the tub (there's often more than one). Never put your head underwater.

Be warned that the water temperature can, for the uninitiated, be extremely hot. Sluice yourself first to get acclimatised, then ease yourself slowly into the bath. Lie back, soak and enjoy.

Onsen

Asakusa Kannon Onsen
2-7-26 Asakusa, Taito-ku (3844 4141). Asakusa station (Asakusa, Ginza lines), Kannosamma exit. **Open** *6.30am-6pm Mon, Tue, Thur-Sun.* **Admission** *¥700.* **Map** *p93. Shiatsu is available for ¥4,000.*
A classic bathhouse located right next to Asakusa Kannon Temple (*see p92*). The waters are supposedly good for sufferers of rheumatism and nervous disorders. Shiatsu is available for ¥4,000.

Azabu Juban Onsen
1-5-22 Azabu-Juban, Minato-ku (3404 2610). Azabu-Juban station (Nanboku line), exit 4. **Open** *Sento 3-11pm Mon, Wed-Sun. Onsen 11am-9pm Mon, Wed-Sun.* **Admission** *Sento ¥400. Onsen ¥1,260.*

The exterior is nothing special, but this is a genuine *onsen* not far from boisterous Roppongi, delivering brownish mineral waters (albeit artificially heated). There's also a *sento* (Koshi no Yu) and a steam sauna.

Oedo Onsen Monogatari

2-57 Omi, Koto-ku (5500 1126/ www.ooedoonsen.jp). Telecom Center station (Yurikamome line). **Open** 11am-9am daily (last entry 2am). **Admission** 11am-6pm ¥2,800; after 6pm ¥1,900; staying past 2am extra charge ¥1,500. **Map** p113.
This 'onsen theme park' in Odaiba (pictured) is one of three recently opened, large-scale *onsen* facilities in Tokyo; the others are LaQua in Tokyo Dome City (*see p202*) and Niwa no Yu in Toshimaen (*see p121*). It does a pretty good job of recreating an Edo-period bathhouse, with traditional snack and souvenir stalls and numerous bathing areas, indoor and out, plus hot sand baths and saunas. The price of admission includes *yukata* and towels.

Seta Onsen

4-15-30 Seta, Setagaya-ku (3707 8228/www.setaonsen.co.jp). Futako Tamagawa station (Tokyu Denentoshi, Tokyu Oimachi, Tokyu Shin-Tamagawa lines), then 10mins walk or shuttle bus. **Open** 10am-11pm daily. **Admission** ¥2,300.
Another large-scale, family-friendly *onsen* in a lovely garden setting. There are indoor and open-air bathing areas, a sauna and restaurants. Swimsuits (which can be rented) must be worn in the 'garden healing pool'.

Sento

The price of all *sento* is set at a standard ¥400.

Aqua

4-9-22 Higashi-Nakano, Nakano-ku (5330 1126). Higashi-Nakano station (Chuo, Oedo lines), east exit. **Open** 3pm-midnight Tue-Sun.
A modern *sento* with a variety of baths, including a *rotenburo* and sauna. Usefully, it stocks cold beers.

Daikoku-yu

32-6 Senju Kotobuki-cho, Adachi-ku (3881 3001). Kita-Senju station (Chiyoda, Hibiya lines), west exit, then 15mins walk. **Open** 3pm-midnight Tue-Sun.

This majestic, temple-like building is probably the most attractive *sento* in Tokyo. Serenely spacious, with its own *rotenburo*, it also has cold beer in stock.

Komparu-yu

8-7-5 Ginza, Chuo-ku (3571 5469). Ginza station (Ginza, Hibiya lines), exit A2. **Open** 2-11pm Mon-Sat. **Map** p60.
A few doors from Kyubei, one of Tokyo's most famous (and famously expensive) sushi restaurants, in ritzy Ginza is this tiny old bathhouse, which dates back to Edo days. There are two baths – *atatakai* (hot) and *nurui* (lukewarm); lukewarm is hot enough for most.

Shimizu-yu

3-12-3 Minami-Aoyama, Minato-ku (3401 4404). Omotesando station (Chiyoda, Ginza, Hanzomon lines), exit A4. **Open** 4pm-midnight Tue-Sun.
Located in the heart of Omotesando.

Tamano-yu

1-13-7 Asagaya-Kita, Suginami-ku (3338 7860). Asagaya station (Chuo line), north exit. **Open** 3.30pm-1am Tue-Sun.
A recently renovated, traditional *sento* with a number of novelty tubs, including a *denkiburo* (electric bath).

The pyschedelic **Ferris wheel**. *See p112.*

Beyond the science museum stands the imposing blue-glass arch of the **Telecom Center**, a major satellite and telecommunications hub, also with an observation deck (open 11.30am-9.30pm daily, admission ¥600). And next to this lies yet another culture shock: the **Oedo Onsen Monogatari** (*see p114* **Getting into hot water**), a hot-spring theme park with customers in *yukata* (dressing gowns) strolling past traditional-looking wooden bathhouses.

Odaiba is also home to **Tokyo Big Sight**, Japan's largest exhibition and convention centre, and another striking architectural creation. There's a scattering of parks too, mainly along the waterfront; the most pleasant is **Odaiba Seaside Park** in front of Decks and Aqua City, which includes a man-made sand beach. This is also where the Suijo Bus boats stop (*see p95* **Take me to the river**).

Fuji TV Building

2-4-8 Daiba, Minato-ku (5500 8888/ www.fujitv.co.jp). Odaiba Kaihin-Koen station (Yurikamome line). **Open** 10am-8pm Tue-Sun. **Admission** *Studios & observation deck* ¥500. **Credit** (gift shop only) AmEx, DC, JCB, MC, V. **Map** p113.

The headquarters of the Fuji TV corporation, one of Japan's nationwide commercial channels, has exhibitions (mostly in Japanese with occasional English subtitles) on popular programmes and guided tours around studios in use. Entrance is free, but you have to pay to get into the studios and observation deck.

Mega Web

1 Aomi, Koto-ku (3599 0808/test drive reservations 0070 800 489 000/www.megaweb.gr.jp/ english/ index.html). Aomi station (Yurikamome line) or Tokyo Teleport station (Rinkai line). **Open** *Futureworld* 11am-11pm daily. *Toyota City Showcase* 11am-9pm daily. *History Garage* 11am-10pm daily. **Admission** free. **Map** p113.

Part of the huge Palette Town development that opened in 1999, Mega Web certainly lives up to its name. Its giant Ferris wheel – at 115m (383ft) one of the tallest in the world – is visible for miles, and lit with amazing kaleidoscopic patterns at night.

Beneath it is the world's largest car showroom, the Toyota City Showcase. Here you can sit in the newest models, take a test drive (¥300) on the two-lap track (Japanese or international driver's licence required) or be ferried around in the company's self-driving electric town-car prototypes (¥200). Expect a queue for tickets, especially at weekends. There's also Futureworld, a virtual reality rollercoaster, and History Garage, a motor museum.

Museum of Maritime Science (Funeno Kagakukan)

3-1 Higashi-Yashio (Odaiba), Shinagawa-ku (5500 1111/www.funenokagakukan.or.jp). Funeno-Kagakukan station (Yurikamome line). **Open** *Winter* 10am-5pm Mon-Fri; 10am-6pm Sat, Sun. *Summer* 10am-6pm daily. **Admission** ¥700 main building; ¥1,000 all areas; ¥400-¥600 concessions. **Credit** (restaurant only) V. **Map** p113.

Attractions include displays on marine exploration, replicas of ancient Japanese ships, and, to crown it all, the replicated bridge of an ocean liner.

National Museum of Emerging Science & Innovation (Nihon Kagaku Miraikan)

2-41 Aomi (Odaiba), Koto-ku (3570 9151/ www.miraikan.jst.go.jp). Funeno-Kagakukan station or Telecom Center station (Yurikamome line). **Open** 10am-5pm Mon, Wed-Sun. **Admission** ¥500; ¥200 concessions; free under-18s Sat. **No credit cards. Map** p113.

Upon entering, the visitor beholds a globe 6.5m (22ft) in diameter above the lobby, with 851,000 LEDs on its surface showing real-time global climatic changes. The museum holds interactive displays on robots, genetic discoveries and space travel and, perhaps most bizarre of all, a model using springs and ball bearings to explain the operating principle of the internet. There are ample explanations in English, and a good gift shop.

Tokyo Metropolitan Waterworks Science Museum

2-4-1 Ariake, Koto-ku (3528 2366/ www.waterworks.metro.tokyo.jp/pp/kagakukan/ kagaku.htm). Kokusai Tenjijo-Seimon station (Yurikamome line). **Open** 9.30am-5pm Tue-Sun. **Admission** free. **Map** p113.

This museum channels a fundamental ingredient of life, water, into exciting displays and interactive games. Witness the cutting power of a high-pressure stream of water and marvel at an enormous underground pump. Take a virtual ride down a river with sound effects, movement and all. If the scientific displays saturate your brain, chill out watching big bubbles pass through huge tubes in a dimly lit room.

Getting there

Odaiba is on the Yurikamome monorail line (a one-day travel pass costs ¥800) and the Rinkai line. You can also get there by water bus (*see p95* **Take me to the river**).

Ikebukuro

Head north for a laid-back vibe and bargain shopping.

Jiyu Gakuen Myonichikan: Frank Lloyd Wright's only building in Tokyo. *See p120.*

Map p119

Ikebukuro, which ranks third behind Shinjuku and Shibuya as one of the main sub-centres of Tokyo, has a resolutely uncool reputation that actually works in its favour, as the resulting lack of pretension gives the whole area a freer, more laid-back atmosphere. Indeed, it has something of a homely feel, because many who come to work, shop or play in Ikebukuro live nearby, and the atmosphere is comparable to that found in Japan's provincial cities. But laid-back doesn't mean quiet: every available square inch is crammed with shops, bars, restaurants, karaoke rooms, cinemas, love hotels and other 'entertainment' establishments.

The nerve centre of Ikebukuro is one of Tokyo's largest train stations, served by two subway lines, two private railways and numerous JR lines. While this makes it an easy place to reach, it can be a difficult place to get around, as the station is devoid of significant landmarks and each of its vast, low-ceilinged underground corridors looks exactly like all the rest. Among more than 40 exits, the most popular meeting spot is the Ike Fukuro ('Lake Owl') statue at the bottom of the stairs inside exit 22. That a statue the size of a beer

barrel should be the most distinctive feature of a station sprawling over many city blocks is damning proof of the station's poor design.

Once you escape the station, though, navigation gets easier. Look north to spot the 30-storey phallic cement chimney of the local garbage incineration plant, and use this as your guide to the **Ikebukuro Sports Centre** (*see p260*) in the building immediately next door to the plant. The centre's tenth-floor gym and 11th-floor swimming pool provide a bird's-eye impression of how Ikebukuro is laid out while you work out. For example, that profusion of neon just below the abdominal benches indicates that the west side of the train tracks between the gym and the station is where you will find the area's largest concentration of love hotels.

Since most of the above-ground railway lines run north–south, Ikebukuro itself divides into east and west. Each side is dominated by a gigantic department store half next to, and half on top of, the train station. This is the result of a feud between wealthy arch-rival half-brothers Tsutsumi Yasujiro and Nezu Kaichiro, who developed the two private rail lines – the Seibu Ikebukuro and Tobu Tojo lines, respectively –

Amlux Toyota: for petrolheads. *See p120.*

that serve the area. Each encouraged local growth by building a department store at the station. Both stores grew to be among the largest in the world.

Confusingly, the **Seibu** department store (*see p174*) – whose name originates from 'west area railway line' – is located on the east side of the station, and **Tobu** (*see p175*) – the 'east area railway line' – has the west side covered. It's advisable to pick up a store map for each, as there's a danger of getting very lost. Outside these two overwhelming stores, east and west Ikebukuro remain distinct.

WEST SIDE

Before World War II, the area west of Ikebukuro station was known in some circles as 'the Montparnasse of Tokyo'. Its cheap homes, built on previously marshy land, were occupied by artists and writers including Edogawa Rampo (1894-1965), the revered detective novelist whose name is a Japanised pronunciation of Edgar Allan Poe.

Even today much of western Ikebukuro consists of quiet residential neighbourhoods, though few pre-war buildings remain. One notable survivor is **Jiyu Gakuen Myonichikan**, a school building designed by Frank Lloyd Wright in 1921. It and the nearby **Mejiro Teien** garden provide an oasis of tranquillity that make a welcome contrast to the bustle of Ikebukuro station. Contributing to that bustle are thousands of students from Rikkyo University, also located to the west of

the station. The campus is unremarkable most of the year, but around Christmas its red-brick buildings are adorned with decorative lights.

Every university needs good bookshops nearby, and for English speakers, that means second-hand specialist **Caravan Books** (*see p177*). For more comprehensive shopping, the other major department store on this side is **Marui**, directly down the street perpendicular to the station's main west exit. Metropolitan Plaza, home to the **Japan Traditional Craft Centre** (*see p188*) – a good place for learning more about Japanese arts and crafts – is right next to Tobu, and can be reached by the Metropolitan exit of the station.

Directly opposite the Metropolitan exit is **Tobu Spice**, a building full of restaurants. In the basement of the next building behind that is the **Dubliners** (*see p159*) – one of Tokyo's ever-expanding number of Irish pubs; it attracts long-time foreign residents and Japanese regulars, as well as musicians keen on Celtic music. The Dubliners' entrance faces a broad stone plaza that is the only significant car-free open space in the area. You're bound to see plenty of old men hunched over *shogi* and *go* boards, and there are likely to be musicians busking or rehearsing nearby. On the west side of the plaza stands the airy, glass-enclosed **Tokyo Metropolitan Art Space** (*see p236*), used for classical concerts, plays and ballets.

EAST SIDE

There are two main exits on this side of the station – the east exit and the Seibu exit. Turn left out of either, and you will come to **Parco**, which is part of the Seibu complex. **P' Parco**, slightly further along, is one source of the wild fashions worn in the trendier parts of Tokyo. One block further up the main street, Meiji Dori, is the Ikebukuro branch of **Bic Camera**, an electronics megastore so big it occupies more than one building.

If you think this area is mobbed, just try making your way to the main centre of Ikebukuro – Sunshine 60 Dori, the wide tree-lined street that heads due east. The thoroughfare is packed with tiny shops, many selling discount clothing, as well as restaurants and cinemas. The **Sanrio** shop is worth a giggle – two whole floors offering Hello Kitty goods, cooed over by seemingly grown women.

Sunshine 60 Dori is so called because it ultimately leads to the **Sunshine 60 Building**, part of the **Sunshine City** complex. In the building's massive mall are all kinds of fashion shops and restaurants, and within the complex, an observatory, an aquarium, a planetarium, a theme park and the Ancient Orient Museum (among other attractions).

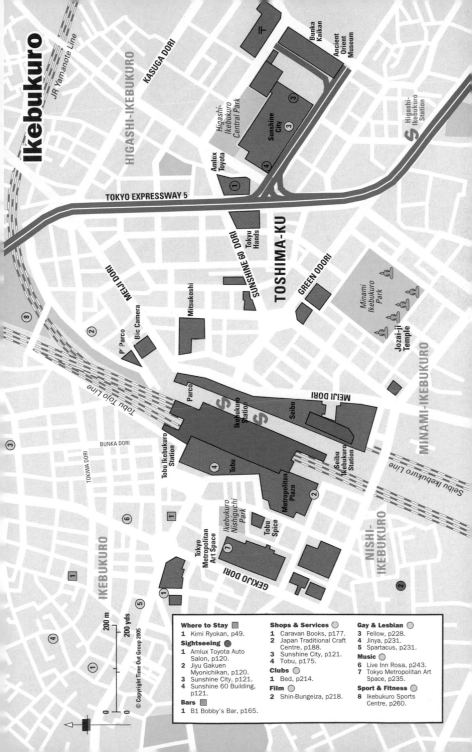

Ikebukuro

JR Yamanote Line

HIGASHI-IKEBUKURO

KASUGA DORI

Bunka Kaikan

Ancient Orient Museum

Higashi-Ikebukuro Central Park

Sunshine City ③

③

Higashi-Ikebukuro Station

Amlux Toyota

① ④

TOKYO EXPRESSWAY 5

TOSHIMA-KU

SUNSHINE 60 DORI

Tokyu Hands

MEIJI DORI

GREEN ODORI

Mitsukoshi

Minami Ikebukuro Park

Bic Camera

P Parco

Jozai-ji Temple

MINAMI-IKEBUKURO

Parco

Tobu Tojo Line

Ikebukuro Station

Seibu

MEIJI DORI

Tobu Ikebukuro Station

BUNKA DORI

Seibu Ikebukuro Station

TOKIWA DORI

④

Tobu

Metropolitan Plaza

②

Seibu Ikebukuro Line

NISHI-IKEBUKURO

③

Ikebukuro Nishiguchi Park

Tobu Spice

IKEBUKURO

⑥

Tokyo Metropolitan Art Space

①

⑦

②

GEKIJO DORI

①

⑤

200 m

200 yds

© Copyright Time Out Group 2005

Where to Stay ▪
1 Kimi Ryokan, p49.
Sightseeing ●
1 Amlux Toyota Auto Salon, p120.
2 Jiyu Gakuen Myonichikan, p120.
3 Sunshine City, p121.
4 Sunshine 60 Building, p121.
Bars ▪
1 B1 Bobby's Bar, p165.

Shops & Services ○
1 Caravan Books, p177.
2 Japan Traditional Craft Centre, p188.
3 Sunshine City, p121.
4 Tobu, p175.
Clubs ○
1 Bed, p214.
Film ○
2 Shin-Bungeiza, p218.

Gay & Lesbian ○
3 Fellow, p228.
4 Jinya, p231.
5 Spartacus, p231.
Music ○
6 Live Inn Rosa, p243.
7 Tokyo Metropolitan Art Space, p235.
Sport & Fitness ○
8 Ikebukuro Sports Centre, p260.

To check out other aspects of modern-day Japan, visit the **Amlux Toyota** car showroom and the **Animate** manga emporium next door.

A few blocks further to the east a more old-fashioned experience awaits, in the form of the **Arakawa Streetcar Line** – one of Tokyo's last two surviving tram lines. Small, one-car trams – *chin-chin densha* ('ding-ding trains') – trundle through picturesque residential areas, sometimes slipping behind rows of houses and sometimes joining cars and buses on the streets, for an unhurried view of non-tourist Tokyo. It's possible to stand behind the driver and look over his shoulder for the best view. There's a flat fare of ¥160, and major stops along the 12-kilometre (eight-mile) route include **Asukayama Park** and its three small museums; **Zoshigaya Cemetery** and the nearby **Zoshigaya Missionary Museum**; and Waseda University. The tram connects with the JR lines at Oji and Otsuka stations, while Sunshine City is only a few blocks' walk from Mukohara station.

FURTHER AFIELD

Thanks to its profusion of railway lines, Ikebukuro is a good staging point for excursions in other areas. Two of Tokyo's main amusement parks are accessible from here: **Toshimaen** (on the Seibu Ikebukuro line, with transfer to the Seibu Toshima spur line; it's also on the Oedo subway line) and **Tokyo Dome City** (on the Marunouchi subway line; *see p202*). A more peaceful option lies next door to Tokyo Dome: **Koishikawa Korakuen**, the oldest garden in the city, laid out in the 17th century.

Amlux Toyota Auto Salon

3-3-5 Higashi-Ikebukuro, Toshima-ku (5391 5900/ www.amlux.jp/english/floor/f1_f.shtml). Ikebukuro station (Yamanote line), east exit; (Marunouchi, Yurakucho lines), exit 35. **Open** *B1F & 1F* 11am-9pm Tue-Sun. *2F-4F* 11am-7pm Tue-Sun. **Admission** free. **Map** p119.
Toyota claimed this was the world's biggest car showroom until it opened an even bigger one in Mega Web (*see p116*) in Odaiba. But Amlux still echoes with the sound of slamming doors as scores of petrolheads gleefully hop in and out of about 70 vehicles on display – essentially Toyota's entire consumer line. More amazing is that you can test drive any vehicle as long as you have a valid driving licence (Japanese or international). Rates start at the absurdly low price of ¥1,000 for 60 minutes.

Asukayama Park

1-1-3 Oji, Kita-ku (3916 1133). Asukayama station (Toden Arakawa line) or Oji station (Keihin Tohoku line), north exit; (Namboku line), exit 1. **Open** *Museums* 10am-5pm Tue-Sun. **Admission** *Individual museum* ¥300; ¥100 concessions. *All museums* ¥720; ¥300 concessions. **No credit cards.**

Sunshine 60 Building: it's tall. See *p121*.

This wooded hilltop park was once the estate of Shibusawa Eiichi (1840-1931), president of Japan's first modern bank. Former US president Ulysses Grant was treated to a *jujitsu* demonstration here in 1879 while staying as Shibusawa's guest. The towering mansion is long gone, but a few outbuildings remain. The park's main attractions are the 'Asukayama Three Museums', which stand in a row at the park's eastern edge.

The Paper Museum (3916 2320, www.paper museum.jp) displays items related to paper art, papermaking technology and the history of paper, and sometimes holds participatory workshops. The Kita City Asukayama Museum (3916 1133) focuses on local archaeological finds, including a dugout canoe from the Jomon period, Japan's stone age. English signage is minimal, but the displays are largely self-explanatory. The Shibusawa Memorial Museum (3910 0005, www.shibusawa.or.jp) praises the achievements of Shibusawa Eiichi. Most of the exhibits are old documents, some in English – including a signed letter from Thomas Edison.

Jiyu Gakuen Myonichikan

2-31-3 Nishi-Ikebukuro, Toshima-ku (3971 7535/ www.jiyu.jp/index-e.html). Ikebukuro station (Yamonote line), Metropolitan exit; (Marunouchi, Yurakucho lines), exit 3. **Open** 10am-4pm Tue-Sun. **Admission** ¥600. **No credit cards.** **Map** p119.
Architect Frank Lloyd Wright's Imperial Hotel in Tokyo was famously demolished in 1968, but few people realise that a smaller Wright building – a private school – still stands in Ikebukuro. Now used as an alumni meeting hall rather than for classes, it is open for tours (but it's wise to call ahead first). Viewed from the outside, the unusual geometry of the window frames is the clearest indication of Wright's signature.

Koishikawa Korakuen

1-6-6 Koraku, Bunkyo-ku (3811 3015). Iidabashi station (Namboku, Oedo lines), exit A1 or Korakuen station (Marunouchi line), exit 2. **Open** 9am-5pm daily. **Admission** ¥300. **No credit cards.**
Koishikawa Korakuen was first laid out in 1629. It's now only a quarter of its original size, but it's still beautiful, with a range of walks, bridges, hills and vistas (often the miniatures of more famous originals) that encourage quiet contemplation. The entrance, tucked away down a side street, can be a little difficult to find.

Mejiro Teien

3-20-18 Mejiro, Toshima-ku (5996 4810). Ikebukuro station (Yamonote line), south exit; Marunouchi, Yurakucho lines), exit 39 or Mejiro station (Yamonote line). **Open** *Jan-June, Sept-Dec* 9am-5pm daily. *July, Aug* 9am-7pm daily. Closed 2nd & 4th Mon of mth. **Admission** free.
This small garden a short walk from Wright's school building creates the illusion of greater space by way of a deep artificial valley with a pond at the bottom. A gazebo over the pond and a grassy area behind some trees are good spots for a picnic lunch.

Sunshine City

3-1-3 Higashi-Ikebukuro, Toshima-ku (3989 3466/ www.sunshinecity.co.jp). Ikebukuro station (Yamanote line), east exit; Marunouchi, Yurakucho lines), exit 35 or Higashi-Ikebukuro station (Yurakucho line), exit 2. **Open** *Aquarium* 10am-6pm Mon-Fri; 10am-6.30pm Sat, Sun. *Planetarium* noon-6pm Mon-Fri; 11am-7pm Sat, Sun. *Ancient Orient Museum* 10am-5pm daily. **Admission** *Aquarium* ¥1,600. *Planetarium* ¥800. *Museum* ¥500. **No credit cards. Map** p119.
Sunshine City occupies the former site of Sugamo Prison, where General Tojo Hideki, Japan's wartime prime minister, was hanged in 1948 (a small monument on the northern corner of the block marks where the gallows stood). As well as the Sunshine 60 Building (*see below*), the complex contains the world's first aquarium in a high-rise building, with more than 20,000 fish and shows by performing seals. There's also a planetarium, located, appropriately enough, in the sky, on the same floor as the aquarium. The Ancient Orient Museum in the Bunka Kaikan building focuses on western Asia, especially Iran and Pakistan – check out the Parthian-era bull-shaped ceremonial drinking vessel with nipple-spouts on its chest.

Sunshine 60 Building

3-1-1 Higashi-Ikebukuro, Toshima-ku (3989 3331/www.sunshinecity.co.jp). Ikebukuro station (Yamonote line), east exit; (Marunouchi, Yurakucho lines), exit 35 or Higashi-Ikebukuro station (Yurakucho line), exit 2. **Open** *Observatory* 10am-8.30pm daily. *Namjatown* 10am-10pm daily. **Admission** *Observatory* ¥620; ¥310 concessions. *Namjatown* ¥300; ¥200 concessions; 1-day passport ¥3,900; ¥3,300 concessions. **No credit cards. Map** p119.

One of the fastest lifts in the world will whisk you to the observatory on the top floor of this 60-storey skyscraper in around 35 seconds. The building's lower floors house the World Import Mart shopping mall and Namjatown, an unbelievably tacky indoor amusement park.

Toshimaen

3-25-1 Koyama, Nerima-ku (3990 8800/ www.toshimaen.co.jp/index.html). Toshimaen station (Oedo line), exit A2. **Open** *Mid July-Aug* 10am-8pm daily. *Sept-mid July* 10am-5pm Fri-Sun. *Toshimaen Garden Spa* 10am-11pm daily. **Admission** *Entry only* ¥1,000. *Entry & ride pass* ¥3,800. *Toshimaen Garden Spa* ¥2,000; ¥1,200 after 9pm.
Every summer this old, usually boring amusement park turns spectacular with the opening of Hydropolis, a waterpark that includes a surf pool and a very elaborate set of waterslides. A year-round attraction next door is an *onsen* mineral water spa.

Zoshigaya Cemetery

4-25-1 Minami-Ikebukuro, Toshima-ku (3971 6868). Zoshigaya station (Toden Arakawa line). **Open** 24hrs daily. **Admission** free.
This tree-shaded cemetery is the final resting place of such notables as John Manjiro (1827-98), the legendary Edo period link between East and West, in plot 1-2-10-1, and writer Lafcadio Hearn (1850-1904), who is buried in plot 1-1-8-35 under his Japanese name, Koizumi Yakumo. In plot 1-14-1-3 lies novelist Natsume Soseki (1867-1916), famous as the face on the old ¥1,000 note (these notes are still in wide circulation as the redesigned ones were introduced only in November 2004). Disgraced general Tojo Hideki is also here, in plot 1-1-12-6.

Zoshigaya Missionary Museum

1-25-5 Zoshigaya, Toshima-ku (3985 4081/ http://humsum.cool.ne.jp/cho-41.html). Higashi-Ikebukuro station (Yurakucho line), exit 5 or Zoshigaya station (Toden Arakawa line). **Open** 9am-4.30pm Tue-Sun. Closed 3rd Sun of mth. **Admission** free.
Very few homes of early foreign residents in Tokyo have escaped the ravages of time and development. This one, built in 1907, belonged to American missionary JM McCaleb. When it was threatened with demolition a few years ago, residents campaigned to save it. Located a couple of blocks south of Zoshigaya Cemetery, the two-storey, white clapboard building is strangely displaced, time-warped from old America to the hubbub of modern Tokyo.

Getting there

Ikebukuro station is on the Yamanote line and the Marunouchi and Yurakucho subway lines, as well as the JR Saikyo, Seibu Ikebukuro and Tobu Tojo train lines. The Toden Arakawa tram line does not serve Ikebukuro station directly, but makes several stops in eastern Ikebukuro, including Higashi-Ikebukuro Yonchome, just outside Higashi-Ikebukuro station on the Yurakucho line.

Sightseeing

Further Afield

There's more to see outside the JR Yamanote line loop.

Outside central Tokyo and the areas covered in earlier Sightseeing chapters lie some funky neighbourhoods that are worth a visit. A few stops from Shibuya station are increasingly fashionable **Naka-Meguro** and the laid-back student hangout of **Shimo-Kitazawa**, while the first handful of stations along the **Chuo line**, one of the city's longest and most crowded commuter lines, offer pockets of interest. We've also included a handful of attractions dotted about the metropolitan area.

Naka-Meguro

To the uninitiated, Naka-Meguro – which lies to the south of Shibuya and east of Ebisu – might seem to be a wholly unremarkable corner of the city. But the generic veneer is part of the appeal: this area doesn't like to advertise the fact that it has recently emerged as Tokyo's hippest hangout. Rents that are relatively cheap for central Tokyo have attracted a hip crowd of young artists, designers and musicians, and, crucially for a land in which shopkeeping is considered an art form, upcoming retailers.

The Meguro river, which defines this funky district, is lined with small cafés, boutiques and interior outfitters catering to image-conscious locals and curious visitors, many of whom wander in from neighbouring shopping haven Daikanyama. These establishments are almost all owned and run by entrepreneurs rather than big corporations – rare for Japan – and the cool spaces they have created are what fuels the hype surrounding this trendy tract.

Naka-Meguro retains a sleepy feel and places of interest are not clustered enough for the area to ever seem crowded, except during *sakura* (cherry blossom) season, and even then, the riverside festivities are a relatively understated affair. Art fans visit at all times of year to view the **Museum of Contemporary Sculpture**.

One of the best places from which to watch this part of the world go by is **Opatoca** (1-25-5 Aobadai, 090 4925 0968, www.mfs11.com/opatoca/opatoca.html, open 11.30am-7.30pm daily), a wholesome riverside café run by the folks behind Naka-Meguro's legendary secret ping-pong lounge (ask a local to find out more).

Fans of café culture should head for **Chano-ma** (Kangyo Bldg 6F, 1-22-4 Kami-Meguro, 3792 9898, open noon-midnight Mon-Thur, Sun, noon-4am Fri, Sat). Located just across from the train station, with a nondescript lift door at ground level, this urban haven has clever lighting, Eames chairs and elevated mattress seating for socks-off sprawling.

For more hearty dining, several rowdy *izakaya* are situated by the river close to the station, such as **Aguri**, as well as pizza specialist **Salvatore** (for both, *see p153*). But to sample the local speciality *nabe* (hot-pot) follow the train tracks away from the river to famed *motsu nabe* (offal hot-pot) restaurant **Torigoya** (3-5-22 Kami-Meguro, 3710 6762, open 11am-midnight Mon-Fri, 11am-1am Sat, Sun), which is run by a camp amateur *enka* singer. On the other side of the tracks is a metalworking factory turned pork *nabe* restaurant, **Butanabe Kenkyushitsu** (3-5-19 Kami-Meguro, 3713 7250, open 6pm-midnight Tue-Fri, 6pm-2am Sat, Sun). Following the tracks a couple of blocks further along on the Torigoya side brings you to the unadvertised entrance of **Depot** (*see p225*), which combines a restaurant with a cavernous gallery space for displaying edgy street art.

Mizuma Art Gallery (*see p225*), whose well-connected curator brings in a steady stream of Tokyo's hottest upcoming artists, is the only venue in this locale that doesn't double up as a shop or eaterie. Visit **Cow Books** (1-14-11 Aobadai, 5459 1747, www.cowbooks.jp, open noon-10pm daily) facing the river to see fashionable kids chuckling over vintage books and magazines, and **Buro-stil** (1-6-19 Higashiyama, 3794 9955, open 1-10pm daily, closed 2nd and 3rd Tue of mth) for wacky retro furniture.

Fashion shopping is what the vast majority of visitors come to Naka-Meguro for, and besides a dozen or so second-hand stores and a handful of posh boutiques pushing upmarket European prêt-à-porter, there are some homegrown labels well worth a potentially mind-broadening browse. Check out the eye-opening oufits on offer at the flagship store of geeky teen favourite **Frapbois** (1-20-4 Aobadai, 6415 4688, www.frapbois.jp, open 11am-8pm daily) and, behind it, **Metal Burger** (MS Bldg B1F, 1-19-7 Aobadai, 5728 4765, www.metalburger.com, open noon-8pm daily), which supplies punk looks to jovial anarchists. The out-there vintage selection at hole-in-the-wall

Shimo-Kitazawa's main shopping street and bar **Heaven's Door** (bottom left).

Waingman Wassa (1-23-5, Aobadai, 5773 5586, open 1-8pm daily) perfectly encapsulates the area's irreverent style.

Museum of Contemporary Sculpture
4-12-18 Naka-Meguro, Meguro-ku (3792 5858/ www.museum-of-sculpture.org). Naka-Meguro station (Hibiya, Tokyu Toyoko lines), central exit.
Open 10am-5pm Tue-Sun. **Admission** free.
The Watanabe Collection includes more than 200 pieces by 56 contemporary Japanese artists. Three outdoor areas filled with large, mostly conceptual works complement two storeys inside of figurative studies. The marble tombstones in the adjacent graveyard provide an interesting counterpoint.

Getting there

Naka-Meguro station is the first stop on the Hibiya subway line and two stops from Shibuya on the Tokyu Toyoko line.

Shimo-Kitazawa

There are not many hippie strongholds left in the world, and you might not expect to find one of them in Tokyo – but come to Shimo-Kitazawa and you will. A small, thriving community a few minutes by train from Shinjuku, it's the happy haunt of various actors, comedians and writers, and numerous students.

The award-winning novelist Ekuni Kaori, author of the recently translated tale of tangled Tokyo relationships *Twinkle, Twinkle*, and the film actor Takenaka Naoto (*Shall We Dance*, *Trick*) have their homes here. The office of the late Itami Juzo, one of Japan's ground-breaking movie directors, is nearby, and legendary theatre directors such as Ninagawa Yukio and Mori Hajime have staged productions on the area's illustrious boards.

The creative impetus behind the area's growth came from the 1960s' *sho-gekijou* (small-theatre) movement, a phenomenon born of frustration with the way theatres were dominated by either Western realism or tradition-bound *kabuki* and *noh*. The *sho-gekijou* movement gave younger actors and directors the freedom to express themselves, and a large number of these came to be concentrated in Shimo-Kitazawa.

As well as theatre, the neighbourhood has become famous for its 'live houses' – the dark, dynamic, box-like venues where Tokyo's aspiring bands hone their skills. Every weekend, these places – particularly the well-known ones, such as **Shelter** (*see p244*), **Club Que** (*see p242*) and **Club 251** (*see p242*) – are rammed full with a body-pierced, leather-wearing crowd moshing politely in front of a tiny stage.

The station has two exits, north and south, both of which lead to areas of interest. From the north exit, turn right and after about 200 metres, you'll come to the first set of crossroads. The street that stretches away to both sides will take you past boutiques selling new and second-hand clothes ranging from cute to bizarre, and all points in-between. There's been in influx of mainstream and chain shops in the past few years, but the area's essential character remains one of quirky individuality.

Keep walking straight, and you'll get to another crossroads. Turning right leads back to the train tracks, and straight ahead down a small alleyway will take you past **fxg** (*see p186*) – the shop that spearheaded the current wave of cheap, stylish opticians – to Ichibangai Dori.

Over on the other side of the station, the south exit crackles with life after dark, as this is where local residents and visitors go to eat, drink and mosh themselves into a happy, eardrum-ringing haze. Directly opposite the south exit is the area's main street, Minami Shotengai, packed full of fast-food shops, *pachinko* parlours and cheap boutiques. Half-way down the street the area's distinctive character starts to reveal itself, with its second-hand book, game and CD shops. A road branching off to the right, with Mr Donuts on the corner, points the way to a quiet, leafy street with one of the best *izakaya* in the area – the stately **Shirube** (3413 3785, open 5.30-11.30pm daily). Right opposite Shirube is English pub **Heaven's Door** (*see p166*), a haven for those looking for a decent pint and UK football.

Going back to the main street and walking right to the bottom, you'll find a knot of streets leading off in five directions. These streets contain numerous little bars and restaurants, many of them serving ethnic food and drink.

Back at the south exit, turn left and head down the nameless street that has a Starbucks on the corner. Halfway down is the basement venue Club Que, while at the end is Chazawa Dori, with Shelter off to the left and Club 251 about ten minutes' walk to the right. The streets between the Minami Shotengai and Chazawa Dori are well worth a wander, as they host several 'natural-food' *izakaya* and the most famous *sho-gekijou* in the area, the **Honda Theatre** (2-10-15 Kitazawa, Setagaya-ku, 3468 0030, www.honda-geki.com).

Arty, lively and occasionally pretentious, Shimo-Kitazawa has the power to restore the faith of those who say Tokyo's losing its soul.

Getting there

Shimo-Kitazawa station is on the Keio Inokashira line (from Shibuya station) and the Odakyu line (from Shinjuku station).

The Chuo line

The JR Chuo line heads west in the evening from its first station, Tokyo, stopping at the key business hubs of Ochanomizu, Yotsuya and Shinjuku before trekking out to the 'bedtowns' and suburbs of western Tokyo and the cities beyond. Its cargo is a mass of sleeping, occasionally drunk, always exhausted commuters heading home. In the morning it all happens in reverse: the Chuo line picks up

Kasai Seaside Park. *See p128.*

the same crew of wage slaves and spits them out again in the bowl of Tokyo central for another day's Japan Inc.

The Chuo line is one of the most important train lines in the capital, and one of the most crowded in all Japan, with commuters jammed in so tightly it's – almost – worth joining in for the experience. But wise travellers avoid it between 7.30am and 9.30am (into the city) and 6pm and 9pm (out of the city). The last train of the night from Shinjuku station, at around 12.30am, is a great way to come face to face, literally, with the locals, and to redefine your concept of personal space .

Living on the government-run Chuo line is more expensive than on privately owned lines, because services run every three minutes at peak times and stop at all the major commercial centres. It's given a high priority by JR, second only to the Yamanote line. Only the occasional platform jumper affects its solid punctuality. It's also famous for gropers (although this is changing, following publicity and increasing prosecution by JR), drunks and cattle-truck conditions at the times outlined above.

The first two stations out of Shinjuku – Okubo and Higashi-Nakano – contain little of note. The most interesting locales are between Nakano and Kichijoji stations; below we describe the highlights of each area.

These stations are served by two types of train: the yellow-coloured local (Sobu line), and the orange-coloured express (Chuo line). The Sobu line starts in Chiba prefecture and stops at all stations (including Shinjuku), but goes no further west than Mitaka. From Shinjuku, the Chuo line plonks down first at Nakano before going station by station out to various termination points, the furthest located deep in the suburbs of west Tokyo. Trains run between roughly 6am and midnight, and their frequency makes it easy to hop from one destination to another; stations are only a few minutes apart.

If you're exploring at the weekend, take the Sobu line – because Chuo trains stop only at Ogikubo, rather than at every station between Nakano and Mitaka. After hours, take a taxi.

Further along the line are more delights, such as the open-air branch of the **Edo-Tokyo Museum** (*see p128*) in Musashi-Koganei.

Nakano

Although best known these days for its cheap shopping, Nakano was once home to 80,000 dogs. The fifth shogun, Tokugawa Tsunaiyasho, was particularly fond of mutts, and in 1695 he built an *inuyashiki* (dog castle) across the whole of Nakano to keep his tens of thousands of canine mates in comfort. Dogs can still be seen today wandering the streets, unaware of their providence.

A must-see for fans of manga, *anime* and cosplay (costume play) is the sprawling empire of **Mandarake**. What was once one shop selling recycled manga comics has slowly spread its Akira-like tentacles across **Nakano Broadway** (*see p177*), the town's main shopping mall next to the station's north exit. Now, 14 shops on three floors of the four-storey centre sell comics, figurines, vintage toys, animation cells, CDs, video games, posters, cosplay costumes – in fact, anything related to Japan's favourite obsession. Start on the third floor at comic HQ, and lose an afternoon wandering around. Key rings and tiny figurines sell from ¥100, and make cheap and unique souvenirs. Japanese schoolgirl dresses can be had for a bigger outlay. Broadway is also home to a host of discount shoe and fashion shops, with prices far below those charged a five-minute train ride away in Shinjuku.

Afterwards, visit the Escher-like confines of Nakano's **Classic** coffee shop (*see p170*) to soak up a ¥400 coffee and a huge sound system playing non-stop classical music. The warren of streets surrounding the Broadway complex has scores of restaurants, bars and *izakaya*, many of them offering food at bargain prices.

Slightly out of Nakano centre are quirky **Tetsugakudo Park** and the **Toy Museum**.

Tetsugakudo Park
1-34-28 Matsugaoka, Nakano-ku (3954 4881). Nakano station (Chuo line), north exit then bus to Tetsugakudo or Arai Yakushi-mae station (Seibu Shinjuku line), north exit then 12mins walk. **Open** 9am-5pm daily.
A hillside park founded by philosopher Inoue Enryo, who wanted to enshrine philosophical theory in physical form. The park contains 77 spots that symbolise different doctrines. On the top of the hill are six Meiji-era buildings that are open to the public during *hanami* (cherry blossom viewing) and in October on public holidays and at weekends.

Toy Museum
2-12-10 Arai, Nakano-ku (3387 5461/www.toy-art.co.jp/museum.html). Nakano station (Chuo line), north exit. **Open** 10.30am-4pm Mon, Wed, Thur, Sat, Sun. **Admission** ¥500; free under-2s. **No credit cards.**
This hands-on, crafts-oriented place has no shortage of local kids busy playing. And there's not a video game or TV in sight.

Koenji

Koenji is home to a youthful live music scene and plenty of students. A cluster of bars and B1 sink pits around both sides of the station exit provide a window into a selection of musical styles – mainly punk/grunge, but also jazz, country and western, and soul. The best of these, **Inaoiza** (2F Sunny Mansion, 2-38-16 Koenjikita, 3336 4480, open 7.30pm-2am daily), is a decades-old bar that could well serve up a treat on a random night. Local talent plays most evenings from 8pm, and entry is ¥1,500, or free if no one is jamming.

Also worth a visit is bar/restaurant **Las Meninas** (*see p166*), run by affable Geordie Johnny Miller and his Japanese wife. Enjoy seasonal dishes with a Mediterranean/tapas focus, supported by an outstanding cast of 30 Spanish wines and 15 sherries. Prices are half what you would pay in central Tokyo. Ask at the police box just outside the north exit for a map – they know all about this place and are used to directing foreigners.

Koenji also has a reputation as Tokyo's centre for all things associated with the southern Japanese island of Okinawa. A new cultural centre directly behind Las Meninas (under construction at time of writing) will feature Okinawan music and dancing. Further down the same street, there is Okinawan food at the Tokyo-famous **Dachibin** (3-2-13 Koenji-Kita, 3377 1352, open 5pm-5am daily). Most of the cooking is *chanpuri* (mixed fried things) and many dishes feature the bitter flavours of the Okinawan vegetable *goya* – *chanpuri goya* is a good start. If you tire of the pedestrian flavours of Orion, the island's own beer, then ask for *awamori* – Okinawan sake. It comes in two strengths: five-year-old 35 per cent and the older 45 per cent. Drink with respect.

Asagaya

Seeing itself as the prince among the kissed toads of the Chuo line, Asagaya strives to match the urbanity of inner Tokyo. This self-confidence is based on both slight and solid cultural connections. The area's well-founded reputation for jazz grows every year as its Jazz Street festival, held in October, continues to mutate both in size and composition. A number of bars showcase local jazz players throughout the year.

Scribblers of all types laid the foundations for Asagaya's self-important world view. The Asagaya-kai was a group of prominent Japanese authors that haunted the area from 1910 to the early 1950s. Its leader, Masuji Ibuse, gained international fame with his novel *Black Rain*, the story of a Hiroshima woman's struggle with radiation poisoning. From the 1970s the area enjoyed an art renaissance when it became a draw for Japan's best manga artists. These days, though, its wealthy

residents spend rather than create, and a little ambulatory effort will unearth good restaurants and homely, cramped bars.

It's worth seeing the aged trees lining Nakasugi Dori, the main street under the railway tracks, which are at their most gloriously green from May to June. Just off this street is **Spicy & Beer Bar** (Watanabe Bldg 1F, 3-31-1 Asagaya-Minami, 3220 7752, open 11.30am-2am Mon-Thur, 11.30am-4am Fri, Sat, 11.30am-midnight Sun), a boozer offering beers from 33 countries and assorted curries. Film buffs note: the square on the south side of the station was a backdrop in the original version of horror movie *The Ring*.

Ogikubo

Key word: ramen. One of Tokyo's best-known ramen shops is in Ogikubo, and people travel from all over Japan to eat there. **Harukiya** (1-4-6 Kami-Ogi, 3391 4868, open 11am-9pm daily) seats only 16 people, and there's usually a small queue. Ask for *chuka soba* or, for extra slices of pork, *chashumen*. Harukiya was established in 1952, on the heels of a black market that sprang up after World War II to offset the poverty of those times. What remains is a good fresh fish, meat and veg market sprawling over the basement floor of the Ogikubo Town 7 shopping centre; it's open daily.

Although not a particularly pretty place, Ogikubo retains a bustling, working-class feel and, more than at most stations on the Chuo line, a sense of history.

Nishi-Ogikubo

In the 1960s peaceful 'Nishi Ogi' rose to heights of civil disobedience as a gathering point for organic, veggie-loving hippies. Two cults have also risen from these nondescript surroundings – most notorious was Aum Shinrikyo, the religious sect responsible for the subway sarin gas attacks in 1995 that killed 12 people.

Now, fortunately, the area is best known only for its antiques and bric-a-brac shops – around 75 of them, in fact. Take the north exit from the station and head for the *koban* (police box). Boldly stride up to the policeman, make no sudden moves, and say 'antiku mapu onegai shimasu'. He'll pull one out of the desk, and you'll be on your way to a pleasant day strolling the backstreets. You'll find both Western and Japanese antiquities on sale, but don't expect bargains. The north-west section of the walk has the best furniture, lighting and antiques shops, and there are also a few eccentric second-hand bookshops which may reward your browsing.

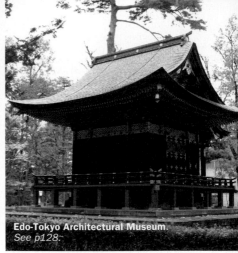
Edo-Tokyo Architectural Museum.
See p128.

Kichijoji

On the edge of Tokyo's 23 wards, Kichijoji is slowly emerging as west Tokyo's own Shibuya. Although lacking the urbane tribalism of Shib, the area attracts large numbers of school and university students, giving a youthful vibe and freshness that other destinations on the Chuo line lack. At weekends, the shopping malls and department stores teem with life, and many people also visit spacious **Inokashira Park**.

Jazz venues and ethnic restaurants are something of a speciality, while digging deep among the streets outside the station's north exit will turn up numerous bars and eateries. This plethora of choice makes Kichijoji an excellent night-time excursion.

An early lunch at **Superbacco** (Frente Kichijoji Bldg B1, 2-1-31 Kichijoji Minami-cho, 0422 49 2005, open 11am-last orders 9.30pm daily) makes a good start to the day. This restaurant is Venetian-themed down to its Italian/Japanese language menu and the unusual standing room-only wine bar by the entrance. Unusually for Tokyo, an intelligent range of wines is available from ¥250 upwards, accompanied by a changing selection of cheap, tapas-style snacks. Great pasta, fish, seafood and meat dishes in the restaurant are also good value. It's located in the basement of the building complex housing Kichijoji station.

The under-lit black interiors of the **Outback Kitchen & Bar** (2-8-1 Kichijoji-honcho, 0422 21 1548, www.sometime.co.jp, open 6pm-2am daily) are popular with couples. This groovy two-storey basement bar has a long cocktail menu, a clued-in selection of wines, and a solid range of spirits and Cuban cigars. Eclectic jazz floats out of two huge speakers, and a sit-down meal can be had on the small second floor. It's a little expensive, but worth the outlay.

Alternatively, modern Japanese presented with flair is served up at **Kin no Saru** ('The Golden Monkey', Inokashira Parkside Bldg 1F, 1-21-1 Kichijoji, 0422 72 8757, open 5.30-11.30pm daily). Traditional floor seating and tables signpost the trim Japanese aesthetics of this upmarket eaterie, situated on the edge of Inokashira Park. Views of bamboo and trees create a romantic ambience. There are no English menus, but staff are young and helpful.

Inside the park itself, groovy café **Pepecafe Forest** (4-1-5 Inokashira-Koen, 0422 42 7081, open noon-10pm Mon, Wed-Sun) lies across from the central bridge over the lake. Its plastic walls roll up in summer, ideal for evening beers.

In between the park and Mitaka (further up the Chuo line) lies the **Ghibli Museum**, a showcase for the Oscar-winning animation studio of the same name.

Ghibli Museum

1-1-83 Shimo-Renjaku, Mitaka-shi (0570 05 5777/www.ghibli-museum.jp). Kichijoji station (Chuo line), north exit then 15mins walk or Mitaka station (Chuo line), south exit then community bus. **Open** (tours only) 10am, noon, 2pm, 4pm Mon, Wed-Sun. **Admission** ¥1,000; ¥400-¥700 concessions. **Credit cards** (gift shop only) AmEx, DC, JCB, MC, V.
Miyazaki Hayao's studio has produced some of Japan's most popular and complex animation classics, from *My Neighbour Totoro* to *Princess Mononoke* and *Spirited Away*. If you want to learn more about the studio's work, be warned that gaining access to this museum is tougher than getting into the Kremlin. You need to purchase tickets in advance (which can be done from overseas; check the website), then show up at the prescribed day and time with your ticket and some ID. You will be escorted into another world: you can view original prints, play in rooms with painted ceilings and walls, and watch short animations in the cinema. The gift shop sells original animation cells.

Inokashira Park

1-18-31 Gotenyama, Musashino-shi (0422 47 6900). Kichijoji station (Chuo line), park exit then 10mins walk. **Open** 24hrs daily.

Located just 15 minutes from the centre of Tokyo, this park has more than enough to occupy you for a full afternoon, including a zoo (not the greatest in the world; *see p203*), a pond with amusingly shaped rental boats, and enough playground facilities to keep the little ones happy. At weekends the park comes alive with street traders, musicians and artists. In late March and early April it fills with people enjoying *hanami* (cherry blossom viewing) and it's worth making the trip to join them.

Other sights

Edo-Tokyo Open-Air Architectural Museum (Edo-Tokyo Tatemono-en)

3-7-1 Sakuracho, Koganei Ishi (042 388 3300/ www.tatemonoen.jp). Musashi Koganei station (Chuo line), north exit then any bus from bus stops 2 or 3 to Koganei Koen Nishi-Guchi. **Open** *Apr-Sept* 9.30am-5.30pm Tue-Sun. *Oct-Mar* 9.30am-4.30pm Tue-Sun. **Admission** ¥400; free-¥200 concessions. **No credit cards.**

Tokyo's façade may be in a never-ending cycle of renewal, but its architectural heritage is well preserved in an unexpectedly rich hoard of buildings at this branch of the Edo-Tokyo Museum (*see p98*). As well as swanky private residences and quaint old town shops, there's a host of one-offs, such as an ornate bathhouse and a mausoleum built for a shogun's wife. Even the visitors' centre once served as a ceremonial pavilion in front of the Imperial Palace. Be prepared for lots of slipping in and out of shoes if you want to visit the interiors.

Kasai Seaside Park

6-2 Rinkai-cho, Edogawa-ku (3686 6911/ www.senyo.co.jp/kasai). Kasai-Rinkai Koen station (Keiyo line) or by Suijo water bus. **Open** *Park* 24hrs daily. *Birdwatching centre & visitor centre* 9.30am-4.30pm daily. *Beach* 9am-5pm daily. *Big wheel* 10am-8pm Mon-Fri; 10am-9pm Sat, Sun. *Tokyo Sea Life Park* 9.30am-5pm Tue-Sun. **Admission** free. *Big wheel* ¥700. *Tokyo Sea Life Park* ¥700. **No credit cards.**

Located by the water at the eastern edge of the city, close to Tokyo Disney Resort (*see below*), this is one of Tokyo's biggest parks and was built to recreate a natural seashore environment. Traces of the metropolis are evident on three sides, but the park still makes a good escape. Inside are the Tokyo Sea Life Park, two small beaches, a Japanese garden and a lotus pond. The birdwatching area includes two ponds and tidal flats.

Museum of Contemporary Art, Tokyo (MoT)

4-1-1 Miyoshi, Koto-ku (5245 4111/www.mot-art-museum.jp). Kiba station (Tozai line), exit 3 then 15mins walk. **Open** 10am-6pm Tue-Sun.

Admission ¥500; ¥250-¥400 concessions; free under-12s; additional charge for special exhibitions. **Credit** (shop only) JCB, MC, V.

This huge, city-owned showpiece opened in 1995 on reclaimed swampland in a distant part of Tokyo. Its collection of 3,500 international and Japanese artworks has its moments, but the temporary exhibitions are the main reason to visit. Visitors can access the database, extensive video library, and magazine and catalogue collection (all available in English).

Sengaku-ji Temple

2-11-1 Takanawa, Minato-ku (3441 5560/ www.sengakuji.or.jp). Sengaku-ji station (Asakusa line), exit A2. **Open** *Temple Apr-Sept* 7am-6pm daily. *Oct-Mar* 7am-5pm daily. *Museum* 9am-4pm daily. **Admission** free.

The most interesting thing about this temple is its connection with one of Japan's most famous stories – that of 47 samurai attached to Lord Ako. After he drew his sword on a rival, Kira Yoshinaka, in Edo Castle (a serious breach of protocol), Ako was ordered to commit *seppuku* (death by ritual disembowelment). He was buried here. His 47 loyal followers then became *ronin*, or samurai without a master, bent on avenging their master's death. They killed Kira and were then themselves permitted to die in the same manner as their master, and to be buried close to him, also at Sengaku-ji. Their tombs are at the top of a flight of steps. Follow the smoke trails from the incense left by well-wishers. The episode is still remembered, with the 47 Ronin Memorial Service at the temple in mid December (*see p199*) and a week of events in April.

Tokyo Disney Resort

1-1 Maihama, Urayasu-shi, Chiba (English information 045 683 3333/www.tokyodisney resort.co.jp/tdr/index_e.html). Maihama station (Keiyo, Musashino lines), south exit. **Open** varies. **Admission** *1-day passport* ¥5,500; ¥3,700-¥4,800 concessions. *2-day passport* ¥9,800; ¥6,700-¥8,600 concessions. *Starlight passport* (after 3pm Sat, Sun) ¥4,500; ¥3,000-¥3,900 concessions; admission to either Disneyland or DisneySea, but not both on same day. **Credit** AmEx, DC, JCB, MC, V.

Sitting on a huge tract of land in Tokyo Bay, the Tokyo Disney Resort comprises two adjacent but separate theme parks: Disneyland and DisneySea. The latter, opened in 2001, has given the whole enterprise a massive shot in the arm, since room for expansion on land is limited here, and the rest of the park was starting to show its age in parts. Disneyland's seven main zones boast 43 attractions, while DisneySea has 23 water-based attractions in its seven zones. Whatever you may feel about the Disney machine, it's virtually impossible not to have a great day out here. The queues can be horrendous, though, so go early, and preferably on a weekday. Also, the restaurants are pricey and there are no vending machines, so bring snacks and drinks at least. It's best to purchase tickets in advance from the Disney ticket office (*see p61*) in central Tokyo.

Eat, Drink, Shop

Features

Restaurants

Chowing, munching, scoffing, slurping – whatever you do, just start eating.

Tokyo is one of the world's great cities for eating out. It boasts more than 300,000 restaurants, taverns, mom-and-pop diners and assorted hole-in-the-wall eateries, serving not only Japanese and Asian foods, but cuisines from all around the globe. Standards are high too: it's hard to eat badly, and many places are world class.

First and foremost, this is the place to explore the remarkable range and depth of Japanese food. Sushi, tempura and sukiyaki need no introduction, but there's much more to sample, from rarefied multi-course banquets of Kyoto-style *kaiseki* to basic streetcorner *yatai* stalls. Unlike in the West, most Japanese restaurants focus on a single style of cuisine, be it grilled eel, blowfish (*fugu*) or sumo stews. However, more generalised restaurants serving

a variety of styles can often be found on the top floors of department stores or in the basements of large office buildings.

In the evenings, look out for *izakaya* (literally, 'sake places'), a catch-all term covering the gamut from raucous, crowded taverns to discreet drinking holes of greater refinement. What they all have in common is their suitability as places to unwind at the end of the day. As in tapas bars, you need only order a couple of dishes at a time with your beer, sake or *shochu*. Some serve food of memorable quality; others are basic yakitori joints. Those with lanterns outside (usually red, sometimes white) are likely to be less expensive.

High-end dining in Tokyo can be staggeringly expensive – although no more so than in London or other European capitals. But eating out doesn't have to break the bank. One strategy is to have your main meal in the middle of the day. Many restaurants offer special lunch discounts and set meals, while noodle shops offer affordable, filling fare. In student areas there are plenty of low-priced eateries, family restaurants and fast-food chains, both Japanese and Western. And if all else fails, drop into one of the ubiquitous convenience stores and pick up a lunch box, sushi roll or *onigiri* rice ball.

ETIQUETTE

You don't have to worry too much about etiquette when dining out, but there are a few no-nos. Don't stick your chopsticks vertically into your rice or use them to pass food directly to another person's chopsticks (both are funerary customs). Don't spear food with your chopsticks or wave them around in the air. Remember to remove your shoes in a Japanese-style restaurant. When leaving, it is polite to say *gochisosama deshita* ('thank you for the meal'). Tipping isn't expected.

TIMINGS AND PRICES

Lunch is taken from shortly before noon to around 1pm. Dinner is a bit more flexible, typically from about 6pm to 11pm, with last orders at around 10.30pm – though things run much later in Roppongi and other central areas.

Prices listed below are for an average meal at lunch excluding drinks (or dinner if the restaurant is not open for lunch). We've noted if you can get a menu in English; many (usually

Eat, Drink, Shop

The best Restaurants

For sky-high gourmet dining
The **New York Grill** is still at the pinnnacle. *See p139*.

For sushi
You won't find fresher fish than at **Sushi Bun**. *See p136*.

For stylish modern Japanese
Enjoy 21st-century *izakaya* food at **Tama**. *See p143*.

For street-level Asian
Phuket Aroina Tabeta for authentic, bargain-priced Thai food. *See p138*.

To escape the madding crowd
For a taste of the country, it's got to be **Ukai Toriyama**. *See p153*.

For busting your budget
Mario Frittoli's super-Tuscan *cucina* at **Luxor**. *See p146*.

For that only-in-Japan experience
The run-down shacks of **Yakitori Yokocho** offer that Blade-Runner-meets-Ozu-movie experience. *See p148* **Street food**.

Daidaiya: beautiful interiors, exotic food, fashionable people.

cheaper) restaurants also display realistic plastic models of dishes in their windows, so you can always point at what you want. All our selections have been checked at the time of writing, but restaurants do change hands, move or close, so if you have a particular destination in mind, call ahead to confirm.

Ginza & around

Japanese

Bird Land

Tsukamoto Sozan Bldg B1F, 4-2-15 Ginza, Chuo-ku (5250 1081). Ginza station (Ginza, Hibiya, Marunouchi lines), exit C6. **Open** 5-10pm Tue-Fri; 5-9pm Sat. **Credit** AmEx, DC, JCB, MC, V. **Average** ¥6,000. **Map** p60.

Bird Land was one of the first places to offer upmarket yakitori, served with imported beers and fine wines. Grill master Wada Toshihiro uses top-quality, free-range bantam chickens that are so tasty you can enjoy their meat raw as sashimi. Start off with the chicken liver pâté and don't miss the superb *sansai-yaki* (breast meat grilled with Japanese pepper). It's a small place – just a few tables and a U-shaped counter – and so popular that reservations are hard to get. But seats usually start freeing up by around 8pm, so it's always worth trying your luck.

Daidaiya

Ginza Nine Bldg No.1 2F, 8-5 Ginza, Chuo-ku (5537 3566/www.chanto.com/matome/restaurant/dai.html). Shinbashi station (Yamanote line), Ginza exit; (Asakusa line), exit A3; (Ginza line), exit 3. **Open** 5pm-1am daily. **Average** ¥5,000. **Credit** AmEx, DC, JCB, MC, V. **English menu**. **Map** p60.

This sprawling multi-section gastrodome is just the kind of place where Tokyo's fashionistas like to graze. The food is a hybrid take on traditional Japanese staples with plenty of exotic imported influences. Choose from spaghetti, *kimchi*, steak or sushi – everything's good, although portions are small. But it's the lavish interior and spectacular lighting that make Daidaiya so special. Definitely worth a detour, if only for a drink and a snack.

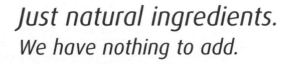

Just natural ingredients.
We have nothing to add.

Discover **KIKKOMAN**
Soy sauce brewed longer to taste better.

Other locations: Shinjuku NOWA Bldg 3F, 3-37-2 Shinjuku, Shinjuku-ku (5362 7173); Belle Vie Akasaka 9F, 3-1-6 Akasaka, Minato-ku (3588 5087).

Little Okinawa

8-7-10 Ginza, Chuo-ku (3572 2930/www.little-okinawa.co.jp). Shinbashi station (Yamanote line), Ginza exit; (Asakusa line), exit A3; (Ginza line), exit 3. **Open** 5pm-3am Mon-Fri; 4pm-midnight Sat, Sun. **Average** ¥3,500. **Credit** AmEx, DC, JCB, MC, V. **English menu**. **Map** p60.

This cheerful, busy hole-in-the-wall serves the foods of Japan's southernmost islands. The Chinese influence is strong, especially in the love for noodles and pork. Among the more accessible dishes are deep-fried chips of *goya* (bitter melon), *jimami-dofu* (a creamy peanut mousse) and *rafuti* (delectable, slow-simmered pork belly). Once you've had a few shots of *awamori*, the rice-based, rocket-fuel local hooch, you'll be ready for the more exotic offerings.

Ohmatsuya

Ail d'Or Bldg 2F, 6-5-8 Ginza, Chuo-ku (3571 7053). Ginza station (Ginza, Hibiya, Marunouchi lines), exit B9. **Open** 5-10pm Mon-Sat. **Average** ¥9,000. **Credit** AmEx, DC, JCB, MC, V. **English menu**. **Map** p60.

Ohmatsuya serves the foods of rural Yamagata prefecture, but does so in swish Ginza style. The decor is faux rustic, with wooden beams and farmhouse furniture. Every table has a charcoal fireplace on which fish, vegetables, mushrooms and delicious *wagyu* beef are grilled as you watch. The rest of the menu features plenty of wild mountain herbs and fresh seafood from the Japan Sea coast, not to mention some of the best sake in the country.

Oshima

Ginza Core Bldg 9F, 5-8-20 Ginza, Chuo-ku (3574 8080). Ginza station (Ginza, Hibiya, Marunouchi lines), exits A3, A4. **Open** 11am-10pm daily. **Average** ¥1,890 set lunch; ¥2,940-¥12,000 set dinner. **Credit** AmEx, DC, JCB, MC, V. **Map** p60.

Oshima offers traditional Japanese food from the Kaga (Kanazawa) area, expertly prepared and beautifully presented. There is a wide range of set meals, including tempura, *shabu-shabu* and *nabe* (hot-pot) courses. The 'ladies afternoon lunch *kaiseki*', served after 2pm, is a bargain. The decor is less exciting than the food: the comfortable and bland 'modern traditional' look.

Other locations: Odakyu Halc Annex 8F, 1-5-1 Nishi-Shinjuku, Shinjuku-ku (3348 8080); Hotel Pacific Tokyo 3F, 3-13-3 Takanawa, Minato-ku (3441 8080).

Robata

1-3-8 Yurakucho, Chiyoda-ku (3591 1905). Hibiya station (Chiyoda, Hibiya, Mita lines), exit A4. **Open** 5-11pm daily. **Average** ¥5,000. **No credit cards**. **Map** p60.

This venerable *izakaya* provides one of the most charming dining experiences in central Tokyo. Sit down at one of the cosy wooden seats and choose from the freshly prepared dishes arrayed in huge bowls on the giant counter. The food is a curious mix of Japanese and Western – salads, pork in cream sauce, tofu dishes and tomato-based vegetable stews – and goes just as well with wine as with sake.

Shichirinya

Ginza Corridor 108 Saki, 7 Ginza, Chuo-ku (3289 0020). Ginza station (Ginza, Hibiya, Marunouchi lines), exit C1 or Shinbashi station (Yamanote line), Ginza exit; (Asakusa line), exit A3; (Ginza line), exit 3. **Open** 5.30pm-4am Mon-Fri; 5.30-11pm Sat, Sun. **Average** ¥6,000. **Credit** AmEx, MC, V. **Map** p60.

Grilling morsels of meat, chicken or fish over *shichirin* braziers was once synonymous with post-war austerity. Now it's the chic way to eat, especially at this sleek Ginza eatery where the name of the game is excellent ingredients, sophisticated service and nary a stray whiff of smoke from the charcoal grills set into your table-top.

Kandagawa Honten.
See p137.

A guide to Japanese cuisine

The staple food in Japan, around which everything else revolves, is rice. Indeed, the word for meal (*gohan*) literally means 'cooked rice'. In farming communities rice is still eaten three times a day (sometimes noodles are substituted), along with a simple side dish, a bowl of miso soup and some pickles. This is a Japanese meal at its most basic.

Until 150 years ago, meat eating (especially from four-legged animals) was shunned, and Japanese cooking is still heavily weighted towards seafood and products made from protein-rich soya beans, such as tofu, *yuba* (soya milk skin), *natto* (fermented beans), soy sauce and miso.

There is a strong emphasis on using fresh ingredients, so the varieties of seafood, vegetables and mushrooms will vary throughout the year, reflecting the season. In addition, each region of the country, from Hokkaido down to Okinawa, has its own specialities – both food and drink – and all are available in Tokyo. Even at the humblest eateries and street stalls, food quality is invariably high and hygiene standards impeccable.

Below is a guide to the most common elements of Japan's amazingly diverse cuisine. For a menu glossary, *see p154*.

Kaiseki ryori

Japan's haute cuisine developed from the highly formalised light meals that were served with the tea ceremony. It consists of a sequence of small dishes, apparently simple but always immaculately prepared and presented to reflect the seasons. Courses follow each other at a slow pace: a one-hour meal would be considered hurried.

The order of the meal is: starter (often highly elaborate); sashimi; clear soup; then a series of dishes prepared in different styles (grilled; steamed; served with a thick dressing; deep-fried; a 'salad' with a vinegar dressing); and finally rice and miso soup, with a light dessert to clear the palate at the end. *Kaiseki* can be very pricey, though some restaurants serve simplified versions for around ¥5,000.

Kushi-age

Pieces of meat, seafood or vegetables are skewered and deep-fried to a golden brown in a coating of fine breadcrumbs. Usually eaten with a sweetened soy-based sauce, salt or even a dab of curry powder, washed down with beer, and rounded off with rice and miso soup.

Nabemono & one-pot cooking

One-pot stews cooked at the table in casseroles (*nabe*) of iron or heavy earthenware are delicious and warming in winter. Everyone is served (or helps themselves) from the one pot: you just pluck out what you want using long chopsticks, and dip into the sauce provided. Favourite *nabe* styles include chicken *mizutaki*; duck meat; *yose* (mixed seafood and vegetables); and *chanko*, the sumo wrestlers' stew into which anything goes.

Noodles: soba, udon & ramen

There are two main indigenous varieties of noodle: soba (thin, grey, made from buckwheat mixed with wheat flour) and udon (chunkier wheat noodles, usually white). These are eaten chilled, served on a bamboo tray with a soy-based dipping sauce, or hot, usually in a soy-flavoured broth. Either way, accompaniments can include tempura, grated daikon (radish) or sweetened tofu. Chinese-style ramen noodles are even more popular. These crinkly, yellowish noodles are served in a rich, meat-based soup flavoured with miso, soy sauce or salt, and topped with vegetables or *cha-shu* (sliced, barbecued pork).

Oden

Fish cakes, tofu, vegetables, whole eggs and *konnyaku* (devil's tongue) are simmered long and slowly in a shoyu-flavoured broth and eaten with a dash of hot mustard. This simple wintertime dish goes wonderfully with sake, and is often served at outdoor *yatai* (street stalls). Cheap versions can smell chokingly pungent, but the subtle flavour of *oden* in fine restaurants can be a revelation.

Sashimi

Raw fish, delicately sliced and artfully arranged, is an essential course in most Japanese meals. Usually it is served with a dip of soy sauce, plus a dab of pungent green wasabi (or sometimes grated ginger). Best appreciated with a few sips of good sake.

Shojin ryori

Japan's long tradition of vegetarian cooking lives on in *shojin ryori* – Buddhist temple cuisine that generally follows the same lines as mainstream *kaiseki*, except that no fish is used in the cooking stocks (shiitake mushrooms and *konbu* seaweed are used instead); garlic and onion are also banned. Tofu and *yuba* (soya milk skin) feature prominently in *shojin* meals and also in *fucha ryori*, a variant style with more Chinese influence. *See p151* **Vegging out**.

Sukiyaki & shabu-shabu

These meat dishes, both cooked at the table, have evolved over the last century to become key parts of Japanese cuisine. Sukiyaki combines tender cuts of meat (usually beef, but sometimes pork, horse or chicken) with vegetables, tofu and other ingredients, such as *shirataki* (jelly-like *konnyaku* noodles), which are lightly cooked in a sweetened soy sauce broth. As they cook, you fish them out and dip them into beaten raw egg.

Shabu-shabu is paper-thin slices of beef quickly dipped into a boiling cooking stock, usually in a special copper pot. The name derives from the sound made as the meat is swished to and fro in the broth.

Sushi

The classic style of arranging raw fish or other delicacies on patties of vinegared rice dates back to the 18th century, when it became a popular street food in Edo. Top sushi shops can be daunting, as they don't post their prices, and customers are expected to know their *uni* (sea urchin) from their *ikura* (salmon roe). The easiest (and cheapest) way to learn your way around the etiquette and vocabulary is to explore the many *kaiten* (conveyor belt) sushi shops, where prices are fixed and you can take what you want without having to order. Another style of sushi popular in Osaka and western Japan is *chirashi-zushi* – large bowls of sushi rice with morsels of fish, egg and vegetables scattered on top.

Tempura

The Portuguese are credited with introducing the idea of deep-frying seafood and vegetables in a light, crisp batter – and also the name itself. But in Japan the technique has been elevated to a fine art. Premium tempura, cooked one morsel at a time in top-quality sesame oil, should never taste too oily.

Teppanyaki, okonomiyaki & monja

Beef is never cheap in Japan, but Japanese beef (especially Kobe *wagyu* beef) is a luxury item. The marbled fat lends itself perfectly to being cooked on a flat *teppan* grill – Japan's contribution to the art of the steak. Seafood and vegetables are also cooked the same way in front of you.

Okonomiyaki ('grilled whatever you like') is a cross between a pancake and an omelette, stuffed with meat, beansprouts, chopped cabbage and other goodies. Many *okonomiyaki* restaurants also do *yaki-soba* (fried Chinese-style noodles). Originally from western Japan (Hiroshima and Osaka both lay claim to it), *okonomiyaki* is cheap, robust and satisfying. The Tokyo version is known as *monja*.

Tofu cuisine

Tofu and other soya bean derivatives are celebrated for their protein content and versatility, and feature strongly in Japanese cooking. Tofu specialist restaurants tend to use small amounts of fish or chicken (often in the soup stocks), so they are classified separately from the strictly vegetarian *shojin* tradition.

Tonkatsu

The *katsu* in *tonkatsu* means cutlet, a very popular dish first introduced during the Meiji period when meat eating began to catch on. The *katsu* is now almost always pork, usually lean cuts of sirloin, dredged in flour, dipped in egg, rolled in breadcrumbs and deep-fried.

Unagi

Another of Japan's great delicacies. Fillets of freshwater eel are basted and very slowly grilled (often over charcoal). The delectably rich, fatty white meat is considered a restorative and is said to improve stamina, eyesight and even virility. That is why it is consumed with extra gusto during the debilitating heat of the summer months.

Yakitori & kushiyaki

Yakitori ('grilled bird') is the Japanese version of the kebab: skewered morsels of chicken cooked over a grill, seasoned either with salt or a slightly sweet soy-based glaze. Most yakitori shops also do wonderful things with vegetables.

Eat, Drink, Shop

Kanda Yabu Soba.
See p137.

Sushi Bun

Chuo Shijo Bldg No.8, 5-2-1 Tsukiji, Chuo-ku (3541 3860/www.sushibun.com). Tsukiji station (Hibiya line), exit A1. **Open** 6.30am-3pm Mon-Sat.
When the fish market (*see p63* **Something fishy**) finally moves out of Tsukiji, Sushi Bun and the other barrow boys' sushi shops will be lost – so go now before it's too late. Like the others, Bun is cramped (the counter seats just 12) and invariably full from first light until its midday closing time. For fish this fresh, the set meal (¥3,500) is great value.

Ten-Ichi

6-6-5 Ginza, Chuo-ku (3571 1949). Ginza station (Ginza, Hibiya, Marunouchi lines), exits C3, B6. **Open** 11.30am-10pm daily. **Average** ¥7,000 lunch; ¥10,000 dinner. **Credit** AmEx, DC, JCB, MC, V. **English menu**. **Map** p60.
Top-quality tempura, served direct from the wok to your plate, is one of the finest delicacies in Japan's cuisine. And you will not find it prepared better than here, at Tokyo's best-known tempura house. The atmosphere is tranquil and pampering, the tempura light and aromatic. A full-course meal also includes sashimi, salad, rice and dessert. This Ginza flagship is the most refined member of the chain (it regularly hosts visiting dignitaries and film stars), but other branches all guarantee similar quality.
Other locations: Imperial Hotel, 1-1-1 Uchisaiwaicho, Chiyoda-ku (3503 1001); Sony Bldg B1F, 5-3-1 Ginza, Chuo-ku (3571 3837); CI Plaza B1F, 2-3-1 Kita-Aoyama, Minato-ku (3497 8465); Mitsui Bldg B1F, 2-1-1 Nishi-Shinjuku, Shinjuku-ku (3344 4706).

Ten-Ichi Deux

Nishi Ginza Depato 1F, 4-1 Ginza (3566 4188). Yurakucho station (Yamanote line), Ginza exit; (Yurakucho line), exit A7 or Ginza station (Ginza, Hibiya, Marunouchi lines), exits C5, C9. **Open** 11am-10pm daily. **Average** ¥1,300-¥2,800. **Credit** AmEx, DC, JCB, MC, V. **English menu**. **Map** p60.
Smart but casual, this offshoot of the reputable Ten-Ichi chain specialises in light (and more affordable) tempura-based meals with simple side dishes. The *ten-don* (tempura prawns on a rice bowl) makes a small but satisfying snack before or after some Ginza window-shopping.

Non-Japanese

Afternoon Tea Baker & Diner

2-3-6 Ginza, Chiyoda-ku (5159 1635/ www.afternoon-tea.net). Ginza-Itchome station (Yurakucho line), exit 4. **Open** 11.30am-2pm, 2-4pm, 5.30-10.30pm Mon-Fri; 11.30am-2.30pm, 5.30-9pm Sat, Sun. **Average** ¥5,000. **Credit** AmEx, DC, JCB, MC, V. **English menu**. **Map** p60.
When it opened, this restaurant brought in British celebrity chef Jamie Oliver to jazz up the menu and generate some buzz. He's no longer involved, but the cooking remains just as good, in the same simple, stylish, contemporary European vein as the decor.

Plenty of good fresh ingredients, organic vegetables and seafood flown in from western Japan.
Other locations: throughout the city.

Kihachi China

2F-4F, 3-7-1 Ginza, Chuo-ku (5524 0761/ www.kihachi.co.jp). Ginza station (Ginza, Hibiya lines), exit A12; (Marunouchi line), exit C8. **Open** 11.30am-4pm, 5-11pm Mon-Fri; 11.30am-4.30pm, 5-11.30pm Sat, Sun. **Credit** AmEx, DC, JCB, MC, V. **Map** p60.

Refined, new-wave Cantonese food that manages to be both subtle and full of flavour. French and Korean influences permeate the cooking, but this is far from fusion territory. The airy fourth-floor dining room is preferable to the dark, cramped second floor, so be sure to phone ahead. Besides lavish set meals, the restaurant also does delectable dim sum lunches.

Marunouchi & around

Japanese

Botan

1-15 Kanda-Sudacho, Chiyoda-ku (3251 0577). Kanda station (Yamanote line), east exit; (Ginza line), exits 5, 6 or Ogawamachi station (Shinjuku line), exit A3 or Awajicho station (Marunouchi line), exit A3. **Open** 11.30am-9pm Mon-Sat. **Average** ¥7,000. **No credit cards**. **Map** p66.

Botan's charm lies in its history and classic wooden premises as much as its food. There's only one thing on the menu, chicken sukiyaki, served in the old style. You will be well taken care of by kimono-clad matrons who bring glowing charcoal to the brazier on your low table, set a small iron dish on top, then begin cooking: chicken, onion, tofu and other vegetables, all simmering in the rich, sweet house sauce.

Isegen

1-11-1 Kanda-Sudacho, Chiyoda-ku (3251 1229). Kanda station (Yamanote line), east exit; (Ginza line), exits 5, 6 or Ogawamachi station (Shinjuku line), exit A3 or Awajicho station (Marunouchi line), exit A3. **Open** 11.30am-2pm, 4-10pm Mon-Fri. **Average** ¥6,000. **No credit cards**. **Map** p66.

Isegen's legendary *anko nabe* (monkfish casserole) is basic but warming – just like the sprawling wooden premises, which are just round the corner from Botan (*see above*) and the same vintage. The *anko* season runs from September to April – the best time of year for a hearty hot-pot. The rest of the year the menu revolves around *ayu* (trout-like sweetfish) and other freshwater fish.

Izumo Soba Honke

1-31 Kanda-Jinbocho, Chiyoda-ku (3291 3005). Jinbocho station (Hanzomon, Mita, Shinjuku lines), exit A7. **Open** 11.30am-8.30pm Mon-Fri; 11.30am-6.30pm Sat. **Average** ¥2,000. **Credit** AmEx, DC, JCB, MC, V. **Map** p66.

The hand-chopped soba noodles here are some of the best in town: wholesome and robust, prepared in the

country style popular in Shimane (western Japan). The classic way to eat them is cold, served in stacks of five small trays with a variety of condiments. A good range of hot soba in broth is also available.

Kandagawa Honten

2-5-11 Soto-Kanda, Chiyoda-ku (3251 5031). Ochanomizu station (Chuo, Marunouchi lines), Hijiribashi exit or Suehirocho station (Ginza line). **Open** 11.30am-2pm, 5-9.30pm Mon-Sat. Closed 2nd Sat of mth. **Average** ¥5,000. **Credit** DC, MC, V.

In a splendid old town house near the business district, kimono-clad waitresses serve succulent, tender eel grilled over charcoal and basted with plenty of thick, sweet soy sauce. Don't miss the *unaju*: eel served on a bed of white rice inside an ornate lacquer box. A classic dish of old Tokyo, in a setting to match. Reservations are essential.

Kanda Yabu Soba

2-10 Kanda-Awajicho, Chiyoda-ku (3251 0287). Kanda station (Yamanote line), east exit; (Ginza line), exits 5, 6 or Ogawamachi station (Shinjuku line), exit A3 or Awajicho station (Marunouchi line), exit A3. **Open** 11.30am-8pm daily. **Average** ¥1,500. **No credit cards**. **English menu**. **Map** p66.

More than merely a soba shop, Yabu is a living museum dedicated to the traditional art of the buckwheat noodle. It's housed in a low Japanese house with a small garden, decorated inside with *shoji* screens, tatami and woodblock prints. Yabu also serves plenty of tasty side dishes if you want to join the locals and settle in with some beer or sake.

Non-Japanese

Brasserie aux Amis

Shin-Tokyo Bldg 1F, 3-3-1 Marunouchi, Chiyoda-ku (6212 1566/www.auxamis.com). Tokyo station (Yamanote, Marunouchi lines), Marunouchi exit or Yurakucho station (Yamanote, Yurakucho lines), International Forum exit. **Open** 11.30am-2pm, 6-10.30pm. **Average** ¥1,300 lunch; ¥5,500 dinner. **Credit** AmEx, DC, JCB, MC, V. **Map** p66.

A slice of Paris in the heart of the Marunouchi business area, down to the red banquettes, brass fittings and menu chalked on large wall mirrors. There's a small bar by the door, for a quick espresso or a glass of *vin ordinaire*, as well as a top-notch wine list to go with the authentically hearty brasserie food.

Dhaba India

2-7-9 Yaesu, Chuo-ku (3272 7160). Kyobashi station (Ginza line), exit 5. **Open** 11.15am-3pm, 5-11pm Mon-Fri; noon-3pm, 5-10pm Sat, Sun. **Average** ¥2,500. **Credit** AmEx, DC, JCB, MC, V. **English menu**. **Map** p60.

The best Indian food in town is found here in the backstreets of Yaesu. Modest and unpretentious, this is one of the few places where you can find South Indian specialities. Delicious masala dosas, curries and thali meals, served with real basmati rice (evenings only), prepared by ever-friendly staff from the subcontinent.

Eat, Drink, Shop

Phuket Aroina Tabeta

3-7-11 Marunouchi, Chiyoda-ku (5219 6099/ www.tabeta.com). Tokyo station (Yamanote, Marunouchi lines), Tokyo Forum exit. **Open** 11am-11pm. **Average** Dishes from ¥630. **No credit cards. English menu. Map** p60.

Nowhere in Tokyo makes Thai food that's as authentic and cheap as this funky little diner wedged in under the train tracks near the International Forum. Simple set meals (including curries, fried noodles and the house speciality, braised pork) are each just ¥630: a veritable bargain, especially for this upwardly mobile stretch of the city.

Shisen Hanten

Zenkoku Ryokan Kaikan 5F-6F, 2-5-5 Hirakawa-cho, Chiyoda-ku (3263 9371). Nagatacho station (Hanzomon, Nanboku, Yurakucho lines), exit 5. **Open** 11.30am-2pm, 5-10pm daily. **Average** ¥2,000 lunch; ¥5,000 dinner. **Credit** AmEx, DC, MC, V. **English menu. Map** p66.

Good Szechuan cuisine, albeit with the spices toned down for Japanese palates, from chef Shin Kenichi, best known for his appearances in the *Iron Chef* TV cooking shows. His classic dish is *mapo-dofu* (spicy minced meat with tofu), but in summer queues form for his *hiyashi chuka*, chilled Chinese-style noodles and chopped vegetables topped with sesame or vinegar sauce.
Other locations: throughout the city.

Shinjuku & around

Japanese

Kitchen Shunju

My City 8F, 3-38-1 Shinjuku, Shinjuku-ku (5369 0377/www.shunju.com/ja/restaurants/ shinjuku). Shinjuku station (Yamanote, Marunouchi, Oedo, Shinjuku lines); My City is above the station. **Open** 11am-3pm, 5-11.30pm. **Average** ¥2,000 lunch; ¥5,000 dinner. **Credit** AmEx, DC, JCB, MC, V. **English menu. Map** p73.

The Shunju ethos – light, creative, modern Japanese food served in a stylish, casual setting – dovetails perfectly with the style of the recently revamped My City mini mall. Sit at the long open kitchen and watch the chefs at work, at tables in the main dining room or tucked away in cosy private alcoves.
Other locations: throughout the city.

Tsunahachi

3-31-8 Shinjuku, Shinjuku-ku (3352 1012/ www.tunahachi.co.jp). Shinjuku station (Yamanote, Marunouchi lines), east exit; (Oedo, Shinjuku lines), exit 1 or Shinjuku-Sanchome station (Marunouchi, Shinjuku lines), exits A1-A5. **Open** 11am-10pm daily. **Average** ¥5,000. **Credit** AmEx, DC, JCB, MC, V. **English menu. Map** p73.

Who says tempura has to be expensive? Surviving amid the gleaming modern buildings of Shinjuku, Tsunahachi's battered wooden premises are a throwback to the early post-war era – as are the

prices. The whole place is filled with the whiff of cooking oil, but the food is perfectly good enough for everyday fare.
Other locations: throughout the city.

Yukun-tei

3-26 Arakicho, Shinjuku-ku (3356 3351/ www.akasakayukun.com). Yotsuya-Sanchome station (Marunouchi line), exit A4. **Open** 11.30am-2pm, 5-10.30pm Mon-Sat. **Average** ¥1,000 lunch; ¥8,000 dinner. **Credit** AmEx, DC, JCB, MC, V.

A friendly *izakaya* with cheerful waitresses and delightful cuisine from Kyushu (Japan's third-largest island). Many of the names on the *washi* menu sound foreign even to locals, and indeed there's something undeniably exotic – and southern – about the food. The lunch sets are absolutely fantastic: *onigiri teishoku* has two enormous *onigiri* (rice balls), while the *inaka udon teishoku* will net you a very generous bowlful of udon with rice and mysterious little side dishes. In the evening, there's sashimi, plus other grilled and simmered goodies. The smooth house-brand sake can only be bought here.
Other locations: Seio Bldg B1F, 2-2-18 Ginza Chuo-ku (3561 6672); Tokyo Tatemono Dai 5 Yaesu Bldg B1F, 1-4-14 Yaesu, Chuo-ku (3271 8231); Akasaka Tokyu Plaza 3F, 2-14-3 Nagatacho, Chiyoda-ku (3592 0393).

Non-Japanese

Angkor Wat

1-38-13 Yoyogi, Shibuya-ku (3370 3019). Yoyogi station (Yamanote line), west exit; (Oedo line), exit A1. **Open** 11am-2pm, 5-11pm daily. **Average** ¥2,500. **No credit cards**.

What this place lacks in ambience it makes up for in the Cambodian cooking. It may look like a cafeteria – and indeed the food comes with amazing speed – but that's probably because so many punters are queuing up to get in; it's a popular spot. Cheerful Cambodian waitresses (daughters of the proprietor) will help you navigate the menu; don't miss the chicken salad and *chahan* (fried rice).

AOC Yoyogi

1-43-2 Yoyogi, Shibuya-ku (5308 7588/ http://home.catv.ne.jp/ss/aoc). Yoyogi station (Yamanote line), west exit; (Oedo line), exit A1 or Minami-Shinjuku station (Odakyu line). **Open** noon-2pm, 6-10pm Mon, Tue, Thur-Sun. **Credit** AmEx, DC, JCB, MC, V. **Average** ¥3,500.

Owner François Dumas and chef Taguchi Naomasa subscribe to the tenets of the Slow Food movement. They also believe in value for money: AOC Yoyogi's ¥3,500 two-course dinner makes this French bistro one of the best bargains in town. All the wines are certified organic, as is much of the meat and produce. Admirable and delicious.

Ban Thai

Dai-ichi Metro Bldg 3F, 1-23-14 Kabuki-cho, Shinjuku-ku (3207 0068). Shinjuku station (Yamanote line), east exit; (Marunouchi line), exits

Tama. *See p143.*

B12, B13; (Oedo, Shinjuku lines), exit 1. **Open** 11.30am-3pm, 5pm-midnight Mon-Fri; 11.30am-midnight Sat, Sun. **Average** ¥3,000. **Credit** AmEx, DC, JCB, MC, V. **English menu. Map** p73. Conveniently situated on the way into raunchy Kabuki-cho, this is one of the longest-standing Thai institutions in town. It's also still one of the best, and there's little on the extensive menu that will disappoint. The curries are especially good.

China Grill – Xenlon

Odakyu Hotel Century Southern Tower 19F, 2-2-1 Yoyogi, Shibuya-ku (3374 2080). Shinjuku station (Yamanote line), south exit; (Marunouchi, Oedo lines), exit A1; (Shinjuku line), exit 6. **Open** 11.30am-11pm daily. **Average** ¥3,500 lunch; ¥7,000-¥15,000 set dinner; ¥7,000 à la carte. **Credit** AmEx, DC, JCB, MC, V. **English menu. Map** p73.
Impeccable service and impressive views of the neon skyline make this stylish Chinese restaurant well worth the splurge. The Cantonese menu, which nods towards Western rather than Japanese influences, includes dim sum at lunchtime.
Other locations: throughout the city.

Hannibal

Urban Bldg B1F, 1-11-1 Hyakunincho, Shinjuku-ku (5389 7313/www.hannibal.cc). Shin-Okubo station (Yamanote line). **Open** 5.30pm-12.30am Mon-Sat. **Average** ¥3,500. **Credit** AmEx, DC, JCB, MC, V. **English menu.**
Chef Mondher Gheribi's Tunisian home cooking adds a further dimension to this colourfully cosmopolitan area. He draws on influences from around the Mediterranean, but the best foods are those from closest to his home – *mechoui* salad, excellent roast chicken stuffed with banana and herbs, and homemade *khobz* bread served with red-hot harissa sauce.

Hyakunincho Yataimura

2-20-25 Hyakunincho, Shinjuku-ku (5386 3320/ www.yataimura.jp). Shin-Okubo station (Yamanote line). **Open** 11.30am-2.30pm, 5pm-2am Mon-Thur; 11pm-4am Fri-Sun. **Average** ¥800. **Credit** AmEx, DC, JCB, MC, V. **English menu** (some stands).
Yataimura ('foodstall village') recently underwent a badly needed face-lift and is no longer quite so anarchic. But the basic layout remains intact: small cooking stands supplying a choice of street foods (Malaysian, Chinese, Thai, Vietnamese and Indian) set around a large central eating area. The proprietors vie aggressively for your custom, so quickly order beer and snacks while you consider the rest of your meal. Fun, funky and cheap.

New York Grill

Park Hyatt Tokyo 52F, 3-7-1-2 Nishi-Shinjuku, Shinjuku-ku (5323 3458/www.parkhyatttokyo.com). Shinjuku station (Yamanote, Marunouchi lines), west exit; (Oedo, Shinjuku lines), exit 6. **Open** 11.30am-2.30pm, 5.30-10.30pm daily. **Average** ¥6,000 brunch; ¥5,000 lunch; ¥10,000 dinner. **Credit** AmEx, DC, JCB, MC, V. **English menu. Map** p73.
The New York Grill offers sky-high power dining, and it's worth every yen for the view from this pinnacle of the Park Hyatt hotel. Service is polished and the cooking is always good, featuring great seafood and meat dishes prepared in modern American style. Sunday brunch is an expat institution, as are evening cocktails in the adjoining New York Bar (the setting for the bar scenes of *Lost in Translation*).

Thien Phuoc

Kotoku Bldg 2F, 3-11 Yotsuya, Shinjuku-ku (3358 6617). Yotsuya-Sanchome station (Marunouchi line), exit 2. **Open** 11am-3pm, 5-11pm Mon-Fri; noon-11pm Sat, Sun. **Average** ¥2,000. **No credit cards.**
Despite the humble location, tucked well back from the street, Thien Phuoc is worth searching out for its excellent Saigon street-stall food. Try crisp *banh xeo* pancakes, spicy Hue-style beef *pho* noodles and memorable *cha gio* (spring rolls). Wash them all down with a 333 beer.

Japanese

Kaisen Dokoro Sushi Tsune

109 Bldg 8F, 2-29-1 Dogenzaka, Shibuya-ku (3477 5137/www.sushitsune.co.jp/shop/01kaisen/37/37.htm). Shibuya station (Yamanote, Ginza, Hanzomon lines), Hachiko exit. **Open** 11am-11pm daily. **Credit** AmEx, DC, JCB, MC, V. **English menu**. **Map** p79.

Unless you're female and under 21, this place is the only reason for visiting the 109 Building. The management call its approach 'New style Edo-mae sushi', which basically means it also serves things like pizza and wine. The main draw is the rock-bottom price of the sushi: ¥109 per piece. The queues are inevitably long, especially at dinner.

Kanetanaka-so

Cerulean Tower Tokyu Hotel 2F, 26-1 Sakuragaoka-cho, Shibuya-ku (3476 3420/www.kanetanaka.co.jp/so/index.html). Shibuya station (Yamanote, Ginza, Hanzomon lines), Tokyu Plaza exit. **Open** 11.30am-2pm, 5.30-9.30pm daily. **Average** ¥3,000 lunch; from ¥8,000 dinner. **Credit** AmEx, DC, JCB, MC, V. **Map** p79.

Kanetanaka is one of Tokyo's most exclusive *ryotei* (traditional restaurants), but this sleek, chic off-shoot is thoroughly modern and totally accessible. Instead of tatami mats and *washi* paper screens, it's furnished with tables and chairs, and blinds of silvery metal. The multi-course *kaiseki* meals are equally inventive, giving Japan's traditional cuisine a brilliant contemporary slant. The restaurant is housed in the Cerulean Tower Hotel, which also contains a *noh* theatre and a jazz club.
Other locations: 7-18-17 Ginza, Chuo-ku (3541 2556).

Myoko

Shinto Bldg 1F, 1-17-2 Shibuya, Shibuya-ku (3499 3450). Shibuya station (Yamanote, Ginza lines), Miyamasusaka (east) exit; (Hanzomon line), exit 11. **Open** 11.30am-2pm, 5-9pm Mon-Fri; 11.30am-2pm Sat. **Average** ¥1,500. **Credit** AmEx, DC, JCB, MC, V. **Map** p79.

Seoul survivors

Not so long ago the only kind of Korean restaurants in Japan were those serving *yakiniku* – a Japanified version of the grilled meat (*pulgogi*) known in the West as 'Korean Barbecue'. Shin-Okubo, to the north of Shinjuku, has long been the 'Koreatown' of Tokyo, but it's only in the past few years that there has been a sea change in attitudes towards Japan's neighbour. Despite ongoing political squabbles between the two countries, young Tokyoites are embracing Korean culture (movies and music, especially) – and food. Here are some of the best places to find that down-home Seoul experience.

Jap Cho Ok

Alteka Belte Plaza Bldg B1F, 4-1-15 Minami-Aoyama, Minato-ku (5410 3408/www.1999group.com/zassouya). Gaienmae station (Ginza line), exit 1A. **Open** 5.30pm-3am Mon-Sat; 5.30-11pm Sun. **Average** ¥5,000 dinner. **Credit** AmEx, MC, V. **English menu**.

This stylish basement restaurant helped to make Korean food fashionable in Tokyo. Medicinal herbs hang from the walls, while paper screens and lamps evoke the spare grandeur of a Korean mountain monastery. You can settle in for a full-course meal (vegetarian options included) in an alcove, or just snack and nurse a drink at one of the central tables. Either way, booking is advised.

Kankoku Shokudo

1-12-3 Okubo, Shinjuku-ku (3208 0209). Shin-Okubo station (Yamanote line) or Higashi-Shinjuku station (Oedo line), exit A1. **Open** 10am-3am Mon-Sat; 10am-2pm Sun. **Average** ¥1,000. **No credit cards**.

Even before Shin-Okubo became known as Koreatown, this was the place to eat the kind of full-on Korean fare you'd find in Pusan or Kwangju. People come to this funky, *izakaya*-style eaterie for the drinking (beer, *makkoli* rice wine and Jinro liquor) as much as for the spicy food.

Kusa no Ie

Mita Bldg 3F, 2-14-33 Akasaka, Minato-ku (3589 0779/www.kusanoie.net/akasaka/index.html). Akasaka station (Chiyoda line), exit 2. **Open** 11.30am-2pm, 5pm-3am Mon-Fri; 5-10pm Sat, Sun. **Average** ¥980. **Credit** AmEx, JCB, MC, V. **English menu**.

Akasaka was one of the areas where the first cluster of Korean barbecue restaurants sprang up, and Kusa no Ie remains one of the best. It offers standard-issue, old-school *yakiniku*, but with decent decor and service, top-quality meat and very little smoke in the air.

Matsuya

1-1-17 Okubo, Shinjuku-ku (3200 5733). Shin-Okubo station (Yamanote line). **Open** 11am-5am Mon-Sat; 11am-2am Sun.

The speciality at Myoko is *houtou*, a hearty mountain-style stew made with flat, wide udon noodles. Other ingredients include oysters, *kimchi*, mushrooms or pork, all cooked in a miso-based broth with plenty of vegetables and served bubbling hot in an iron kettle. You'll also find a wide selection of cold dishes, such as 'salad udon' (chilled noodles and vegetables), plus good-value set lunches. A large picture menu makes ordering simple for those who don't speak Japanese.

Non-Japanese

Ankara
Social Dogenzaka B1F, 1-14-9 Dogenzaka, Shibuya-ku (3780 1366/www.ankara.jp). Shibuya station (Yamanote, Ginza, Hanzomon lines), Hachiko exit. **Open** 5-11.30pm daily. **Average** ¥3,000. **Credit** MC, V. **English menu. Map** p79.
Tucked away in the backstreets of Shibuya, this cheerful little Turkish restaurant serves up a surprisingly extensive array of delicious and healthy meze and other Turkish delicacies.

Legato
E Space Tower 15F, 3-6 Maruyama-cho, Shibuya-ku (5784 2121/www.global-dining.com). Shibuya station (Yamanote, Ginza, Hanzomon lines), Hachiko exit. **Open** 11.30am-2pm, 5.30-10.30pm (last orders) Mon-Fri; 5.30-10.30pm (last orders) Sat, Sun. **Average** ¥7,000. **Credit** AmEx, DC, JCB, MC, V. **English menu. Map** p79.
Trust the Global Dining Group – which is also behind Tableaux and Stellato (for both, *see p146*) – to do things in style. Legato occupies the top floor of a new tower on Dogenzaka, and its food is as theatrical as the lavish decor. The menu mixes Asian and Western influences, in accordance with Tokyo's current vogue, and features Vietnamese spring rolls and Chinese noodles alongside lamb chops and pizza. There's also a bar/lounge open until 4am on Friday and Saturday nights.

Raj Mahal/Raj Palace
Jow Bldg 5F, 30-5 Udagawa-cho, Shibuya-ku (3770 7677). Shibuya station (Yamanote, Ginza, Hanzomon lines), Hachiko exit. **Open** 11.30am-11pm

Average ¥1,500. **No credit cards.**
The name may be Japanese, but the food is 100% Korean home-style cooking. Kick off your shoes, sit on the floor and tuck into *kamjatang* – a delectable chilli-rich stew of spuds and massive pork backbones. Subtle fare this isn't, but it's a fine way to keep out the winter chill.

Saikabo
3-10-25 Yotsuya, Shinjuku-ku (3354 0100/www.saikabo. com). Yotsuya-Sanchome station (Marunouchi line), exit 2. **Open** 11.30am-11pm daily. **Average** ¥1,000-¥1,600. **Credit** JCB, MC, V.
Besides the standard *kalbi* (beef) grill and *ishiyaki-bibimbap* (rice served in a sizzling-hot stone pot), many aficionados believe Saikabo (pictured) produces the best *kimchi* pancakes in Tokyo. There are now several branches, but the full-blown flavours at this original restaurant make it the best of the lot. Korean staples are sold on the ground floor. **Other locations**: throughout the city.

Shinmasan-ya
Namiki Bldg 1F, 3-12-5 Akasaka, Minato-ku (3583 6120). Akasaka-Mitsuke station, Belle Vie exit. **Open** 11.30am-3am Mon-Sat. **Average** ¥3,500. **Credit** JCB, MC, V.
This Akasaka outfits serves home-style Korean cooking with plenty of other dishes besides *yakiniku* – including some of the best *bibimap* in Tokoyo. Ask to be seated on the ground; your legs can dangle under the table, while the heated floor warms those parts that the food can't reach.

Eat, Drink, Shop

A luxurious setting for high-class Italian food at **Luxor**. *See p146.*

daily. **Average** ¥2,500. **Credit** AmEx, DC, JCB, MC, V. **English menu**. **Map** p79.

Despite their chain status, the Raj Mahal/Palace restaurants are known for their good service, extensive menus and above-average Moghul-style food. **Other locations**: Urban Bldg 4F, 7-13-2 Roppongi, Minato-ku (5411 2525); Peace Bldg 5F, 3-34-11 Shinjuku, Shinjuku-ku (5379 2525); Hakuba Bldg 4F, 26-11 Udagawa-cho, Shibuya-ku (3780 6531).

Sonoma

Kasumi Bldg, 2-25-17 Dogenzaka, Shibuya-ku (3462 7766/www.sonomatokyo.com). Shibuya station (Yamanote, Ginza, Hanzomon lines), Hachiko exit. **Open** 6.30pm-midnight Mon-Thur, Sun; 6.30pm-4am Fri, Sat. **Average** ¥3,000. **Credit** AmEx, DC, JCB, MC, V. **English menu**. **Map** p79.

Grilled salmon with Szechuan glaze; beef fajitas with guacamole; seared tuna on baba ganoush: these are just a few of the Californian-fusion items on the menu at Sonoma. Execution can be hit or miss, but there's always a mellow, laid-back atmosphere at this favourite *gaijin* hangout. Upstairs is the Ruby Room lounge (*see p211*), successor to the fabled Sugar High club, where the emphasis is on snacking rather than full-scale dining.

Harajuku & Aoyama

Japanese

Crayon House Hiroba

3-8-15 Kita-Aoyama, Minato-ku (3406 6409/ www.crayonhouse.co.jp). Omotesando station (Chiyoda line), exit A1; (Ginza, Hanzomon lines), exit B2. **Open** *Home* 11am-2pm, 2-5.30pm (tea), 5.30-9pm (last orders) daily. *Hiroba* 11am-2pm, 5-9.30pm (last orders) daily. **Average** ¥2,000. **Credit** AmEx, DC, JCB, MC, V. **Map** p85.

Sitting next to a natural food shop, Crayon House is not exclusively vegetarian, but offers a good selection of wholesome, well-prepared dishes, many with organic ingredients. It consists of two mini restaurants: Hiroba, offering Japanese food, and Home, offering Western.

Kyushu Jangara Ramen

Shanzeru Harajuku Ni-go-kan 1F-2F, 1-13-21 Jingumae, Shibuya-ku (3404 5572/ www.kyusyujangara.co.jp). Harajuku station (Yamanote line), Omotesando exit or Meiji-Jingumae station (Chiyoda line), exit 3. **Open** 11am-2am Mon-Thur, Sun; 11am-3.30am Fri, Sat. **Average** ¥1,000. **No credit cards**. **Map** p85.

This colourfully decorated ramen restaurant always has queues snaking down the stairs. Don't worry: with 73 seats, an opening will soon appear. Kyushu ramen from Fukuoka city is the speciality, but it comes with a little twist: the customer selects whether they want the broth light or heavier; the noodles thin, thick or in between; the quantity big or small; and what toppings to add. **Other locations**: 3-11-6 Soto Kanda, Chiyoda-ku (3512 4059); 7-11-10 Ginza, Chuo-ku (3289 2307); 2-12-8 Nagata-cho, Chiyoda-ku (3595 2130); 1-1-7 Nihonbashi, Chuo-ku (3281 0701).

Maisen

4-8-5 Jingumae, Shibuya-ku (3470 0071/ http://members.aol.com/maisenpr). Omotesando station (Chiyoda, Ginza, Hanzomon lines), exit A2. **Open** 11am-9pm daily. **Average** ¥2,000. **Credit** DC, JCB, MC, V. **English menu**. **Map** p85.

This branch of the chain *tonkatsu* shop is a converted bathhouse. If you're able to get a seat in the huge and airy dining room in the back, you'll notice several tell-tale signs of its origins: very high ceilings and a small garden pond. You can't miss with any of the *teishoku* (set meals); standard *rosu katsu*

or lean *hire katsu* are both good choices, and each comes with rice, soup and pickled daikon.
Other locations: 1-1-5 Yurakucho, Chiyoda-ku (3503 1886).

Tama

5-9-8 Minami-Aoyama, Minato-ku (3406 8088/ www.bigriver.co.jp). Omotesando station (Chiyoda, Ginza, Hanzomon lines), exit B1. **Open** 11.30am-2pm, 6-11pm Mon-Thur; 11.30am-2pm, 6-midnight Fri; noon-3pm, 6-11pm Sat; noon-3pm, 5-11pm Sun. **Average** ¥3,500. **Credit** AmEx, DC, JCB, MC, V. **English menu**.
Tama serves inventive *izakaya* food rejigged for the new century. It's a small place and highly popular with the well-dressed Aoyama set on account of its sleek minimalism and reasonable prices. The bar stays open until 2am except on Sunday.
Other locations: CI Plaza 2F, 2-3-1 Kita-Aoyama, Minato-ku (5772 3933).

Non-Japanese

Las Chicas

5-47-6 Jingumae, Shibuya-ku (3407 6865/ www.vision.co.jp/2004/h_lc.html). Omotesando station (Chiyoda, Ginza, Hanzomon lines), exit B2. **Open** 11am-11pm Mon-Fri; 11am-11.30pm Sat, Sun. **Average** ¥1,000 lunch; ¥4,000 dinner. **Credit** AmEx, DC, JCB, MC, V. **English menu**. **Map** p79.
One of the most creative and foreigner-friendly spaces in town, Las Chicas is part of a complex that encompasses various restaurants and bars hosting revolving exhibitions of local talent. The bilingual staff (mostly Australian) are friendly and helpful, though not always very organised. In the main restaurant, dishes such as potato wedges with sour cream and Thai chilli sauce, cheesy polenta chips, or home-made bread with real butter, are all meals in themselves, and make perfect mates for the earthy Australian wines. *See also p223.*

Fonda de la Madrugada

Villa Bianca B1, 2-33-12 Jingumae, Shibuya-ku (5410 6288/www.fonda-m.com). Meiji-Jingumae station (Chiyoda line), exit 5 or Harajuku station (Yamanote line), Omotesando exit. **Open** 5.30pm-2am Mon-Thur, Sun; 5.30pm-5am Fri, Sat. **Average** ¥3,500. **Credit** AmEx, DC, JCB, MC, V. **Map** p85.
This basement hacienda has some of the best Mexican food in Tokyo, and the most authentic atmosphere too. Chugging on a bottle of Dos Equis, serenaded by mariachi singers, with tortillas and chicken in mole cooked and served by Latinos – you'll feel that you really could be in Cancun.

Fujimamas

6-3-2 Jingumae, Shibuya-ku (5485 2262/ www.fujimamas.com). Harajuku station (Yamanote line), Omotesando exit or Meiji-Jingumae station (Chiyoda line), exit 4. **Open** 11am-11pm daily. **Average** ¥3,000. **Credit** AmEx, DC, JCB, MC, V. **English menu**. **Map** p85.

Chef Mark Vann and his polyglot crew produce confident, accessible East-West fusion cuisine in a converted two-storey wooden Japanese house (once an old tatami workshop). Servings are large and prices reasonable given the swanky address and sunny decor. The well-stocked bar draws a gregarious mix of locals and expats.

Fumin

Aoyama Ohara Bldg B1F, 5-7-17 Minami-Aoyama, Minato-ku (3498 4466). Omotesando station (Chiyoda, Ginza, Hanzomon lines), exit B1. **Open** 11.45am-2.30pm, 5-9pm Mon-Fri; 11.45am-2.30pm, 5-8.30pm Sat, Sun. Closed 1st Mon of mth. **Average** ¥4,000. **No credit cards**.
This long-established Chinese restaurant has always been popular. The simple home-style cooking is characterised by large servings, liberally seasoned and worth any wait. Don't miss the *negi* (spring onion) wonton, the *kaisen gyoza* (seafood dumplings) or the house special Fumin noodles.

Ghungroo

Seinan Bldg 2F, 5-6-19 Minami Aoyama, Minato-ku (3406 0464/www.ghungroo-jp.com). Omotesando station (Chiyoda, Ginza, Hanzomon lines), exit B1. **Open** 11.30am-10.30pm Mon Thur; 11.30am-11pm Fri; noon-11pm Sat; noon-9.30pm Sun. **Average** ¥1,500. **Credit** AmEx, DC, JCB, MC, V. **English menu**. **Map** p85.
This restaurant may offer the closest experience in Tokyo to a (classy) British-style Indian curry. The place is divided into two rooms, the one further from the door being the more inviting. The menu contains few surprises, but the chicken dishes and okra curry are especially good. Like most Indian places in Tokyo, it lets itself down by serving only Japanese rice. You're better off sticking with the naan, fresh from the tandoor.

La Grotta Celeste

Aoyama Centre Bldg 1F, 3-8-40 Minami-Aoyama, Minato-ku (3401 1261). Omotesando station (Chiyoda, Ginza, Hanzomon lines), exit A4. **Open** 11.30am-3pm, 5.30-11pm daily. **Average** ¥1,500 lunch; ¥5,000 dinner. **Credit** AmEx, DC, JCB, MC, V. **Italian menu**. **Map** p85.
A place for a special-occasion splurge, with excellent service and exquisite Italian food in a delightful, pink-hued setting. It's hard to decide which is better: the grotto room with its brick lattice walls and ceiling fresco or the central room, complete with a view of the open kitchen and its wood-burning stove.

Harem

Aoyama Bianca Bldg B1, 3-1-26 Jingumae, Shibuya-ku (5786 2929). Gaienmae station (Ginza line), exit 3. **Open** 5.30-11.30pm Mon, Tue, Thur-Sun; 11.30am-12.30pm Wed. **Average** ¥5,000. **Credit** AmEx, DC, JCB, MC, V. **English menu**. **Map** p85.
With its chic and stylish furniture, Harem offers a much more sophisticated experience than the regular mom-and-pop Turkish eateries elsewhere in town.

The food is equally refined: excellent meze meat dishes, especially the imam bayildi (aubergine) and *hunkar gebendi* ('His Majesty's favourite') lamb. Food fit for a sultan.

Kaikatei

7-8-1 Minami-Aoyama, Minato-ku (3499 5872). Omotesando station (Chiyoda, Ginza, Hanzomon lines), exit B1. **Open** 11am-2pm, 6-11pm Mon-Sat. **Average** ¥3,500. **No credit cards.**

Visiting Kaikatei is like stepping back in time to 1930s Shanghai: old beer posters, wooden clocks, dated LPs and odd murals of barbarian foreigners lend an air of wartime mystery to this atmospheric Chinese restaurant. Shrimp in crab sauce is delicately flavoured, and a good match for mildly spicy Peking-style chicken with cashew nuts and rich black bean sauce.

Kizakura

Scene Akira Bldg B1F, 5-8-1 Minami-Aoyama, Minato-ku (5468 3636). Omotesando station (Chiyoda, Ginza, Hanzomon lines), exit B1. **Open** 6pm-2am daily. **Average** ¥4,500. **Credit** AmEx, DC, JCB, MC, V.

With its plush furniture, low ceilings and tables lit with oil lamps, this is clearly a place aimed at dating couples and romantic evenings *à deux*. The cuisine (French with a few extra tweaks) is surprisingly good and, with four-course set meals from ¥4,500, quite affordable for this part of town. Just the place for a celebratory meal.

Nataraj

Sanwa-Aoyama Bldg B1 F, 2-22-19 Minami-Aoyama, Minato-ku (5474 0510/www.nataraj.co.jp/ en/aoyama). Gaienmae station (Ginza line), exit 1B. **Open** 11.30am-3pm, 5.30-11pm Mon-Fri; 11.30am-11pm Sat, Sun. **Average** ¥3,500. **Credit** AmEx, DC, JCB, MC, V.

Enjoy sophisticated, vegetarian Indian delicacies courtesy of chef Sadananda and his team. The original restaurant in Ogikubo may be funkier and more casual, but this newer branch near Gaienmae is far more accessible – it's also less impersonal than the latest outlet in Ginza. **Other locations**: Ginza Kosaka Bldg 7F-9F, 6-9-4 Ginza, Chuo-ku (5537 1515); Hukumura-Sangyou Bldg B1F, 5-30-6 Ogikubo, Suginami-ku (3398 5108).

Natural Harmony Angoro

3-38-12 Jingumae, Shibuya-ku (3405 8393). Gaienmae station (Ginza line), exits 2, 3. **Open** 11.30am-2.30pm, 6-10pm Tue-Sun. **Average** ¥1,200-¥1,500. **No credit cards. English menu. Map** p85.

Still Tokyo's best natural food restaurant, this no-smoking venue boasts a simple, wood-clad interior and an additive-free menu. The food is very tasty, and although some fish is served, the ethos is strongly vegetarian. The baked aubergine is great; the whole-wheat pizzas less so. There's also a good range of organic beer, sake and wine.

Nobu Tokyo

6-10-17 Minami-Aoyama, Minato-ku (5467 0022/ www.soho-s.co.jp). Omotesando station (Chiyoda, Ginza, Hanzomon lines), exit B1 then 10mins walk. **Open** *Restaurant* 11.30am-3.30pm Mon-Fri; 6-11.30pm (doors close 10pm) Mon-Sat. *Bar* 6pm-4am Mon-Sat; 6-11pm Sun. **Average** ¥5,000 lunch; ¥8,000 dinner. **Credit** AmEx, DC, JCB, MC, V. **English menu.**

Nobu Matsuhisa started his career as a sushi chef in Tokyo before striking out for Peru, Argentina and the US. Since opening his first eponymous restaurant in New York, he has gone on to set the standard for nouvelle Japanese cuisine throughout the world. Now back home, he has an elegant, sophisticated setting in which to serve his world-class fusion cuisine – and those celebrated sushi rolls.

Rojak

B1F, 6-3-14 Minami-Aoyama, Minato-ku (3409 6764). Omotesando station (Chiyoda, Ginza, Hanzomon lines), exit B1. **Open** noon-4pm, 6pm-midnight daily. **Average** ¥1,000-¥2,500. **Credit** AmEx, DC, JCB, MC, V. **English menu.**

Western-influenced Asian food in a lovely basement with candlelit nooks and crannies, high ceilings and jungle-motif wall coverings. Next to the dining room is a comfy bar area with soft sofas and a cigar humidor. Fantastic salads are served in large, dark wood bowls that match the tables. Noodles, curries and seafood, especially sashimi, get reinvented at Rojak in sublime ways. And to top all this, there's a fair choice of wines (mostly Australian), as well as beers. **Other locations**: Roppongi Hills B2F, 6-10-1 Roppongi, Minato-ku (5770 5831).

Roy's Aoyama

Riviera Minami-Aoyama Bldg 1F, 3-3-3 Minami-Aoyama, Minato-ku (5474 8181/www.soho-s.co.jp). Gaienmae station (Ginza line), exits 1A, 1B. **Open** 11.30am-3.30pm, 5.45-11.30pm daily. **Average** ¥1,400-¥1,800. **Credit** AmEx, DC, JCB, MC, V. **English menu.**

Hawaii-based Roy Yamaguchi's fabulous Euro-Asian-Pacific cuisine is fusion food at its best: simple, attractive and stylish. He melds traditional Japanese flavours – shoyu, ginger, wasabi – into exquisitely arranged masterpieces such as seared shrimp with a spicy miso butter sauce or Mediterranean-style seafood frittata accompanied by pickled ginger and spicy sprouts. The weekend brunch is a fantastic way to start your Saturday.

Soho's

V28 Bldg 4F, 6-31-17 Jingumae (5468 0411/ www.soho-s.co.jp). Harajuku station (Yamanote line), Omotesando exit or Meiji-Jingumae station (Chiyoda line), exit 4. **Open** 11.30am-4am Mon-Sat; 11.30am-11.30pm Sun. **Average** ¥980-¥1,280. **Credit** AmEx, DC, JCB, MC, V. **English menu. Map** p85.

The impressive space-age setting rather outshines the Italian-lite food, but a meal at Soho's is always enjoyable. Pasta and pizza go for around ¥1,500 (the

pumpkin and prosciutto risotto is highly recommended), but other main courses are rather pricier. The bar area is equally impressive. You can drink here without eating (though there's a snack menu), and gaze through the curved windows to the shopping mecca of Omotesando four floors below.
Other locations: Soho's Vino Rosso, 35-4 Udagawacho, Shibuya-ku (3462 5646).

Ebisu & Daikanyama

Japanese

Chibo
Yebisu Garden Place Tower 38F, 4-20-3 Ebisu, Shibuya-ku (5424 1011). Ebisu station (Yamanote line), east exit; (Hibiya line), exit 1. **Open** 11.30am-3pm, 5-11pm Mon-Fri; 11.30am-10pm Sat, Sun. **Average** ¥1,000. **Credit** AmEx, DC, JCB, MC, V. **English menu.**
This branch of one of Osaka's top *okonomiyaki* restaurants replicates the original Kansai-style recipes. In addition to the usual meats and seafood, stuffings include asparagus, *mochi* (rice cakes), cheese and, of course, mayonnaise. Friendly staff, reasonable prices, a large menu and a gorgeous view make this a popular place.
Other locations: 108-7 Ginza, Chuo-ku (5537 5900); BIC Camera 6F, 1-11-1 Yurakucho, Chiyoda-ku (5288 8570); Seibu department store 8F, 1-28-1 Minami-Ikebukuro, Toshima-ku (3980 3351).

Ippudo
1-3-13 Hiroo, Shibuya-ku (5420 2225/ www.ippudo.com). Ebisu station (Yamanote line), west exit; (Hibiya line), exit 1. **Open** 11am-4am daily. **Average** ¥800. **No credit cards.**
Once you get past all the ordering choices – red or white pork broth; noodles soft-cooked, medium or al dente; with or without *chashu* pork – you can settle in and appreciate all the little touches that make Ippudo different from other ramen shops. The layout is simple and open, with lots of plain wood; you can add your own condiments (spicy beansprouts, sesame seeds and garlic that you grind yourself); and there are unlimited pots of Rooibos (red bush) tea to quench your thirst.
Other locations: throughout the city.

Jinroku
6-23-2 Shirokane, Minato-ku (3441 1436). Hiroo station (Hibiya line), exits 1, 2. **Open** 6pm-3am (last food order 1.30am) Tue-Sat; 6-11pm Sun. **Average** ¥4,500. **Credit** AmEx, MC, V. **English menu.**
Okonomiyaki raised to a new level, in gleaming, modern, upmarket surroundings. Besides the standard pancakes, the chefs at Jinroku also fry up great *gyoza* dumplings, *teppanyaki* seafood, tofu steaks and *yaki-soba* (fried noodles). Be sure to try the *negi-yaki*, which substitutes chopped green leeks in place of the more usual Chinese cabbage. Help it all down with cheap Chilean cabernet.

The Terrace Restaurant, Hanezawa Garden
3-12-15 Hiroo, Shibuya-ku (3400 2013/ www.thehanezawagarden.com). Ebisu station (Yamanote line), west exit; (Hibiya line), exit 1. **Open** *Summer* 11am-1.30pm (BBQ). *Year round* 6-11pm daily. **Average** ¥1,600-¥2,500. **Credit** AmEx, MC, V. **English menu.**
Once a mouldering but atmospheric old-style beer garden, now a smooth and rather soulless al fresco restaurant – though still a great place to nurse a beer in the muggy heat of a Tokyo summer. The menu is Asian-tinged Japanese, with a few pastas and other Western-style dishes. The DIY table-top barbecue grill is fun; the sushi is best avoided. In winter, the menu features *nabe* casseroles, and staff give you blankets and heaters; there are also tables indoors.

Non-Japanese

Cardenas Charcoal Grill
1-12-14 Ebisu-Nishi, Shibuya-ku (5428 0779/ www.cardenas.co.jp/chacoal). Ebisu station (Yamanote line), west exit; (Hibiya line), exit 4. **Open** 5.30pm-2am daily. **Average** ¥5,000 dinner. **Credit** AmEx, JCB, MC, V. **English menu.**
This is the most stylish and satisfying of the three Californian-style restaurants that share the Cardenas name and its distinctive take on Pacific Rim fusion food. The centrepiece is the grill, which serves up chicken, steak, fish and seafood, backed up by a strong selection of US West Coast wines.
Other locations: Cardenas Ginza Kanematsu Bldg 7F, 6-9-9 Ginza, Chuo-ku (5537 5011); **Cardenas Chinois** 22-3 Hiroo, Shibuya-ku (5447 1287).

La Casita
Selsa Daikanyama 2F, 13-4 Daikanyama, Shibuya-ku (3496 1850/www.lacasita.co.jp). Daikanyama station (Tokyu Toyoko line). **Open** 5-11pm Mon; noon-11pm Tue-Sun. **Average** ¥2,000. **No credit cards.** **English menu.**
Like most of Tokyo's south-of-the-border restaurants, La Casita isn't authentically Mexican. But the heady aroma of corn tortillas grabs you upon entering this airy 'little house' and won't let go until you've sampled the near-perfect *camarones al mojo de ajo* (grilled shrimp with garlic, Acapulco-style) or the *enchiladas rojas* bathed in spicy tomato sauce.

Good Honest Grub
1-11-11 Ebisu-Minami, Shibuya-ku (3710 0400/ www.goodhonestgrub.com). Ebisu station (Yamanote line), west exit; (Hibiya line), exit 5. **Open** 11.30am-11.30pm Mon-Fri; 9am-11.30pm Sat, Sun. **Average** ¥1,000. **No credit cards. English menu.**
No-nonsense North American comfort food in a friendly, pavement-café setting. Portions are generous and there are plenty of options for vegetarians. The weekend brunch (including a great eggs benedict) runs until 4.30pm.
Other locations: 6-6-2 Jingumae, Shibuya-ku (3406 6606).

Luxor

Barbizon 25 2F, 5-4-7 Shirokanedai, Minato-ku (3446 6900/www.luxor-r.com). Shirokanedai station (Nanboku line), exit 1. **Open** 11.30am-2pm, 5.30-10.30pm daily. **Average** ¥1,500. **Credit** AmEx, MC, DC, JCB, V. **English menu.**

Mario Frittoli takes the *cucina* of his native Tuscany and dresses it up to match the ritzy setting in up-market Shirokanedai. There is more than a whiff of celebrity here (from both Frittoli and his well-heeled clientele), but the cooking is creative and confident, and the home-made pasta is outstanding.

Ninniku-ya

1-26-12 Ebisu, Shibuya-ku (3446 5887). Ebisu station (Yamanote line), west exit; (Hibiya line), exit 1. **Average** ¥5,000 dinner. **Credit** AmEx, MC, JCB, V. **English menu.**

Ninniku is the Japanese word for garlic, and everything on the menu, with the possible exception of the drinks, is laced with it. The odours of towering garlic bread, vicious curries and mouth-watering pasta and rice dishes, with Chinese, Thai, Indian and other ethnic twists, waft out on the street.

Ricos Kitchen

4-23-7 Ebisu, Shibuya-ku (5791 4649). Ebisu station (Yamanote line), east exit; (Hibiya line), exit 1. **Open** 11.30am-3pm, 5.30-11pm daily. **Average** ¥1,000-¥2,500 lunch; ¥6,000 dinner. **Credit** AmEx, MC, V. **English menu.**

Chef Haruki Natsume produces a suave and satisfying 'cucina nueva americana', served in a chic, airy space. Perhaps these are the reasons why Ricos has been full virtually every day since it opened. **Other locations**: 1-20-3 Higashi-Azabu, Minato-ku (3588 8777).

Stellato

4-19-17 Shirokanedai, Minato-ku (3442 5588/ www.global-dining.com). Shirokanedai station (Mita, Nanboku lines), exit 2. **Open** 11.30am-3pm Mon-Fri; 5.30pm-midnight daily. **Average** ¥2,500 lunch; ¥7,000 dinner. **Credit** AmEx, DC, JCB, MC, V. **English menu.**

Stellato combines a flair for the dramatic – huge chandeliers, a blazing log fire and an immodest faux-Moorish façade – with modern American cooking that is always interesting and frequently exceptional. The nicest touch is the rooftop lounge with a view of Tokyo Tower. Perfect for a special occasion.

Tableaux

11-6 Sarugakucho, Shibuya-ku (5489 2201/ www.global-dining.com). Daikanyama station (Tokyu Toyoko line). **Open** 5.30pm-1am daily (last orders 11pm). **Average** ¥5,000-¥10,000. **Credit** AmEx, MC, V. **English menu.**

There is more than a touch of kitsch to the decor, but the eclectic Pac-Rim fusion food is entirely serious. Tableaux has become a favourite port of call with the well-heeled Daikanyama set, many of whom drop by for a Havana and cognac in the cigar bar.

Roppongi & Nishi-Azabu

Japanese

Bincho

Marina Bldg 2F, 3-10-5 Roppongi, Minato-ku (5474 0755/www.headrock.co.jp). Roppongi station (Hibiya, Oedo lines), exit 5. **Open** 6-11.30pm Mon-Sat; 6-9.30pm Sun. **Average** ¥5,000 dinner. **Credit** AmEx, DC, JCB, MC, V. **English menu. Map** p109.

Settle back in the dark, romantic, Japanese-style interior and enjoy the heady aroma of top-quality yakitori chicken and seasonal vegetables – grilled over Bincho charcoal, of course – complemented with an array of side dishes and sake from all over Japan.

Other locations: Jyuko Bldg, 8-12-12 Ginza, Chuo-ku (5537 6870).

Fukuzushi

5-7-8 Roppongi, Minato-ku (3402 4116/ www.roppongifukuzushi.com). Roppongi station (Hibiya, Oedo lines), exit 3. **Open** 11.30am-2pm, 5.30-11pm Mon-Sat. **Average** ¥3,500. **Credit** AmEx, DC, JCB, MC, V. **English menu. Map** p109.

Tokyo may have more exclusive (and even pricier) sushi shops than Fukuzushi, but few are as welcoming or accessible. Superlative seafood in an elegant yet casual setting that feels miles away from the gritty hubbub of Roppongi.

Gonpachi

1-13-11 Nishi-Azabu, Minato-ku (5771 0170/sushi restaurant 5771 0180/www.global-dining.com). Roppongi station (Hibiya, Oedo lines), exit 1. **Open** 11.30am-5am daily. **Average** ¥1,500. **Credit** AmEx, DC, JCB, MC, V. **English menu. Map** p109.

Dominating the Nishi-Azabu crossing like a feudal Japanese castle, Gonpachi was supposedly an inspiration behind *Kill Bill*. Sit at rustic wooden tables or in private booths, supping on simple country-style cooking, such as yakitori, grilled pork or soba noodles. The waiters dress in folksy *happi* coats and traditional festival music plays over the speakers. The separate third-floor sushi restaurant is more sophisticated, in both atmosphere and food, and has an open-air terrace. When President George W Bush was in town, this is where Prime Minister Koizumi Junichiro took him for a little local colour.

Other locations: Mediage 4F, 1-7-1 Daiba, Minato-ku (3599 4807); E Spacetower 14F, 3-6 Maruyamacho, Shibuya-ku (5784 2011); 1-23 Ginza, Chuo-ku (5524 3641).

Jidaiya

Naritaya Bldg 1F, 3-14-3 Akasaka, Minato-ku (3588 0489). Akasaka station (Chiyoda line), exit 1. **Open** 11.30am-2.30pm, 5pm-3am Mon-Fri; 5-11pm Sat, Sun. **Average** ¥880 lunch; ¥5,000 dinner. **Credit** AmEx, DC, JCB, MC, V.

Jidaiya recreates a rustic Japanese farmhouse, complete with tatami mats, dried ears of corn, fish-shaped hanging fireplace fixtures and heaps of

Gonpachi.
See p146.

Eat, Drink, Shop

old-looking wooden furniture. The atmosphere is a bit contrived, but fun nevertheless, and large shared tables contribute to the conviviality. The food is all Japanese, with an emphasis on seafood, meat and vegetables cooked at the table.

Maimon

3-17-29 Nishi-Azabu, Minato-ku (3408 2600/ www.maimon.jp). Roppongi station (Hibiya, Oedo lines), exit 1. **Open** 6pm-4am Mon-Thur; 6pm-5am Fri, Sat; 6pm-midnight Sun. **Average** ¥8,000 dinner. **Credit** AmEx, MC, JCB, DC, V. **English menu**. **Map** p109.

A stylish oyster bar that stocks an astounding 40 varieties of the molluscs, served either raw in the shell or cooked in numerous ways. Alternatives include yakitori and other charcoal-grilled delicacies (beef tongue, pork, shellfish and more), with a great range of sake and *shochu*.
Other locations: 1-1-10 Ebisu-Minami, Shibuya-ku (3715 0303).

Nodaiwa

1-5-4 Higashi-Azabu, Minato-ku (3583 7852/ www.geocities.co.jp/Milkyway/8859/nodaiwa). Kamiyacho station (Hibiya line), exit 1 or Akabanebashi station (Oedo line), Akabanebashi exit. **Open** 11am-1.30pm, 5-8pm Mon-Sat. **Average** ¥3,000. **Credit** MC, V. **English menu**. **Map** p109.

Housed in an old *kura* storehouse transported from the mountains, Nodaiwa is arguably the best *unagi* shop in the city. It only uses eels that have been caught in the wild, and the difference is noticeable in the texture, especially if you try the *shirayaki* (grilled without any added sauce and eaten with a dip of shoyu and wasabi).

Shunju

House 530 B1, 5-16-47 Roppongi, Minato-ku (3583 2611/www.shunju.com/ja/restaurants/ toriizaka). Roppongi station (Hibiya, Oedo lines), exit 3. **Open** 6-11pm daily. **Average** ¥6,000 dinner. **Credit** AmEx, DC, JCB, MC, V. **English menu**. **Map** p109.

Shunju is the typical modern *izakaya* – a sophisti-cated blend of modern and traditional, farmhouse and urban, Japanese and imported. You'll find good food with many creative touches; a stylish design sense; and a young (but not too young) and casual crowd. It can get smoky and noisy, but never bois-terous or out of hand. It's part of the same group as Kitchen Shunju (*see p138*) in Shinjuku.
Other locations: throughout the city.

Zakuro

TBS Kaikan Bldg B1F, 5-3-3 Akasaka, Minato-ku (3582 6841). Akasaka station (Chiyoda line), exit 1. **Open** 11am-11pm daily. **Average** ¥2,000. **Credit** AmEx, DC, JCB, MC, V. **English menu**.

A casual restaurant that captures the best of Japan's traditional haute cuisine – *shabu-shabu*, sukiyaki, tempura and dishes inspired by seasonal bounties – served in private or communal Western-style dining rooms, a tempura bar or private tatami rooms. **Other locations**: Ginza Sanwa Bldg B1F, 4-6-1 Ginza, Chuo-ku (3535 4421); Nihon Jitensha Kaikan B1F, 1-9-15 Akasaka, Minato-ku (3582 2661); Shin Nihonbashi Bldg B1F, 3-8-2 Nihonbashi, Chuo-ku (3271 3791); Shin Yaesu Bldg B1F, 1-7-1 Kyobashi, Chuo-ku (3563 5031).

Non-Japanese

L'Atelier de Joel Robuchon

Roppongi Hills Hillside 2F, 6-10-1 Roppongi, Minato-ku (5772 7500/www.robuchon.com). Roppongi station (Hibiya, Oedo lines), exit 1. **Open** 11am-midnight (last orders 10pm) daily. **Average** ¥2,900. **Credit** AmEx, DC, JCB, MC, V. **Map** p109.
Robuchon's new 'casual' French restaurant fits in well in glitzy Roppongi Hills. As at the identical sister operation in Paris, diners sit at a long counter looking in at the open kitchen, ordering one or two dishes at a time as if it were a sushi counter or tapas bar (the Spanish influence is also strong). Courses start from ¥6,300. Reservations are accepted, but only for the ridiculously early hour of 6pm; after that it's first come, first served.

Bangkok

Woo Bldg 2F, 3-8-8 Roppongi, Minato-ku (3408 7353). Roppongi station (Hibiya, Oedo lines), exit 1. **Open** 11.30am-2pm Mon-Fri; 5-11pm Mon-Sat; 11.30am-9pm Sun. Closed 3rd Sun of mth. **Average** ¥980. **No credit cards. English menu. Map** p109.

Street food

Eat, Drink, Shop

Compared to other Asian cities, Tokyo does not have much street food. This is due more to government regulation than national temperament. In Edo times, street peddlers used to dispense tempura, sushi and all manner of noodles. That tradition lives on in the *yatai* – small food stalls found outside many train stations late at night, serving oden, ramen or (sometimes) yakitori. Equipped with basic cooking equipment, they offer stools or a bench for half a dozen customers to huddle elbow-to-elbow, sipping beer or cheap sake.

One step up, in terms of permanence if not quality, is the food served in smoky, open-fronted eateries found under railway tracks or tucked away in Tokyo's old-style districts. Try **Yakitori Yokocho** outside the north-west exit of Shinjuku JR station. Referred to (unfairly) by most resident *gaijins* as 'Piss Alley', this block of shabby shacks is a time warp to the 1950s. Or join the red-faced salarymen at the tiny stalls under the arches of the JR Yamanote line at **Yurakucho** station, for basic yakitori and other titbits.

Other popular street stall foods are:
Grilled mochi: squares of chewy rice, cooked on flat *teppanyaki* grills, seasoned with soy sauce and usually wrapped in a small sheet of savoury nori seaweed.
Taiyaki: sweet, pancake-like batter cooked in fish-shaped moulds (*tai* means sea bream) with a stuffing of sweet red bean jam.
Takoyaki: an Osaka speciality: diced octopus cooked in egg batter and moulded into balls, often with pickled ginger and a sweet glaze

sauce. Look for stalls with banners featuring a cheerful-looking red octopus.
Yaki-imo: sweet potatoes roasted until the skin is flaky and the yellow flesh inside is soft, moist and very hot. A winter speciality, often sold from small trucks cruising slowly through the streets, advertising their presence with a distinctive plaintive cry.
Yakisoba: noodles fried on a wide *teppan* grill with shredded cabbage, beansprouts and bits of pork, then doused with sweet sauce and sprinkled with red pickled ginger and nori. Nothing like the fried noodles served in Chinese restaurants.

This funky second-floor diner is worth tracking down, as it turns out good Thai street food without fuss or delay. Among the highlights are *tom kha kai* soup in traditional clay pots, and the minced meat *larb* 'salads', generously seasoned with lemongrass, mint and onion.

Cicada

5-2-40 Minami-Azabu, Minato-ku (5447 5522/ www.cicada.co.jp). Hiroo station (Hibiya line), exit 3. **Open** 6-11pm Mon, Sun; noon-3pm, 6pm-3am Tue-Sat. **Average** ¥1,500. **Credit** AmEx, DC, JCB, MC, V. **English menu.**

Spain is the inspiration, but the whole Mediterranean is reflected in the excellent modern cooking of American chef David Chiddo and his crew. Hugely popular with the expat community (and deservedly so), Cicada always generates a great atmosphere. The large dining room is smoke-free, though the bar is anything but. Booking essential.

Coriander

B1F, 1-10-6 Nishi-Azabu, Minato-ku (3475 5720/ www.simc-jp.com/coriander). Roppongi station (Hibiya, Oedo lines), exit 2. **Open** 11.30am-2pm Mon-Fri; 6-11pm Mon-Sat. **Average** ¥1,000. **Credit** AmEx, DC, JCB, MC, V. **English menu. Map** p109.

A cosy basement restaurant that markets itself as 'new Thai', Coriander serves tasty dishes that are lighter on the chillies than its more authentic cousins, and often contain unusual ingredients, as with the carrot *tom yam* soup. The decor is pleasant, heavy on the cushions, greenery and incense, and service is keen if not always very efficient.

Erawan

Roi Bldg 13F, 5-5-1 Roppongi, Minato-ku (3404 5741/www.gnavi.co.jp/gn/en/g038502h.htm). Roppongi station (Hibiya, Oedo lines), exit 3. **Open** 5.30-11.30pm Mon-Fri; 5-11.30pm Sat, Sun. **Average** ¥4,000 dinner. **Credit** AmEx, DC, JCB, MC, V. **English menu. Map** p109.

Following its well-overdue refurbishment, with lots of teakwood and tropical artefacts, Erawan has become one of the classiest Thai restaurants in town. The chefs don't stint on the spices, and the Thai waitresses serve it all with customary grace. **Other locations**: 1-1-39 Hiroo, Shibuya-ku (3409 8001); 3-28-10 Shinjuku, Shinjuku-ku (3341 5127).

Hainan Jeefan Shokudo

6-11-16 Roppongi, Minato-ku (5474 3200). Azabu-Juban station (Nanboku, Oedo lines), exit 7. **Open** 11.30am-2pm, 6-11pm Mon-Fri; 11.30am-3pm, 6-11pm Sat, Sun. **Average** ¥900. **Credit** MC, V. **English menu. Map** p109.

The lunch speciality at this friendly little diner is Hainan-style soft-simmered chicken served with rice. At dinner, the kitchen also turns out an extensive range of Singapore-style street-stall staples, including curries, stir-fries and spicy *laksa lemak* noodles. The small terrace is a popular spot during the heat of summer.

Harmonie

4-2-15 Nishi-Azabu, Minato-ku (5466 6655). Hiroo station (Hibiya line), exit 1 or Roppongi station (Hibiya, Oedo lines), exit 1. **Open** noon-1.30pm, 6pm-2am Mon-Sat. **Average** ¥1,600-¥3,000. **Credit** AmEx, JCB, MC, V. **Map** p109.

Chef Yamada Jitsuhiro was a pioneer in matching top-notch French food with top wine – he has an astounding cellar of Burgundies. His winter menu features *gibier* (boar, venison and wild fowl), much of which he hunts himself. The cosy, wood-clad, second-floor dining room is no-smoking, but you can repair to the intimate stand-up bar downstairs for a Cohiba and rare armagnac.

Hong Kong Garden

4-5-2 Nishi-Azabu, Minato-ku (3486 8611/ www.hongkong-garden.co.jp). Hiroo station (Hibiya line), exit 3. **Open** *Dim sum* 11.30am-3pm Mon-Fri; 11.30am-4.30pm Sat, Sun. *Dinner* 5.30-10.30pm daily. **Average** ¥3,150. **Credit** AmEx, JCB, MC, V. **English menu.**

Huge gastrodome (seating 800-plus) devoted to the pleasures of Hong Kong-style cooking. The main dishes are Cantonese-lite, but very pleasant, especially the stir-fried organic beef with subtle hints of star anise. The trolley-borne dim sum are not totally authentic, but as good as you can expect in Tokyo.

Oak Door

Grand Hyatt Hotel 6F, 6-10-3 Roppongi, Minato-ku (4333 8784/www.grandhyatttokyo.com). Roppongi station (Hibiya, Oedo lines), exit 1. **Open** 11.30am-6pm (last orders 2.30pm), 6-11.30pm daily. **Average** ¥2,900-¥4,000. **Credit** AmEx, DC, JCB, MC, V. **English menu. Map** p109.

A huge selection of premium steaks (each *wagyu* steer individually identified), grilled to order in wood-burning ovens, and a gleaming cellar of New World wines: no wonder Oak Door is so popular with the expense-account expat community.

Olives

West Walk 5F, 6-10-1 Roppongi, Minato-ku (5413 9571/www.toddenglish.com/restaurants/ olives.html). Roppongi station (Hibiya, Oedo lines), exit 1. **Open** 11am-4pm, 5.30-11.30pm daily. **Average** ¥2,000-¥3,500. **Credit** AmEx, DC, JCB, MC, V. **English menu. Map** p109.

Roppongi Hills is a suitably larger-than-life venue for US celebrity chef Todd English's 'interpretive Mediterranean' cuisine. From his signature tuna tartare and Riso Crabonara (sic) to his juicy marinated *wagyu* steaks, this is ultra-confident cooking, Italian-based but utterly New World in its bold execution. The view is fantastic, so reserve a window seat if you can.

Roti

Piramide Bldg 1F, 6-6-9 Roppongi, Minato-ku (5785 3672/www.rotico.com). Roppongi station (Hibiya, Oedo lines), exit 1. **Open** 11.30am-2.30pm, 2.30-5pm, 6-10pm Mon-Fri; 11.30am-5pm, 6-11pm Sat; 11am-3pm, 3-5pm, 6-10pm Sun. **Average** ¥1,500. **Credit** AmEx, DC, JCB, MC, V. **Map** p109.

Eat, Drink, Shop

The speciality at this casual, self-styled 'modern American brasserie' is the rotisserie chicken. There's a good selection of New World wines and American microbrews to provide appropriate lubrication.

Vietnamese Cyclo

Piramide Bldg 1F, 6-6-9 Roppongi, Minato-ku (3478 4964/http://r.gnavi.co.jp/g222004). Roppongi station (Hibiya, Oedo lines), exit 3. **Open** 11.30am-3pm, 5-10.30pm daily. **Average** ¥1,500. **Credit** AmEx, DC, JCB, MC, V. **English menu. Map** p109.

There is more style than content to this Saigon eaterie, down to the cyclo trishaw parked at the door. Flavours have been toned down for Japanese tastes, but the *goi cuon* spring rolls are undeniably tasty.

Asakusa

Japanese

Hatsuogawa

2-8-4 Kaminarimon, Taito-ku (3844 2723). Asakusa station (Asakusa, Ginza lines), exits 1, 2, 3, A3, A4. **Open** noon-2pm, 5-8pm Mon-Sat; 5-8pm Sun. **Average** ¥1,365-¥3,000. **No credit cards. Map** p93.

Stones, plants, bamboo latticework and a white *noren* (curtain) emblazoned with the word 'unagi' mark the entrance to this venerable eel shop in historic Asakusa. Step into this minute world of wooden beams and traditional Japanese decor and savour the taste of succulent grilled eel. The *unaju* box set is delicious, or try *kabayaki* – skewered eel with the rice served separately.

Komagata Dojo

1-7-12 Komagata, Taito-ku (3842 4001/ www.dozeu.co.jp). Asakusa station (Asakusa, Ginza lines), exit A1. **Open** 11am-9pm daily. **Average** ¥2,400. **Credit** AmEx, DC, JCB, MC, V. **English menu. Map** p93.

You dine here much as you would have done a century ago – sitting on thin cushions at low tables that are little more than polished planks on the rush-matting floor. The menu revolves around *dojo* – small, plump, eel-like fish served (in ascending order of delectability) as *nabe* hotpots; *yanagawa* (in a runny omelette); or *kabayaki* (grilled, like eel). Not a gourmet delicacy, perhaps, but an absolute Asakusa institution.

Mugitoro

2-2-4 Kaminarimon, Taito-ku (3842 1066/ www.mugitoro.co.jp). Asakusa station (Asakusa, Ginza lines), exits A1, A3, A4. **Open** 11.30am-10.30pm (last orders 9pm) daily. **Average** ¥1,500-¥3,500. **Credit** AmEx, DC, JCB, MC, V. **Map** p93.

The speciality at this Japanese restaurant is rice cooked with barley and served with a bowl of grated yam (so gooey it must be healthy). There are plenty of other options too, ranging from simple lunches to full evening meals.

Otafuku

1-6-2 Senzoku, Taito-ku (3871 2521/ www.otafuku.ne.jp). Iriya station (Hibiya line), exits 1, 3. **Open** *Apr-Sept* 5-11pm Tue-Sat; 5-10pm Sun. *Oct-Mar* 5-11pm Mon-Sat; 4-10pm Sun. **Average** ¥100-¥500 per piece. **Credit** AmEx, DC, JCB, MC, V. **English menu.**

This place has been serving *oden* since the Meiji era. The chef takes great pride in his special Kansai-style version (with a much lighter broth than the Tokyo version). Otafuku also specialises in sake, which complements the delicate flavour of the vegetables and fish cakes that make up *oden*.

Sometaro

2-2-2 Nishi-Asakusa, Taito-ku (3844 9502). Tawaramachi station (Ginza line), exit 3. **Open** noon-10.30pm daily. **Average** ¥1,000. **No credit cards. English menu. Map** p93.

Comfort food in a funky wooden shack, within easy walking distance of Asakusa's tourist sights. It can get incredibly sweaty in summer, but when you're sitting round the *okonomiyaki* pan, the intimate atmosphere is wonderfully authentic.

Yoshiba

2-14-5 Yokoami, Sumida-ku (3623 4480). Ryogoku station (Oedo line), exit A1; (Sobu line), east exit. **Open** 11.30am-1.30pm, 5-10pm Mon-Sat; also during sumo tournaments. **Average** ¥2,400. **No credit cards.**

Chanko-nabe is the legendary food of sumo wrestlers, said to help them put on those extra tonnes – but only if eaten in huge amounts late at night. For the rest of us, it's just a warming, mixed casserole. Nowhere makes a more atmospheric sampling spot than Yoshiba, a former sumo stable where you sit around the hard-packed mud of the ring where wrestlers used to practise.

Non-Japanese

Vin Chou

2-2-13 Nishi-Asakusa, Taito-ku (3845 4430). Tawaramachi station (Ginza line), exit 3. **Open** 5pm-midnight Mon, Tue, Thur-Sat; 4-10pm Sun. **Average** ¥4,000 dinner. **Credit** MC, V. **Map** p93.

This five-star yakitori shop is an offshoot of the nearby French bistro La Chevre. This explains why it offers charcoal-grilled Bresse chicken, quail and a range of wines and cheese. Casual and simple, this is some of the best food in the neighbourhood.

Ueno

Japanese

Goemon

1-1-26 Hon-Komagome, Bunkyo-ku (3811 2015). Hon-Komagome station (Nanboku line), exit 2 or Hakusan station (Mita line), exit A2. **Open** noon-2pm, 5-10pm Tue-Fri; noon-8pm Sat, Sun. **Average** ¥2,700-¥3,500. **No credit cards.**

Vegging out

Committed vegetarians can have a hard time of it in Japan, since fish stock is used in almost every Japanese dish. However, some sects of Buddhism shun the consumption of animal products, especially red meat, and thanks to the temples and monasteries, the Buddhist vegetarian temple cuisine known as *shojin ryori* survives. Meals range from the basic rice gruel served in Zen refectories to numerous courses of utter delicacy. Many foreign restaurants (Indian, Italian, Thai and so on) are also veggie-friendly, of course. Here are some options.

Bon

1-2-11 Ryusen, Taito-ku (3872 0375/ www.fuchabon.co.jp). Iriya station (Hibiya line), exit 3. **Open** *noon-3pm, 5-9pm Mon-Fri; noon-9pm Sat; noon-8pm Sun.* **Average** *¥3,800-¥5,000.* **Credit** *AmEx, DC, JCB, MC, V.* **English menu**.
Compared with Daigo (*see below*), Bon is almost rustic in its simplicity, but the food is no less beautifully presented. Only one set menu is served, though individual dishes change according to the season. The style of cooking, called *fucha ryori*, is similar to *shojin*, but with a few more echoes of its Chinese origins. Last orders are two hours before closing.

Brown Rice Café

Green Bldg 1F, 5-1-17 Jingumae, Shibuya-ku (5778 5416/www.brown.co.jp). Omotesando station (Chiyoda, Ginza, Hanzomon lines), exit A1. **Open** *noon-9pm daily.* **Average** *¥1,680.* **No credit cards**. **English menu**. **Map** *p85.*
Adhering to the macrobiotic philosophy of quality and balance, this small, stylish café serves simple, light meals that are wholesome and good value. The thick, multi-grain potage is excellent, as is the fried tempeh (strictly vegan, but not strictly Japanese). The decor is Scandinavian minimalist, and there's a fine outdoor patio for relaxing in the warmer months.

Daigo

Forest Tower 2F, 2-3-1 Atago, Minato-ku (3431 0811/www.shiba-daigo.com). Kamiyacho station (Hibiya line), exit 3 or Onarimon station (Mita line), exit A5. **Open** *noon-3pm, 5-9.30pm daily.* **Average** *¥10,000.* **Credit** *AmEx, DC, JCB, MC, V.*

Tokyo's top *shojin* restaurant serves cuisine as complex and subtle as the finest *kaiseki ryori*. Each meal comprises a dozen or more exquisite dishes presented one at a time like edible brush paintings to be savoured with the eyes no less than with the mouth. A meal can last as long as three hours and linger in your memory for months afterwards, making it well worth the substantial outlay. Booking essential.

Gesshinkyo

4-24-12 Jingumae, Shibuya-ku (3796 6575). Meiji-Jingumae station (Chiyoda line), exit 5 or Harajuku station (Yamanote line), Omotesando exit. **Open** *6-11pm Mon-Sat.* **Average** *¥12,000 dinner.* **No credit cards**. **English menu**. **Map** *p85.*
Tanahashi-san, the master of Gesshinkyo, studied *shojin ryori* with Zen nuns in Kyoto, but has gone on to develop his own unorthodox, vegetable-intense version of the genre. The interior is classy and intimate, but the food is rough hewn, intense on the palate (especially the green *sansho* pepper sorbet) and very filling. Reservations essential.

Kushi Garden Deli & Café

Palace Side Building 1F, 1-1-1 Hitotsubashi, Chiyoda-ku (3215 9455/www.kushi-garden.com). Takebashi station (Tozai line), exit 1B. **Open** *11am-2pm, 5-9pm Mon-Sat.* **Average** *¥1,000.* **No credit cards**. **Map** *p66.*
This self-service café serves a good variety of salads, baked goods and wholesome light meals. It's a bit dark and earnest, but the food is tasty, the room is no-smoking, and it's handy for the Modern Art Museum and Imperial Palace gardens.

Pure Café

5-5-21 Minami-Aoyama, Minato-ku (5466 2611/www.pure-cafe.com). Omotesando station (Chiyoda, Ginza, Hanzomon lines), exit B3. **Open** *8.30am-10.30pm daily.* **Average** *¥1,050.* **No credit cards**. **Map** *p85.*
Set in the heart of fashionable Aoyama, Pure Café melds its health-conscious, near-vegan principles with a bright, contemporary interior – it's part of the glass-fronted Aveda spa complex. The menu offers a mix of East and West, and the early opening hours make it just the place for a healthy breakfast.

The entrance to this Kyoto-style tofu restaurant is lined with bamboo, while the garden has a waterfall, carp ponds and a couple of rustic bowers where you can sit outside in clement weather. The winter speciality is *yudofu* (piping hot tofu in broth); in summer, order the chilled *hiya yakko*. One of Tokyo's best-kept secrets. This is not the place for a rushed meal; last orders are taken two hours before closing time.

Hantei

2-12-15 Nezu, Bunkyo-ku (3828 1440). Nezu station (Chiyoda line), exit 2. **Open** noon-2.30pm, 5-10pm Tue-Sat; 4-9.30pm Sun. **Average** ¥3,500. **No credit cards. English menu. Map** p103.

Kushi-age (skewers of meat, fish or vegetables) is not gourmet fare, but Hantei almost makes it refined. This is partly due to the care that goes into the preparation, but mostly because of the beautiful old wooden building. There's no need to order: staff will bring course after course, stopping after every six to ask if you want to continue.

Ikenohata Yabu Soba

3-44-7 Yushima, Bunkyo-ku (3831 8977). Yushima station (Chiyoda line), exit 2. **Open** 11.30am-2pm, 4.30-8pm Mon, Tue, Thur-Sat; 11.30am-8pm Sun. **Average** ¥1,500. **No credit cards. English menu. Map** p103.

Kanda Yabu Soba (*see p137*) has spawned numerous shops run by former apprentices. This one does predictably good noodles at reasonable prices in a simple Japanese setting. The menu also includes a range of snacks, and in winter it offers suitably warming *nabe* hot-pots.

Yanaka

Nezu Club

2-30-2 Nezu, Bunkyo-ku (3828 4004/ www.nezuclub.com). Nezu station (Chiyoda line), exit 1. **Open** 6-10pm Wed-Sat. **Average** ¥6,500. **Credit** AmEx, DC, JCB, MC, V. **Map** p103.

Chef Yamada Etsuko's stylish Japanese cuisine is not as formal as *kaiseki*, but far more sophisticated than regular home cooking. She has a very creative modern touch that reflects the restaurant's innovative setting: a converted 30-year-old, metal-frame workshop tucked away down a narrow alley in a very traditional neighbourhood.

Sasanoyuki

2-15-10 Negishi, Taito-ku (3873 1145). Uguisudani station (Yamanote line), north exit. **Open** 11am-9.30pm Tue-Sun. **Average** ¥4,500. **Credit** AmEx, DC, JCB, MC, V. **English menu.**

Tokyo's most famous tofu restaurant was founded way back in the Edo period by a tofu-maker lured from Kyoto by the Kanei-ji temple's imperial abbot. Despite its illustrious past, Sasanoyuki is as down-home as the Nippori neighbourhood it sits in, with very reasonable prices.

Ikebukuro

Non-Japanese

A Raj

2-42-7 Minami-Ikebukuro, Toshima-ku (3981 9688). Higashi-Ikebukuro station (Yurakucho line), exit 3. **Open** 11am-2.30pm, 6-11pm Mon, Wed-Sun. **Average** ¥800. **No credit cards. English menu.**

With its colourful wall hangings of Ganesha, Hanuman and Shiva, this modest Indian diner is a welcome find on such a barren location, under an expressway overpass. Besides the fine range of well-priced curries, chef A Raj also delivers good dosas, idli, uppama and other South Indian exotica. Not worth crossing town for, but a gem if you're nearby.

La Dinette

2-6-10 Takadanobaba, Shinjuku-ku (3200 6571). Takadanobaba station (Yamanote line), Waseda exit; (Tozai line), exit 2. **Open** 11.30am-1.30pm, 6-9pm Mon, Wed-Sun. **Average** ¥1,050. **No credit cards. French menu.**

This low-budget joint looks very tatty round the edges, but it still serves some of the cheapest French bistro food in Tokyo, and is hugely popular with the local student population. Booking advisable.

Shilingol

4-11-9 Sengoku, Bunkyo-ku (5978 3837). Sugamo station (Yamanote line), south exit; (Mita line), exit A2 or Sengoku station (Mita line), exit A4. **Open** 6-10.30pm daily. **Average** ¥3,000 dinner. **No credit cards. English menu.**

As much a Mongolian cultural centre as a restaurant, this converted coffee shop serves little that isn't made with mutton. You can have it stuffed in dumplings, skewered on kebabs, stewed with spuds, swished in *shabu-shabu* style or simply boiled on the bone. To help it down, there's Genghis Khan vodka and live performances of folk music on the two-stringed 'horse-head' cello. Totally transporting.

Elsewhere in central Tokyo

Japanese

Ninja

Akasaka Tokyu Plaza 1F, 2-14-3 Nagatacho, Chiyoda-ku (5157 3936/www.ninja.tv). Akasaka-Mitsuke station (Ginza, Marunouchi lines), Sotobori Dori exit. **Open** 5.30pm-2am Mon-Sat; 5-11pm Sun. **Average** ¥4,000. **Credit** AmEx, DC, JCB, MC, V. **English menu.**

Waiters dressed as *ninja* (spies trained in martial arts) usher you through a series of winding wooden corridors designed to evoke the interior of an ancient Japanese castle. Others sneak up with menus and food, and there's also an itinerant magician. It's good harmless fun that is just as popular with most adults as with kids. The food is Japanese with plenty of Western tweaks – and the sushi rolls are great.

Torijaya

*4-2 Kagurazaka, Shinjuku-ku (3260 6661/
www.bolanet.ne.jp/torijaya). Iidabashi station
(Chuo, Sobu lines), west exit; (Nanboku, Yurakucho
lines), exit B3 or Kagurazaka station (Tozai line),
Kagurazaka exit or Ushigome-Kagurazaka station
(Oedo line), exit A3.* **Open** *11.30am-2.30pm,
5-10.30pm Mon-Sat; 11.30am-3pm, 4-10pm Sun.*
Average *¥950 lunch a la carte; ¥2,500-¥4,000
lunch set.* **Credit** *AmEx, JCB, MC, V.*

Kyoto-style cuisine is the focus of this traditional
restaurant. They call it *udon kaiseki*, but things
never get too formal. The centrepiece of any meal
here is *udon-suki* – a hearty hot-pot of chicken, vegetables and thick-cut wheat noodles.

Non-Japanese

Stefano

*Terui Bldg 1F, 6-47 Kagurazaka, Shinjuku-ku
(5228 7515/www.stefano-jp.com). Kagurazaka
station (Tozai line), exit 1 or Ushigome-Kagurazaka
station (Oedo line), exit A3.* **Open** *11.30am-2pm,
5.30-11pm Tue-Sun.* **Average** *¥1,260-¥2,350.*
Credit *AmEx, DC, JCB, MC, V.*

Chef Stefano Fastro hails from the Veneto, and his
repertoire ranges from Venetian seafood to the
meaty, almost Austrian fare of the mountains. It's a
modest place and rather off the beaten track, but
many rate Stefano among their favourite Italian
restaurants in Tokyo. The gnocchi alone are worth
the effort to find it.

Vietnam Alice

*Belle Vie Akasaka 2F, 3-1-6 Akasaka, Minato-ku
(3588 5020). Akasaka-Mitsuke station (Ginza,
Marunouchi lines), Belle Vie exit.* **Open** *11am-
11pm Mon-Fri; 11am-9pm Sat, Sun.* **Average**
¥1,000-¥1,500. **Credit** *AmEx, DC, JBC, MC, V.*
English menu.

Neo-colonial decor, bamboo furniture, waitresses
dressed in traditional *aodai* outfits and a tasty menu
of light Vietnamese dishes delicately prepared with
plenty of authentic seasoning. Not hearty enough for
winter, but just the ticket in midsummer.

Further afield

Japanese

Aguri

*1-6-7 Kami-Meguro, Meguro-ku (3792 3792).
Naka-Meguro station (Hibiya line).* **Open** *5.45pm-
1am daily.* **Average** *¥4,000.* **Credit** *AmEx, MC, V.*
Friendly, casual and inexpensive, this large *izakaya*
not far west of Ebisu has just enough style to raise
it above the average. Platters of prepared foods line
the counter in tapas style, while short-order cooks
stand ready to rustle up grilled fish and *teppanyaki*
meat or vegetables. Just point at whatever you fancy
– and that applies to the sake and *shochu*.
Other locations: throughout the city.

Ukai Toriyama

*Minami-Asakawa 3426, Hachioji-shi (0426 61
0739/www.ukai.co.jp/toriyama). Takaosan-Guchi
station (Keio line) then free shuttle bus.* **Open** *11am-
9.30pm Mon-Sat; 11am-8.30pm Sun.* **Average**
¥5,000-¥8,000. **Credit** *AmEx, DC, JCB, MC, V.*
English menu.

You sit in quaint teahouse-style cottages in a large,
manicured garden with ponds, grilling your own
jidori chicken over charcoal, or dining on other seasonal Japanese delicacies. Anyone visiting Mt Takao
should make a special detour for a meal here. In fact,
it's worth making a special trip, despite the long
journey (50 minutes from Shinjuku by Keio line
express train, plus ten minutes by bus). Reservations
are highly recommended. Note that last orders is an
hour and a half before closing time.

Non-Japanese

Jiang's

*Kurokawa Bldg 3F, 3-5-7 Tamagawa, Setagaya-ku
(3700 2475). Futako-Tamagawa station
(Tokyu Denentoshi line).* **Open** *5-10pm Tue-Sun.*
Average *¥3,500.* **Credit** *AmEx, JCB, MC, V.*
English menu.

Nguyen Thi Giang was born in Hanoi and raised in
the south of Vietnam, and the menu in her spotless
little restaurant reflects both influences. The hearty
cha gio rolls are cooked in northern style, full of tasty
pork, while the delicate *banh xeo* pancakes are as
sweet and satisfying as you'd find in Hue. The best
home-style Vietnamese food in Tokyo and worth the
train ride (six stops) from Shibuya.

Salvatore

*1-22-4 Kami-Meguro, Meguro-ku (3719 3680).
Naka-Meguro station (Hibiya line).* **Open** *noon-2pm,
6-10pm daily.* **Average** *¥2,000-¥3,000.* **Credit**
AmEx, DC, JCB, MC, V. **English menu.**
The wood-fired ovens on the ground floor are the
best enticement to head upstairs to sample the cooking at this affordable Italian overlooking the Meguro
river. The pizzas are excellent, as is the rest of the
trattoria-style menu. Salvatore also has a couple of
upmarket restaurants, but this one just west of
Ebisu has the fewest pretensions.
Other locations: 5-6-24 Minami-Aoyama,
Minato-ku (3797 3790).

TY Harbor Brewery

*2-1-3 Higashi-Shinagawa, Shinagawa-ku
(5479 4555/www.tyharborbrewing.co.jp). Tennozu
Isle station (Tokyo monorail), central exit.* **Open**
*11.30am-2pm, 5.30-10.30pm Mon-Fri; 11.30am-3pm,
5.30-10.30pm Sat, Sun.* **Average** *¥2,000.* **Credit**
AmEx, DC, JCB, V. **English menu.**
Tokyo's best brewpub produces a good range of
Californian-style ales and porters, and the attached
restaurant serves up straightforward diner fare that
is adequate if uninspired. The canalside location is
hardly convenient, but it is one of the few places
where you can sit outside on the waterfront.

Eat, Drink, Shop

Menu Reader

MAIN TYPES OF RESTAURANT

寿司屋 *sushi-ya*
sushi restaurants

イクラ *ikura* salmon roe

タコ *tako* octopus

マグロ *maguro* tuna

こはだ *kohada* punctatus

トロ *toro* belly of tuna

ホタテ *hotate* scallop

ウニ *uni* sea urchin roe

エビ *ebi* prawn

ヒラメ *hirame* flounder

アナゴ *anago* conger eel

イカ *ika* squid

玉子焼き *tamago-yaki* sweet egg omelette

かっぱ巻き *kappa maki* rolled cucumber

鉄火巻き *tekka maki* rolled tuna

お新香巻き *oshinko maki* rolled pickles

蕎麦屋（そば屋）*soba-ya*
Japanese noodle restaurants

天ぷらそば うどん *tempura soba, udon*
noodles in hot broth with prawn tempura

ざるそば うどん *zaru soba, udon*
noodles served on a bamboo rack in a lacquer box

きつねそば うどん *kitsune soba, udon*
noodles in hot broth topped with spring onion and fried tofu

たぬきそば うどん *tanuki soba, udon*
noodles in hot broth with fried tempura batter

月見そば うどん *tsukimi soba, udon*
raw egg broken over noodles in hot broth

あんかけうどん *ankake udon*
wheat noodles in a thick fish bouillon/soy sauce soup with fishcake slices and vegetables

鍋焼きうどん *nabeyaki udon*
noodles boiled in an earthenware pot with other ingredients and stock. Mainly eaten in winter.

居酒屋 *izakaya*
Japanese-style bars

日本酒 *nihon-shu* sake

冷酒 *rei-shu* cold sake

焼酎 *shoochuu* barley or potato spirit

チュウハイ *chuuhai*
shoochuu with juice or tea

生ビール *nama-biiru* draught beer

黒ビール *kuro-biiru* dark beer

梅酒 *ume-shu* plum wine

ひれ酒 *hirezake*
hot sake flavoured with blowfish fins

焼き魚 *yaki zakana* grilled fish

煮魚 *ni zakana*
fish cooked in various sauces

刺し身 *sashimi*
raw fish in bite-sized pieces, served with soy sauce and wasabi

揚げ出し豆腐 *agedashi doofu*
deep fried plain tofu served with savoury sauce

枝豆 *edamame*
boiled green soybeans in the pod

おにぎり *onigiri*
rice parcel with savoury filling

焼きおにぎり *yaki onigiri*
grilled rice balls

フグ刺し *fugusashi*
thinly sliced sashimi, usually spectacularly arranged and served with ponzu sauce

Eat, Drink, Shop

フグちり *fuguchiri*
chunks of fugu in a vegetable stew

雑炊 *zosui*
rice porridge cooked in fuguchiri broth

焼き鳥屋 **yakitori-ya**
yakitori restaurants

焼き鳥 *yakitori*
barbecued chicken pieces seasoned with
sweet soy sauce

つくね *tsukune* minced chicken balls

タン *tan* tongue

ハツ *hatsu* heart

シロ *shiro* tripe

レバー *reba* liver

ガツ *gatsu* intestines

鳥皮 *tori-kawa* skin

ネギ間 *negima* chicken with leek

おでん屋 **oden-ya**
oden restaurants or street stalls

さつま揚げ *satsuma-age* fish cake

昆布 *konbu* kelp rolls

大根 *daikon* radish

厚揚げ *atsu-age* fried tofu

OTHER TYPES OF RESTAURANT

料亭 *ryotei*
high-class, traditional restaurants

ラーメン屋 *ramen-ya*
ramen noodle shop

天ぷら屋 *tempura-ya* tempura restaurants

すき焼き屋 *sukiyaki-ya*
sukiyaki restaurants

トンカツ屋 *tonkatsu-ya*
tonkatsu restaurants

お好み焼き屋 *okonomi yaki-ya*
okonomiyaki restaurants

ESSENTIAL VOCABULARY

A table for..., please *...onegai shimasu*

one/two/three/four
hitori/futari/san-nin/yo-nin

Is this seat free? *kono seki aite masu ka*

Could we sit...? *...ni suware masu ka*

over there *asoko*

outside *soto*

in a non-smoking area *kin-en-seki*

by the window *madogiwa*

Excuse me
sumimasen/onegai shimasu

May I see the menu, please
menyuu o onegai shimasu

Do you have a set menu?
setto menyuu/teishoku wa arimasu ka

I'd like... *...o kudasai*

I'll have... *...ni shimasu*

a bottle/glass...
...o ippon/ippai kudasai

I can't eat food containing...
...ga haitte iru mono wa taberare masen

Do you have vegetarian meals?
bejitarian no shokuji wa arimasu ka

Do you have a children's menu?
kodomo-yoo no menyuu wa arimasu ka

The bill, please
o-kanjyoo onegai shimasu

That was delicious, thank you
gochisou sama deshita

We'd like to pay separately
betsubetsu ni onegai shimasu

It's all together, please
issho ni onegai shimasu

Is service included?
saabisu-ryoo komi desu ka

Can I pay with a credit card?
kurejitto caado o tsukae masu ka

Could I have a receipt, please?
reshiito onegai shimasu

Eat, Drink, Shop

Bars

In a city that enjoys its booze, you can drink the night – every night – away.

Alcohol makes the world go round – at least in Tokyo, where after-work drinking with office colleagues is mandatory for many Japanese salarymen (and women). People rarely entertain at home, so most socialising is also done in public places – hence the importance, and plethora, of bars and restaurants.

But defining a 'bar' is quite a challenge. Drinking and eating are such inseparable activities for Tokyoites that some of the best boozing spots are technically restaurants – such as **Hanezawa Garden** (*see p145*) or the **TY Harbor Brewery** (*see p153*) – and many of the places listed below have kitchens attached. Even venues that consider themselves strictly bars will probably place a small bowl of snacks before you – an indication that you've just incurred a seating charge (usually ¥500-¥1,000). Bars that don't charge will almost always say so outside (in English).

The cheapest and most popular way to eat and drink is still the *izakaya* – rowdy venues serving cheap Japanese food alongside staple drinks such as beer and *shochu* (*see p158* **Drink up**). There has been a steady growth

in the popularity of British- and Irish-style pubs, although the stand-and-sip mode of socialising is still rare for Tokyo.

Each area of the city has a discernible character reflected in its bars. Harajuku, Aoyama and Nishi-Azabu are the best places for sleek lounges and designer bars. Roppongi offers the complete opposite: tatty, noisy joints with drinks as cheap as the pick-up lines. In Shibuya and outlying Shimo-Kitazawa you'll find quaint, affordable bars, while Ginza is best avoided if you're on a tight budget.

Take care if you see the words 'pub' and 'snack' outside a small Japanese bar; these two words are misleading for foreigners in search of a drink. Such places are often tamer versions of hostess bars, where staff will drink merrily away on your bar tab. Prices are rarely displayed, so if you aren't the guest of a regular customer you can expect to pay an arbitrary sky-high sum at the end of the night.

But this is an exception. In general, you'll find Tokyo's bars welcoming, even if you don't speak the language. Generous licensing laws mean that many places don't close until the

Trip the light fantastic at **Hajime** in Ginza. *See p157.*

The best Bars

Best in summer
Nowhere else in Tokyo comes close to the beautiful, verdant setting of historic **Sekirei**. *See p161.*

Best view
It's easy to find booze with a view in Tokyo, but the **Museum Café** offers almost 360° of viewing pleasure. *See p164.*

Best for romance
Xex Daikanyama is the place. Don't bring your mates. *See p162.*

Best for relaxing
Massage chairs, aromatherapy scents, projectors beaming aquatic images; **Seabed** is probably the most chilled-out bar in the world. *See p164.*

Best for the unexpected
Something different is going on every time you enter **Super-deluxe**. *See p164.*

trains begin running at 5am – which means the first few trains of the day often carry a jumble of sleepy-eyed salarymen heading for work, and baggy-eyed souks (who may or may not also be office-bound). Fortunately, public drunkenness is treated with tolerance. For advice on drinking etiquette, *see p98* **Etiquette**.

Ginza

Cabaret
Ginzazetton Bldg B1F, 5-14-15 Ginza, Chuo-ku (5148 3600). Higashi-Ginza station (Asakusa, Hibiya lines), exit 4. **Open** 8pm-5am daily. **Credit** AmEx, DC, JCB, MC, V. **Map** p60.
Descend the red velvet-draped spiral staircase and… that's pretty much where the cabaret theme ends. But you'll find yourself in the sleek basement of Zetton, a Korean/Japanese restaurant in the back-streets of Ginza. Be warned, though. A seat at the bar costs ¥500, but a spot on the sofa bears a hefty ¥1,500 charge.

Hajime
Iraka Ginza Bldg B1F, 6-4-7 Ginza, Chuo-ku (5568 4552/www.ginza-hajime.com). Ginza station (Ginza, Hibiya, Marunouchi lines), Sotobori Dori exit. **Open** 6pm-3am Mon-Fri; 6-11pm Sat. **Credit** AmEx, DC, JCB, MC, V. **Map** p60.
What looks like an old apartment from the outside turns out to be a sleek, modern designer bar. The yellow light that snakes its way around the room and across the bar counter gives a warm glow to this

tiny basement. The menu focuses on wines – both grape and rice varieties. This being Ginza, there's a predictable ¥1,000 seating charge.

Hibiki
Caretta Shiodome 46F, 1-8-1 Higashi-Shinbashi, Minato-ku (6215 8051). Shiodome station (Oedo line), exit A1; (Yurikamome line), Dentsu exit. **Open** 11am-4pm, 5-11.30pm daily. **Credit** AmEx, DC, JCB, MC, V.
A pleasantly upmarket *izakaya* with great Japanese food and even better views, near the top of one of the towers in the Shiodome complex. The food is freshly prepared Japanese grill fare, at around ¥800 a dish, while drinks cost around ¥700. The view over the river towards Odaiba is spectacular, taking in both Rainbow Bridge and the Odaiba Ferris wheel, but window tables should be reserved in advance.

Ieyasu Hon-jin
1-30 Kanda-Jinbocho, Chiyoda-ku (3291 6228). Jinbocho station (Hanzomon, Mita, Shinjuku lines), exit A7. **Open** 5-10pm Mon-Fri. **No credit cards.** **Map** p66.
Genial host Taisho bangs the drum behind the bar to greet each new customer to this cosy, top-class *yakitori* bar named after the first of the Tokugawa shoguns. There are only a dozen seats, so everyone crowds around the counter, where a wide choice of food lies in glass cases, already on sticks, ready to be popped on the coals and grilled. The food is excellent, as is the beer and sake, which Taisho dispenses with natural flair, pouring into small cups from a great height. Not cheap (expect around ¥4,000-¥7,000 for a couple of hours' eating and drinking), but still good value. Avoid the 6-8pm after-work rush and don't go in a group of more than three.

Kagaya
B1F, 2-15-12 Shinbashi, Minato-ku (3591 2347/ www1.ocn.ne.jp/~kagayayy). Shinbashi station (Yamanote line, Asakusa line), Karasumori exit; (Ginza line), exit 8; (Yurikamome line), exit 6. **Open** 5.30pm-midnight/empty Mon-Sat; by appointment only Sun. **No credit cards.**
A warm, eccentric welcome is guaranteed to all by Mark, the Japanese crackpot host of this Shinbashi institution. When you arrive, choose a country-themed drink from a list, and Mark will disappear into his magic cupboard to re-emerge in a costume that reflects your choice. Drinks come in glasses that move, shake or make noises, and serve as the pre-lude to games such as table football or Jenga. You can also, if you wish, dress as a frog or giant teddy bear. The billing system is just as unique; it always seems to come to ¥2,500 a head, no matter how much you eat or drink. Delicious (often vegetarian) food is prepared by Mark's very tolerant mother.

Lion Beer Hall
7-9-20 Ginza, Chuo-ku (3571 2590/www.ginzalion.jp). Ginza station (Ginza, Hibiya, Marunouchi lines), exit A4. **Open** 11.30am-11pm Mon-Sat; 11.30am-10.30pm Sun. **Credit** AmEx, MC, V. **Map** p60.

Eat, Drink, Shop

This 1930s beer hall, part of the Sapporo Lion chain, is a tourist attraction in itself. The tiled and wood-panelled interior looks as if it's been transplanted from Bavaria, and a menu laden with sausages adds to the effect. Friday night sessions have been known to descend into mass karaoke demonstrations. There is also a cheap and cheerful restaurant upstairs serving both Japanese and Western dishes.

Shinjuku

Albatross

1-2-11 Nishi-Shinjuku, Shinjuku-ku (3342 5758). Shinjuku station (Yamanote, Shinjuku lines), west exit; (Marunouchi, Oedo lines), exit B16. **Open** 5pm-2am daily. **No credit cards. Map** p73.
Hidden among the tiny, time-worn *yakitori* stalls of Omoide Yokocho, beside Shinjuku station, Albatross is a tiny three-storey salon that seats, in total, around 30 people. The bar occupies most of the red-lit ground-floor space, with up to ten patrons squeezed between the counter and the back wall. The floor above is officially a gallery, more accurately a Japanese-style room with a few pictures on the walls. First-floor customers place their orders and receive their drinks through a hole in the floor; an operation that becomes increasingly perilous as the night progresses and senses diminish. Up top, in lenient weather, a rickety roof accommodates half a dozen more drinkers. The crowd is a genuinely eclectic mix of suits, artists, expats and students.

Café Hoegaarden

2-20-16 Yoyogi, Shibuya-ku (5388 5523/ www.brussels.co.jp/index.html). Shinjuku station (Yamanote line), south exit; (Shinjuku line), exit A1; (Shinjuku line), exit 6. **Open** 5.30pm-2am Mon-Fri; 5.30-11pm Sat. **Credit** AmEx, DC, JCB, MC, V. **Map** p73.
An upmarket cousin of the local Brussels chain, this light and airy bar, done out in pine, is popular with local office ladies. On draught, as well as the epony-mous wheat beer, is Kriek cherry beer and a guest beer that changes weekly. The bottled beer menu contains over 50 highly priced but popular Belgian brews. Food is standard pub stuff, with a Belgian twist in the form of sausages and great frites.
Other locations: 3-16-1 Kanda Ogawacho, Chiyoda-ku (3233 4247); 75-1 Yaraicho, Shinjuku-ku (3235 1890); 1-10-23 Jingumae, Shibuya-ku (3403 3972); 3-21-14 Nishi-Azabu, Minato-ku (5413 5333).

Clubhouse Tokyo

Marunaka Bldg 3F, 3-7-3 Shinjuku, Shinjuku-ku (3359 7785/www.clubhouse-tokyo.com). Shinjuku-Sanchome station (Marunouchi, Shinjuku lines), exits C3, C4. **Open** 5pm-midnight daily. **No credit cards. Map** p73.
Clubhouse is the only specialist sports bar in Shinjuku and can get phenomenally crowded on big game nights. Premiership football is also screened. Monday night is darts night. There are British and Irish beers on tap.

Drink up

The bestselling form of alcohol in Japan is **beer** (almost invariably lager), which overtook sake as the nation's drink of choice in the early 20th century. Japan's major brewers Kirin, Asahi, Suntory and Sapporo are recognised the world over, but since a 1994 liberalisation of relevant laws, there has been an explosion in local microbrews, known in Japanese as *ji-biru*. Many of the city's better bars will carry some of these; brands to look for include Akagi Jibeer, Akasaka Beer, Tama no Megumi and Tokyo Ale. **TY Harbor Brewery** (*see p153*) sells only its own brewed-on-the-premises concoctions.

To dodge the beer tax, Japanese brewers invented a drink called *happoshu*, designed to look and taste like beer but with barley in place of malt. When the government recently caught up with the practice and levied a *happoshu* tax, the brewers created *zasshu*, this time made from beans rather than barley. Both drinks resemble beer in looks – but the taste is a different matter.

Japanese **sake**, more commonly referred to as *nihonshu* since 'sake' also means 'booze', is rice wine (though it's actually brewed), and connoisseurs exist in much the same way as they do for wine in the West. There are good years and bad years, renowned regions and different grades. *Nihonshu* is delicious hot or cold, typically 10-20 per cent alcohol by volume, and drinking cheap stuff to excess produces phenomenal hangovers.

Japan's very own distilled spirit is called **shochu**. It can be made from rice, but also from barley, buckwheat, potatoes or even brown sugar, and typically contains 25-40 per cent alcohol by volume. *Shochu* is rarely drunk straight, but mixed with fruit juices and soda water, or with Oolong tea to form an Oolong *hai*.

If you want to try a *shochu* drink, first ask if it's possible to have a *nama fruit hai*, meaning (usually) that the customer gets to squeeze his own juice out of the fruit. Cheaper *izakaya* do not offer this option, and the juice is likely to come from a box. Fruit *hai* do not taste alcoholic, but have the curious effect of getting you drunk from the ankles up, so be careful when getting to your feet.

The Dubliners

Shinjuku Lion Hall 2F, 3-28-9 Shinjuku, Shinjuku-ku (3352 6606/www.gnavi.co.jp/lion/05.html). Shinjuku station (Yamanote line), east exit; (Marunouchi, Oedo, Shinjuku lines), exit A8. **Open** noon-1am Mon-Sat; noon-11pm Sun. **Credit** AmEx, MC, V. **Map** p73.

The oldest and scruffiest of the growing chain of Irish pubs owned by Sapporo, one of Japan's largest brewers and also Japan's Guinness importer. Draught Guinness and cider (little known in Japan) accompany standard domestic beers, while the menu offers semi-authentic fish and chips. The Shibuya branch is the cosiest, the Ikebukuro branch tends to be the most raucous, and the Sanno Park Tower branch the quietest.

Other locations: 2-29-8 Dogenzaka, Shibuya-ku (5459 1736); Sun Grow Bldg B1F, 1-10-8 Nishi-Ikebukuro, Toshima-ku (5951 3614); Sanno Park Tower B1F, 2-11-1, Nagatacho, Chiyoda-ku (3539 3615); 1-1-18 Toranomon, Minato-ku (5501 1536); Imonnishi Azabu Bldg 1F, 1-14-1 Nishi-Azabu, Minato-ku (3479 0345).

The Fiddler

Tajima Bldg B1F, 2-1-2 Takadanobaba, Shinjuku-ku (3204 2698/www.thefiddler.com). Takadanobaba station (Yamanote line), Waseda exit; (Tozai line), exit 3. **Open** 6pm-3am Mon-Thur, Sun; 6pm-5am Fri, Sat. **No credit cards**.

Run by UK expats, this place smells like pubs back home, only it's open until the wee hours. There's free live music or comedy on many nights. Most acts are local foreign groups, but the odd Japanese band plays too. The menu features ploughman's lunch, and the kitchen stays open until midnight. Takadanobaba is a couple of stops north of Shinjuku on the Yamanote line.

Living Bar

Shinjuku Nomura Bldg 49F, 1-26-2 Nishi-Shinjuku, Shinjuku-ku (3343 8101/www.j-group.jp). Shinjuku station (Yamanote line), west exit; (Marunouchi, Oedo, Shinjuku lines), exits A17, A18. **Open** 11.30am-2pm, 5-11pm Mon-Fri; 5-11pm Sat; 5-10pm Sun. **Credit** AmEx, DC, JCB, MC, V. **Map** p73.

Living Bar is an unremarkable chain of Japanese-style *izakaya*, but the cheap food and great views at the Shinjuku branch make it noteworthy. The dining room is surrounded by huge windows offering a vista over neighbouring skyscrapers towards the neon lights of east Shinjuku. There are also four private rooms, all with their own windows, which can be booked for parties of six to 25 people.

Other locations: 2-1-20 Hamamatsu-cho, Minato-ku (5472 3808); 5-2-1 Roppongi, Minato-ku (3423 3808).

Shibuya

Bello Visto

Cerulean Tower Tokyu Hotel 40F, 26-1 Sakuragaoka-cho, Shibuya-ku (3476 3000/www.ceruleantower-hotel.com). Shibuya station (Yamanote, Ginza, Hanzomon lines), south exit. **Open** 4pm-midnight Mon-Fri; 3pm-midnight Sat, Sun. **Credit** AmEx, DC, JCB, MC, V. **Map** p79.

Enormous glass windows open up the city before you, with the surprisingly low-rise skyline of Shibuya particularly impressive at night. The focus at this hotel bar is on wine, with a frankly terrifying list of expensive wines from all over the world. Prices start at ¥900 a glass, and a 10% service charge will be added to your bill. To ensure a seat by the window, booking is advisable.

Eat, Drink, Shop

Tiny **Albatross**. *See p158.*

Xex appeal.
See p162.

Chandelier Bar/Red Bar

1-12-24 Shibuya, Shibuya-ku. Shibuya station (Yamanote, Ginza, Hanzomon lines), east exit. **Open** 8pm-5am Mon-Thur, Sun; 8pm-11am Fri, Sat. **Map** p79.

This is *the* new late-late-night place for beautiful people and drunks alike. The bar is, appropriately, stuffed with chandeliers, adding a touch of surreal vibe and superficial class. The endless hours make it the perfect hangout for the all-night, all-morning and all-night again set. Shame about the snotty staff, who refuse to release the bar's phone number, let alone answer it. From Shibuya station, walk up the Miyamasuzaka hill towards the post office, turn left at the first corner past the lights and then take the first right; it's on the left past Concombre restaurant.

Insomnia Lounge

Ikuma Bldg B1F, 26-5 Udagawacho, Shibuya-ku (3476 2735/www.gnavi.co.jp/miwa). Shibuya station (Yamanote, Ginza, Hanzomon lines), Hachiko exit. **Open** 6pm-5am daily. **Credit** AmEx, DC, JCB, MC, V. **Map** p79.

Welcome back to the womb. This spacious basement bar, tucked away opposite the 109 building, is covered from floor to ceiling in soft red fabric, the cushioned walls reminiscent of a padded cell. For the ultimate queasy experience, try sitting at the bar and gazing into the mirrored lights above it. And don't miss a trip to the toilet. There's an extensive food and cocktail menu, and a cover charge of ¥525. Remove your shoes when you enter.

Pink Cow

Villa Moderna B1F, 1-3-18 Shibuya, Shibuya-ku (3406 5597/www.thepinkcow.com). Shibuya station (Yamanote, Ginza, Hanzomon lines), Hachiko exit. **Open** 5pm-late Tue-Thur, Sun; 5pm-3am Fri, Sat. **Credit** (over ¥5,000) AmEx, DC, JCB, MC, V. **Map** p79.

American owner Traci Consoli envisioned this snazzy little bar and restaurant to be a space where foreign artists could meet and work. The original Harajuku locale had more rooms and more funk, but these new digs aren't bad either. Art from local artists adorns the walls and events include a monthly short film festival. The grub is good too and each Friday and Saturday there is a buffet spread for a very reasonable ¥2,500.

Soft

B1F, 3-1-9 Shibuya, Shibuya-ku (5467 5817/ www.soft-tokyo.com). Shibuya station (Yamanote, Ginza, Hanzomon lines), east exit. **Open** 7pm-4am Mon-Fri; 9pm-4am Sat. **No credit cards**. **Map** p79.

The only bar in town where the toilet gets more comments than the drinks. A 60cm-high (2ft) door leads to a spacious water closet where the loo paper is way above your head and the tap water plummets through a tube from the ceiling. Soft also boasts a wide range of imported beers (weekdays only) and DJs playing everything from 1950s show tunes to breakbeats.

Tantra

Ichimainoe Bldg B1F, 3-5-5 Shibuya, Shibuya-ku (5485 8414). Shibuya station (Yamanote, Ginza, Hanzomon lines), east, new south exits. **Open** 8pm-5am daily. **Credit** AmEx, DC, JCB, MC, V. **Map** p79.

Blink and you'll miss the entrance to Tantra– the only sign is a small, dimly lit 'T' above a nondescript stairwell on the corner of a nondescript office building on the south side of Roppongi Dori near Shibuya. But heave open the imposing metal door and, amazingly, you'll find yourself in what resembles a secret, subterranean drinking club, decorated with stone pillars, veiled alcoves, flickering candles and statues depicting scenes from the *Kama Sutra*. On your first visit you'll feel like you've gatecrashed a very private party, but have courage and don't be put off by the ice-cool staff. The ¥1,000 cover charge is a warning not to enter without a substantial wad waiting in your wallet.

Harajuku & Aoyama

Bar Ho

Backborn House B1F, 6-2-10 Minami-Aoyama, Minato-ku (5774 4390). Omotesando station (Chiyoda, Ginza, Hanzomon lines), exit B1. **Open** 6pm-2am Mon-Thur, Sun; 6pm-5am Fri, Sat. **Credit** AmEx, DC, JCB, MC, V.

A pleasant little bar that specialises in single-malt Scotch whiskies, of which it has over 70 on the menu, with many more exotic and expensive ones off it. The atmosphere is olde worlde calm, with soft jazz and soft furnishings making Bar Ho the perfect place to unwind after a hard day. Head upstairs, flop down on a sofa with a double Macallan and let your worries drift away.

Den Aquaroom

FIK Bldg B1F, 5-13-3 Minami-Aoyama, Minato-ku (5778 2090). Omotesando station (Chiyoda, Ginza, Hanzomon lines), exit B1. **Open** 6pm-2am Mon-Thur, Sat; 6pm-4am Fri; 6-11pm Sun. **Credit** AmEx, DC, JCB, MC, V.

Fish tanks, and lots of them, are the defining feature of this fashionable yet comfortable bar. Before you sink into one of the red armchairs or perch at the crowded bar, be aware of the ¥500 cover charge. To soften the blow, there's a wide selection of cocktails and an intriguing menu (in English) of reasonably priced Asian-influenced food.

Office

Yamazaki Bldg 5F, 2-7-18 Kita-Aoyama, Minato-ku (5786 1052). Gaienmae station (Ginza line), exit 2. **Open** 7pm-3am daily. **No credit cards.**

You'll find that theme bars of all description abound in Tokyo, but none has quite the same bizarrely unattractive concept as Office. With a photocopier by the window, power points for workaholics and bookshelves against the wall, the management seems not to have noticed that its bar offers the best view in the area.

Oh God!

B1F, 6-7-18 Jingumae, Shibuya-ku (3406 3206/ www.oh-god-jp.com). Harajuku station (Yamanote line), Omotesando exit or Meiji-Jingumae station (Chiyoda line), exit 4. **Open** 6pm-6am daily. **Credit** AmEx, DC, JCB, MC, V. **Map** p85.

Come here for an atmosphere reminiscent of Bangkok's Khao San Road, with nightly movie screenings, pool and pinball tables and a cheap 'n' cheerful vibe. A schedule for the week's roster of films is posted outside.

Sekirei

Meiji Kinenkan, 2-2-23 Moto-Akasaka, Minato-ku (3746 7723/www.meijikinenkan.gr.jp/sekirei). Shinanomachi station (Chuo, Sobu lines). **Open** June-Aug 4.30-10.30pm Mon-Fri; 5.30-10.30pm Sat, Sun. Closed Sept-May. **Credit** AmEx, DC, JCB, MC, V.

Kimono-clad traditional *buyou* dancers perform nightly on the spot where Emperor Meiji once signed the Japanese constitution. Meanwhile, a predominantly suit-wearing crowd sink beers and wine as they lounge in grand wicker chairs skirting the immaculate lawn. Any place this beautiful ought to be prohibitively expensive. Luckily, it's not. Beer clocks in at just ¥700 a jug and the *izakaya*-style food is equally reasonable. Shinanomachi is a few stops east from Shinjuku.

Sign

2-7-18 Kita-Aoyama, Minato-ku (5474 5040). Gaienmae station (Ginza line), exit 3. **Open** 10am-3am Mon-Fri; 11am-midnight Sat, Sun. **No credit cards.**

An unashamedly artistic and artsy bar-cum-restaurant-cum-gallery a stone's throw from the station, Sign manages the difficult trick of being all things to all punters. While nearby office workers drop in and treat it as their local, artistic or creative types flock to the basement gallery, and clubbers come to listen to the occasional shows by local DJs.

Ebisu & Daikanyama

Bar

1-9-11 Ebisu-Minami, Shibuya-ku (5704 0186). Ebisu station (Yamanote, Hibiya lines), west exit. **Open** 6pm-1am Mon; 6pm-5am Tue-Sat. **Credit** AmEx, DC, JCB, MC, V.

Perhaps the owners couldn't think of a better name for this ethereal drinking den, or perhaps they used up all their imagination on the interior, where glass beads on the pillars twinkle like distant stars amid the orange glow of Japanese paper lanterns, all to a backdrop of space-like sounds. The speciality is Scotch, with a staggering 200 single malts on offer at around ¥600 a throw.

Bar Kitsune

Chatolet Shibuya B1F, 2-20-13 Higashi, Shibuya-ku (5766 5911/www.usen.com/tenpo/kitsune/shibuya. html). Ebisu station (Yamanote, Hibiya lines), west exit. **Open** 6pm-midnight Mon; 6pm-3am Tue-Thur, Sun; 6pm-5am Fri, Sat. **Credit** AmEx, DC, JCB, MC, V.

Eat, Drink, Shop

Situated on Meiji Dori between Ebisu and Shibuya, this bar pushes back the boundaries between restaurant, DJ bar and club, but stops short of providing a dancefloor. It's rare to see a foreign face here, as Kitsune hasn't been colonised by bar and club hoppers. The most striking aspect of the slick interior is the phenomenal, ever-changing light radiating from all four walls.

Dagashi

1-13-7 Ebisu-Nishi, Shibuya-ku (5458 5150). Ebisu station (Yamanote, Hibiya lines), west exit. **Open** 6.30pm-4.30am Mon-Sat; 6.30pm-1am Sun. **Credit** AmEx, DC, MC, V.

A beautiful, dark wooden *izakaya* serving standard drinks alongside steaming dishes of Asian faves. The twist is the all-you-can-eat candy (*dagashi*), free for every customer. Sweet-toothed boozers can plunge their hand into the numerous buckets of trad Japanese candies and crispy snacks. For an extra ¥500 you can take a bag home. The name outside is only in Japanese, so look for the blazing orange signs.

Kissa Ginza

1-3-9 Ebisu-Minami, Shibuya-ku (3710 7320/ www8.plala.or.jp/dj/index.html). Ebisu station (Yamanote, Hibiya lines), west exit. **Open** 6pm-2am Mon-Sat. **Credit** AmEx, DC, JCB, MC, V.

Here's a recipe for postmodern kitsch, Tokyo-style. Take a 40-year-old coffee shop that hasn't seen a decorator in 30 years, install a glitter ball and two turntables and… absolutely nothing else. Result: the blue-rinse set still comea for coffee in the daytime, but the evening brings lounge-loving urban hipsters who come for the laid-back grooves. Arrive around 6pm to watch the crowds collide.

What the Dickens

Roob 6 Bldg 4F, 1-13-3 Ebisu-Nishi, Shibuya-ku (3780 2099). Ebisu station (Yamanote, Hibiya lines), west exit. **Open** 5pm-1am Tue, Wed; 5pm-2am Thur-Sat; 3pm-midnight Sun. **No credit cards**.

At the top of the building that houses nightclub Milk (*see p213*) is this popular British-style pub. The walls are decorated with Dickens manuscripts (which have been liberally recaptioned in the gents' toilets). Unfortunately, food is of genuine British pub standard. Local bands play nightly.

Xex Daikanyama

La Fuente Daikanyama 3F, 11-1 Sarugakucho, Shibuya-ku (3476 0065/www.ystable.co.jp/ restaurant/xexdaikanyama/bar.html). Daikanyama station (Tokyu Toyoko line). **Open** 2.30pm-4am Mon-Fri; 11.30am-4am Sat, Sun. **Credit** AmEx, DC, JCB, MC, V.

This restaurant/bar complex offers two great spots for red-blooded romantics. The bar is all sultry jazz ambience and quality cocktails, while outside on the terrace a reflecting pool and flickering lanterns create a Balinese-style look. Take note: while anyone is welcome to enter, Xex operates a membership system that reserves many of the best seats for those willing to shell out a ¥30,000 joining fee plus ¥7,000 per month.

Roppongi

Agave

Clover Bldg B1F, 7-15-10 Roppongi (3497 0229/ www.lead-off-japan.co.jp/tempo/agave/index.html). Roppongi station (Hibiya, Oedo lines), exit 4B. **Open** 6.30pm-2am Mon-Thur; 6.30pm-4am Fri, Sat. **Credit** AmEx, DC. **Map** p109.

From the orange stone walls to the snifters and sangritas, Agave is a perfect replica of an upmarket Mexican cantina in all ways but two: few cantinas stock 400 varieties of tequila and mescal, and no joint in Mexico would charge so much for them. With single measures costing from ¥800 to an impressive ¥9,400, this is the only place in Roppongi where customers don't hurl their cactus juice straight into their bloodstream.

Paddy Foley's. *See p164.*

Golden Gai

While the skyline all around rises ever higher, this tiny section of east Shinjuku between Kuyakusho Dori and Hanazono shrine remains resolutely stuck in the 1950s. The four streets that constitute this fascinating little area host some 200 tiny drinking dens, most of which cannot accommodate more than eight customers at a time. The area is incredibly popular with Japanese salarymen in their 40s and 50s; many bars cater to them exclusively, and do not welcome foreign customers – so don't just wander in at random. The bars below are all foreigner-friendly.

Many bar leases came up for renewal in late 2002 and early 2003, and some have been taken over by a younger breed of master, who are introducing rock music and DJs, much to the chagrin of older regulars.

La Jetée

1-1-8 Kabuki-cho, Shinjuku-ku (3208 9645). Shinjuku station (Yamanote, Chuo lines), east exit; (Marunouchi line), exits B6, B7; (Oedo, Shinjuku lines), exit 1. **Open** 7pm-empty Mon-Sat. **No credit cards**. **Map** p73.
A tiny Golden Gai institution, owned by a film fanatic (the place gets its name from the Chris Marker classic) who speaks fluent French but no English. Popular with French expatriates and creative types.

J Fox R&R Bar

1-1-9 Kabuki-cho, Shinjuku-ku (090 1502 5547). Shinjuku station (Yamanote, Chuo lines), east exit; (Marunouchi line), exits B6, B7; (Oedo, Shinjuku lines), exit 1. **Open** 7pm-late daily. **No credit cards**. **Map** p73.
Probably the friendliest bar in Golden Gai. If you want to chat with the staff or regulars, take any seat at the bar. For a more peaceful drink, the second floor is a beautiful Japanese-style hideaway. Bar owner Higuchi Hirotaka would like it to be known that he'll waive the ¥1,000 seating charge for anyone bringing in this edition of the guide.

Shot Bar Shadow

1-1-8 Kabuki-cho, Shinjuku-ku (3209 9530). Shinjuku station (Yamanote, Chuo lines), east exit; (Marunouchi line), exits B6, B7; (Oedo, Shinjuku lines), exit 1. **Open** 5pm-midnight Mon-Fri; 6pm-midnight Sat (members only after midnight). **No credit cards**. **Map** p73.
The master of this tiny bar speaks Arabic, German, Russian and French, thanks to his time in the Foreign Legion. For you to become a member, and be allowed in after midnight, he must be able to remember your name, which is not as easy a feat as it might sound. A friendly place where six is a crowd, typical in Golden Gai.

Bauhaus

Reine Roppongi Bldg 2F, 5-3-4 Roppongi (3403 0092/www.e-bauhaus.jp). Roppongi station (Hibiya, Oedo lines), exit 3. **Open** 7pm-1am Mon-Sat. **Credit** AmEx, DC, JCB, MC, V. **Map** p109.
One of those 'only in Japan' experiences, this is a music venue that has featured the same band for over 20 years. Nowhere else in the world can you jam to flawless covers of the Rolling Stones, Pink Floyd or Madonna performed by men and women who can't speak three words of English, and then have them serve you food and drink in between sets. It's on the pricey side, though, with a ¥2,700 music charge. Sets every hour.

Bernd's Bar

Pure 2F, 5-18-1 Roppongi, Minato-ku (5563 9232/ www.berndsbar.com). Roppongi station (Hibiya, Oedo lines), exit 3. **Open** 5-11pm/empty Mon-Sat. **Credit** AmEx, MC. **Map** p109.
A small corner of Germany, with fresh pretzels on the tables, and Bitburger and Erdinger on tap for washing down your Wiener schnitzel. Try to get a window table for the view over the nightlife area of Roppongi. If you happen to meet owner Bernd Haag, you'll find he can chat with you in English, German and Spanish, as well as Japanese.

Cavern Club

Saito Bldg 1F, 5-3-2 Roppongi (3405 5207/ www.kentos-group.co.jp/cavern). Roppongi station (Hibiya, Oedo lines), exit 3. **Open** 6pm-2.30am Mon-Sat; 6pm-midnight Sun. **Credit** AmEx, DC, JCB, MC, V. **Map** p109.
Tokyo's famous Beatles imitators play here most nights – look for the Silver Beats on the schedule. Some say they sound better live than the originals. In low light, if you're very drunk and wearing dark enough glasses, you might convince yourself you're back in Liverpool. Music fee is ¥1,500.

Gas Panic

2F-3F, 3-15-24 Roppongi, Minato-ku (3405 0633/ www.gaspanic.co.jp). Roppongi station (Hibiya, Oedo lines), exit 3. **Open** 6pm-5am daily. **No credit cards**. **Map** p109.
Gas Panic is a Roppongi institution, where young people go to grope other young people. The chart classics and Eurobeat play at such high volume that

Eat, Drink, Shop

your mating ritual needs to be physical rather than verbal. To give an idea of what it's like, note that you must have an alcoholic drink in your hand at all times, and drinking water is not in evidence. Every drink costs ¥400 at happy hour (6-9.30pm daily) and all night on Thursday. There are three other Gas Panic outfits in Roppongi, two in Shibuya and another in Yokohama; check the website for details.

George's Bar

9-7-55 Akasaka, Minato-ku (3405 9049/ www2.ocn.ne.jp/~hasshi/soul4.htm). Roppongi station (Hibiya, Oedo lines), exit 7. **Open** 8pm-5am daily. **No credit cards. Map** p109.

If the Tokyo government gave out blue plaques for historic monuments, then this tiny place would definitely get one. George's has been around since the early 1960s, and the jukebox contains many songs from the period to prove it. It can get very raucous indeed at weekends, with frequent impromptu karaoke demonstrations. Note that opening times vary at the whim of the master.

Heartland

West Walk Roppongi Hills, 6-10-1 Roppongi, Minato-ku (5772 7660/www.heartland.jp). Roppongi station (Hibiya line, exit A1; (Oedo line), exit 3. **Open** 11am-5am daily. **Credit** AmEx, DC, JCB, MC, V. **Map** p109.

A recent addition to the Roppongi drinking stable, Heartland is a chrome and glass, standing-room-only DJ bar serving the eponymous Heartland beer. It's also a meat market for very expensive meat. There's an open-air courtyard for warm weather.

Maduro

Grand Hyatt Tokyo 4F, 6-10-3 Roppongi, Minato-ku (4333 1234/freephone 0120 588 288/www.grand hyatttokyo.com). Roppongi station (Hibiya line), exit 1C; (Oedo line), exit 3. **Open** 5pm-2am Mon-Thur, Sun; 5pm-3am Fri, Sat. **Credit** AmEx, DC, JCB, MC, V. **Map** p109.

The luxurious bar of the five-star Grand Hyatt Tokyo, Maduro is the place to go once the business deals are sealed. The jet-set clientele won't mind the ¥1,575 seating charge; they come for the spacious lounge setting and superior drinks menus. If you know your Speysides from your Islays and your Krugs from your cavas, this is your spot.

Museum Café

Mori Tower 52F, 6-10-1 Roppongi, Minato-ku (6406 6652/www.tokyocityview.com/en/index.html). Roppongi station (Hibiya line), exit 1C; (Oedo line), exit 3. **Open** 10am-11pm Mon-Thur, Sun; 10am-midnight Fri, Sat. **Credit** AmEx, DC, JCB, MC, V. **Map** p109.

Roppongi Hills' Tokyo City View (*see p110*) is not just the most attractive observation deck in Tokyo, it's also the only one that sells booze (beer and wine only). ¥1,500 gets you up to the 52nd floor, plus entrance to the Mori Art Museum, which resides in the centre. It's not the most atmospheric of bars, but the views are spectacular.

Paddy Foley's Irish Pub

Roi Bldg B1F, 5-5-1 Roppongi, Minato-ku (3423 2250/www.paddyfoleystokyo.com). Roppongi station (Hibiya, Oedo lines), exit 3. **Open** 5pm-1am daily. **Credit** AmEx, MC, V. **Map** p109.

One of Tokyo's first Irish pubs, still offering the best *craic*, despite increasing competition. Guinness, naturally, is the house speciality and the food is good. It can get as crowded as a London pub at weekends, something the locals (who always sit down to drink) regard with mild bemusement.

Seabed

Dear Nishi-Azabu Bldg 3F, 3-1-20 Nishi-Azabu, Minato-ku (5411 5664/www.seabed.jp). Roppongi station (Hibiya, Oedo lines), exit C1. **Open** 9pm-5am Tue-Sat (last orders 4am). **Credit** MC, V. **Map** p109.

An aquatic-themed relaxation salon by day, Tokyo's mellowest bar by night. The fragrance of massage oils linger as the bartenders take over from the therapists at 9pm. You'll find cocktails, as well as Corona, Guinness and other bottled beers. So sink into a massage chair or sofa, relax and imbibe. Don't forget to swap your shoes for slippers at the door.

Shanghai Bar

6-2-31 Roppongi, Minato-ku (5772 7655). Roppongi station (Hibiya, Oedo lines), exit 1. **Open** 11am-4am Mon-Sat; 11am-11pm Sun. **Credit** AmEx, DC, JCB, MC, V. **Map** p109.

Forget the clichéd images of Chinese pagodas and lion statues. The city to which this bar pays tribute with its sleek, polished decor is the Shanghai of the 21st century. House specialities are cocktails and champagne, costing around ¥1,000 per glass, and there's a good menu of Japanese- and Chinese-style dishes. Non-drinkers will be heartened by some inventive, alcohol-free cocktails.

Super-deluxe

B1F, 3-1-25 Nishi-Azabu, Minato-ku (5412 0515/ www.super-deluxe.com). Roppongi station (Hibiya, Oedo lines), exit 1B. **Open** 6pm-2am Mon-Sat. **Credit** V. **Map** p109.

Picked up by *Time* magazine as Asia's best spot for 'avant-garde idling', Super-deluxe is the brainchild of a pair of architects who envisaged the spot as 'a bar, a gallery, a kitchen, a jazz club, a cinema, a library, a school…' and so on. Closer in atmosphere to an artists' salon than a bar, every night offers something different, from slide shows to club nights. If you want to meet the creative cream of Tokyo, this is the place. Also the home of Tokyo Ale – the city's finest microbrew.

These

2F, 2-13-19 Nishi-Azabu, Minato-ku (5466 7331/ www.these-jp.com). Roppongi station (Hibiya, Oedo lines), exit 1. **Open** *Café* noon-5pm Mon-Fri. *Bar* 7pm-4am daily. **Credit** MC, V. **Map** p109.

As much library as bar – and pronounced 'tay-zay' – this strange spot exudes the feel of a British gentlemen's club, but with superior service. The bar has shelves and shelves of magazines and books for browsing, both foreign and Japanese, and a large central room where you are free to chat while indulging in one of the long list of whiskies. Harry Potter fans, watch out for the secret room.

Tokyo Sports Café
7-15-31 Roppongi, Minato-ku (3404 3675/ www.tokyo-sportscafe.com). Roppongi station (Hibiya, Oedo lines), exits 2, 4. **Open** 6pm-6am Mon-Sat (closing time depends on matches). **Credit** DC, JCB, MC, V. **Map** p109.

One of the longest-established and largest sports bars in Tokyo, this place screens all major sporting events from around the world, with space to show two things at once. It offers an extensive range of beers, both domestic and imported, and cocktails. The generous happy hour lasts from 6-8pm daily.

Asakusa

Flamme d'Or
Asahi Super Dry Hall 1F-2F, 1-23-36 Azumabashi, Sumida-ku (5608 5381/www.asahibeer.co.jp/ restaurant/azuma/flamdoll1.html). Asakusa station (Asakusa line) exit A5; (Ginza line), exits 4, 5. **Open** *June-Aug* 11.30am-11pm daily. *Sept-Mar* 11.30am-10pm daily. **Credit** AmEx, MC, V. **Map** p93.

One of Tokyo's quirkier landmarks, the enormous golden object atop Philippe Starck's ultra-modern building across the river from the temples of Asakusa is most often compared with an unknown root vegetable. Or a golden turd. The beer hall inside is also distinctive: oddly shaped pillars, tiny porthole windows high overhead and sweeping curved walls covered in soft grey cushioning. English

menus are available, as is a choice of German-style bar snacks and Asahi draught beers. On the 22nd floor of the building next door is another bar, the Asahi Sky Room, serving beer and soft drinks from 10am to 9pm.

Kamiya Bar
1-1-1 Asakusa, Taito-ku (3841 5400/www.kamiya-bar.com). Asakusa station (Asakusa line), exit A5; (Ginza line), exit 3. **Open** 11.30am-10pm Mon, Wed-Sun. **No credit cards**. **Map** p93.

Established in the late 1800s, Kamiya is the oldest Western-style bar in Tokyo and quintessential Asakusa. The crowds aren't here for the decor (Formica-table coffee shop and too-bright lighting), but the atmosphere – loud, smoky and occasionally raucous – is typical of this working-class neighbourhood. Try the house Denki Bran (Electric Brandy) – not so much for the taste, but for the experience. It imparts amazing hangovers and also makes a dubious souvenir.

Ikebukuro

Bobby's Bar
Milano Bldg 3F, 1-18-10 Nishi-Ikebukuro, Toshima-ku (3980 8875/http://plaza.rakuten.co.jp/bobbysbar). Ikebukuro station (Yamanote, Marunouchi, Yurakucho lines), west exit. **Open** 6pm-empty Mon-Thur, Sun; 6pm-5am Fri, Sat. **No credit cards**. **Map** p119.

A small, foreigner-friendly bar on the west side of Ikebukuro station, offering a fine selection of imported beers with live music most nights. It shares a building with the New Delhi Indian restaurant, which offers good food at reasonable prices, and is a conveniently placed bolthole after a few lagers.

Mother.
See p166.

Elsewhere in central Tokyo

Artist's Café

Tokyo Dome Hotel 43F, 1-3-61 Koraku, Bunkyo-ku (5805 2243/www.tokyodome-hotels.co.jp). Suidobashi station (Chuo line), west exit; (Mita line), exits A3, A4 or Korakuen station (Marunouchi, Nanboku lines), exit 2 or Kasuga station (Mita, Oedo line), exit A1. **Open** 11.30am-11pm daily. **Credit** AmEx, DC, JCB, MC, V.

A pleasant jazz-themed bar and restaurant on the 43rd floor of a swanky hotel. The nice feature is that the two main windows to the left and right of the lift offer totally different views. To the right, you tower over houses and small local businesses, while to the left the monoliths of Shinjuku heave into view.

Shunju

Sanno Park Tower 27F, 2-11-1 Nagatacho, Chiyoda-ku (3592 5288/www.shunju.com/top.html). Tameike-Sanno station (Ginza, Nanboku lines), exit 7. **Open** 11.30am-2.30pm, 5-11pm Mon-Sat. **Credit** AmEx, DC, JCB, MC, V.

From this upmarket whisky and cigar bar high in the Sanno Park Tower you get a good view of the jumbled cityscape towards Shibuya. The illuminated glass wine cellar and shelves of whisky (from ¥1,200 a glass) stand out amid the bar's dark elegance, and you feel a world away from the buzzing chaos 27 floors below. Staff also serve a mean Martini and good seasonal cocktails.

Further afield

A-Sign Bar

3F, 5-32-7 Daizawa, Setagaya-ku (3413 6489). Shimo-Kitazawa station (Keio Inokashira, Odakyu lines), south exit. **Open** 8pm-4am Tue-Sun. **No credit cards.**

The name of this Okinawa-style bar refers to the 'Approved for US Military' signs that appeared outside select drinking holes on the southern Japanese island during its American occupation. An interesting drinks policy means that the per-glass price for spirits gets cheaper if you bulk order. As well as the island's own Orion beer, on offer are 47 types of *awamori* (Okinawan sake, notorious for its strength). Food from the Okinawan restaurant below can be ordered at the bar.

Heaven's Door

Takimoto Bldg 2F, 2-17-10 Kitazawa, Setagaya-ku (3411 6774/http://heavensdoortokyo.fc2web.com). Shimo-Kitazawa station (Keio Inokashira, Odakyu lines), south exit. **Open** 6pm-2am daily. **No credit cards.**

An extremely comfortable bar near Shimo-Kitazawa station run by charismatic Brit expat Paul Davies. Comfy sofas, a Joe Orton-style approach to interior design, a crowd of friendly regulars and a complete absence of food mark this place out. One of the best places in town to watch live football; call ahead to confirm that it's on.

Meguro Tavern

Sunwood Meguro 2F, 1-3-28 Shimo-Meguro, Meguro-ku (3779 0280/www.themegurotavern.com). Meguro station (Yamanote line) west exit; (Mita, Nanboku lines), Chuo exit. **Open** 6pm-1am Mon-Fri; 5pm-1am Sat; noon-11pm Sun. **No credit cards.**

An above-average English pub with a menu designed to reassure expats. The Sunday lunch roast beef and Yorkshire pud is a local institution. One of the best places too for traditional Christmas dinner, if you happen to be in town at the time.

Las Meninas

Plaza Koenji 2F, 3-22-7 Koenji-Kita, Suginami-ku (3338 0266). Koenji station (Chuo line), north exit. **Open** 6pm-late Tue-Sun. **Credit** AmEx, DC, JCB, MC, V.

Johnny the giant Geordie is the unlikely manager of this elegant, spotless tapas bar. Among the myriad late-night drinking spots of Koenji, Las Meninas stands out for both the banter of the big man, and his cooking. A one-time chef, Johnny serves such reliably high-class, home-cooked fare that most customers ignore the menu and simply ask for 'food'. In an area noted for cheap, friendly bars, this is notable on both counts. Cocktail lovers, be advised: it's strictly beer or wine here.

Mother

5-36-14 Daizawa, Setagaya-ku (3421 9519). Shimo-Kitazawa station (Keio Inokashira, Odakyu lines), south exit. **Open** 6pm-2am Mon-Sat; 5pm-2am Sun. **No credit cards.**

The extreme kitsch of this Shimo-Kitazawa bar, which resembles a mix of gingerbread house, treehouse and pub, betrays what it is about a classy establishment. The no-hard-edges interior is difficult to describe, with ceramic mosaic walls dotted with glowing blue 'stone' lights, and faux wood seating. There's a wide selection of bottled beers, as well as a high-quality menu of freshly made Okinawan and Thai dishes. The playlist consists mostly of legends such as Sly and the Family Stone, the Rolling Stones, Bob Dylan and the like, but you can bring your own CDs and staff will play them.

Pierrôt

2-1-8 Kitazawa, Setagaya-ku (090 8042 7014/ http://members.tripod.co.jp/shimokitapierrot/top.htm). Shimo-Kitazawa station (Keio Inokashira, Odakyu lines), south exit. **Open** 8.30pm-late daily. **No credit cards.**

By day a second-hand clothes shop, at 8pm the racks are wheeled away and this shack at the bottom of the main shopping street in Shimo-Kitazawa turns into an open-air bar. Tokyo needs far more al fresco watering holes like this in summer, but in winter Pierrôt is rather left out in the cold. Still, it's worth stopping by any time of the year for the almost always excellent free live music. In winter, warm cocktails are on offer, as well as the usual range of beers. The coffee is best avoided. There's no toilet, but customers can use the 'Toilet Express' bike to speed themselves to the nearest convenience.

Coffee Shops

Tokyo's multifaceted refuelling stops.

The Japanese love their caffeine. The country is the world's third-biggest importer of coffee and its love affair with the noble bean stretches back to the 19th century. Forget for a moment Tokyo's mushrooming number of franchise outlets offering a Seattle-style quick caffeine fix. Long before Starbucks landed in 1996, the capital already boasted a vast profusion of coffee shops (*kissaten*), with wood-panelled traditionalists and cosy, family-run operations jostling for attention alongside grand cafés and an eclectic mix of strange specialists.

Café society has bowed to the winds of change in Tokyo since the city's first coffee shop opened in Ueno back in 1888. That was during the Meji Restoration when all things Western were embraced with enthusiasm. Later, jazz cafés came to prominence, while the past decade has seen – along with the arrival of the big multinationals – the emergence of 24-hour *manga kissaten* offering comic books, online access and a convenient place to crash for night owls awaiting the first morning train.

For those running stand-alone operations in Tokyo, fierce competition from well-heeled chain operators and the effects of the endless recession can mean a continuing struggle just to survive. Even so, the *kissaten* remains an essential part of daily life, and many independents continue to hold out against the odds: in an era of globalisation, they retain their own unique characters and styles. Of the numerous chains, look out for Excelsior Caffe, a smart offshoot of local market leader Doutor.

Expense is always a consideration in Tokyo. The price of a cup of coffee in a non-franchise *kissaten* may average ¥500-¥600, but you're free to sit all day on some of the world's most expensive real estate. With the city rushing by outside, pleasant surroundings, constantly replenished iced water and unlimited sitting time, the price of that single cup soon seems to be a bargain.

Ginza

Benisica

1-6-8 Yurakucho, Chiyoda-ku (3502 0848). Hibiya station (Chiyoda, Hibiya, Mita lines), exit A4. **Open** 9.30am-11pm daily. **No credit cards. Map** p60.
The traditional neighbourhood café is realised in ideal form just across the railway tracks from Ginza, with an extensive selection of meal-and-cake sets to

boot. Benisica claims to be the original inventor of 'pizza toast', a near cousin of Welsh rabbit now featured on coffee shop menus all over Japan.

Le Café Doutor Ginza

San'ai Bldg 1F, 5-7-2 Ginza, Chuo-ku (5537 8959). Ginza station (Ginza, Hibiya, Marunouchi lines), exits A1, A3. **Open** 7.30am-11pm Mon-Fri; 8am-11pm Sat; 8am-10pm Sun. **No credit cards. Map** p60.
A one-off upmarket branch of the cheap 'n' cheerful chain that proliferated across Tokyo during the recession-hit 1990s. Located on one of the city's most famous intersections, at Ginza 4-chome crossing, its drinks and sandwiches move beyond the standard Doutor fare. Outside tables (an unusual feature) and the highly prized upstairs window seats provide perfect places for watching the bustling crowds and checking out the famous Wako clock tower across the street.
Other locations: throughout the city.

Café Fontana

Abe Bldg B1, 5-5-9 Ginza, Chuo-ku (3572 7320). Ginza station (Ginza, Hibiya, Marunouchi lines), exits B3, B5. **Open** noon-midnight Mon-Fri; 2-11pm Sat; 2-9pm Sun. **No credit cards. Map** p60.
A typically genteel Ginza basement establishment, but one where the individually served apple pies come in distinctly non-dainty proportions. Each steaming specimen contains a whole fruit, thinly covered in pastry, then doused thoroughly in cream.

Café Paulista

Nagasaki Centre, 8-9-16 Ginza, Chuo-ku (3572 6160/www.paulista.co.jp). Ginza station (Ginza, Hibiya, Marunouchi lines), exits A3, A4, A5. **Open** 8.30am-10pm Mon-Sat; noon-8pm Sun. **No credit cards. Map** p60.
This Brazil-themed, veteran Ginza establishment was founded back in 1914. The all-natural beans are imported directly from Brazil, keeping blend coffee prices down to ¥498, a bargain for the area. Low leather seats, plants and wall engravings catch the eye amid a general brown and green motif.

Ki No Hana

4-13-1 Ginza, Chuo-ku (3543 5280). Higashi-Ginza station (Asakusa, Hibiya lines), exit 5. **Open** 10am-8pm Mon-Fri. **No credit cards. Map** p60.
The pair of signed John Lennon cartoons on the walls is the legacy of a chance visit by the former Beatle one afternoon in 1978. With its peaceful atmosphere, tasteful floral decorations, herbal teas and lunchtime vegetarian curries, it isn't too difficult to understand Lennon's appreciation of the place. Apparently, the overawed son of the former

Eat, Drink, Shop

For a taste of island life: **Saboru**.

for canned coffee dispensed from vending machines, but it's difficult to argue with the price (¥120). While the surroundings are less spacious than the former premises across the street, internet access and magazines are still available.

Mironga
1-3 Kanda-Jinbocho, Chiyoda-ku (3295 1716).
Jinbocho station (Hanzomon, Mita, Shinjuku lines),
exit A7. **Open** 10.30am-11pm Mon-Fri; 11.30am-7pm
Sat, Sun. **No credit cards. Map** p66.
Probably the only place in Tokyo where non-stop (recorded) tango provides seductive old-style accompaniment to the liquid refreshments. Argentina's finest exponents feature in the impressive array of fading monochromes on the walls, and there's also a selection of printed works on related subjects lining the bookshelves. Of the two rooms, the larger and darker gets the nod for atmosphere. As well as a wide range of coffees, Mironga proffers a good selection of imported beers and reasonable food.

Saboru
1-11 Kanda-Jinbocho, Chiyoda-ku (3291 8404).
Jinbocho station (Hanzomon, Mita, Shinjuku lines),
exit A7. **Open** 9am-11pm daily. **No credit cards.**
Map p66.
Wooden masks on the walls, tree pillars rising to the ceiling and a menu that features banana juice all lend a South Sea island air to this cosy, triple-level establishment squeezed into a brick building reverting to jungle on a Jinbocho backstreet. It's cheap too, with blend coffee a snip at ¥400. Next door is the less extravagantly furnished sequel, Saboru 2 (3291 8404).

Shinjuku

Ben's Café
1-29-21 Takadanobaba, Shinjuku-ku (3202 2445/
www.benscafe.com/en). Takadanobaba station
(Yamanote line), Waseda exit; (Tozai line), exit 3.
Open 11.30am-11.30pm Mon-Thur, Sun; 11.30am-
12.30am Fri, Sat. **No credit cards.**
A New York-style café famed locally for its cakes, bagels and easygoing ambience, Ben's also hosts occasional art shows, comedy evenings and weekend poetry readings. The friendly staff speak English and the coffee is great.

Bon
Toriichi Bldg B1, 3-23-1 Shinjuku, Shinjuku-ku
(3341 0179). Shinjuku station (Yamanote, Chuo,
Sobu lines), east exit; (Marunouchi line), exit A5;
(Oedo, Shinjuku lines), exit 1. **Open** 12.30-11.30pm
daily. **No credit cards. Map** p73.
The search for true coffee excellence is pursued with surprising vigour at this pricey but popular Shinjuku basement. The cheapest choice from the menu will set you back a cool ¥1,000, but at least the cups will be bone china – selected from an enormous collection. Special tasting events are held periodically for connoisseurs.

owner also preserved the great man's full ashtray, including butts. Alas, he kept this as a personal memento, so it isn't on display.

Marunouchi

Marunouchi Café
Shin Tokyo Bldg 1F, 3-3-1 Marunouchi, Chiyoda-ku
(3212 5025/www.marunouchicafe.com). Yurakucho
station (Yamanote line), Tokyo International Forum
exit; (Yurakucho line), exit A1 or Nijubashimae
station (Chiyoda line), exit B7. **Open** 8am-9pm Mon-
Fri; 11am-8pm Sat, Sun. **No credit cards. Map** p66.
If the Japanese coffee shop is essentially a place to hang out, this popular innovator could be a glimpse of a new, low-cost future. Connoisseurs may not care

Danwashitsu Takizawa

*B1, 3-36-12 Shinjuku, Shinjuku-ku (3356 5661).
Shinjuku station (Yamanote, Chuo, Sobu lines),
east exit; (Marunouchi line), exit A5; (Oedo,
Shinjuku lines), exit 1.* **Open** 9am-9.50pm Mon-
Sat; 9am-9.30pm Sun. **No credit cards.**
Map p73.

Another spot where you can experience the perverse
pleasure of blowing ¥1,000 on a single cup of coffee.
Artfully simple yet completely comfortable, it's the
kind of place you could stay all day: water trickles
over rocks, creating a vaguely Zen-like sense of
tranquillity, and staff bow with quite extraordinary
politeness. Once you've paid the bill, you'll get a
discount ticket for your next visit.

GeraGera

*B1& B2, 3-17-4 Shinjuku, Shinjuku-ku (3350 5692/
www.geragera.co.jp). Shinjuku station (Yamanote,
Chuo, Sobu lines), east exit; (Marunouchi line), exit
A5; (Oedo, Shinjuku lines), exit 1.* **Open** 24hrs daily.
No credit cards. Map p73.

Manga coffee shops spread rapidly after emerging
in the mid 1990s with a winning formula of coffee
and Japanese comic books. More recently, computer
games and internet access have been added as regular features. This branch of one of the main chains
has 250 seats, with facilities available at ¥200 per
30 minutes or ¥880 for three hours (or five hours
between 10pm and 6am). Self-service hot and cold
drinks cost ¥180.
Other locations: throughout the city.

New Dug

*B1, 3-15-12 Shinjuku, Shinjuku-ku (3341 9339/
www.dug.co.jp). Shinjuku station (Yamanote, Chuo,
Sobu lines), east exit; (Marunouchi line), exit B10;
(Oedo, Shinjuku lines), exit 1.* **Open** noon-2am
Mon-Sat; noon-midnight Sun (bar from 6.30pm).
Credit AmEx, DC, JCB, MC, V. **Map** p73.

Way back in the 1960s and early '70s, Shinjuku was
sprinkled with jazz coffee shops. Celebrated names
of that bygone era included Dug, an establishment
whose present-day incarnation is a cramped brick-
lined basement on Yasukuni Dori. Everything about
the place speaks serious jazz credentials, with carefully crafted authenticity and assorted memorabilia.
A basement bar annexe below the nearby KFC is
used for live performances.

Tajimaya

*1-2-6 Nishi-Shinjuku, Shinjuku-ku (3342 0881/
www.shinjuku.or.jp/tajimaya). Shinjuku station
(Yamanote, Chuo, Sobu lines), west exit;
(Marunouchi line), exit A17; (Oedo, Shinjuku
lines), exit 3.* **Open** 10am-11pm daily. **No credit
cards. Map** p73.

Caught between the early post-war grunge of its
immediate neighbours and the skyscraper bustle of
the rest of west Shinjuku, Tajimaya responds with
abundant bone china, coffees from all over the
world, non-fetishist use of classical music, and milk
in the best copperware. Scones on the menu and the
unusual selection of ornaments provide further

evidence of advanced sensibilities, but the deeply
yellowed walls and battered wood suggest a struggle to keep up appearances.

Shibuya

Coffee 3.4 Sunsea

*Takano Bldg 1F, 10-2 Udagawacho, Shibuya-ku
(3496 2295/www.coffee-sunsea.com). Shibuya station
(Yamanote, Ginza, Hanzomon lines), Hachiko exit.*
Open noon-11pm Tue-Sat; noon-midnight Sun.
No credit cards. Map p79.

Kathmandu hippie chic and postmodern Shibuya
cool meet in this laid-back retreat, with classical
Indian sitar and tabla on soundtrack. Cushion-
strewn sofas, ethnic wood carvings and a large tank
of hypnotic tropical fish all add to the dreamy effect.
Self-indulgent sensory overload is guaranteed from
the sensational coffee float. It's somehow in keeping
with the mood of the place that the owners don't
have fixed days off; they close whenever they feel
like it, so call ahead before you visit.

Lion

*2-19-13 Dogenzaka, Shibuya-ku (3461 6858/
http://lion.main.jp). Shibuya station (Yamanote,
Ginza, Hanzomon lines), Hachiko exit.* **Open** 11am-
10.30pm daily. **No credit cards. Map** p79.

There's a church-like air of reverence at this sleepy
shrine to classical music. A pamphlet listing stereo-
phonic offerings is laid out before the customer,
seating is in pew-style rows facing an enormous
pair of speakers, and conversations are discouraged. If you must talk, then do so in whispers. The
imposing grey building is an unexpected period
piece amid the gaudy love hotels of Dogenzaka.

Satei Hato

*1-15-19 Shibuya, Shibuya-ku (3400 9088). Shibuya
station (Yamanote line), east exit; (Ginza line),
Toyoko exit; (Hanzomon line), exit 9.* **Open** 11am-
11.30pm daily. **No credit cards. Map** p79.

Step through the marble-tiled entrance and into top-
grade *kissaten* territory of a traditionalist bent. A
huge collection of china cups stands behind the
counter, while sweeping arrangements of seasonal
blooms add colour to a dark wood interior that
recalls an earlier age. The most expensive coffee on
the menu is Blue Mountain at ¥1,000.

Harujuku & Aoyama

Daibo

*2F, 3-13-20 Minami-Aoyama, Minato-ku (3403
7155). Omotesando station (Chiyoda, Ginza,
Hanzomon lines), exits A3, A4.* **Open** 9am-10pm
Mon-Sat; noon-8pm Sun. **No credit cards.**
Map p85.

The biggest treat at this cosy, wood-bedecked outpost is the excellent milk coffee, which comes lov-
ingly hand-dripped into large pottery bowls. Even
the regular blend coffee reveals a true craftsman's
pride and comes in four separate varieties. There's

just one long wooden counter plus a couple of tables, but the restrained decoration and low-volume jazz soundtrack combine to soothing and restful effect.

Volontaire
2F, 6-29-6 Jingumae, Shibuya-ku (3400 8629). Meiji-Jingumae station (Chiyoda line), exit 4. **Open** noon-7pm (bar 7pm-midnight) Mon-Sat. **No credit cards. Map** p85.
A hole-in-the-wall, old-style coffee and jazz joint handily placed near Omotesando crossing. There's only a single counter for seating, but the area behind the bar bulges with old vinyl. It switches to bar mode in the evening, with a hefty cover charge.

Roppongi

Almond Roppongi
6-1-26 Roppongi, Minato-ku (3402 1870/ www.roppongi-almond.jp). Roppongi station (Hibiya, Oedo lines), exit 3. **Open** 9am-5am Mon-Sat; 10am-3pm Sun. **No credit cards. Map** p109.
A pink-hued landmark at the main Roppongi intersection that has provided an instantly recognisable meeting spot for generations of revellers, and is possibly the single best-known coffee shop in Tokyo. Relatively few venture inside, however, where the coffee and cakes are pretty standard fare – it's part of a unremarkable coffee shop chain.
Other locations: throughout the city.

Asakusa

Angelus
1-17-6 Asakusa, Taito-ku (3841 2208). Asakusa station (Asakusa, Ginza lines), exits 1, 3. **Open** 10am-9.30pm Tue-Sun. **No credit cards. Map** p93.
Perhaps, at some point in the distant past, this was the way local upmarket operations got to grips with handling new-fangled foreign delicacies. Out front is a smart counter selling a fancy selection of Western-style cakes; further inside, the coffee shop section is a more spartan affair of plain walls and dark wood trimmings.

ef
2-19-18 Kaminarimon, Taito-ku (3841 0114/ gallery 3841 0442/www.gallery-ef.com). Asakusa station (Asakusa line, exit A5; (Ginza line), exit 2. **Open** 11am-7pm (café & gallery), 6pm-midnight (bar) Mon, Wed, Thur, Sat; 11am-2am Fri; 11am-10pm Sun. **No credit cards. Map** p93.
This retro-fitted hangout is a welcome attempt to inject a little Harajuku-style cool into musty Asakusa, but among its own more surprising attractions is a small art gallery (*see p225*) converted from a 130-year-old warehouse. Duck through the low entrance at the back and suddenly you're out of 1950s Americana and into *tatami* territory, with admittance to the main exhibits up a steep set of traditional wooden steps. A place to try when you're tired of the local temples.

Ueno

Miro
2-4-6 Kanda-Surugadai, Chiyoda-ku (3291 3088). Ochanomizu station (Chuo, Sobu lines), Ochanomizu exit; (Marunouchi line), exit 2. **Open** 9am-11pm Mon-Sat. **No credit cards.**
Named after Catalan surrealist Joan Miró, several of whose works adorn the walls. Both ambience and decor appear untouched by the passing decades. The location is pretty well hidden, down a tiny alley opposite Ochanomizu station.

Further afield

Café Bach
1-23-9 Nihonzutsumi, Taito-ku (3875 2669/ www.bach-kaffee.co.jp.). Minami-Senju station (Hibiya line), south exit. **Open** 8.30am-9pm Mon-Thur, Sat, Sun. **No credit cards.**
All the beans are roasted on the premises of this dedicated *shitamachi* coffee specialist in suburban Minami-Senju in northern Tokyo. Café Bach supplied the coffee for the G8 summit in Okinawa in 2000, a meeting that is commemorated on the Japanese ¥2,000 note.

Classic
5-66-9 Nakano, Nakano-ku (3387 0571). Nakano station (Chuo, Tozai lines), north exit. **Open** noon-9.30pm Tue-Sun. **No credit cards.**
This ramshackle relic of eccentricity in Nakano (just outside the Yamanote line loop) is a creaky one-off that's withstood the passage of time since 1930. Classical music drifts eerily over the sound system as the ill-lit Gothic gloom slowly reveals strangely sloping floors, ancient leather chairs and long-deceased and undusted clocks. The paintings that adorn the walls are all by the shop's original (now dead) owner. Tickets for coffee, tea or juice cost ¥400 and are purchased at the entrance.

Jazz Coffee Masako
2-20-2 Kitazawa, Setagaya-ku (3410 7994). Shimo-Kitazawa station (Keio Inokashira, Odakyu lines), south exit. **Open** 11.30am-11pm daily. **No credit cards.**
This Shimo-Kitazawa spot has a really homely feel, in addition to all the jazz coffee shop essentials such as an excellent sound system, an enormous stack of records and CDs behind the counter, and walls and low ceiling painted black and plastered in posters and pictures. The noticeboard at the flower-filled entrance proudly announces newly obtained recordings; inside, there are bookcases and sofas among the well-lived-in furnishings.

Mignon
2F, 4-31-3 Ogikubo, Suginami-ku (3398 1758/ http://members.jcom.home.ne.jp/stmera/mignon). Ogikubo station (Chuo line), south exit; (Marunouchi line), exit 2. **Open** 11am-10pm Mon-Tue, Thur-Sat; 11am-7pm Sun. **No credit cards.**

Classical music is the name of the game here, with an awesome collection of vinyl lining the shelves behind the counter. There's just one room, plus a small side gallery of pottery items, but it's comfortable and doesn't feel cramped.

Pow Wow

2-7 Kagurazaka, Shinjuku-ku (3267 8324). Iidabashi station (Chuo, Sobu lines), west exit; (Oedo, Namboku, Tozai, Yurakucho lines), exit B3.

Open 10.30am-10.30pm Mon-Sat; 12.30-7pm Sun. **No credit cards**.

Heavy on the old-fashioned virtues of dark wood and tastefully chosen pottery, this spacious traditionalist near the British Council features an extraordinary coffee-brewing performance in its narrow counter section, where large glass flasks bubble merrily away over tiny glass candles in the manner of some mysterious chemistry experiment. There's also an upstairs gallery space.

Tea time

Tea usually comes a poor second to coffee at standard *kissaten*. Recently, however, new chain operators such as **Ony** (www.ony.jp) and **Koots** (www.koots.co.jp) have targeted a fashionable female market with health-conscious menus based on green tea, including strange hybrids such as *matcha* latte. Meanwhile, older specialist shops continue to serve up a wide variety of Japanese, Chinese and English-style teas. Those in search of a tea ceremony experience may wish to try one of the larger hotels.

Hua Tai Tea (Hua Tai Cha So)

3F, 1-18-6 Dogenzaka, Shibuya-ku (5728 2551/www.chinatea.co.jp). Shibuya station (Yamanote, Ginza, Hanzomon lines), Hachiko exit. **Open** 10.30am-8pm daily. **Credit** DC, MC, V. **Map** p79.

Upstairs from the Chinese tea and assorted utensils sold on the first two floors is a room where Taiwanese teas and snacks are served. Pour from the pot into the taller cup and savour the aroma, then decant again for drinking. Virtually unlimited pot refills from the huge kettle boiling away on the table.

Mariage Frères

2F & 3F, 5-6-6 Ginza, Chuo-ku (3572 1854/www.mariagefreres.co.jp). Ginza station (Ginza, Hibiya, Marunouchi lines), exit A1. **Open** 11.30am-8pm daily. **Credit** AmEx, DC, JCB, MC, V. **Map** p60.

The oddly colonial atmosphere is heightened by linen-clad waiters and wicker chairs. There are literally hundreds of different teas on the menu, from Russian to Earl Grey (from ¥850). The tea rooms are upstairs from a street-level shop that sells tea and related paraphernalia.

Uogashi Meicha

2F & 3F, 5-5-6 Ginza, Chuo-ku (3571 1211/www.uogashi-meicha.co.jp/shop_01.html). Ginza station (Ginza, Hibiya, Marunouchi lines), exit B3. **Open** 11am-7pm Tue-Sun. **No credit cards**. **Map** p60.

Collect a ¥500 ticket at the counter downstairs, for servings of either *sencha* (green leaf tea) on the second floor or *matcha* (powdered green tea, as used in the tea ceremony) on the third. Furnishings are minimalist, with bench seating along the walls. The third floor is recommended for its semi-outdoor feel.

Shops & Services

Hey, big spender.

Welcome to shopping nirvana. Years of recession seem to have had little impact on consumer spending in Tokyo – if the crowded shops and streets of Ginza, Shibuya, Shinjuku, Omotesando, Ikebukuro and other retail centres are anything to go by. You'll find an extraordinary range of shops and products, from ritzy department stores and high-end international designer flagships to multi-storey electronics emporiums and tiny outlets specialising in traditional crafts.

Long a city with luxury tastes, Tokyo has experienced an incredible change in shopping habits since the end of the Bubble era. Hundred-yen shops (where toiletries, household goods, toys and the like cost ¥100) proliferated, as did 'pile 'em high, sell 'em cheap' chain **Don Quixote** (*see p192*). Budget clothing brand **Uniqlo** (*see p182*) has exploded in the past five years, and second-hand shops have become more popular (just look for the word 'recycle') – in a nation that has never previously taken to the idea of used goods. Yet none of this has affected the popularity of the top brands, whose fortunes have soared in parallel with the bargain-shopping boom.

OPENING HOURS, SALES AND TAX

Shops usually open at 10am or sometimes 11am, and close at 8pm or occasionally 9pm daily. Smaller shops may close for one day, usually Monday or Wednesday. Sunday trading is the norm as the day has no religious significance in Japan – in fact, it's one of the busiest shopping days. Department stores do have the occasional day off; look for large notices inside the store announcing which day (if any) they are closed that month.

Most shops (except the traditional, craft-oriented shops) are open on national holidays – but if you're heading for a specific place, it's wise to call ahead before you go. Christmas is not a holiday in Japan; 25 December is a normal working day with ordinary office hours. What's more, the Christmas decorations come down on the stroke of midnight on the 24th, to make space for the more traditional New Year celebrations – a practice that can be bemusing for foreign visitors. Sales are held seasonally – with the biggest at New Year and around the beginning of July.

Prices include a consumption tax of five per cent, which is levied on all goods and services. For information on tax refunds, *see p174* **Duty-free goods**.

One-stop shopping

Department stores

All Japanese *depato* share certain basic features. Food halls (*depa-chika*) – hectic places featuring branches of internationally famous pâtisseries, confectioners and delis – are always in the basement, along with some restaurants and cafés. The first two or so floors sell women's clothing and accessories, with menswear beginning on the third floor (or higher). The top levels include restaurants (*depa-res*) that stay open at night after the main store has closed, and many of the rooftops are used as beer gardens in the summer. Most *depato* have Japanese craft and souvenir sections, and some offer worldwide delivery services. Almost all stores offer a tax-exemption service for purchases (mainly clothing, kitchenware and electrical goods) that total over ¥10,000 – you'll need your passport. Floor guides in English are available at the information desk.

Daimaru

1-9-1 Marunouchi, Chiyoda-ku (3212 8011/ www.daimaru.co.jp/english/tokyo.html). Tokyo station (Yamanote, Chuo lines), Yaesu central exit; (Marunouchi line), exits 1, 2. **Open** 10am-9pm Mon-Fri; 10am-8pm Sat, Sun. **Credit** AmEx, DC, JCB, MC, V. **Map** p66.

Conveniently located inside Tokyo railway station. The first six floors are devoted to fashion and accessories, Japanese souvenirs on the seventh and tenth, restaurants on the eighth, and the Daimaru Museum on the 12th. 'Gochiso Paradise', on floor B1 by the Yaesu central exit, contains Japanese confectionery shop Shirotae, and Kihachi, a hugely popular cake outlet. The currency exchange and tax exemption counters are on the seventh floor. A shipping service is also available.

Isetan

3-14-1 Shinjuku, Shinjuku-ku (3352 1111/ www.isetan.co.jp/iclub). Shinjuku-Sanchome station (Marunouchi, Shinjuku lines), exits B3, B4, B5 or Shinjuku station (Yamanote, Chuo lines), east exit; (Oedo line), exit 1. **Open** 10am-8pm daily. **Credit** AmEx, DC, JCB, MC, V. **Map** p73.

This mammoth Shinjuku enterprise is split into eight buildings very close to one another, the most noteworthy being the Main Building and the Men's Building. The overseas shipping service is in the basement of the Main Building, and the tax exemption counter is on the eighth floor of the Annex Building. BPQC – an eclectic selection of Japanese and foreign concession shops selling cosmetics, perfumes, CDs and household goods – is on the B2 floor of the Main Building. Isetan also runs the I-Club, a free service for foreign residents in Japan; ask for membership details at the foreign customer desk on the eighth floor of the Men's Building. The club's monthly newsletter contains news of sales, discounts and special promotions, plus details of the Clover clothing range, available in larger sizes than standard Japanese ones.
Other locations: 1-11-5 Kichijoji Honcho, Musashino-shi (0422 211 111).

Keio

1-1-4 Nishi-Shinjuku, Shinjuku-ku (3342 2111/ www.keionet.com). Shinjuku station (Yamanote line), west exit; (Marunouchi line), exits A12, A13, A14; (Oedo, Shinjuku lines), exit 3. **Open** 10am-8pm daily. **Credit** AmEx, DC, JCB, MC, V. **Map** p73.

Shops

For the traditional department store experience
Mitsukoshi in Ginza. *See right.*

For a vision of the future of shopping
Roppongi Hills. *See p176.*

For an overdose of cuteness
Kiddyland. *See p193.*

For keeping up with the teenage fashion queens
109. *See p180.*

For gimmicks and gadgets
Laox: Duty Free Akihabara. *See p179.*

For cheap reads in English
Good Day Books. *See p177.*

For a taste of home
National Azabu. *See p187.*

For one-stop souvenir shopping
Oriental Bazaar. *See p190.*

For all those things you never knew you didn't need
Tokyu Hands. *See p192.*

Situated next to Odakyu (*see p174*) and with entrances leading directly from Shinjuku station, Keio has womenswear and accessories on the first four floors, menswear on the fifth, kimono, jewellery and furniture on the sixth, children's clothes and sporting goods on the seventh, and office supplies on the eighth. The Lilac range of clothing is available in Westerner-friendly larger sizes. The tax exemption counter is on the sixth floor.
Other locations: Keio Seiseki-Sakuragaoka, 1-10-1 Sekido, Tama-shi (042 337 2111).

Matsuya

3-6-1 Ginza, Chuo-ku (3567 1211/www.matsuya. com). Ginza station (Ginza, Hibiya, Marunouchi lines), exits A12, A13. **Open** 10am-8pm daily. **Credit** AmEx, DC, JCB, MC, V. **Map** p60.
Clothing at Matsuya includes menswear and womenswear by Issey Miyake on the third floor. Traditional Japanese souvenirs are on the seventh, with shopping services for foreigners – tax exemption and overseas delivery – can be found on the third floor. The money exchange counter is on the first floor.
Other locations: 1-4-1 Hanakawato, Taito-ku (3842 1111).

Matsuzakaya

10-1 Ginza, Chuo-ku (3572 1111/www.matsuzakaya. co.jp/ginza/index.shtml). Ginza station (Ginza, Hibiya, Marunouchi lines), exits A1-A4. **Open** 10.30am-7.30pm Mon-Wed; 10.30am-8pm Thur-Sat; 10.30am-7pm Sun. **Credit** AmEx, DC, JCB, MC, V. **Map** p60.
The main branch of Matsuzakaya is actually in Ueno, but foreign visitors are usually more familiar with this branch, located on Ginza's main drag near Mitsukoshi and Matsuya. The tax exemption and currency exchange counters are on the basement second floor, and kimono are sold on the sixth. The annex contains a beauty salon, art gallery and even a ladies' deportment school.
Other locations: 3-29-5 Ueno, Taito-ku (3832 1111).

Mitsukoshi

4-6-16 Ginza, Chuo-ku (3562 1111/www.mitsukoshi. co.jp). Ginza station (Ginza, Hibiya, Marunouchi lines), exits A7, A8, A11. **Open** 10am-7.30pm daily. **Credit** AmEx, DC, JCB, MC, V. **Map** p60.
The oldest surviving department store chain in Japan (founded 1673), Mitsukoshi's flagship store is in Nihonbashi. This Ginza outlet (opposite Wako) has womenswear and accessories on the first five floors, menswear on the sixth, and household goods on the seventh. The B3 floor has toys, childrenswear and the tax exemption counter. Note that the bronze lion outside Mitsukoshi's main entrance is a popular meeting place.
Other locations: 1-4-1 Muromachi, Nihonbashi, Chuo-ku (3354 1111); 1-5-7 Higashi-Ikebukuro, Toshima-ku (3987 1111); 4-20-7 Ebisu, Shibuya-ku (5423 1111); 1-19-1 Honcho, Kichijoji, Musashino-shi (0422 29 1111).

Eat, Drink, Shop

My City

*3-38-1 Shinjuku, Shinjuku-ku (5269 1111/
www.e-mycity.co.jp). Shinjuku station (Yamanote,
Chuo lines), east exit; (Marunouchi line), exit A9;
(Oedo, Shinjuku lines), exit 1.* **Open** 10.30am-9.30pm
daily. **Credit** AmEx, DC, JCB, MC, V. **Map** p73.
Situated above the east exit of Shinjuku station, My
City is chiefly notable for the Shunkan gourmet
restaurant area, created by celebrated designer
Sugimoto Takashi, on the seventh and eighth floors.
The lower floors have also been revamped recently
to move the image upmarket.

Odakyu

*1-1-3 Nishi-Shinjuku, Shinjuku-ku (3342 1111/
www.odakyu-dept.co.jp). Shinjuku station (Yamanote,
Chuo lines), west exit; (Marunouchi line), exits A12-
A14; (Oedo, Shinjuku lines), exit 3.* **Open** 10am-8pm
daily. **Credit** AmEx, DC, JCB, MC, V. **Map** p73.
Odakyu is split into two buildings, the Main
Building and the Annex (Halc) Building, which are
connected by an elevated walkway and underground passageways. The Main Building has
women's clothing on the first five floors, kimono on
the sixth and furniture on the eighth, while the Halc
offers menswear, sportswear, four floors of the electronics retailer Bic Camera and a Troisgros deli-
catessen in the basement food hall. The top three
floors of the Main Building contain restaurants; the
fifth holds the tax exemption counter.

Seibu

*21-1 Udagawa-cho, Shibuya-ku (3462 0111/
www.seibu.co.jp). Shibuya station (Yamanote, Ginza
lines), Hachiko exit; (Hanzomon line), exits 6, 7.*
Open 10am-8pm Mon-Wed, Sun; 10am-9pm Thur-
Sat. **Credit** AmEx, DC, JCB, MC, V. **Map** p79.
The Shibuya main store is split into two buildings,
Annexes A and B, which face each other across the
street. Annex A sells mainly womenswear; Annex
B menswear, children's clothes and accessories. The
tax exemption counter is on the M2 (mezzanine) floor
of Annex A. Seibu also runs retailers Loft and
Movida, both of which are within easy walking dis-
tance of the Shibuya store. Aimed at 18-35s, Loft
sells household and beauty products, while Movida
contains a number of designer boutiques.
Other locations: 1-28-1 Minami-Ikebukuro,
Toshima-ku (3981 0111); 2-5-1 Yurakucho, Chiyoda-
ku (3286 0111); Shinjuku Loft, 4F-6F Mitsukoshi
Bldg, 3-29-1 Shinjuku, Shinjuku-ku (5360 6210).

Takashimaya

*2-4-1 Nihonbashi, Chuo-ku (3211 4111/
www.takashimaya.co.jp). Nihonbashi station
(Asakusa line), exit D3; (Ginza, Tozai lines),
exits B1, B2.* **Open** 10am-8pm daily. **Credit**
AmEx, DC, JCB, MC, V. **Map** p66.
The Nihonbashi branch of Takashimaya has based
much of its interior style on Harrods of London.
Menswear is on the first and second floors, womenswear on the third and fourth, children's clothes on
the fifth, furniture on the sixth and kimono on the
seventh. The tax exemption counter is on the first

floor and the overseas shipping service on floor B1.
The massive Shinjuku branch – Takashimaya
Times Square – contains a host of boutiques and
restaurants, a branch of hardware shop Tokyu
Hands, Kinokuniya International Bookshop in the
annex building and the Times Square Theatre on
the 12th floor.
Other locations: Takashimaya Times Square,
5-24-2 Sendagaya, Shibuya-ku (5361 1111).

Duty-free goods

Foreign visitors can reclaim the five per
cent sales tax at shops that have duty-free
counters. These include most department
stores and many electrical goods shops
in Akihabara (*see p181* **Electric Town**).
Exempted items include food, beverages,
tobacco, pharmaceuticals, cosmetics,
film and batteries. To qualify, your total
purchases must cost more than ¥10,000,
and your passport must show that you
have been in Japan for less than six
months. Take the paid-for goods and
receipts to the store's tax-refund counter,
along with your passport; the refund will
be paid on the spot. When you leave
Japan, make sure you have your purchases
with you (preferably in your carry-on bag –
Customs may ask you to show them).

Wako, in the heart of Ginza.

Tobu

1-1-25 Nishi-Ikebukuro, Toshima-ku (3981 2211/ www.tobu-dept.jp). Ikebukuro station (Yamanote line), west exit; (Marunouchi, Yurakucho lines), exits 4, 6. **Open** 10am-8pm daily. **Credit** AmEx, DC, JCB, MC, V. **Map** p119.

The Main Building houses clothing for all occasions on the lower floors (including kimono on the ninth), with an enormous selection of restaurants from the 11th to 17th floors. The Central Building sells clothing in larger sizes, plus a good range of interior goods and office supplies. The Plaza Building contains the designer collection. The currency exchange and tax exemption counters are on the basement first floor of the Central Building.

Tokyu Honten

2-24-1 Dogenzaka, Shibuya-ku (3477 3111/ www.tokyu-dept.co.jp/honten). Shibuya station (Yamanote, Ginza lines), Hachiko exit; (Hanzomon line), exits 3, 3A. **Open** 11am-7pm daily. *Tokyu Food Show (B1F)* 11am-8pm daily. **Credit** AmEx, DC, JCB, MC, V. **Map** p79.

Tokyu Honten sells designer fashions for men and women and interior goods for the home. The Tokyu Toyoko store is situated directly above Shibuya JR station. The gourmet food hall in the basement holds branches of the extremely popular delis Seijo Ishii and Dean & DeLuca. The Tokyu Plaza store, behind Shibuya station, sells women's fashion, cosmetics and accessories, and has a CD shop and a branch of the Kinokuniya bookshop (but it does not sell books in English). All the stores are close to one another. **Other locations**: 2-3-1 Honcho, Kichijoji, Musashino-shi (0422 21 5111).

Wako

4-5-11 Ginza, Chuo-ku (3562 2111/www.wako. co.jp). Ginza station (Ginza, Hibiya, Marunouchi lines), exits A9, A10, B1. **Open** 10.30am-6pm Mon-Sat. **Credit** AmEx, DC, JCB, MC, V. **Map** p60.

The most famous department store in Japan, located on the corner of Ginza 4-chome. The building's grand exterior – with its landmark clock tower – is matched only by the hushed ambience of the interior. As well as fine jewellery, it sells designer apparel and accessories.

Other locations: 5-6-6 Hiro, Shibuya-ku (3473 0200).

Shopping malls

'Mall' is an inadequate description for the new shopping sites that have sprung up in the metropolis. They are theme parks of conspicuous consumption, with breathtaking exteriors designed by internationally renowned architects. The centrepiece of the new movement, **Roppongi Hills**, has been devised by the Mori Corporation as more than a mere shopping area, but as a visionary project combining business, culture, education and apartments. It will soon have a rival in the form of the **Aoyama Complex** on Omotesando, designed by world-famous architect Tadao Ando; under construction at the time of writing, completion is scheduled for late 2005.

Caretta Shiodome

1-8-2 Higashi-Shinbashi, Minato-ku (6218 2100/ www.caretta.jp). Shiodome station (Oedo line), exits 5, 6. **Open** varies.

One of the recent wave of micro-malls that are providing Roppongi Hills with competition. Designed by US architect Jon Jerde, the Caretta building in the new Shiodome complex holds an eclectic mix of more than 60 shops, cafés and restaurants, plus more restaurants on the first three floors of the Canyon Terrace building. The 51-floor skyscraper houses the main offices of advertising giant Dentsu, the ADMT Advertising Museum (*see p61*) and the Dentsu Shiki Theatre (*see p248*).

Mark City

1-12-1 Dogenzaka, Shibuya-ku (3780 6503/ www.s-markcity.co.jp). Shibuya station (Yamanote, Ginza lines), Hachiko exit; (Hanzomon line), exits 5, 8. **Open** varies. **Map** p79.

A major addition to the Shibuya shopping scene, Mark City contains a number of boutiques and 'lifestyle' stores in one building, opposite Shibuya station. Restaurants and cafés are on the fourth and third floors, women's clothing is on the second, accessories and cosmetics are on the first.

Marunouchi Building

2-4-1 Marunouchi, Chiyoda-ku (5218 5100/ www.marubiru.jp/index2.html). Tokyo station (Yamanote, Chuo lines); (Marunouchi line), exit 5. **Open** *Shops* 11am-9pm Mon-Sat; 11am-8pm Sun. *Restaurants* 11am-11pm Mon-Sat; 11am-10pm Sun. **Map** p66.

The 'Marubiru', as it's affectionately known, devotes its first four floors and basement to the Shopping Zone, while the fifth, sixth, 35th and 36th floors belong to the Restaurant Zone. The rest are occupied by offices. The basement food hall has an emphasis on big-name gourmet products, and there are also branches of American Pharmacy and upmarket grocery store Meidi-ya.

Oazo

1-6-4 Marunouchi, Chiyoda-ku (5218 5100/ www.oazo.jp). Tokyo station (Yamanote, Chuo lines), Marunouchi north exit; (Marunouchi line), exits 10, 12, 14. **Open** *Shops* 11am-9pm daily. *Restaurants* 11am-11pm daily. **Map** p66.

This brand-new gleaming glass complex of shops, restaurants and offices opposite Tokyo station is affiliated to the nearby Marunouchi Building and, according to one claim, named (bizarrely) after the Esperanto word for 'oasis'. Pride of place goes to Maruzen's new flagship bookstore (with a good English-language section; *see p178*), but other new shops are being added. You'll also find the showroom of the Japan Aerospace Exploration Agency.

Roppongi Hills

6-10 Roppongi, Minato-ku (6406 6000/ www.roppongihills.com). Roppongi station (Hibiya line), exit 1C; (Oedo line), exit 3. **Open** varies. **Map** p109.

Opened in 2003, this mammoth shopping and entertainment development received more than 49 million visitors in its first year. The brainchild of Tokyo property magnate Mori Minoru, it's a mini city – with 200 shops and restaurants, the Grand Hyatt hotel, private apartment buildings, a multiplex cinema, a TV studio, and the colossal Mori Tower, which is topped by the Mori Art Museum and Tokyo City View observation deck. *See also p110*.

Sunshine City

3-1 Higashi-Ikebukuro, Toshima-ku (3989 3331/ www.sunshinecity.co.jp). Ikebukuro station (Yamanote line), east exit; (Marunouchi, Yurakucho lines), exits 43, 44 or Higashi-Ikebukuro station (Yurakucho line), exit 2. **Open** 10am-8pm daily. *Restaurants* 11am-10pm daily. **Map** p119.

The prototype for the huge malls that dominate Tokyo's retail scene, Sunshine City has most of its shops and restaurants in the Alpa Shopping Centre. The complex also hosts the Ancient Orient Museum, indoor theme park Namja Town and Gyoza Stadium (a collection of restaurants devoted to *gyoza*, the Chinese dumplings that the Japanese adore). *See also p121*.

Venus Fort

Palette Town, 1 Aomi, Koto-ku (3599 0700/ www.venusfort.co.jp). Aomi station (Yurikamome line) or Tokyo Teleport station (Rinkai line). **Open** *Shops* 11am-9pm Mon-Fri, Sun; 11am-10pm Sat. *Restaurants* 11am-11pm daily. **Map** p113.

Widely touted as the 'first theme park exclusively for women', this unusual mall is decorated in a faux-classic Greco-Roman style designed to evoke the feeling of strolling through Florence or Milan (it even has an artificial sky that changes colour with the time of day outside). It contains mainly European-style boutiques and pâtisseries, and is part of the giant Odaiba bayfront complex (*see pp112-16*).

Yebisu Garden Place

4-20 Ebisu, Shibuya-ku & 13-1/4-1 Mita, Meguro-ku (5423 7111/www.gardenplace.co.jp/english). Ebisu station (Yamanote line), east exit; (Hibiya line), exit 1. **Open** *Shops* 11am-8pm Mon-Sat; 11am-7.30pm Sun. *Restaurants* varies.

Within the spacious precincts of Yebisu Garden Place can be found the Atre shopping arcade, Westin Hotel, Tokyo Metropolitan Museum of Photography and Yebisu Beer Museum. A large number of boutiques are located in the stylish, self-enclosed shopping centre called Glass Square.

Shopping streets

Shopping streets, or *shotengai*, exist in various forms around Tokyo. Often near railway stations, they are home to long-established shopkeepers and marketeers, and provide a livelier, less-sanitised retail experience than the super-shiny, air-conditioned malls. Here are some of the best.

Ameyoko Plaza Food & Clothes Market

www.ameyoko.net. Ueno station (Yamanote, Ginza lines), Shinobazu exit; (Hibiya line), exits 6, 7 or Okachimachi station (Yamanote line), north exit. **Open** varies. **No credit cards.** **Map** p103.

This maze of streets next to the railway tracks between Ueno and Okachimachi stations comprises two markets, covered Ueno Centre Mall and open-air Ameyoko itself. The mall sells souvenirs and clothes, while the 500 stalls of jam-packed Ameyoko – one of Tokyo's great street markets – specialise in fresh food, especially fish. Vendors knock down their prices towards the end of the day. *See also p101.*

Kappabashi Dogu-gai Dori

Tawaramachi station (Ginza line), exit 1 or Asakusa station (Asakusa, Ginza lines), exits 1, 2, 3, A4. **Open & credit** varies. **Map** p93.

If you're visiting Asakusa's Senso-ji temple (*see p92*) and Nakamise Dori, take a short detour to this area devoted to wholesale kitchenware shops. You'll find low-cost crockery, rice cookers, knives, grills – everything you need to set up a restaurant – including, of course, the realistic-looking plastic models of dishes that are displayed in restaurant windows. The shops run along Shinbori Dori, from the corner of Asakusa Dori; look for the giant chef's head on the top of the Niimi store.

Nakamise Dori

www.asakusa-nakamise.jp. Asakusa station (Asakusa, Ginza lines), exits 1, 3, A4. **Open** 8am 8pm daily. **No credit cards.** **Map** p93.

This avenue of stalls and tiny shops leading up to the entrance of Senso-ji temple in Asakusa sells all sorts of Japanese souvenirs, some dating back to the Edo era. It also sells the kind of food that is associated with festivals, and traditional snacks such as *kaminari-okoshii* (toasted rice crackers) and *ningyo-yaki* (red bean-filled buns moulded into humorous shapes). *See also p94.*

Nakano Broadway

3387 1610/3388 7004/www.nbw.jp. Nakano station (Chuo, Tozai lines), north exit. **Open & credit** varies.

Walk down this cathedral-like *shotengai* and you'll reach the covered Broadway section. This contains numerous outlets of Mandarake (*see p193*), specialising in new and second-hand manga; branches of Fujiya Avic, a second-hand CD/DVD/*anime* store where rarities and bootlegs can invariably be found; and a large number of shops selling a vast range of collectable action figures.

Nishi-Ogikubo

www.sugishoren.com/street/400.htm. Nishi-Ogikubo station (Chuo, Sobu lines), north exit. **Open & credit** varies.

The area around the four main roads that cross at the Zenpukuji river is home to around 75 antique, second-hand and 'recycle' shops. These sell everything from Japanese ceramics to 1950s American

memorabilia. Go out of the station's north exit, stop at the *koban* (police box) and ask for a copy of the 'an-tik-ku map-pu'.

Takeshita Dori

www.harajuku.jp/takeshita. Harajuku station (Yamanote line), Takeshita exit or Meiji-Jingumae station (Chiyoda line), exit 2. **Open & credit** varies. **Map** p85.

Takeshita Dori stands as a symbol of Tokyo's collision of street cultures. Along this narrow sloping street (which starts opposite old-fashioned Harajuku station and curves down to join Meiji Dori) you'll find stalls selling photos of fresh-faced *idoru* to starstruck schoolgirls in uniforms while the hip hop boutique next door pumps out gangster rap. Shops specialising in 'Gothic Lolita' nurse and maid uniforms stand next to those selling retro-punk fashions and Beatles bootlegs. A must-see. Visit at the weekend for the full-on experience.

Books

The shops listed below are the best sources for books in English and other languages, on any subject. If you're looking for curiosities or bargains and have a day to spare, head for the **Kanda-Jinbocho** area (Jinbocho station) and browse among the second-hand bookshops that line Yasukuni Dori.

English-language newspapers are available from kiosks outside or inside train stations. Some branches of AM/PM, Family Mart and other convenience stores stock them too.

Caravan Books

2-21-5 Ikebukuro, Toshima-ku (5951 6406/www.booksatcaravan.com). Ikebukuro station (Yamanote line), west exit; (Marunouchi, Yurakucho lines), exit C1. **Open** 11am-8pm Mon-Thur; 11am-9pm Fri, Sat; noon-6pm Sun. **No credit cards.** **Map** p119.

Thousands of titles on every conceivable subject line the shelves of this second-hand English book specialist, with prices starting at ¥200. Books can be exchanged for cash or credit, and there's an online service too. There's also a café, and events such as signings, poetry readings, and cheese and wine parties on the last Friday of every month.

Fiona's Books

5-41-5 Okusawa, Setagaya-ku (3721 8186/www.fiona.co.jp). Jiyugaoka station (Tokyu Toyoko line), central exit. **Open** 11am-8pm Mon,Wed-Sun. **Credit** AmEx, DC, JCB, MC, V.

Fiona specialises in English teaching materials for children, and stocks a large range of books, videos and educational toys.

Good Day Books

3F, 1-11-2 Ebisu, Shibuya-ku (5421 0957/www.gooddaybooks.com). Ebisu station (Yamanote line), east exit; (Hibiya line), exit 1. **Open** 11am-8pm Mon, Wed-Sat; 11am-6pm Sun. **No credit cards.**

Eat, Drink, Shop

For all your reading requirements: **Caravan Books**. *See p177.*

Tokyo's oldest and best-known used English bookshop stocks more than 35,000 second-hand books and 7,000 new ones, most of them in English. There's also an extensive selection of second-hand books on Japan and Japanese-language texts. You can also sell/trade your own second-hand books and DVDs.

The Intelligent Idiot

5-47-6 Jingumae, Shibuya-ku (5467 5866/ www.vision.co.jp). Omotesando station (Chiyoda, Ginza, Hanzomon lines), exit B2. **Open** 2-8pm Mon, Wed-Fri; noon-8pm Sat, Sun. **No credit cards.** **Map** p79.

Part of the eclectic Vision Network empire and located above the Las Chicas café (*see p143*), this shop sells new books in English at discount prices, and is also a showroom for furniture company Kyozon.

Kinokuniya Bookstore

3-17-7 Shinjuku, Shinjuku-ku (3354 0131/ www.kinokuniya.co.jp). Shinjuku station (Yamanote, Chuo lines), east exit; (Marunouchi line), exits B7, B8; (Oedo, Shinjuku lines), exit 1. **Open** 10am-8pm daily. **Credit** AmEx, DC, JCB, MC, V. **Map** p73.

The main branch of this chain is near Studio Alta, though the branch behind nearby Takashimaya (on the south side of Shinjuku station) is much larger. Kinokuniya has perhaps the largest selection of new books in Tokyo, in French and German as well as English, with numerous specialised academic titles. It also carries videos, audio-visual software and CD-Roms. Not all branches sell English books.
Other locations: throughout the city.

Maruzen

Oazo 1F-4F, 1-6-4 Marunouchi, Chiyoda-ku (5288 8881/www.maruzen.co.jp). Tokyo station (Yamanote, Chuo lines), Marunouchi north exit; (Marunouchi line), exits 10, 12, 14. **Open** 9am-9pm daily. **Credit** AmEx, DC, JCB, MC, V. **Map** p66.

This recently opened flagship store inside the Oazo shopping complex (*see p176*) holds 200,000 books in English and other languages. There are bilingual book advisors on the staff and a touch-screen computer search facility, also in English.
Other locations: throughout the city.

Nellie's English Books

Sunbridge Bldg 1F-2F, 1-26-6 Yanagibashi, Taito-ku (3865 6210/0120 071 329/www.nellies.jp). Asakusabashi station (Asakusa line), exit A3; (Sobu line), east exit. **Open** 10am-7pm Mon, Tue, Thur, Fri; 10am-6pm Wed, Sat. **Credit** AmEx, DC, JCB, MC, V.

Nellie's stocks a wide selection of materials useful for English-language teachers working in Japan. The range includes books, readers, videos, songbooks and software.

Manga

Manga is an art form that has seeped into global consciousness – and is a valuable tool for understanding Japanese language and culture. The garish covers of the magazines and collected paperback volumes can be found anywhere, but here are a couple of specialist shops worth visiting – as is Mandarake in **Nakano Broadway** mall (*see p177*). *See also p82* **Manga mania**.

COMIX by Manga no Mori

12-10 Udagawa-cho, Shibuya-ku (5489 0257/ www.manganomori.net). Shibuya station (Yamanote, Ginza lines), Hachiko exit; (Hanzomon line), exits 3, 6, 7. **Open** noon-9pm Mon-Fri; 11am-9pm Sat, Sun. **Credit** AmEx, DC, JCB, MC, V. **Map** p79.

In the Shibuya store, as well as collected editions of classic manga and action figures, you'll find the latest imported titles from Marvel, DC and various independent publishers.

Other locations (Manga no Mori): 6-16-16 Ueno, Taito-ku (3833 3411); 3-10-12 Takada, Toshima-ku (5292 7748); 1-28-1 Higashi-Ikebukuro, Toshima-ku (5396 1245).

Tora no Ana

B1F-4F, 4-3-1 Soto-Kanda, Chiyoda-ku (5294 0123/ www.toranoana.co.jp). Akihabara station (Yamanote, Sobu lines), Electric Town exit; (Hibiya line), exit 3. **Open** 11am-9pm Mon-Thur; 10am-9pm Fri-Sun. **Credit** DC, JCB, MC, V.

Look out for the giant cartoon mascot painted on the top of this flagship store in Akihabara. Inside the six-floor building it's a hive of activity as Japan's *otaku* (nerds) flip through the latest releases. In addition to the nation's bestselling new comics, the shop sells a selection of *dojinshi*, fanzines created by devoted manga amateurs and showcasing everything from Disneyesque fantasies to hardcore porn. **Other locations**: 1-18-1 Nishi-Shinjuku, Shinjuku-ku (5908 1681); 1-13-4 Higashi-Ikebukuro, Toshima-ku (5957 7138); Akihabara Part 2, Kimura Bldg 2F-4F, 1-9-8 Soto-Kanda, Chiyoda-ku (5256 2055); Akihabara Part 3, Kyoeki Soto Kanda Bldg 4F-6F, 4-4-2 Soto-Kanda, Chiyoda-ku (3526 7211).

Electronics

For the visitor, the best place to buy electronics is Akihabara, the main area outside the airport for duty-free shopping. Tax exemption is available on purchases of ¥10,000 and over; take your passport, which needs to show that you've been in Japan for less than six months. *See p181* **Electric Town**.

There are also some chain stores with prices that almost match those of Akihabara. The most notable – with near-identical logos, layouts and products – are **Bic Camera** (1-41-5 Higashi-Ikebukuro, Toshima-ku, 5396 1111, www.biccamera.co.jp); **Sakuraya** (1-1-1 Nishi-Shinjuku, Shinjuku-ku, 5324 3636, www.sakuraya.co.jp); and **Yodobashi Camera** (1-11-1 Nishi-Shinjuku, Shinjuku-ku, 3346 1010, www.yodobashi.co.jp). They're geared to domestic consumption, so some knowledge of Japanese is useful. All have branches throughout the city; check their websites to find your nearest.

Photography enthusiasts should take a stroll around the backstreets of Shinjuku near Studio Alta, where there's a host of second-hand camera shops.

Akky

1-12-1 Soto-Kanda, Chiyoda-ku (5207 5027). Akihabara station (Yamanote, Sobu lines), Electric Town exit; (Hibiya line), exit 3. **Open** 9.30am-8pm daily. **Credit** AmEx, DC, JCB, MC, V.

A well-presented store that sells all kinds of electrical appliances. All products are export models, sold with an international warranty and English instructions, at duty-free prices. An overseas delivery service is also available. The expert staff speak a variety of languages.

Laox: Duty Free Akihabara

1-15-3 Soto-Kanda, Chiyoda-ku (3255 5301/ www.laox.co.jp). Akihabara station (Yamanote, Sobu lines), Electric Town exit; (Hibiya line), exit 3. **Open** 10am-8pm Mon-Sat; 10am-7.30pm Sun. **Credit** AmEx, DC, JCB, MC, V.

One of Japan's biggest suppliers of duty-free overseas-model electronics and appliances. There are English-language catalogues and instruction manuals for most products. This branch is near the station, and there's a big sign outside, so it's pretty hard to miss.

Other locations: throughout the city.

Sony Building

5-3-1 Ginza, Chuo-ku (3573 2563/www.sony building.jp). Ginza station (Ginza, Hibiya, Marunouchi lines), exit B9. **Open** 11am-7pm daily. **Credit** AmEx, DC, JCB, MC, V. **Map** p60.

This eight-floor building – a landmark in Ginza – contains showrooms for Sony's world-famous products, including the AIBO robot hound, PlayStation 2, VAIO, Cyber-Shot, Handy cam and others. In addition, the Sony Building contains a number of cafés and restaurants, and even an English pub. *See also p59.*

Takarada Musen

1-14-7 Soto-Kanda, Chiyoda-ku (3253 0101/ www.takarada-musen.com). Akihabara station (Yamanote, Sobu lines), Electric Town exit; (Hibiya line), exit 3. **Open** 11am-8.30pm daily. **Credit** AmEx, DC, JCB, MC, V.

This small but very busy shop is close to Akihabara station, and has a number of bilingual staff to help you find what you want. Takarada specialises in overseas models of Sony products – digital cameras, video cameras, TVs, Walkmans and so on. English manuals are available.

Tokyo IT Services

Hibino Bldg 3F, 5-8-6 Toranomon, Minato-ku (5733 4279/www.tokyo-it.com). Kamiyacho station (Hibiya line), exits 1, 2. **Open** 9am-6pm Mon-Fri. **Credit** AmEx, DC, JCB, MC, V. **Map** p109.

Tokyo IT Services, as the name suggests, offers English-language support to computer users in Tokyo, plus wireless network installation, notebook computer rental from ¥500 a day, and a computer repair service. For Macs and PCs.

User's Side 2

K&S Ebisu Bldg 2F-4F, 1-16-2 Hiroo, Shibuya-ku (5447 7011/www.users-side.co.jp/2/index.php). Ebisu station (Yamanote line), west exit; (Hibiya line), exit 1. **Open** 11am-7pm Mon-Sat. **Credit** AmEx, DC, JCB, MC, V.

User's Side 2 sells export models of Japanese technology, with English software. It also has an affordable repair and troubleshooting service, with English-language technical support and bilingual shop staff.
Other locations: Suehiro Bldg 1F, 3-9-2 Sotokanda, Chiyoda-ku (5295 1011).

Fashion

'If there's a recession on,' said one noted visitor to Japan a few years back, 'how come everyone's so well dressed?' To say that the Japanese take fashion seriously is a huge understatement. Grooming, cosmetics, accessories, brand names – all are pursued with a casual-seeming efficiency that constantly impresses and bewilders visitors.

Every area has its own character: for established upmarket brands like Chanel and Hermès, head to Ginza; for big names with more of an edge like Dior and Prada, hit the main drag in Harajuku, while the surrounding side streets are crammed with tiny one-off boutiques; for the latest teen trends, Shibuya is the place. Below is just a taste of what's on offer; you'll find scores of fashion outlets down almost any street.

All Japanese clothing sizes are measured in centimetres. Foreigners often find Japanese sizes too small, though **Isetan** (*see p172*) in Shinjuku caters for larger frames.

Boutiques

Banana Fish
3-3-17 Jingumae, Shibuya-ku (3405 8310/ www.smiths-web.com). Meiji-Jingumae station (Chiyoda line), exit 5. **Open** 11.30am-8pm daily. **Credit** AmEx, DC, JCB, MC, V. **Map** p85.
A cheery and chaotic store selling retro, bohemian clothes and costume jewellery for young girls. Named after the famous manga by Yoshida Akimi.

Candy Stripper
4-26-27 Jingumae, Shibuya-ku (5770 2200/ www.candystripper.net). Meiji-Jingumae station (Chiyoda line), exit 5. **Open** 11am-8pm daily. **Credit** AmEx, DC, JCB, MC, V. **Map** p85.
The exterior is reminiscent of the Tardis from *Dr Who*. The shop isn't bigger on the inside, but it does boast some eye-catching and original clothes, accessories and jewellery for girls.
Other locations: Shibuya Parco Part 3 2F, 15-1 Udagawa-cho, Shibuya-ku (3477 8816).

Comme Ça
3-26-6 Shinjuku, Shinjuku-ku (5367 5551). Shinjuku station (Yamanote, Chuo lines), east exit; (Marunouchi lines), exit A9; (Oedo, Shinjuku lines), exit 1. **Open** 11am-9pm Mon-Sat; 11am-8pm Sun. **Credit** AmEx, DC, JCB, MC, V. **Map** p73.

The company's name is 'FIVE FOXes' (sic), its brand's name is 'Mono Comme Ça' – and it is no relation to Comme des Garçons. As well as affordable fashions in warm colours and fabrics, you'll find toys, stationery and household goods. *See also p192* **Three Minutes Happiness**.
Other locations: throughout the city.

Final Home
3-27-1 Jingumae, Shibuya-ku (5412 1345/ www.finalhome.com). Meiji-Jingumae station (Chiyoda line), exit 5. **Open** 11am-8pm daily. **Credit** AmEx, DC, JCB, MC, V. **Map** p85.
Futuristic men's urbanwear with an understated techno influence. Affiliated to the label owned by Japanese trip hop legend DJ Krush.
Other locations: La Fuente, 11-1 Sarugaku-cho, Shibuya-ku (5728 2923); 5F, 15-1 Udagawa-cho, Shibuya-ku (3477 5922); 3F, 1-50-35 Higashi-Ikebukuro, Toshima-ku (5391 8578).

Laforet Harajuku/ Foret Harajuku
1-11-6 Jingumae, Shibuya-ku (3475 0411/www. laforet.ne.jp/harajuku). Harajuku station (Yamanote line), Takeshita exit or Meiji-Jingumae station (Chiyoda line), exit 5. **Open** *Laforet* 11am-8pm daily. *Foret* 11am-9pm daily. **Credit** varies. **Map** p85.
One of teenage Tokyo's hallowed sites, Laforet is located in the heart of Harajuku, on the corner of Omotesando and Meji Dori; look for the flower sculptures outside. This multi-level emporium contains numerous small boutiques selling clothes and accessories aimed at young wearers of garish, eccentric fashion. Exhibitions and multimedia events are also held here. Sister outfit Foret is down the street.

Loveless
3-17-11 Minami-Aoyama, Minato-ku (5474 5934). Omotesando station (Chiyoda, Ginza, Hanzomon lines), exit A4. **Open** noon-10pm Mon-Sat; noon-8pm Sun. **Credit** AmEx, DC, JCB, MC, V. **Map** p85.
This newish megastore offers a wealth of luxury items for ladies: bags, coats, shoes and much more.

Neighborhood
4-32-5 Jingumae, Shibuya-ku (3401 1201). Meiji-Jingumae station (Chiyoda line), exit 4. **Open** noon-8pm daily. **Credit** AmEx, DC, JCB, MC, V. **Map** p85.
'Death from Above' declare the red neon signs outside this minimalist urban fashion shop. Inside are men's jackets, shirts, jeans and accessories.

109
2-29-1 Dogenzaka, Shibuya-ku (3477 5111/ www.shibuya109.jp). Shibuya station (Yamanote, Ginza lines), Hachiko exit; (Hanzomon line), exit 3A. **Open** 10am-9pm daily. **Credit** varies. **Map** p79.
This landmark Shibuya store is the domain of the *joshikousei* – the fashion-obsessed teenage girls who don't just follow trends but start them. Take a stroll around and indulge in some amateur anthropology. Nearby 109-2 caters to pre-teens.
Other locations: **109-2** 1-23-10 Dogenzaka, Shibuya-ku (3477 8111).

Electric Town

Science fiction author William Gibson once famously described Japan as being 'the global imagination's default setting for the future'. Go to Akihabara, and you'll know exactly what he means. Walk out of Akihabara station and you'll find yourself surrounded by garish Chinese characters flashing from video screens and fluttering from banners above the shopfronts; stalls and street vendors selling compact high-tech devices; tomorrow's computer technology fighting for space among bicycles, *pachinko* parlours and cheap noodle bars.

Akihabara got its reputation as the electronics capital of Japan just after World War II, when a large black market for radio parts sprang up. In the economic boom following the 1964 Tokyo Olympics, the range of products increased, led by the government's single-minded drive to ensure that consumer spending became the engine of economic recovery. It was then that the area became known as Electric Town, and even today retailers regard it as the ultimate testing ground for new technologies before they enter national and world markets.

Almost 600 electronics retailers can be found here, clustered in a few small blocks centred around Chuo Dori. For foreign visitors, the main attraction is the variety of overseas models of Japanese-made goods at duty-free prices. The duty-free shops are clearly signposted outside, and have English-speaking staff (for the best stores, *see p179*). To qualify for tax-exempt goods, you must have been in Japan for less than six months and be buying items worth over ¥10,000. Bring your passport with you. If you want to check voltage requirements and how they differ before you buy, take a look at the World Electric Power Guide (http://kropla. com/electric.htm).

Akihabara is also a haven for the young adult males generally referred to as *otaku* (nerd), and consequently various shops and services have sprouted to cater for their tastes. There are numerous large retailers of manga, *anime* and comic-related action figures, most with sections devoted to pornography in every format. You might even stumble across some of the *cosplay* ('costume play') cafés in the side streets. These are establishments where the waitresses wear the uniforms of 19th-century European maids – a fashion supposedly inspired by *Emma*, a best-selling manga written by Kaoru Mori.

Welcome to Akihabara: where science fact and science fantasy converge.

Parco

15-1 Udagawa-cho, Shibuya-ku (3464 5111/
www.parco.co.jp). Shibuya station (Yamanote,
Ginza lines), Hachiko exit; (Hanzomon line),
exits 6, 7. **Open** 10am-9pm daily. **Credit** AmEx,
DC, JCB, MC, V. **Map** p79.

The main branch of this mid-range clothing store is
split into three nearby buildings. Part 1 also houses
a theatre on the top floor and an art bookshop, while
Part 2 specialises in fashion. Part 3 has an exhibition space that hosts frequent shows by artists and
designers from Japan and abroad. Another branch
is the home of the concert hall Club Quattro (*see*
p242). Parco has also opened the innovative Zero
Gate building in Shibuya, containing cafés, boutiques and the Rolling Stones memorabilia shop,
Gimme Shelter.

Other locations: 1-28-2 Minami-Ikebukuro,
Toshima-ku (5391 8000); 1-5-1 Kichijoji-Honcho,
Musashino-shi (0422 21 8111).

Perfect Suit Factory

3-17-5 Shinjuku, Shinjuku-ku (3358 4401/
www.perfect-s.com). Shinjuku station (Yamanote,
Chuo lines), east exit; (Marunouchi line), exit B7;
(Oedo, Shinjuku lines), exit 1. **Open** 11am-9pm
daily. **Credit** AmEx, DC, JCB, MC, V. **Map** p73.

This chain sells well-tailored, fashionably cut men's
suits at reasonable prices, and has frequent sales.
Other locations: throughout the city.

Uniqlo

6-10-8 Jingumae, Shibuya-ku (5468 7313/
www.uniqlo.co.jp). Harajuku station (Yamanote
line), Omotesando exit or Meiji-Jingumae station
(Chiyoda line), exit 4. **Open** 11am-9pm daily.
Credit AmEx, DC, JCB, MC, V. **Map** p85.

UK residents will already be familiar with the name
Uniqlo. This is the chain store that revolutionised
retail and distribution practices in Japan with its cut-
price but reasonably high-quality apparel.
Other locations: throughout the city.

Children

Also try the casualwear chains such as **Gap**,
Comme Ça (*see p180*), **Muji** (*see p192*) and
Uniqlo (*see above*), all of which have outlets
throughout the city.

Familiar

New Melsa Bldg B1F, 5-7-10 Ginza, Chuo-ku
(3574 7111/www.familiar.co.jp). Ginza station
(Ginza, Hibiya, Marunouchi lines), exit A2. **Open**
11am-8pm Mon, Tue, Thur-Sun. **Credit** AmEx, DC,
JCB, MC, V. **Map** p60.

This upscale children's goods shop in Ginza handles
everything from clothes, shoes and umbrellas to
desks, beds, strollers and skin care. Prices are hefty,
but all items are of good quality.

Mont-Bell

Mont-Bell Shibuya Bldg, 11-5 Udagawa-cho, Shibuya-
ku (5784 4005/www.montbell.com). Shibuya station

(Yamanote, Ginza, Hanzomon lines), Hachiko exit.
Open 10.30am-9pm daily. **Credit** AmEx, DC, JCB,
MC, V. **Map** p79.

Winter in Tokyo may not be as cold as in London or
New York, but durable, warm and lightweight clothing is always handy. This outdoor equipment chain,
founded by a Japanese mountaineer, provides
sturdy but fashionable jackets, coats, mittens and
boots for children.
Other locations: throughout the city.

Designer: Japanese

You'll also find outlets at department stores.

A Bathing Ape

5-5-8 Minami-Aoyama, Minato-ku (5464 0335).
Omotesando station (Chiyoda, Ginza, Hanzomon
lines), exit A5. **Open** 11am-7pm daily. **Credit**
AmEx, DC, JCB, MC, V. **Map** p85.

Founded by designer Nigo in 1993, this pseudo-retro
brand has evolved into the epitome of Japanese cool.
You'll have to search for the entrances to both shops
very carefully; they're so hip they don't bother with
stuff like signs or publicity.
Other locations: **BAPY Aoyama** 3-8-5 Kita-
Aoyama, Minato-ku (5766 9177).

Comme des Garçons

5-2-1 Minami-Aoyama, Minato-ku (3406 3951).
Omotesando station (Chiyoda, Ginza, Hanzomon
lines), exit A5. **Open** 11am-8pm daily. **Credit**
AmEx, DC, JCB, MC, V. **Map** p85.

Comme des Garçons' Rei Kawakubo is one of the
pioneers who put Japanese designers on the fashion
map. The extraordinary exterior of the main store
beckons the shopper into a maze of psychedelic
prints, classically themed suits and smart formal
wear. Tax exemption service available.

Hanae Mori

3-6-1 Kita-Aoyama, Minato-ku (3499 1601).
Omotesando station (Chiyoda, Ginza, Hanzomon
lines), exit A1. **Open** 10.30am-7pm daily. **Credit**
AmEx, DC, JCB, MC, V. **Map** p85.

Bouncing back from rough times at the beginning
of the millennium, Hanae Mori is the designer who
first put Japan on the international haute couture
map. Her flagship store in Aoyama offers her trademark designs, a blend of Euro-Asian influences.

Issey Miyake

3-18-11 Minami-Aoyama, Minato-ku (3423 1407/
1408/www.isseymiyake.com). Omotesando station
(Chiyoda, Ginza, Hanzomon lines), exit A4. **Open**
11am-8pm daily. **Credit** AmEx, DC, JCB, MC, V.
Map p85.

Issey Miyake is one of the big three designers, along
with Yohji Yamamoto and Rei Kawakubo, who
transformed Japanese fashion back in the late
1980s. In his Tokyo store, you'll find original creations and collaborations between designers and
artists that can't be seen anywhere else. Tax exemption service available.

UnderCover

*5-3-18 Minami-Aoyama, Minato-ku (3407 1232).
Omotesando station (Chiyoda, Ginza, Hanzomon
lines), exit A5.* **Open** 11am-8pm daily. **Credit**
AmEx, DC, JCB, MC, V. **Map** p85.
Designer Takashi Jun has walked the thin line
between the anarchy of punk and the security of the
mainstream for over ten years; visit his stores to
judge whether he's still the angry young man of
Japanese fashion.

Yohji Yamamoto

*5-3-6 Minami-Aoyama, Minato-ku (3409 6006/
www.yohjiyamamoto.co.jp). Omotesando station
(Chiyoda, Ginza, Hanzomon lines), exit A5.*
Open 11am-8pm daily. **Credit** AmEx, DC, JCB,
MC, V. **Map** p85.
It was largely due to Yamamoto's innovative fashion shows in the 1980s that the colour black became
the cool, timeless choice of clothing that it is today.
Fittingly enough, the dark, anonymous concrete
of his shop's exterior blends in well with the
surrounding buildings. The clothes, however,
shine with originality. Note that a tax exemption
service is available.

Designer: international

Over the past decade, the Japanese have
made a name for themselves as devotees of
foreign fashion brands. They have rejuvenated
the fortunes of Burberry and Louis Vuitton,
and changed the retail landscape of Tokyo
by adding more and more gorgeous, high-
profile outlets to most shopping areas.
Foreign design brands are omnipresent, with
key areas being the upmarket neighbourhoods
of Ginza, Omotesando and Roppongi Hills;
many also have outlets inside the main
department stores.

Recent, highly publicised additions include
flagship stores for **Chanel** and **Hermès**, as
well as the arrival of **Barneys of New
York** – all in Ginza – plus the stunning
Prada building in Omotesando, designed
by Swiss duo du jour Herzog & de Meuron.

Fashion accessories

Hats

Override 9999

*5-17-25 Jingumae, Shibuya-ku (5766 0575/
www.override9999.com). Meiji-Jingumae
station (Chiyoda line), exit 4.* **Open** 11am-
8pm daily. **Credit** AmEx, DC, JCB, MC, V.
Map p85.
Eye-catching headgear, as worn by many of the
young bucks prowling around Harajuku.
Other locations: 6-29-3 Jingumae, Shibuya-ku
(5467 0047); 7-5 Daikanyama-cho, Shibuya-ku
(5428 5085).

Yamada Boushiten

*1-1-10 Shibuya, Shibuya-ku (3400 5883). Shibuya
station (Yamanote line), south exit; (Ginza line),
Toyoko exit; (Hanzomon line), exit 9.* **Open** 10am-
7pm Mon-Sat. **Credit** AmEx, DC, JCB, MC, V.
Map p79.
For more traditional hats. This family-owned shop
has every kind of bowler, topper, boater or hat that
you might need for formal wear or fancy dress.

Jewellery

Atelier Shinji

*5-6-24 Minami-Aoyama, Minato-ku (3400 5211/
www.ateliershinji.com). Omotesando station (Chiyoda,
Ginza, Hanzomon lines), exit A5.* **Open** 11am-7pm
daily. **Credit** AmEx, DC, JCB, MC, V. **Map** p85.
This small Aoyama shop, located behind the
Spiral building, sells the original creations of noted
jeweller Shinji Naoi.
Other locations: (factory store) 2-2-2 Iriya,
Taito-ku (3872 7201).

4°C

*2-6-4 Ginza, Chuo-ku (3538 2124/www.fdcp.co.jp).
Ginza-Itchome station (Yurakucho line), exit 8.*
Open 10am-8pm daily. **Credit** AmEx, DC, JCB,
MC, V. **Map** p60.
The name of this upmarket shop is pronounced *yon-
do-shi*. You'll find a stylish, modern range of gold,
silver and platinum jewellery made by Japanese
designers, as well as its own brand of watches, per-
fume, apparel and accessories.
Other locations: throughout the city.

Mikimoto

*4-5-5 Ginza, Chuo-ku (3535 4611/www.mikimoto.com).
Ginza station (Ginza, Hibiya, Marunouchi lines), exit
A9.* **Open** 11am-7pm daily. **Credit** AmEx, DC, JCB,
MC, V. **Map** p60.
The story of how the world's first cultured pearls
were developed is the story of Kokichi Mikimoto,
founder of this world-famous store. This flagship
branch has a magnificent range of pearl jewellery on
display, plus a museum. Not for the faint of wallet.
Other locations: throughout the city.

Tasaki Shinju

*5-7-5 Ginza, Chuo-ku (3289 1111/www.tasaki.co.jp).
Ginza station (Ginza, Hibiya, Marunouchi lines),
exit A2.* **Open** 10.30am-7.30pm daily. **Credit** AmEx,
DC, JCB, MC, V. **Map** p60.
The flagship Ginza shop is known (with good reason) as the Jewellery Tower. Each floor of this huge
building is devoted to a particular jewellery theme;
the museum on the fifth floor is worth a look.
Other locations: throughout the city.

Opticians

Recent years have seen an explosion of shops
specialising in stylish eyewear at discount
prices. This development is partly due to the

Eat, Drink, Shop

Present perfect

There's a vast range of gifts and souvenirs, both ancient and modern, classy and kitsch, available in Tokyo: here are a few ideas. We list numerous specialist retailers throughout this chapter; for one-stop shopping, **department stores** (*see p172*) are a good bet. If you're short of time and/or money, the must-visit spot is **Oriental Bazaar** (pictured; *see p190*) on Omotesando. But probably the first thing you should buy is an extra suitcase in which to carry your spoils home.

Clothing

The obvious garment is a **kimono**, new or second-hand, which can be found for as little as ¥4,000, but are often much more expensive. A cheaper and easier-to-wear option is the **yukata**, a cotton gown that is used by both sexes. Designs are highly detailed and use seasonal motifs such as cherry blossom, plum blossom, maple and pine. For men, the **happi** coat is a short tunic used in festivals, and for both sexes there are **tabi** (split-toed socks) and **tenugui** (towel worn around the head at festivals, often decorated with some form of heraldic symbol). Accessories include the **netsuke**, a small carved pouch that is hung from the kimono.

Kitchenware

Ceramic and pottery **tableware** comes in all shapes and sizes, and at all price ranges; or there's (often expensive) **lacquerware** (*urushi-nuri*) and, of course, **chopsticks** – all vary according to their region of origin.

Cultural and traditional

Myriad antiques shops specialise in everything from **samurai swords** and **helmets** to **screens** – but you'll need a fat wallet, and they're difficult to transport. *Ukiyo-e* woodblock **prints** by Hiroshige, Hokusai or lesser-known artists are always popular; you can pay as little as ¥1,500 for a modern reproduction to many thousands for an original work. Head for a stationery/paper specialist for seasonal **greeting cards** and **calligraphy sets**; or for lanterns, fans, boxes and other ornamental goods made with colourful, handmade **washi** paper.

   Fuuring (wind chimes) are a reminder of the cooling, melodic sound heard in the heat of the Japanese summer, while **hagoita** (battledores), painted with decorative scenes from *kabuki* plays, are sold in November as household decorations for the New Year. Then there are the numerous implements used in the **tea ceremony**, and the *karuta* **card games** Hyakunin Isshu and Hanafuda (each has a long and fascinating history).

Food and drink

There is a bewildering variety of edible/drinkable items to choose from, but **sake** and **green tea** are always reliable choices; go to a specialist for the best advice and largest range. Boxed **wagashi** (traditional Japanese sweets) are a thing of beauty, but check how quickly they should be eaten.

Toys and novelties

Japan's love of the cute and bizarre means there's no end of options, from traditional **dolls** to **retro action toys** to **kitsch** galore: visit one of the large toyshops or **manga** emporiums for ideas. Traditional Japanese dolls come with a surprising variety of faces, figures and hairstyles, from stylised wooden *kokeshi* to the delicate Imperial Doll Family displayed in every Japanese house on Girls' Day. **Incense** sets are widely available, while inexpensive **hokaron** heat pads are sold in pharmacies and most convenience stores. Stalls near shrines and temples sell all sorts of small, cheap **good-luck charms**. Look for the omnipresent *maneki neko* (lucky cat); a raised left paw is for business success; a raised right paw is for money – or hedge your bets and get one with both paws raised.

deflationary economy, and partly to a self-conscious nation always hungry for a new trend. Below is a selection of the best of these new-wave opticians. All employ the latest technology for their speedy, convenient – and often free – eye tests.

fxg (Face By Glasses)

2-35-14 Kitazawa, Setagaya-ku (5790 8027/ www.fxg.co.jp). Shimo-Kitazawa station (Keio Inokashira, Odakyu lines), north exit. **Open** *Jan-June, Aug-Nov* 11am-8pm Mon, Tue, Thur-Sun. *July, Dec* 11am-8pm daily. **Credit** AmEx, DC, JCB, MC, V.

Hatch

2-5-8 Dogenzaka, Shibuya-ku (5784 3888/ www.e-hatch.jp). Shibuya station (Yamanote, Ginza lines), Hachiko exit; (Hanzomon line), exits 2, 4. **Open** 11am-8pm daily. **Credit** AmEx, DC, JCB, MC, V. **Map** p79.
Other locations: throughout the city.

Zoff

Mark City 4F, 1-12-5 Dogenzaka, Shibuya-ku (5428 3961/www.zoff.co.jp). Shibuya station (Yamanote, Ginza lines), Hachiko exit; (Hanzomon line), exits 5, 8. **Open** 10am-9pm daily. **Credit** AmEx, DC, JCB, MC, V. **Map** p79.
Other locations: throughout the city.

Shoes

ABC Mart

1-11-5 Jinnan, Shibuya-ku (3477 0602/www.abc-mart.com). Shibuya station (Yamanote, Ginza lines), Hachiko exit; (Hanzomon line), exits 6, 7. **Open** 11am-9pm daily. **Credit** AmEx, DC, JCB, MC, V. **Map** p79.
An incredibly cheap and incredibly busy chain of shops selling brand-name footwear and sportwear with discounts of 50% or more.
Other locations: throughout the city.

Ginza Kanematsu

6-9-9 Ginza, Chuo-ku (3573 0077/www.ginza-kanematsu.co.jp). Ginza station (Ginza, Hibiya, Marunouchi lines), exit A4. **Open** 11am-9pm Mon-Sat; 11am-8pm Sun. **Credit** AmEx, DC, JCB, MC, V. **Map** p60.
Stylish shoes for both men and ladies, available in larger than the usual Japanese sizes.
Other locations: throughout the city.

Food & drink

The basement food halls in **department stores** (*see p172*) are always worth a visit.

Confectionery

Wagashi – traditional Japanese sweets – originated in Kyoto and are steeped in culture. Types of *wagashi* most palatable to the

Westerner's sweet tooth are *yokan* (thick jellied candies made from gelatin, sugar and adzuki beans), *monaka* (adzuki bean paste sandwiched between two crisp wafers), *zangetsu* (ginger-flavoured, round pancakes folded in half) and *wasonbon* (a luxury powdery sugar pressed into tablets). Products vary according to the season and most are meant to be eaten quickly, so ask how long they'll keep.

Akebono

5-7-19 Ginza, Chuo-ku (3571 3640/www.ginza-akebono.co.jp/top.html). Ginza station (Ginza, Hibiya, Marunouchi lines), exit A1. **Open** 9am-9pm Mon-Sat; 9am-8pm Sun. **Credit** AmEx, DC, JCB, MC, V. **Map** p60.
This small but lively shop's variety of traditional Japanese sweets is also available in the basement food halls of all Tokyo's major department stores (*see p172*).
Other locations: throughout the city.

Kihachi Patisserie

Flags Bldg 3F, 3-37-1 Shinjuku, Shinjuku-ku (5366 6384/www.kihachi.co.jp). Shinjuku station (Yamanote, Chuo lines), east-south exit; (Marunouchi line), exits A7, A8; (Oedo, Shinjuku lines), exit 1. **Open** 11am-9pm daily. **Credit** AmEx, DC, JCB, MC, V. **Map** p73.
This popular store makes and sells highly original cakes. They are often a fusion of Western and Japanese elements, using ingredients such as green tea or chestnuts.
Other locations: throughout the city.

Toraya. *See p187.*

Kimuraya

4-5-7 Ginza, Chuo-ku (3561 0091/www.kimuraya-sohonten.co.jp). Ginza station (Ginza, Hibiya, Marunouchi lines), exits A9, B1. **Open** 10am-9.30pm daily. **No credit cards. Map** p60.
This venerable shop one door away from Wako is historically and culturally significant for being the first in Tokyo to sell *anpan* – bread rolls filled with adzuki bean paste.
Other locations: throughout the city.

Toraya

4-9-22 Akasaka, Minato-ku (3408 4121/ www.toraya-group.co.jp). Akasaka-Mitsuke station (Ginza, Marunouchi lines), exit A. **Open** 8.30am-8pm Mon-Fri; 8.30am-6pm Sat, Sun. **Credit** AmEx, DC, JCB, MC, V.
This highly distinguished shop provides *wagashi* to the Imperial Family. It has 70 shops throughout Japan and a branch in Paris.
Other locations: throughout the city.

Japanese tea

There are a number of reasons why drinking green tea is good for your health. Catechin, the ingredient responsible for the bitter taste, is known to kill bacteria that can cause food poisoning. It's also believed to reduce the risk of cancer, prevent the build-up of cholesterol and even make your breath smell sweeter.
For places to drink tea, *see p171* **Tea time**.

Yamamoto Yama

2-5-2 Nihonbashi, Chuo-ku (3281 0010/www. yamamotoyama.co.jp). Nihonbashi station (Asakusa line), exit D3; (Ginza, Tozai lines), exit B4. **Open** 9.30am-7pm daily. **Credit** AmEx, DC, JCB, MC, V. **Map** p66.
Sells a wide selection of Japanese and Chinese teas and implements for *chado* – the tea ceremony.
Other locations: throughout the city.

Imported food

If you're staying in Japan for more than a few weeks, you may start to miss the tastes and comforts of home. The shops below cater to expats, and to Japanese people looking for something a bit different. Prices tend to be high.

Kinokuniya International

3-11-13 Minami-Aoyama, Minato-ku (3409 1231/ www.e-kinokuniya.com). Omotesando station (Chiyoda, Ginza, Hanzomon lines), exit A3. **Open** 9.30am-8pm daily. **Credit** AmEx, DC, JCB, MC, V. **Map** p85.
Currently based in an interim store until it moves into a new building in 2007, Kinokuniya has no connection with the Shinjuku bookshop of the same name. The best-known and most prestigious of Tokyo's foreign food specialists, it also sells English-language newspapers, magazines and cards.
Other locations: outlets in department stores.

Meidi-ya

2-6-7 Ginza, Chuo-ku (3563 0221/www.meidi-ya-store.com). Ginza-Itchome station (Yurakucho line), exit 8. **Open** 10am-9pm Mon-Sat; 10am-8pm Sun. **Credit** AmEx, DC, JCB, MC, V. **Map** p60.
An attractive array of imported foods from all over the world and an impressive wine cellar. Meidi-ya also holds regular themed fairs at discount prices.
Other locations: throughout the city.

National Azabu

4-5-2 Minami-Azabu, Minato-ku (3442 3181). Hiroo station (Hibiya line), exit 1. **Open** 9.30am-8pm daily. **Credit** AmEx, DC, JCB, MC, V.
This Hiroo supermarket has a long history of serving the international community, with imported fruit and veg, cheeses, wines – pretty much all you could want. There's also a bookstore and stationery shop on the second floor.

Nissin

2-34-2 Higashi-Azabu, Minato-ku (3583 4586). Azabu-Juban station (Nanboku line), exit 3; (Oedo line), exit 6. **Open** 9am-9pm daily. **Credit** AmEx, DC, JCB, MC, V.
This huge outlet in Azabu-Juban specialises in imported meat – rabbit, kangaroo, pheasant and lots of sausages – but also sells groceries and beers. The third-floor wine department is impressive.

Yamaya

3-2-7 Nishi-Shinjuku, Shinjuku-ku (3342 0601/ www.yamaya.jp). Shinjuku station (Yamanote, Chuo lines), south exit; (Marunouchi line), exits A16, A17; (Oedo, Shinjuku lines), exit 6. **Open** 10am-10pm daily. **Credit** AmEx, DC, JCB, MC, V. **Map** p73.
A medium-sized foreign food and booze specialist with one unique feature for Tokyo: it's cheap. It has a vast selection of imported wines priced from a budget-beating ¥280, along with cheap cheeses and snack foods. Delivery of large orders within the 23 wards of central Tokyo costs an extra ¥500.
Other locations: throughout the city.

Sake

Sake (pronounced 'sah-kei') is, to put it simply, a spirit brewed from rice. There are many different types, based on location, brewing method, amount of rice polished away and amount of distilled alcohol added. The broad categories are *amakuchi* (sweet sake) and *karakuchi* (dry sake). In addition, some varieties are meant to be heated and served in a special ceramic jug (*tokkuri*). Premium brands of rice wine known as *jizake* are more expensive and highly sought after by connoisseurs. Sake shops can be found in the basements of most department stores.

Shinanoya

1-12-9 Kabuki-cho, Shinjuku-ku (3204 2365/ www.shinanoya.co.jp). Shinjuku station (Yamanote, Chuo lines), east exit; (Marunouchi line), exit B12;

(Oedo, Shinjuku lines), exit 1. **Open** 11am-4am Mon-Sat; 11am-9pm Sun. **Credit** MC, V.

Sake and whisky from all over Japan, plus hundreds of Scotch single malts, at prices cheaper than in the UK. There's also a small selection of foreign foods and snacks, and some imported beers.

Other locations: Daida Wine House 1-42-1 Daida, Setagaya-ku (3412 2418); 8-6-22 Ginza, Chuo-ku (3571 3315).

Suzuden

1-10 Yotsuya, Shinjuku-ku (3351 1777). Yotsuya station (Chuo, Sobu lines), Yotsuya exit; (Marunouchi line), exit 1; (Nanboku line), exit 2. **Open** 9am-9pm Mon-Fri; 9am-6pm Sat. **Credit** AmEx, DC, JCB, MC, V.

A homely shop offering a wide selection of rare sake brands, with an area set aside for tasting.

Gift & craft shops

Many department stores also sell kimono, ceramics, chopsticks and other souvenirs, while some of the shopping streets (*see p176*) – notably **Nakamise Dori** and **Kappabashi**, both in Asakusa – are good places for gifts. *See also p192* **Novelties & toys.**

Bingo-Ya

10-6 Wakamatsu-cho, Shinjuku-ku (3202 8778/ www.quasar.nu/bingoya). Wakamatsu-Kawada station (Oedo line), Kawada exit. **Open** 10am-7pm Tue-Sun. **Credit** AmEx, DC, JCB, MC, V.

Six floors of handmade traditional crafts, including pottery, fabrics, bamboo, lacquerware, glassware, dolls and folk art.

Ebisu-Do Gallery

Kamesawa Bldg 2F, 1-12 Kanda-Jinbocho, Chiyoda-ku (3219 7651/www.ebisu-do.com). Jinbocho station (Hanzomon, Mita, Shinjuku lines), exit A5. **Open** 11am-6.30pm Mon-Sat. **Credit** AmEx, DC, JCB, MC, V. **Map** p66.

Here you can buy original *ukiyo-e* prints (from around ¥20,000) and reproductions (from ¥3,000) by masters such as Hiroshige, Hokusai and Harunobu.

Fuji Torii

6-1-10 Jingumae, Shibuya-ku (3400 2777/ www.fuji-torii.com). Harajuku station (Yamanote line), Omotesando exit or Meiji-Jingumae station (Chiyoda line), exit 4 or Omotesando station (Chiyoda, Ginza, Hanzomon lines), exit A1. **Open** 11am-6pm Mon, Wed-Sun. **Closed** 3rd Mon of mth. **Credit** AmEx, DC, JCB, MC, V. **Map** p85.

Fuji Torii sells a wide variety of Japanese antiques (screens, ceramics, sculptures), as well as designing and selling its own original artwork and crafts.

Gallery Samurai

Aoyama TIM Bldg 3F, 3-13-20 Minami-Aoyama, Minato-ku (5474 6336/www.nihonto.co.jp). Omotesando station (Chiyoda, Ginza, Hanzomon lines), exits A3, A4. **Open** 11am-7pm daily. **Credit** AmEx, DC, JCB, MC, V. **Map** p85.

A small shop in the heart of Aoyama, crowded with antique swords, guns, armour and helmets, not to mention screens, statues, woodblock prints and less classifiable curios. Staff speak fluent English.

Ginza Natsuno

6-7-4 Ginza, Chuo-ku (3569 0952/www.e-ohashi. com/natsuno/index.html). Ginza station (Ginza, Hibiya, Marunouchi lines), exit A5. **Open** 10am-8pm Mon-Sat; 10am-7pm Sun. **Credit** AmEx, DC, JCB, MC, V. **Map** p60.

Chopsticks are affordable and easily portable souvenirs – and this shop has an amazing and eclectic collection packed into its small premises.

Other locations: 4-2-17 Jingumae, Shibuya-ku (5785 4721).

Hara Shobo

2-3 Kanda-Jinbocho, Chiyoda-ku (5212 7801/ www.harashobo.com). Jinbocho station (Hanzomon, Mita, Shinjuku lines), exit A6. **Open** 10am-6pm Tue-Sat. **Credit** AmEx, DC, JCB, MC, V. **Map** p66.

Hara Shobo sells all kinds of woodblock prints, both old and new. The company issues a catalogue, 'Edo Geijitsu' ('Edo Art'), twice a year. The staff speak good English.

Ito-ya

2-7-15 Ginza, Chuo-ku (3561 8311/www. ito-ya.co.jp). Ginza station (Ginza, Hibiya, Marunouchi lines), exit A13. **Open** 10am-7pm Mon-Sat; 10.30am-6pm Sun. **Credit** AmEx, DC, JCB, MC, V. **Map** p60.

This huge, very busy store in Ginza specialises in Japanese paper. The main shop (Ito-ya 1 Bldg) sells conventional stationery and calligraphic tools, while the annexe (Ito-ya 3 Bldg), directly behind it and reached by walking through the main store, has origami, traditional handmade paper (*washi*), letter paper and ink, and many other paper-related crafts.

Japan Traditional Craft Centre

Metropolitan Plaza 1F-2F, 1-11-1 Nishi-Ikebukuro, Toshima-ku (5954 6066/www.kougei.or.jp/english/ center.html). Ikebukuro station (Yamanote line), Metropolitan exit; (Marunouchi, Yurakucho lines), exit 3. **Open** 11am-7pm daily (11am-5pm every other Tue; closed occasional Wed). **Admission** free. **Credit** AmEx, MC, V. **Map** p119.

This organisation was founded with the aim of promoting awareness of Japan's traditional crafts. Learn about, then shop for, a broad cross-section of crafts (lacquer, ceramics, paper, kimono, knives, textiles, stonework, household Buddhist altars and so on) at this showroom-cum-museum. There are permanent and temporary exhibitions, a reference library and even classes. The gift shop sells the work of living craftspeople (who sometimes give demonstrations) from across the country.

Kimono Arts Sunaga

2-1-8 Azabu-Juban, Minato-ku (3457 0323). Azabu-Juban station (Oedo, Nanboku lines), exit 4. **Open** 11am-8pm Mon, Wed-Sun. **Credit** AmEx, DC, JCB, MC, V.

Eat, Drink, Shop

Kimono Arts Sunaga sells new and second-hand kimono, plus crafts and ornaments made from recycled kimono material.

Kyukyodo

5-7-4 Ginza (3571 4429/www.kyukyodo.co.jp). Ginza station (Ginza, Hibiya, Marunouchi lines), exit A2. **Open** 10am-7.30pm Mon-Sat; 11am-7pm Sun. **Credit** AmEx, DC, JCB, MC, V. **Map** p60.

Another Japanese paper specialist, Kyukyodo opened its first shop in Kyoto in 1663 and supplied incense to the Imperial Palace during the Edo period. Still run by the Kumagai family that founded it, it moved to Tokyo in 1880. This branch in Ginza, with its distinctive arched brick entrance, still sells incense, alongside a selection of seasonal gift cards and lots of small, moderately priced items (boxes, notebooks, picture frames) made from colourful *washi*.
Other locations: 2-24-1 Shibuya, Shibuya-ku (3477 3111); 1-1-25 Nishi-Ikebukuro, Toshima-ku (3981 2211).

Noritake Shop Akasaka

7-8-5 Akasaka, Minato-ku (3586 0059/ www.noritake.co.jp/shopping/). Akasaka station (Chiyoda line), exit 7. **Open** 10am-6pm Mon-Fri. **Credit** AmEx, DC, JCB, MC, V.

Noritake is the name of one of Japan's oldest and most distinctive forms of pottery and china, and this is its flagship store.

Vending machines

The Japanese vending machine (*jidohanbaiki*) has acquired an almost legendary status. It's taken for granted by the average Japanese, but the first-time visitor will be impressed by their ubiquity, the fact that they always work (and are never vandalised – unthinkable in most major cities elsewhere in the world), and by the range of products sold.

The vast majority of vending machines in Tokyo sell soft drinks (hot and cold) or cigarettes, with a smaller number selling alcohol (usually beer, whisky or sake). Found on almost every street corner, singly or clustered in groups, most machines operate 24 hours, but those selling tobacco switch themselves off from 11pm until 7am (in an attempt to combat under-age smoking). The drinks machines tend to stop dispensing hot coffee or tea in the summer. ID (a driver's licence, usually) may be required to operate those carrying alcohol.

If you venture further afield, outside the main shopping areas, you may find machines that sell more esoteric products. Batteries, condoms, rice, tights, 'stamina' drinks, ice-cream, pornography – all have vending machines devoted to them somewhere in Japan. The saucier machines that sell 'used' schoolgirls' knickers are not an urban legend; they did exist, until the Mayor of Tokyo ordered a crackdown on sleaze, forcing them off the streets – though a few can still be found.

The first wave of *jidohanbaiki* arrived during the Tokyo Olympics in 1964; by the end of 2003, according to the Japan Vending Machine Manufacturers Association, there were over six million machines across Japan. All accept coins and ¥1,000 notes, but some do not accept ¥500 yen coins, thanks to a run of fake coin scams across the country.

What does the future hold for these big metal monsters? Some sectors of industry are touting 'digital kiosks' – combining the *jidohanbaiki* with the ATM or mobile phone to offer services such as online ordering of goods, paying bills and reading email.

Eat, Drink, Shop

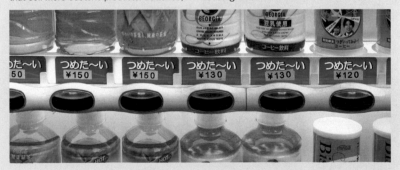

Three Minutes Happiness. *See p192.*

Oriental Bazaar

5-9-13 Jingumae, Shibuya-ku (3400 3933). Harajuku station (Yamanote line), Omotesando exit or Meiji-Jingumae station (Chiyoda line), exit 4 or Omotesando station (Chiyoda, Ginza, Hanzomon lines), exit A1. **Open** 10am-7pm Mon-Wed, Fri-Sun. **Credit** (over ¥2,000) AmEx, DC, JCB, MC, V. **Map** p85.
Probably the best-known gift shop in Tokyo, this is a useful one-stop outlet for almost everything: dolls, chinaware, kimono, *yukata*, woodblock prints, furniture, antiques and books on Japan. Prices are generally moderate, and staff speak English.
Other locations: No.1 Terminal Building 4F, Narita Airport (0476 32 9333).

Sagemonoya

Palais Eternal Bldg 702 & 703, 4-28-20 Yotsuya, Shinjuku-ku (3352 6286/www.netsuke.com). Shinjuku-Gyoenmae station (Marunouchi line), Ookidomon exit or Yotsuya-Sanchome station (Marunouchi line), exits 1, 2. **Open** 1.30-6pm Wed-Sat or by appointment. **Credit** AmEx, DC, JCB, MC, V.
Sagemonoya specialises in *netsuke* and *sagemono* – the tiny, ornate accessories designed to hang from the belt of a kimono and to hold tobacco, medicines and other small objects. This shop holds hundreds of collectibles, and staff can answer enquiries in English, French or German.

Tanagokoro

1-8-15 Ginza, Chuo-ku (3538 6555/www.tanagokoro. com). Ginza-Itchome station (Yurakucho line), exits 7, 9. **Open** 11am-8pm Mon-Fri; 11am-7pm Sat, Sun. **Credit** AmEx, DC, JCB, MC, V. **Map** p60.
Binchotan, a highly refined form of Japanese charcoal, has the power to purify, dehumidify and deodorise the air of a room it's placed in. This shop, whose name means 'palm of the hand', sells products made from *binchotan*. Shoppers can also indulge in the curative powers of *binchotan*'s fragrance in the basement healing room.

Health & beauty

Beauty salons

Boudoir

Mansion Kawai 101, 2-25-3 Jingumae, Shibuya-ku (3478 5898/www.boudoirtokyo.com). Harajuku station (Yamanote line), Takeshita exit or Meiji-Jingumae station (Chiyoda line), exit 5. **Open** 10am-8pm daily. **Credit** AmEx, DC, JCB, MC, V. **Map** p85.
Mostly non-Japanese beauticians offer a full range of beauty and body treatments, including massages, facials, manicures, waxing and relaxation therapy.

Jennifer Hair & Beauty International

Roppongi Hills West Walk 6F, 6-10-1 Roppongi, Minato-ku (5770 3611). Roppongi station (Hibiya line), exit 1; (Oedo line), exit 3. **Open** 10am-9pm daily. **Credit** AmEx, DC, JCB, MC, V. **Map** p109.

Extensive hair, make-up and nail services, plus massages and relaxing treatments. The salon uses Kérastase products from Paris, and the staff can speak Japanese, Korean and English.

Nail Bee

Keitoku Bldg 3F, 3-3-14 Ginza, Chuo-ku (5250 0018/www.nailbee.com). Ginza station (Ginza, Hibiya, Marunouchi lines), exit C8. **Open** 11am-8pm daily. **Credit** AmEx, DC, JCB, MC, V. **Map** p60.

Tokyo's leading nail salon has been serving the international community for over a decade. In addition to manicures and nail art, Nail Bee offers the likes of facials, massages, waxing, pedicures and eyelash perms.

Other locations: Minochi Bldg 4F, 3-11-8 Roppongi Minato-ku (3470 9665); Marui-City Shibuya Bldg 3F, 1-21-3 Jinnan, Shibuya-ku (5458 0026).

Cosmetics

Japan's three biggest cosmetics companies are **Kanebo** (www.kanebo.com), **Shiseido** (www.shiseido.co.jp) and **Shu Uemura** (www.shu-uemura.com), whose products can be found in standalone shops and on the shelves of all department stores.

Aizu Tulpe

1-13-14 Jingumae, Shibuya-ku (5775 0561). Harajuku station (Yamanote line), Meiji-Jingumae exit or Meiji Jingumae station (Chiyoda line), exit 3. **Open** 9am-11pm daily. **Credit** AmEx, DC, JCB, MC, V. **Map** p85.

Aizu is a boon for late-night shoppers and a bedazzling introduction to the world of Japanese cosmetics and medicine. Two floors of every conceivable kind of beauty and health product.

Other locations: Seibu 7F, 1-28-1 Minami-Ikebukuro, Toshima-ku (5949 2745).

Kampo Boutique Aoyama

3-3-13 Minami-Aoyama, Minato-ku (5775 6932/ www.nihondo.co.jp). Omotesando station (Chiyoda, Ginza, Hanzomon lines), exit A4. **Open** 10am-7pm daily. **Credit** AmEx, DC, JCB, MC, V. **Map** p85.

This shop is the brainchild of the Nihondo corporation and employs the *kampo* (traditional Chinese medicine) method of product development. It sells a wide range of products including natural cosmetics, health foods and herbal teas.

Other locations: throughout the city.

Hairdressers

Peek-a-Boo Ext

4-3-15 Jingumae, Shibuya-ku (5411 0848/www.peek-a-boo.co.jp). Omotesando station (Chiyoda, Ginza, Hanzomon), exit A2. **Open** 10am-10pm Tue-Fri; 10am-9pm Sat; 10am-7.30pm Sun. **Credit** AmEx, DC, JCB, MC, V. **Map** p85.

This stylish chain of unisex salons has been an indispensable feature of Tokyo's style centre Aoyama since 1978. All forms of hair treatment are available here.

Other locations: throughout Harajuku and Aoyama.

Serendipity

Powerhouse Bldg B2F, 7-12-3 Roppongi, Minato-ku (5414 1717). Nogizaka station (Chiyoda line), exit 3 or Roppongi station (Oedo line), exit 7; (Hibiya line), exit 4A. **Open** noon-4am Mon-Sat; noon-8pm Sun. **Credit** AmEx, DC, JCB, MC, V. **Map** p109.

As well as reasonable prices, this hair salon near Roppongi has a unique selling point: it's open until 4am six days of the week.

Who-Ga

Akasaka Kyo Bldg 1F, 2-16-13 Akasaka, Minato-ku (5570 1773/www.who-ga-newyork.com). Akasaka station (Chiyoda line), exits 5A, 5B. **Open** 11am-9pm Mon, Wed-Fri; 10am-7pm Sat, Sun. **Credit** AmEx, DC, JCB, MC, V.

The bilingual staff here all trained at Who-Ga's New York salon. There's a membership system for female customers; privileges include discounts for haircuts, perms and colouring, and further discounts if reservations are made one week in advance.

Opticians

Fuji Optical

Otemachi Bldg 1F, 1-6-1 Otemachi, Chiyoda-ku (3214 4751/www.fujimegane.co.jp/index2.html). Otemachi station (Hanzomon, Marunouchi, Tozai lines), exit E2; (Chiyoda, Mita lines), exit C7. **Open** 10am-7pm Mon-Fri; 10am-6pm Sat. **Map** p66.

An appointment may be required for a consultation with an English-speaking optician.

Pharmacies

Basic items, such as sanitary towels, condoms or sticking plasters, can be purchased at any convenience store (usually open 24 hours daily), but these are forbidden by law from selling pharmaceuticals – though some branches of the AM-PM chain have in-store pharmacies.

The following pharmacies all have English-speaking staff (except Roppongi Pharmacy, which does, however, have a late-night service, until 1am daily). Under Japanese law, Western medicines are not generally available, but staff will usually try to find the best Japanese remedy for any complaint. For emergency medical information, *see p290*.

American Pharmacy

Marunouchi Bldg B1F, 2-4-1 Marunouchi, Chiyoda-ku (5220 7716/www.tomods.jp/). Tokyo station (Yamanote, Chuo lines), Shin Marubiru, south exits; (Marunouchi line), Marunouchi Bldg exit. **Open** 9am-9pm Mon-Fri; 10am-9pm Sat; 10am-8pm Sun. **Credit** AmEx, DC, JCB, MC, V. **Map** p66.

Eat, Drink, Shop

Koyasu Drug Store Hotel Okura

Hotel Okura Main Bldg B1F, 2-10-4 Toranomon, Minato-ku (3583 7958). Roppongi-Itchome station (Nanboku line), exit 3. **Open** 8.30am-9pm Mon-Sat; 10am-9pm Sun. **Credit** AmEx, DC, MC, V. **Map** p109.

Roppongi Pharmacy

6-8-8 Roppongi, Minato-ku (3403 8879). Roppongi station (Hibiya,Oedo lines), exit 3. **Open** 10am-1am daily. Closed 2nd Sun of mth. **No credit cards**. **Map** p109.

Tattooing

Inkrat Tattoo

Linebuild Koenji 201, 4-27-7 Koenji-Minami, Suginami-ku (3317 0252/www.inkrattattoo.com). Koenji station (Chuo line), south exit. **Open** noon-8pm daily. **Credit** AmEx, DC, JCB, MC, V.

If you're after a tattoo, and are interested in traditional Japanese designs or *kanji* Chinese characters, try Inkrat. It has a number of expert Japanese artists available, and non-Japanese 'guest' artists frequently do shows and residencies at the studio.

Home & garden

The **Jiyogauka** area on the Tokyu Toyoko line has a multitude of interior and houseware shops clustered around the station.

Bell Commons

2-14-6 Kita-Aoyama, Minato-ku (3475 8121/ www.bellcommons.co.jp). Gaienmae station (Ginza line), exit 3. **Open** 11am-8pm daily. **Credit** AmEx, DC, JCB, MC, V. **Map** p85.

Shop for an immense range of medium- to high-priced furniture and household goods, both modern and old-fashioned, in sumptuous surroundings.

Franc Franc

Shinjuku Southern Terrace, 2-2-1 Yoyogi, Shibuya-ku (5333 7701/www.francfranc.com). Shinjuku station (Yamanote, Chuo, Marunouchi lines), south exit; (Oedo, Shinjuku lines), exit A1. **Open** 11am-10pm daily. **Credit** AmEx, DC, JCB, MC, V. **Map** p73.

A popular and reasonably priced interiors shop, with a wide range of candles, incense, lamps, bathroom goods, and furniture. It also has its own brand of compilation CDs, catering to the massive market for bossa nova music.

Other locations: throughout the city.

Mujirushi Ryohin

3-8-3 Marunouchi, Chiyoda-ku (5208 8241/ www.muji.net). Yurakucho station (Yamanote line), Kyobashi exit; (Yurakucho line), exit A9. **Open** 10am-9pm daily. **Credit** AmEx, DC, JCB, MC, V. **Map** p60.

The shop better known as Muji – the original no-brand designer brand. This is the biggest Tokyo outlet of the all-purpose, one-stop store that went on to conquer London and Paris.

Other locations: throughout the city.

Sputnik Pad

1F-3F, 5-46-14 Jingumae, Shibuya-ku (6418 1330/ www.gosputnik.com). Omotesando station (Chiyoda, Ginza, Hanzomon lines), exit B2. **Open** 11am-7pm daily. **Credit** AmEx, DC, JCB, MC, V. **Map** p85.

Sputnik Pad is part of Idée, the furniture conglomerate run by Teruo Kurosaki, 'the Terence Conran of Japan', and specialises in innovative, postmodern housewares. It's located opposite restaurant Las Chicas (*see p143*).

Three Minutes Happiness

3-5 Udagawa-cho, Shibuya-ku (5459 1851). Shibuya station (Yamanote, Ginza lines), Hachiko exit; (Hanzomon line), exits 6, 7. **Open** 11am-9pm daily. **Credit** AmEx, DC, JCB, MC, V. **Map** p79.

Think of this as a high-class 100-yen shop, selling a large and eclectic mix of original household goods, most costing less than ¥1,000. It's owned by the Comme Ça fashion chain (*see p180*).

Tokyu Hands

12-18 Udagawa-cho, Shibuya-ku (5489 5111/ www.tokyu-hands.co.jp). Shibuya station (Yamanote, Ginza lines), Hachiko exit; (Hanzomon line), exits 6, 7. **Open** 10am-8pm daily. **Credit** AmEx, DC, JCB, MC, V. **Map** p79.

From stationery to wooden boxes, this is the largest household goods store in Tokyo, packed with knick-knacks for the home. Particularly interesting is the party supplies section, which gives a unique glimpse into the Japanese sense of humour. It can be difficult to find your way around the multitude of floors.

Other locations: Takashimaya Times Square, 5-24-2 Sendagaya, Shibuya-ku (5361 3111); 1-28-10 Higashi-Ikebukuro, Toshima-ku (3980 6111).

Novelties & toys

BorneLund

Hara Bldg 1F, 6-10-9 Jingumae, Shibuya-ku (5485 3430/www.bornelund.co.jp). Harajuku station, (Yamanote line), Omotesando exit or Meiji-Jingumae station (Chiyoda line), exit 4. **Open** 11am-7.30pm daily. **Credit** AmEx, DC, JCB, MC, V. **Map** p85.

No electric or 'character' toys are sold at this small shop near Omotesando, which specialises in imported wooden toys. You can touch and play with most of the items on display. Sofas and nursing/nappy-changing facilities are also provided.

Don Quixote

1-16-5 Kabuki-cho, Shinjuku-ku (5291 9211/ www.donki.com). Shinjuku station (Yamanote, Chuo lines), east exit; (Marunouchi line), exits B12, B13; (Oedo, Shinjuku lines), exit 1. **Open** 24hrs daily. **No credit cards**. **Map** p73.

The concept is roughly the same as in the 100-yen stores. You'll find snacks, liquor, toys, 'character goods', kitchen utensils and designer brands, all at bargain prices.

Other locations: throughout the city.

ranKing ranQueen: strange name, even stranger products.

Hakuhinkan

8-8-11 Ginza, Chuo-ku (3571 8008/www.hakuhinkan. co.jp). Shinbashi station (Yamanote line), Ginza exit; (Asakusa line), exit A3; (Ginza line), exit 1. **Open** 11am-8pm daily. **Credit** AmEx, JCB, MC, V. **Map** p60.

This multi-storey emporium in Ginza, one of Tokyo's biggest toy shops, is a showcase for the wacky, the cuddly and the cute, all with a Japanese twist. The basement is the headquarters of the Licca-chan Club (the Japanese equivalent of Barbie). There is a tax exemption counter on the fourth floor.

Kiddyland

6-1-9 Jingumae, Shibuya-ku (3409 3431/www. kiddyland.co.jp). Harajuku station, (Yamanote line), Omotesando exit or Meiji-Jingumae station (Chiyoda line), exit 4. **Open** 10am-8pm daily. Closed 3rd Tue of mth. **Credit** AmEx, DC, JCB, MC, V. **Map** p85.

Kiddyland is a Tokyo institution. The main Harajuku shop is a noisy, heaving maze of mascots, dolls, cuddly toys, furry toys, action figures, Disney, Snoopy, Kitty, Doraemon, Godzilla, Ultraman and more. Warning: too much cuteness can damage your mental health. **Other locations**: throughout the city.

Mandarake

5-52-15 Nakano, Nakano-ku (3228 0007/ www.mandarake.co.jp). Nakano station (Chuo, Tozai lines), north exit. **Open** noon-8pm daily. **Credit** AmEx, DC, JCB, MC, V.

Mandarake (pronounced 'Mandala-K') is the place to go for action figures related to obscure Japanese *anime*, retro US toys from the 1960s and '70s, manga, *dojinshi* (fanzines) and any kind of kitsch weirdness you care to name. It has numerous outlets in the Broadway shopping centre, at the end of the Nakano *shotengai*. The Shibuya branch is pretty large too. **Other locations**: throughout the city.

Pokemon Centre

3-2-5 Nihonbashi, Chuo-ku (5200 0707/www. pokemoncenter-online.com). Nihonbashi station (Asakusa line), exit D3; (Ginza, Tozai lines), exits B1, B2 or Tokyo station (Yamanote, Chuo, Marunouchi lines), Yaesu (north) exit. **Open** 10am-7pm daily. **Credit** AmEx, DC, JCB, V. **Map** p66.

'Pocket Monster' may have lost ground to Yu-Gi-Oh and a variety of other games, but Pikachu's furry yellow paw still has an iron grip on Japanese pop culture. Come and see the monster-masters in their central Tokyo stronghold.

ranKing ranQueen

West Bldg 2F, Tokyu Department Toyoko branch, 2-24-1 Shibuya, Shibuya-ku (3770 5480/ www.ranking-ranqueen.net). Shibuya station (Yamanote, Ginza, Hanzomon lines). **Open** 10am-11.30pm daily. **Credit** AmEx, DC, JCB, MC, V. **Map** p79.

In recent years, the Japanese have become obsessed with making lists and charts of what's popular, which they call 'rankings' – hence the puns in this shop's name. At ranKing, ranQueen, a shop inside Shibuya JR station, you'll find the top ten products for CDs, cosmetics, dieting aids, magazines and so on. It's an intriguing insight into the mind of the Japanese consumer.

Other locations: Shinjuku station, east exit (5919 1263); Jiyuugaoka station, central exit (3718 8890).

Records & CDs

HMV (www.hmv.co.jp) and **Tower Records** (www.towerrecords.co.jp) have various branches in Tokyo; the Shibuya outlet of **Tower** (1-22-14 Jinnan, Shibuya-ku, 3496 3661) is a fave with expats, partly because it's got one of the city's best foreign bookshops, selling magazines and newspapers that are unavailable elsewhere. The Japanese are notoriously obsessive when it comes to collecting music, so there's also an abundance of specialist music shops. Rock fans should head to the alleyways off Otakibashi Dori in Shinjuku, a short walk from Odakyu department store. For hip-hop, house or techno, try Shibuya; while, away from the centre, Shimo-Kitazawa and Kichijoji are rich in quirky, independent stores where you can find more obscure offerings.

As for new releases, domestic CDs are actually more expensive than foreign ones; thus it's possible to buy imported, big-name CDs for ¥1,500 to ¥2,500, while albums produced by Japanese artists usually sell for ¥3,000 or more.

Cisco

11-1 Udagawa-cho, Shibuya-ku (3462 0366/ www.cisco-records.co.jp). Shibuya station (Yamanote, Ginza lines), Hachiko exit; (Hanzomon line), exits 3, 6. **Open** noon-10pm Mon-Sat; 11am-9pm Sun. **Credit** AmEx, DC, JCB, MC, V. **Map** p79.
Cisco is at the cutting edge of dance music. Its Shibuya branch comprises five buildings close to one another, divided according to sub-genre of techno. This is the place to see well-known DJs holding earnest discussions with shop owners across the in-store turntables.
Other locations: Studio Alta 6F, 3-24-3 Shinjuku, Shinjuku-ku (3341 7495).

Dance Music Record

36-2 Udagawa-cho, Shibuya-ku (3477 1556/ www.dmr.co.jp). Shibuya station (Yamanote, Ginza lines), Hachiko exit; (Hanzomon line), exits 3, 6. **Open** noon-10pm daily. **Credit** AmEx, DC, JCB, MC, V. **Map** p79.
Dance Music Record is the name and, indeed, dance music records are what this shop sells. The first floor is a wide, open space with a comprehensive collection of the latest vinyl releases, both domestic and international. All genres of house, as well as jazz re-releases and loungecore, are catered for.

Disk Union

3-31-4 Shinjuku, Shinjuku-ku (3352 2691/ www.diskunion.co.jp/top.html). Shinjuku station (Yamanote, Chuo lines), east, central exits; (Marunouchi line), exit A6; (Oedo, Shinjuku lines), exit 1. **Open** 11am-9pm Mon-Sat; 11am-8pm Sun. **Credit** AmEx, DC, JCB, MC, V. **Map** p73.
Stocking thousands of items, Disk Union deals mainly in second-hand CDs and vinyl. The Shinjuku main store is a tall, narrow building where each floor is devoted to a different genre, including world music, soundtracks and electronica. Branches nearby specialise in dance music, jazz, funk and that much-maligned genre, progressive rock.
Other locations: throughout the city.

Recofan

Shibuya Beam 4F, 31-2 Udagawa-cho, Shibuyaku (3463 0090/www.recofan.co.jp). Shibuya station (Yamanote, Ginza lines), Hachiko exit; (Hanzomon line), exit 3A. **Open** 11.30am-9pm daily. **Credit** AmEx, DC, JCB, MC, V. **Map** p79.
Recofan has a policy of selling new releases at bar-gain rates – in some cases, half the retail price. Each branch also has a large selection of second-hand CDs in all genres. Regular shoppers receive a loyalty card that gives even bigger discounts.
Other locations: throughout the city.

Sports

High-street shops and department stores offer most brands of sportswear and equipment. In addition, Yasukuni Dori near Ochanomizu station on the Chuo line has numerous sports outlets, notably ski and snowboard shops. For cut-price goods, look for the Victoria chain (www.victoria.co.jp).

Oshmans

1-14-29 Jingumae, Shibuya-ku (3478 4888/ www.oshmans.co.jp). Harajuku station (Yamanote line), Omotesando exit or Meij-Jingumae station (Chiyoda line), exit 2. **Open** 10.30am-9.30pm daily. **Credit** AmEx, DC, JCB, MC. V. **Map** p85.
A useful chain, stockist of sports equipment galore, plus kit by Patagonia, Gramicci, Merrell, Maxim and many other brands.
Other locations: throughout the city.

Travel agents

No.1 Travel

Don Quixote Bldg 7F, 1-16-5 Kabuki-cho, Shinjuku-ku (3200 8871/www.no1-travel.com). Shinjuku station (Yamanote, Chuo lines), east exit; (Marunouchi line), exit B13 or Shinjuku-Nishiguchi station (Oedo line), exit D1. **Open** 10am-6.30pm Mon-Fri; 11am-4.30pm Sat. **Credit** AmEx, DC, JCB, MC. V. **Map** p73.
No.1 has been in business for 20 years and specialises in last-minute, discounted tickets. Staff speak a number of European and Asian languages.
Other locations: throughout the city.

Arts & Entertainment

Festivals & Events

It's party time all year round in Tokyo.

Tokyo hosts innumerable festivals celebrating all manner of seasonal events from flower-blossoming to the harvest, religious ceremonies, historical events and cultural happenings, alongside key sports tournaments and major trade fairs. That's not to mention more family-oriented celebrations that visitors are less likely to witness. Below we list the highlights of the annual calendar, but there are plenty of other festivities along the way; contact the tourist offices (*see p297*) for more info on what's happening when you're in town.

The two big holiday periods are **Golden Week** (29 April to 5 May) and over **New Year** (28 December to 4 January). The former contains three public holidays (Greenery Day, Constitution Day and Children's Day); people flee the city en masse, then all head home again at the same time. Tokyo remains relatively quiet, with many smaller shops and restaurants shut for the duration. Avoid travelling at this time as prices increase and accommodation vacancies throughout Japan decrease. It's a similar problem at New Year, when many attractions, museums, shops and businesses are shut until 5 January.

For information on rock and pop music festivals, *see p241* **Feeling festive**. For information on Tokyo's climate and dates of Japan's 14 public holidays, *see p298*.

Spring

Fire-Walking Ceremony (Hi-watari)
0426 61 1115/www.takaosan.com. Kotsu Anzen Kitosho, near Takaosan-guchi station (Keio line). **Date** 2nd Sun in Mar.
At the foot of Mt Takao, *yamabushi* (hardcore mountain monks) from Yakuoin Temple walk bare-foot across burning coals while chanting incantations. Brave members of the public are then invited to test their own toughness of soul and sole by following in their footsteps (literally).

White Day
Date 14 Mar.
Invented by confectionery companies to make up for the fact that in Japan on Valentine's Day (*see p200*) only guys receive chocs, this attempts to restore the balance by being only for the ladies. And it also helps sell more chocolate, of course.

St Patrick's Day Parade
www.inj.or.jp. **Date** 17 Mar or nearest Sun.

Enthusiastic local devotees of Gaelic culture demonstrate their baton-twirling, drumming, pipe-playing and dancing skills at this popular parade along Omotesando (*see p83*), led by Ireland's ambassador. The celebrations at Tokyo's many Irish pubs continue into the wee hours.

Geisai
www.geisai.net. **Date** Mar, Sept.
Started by artist Murakami Takashi, Geisai, like its older brother Design Festa (*see p197*), is a twice-yearly art fair for little-known and young artists to show their wares. Geisai has a slight professional edge because a few major galleries appear, and it runs a competition where winners are given a chance to break into the commercial art market.

Cherry Blossom Viewing (Hanami)
3201 3331. Ueno Park, Sumida Park, Yasukuni Shrine, Shinjuku Gyoen, Aoyama Cemetery & other locations. **Date** late Mar-early Apr.
The great outdoor event of the year sees popular viewing spots invaded by hordes of nature-loving locals. The ideal time is when the petals have fully bloomed and are starting to fall off in the breeze like pink snow – but as this is also a big drinking occasion, by late afternoon many party-goers no longer notice. Cases of alcohol poisoning are not unknown and ambulance crews remain on alert, as do the pizza delivery boys trying to find the right customers amid the sea of people.

New Fiscal Year
Date 1 Apr.
April Fool's Day marks the start of Japan's financial and academic calendars. Big firms hold speech-filled ceremonies to welcome the year's graduate intake to the rigours of corporate life. Universities do the same for their students. All very boring, but designed to make the new recruits feel part of the group.

Tokyo Motorcycle Show
5457 2106/www.motorcycleshow.org. **Date** early Mar.
Plenty of stuff to set any biker's pulse racing, with the latest models from Japan and the rest of the world, as well as some classics. Held at Tokyo Big Sight (*see p288*), the event celebrated its 32nd anniversary in 2005.

Nippon International Contemporary Art Fair
5212 1925/www.nicaf.com. **Date** early Apr.
The largest art fair in Asia is held at Tokyo International Forum (*see p235*) every couple of years or so, featuring galleries from across Japan and Asia.

Start of the baseball season

Date early Apr.

The long and winding road to the October play-offs usually gets under way with a three-game Central League series featuring the Giants, the city's perennial favourite. There's extra spice if the opposition is the Swallows, the capital's other big team, or the Giants' oldest and deadliest rivals, the Hanshin Tigers. It's held at either Tokyo Dome or Jingu Baseball Stadium (*see p253*).

Horseback Archery (Yabusame)

5246 1111. **Date** mid Apr.

Mounted riders in full medieval samurai gear fire their bows at three stationary targets while galloping at full speed. It's held at Sumida Park in Asakusa. There's also a big *yabusame* festival at Tsurugaoka Hachiman-gu in Kamakura (*see p273*) in September, and the practice can be seen during the Meiji Shrine's autumn festival (*see p199*).

Design Festa

3479 1433/www.designfesta.com. **Date** Apr, Nov.

A twice-yearly showcase for young designers, artists, musicians and performers, hundreds of whom rent booths, turning the Tokyo Big Sight convention centre (*see p288*) into one big art fair.

Meiji Jingu Spring Festival (Haru no Taisai)

3379 5511. **Date** 29 Apr-early May.

Free daily performances of traditional entertainment at the large Meiji Shrine complex (*see p88*) in Harajuku, including *gagaku* and *bugaku* imperial court music and dance, plus *noh* and *kyogen* drama.

Thai Festival

3447 2247/www.thaiembassy.jp. **Date** Sat, Sun in mid May.

An annual festival of Thai food, drink, arts and culture in the southern part of Yoyogi Park (*see p87*), near the NHK Hall. The stage has demos of Muay Thai boxing, dancing and some Thai bands too.

Summer

Iris Viewing

3201 3331. Meiji Shrine Inner Garden, Horikiri Iris Garden, Mizumoto Park & other locations. **Date** mid June.

The annual blooming of the beautiful purple and white flowers falls during the not so beautiful rainy season, but is no less popular for such bad timing.

Ground-Cherry Market (Hozuchi-ichi)

Date 9-10 July.

On these two days in July, prayers at Asakusa Kannon Temple (aka Senso-ji; *see p97*) are said to carry the spiritual equivalence of 46,000 days' worth at other times. Big crowds are attracted by this spiritual bargain. A ground-cherry market takes place at the temple over the same period.

Tokyo International Lesbian & Gay Film Festival

5380 5760/http://l-gff.gender.ne.jp. **Date** mid July.

Sumida River Fireworks. *See p198.*

Arts & Entertainment

Cameras out, it's **Hanami**. *See p196.*

Launched in 1992, the annual LGFF lasts around five days and offers a rare chance for locals to catch up on the best of gay cinema. The main venue is the Spiral building (*see p224*) in Harajuku.

Sumida River Fireworks

5246 1111. **Date** last Sat in July.
First held in 1733, this is the oldest of Tokyo's many summer firework events, and also the biggest and most crowded. Up to a million people pack the river-bank area in Asakusa (*see p92*) to see around 20,000 *hanabi* ('flower-fires') light up the night skies. Waterfront locations are popular, but not for the claustrophobic.

Obon

Date 13-15 Aug.
The souls of the departed are supposed to return to the world of the living during this Buddhist festival honouring ancestral spirits. Observances include welcoming fires, Bon dances, night-time floating of lanterns on open water and the placing of horses made from vegetables on the doorsteps of rural homes to carry and sustain the souls of the ances-tors. Although there's no public holiday, many firms give workers time off to visit the folks back home, leaving the capital unusually quiet for a few days.

War-End Anniversary

Date 15 Aug.
The annual anniversary of Japan's surrender to the Allied forces is still a source of diplomatic friction with neighbouring countries, as many leading politi-cians mark the day by visiting Yasukuni Shrine (*see p68*), where the souls of Japan's war-dead, including those executed as war criminals, are honoured.

Asakusa Samba Carnival

3842 5566. **Date** late Aug.
Thousands of brilliantly plumed dancers, some of whose costumes leave little to the imagination, shake their stuff in the streets of old Asakusa (*see p92*). It's a startling and colourful spectacle, with a competition for the parade's top troupe, some of whom may be Brazilian. The sides of the route are very busy, so only tall latecomers get a good view.

Awa Odori

3312 2728. **Date** late Aug.
Street carnival Japanese-style. This annual shindig in Koenji (*see p125*) features a form of traditional Tokushima folk dance known as the Fool's Dance. As the raucous refrain of its lighthearted song puts it, 'You're a fool whether you dance or not, so you may as well dance.'

Autumn

Tokyo Game Show

3591 1421/www.cesa.or.jp. **Date** late Sept.
The biggest computer and video game show on the planet is now held on just one weekend a year, at Makuhari Messe convention centre (*see p239*), and launches plenty of eagerly awaited new releases.

Moon Viewing (Tsukimi)

Date late Sept.
Parties to view the harvest moon have been held in the city since the Edo era, but the search for clear night skies means that somewhat less urban venues are favoured nowadays. Those not wishing to travel may find solace in the annual *tsukimi* burger promo-tion, recognising a distinctly lunar quality to the fried egg that comes as a seasonal extra.

Art-Link Ueno-Yanaka

5685 7685. **Date** late Sept-mid Oct.
An annual art fair that includes exhibitions and events in galleries, shops and temples around the old cultural centre of Ueno and the artists' district of Yanaka. Keep an eye out for flyers or announce-ments in the media.

Takigi Noh

Date Sept-Oct.
Atmospheric outdoor performances of medieval *noh* drama are staged at a number of shrines, temples and parks, illuminated by flickering flames from bonfires and torches.

CEATEC Japan

5402 7603/www.ceatec.com/index.html.
Date early Oct.
The best place to check out all the latest gadgets before they hit the shops, and also an opportunity to see cutting-edge Japanese communications and

information technology in action. The fair is held at Makuhari Messe convention centre (*see p239*).

Tokyo Designer's Block/ Designer's Week/Swedish Style

www.tokyodesignersblock.com/www.tdwa.com/ www.swedishstyle.net. **Date** early Oct.

These three big annual design events usually happen around the same time at various venues around town. Though not directly related, each draws product, fashion and other designers from around the world. The Swedish event also usually includes artists and musicians.

Japan Tennis Open

3481 2321. **Date** early Oct.

The international tennis circus hits town for Japan's premier event, held at Ariake Tennis Forest (*see p260*). Local interest tends to focus on the women's section of the tournament.

Tokyo Motor Show

3211 8829/www.tokyo-motorshow.com. **Date** late Oct-early Nov.

Held at the Makuhari Messe (*see p239*) and one of the major events in the automobile world's calendar, this is a showcase for swish new products from car manufacturers both domestic and foreign. Passenger cars and motorbikes are featured in odd-numbered years; commercial vehicles in even ones.

Chrysanthemum Festival

3379 5511. **Date** late Oct-late Nov.

The start of autumn was traditionally marked by the Chrysanthemum Festival on the ninth day of the ninth month of the old lunar calendar. The delicate pale blooms are also represented on the crest of Japan's imperial family. The Meiji Shrine Inner Garden (*see p88*) is one of the places displaying chrysanthemums.

Meiji Jingu Grand Autumn Festival (Reisai)

3379 5511. **Date** 3 Nov.

In former times, Culture Day (3 November) celebrated the birthday of the Meiji emperor, and the biggest annual festival at the Meiji Shrine (*see p88*) still takes place on the same date. There are performances of traditional music, theatre and *yabusame*, horseback archery.

Tokyo International Film Festival

3563 6305/www.tiff-jp.net. **Date** early Nov.

The largest film fest in Japan attracts a glittering influx of international movie talent, gathered for the serious business of competitions and special screenings of forthcoming Hollywood blockbusters. Most new films arrive in Japan months after their US premières, so this makes a welcome change. There are also showings of Japanese cinema classics, an Asian film award, Women's Film Week and the sci-fi and horror International Fantastic Film Festival (5777 8600, http://tokyofanta.com). The main venue is Le Cinema (*see p217*) in the Bunkamura complex.

Seven-Five-Three Festival (Shichi Go San)

3201 3331. **Date** 15 Nov.

During the Heian period (710-1185) children had their heads shaved from birth until they were three, when they were allowed to grow their hair. From age five boys could wear *hakama* and *haori* (traditional dress for men) and from age seven girls could wear kimono. These, then, were children's special birthdays. Nowadays the third birthday is celebrated only by girls, with the fifth and seventh following the traditional pattern. All kids of these ages go to their local shrine on 15 November in their finest outfits. Important shrines are besieged by junior hordes from well-to-do families.

Autumn Leaves (Koyo)

3201 3331. Shinjuku Gyoen, Ueno Park, Meiji Shrine Inner Garden & other locations. **Date** 2nd half of Nov.

The spectacular autumnal colours of maple and gingko trees transform many of Tokyo's parks and gardens into a blaze of reds and yellows.

Japan Cup

042 363 3141. Tokyo Racecourse, 1-1 Hiyoshi-cho, Fuchu-shi. Seimonmae station (Keio line). **Date** late Nov.

Top horses and jockeys from around the world race over 2,400m (1.5 miles) in Japan's most famous horse race, held about half an hour by train from Tokyo.

Winter

FIFA Club World Championship

www.fifa.com. **Date** mid Dec.

What was the Toyota Cup, a one-off match between the winners of Europe's Champion's League and South America's Copa Libertadores, has been replaced by a new tournament involving the club champions from all six continents. The inaugural 2005 event is at Tokyo's National Stadium (*see p254*).

47 Ronin Memorial Service (Ako Gishi-sai)

3441 5560. **Date** 14 Dec (also 1-7 Apr).

The famous revenge attack by the masterless samurai known as the 47 *ronin* (*see p14*) took place in the early hours of 31 January 1703, or 15 December 1702 by the old Japanese calendar. Two days of events, including dances, a parade in period costume and a Buddhist memorial ceremony, take place at Sengaku-ji temple (*see p128*), where the warriors are buried alongside their former master. There's also a parade in Ginza, with participants in samurai outfits. There's also a whole week of services in April to honour the *ronin*.

Battledore Market (Hagoita Ichi)

3842 0181. **Date** 17-19 Dec.

Hagoita are paddle-shaped bats used to hit the shuttlecock in *hanetsuki*, the traditional New Year game. Ornamental versions come festooned with

Arts & Entertainment

colourful pictures, and many temples hold markets selling them in December. The one at Asakusa Kannon Temple (*see p97*) is Tokyo's largest.

Emperor's Birthday (Tenno Tanjobi)

Date 23 Dec.
The only day apart from 2 January when the public is allowed to enter the inner grounds of the Imperial Palace (*see p67*).

Christmas Eve & Christmas Day

Date 24, 25 Dec.
Christmas Eve is the most romantic day of the year in Japan: couples celebrate with extravagant dates involving fancy restaurants and love hotels. Few locals mark the following day, despite the battery of fairylights, decorated trees and piped carols deployed by department stores. Neither day is an actual public holiday.

Year End

Date 28-31 Dec.
The last official day of work is 28 December, but all through the month companies have *bonenkai* (work-organised drinking parties to celebrate the end of the year). After work on the 28th people begin a frantic round of last-minute house-cleaning, decoration-hanging and food preparation ready for the New Year's Eve festivities. Many stay at home to catch NHK's eternally popular TV show *Red & White Singing Contest*, although huge crowds also go out to shrines and temples for midnight, when bells are rung 108 times to dispel the 108 earthly desires that plague us all, according to Buddhist teachings.

New Year's Day (Ganjitsu)

3201 3331. Date 1 Jan.
Japan's most important annual holiday sees large crowds fill temples and shrines for that all-important first visit of the year; some of the more famous spots are rammed from midnight onwards. Otherwise, New Year's Day tends to be a quiet family affair, except for postmen staggering under enormous sacks of New Year cards (*nengajo*), which all Japanese people send to friends and colleagues. Only the first day of the year is an official holiday, but people stay away from work for longer, with most shops and businesses shut until 4 January.

Emperor's Cup Final

Date 1 Jan.
The showpiece event of Japan's domestic football season is the climax of the main cup competition, at the National Stadium (*see p254*). It's become more popular since the 2002 World Cup was held in Japan.

New Year Congratulatory Visit (Ippan Sanga)

Date 2 Jan.
The public is allowed into the inner grounds of the Imperial Palace (*see p67*) on two days a year, and this is one of them (the emperor's birthday in December is the other; *see above*). Seven times during the day, between 9.30am and 3pm, the public face of

the state appears on the palace balcony with other members of the royal family to wave to the crowds from behind bulletproof glass.

Tokyo Metropolitan Fire Brigade Parade (Dezome-shiki)

3201 3331. Date 6 Jan.
The highlight of this day, which celebrates the work of the city's firefighters, is a display by members of the Preservation Association of the old Edo Fire Brigade, at Tokyo Big Sight (*see p288*). They dress in traditional *hikeshi* firefighters' garb and perform acrobatic stunts at the top of long ladders.

New Year Grand Sumo Tournament (Ozumo Hatsu Basho)

3623 5111/www.sumo.or.jp/eng/index.html.
Date mid Jan.
The first of the year's three full 15-day sumo tournaments (*basho*) held in Tokyo. The tournaments take place at the Kokugikan (*see p257*) from the second to the fourth Sunday of January, May and September. The other three *basho* take place in Osaka, Nagoya and Kyushu in March, July and November respectively.

Coming of Age Day (Seijin no Hi)

3201 3331. Meiji Shrine & other locations.
Date 2nd Mon of Jan.
Those reaching the age of 20 in the 12 months up to April make their way to shrines in their best kimono and suits for blessings and photos. Some areas organise a ceremony at local school halls; in recent years these have been interrupted by drunken youngsters (20 is the legal drinking age). The traditional date of 15 January generally coincides with New Year's Day under the old lunar calendar, so the ceremonies are held around this time to try to maintain a connection with the old system.

Setsubun

3201 3331. Date 3 Feb.
Much hurling of soybeans to cries of '*oni wa soto, fuki wa uchi*' ('demons out, good luck in') as the last day of winter – according to the lunar calendar – is celebrated in homes, shrines and temples. The tradition is to eat one bean for every year of one's age. Sumo wrestlers and other celebrities are among those doing the casting out in ceremonies at well-known Tokyo shrines, including Senso-ji (*see p97*) and Zojo-ji (*see p111*).

Toray Pan Pacific Open Tennis Tournament

www.toray-ppo.co.jp/web/pc/outline.
Date late Jan (qualifying)-mid Feb.
This women-only indoor tennis tournament, played at the Tokyo Metropolitan Gymnasium (*see p257*), is usually well attended by the biggest names in the women's game. Maria Sharapova beat Lindsay Davenport in the final of the 2005 event.

Valentine's Day

Date 14 Feb.

The big three

Tokyo has three major Shinto matsuri (festivals) that date back to the Edo period. Don't miss them if you're in town at the right time – they're a great sight. Elaborate, colourful, noisy affairs, with a cast of thousands, they always involve a grand procession with the kami (Shinto spirits) being carried through the streets in highly ornate mikoshi (portable shrines), accompanied by a procession of performers, musicians, dancers and decorated floats. Participants wear traditional costume, and huge crowds come to gaze and cheer and make merry. Numerous stalls sell snacks, toys and games.

The biggest festival of all is the **Sanja Matsuri**, held every year on the third weekend in May. It attracts enormous crowds of up to two million to Asakusa to honour the three seventh-century founders of Asakusa shrine and temple (see p97). It climaxes after several days of events with three huge mikoshi, which hold the spirits of the three men, being paraded around local streets (pictured). Each shrine needs dozens of people to carry it.

Then comes the **Kanda Matsuri**, which is held on odd-numbered years on the weekend before 15 May and alternates with the **Sanno Matsuri**, held on even-numbered years around mid June. The Kanda festival was a particular favourite of the local townspeople in Edo days, thanks to Kanda Myojin shrine's links with the popular tenth-century rebel Taira no Masakado. Events include participants parading in Heian-period costume, displays from local martial arts groups, and a gala procession involving

festival floats and portable shrines that criss-crosses the Kanda area.

The Sanno festival, organised by Hie shrine, which had close links with the Tokugawa shoguns, is held near today's central government district. The main procession goes round the edge of the Imperial Palace, with participants in Heian costumes and priests riding on horses, plus all the usual festival floats and mikoshi.

For more details of all three, contact the local tourist offices (see p297).

Introduced into Japan by confectionery companies as the day when women give chocolates to men: there are heart-shaped treats for that special someone, plus giri choko (obligation chocs) for a wider circle of male associates. These are reciprocated by the men giving women chocolates on White Day (see p196) a month later.

Plum Blossoms
3836 0753. Yushima Tenjin Shrine, 3-30-1 Yushima, Bunkyo-ku. Yushima station (Chiyoda line), exit 3. **Date** mid Feb-mid Mar.
The delicate white blooms arrive a little earlier than the better-known cherry blossoms, and are usually celebrated in a more restrained fashion, possibly because the weather is still on the cold side. Yushima Tenjin Shrine, a prime viewing spot south of Ueno

Park, holds a month-long festival featuring traditional arts such as *ikebana* and tea ceremonies.

Daruma Fair
0424 86 5511. Jindai-ji Temple, 5-15-1 Jindaiji Motomachi, Chofu-shi. Bus from Chofu station (Keio line), north exit to terminus at Jindai-ji Temple. **Date** 3-4 Mar.
After meditating in a cave for nine years, Bodhidharma, a Zen monk from ancient India, is reputed to have lost the use of all four limbs. The cuddly red figure of the Daruma doll, which is modelled after him, also lacks eyes as well as limbs. The first eye gets painted in when a difficult task is undertaken for good luck, the second when the task is successfully completed. Jindai-ji's Daruma fair is one of the biggest.

Children

Start kidding about.

There's no shortage of stimulus for children in Tokyo. From amusement parks to zoos, and playgrounds to toy emporiums, there are myriad outlets aimed specifically at youngsters. With the falling birth rate – Japan's was 9.56 per 1,000 population in 2004, compared with 14.13 per 1,000 in the United States, for example – parents, businesses and the government are all becoming more child-focused.

Large stores provide small (unstaffed) play areas, so that parents can shop without worrying that their brood might be getting bored. Government-run children's halls provide purpose-built, free entertainment, and Tokyo's restaurants increasingly welcome families. It seems that the Japanese are realising that children cannot be happy unless their parents are happy in the first place.

Tokyo has also become much more accessible for families. Public transport is free for kids under six and half-price for under-12s. Most stations and major commercial facilities in the downtown areas are equipped with lifts and escalators – although you may need help to locate them, particularly in the large and crowded terminal stations.

Nappy-changing facilities are available in indoor public toilets, although not in parks and playgrounds. Most commercial outlets have nursing facilities. You should be aware, however, that the Japanese do not breastfeed in public, so be prepared to brave curious stares if you do.

If you have to carry a pushchair up a long flight of steps, it's best to ask a woman for help. Japanese men are apparently too timid to offer such assistance, particularly to foreigners. Avoid the weekday rush hours, when trains and stations are usually horribly packed. Facilities for kids can get very crowded at weekends and during school holidays (21 March-7 April, 20 July-31 August and 23 December-7 January), especially on wet or cold days.

For useful information and child-oriented tips, visit **www.tokyowithkids.com**, an online forum for English-speaking families living in Japan. Click on 'Discussions' at the top of the home page to link to a decent list of topics that includes shopping, education and playgroups.

For children's clothes and toy shops, *see* chapter **Shops & Services**, starting on p172.

Amusement parks

Visiting amusement parks can be a pricey business, so it's worth noting that tickets are often available cheaply at *kinken* shops – discount ticket stores – sometimes at a fraction of the regular prices. In addition to the places listed below, the **Hanayashiki** park (*see p98*) is small with old-fashioned charm and a 1953 rollercoaster, while **Toshimaen** (*see p121*) offers hours of splashing fun at its water park in summer and a spa in winter. For the **Tokyo Disney Resort**, out in Tokyo Bay, *see p128*.

Joypolis

Decks Tokyo 3F-5F, 1-6-1 Daiba, Minato-ku (5500 1801/www.sega.co.jp/joypolis/tokyo_e.html). Odaiba Kaihin Koen station (Yurikamome line) or Tokyo Teleport station (Rinkai line). **Open** 10am-11pm daily (last entry 10.15pm). **Admission** *1-day passport* ¥3,300; ¥3,100 7-14s. *Entry only* ¥500; ¥300 7-14s; each ride then costs ¥300-¥600. **Credit** AmEx, DC, JCB, MC, V. **Map** p113.

You can dive from the sky, raft down a turbulent river, snowboard on a mountain or drive in a jungle at this indoor park in Odaiba that is packed with Sega's virtual reality games. Bilingual instructions are provided for each game. The – non-virtual – highlight is the Sky Border sideways rollercoaster.

Tamatech

5-22-1 Hodokubo, Hino-shi (042 591 0820/ www.tamatech.com). Bus from Tama Dobutsu Koen station (Keio line). **Open** 9.30am-5.30pm daily. **Admission** *All rides* ¥4,000; ¥3,000 7-12s; ¥2,200 3-6s. *Entry only* ¥1,600; ¥800 3-12s; each ride then costs ¥200-¥800. **Credit** JCB, MC, V.

Children can drive a train, a car or a motorcycle at this Honda-run amusement park an hour from the city centre. There are 700m and 1,200m go-kart loops and a 500m racing circuit; kids need to be nine years old to participate. Other standard amusement park fare includes a free fall and a rollercoaster.

Tokyo Dome City

1-3-61 Koraku, Bunkyo-ku (5800 9999/www.tokyo-dome.co.jp). Suidobashi station (Chuo line), west exit; (Mita line), exits A3, A4 or Korakuen station (Marunouchi, Nanboku lines), exit 2 or Kasuga station (Mita, Oedo lines), exit A1. **Open** *Dome City* 10am-10pm daily. *LaQua Spa* 11am-9am daily. *Toys Kingdom* 10am-6pm Mon-Fri; 9.30am-7pm Sat, Sun. **Admission** *Dome City* Multi-ride ticket ¥3,000; individual rides ¥200-¥1,000. *LaQua Spa* ¥2,800; ¥3,100 Sat, Sun; ¥4,600 midnight-6am. *Toys Kingdom* 1st 3hrs ¥700-¥1,000; every subsequent 30mins ¥300-¥400. **No credit cards.**

The amusement park formerly known as Korakuen reopened in 2003 as part of an amusement complex with baseball stadium Tokyo Dome (*see p253*) at its centre. The ultra-modern section, called LaQua, comprises a shopping centre, restaurants, the world's first spokeless Ferris wheel and a hot mineral bath theme park where spring water is pumped up from an incredible 1,700m (5,670ft) below ground. Restaurants include a Hawaiian-Japanese place run by retired sumo star Konishiki. Topping it all off is the Thunder Dolphin, a stunning urban rollercoaster that starts off higher than the Dome, leaps to the roof of the main LaQua building and plunges through the centre of the Ferris wheel: a must for thrill-seekers. For small kids, there is Toys Kingdom, providing room after room of toys and educational equipment, making the place a great rainy-day solution.

Tokyo Sesame Place
600 Kamiyotsugi, Akiruno-shi (042 558 6511/ www.sesameplace.co.jp). Akikawa station (Itsukaichi line) then bus or taxi. **Open** *July-Sept daily. Oct, Nov, Mar-June Mon-Wed, Fri-Sun. Dec-Feb Sat, hols. Hrs vary.* **Admission** *Summer* ¥2,200; ¥1,200 2-12s. *Winter* ¥2,000; ¥1,000 2-12s. **No credit cards**.
This theme park based on the *Sesame Street* TV series has reproduced some of the most exciting attractions of the original park in Pennsylvania, including big ball pools, a gigantic air mattress, cargo nets, tunnels and climbs. Various interactive shows, including English play-along and musical revues, will keep the kids entertained. A small water section (open in summer) includes a paddling pool and a water maze. It's about an hour by train from Shinjuku station.

Aquariums & zoos

There's also an aquarium inside **Sunshine City** in Ikebukuro; *see p121* for details.

Inokashira Nature & Culture Park
1-17-6 Gotenyama, Musashino-shi (042 246 1100/ www.tokyo-zoo.net). Kichijoji station (Chuo line), park (south) exit. **Open** *9.30am-5pm Tue-Sun (last entry 4pm).* **Admission** ¥400; ¥200 over-65s; ¥150 13-15s; free under-13s. **No credit cards**.
A five-minute walk from Kichijoji station, this zoo is set in splendid Inokashira Park (*see p128*), with a pond, woods, playground and outdoor pool all close by. The zoo comprises two sections, one near the pond housing an aviary and freshwater aquarium; the other near the wood and containing a zoo with a petting area, greenhouse and small amusement park. The entrance fee gets you tickets for both sections, which can be used separately. If you tire of watching animals, take a boat ride on the pond.

Shinagawa Aquarium
3-2-1 Katsushima, Shinagawa-ku (3762 3431/ www.aquarium.gr.jp). Omori Kaigan station (Keihin Kyuko Line), east exit/Sujo water bus from

Hinode Pier. **Open** *10am-5pm Mon, Wed-Sun (last entry 4.30pm).* **Admission** ¥1,100; ¥600 7-12s; ¥300 4-6s. **No credit cards**.
Tokyo's best aquarium is in a rather inconvenient location, on the western edge of Tokyo Bay. The best feature is the water tank tunnel, which lets you walk under swimming green turtles, stingrays and scores of other fish. From another tank, huge sand tiger sharks peer out with cold, steely eyes. The aquarium also offers Tokyo's only dolphin shows, which take place at the outdoor stadium four or five times a day. They always attract huge crowds, so check the show schedule on arrival.

Tama Zoo
7-1-1 Hodokubo, Hino-shi (042 591 1611/ www.tokyo-zoo.net). Tama Dobutsu Koen station (Keio line). **Open** *9.30am-5pm Mon, Tue, Thur-Sun (last entry 4pm).* **Admission** ¥600; ¥300 over-65s; ¥200 13-15s; free under-13s. Free 29 Apr, 5 May, 1 Oct. **No credit cards**.
The animals at this zoo in Hino City (an hour by train from central Tokyo) are displayed in a more natural setting than at Ueno Zoo (*see below*). Built over several low hills, it's divided into three ecological areas: Asiatic, African and Australian. The main attractions include koalas, lions in a 'safari' setting and, above all, a huge insectarium with butterflies, beetles and other creepy-crawlies. Enjoy the sensation of butterflies coming to rest their weary wings on your hand.

Tokyo Sea Life Park
6-2-3 Rinkai-cho, Edogawa-ku (3869 5152/ www.tokyo-zoo.net). Kasai Rinkai Koen station (Keiyo line)/Sujo water bus from Hinode Pier. **Open** *9.30am-5pm Mon, Tue, Thur-Sun (last entry 4pm).* **Admission** ¥700; ¥350 over-65s; ¥250 13-15s; free under-13s. Free for all 29 Apr, 1 Oct, 10 Oct. **Credit** (giftshop only) JCB, MC, V.
Newer than Shinagawa Aquarium and located on the other side of Tokyo Bay, this place was built on the 77ha (190 acres) of reclaimed land that constitute Kasai Seaside Park. The main attraction is a large doughnut-shaped water tank, home to 200 tuna. Tokyo Disney Resort (*see p128*) is nearby.

Ueno Zoo
9-83 Ueno Koen, Taito-ku (3828 5171/www.tokyo-zoo.net). Ueno station (Yamanote, Ginza, Hibiya lines), park exit. **Open** *9.30am-5pm Tue-Sun (last entry 4pm).* **Admission** ¥600; ¥300 over-65s; ¥200 13-15s; free under-13s. Free 20 Mar, 29 Apr, 1 Oct. **Map** p103.
Japan's oldest zoo, established in 1882, is also Tokyo's most popular, thanks mainly to its central location in Ueno Park and its giant panda (Ling Ling). You'll find the panda in the eastern section, along with elephants, lions, gorillas, sea lions and assorted bears. Don't be discouraged by the crowds, though; the western section across the bridge is less busy and offers opportunities to interact with animals in a petting zoo and watch a huge alligator relaxing in the reptile house.

Children's halls

Run by the local authorities, children's halls (*jidokan*) are free indoor play facilities for residents (not short-term visitors). Designed to supplement formal education, they provide weekly play classes for pre-schoolers, and daily after-school programmes for school-age children of working parents. There are more than 500 *jidokan* within Tokyo's 23 wards, including one run by the Tokyo Metropolitan Government, and another built by the welfare ministry, the National Children's Castle (the only one that charges a fee). For information about other *jidokan*, contact the Tokyo Metropolitan Government Foreign Residents' Advisory Centre (*see p291*).

National Children's Castle (Kodomo no Shiro)

5-53-1 Jingumae, Shibuya-ku (3797 5666/ www.kodomono-shiro.or.jp). Shibuya station (Yamanote, Ginza, Hanzomon lines), Miyamasuzaka (east) exit or Omotesando station (Chiyoda, Ginza, Hanzomon lines), exits B2, B4. **Open** 12.30-5.30pm Tue-Fri; 10am-5.30pm Sat, Sun. **Admission** ¥500; ¥400 3-17s. **No credit cards**. **Map** p79.

A fabulous play hall halfway between Shibuya and Omotesando. Facilities include climbing equipment and a playhouse on the third floor, and a music lobby on the fourth floor where children can indulge their love of noise. The playport on the fifth-floor roof garden is the biggest attraction, combining a jungle gym with large ball pools. Kids must be over three to use the playport, which closes on rainy days.

0123 Kichijoji

2-29-12 Kichijoji Higashi, Musashino-shi (0422 20 3210/www.parkcity.ne.jp/~m0123hap/kitijyouzi/ k_index.htm). Kichijoji station (Chuo line), north exit. **Open** 9am-4pm Tue-Sat. **Admission** free.

This *jidokan* caters specifically for under-threes. Converted from a former kindergarten, it's a spacious building with a garden and a sand box. Children can paint, and play with clay and a variety of toys handmade by the staff.

Tokyo Metropolitan Children's Hall

1-18-24 Shibuya, Shibuya-ku (3409 6361/ www.jidokaikan.metro.tokyo.jp). Shibuya station (Yamanote, Ginza, Hanzomon lines), Miyamasuzaka (east) exit. **Open** *July, Aug* 9am-6.30pm daily. *Sept-June* 9am-5pm daily. Closed 2nd & 4th Mon of mth. **Admission** free. **Map** p79.

Handily located not far from Shibuya station, this six-storey hall is packed with recreational and educational facilities. The second floor is reserved for pre-schoolers, with large climbing frames and wooden toys. The third floor has a handicraft section, the 'human body maze' and a ball pool. There's a library on the fifth floor, while on the roof kids can try roller-skating and unicycling. Each floor has plenty of lockers to stash belongings.

Museums

Other child-friendly museums include the **Transportation Museum** (*see p69*), **Japan Science Foundation Science Museum** (*see p67*) and **Fire Museum** (*see p74*).

National Science Museum

7-20 Ueno Koen, Taito-ku (3822 0111/www.kahaku. go.jp/english/index.html). Ueno station (Yamanote line), park exit; (Ginza, Hibya lines) Shinobazu exit. **Open** 9am-4.30pm Tue-Thur; 9am-8pm Fri; 9am-6pm Sat, Sun. **Admission** ¥420; ¥70 concessions; free under-18s Sat. **No credit cards**. **Map** p103.

At this museum inside Ueno Park, the exhibits of fossils, specimens and asteroids are now supplemented with touchscreens providing videos and multilingual explanations. After checking out dinosaur bones and a prehistoric house built with mammoth tusks, you may want to taste the speciality of the museum's Musée Basara restaurant: a 'dinosaur's egg' croquette. All displays are currently in the new building, which opened in November 2004, while the main building is being refurbished.

Tama Rokuto Kagakukan

5-10-64 Shibakubo, Nishi-Tokyo-shi (042 469 6100/ www.tamarokuto.or.jp). Hana-Koganei station (Seibu Shinjuku Line), north exit then 18mins walk, or take bus bound for Tama Rokuto Kagakukan from Hana-Koganei station (Seibu Shinjuku line), south exit (Sat, Sun & holidays) or Kichijoji station (Chuo line), north exit (Sun & holidays). **Open** 9.30am-5pm Tue-Sun. **Admission** ¥500; ¥200 4-18s. *Planetarium shows* ¥500; ¥200 4-18s. **No credit cards**.

Visitors can climb inside the life-size model of a space shuttle that stands upright in the middle of this science museum an hour from Shinjuku. You

Ferris wheel and Toys Kingdom at
Tokyo Dome City. *See p202.*

can practise moving cargo with a robot arm simulator, while a moonwalker simulator recreates the low-gravity environment of the moon's surface. Star shows are held at the planetarium, one of the world's largest. While astronomy is the major focus, there are also geology and biology sections too. The major drawback is poor public transport access, with infrequent bus services from local train stations.

Parks & playgrounds

Apart from **Yoyogi Park** (*see p87*) and **Shinjuku Gyoen** (*see p75*), parks in central Tokyo are few and far between. Furthermore, they are often not ideal for picnics or playing – Ueno Park is more concrete than grass, for example. To find the best green spaces, you're better off grabbing a map and a rail pass and heading to the suburbs.

Koganei Park

1-13-1 Sekino-machi, Koganei-shi (042 385 5611/ www.tokyo-park.or.jp/english). Musashi Koganei station (Chuo line), north exit then any bus from bus stop 2 or 3; get off at Koganei Koen Nishi-Guchi. **Open** 24hrs daily. **Admission** free.

You can explore the central part of this spacious park in western Tokyo by bicycle; about 120 bikes are available for pre-schoolers and their parents (¥100-¥200/hr). If your child tires of pedalling, they can try sledging down an artificial, turf-covered slope, built into one of the park's grassy knolls. The 17° slope is wide enough for at least a dozen sledges to race down at the same time. You can buy a sledge or borrow one of the park's by queuing at the bottom of the slope. The park also houses the open-air branch of the Edo-Tokyo Museum (*see p98*).

Nogawa Park

6-4-1 Osawa, Mitaka-shi (042 231 6457). Shin-Koganei station (Seibu Tamagawa line) then 15mins walk (follow railway tracks south until you reach Nogawa river). **Open** *Park* 24hrs daily. *Nature centre* 9.30am-4.30pm Tue-Sun. **Admission** free.

A natural spring on the northern side of the Nogawa river bisects this picturesque park. The area around the spring is a popular paddling spot in summer. Upstream is a small nature centre where you can listen to recorded sounds of birds in Tokyo and learn about various insects. Climbing frames and other wooden play equipment dot the extensive grassy areas. It's a half-hour train ride from Shinjuku, followed by an easy walk.

Showa Kinen Park

3173 Midori-machi, Tachikawa-shi (042 528 1751/ www.showapark.jp). Nishi-Tachikawa station (Ohme line). **Open** 9.30am-4.30pm/7pm daily (last entry 1hr before closing); closing time varies during year. **Admission** *Park* ¥400; ¥80 6-14s. *Park & Rainbow Pool* ¥2,200; ¥1,200 6-14s; ¥300 4-5s. **No credit cards.**

A paradise for athletic children, this 180ha (445-acre) park 40 minutes from Shinjuku has a large play area called Children's Forest, with giant trampoline nets, bouncy domes and 'foggy woods' that – as the name implies – get covered by clouds of artificial fog. The Forest House in the centre sells snacks and drinks and provides a resting space. If it's too hot to walk to the Children's Forest from the main gate, pop into the Rainbow Pool for a paddle. Three pools contain waterfalls and squirt fish; bigger children have the choice of a current pool, a wave pool and water slides. The park also has some lengthy cycling tracks; bike rental for three hours costs ¥250 for under-15s, ¥410 for adults.

Arts & Entertainment

Trim Sports Centre
(Jingu Gaien 'Jido Yuen')

1-7-5 Kita-Aoyama, Minato-ku (3478 0550/
www.meijijingugaien.jp/child/index.html).
Shinanomachi station (Sobu line). **Open** 9.30am-
4.30pm/5pm daily (last entry 30mins before closing);
closing time varies during year. **Admission** ¥200;
¥50 2-12s. **No credit cards.**

Despite its compact size and central location, this
popular playground within the Outer Garden of the
Meiji Jingu has more play equipment than any other
park in Tokyo. Children can try swings, slides and
climbs of various sizes and shapes, and picnic at
beautiful log houses equipped with large tables and
chairs. The park has three areas, each for a different
age group, but children are allowed to wander anywhere under parental supervision.

Resources

Babysitting & nurseries

Staff at more reputable hotels may be able
to arrange babysitting. Alternatively, the
following outfits come highly recommended by
Tokyo parents. Expect to pay between ¥1,500
and ¥2,800 per hour. Some agencies demand a
minimum of two hours at a set rate; you then
pay for each additional hour, with different
rates for late-night and early-morning services.

Japan Baby Sitter Service

3423 1251/www.jbs-mom.co.jp. **Open** 5am-noon
daily. **No credit cards.**
One of the oldest services in Tokyo, specialising in
grandmotherly types. Bookings must be made by
5pm on the preceding day.

Kids Square

West Walk 6F, Roppongi Hills, 6-10-1 Roppongi,
Minato-ku (5772 1577/toll-free 0120 086 720/
www.alpha-co.com/english/index.html). Roppongi
station (Hibiya, Oedo lines), exit 1. **Open** 11am-7pm
daily. **No credit cards. Map** p109.
Located conveniently in the middle of the Roppongi
business district, this is a spacious, well-equipped
nursery. You can check your child via mobile phone
or computer by hooking up to video cameras
installed in the nursery. Book by 4pm the day before.
Other locations: Ark Hills Side 3F, 1-3-41
Roppongi, Minato-ku (3583 9320); Tokyo Dome Hotel
7F, 1-3-61 Koraku, Bunkyo-ku (5805 2272).

Kids World

Pigeon Shoto Takada Bldg 2F, 1-28-11 Shoto,
Shibuya-ku (5428 3630/www.pigeonhearts.co.jp/
kidsworld). Shibuya station (Yamanote, Ginza,
Hanzomon lines), Hachiko exit or Shinsen station
(Keio Inokashira line). **Open** 9am-6pm Mon-Fri.
No credit cards. Map p79.
This English-language school for children also pro-
vides nursery care at its many branches in the city,
including this one in Shibuya. Pigeon Hearts, which

runs the school, can also arrange a babysitting service for those able to communicate in Japanese;
phone for more details on freephone 0120 764 154.
Other locations: throughout the city; details on
0120 001 537.

Little Mate

045 712 3253/www.tokyolm.co.jp. Nurseries at
Hotel Okura, Roppongi (3586 0360), Keio Plaza
Intercontinental, Shinjuku (3345 1439), Sheraton
Grande Tokyo Bay Hotel, near Tokyo Disneyland
(047 355 5720). **Open** 10am-6pm daily.
No credit cards.
You can drop off your kids for an hour or more at a
day nursery at one of the three hotels listed above.
Reservations are required by 6pm the previous day
(4pm at the Hotel Okura).

Poppins Service

3447 2100/www.poppins.co.jp/english/index.html.
Open 7am-9pm Mon-Sat. **No credit cards.**
Expect either a young lady trained in early child-
hood education or a retired veteran teacher when
you request a sitter from Poppins. Non-members
pay a flat rate of ¥2,500 per hour (¥3,200 6-10pm),
and bookings must be made two days in advance. If
Japanese is not your – or your children's – strong
point, foreign-language speakers can be provided.

Royal Baby Salon

Ginza Kosumion Bldg 7F, 1-5-14 Ginza, Chuo-ku
(3538 3238/www.royalbaby.co.jp). Ginza-Itchome
station (Yurakucho line), exit 6. **Open** 10am-6pm
daily. **Credit** (incurs extra charge) AmEx, DC, JCB,
MC, V. **Map** p60.
An upmarket nursery in Ginza that also offers a
babysitting service. Bookings must be made by 5pm
on the preceding day.

Equipment rental

Duskin Rent-All

0120 100 100/www.kasite.net.
If you don't have access to second-hand childcare
equipment, try Duskin. It hires out all sorts of kit,
from car seats to cots, at very reasonable rates, and
will deliver to your home. There are also ten central
outlets, but you'll need to speak Japanese.

Hairdressing

Choki Choki

Aqua City Odaiba 6F, 1-7-1 Minato-ku (3528 4005/
www.choki-choki.com). Daiba station (Yurikamome
line). **Open** 11am-9pm daily (last appointment
7.30pm). **Credit** AmEx, DC, JCB, MC, V. **Map** p113.
Located in the Aqua City shopping mall in Odaiba,
this is Japan's largest hair salon for children. Junior
customers are covered in a plastic cape printed with
cartoon pictures, and sit on a chair that's actually a
pedal car. While they are 'steering' and watching a
video shown in a side mirror, the hairdressers go
about their business. Clever, huh?

Clubs

Dance and trance, funk and punk, soul and rock 'n' roll. Take your pick.

The Orient. *See p212.*

Though Tokyo's nightlife might not be as crazy as the heady days of the mid 1990s, when Bubble-economy yen sponsored luxurious clubs, the patrons all had money to spend and the vibrant electronic music/rave culture was just taking root, things are still pulsing on the scene. Tokyo has a nightlife and party culture to rival any city, comparable to London and New York in terms of intensity and late-night ethos; it's safe and relatively friendly, and the level of DJ talent is excellent. New clubs with even better sound systems have been appearing and Tokyo's reputation as a world-class party city is beginning to grow.

The main clubbing areas are the youth playground of Shibuya and trendy hangout Aoyama, but Roppongi has its fair share of hotspots too, and there's a smattering of venues in Shinjuku's Kabuki-cho and around Harajuku.

Clubs come in all shapes and sizes – with prices to match. The smaller ones are usually dark but cosy, with entrance costing around ¥2,000 including one or two drinks tickets. If your stay is short, you might be better off hitting one of the larger clubs, such as **Womb** (*see p211*), **Space Lab Yellow** (*see p214*), **Ageha** (*see p214*) or the **Orient** (*see p212*).

Although more expensive – around ¥3,500 with one drink ticket – you will definitely know where your money has gone.

Newcomers to Japan should also take the opportunity to observe the subtle cultural differences between clubbing in the East and West. You will notice a lack of security at the door, the issuing of tickets for drinks after paying for entry, the far-out fashion and the relaxed attitude on and off the dancefloor. People are genuinely friendly, and fights in clubs are almost unheard of.

Although Japan is considered a drug-free society and open talk about drugs is taboo for practically all Japanese, the use of dance-enhancing drugs has been well established since the trance scene took off here circa 1995. It is still a delicate matter, however, and most clubbers as well as clubs do not want to draw attention to it. If this is part of your scene, a cautious approach is advisable.

The last ten years have seen a steady influx of foreign DJs living in Japan. Check out Brit Mike McKenna (house/breaks) – interestingly, voted Best Japanese DJ in 2004 by national clubbing magazine *Loud*; Canadian Robert Palmer (house/techno); Australian

Jaybee (house); American Makyo (Indo/Middle Eastern beats); and Frenchman Cyril (world/Mediterranean beats). Local talent to look out for includes Kaoru Inoue (house, world beat), DJ Hasebe (hip hop) and Duck Rock (rock/breaks crossover), while among the internationally known Japanese DJs are EYE (experimental techno, breaks), Takkyu Ishino (techno), DJ Krush (hip hop) and Ken Ishii (techno, electronica).

INFORMATION AND HOURS
For club listings and recommendations, check out *Metropolis* and webzine Tokyo Q. Record shops such as Tower and HMV have heaps of flyers (sometimes offering discounted admission). If your Japanese is up to scratch, get hold of *Floor* or *Juice* magazines (the latter with rock and club-versions) or visit www.ciajapan.com. For gay clubs, *see p230*.

Most clubs don't really get going until midnight or 1am, and are at their busiest (as you might expect) on Friday and Saturday. Standard closing times are around 4am or 5am – despite a ridiculous law that supposedly prohibits dancing after midnight. The law is universally ignored, though a few places, when asked, may claim to close at midnight.

Shinjuku

Club Complex Code
Shinjuku Toho Kaikan 4F, 1-19-2 Kabuki-cho, Shinjuku-ku (3209 0702/www.clubcomplexcode.com). Shinjuku station (Yamanote, Chuo, Sobu lines), east exit; (Marunouchi line), exit B12; (Oedo, Shinjuku lines), exit 1. **Open** from 8pm daily. **Admission** ¥3,000 (incl 2 drinks) Mon-Thur, Sun; ¥3,500 (incl 2 drinks) Fri, Sat. **No credit cards.**
With three dancefloors (one huge, two small), this is a monster nightclub that can host a variety of events and special nights (sometimes at the same time). Its location, on the fourth floor of a Kabuki-cho building, means that from the outside you get no idea of its size: it's one of the biggest clubs in Japan, with room for 2,000 people. The largest dancefloor, En-Code, can hold 1,000 and has four gigantic screens for VJs. Sub-floor De-Code holds 120. There's also a main bar and lounge, Ba-Code, and a snack bar next to the main floor.

Garam
Dai-Roku Polestar Bldg 7A, 1-16-6 Kabuki-cho, Shinjuku-ku (3205 8668). Shinjuku station (Yamanote, Chuo, Sobu lines), east exit; (Marunouchi line), exit B12; (Oedo, Shinjuku lines), exit 1. **Open** 8pm-5am daily. **Admission** ¥1,000-¥1,500 (incl 1 drink). **No credit cards. Map** p73.
This swinging, foreign-owned Jamaican dance hall and reggae club could double as a walk-in closet. Still, the staff are very friendly and it's become something of an institution, with Japanese MCs, sharp DJs

C'est chic, **La Fabrique**. *See p210.*

and pounding vibes. To find it, head out of the east exit of Shinjuku station and down the pedestrianised street next to the Studio Alta TV screen. Cross over Yasukuni Dori and it's the third building on the right. Take the lift to the eighth floor.

Izm
J2 Bldg B1F-B2F, 1-7-1 Kabuki-cho, Shinjuku-ku (3200 9914/www.clubizm.net). Shinjuku station (Yamanote, Chuo, Sobu lines), east exit; (Marunouchi line), exit B12; (Oedo, Shinjuku lines), exit 1. **Open** 10pm-5am daily. **Admission** ¥2,000 Mon-Thur, Sun (incl 1 drink); ¥2,500 Fri, Sat (incl 1 drink). **No credit cards. Map** p73.
Hidden in the seediest part of Kabuki-cho, this small venue attracts a teenage clientele. The music is mainly hip hop, with a touch of R&B and reggae.

Open
2-5-15 Shinjuku, Shinjuku-ku (3226 8855/ http://club-open.hp.infoseek.co.jp). Shinjuku-Gyoenmae station (Marunouchi line), Shinjuku Gate exit. **Open** 5pm-5am Mon-Sat. **Admission** ¥1,000-¥1,500 (incl 1 drink). **No credit cards. Map** p73.
Open is the proud inheritor of the roots reggae tradition in Japan – and it holds fast to those roots. It was set up by the staff of 69, the country's very first reggae bar/club, when that bar closed down about a decade ago. The music is strictly roots, and the atmosphere friendly.

Oto

2F, 1-17-5 Kabuki-cho, Shinjuku-ku (5273 8264/ www.club-oto.com). Shinjuku station (Yamanote, Chuo, Sobu lines), east exit; (Marunouchi line), exit B12; (Oedo, Shinjuku lines), exit 1. **Open** 10pm-5am daily. **Admission** ¥2,000 (incl 1 drink) Mon-Thur, Sun; ¥2,500 (incl 1 or 2 drinks) Fri, Sat. **No credit cards. Map** p73.

Oto (meaning 'sound' in Japanese) lives up to its name, with a PA that would do a much larger place credit. Music runs from hip hop to techno, and all drinks cost ¥700.

Rags Room Acid

Kowa Bldg B1F, 2-3-12 Shinjuku, Shinjuku-ku (3352 3338/www.acid.jp). Shinjuku-Gyoenmae station (Marunouchi line), Shinjuku Gate exit. **Open** from 10pm; days vary. **Admission** usually ¥2,000 (incl 2 drinks). **No credit cards. Map** p73.

Finding the entrance to Rags Room Acid (formerly Club Acid) is a challenge in itself – a small sign on Shinjuku Dori provides the only hint of its existence. The best method is to pay attention to the stairways of neighbouring buildings and follow your ears: you can hear anything booming out of here, from ska to rock, hip hop to Latin, R&B to techno to drum 'n' bass. It's not always open, so check before you go.

Shibuya

Ball

Kuretake Bldg 4F, 4-9 Udagawacho, Shibuya-ku (3476 6533/www.club-ball.com). Shibuya station (Yamanote, Ginza lines), Hachiko exit; (Hanzomon line), exits 3, 6. **Open** 10pm-5am Mon-Sat; varies Sun. **Admission** ¥2,000 (incl 2 drinks). **No credit cards. Map** p79.

There's a great night view of Shibuya to be had from this little venue, but sadly that is its best feature, despite the moderately priced bar (drinks from ¥600). The sound system simply isn't up to scratch – and given that the choice of music is house, this is a very serious shortcoming indeed. The tiny dancefloor is another drawback.

Club Asia

1-8 Maruyamacho, Shibuya-ku (5458 1996/ www.clubasia.co.jp). Shibuya station (Yamanote, Ginza lines), Hachiko exit; (Hanzomon line), exit 3A. **Open** usually from 11pm. **Admission** ¥2,000-¥2,500 (incl 1 drink). **No credit cards. Map** p79.

Club Asia is a favourite space with private-party organisers, so for individual events check the schedule by the door. You'll find a bar on the first floor, a small dancefloor and bar on the second, and another, moderately spacious dancefloor and bar next to the stairs that lead from the second floor. The stairway to the main hall is an unusual feature, but it can get very crowded, especially on Friday nights. The main hall's high ceiling looks fab, but can result in an uneven sound.

Club Atom

Dr Jeekahn's 4F-6F, 2-4 Maruyamacho, Shibuya-ku (5428 5195/www.clubatom.com). Shibuya station (Yamanote, Ginza lines), Hachiko exit; (Hanzomon line), exit 3A. **Open** 9pm-5am Thur-Sat. **Admission** ¥3,000 (incl 2 drinks). **No credit cards. Map** p79.

There are two reasonably open dancefloors at this roomy venue. The one on the fifth floor focuses on mainstream trance or house, while the cave-like fourth-floor one offers R&B and hip hop.

Club Bar Family

Shimizu Bldg B1F, 1-10-2 Shibuya, Shibuya-ku (3400 9182). Shibuya station (Yamanote line), Miyamasuzaka (east) exit; (Ginza line), Tamagawa, Inokashira exits; (Hanzomon line), exit 11. **Open** 10.30pm-4am Mon-Thur; 10.30pm-5am Fri, Sat. **Admission** ¥2,000 (incl 1 drink). **No credit cards. Map** p79.

A tiny space pouring out heavy bass sounds, this all-Japanese club is ground-level hip hop at its best. Perfect if you like thundering rap beats. Grab a flyer at a record shop or even outside the venue to get ¥500 off the price of admission. Drinks are a good deal at around ¥600.

Club Chu

Oba B-Bldg B1F, 28-4 Maruyamacho, Shibuya-ku (3770 3780/www.fbi-tyo.com). Shibuya station (Yamanote, Ginza lines), Hachiko exit; (Hanzomon line), exit 1. **Open** 10pm-5am daily. **Admission** ¥2,000 (incl 2 drinks). **No credit cards. Map** p79.

Chu means 'sky' or 'space' in Japanese, and the decor here is designed to give you the feeling that you're floating in space. The cool ambience tends to attract an older clientele than you'll find in many other venues; in other words, people seeking a lounge space with good music and drinks, rather than serious dance freaks or date-hunters.

Club 49

Yuzawa Bldg 2F-3F, 3-26-25 Shibuya, Shibuya-ku (5485 4011/www.club49.jp). Shibuya station (Yamanote line), Miyamasusaka (east), south exits; (Ginza line), Toyoko exit; (Hanzomon line), exit 9. **Open** 9pm-5am Tue-Sat. **Admission** ¥500 Tue-Thur; ¥2,500 (incl 1 drink) Fri, Sat. **No credit cards.**

Formerly Club Fura, Club 49 has a slightly more progressive vibe and a somewhat cooler crowd. The emphasis is now on dance hall, reggae and hip hop, with some house nights and a little of the trashy trance left over from Fura. The second floor has a relatively roomy dance area, while the floor above takes the shape of a bar-cum-lounge.

Club Hachi

Aoyama Bldg 1F-4F, 4-5-9 Shibuya, Shibuya-ku (5766 4887). Shibuya station (Yamanote line), Miyamasusaka (east) exit; (Ginza line), Tamagawa, Inogashira exits; (Hanzomon line), exit 11. **Open** 10pm-5am Mon-Sat; 5-11pm Sun. **Admission** ¥2,000 (incl 1 drink) Mon-Thur, Sun; ¥2,500 (incl 1 drink) Fri, Sat. **No credit cards. Map** p79.

This dingy but funky club occupies the whole of a run-down, four-storey building on Roppongi Dori. The first floor contains a yakitori bar, the second a DJ bar, the third the main dance area, and the fourth a lounge bar. The monthly schedule ranges widely, from drum 'n' bass to R&B, house, techno, hip hop and jazz. It was once the regular haunt of globally fêted DJ Ken Ishii.

La Fabrique

Zero Gate B1F, 16-9 Udagawacho, Shibuya-ku (5428 5100/www.lafabrique.jp). Shibuya station (Yamanote, Ginza lines), Hachiko exit; (Hanzomon line), exit 6. **Open** 11am-5pm Fri, Sat. **Admission** ¥3,000-¥4,000 (incl 1 drink). **No credit cards.** **Map** p79.

Both a French restaurant and a happening club, this place transforms into a spacious dance venue after 10pm. Resident DJs start playing at about 6pm, but guest DJs don't begin their sets before 11pm. Downtempo sounds are usually played during the week; but by the weekend the music speeds up to include a mix of house and disco. The sibling of a well-known Paris venue, La Fabrique has another branch in Shanghai.

Harlem

Dr Jeekahn's Bldg 2F-3F, 2-4 Maruyamacho, Shibuya-ku (3461 8806/www.harlem.co.jp). Shibuya station (Yamanote, Ginza lines), Hachiko exit; (Hanzomon line), exit 3A. **Open** 10pm-5am Tue-Sat. **Admission** ¥2,000 (incl 2 drinks) Tue-Thur; ¥3,000 (incl 2 drinks) Fri. Sat. **No credit cards.** **Map** p79.

Located in the same building as Club Atom (*see p209*), Harlem has been the mecca of hip hop culture in Japan since the mid 1990s. If you want to see B-bwoys and fly girls shakin' it, as well as some of Japan's up-and-coming MCs, this is the spot. The tunes are basically straight-up rap with a little R&B mixed in. DJ Hasebe and other well-known Japanese spinners often play here. At the time of writing, unaccompanied foreign men won't be admitted.

Ism Shibuya

Social Dogenzaka Bldg 2F, 1-14-9 Dogenzaka, Shibuya-ku (3780 6320/http://club-ism.com). Shibuya station (Yamanote, Ginza lines), Hachiko exit; (Hanzomon line), exit 3A. **Open** from 10pm daily. **Admission** varies. **No credit cards.** **Map** p79.

Sister venue of Rockwest (*see p211*), located in the area between Mark City and 246 Street. Ism takes the old Rockwest ethos of pulling in the crowds by hosting a variety of events, so expect a mix of techno, house, trance and happy hardcore parties.

Loop

B1F, 2-1-13 Shibuya, Shibuya-ku (3797 9933/www.club-loop.com). Shibuya station (Yamanote line), Miyamasusaka (east) exit; (Ginza line), Tamagawa, Inokashira exits; (Hanzomon line), exit 11 or Omotesando station (Chiyoda, Ginza, Hanzomon lines), exit B1. **Open** 10pm-5am daily. **Admission** ¥2,000 (incl 1 drink) Mon-Thur; ¥2,500 (incl 1 drink) Fri-Sun. **No credit cards.** **Map** p79.

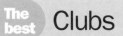

The best Clubs

Best superclub
Womb. *See p211.*

Best midsized club
Simoon. *See p211.*

Best small club
Loop. *See below.*

Best for international DJs
Space Lab Yellow. *See p214.*

Friendliest club
Secobar. *See p211.*

Best chill-out club
Bullet's. *See p213.*

Best sound system
Ageha. *See p214.*

Located between Shibuya and Omotesando stations, Loop has a stylish, bare-concrete interior and is an ideal hideout for true dance music aficionados into progressive house, deep house, tech house and some techno. The dancefloor has moody lighting, an excellent sound system and a friendly vibe. For local talent, check out 'Smoker' (Wednesday) and 'Fantasize' with DJ Jun (Friday). Well-known foreign DJs play occasionally.

Module

M&I Bldg B1F-B2F, 34-6 Udagawacho, Shibuya-ku (3464 8432/www.clubmodule.com). Shibuya station (Yamanote, Ginza lines), Hachiko exit; (Hanzomon line), exits 3, 6. **Open** from 10pm Mon-Sat. **Admission** ¥2,000 (incl 1 drink) Mon-Thur; ¥2,500 (incl 1 drink) Fri, Sat. **No credit cards.** **Map** p79.

There's a relaxing split-level bar on the first floor of the basement. You'll find a marked contrast when you get downstairs to the second level: a loud sound system causes the foundations to shudder below the small, pitch-black dancefloor, which has only a glitter ball for light.

Neo

TLC Building 5F, 2-21-7 Dogenzaka, Shibuya-ku (5459 7230/www.clubasia.co.jp). Shibuya station (Yamanote, Ginza lines), Hachiko exit; (Hanzomon line), exit 3A. **Open** 11pm-5am; days vary. **Admission** ¥3,000-¥3,500. **No credit cards.** **Map** p79.

More a deluxe lounge than a club, Neo's location among Shibuya's biggest clubs (Womb, Vuenos, Club Asia) means it's often overlooked by clubbers, but it can offer a more chilled-out experience. The venue has no music policy – so you could be listening to deep soul or progressive house.

Organ Bar

Kuretake Bldg 3F, 4-9 Udagawacho, Shibuya-ku (5489 5460/www.organ-b.net). Shibuya station (Yamanote, Ginza lines), Hachiko exit; (Hanzomon line), exit 6. **Open** 9pm-5am daily. **Admission** ¥2,000 (incl 1 drink) Mon-Sat; ¥1,000 Sun. **No credit cards. Map** p79.

Another small joint in the same building as Ball (*see p209*). What the tiny dancefloor lacks in space, it makes up for in atmosphere. The focus is on soul, jazz and bossa nova, all of which attract a slightly older crowd. All drinks cost ¥700.

Rockwest

Tosen Udagawacho Bldg 7F, 4-7 Udagawacho, Shibuya-ku (5459 7988/www.rock-west.com). Shibuya station (Yamanote, Ginza lines), Hachiko exit; (Hanzomon line), exit 6. **Open** 10pm-5am daily. **Admission** ¥2,000-¥2,500. **No credit cards. Map** p79.

Rockwest was once one of the best places in town for a happy hardcore night. It's still a good night out – if you want to listen to a mixture of hip hop and soul. Plus points are the air-conditioning, good sound system and a relatively roomy dancefloor. Re-entry to the club is allowed.

The Room

Daihachi Tohto Bldg B1F, 15-19 Sakuragaoka, Shibuya-ku (3461 7167/www.theroom.jp). Shibuya station (Yamanote line), south exit; (Ginza line), central exit; (Hanzomon line), exit 8. **Open** 10pm-5am Mon-Sat. **Admission** ¥1,000-¥2,000 (incl 1 drink) Mon-Thur; ¥2,500 (incl 1 drink) Fri, Sat. **No credit cards. Map** p79.

The Room is well hidden, so look for a red street light poking out from the basement. Owned by members of Kyoto Jazz Massive, it's a small venue split in two: one half is a concrete-walled bar, the other a pitch-black dancefloor. The flavour is available house, jazz, crossover or breakbeats. Top DJs sometimes come here to practise new routines on their nights off.

Ruby Room

Kasumi Bldg 4F, 2-25-17 Dogenzaka, Shibuya-ku (3780 3022/www.rubyroomtokyo.com). Shibuya station (Yamanote, Ginza lines), Hachiko exit; (Hanzomon line), exit 3A. **Open** 7pm-5am daily. **Admission** free Mon-Thur, Sun; ¥1,500 (incl 1 drink) Fri, Sat. **No credit cards. Map** p79.

This is a little box of a room that succeeds by staging top-quality, innovative nights. The American owners have lured some of Tokyo's top DJs to a venue that struggles to hold 150 people. From the flagship Deck 'n' Effect breaks party to the surprisingly decent open-stage nights, the styles vary greatly, but the atmosphere never disappoints. Restaurant Sonoma downstairs is under the same ownership.

Secobar

3-23-1 Shibuya, Shibuya-ku (5778 4571/ www.secobar.jp). Shibuya station (Yamanote line), Miyamasuaka (east) exit; (Ginza line), Toyoko exit; (Hanzomon line), exit 9. **Open** *Café* 11am-5am

Mon-Sat; 11.30am-1am Sun. *Club* 7pm-5am daily. **Admission** from ¥1,000 (incl 1 drink). **No credit cards. Map** p79.

Neatly located under the railway tracks, this lounge café doubles up as a dance venue in the evenings, with room for around 200 people. Music ranges from bossa nova to house. Check out the monthly 'electronic pub' night, where electronica, breaks and electro funk is played until early in the morning.

Simoon

3-26-16 Shibuya, Shibuya-ku (5774 1669/ www.simoon.net). Shibuya station (Yamanote line), east exit; (Ginza line), Toyoko exit; (Hanzomon line), exit 9. **Open** 10pm-5am daily. **Admission** ¥2,500-¥4,000 (incl 1 drink). **No credit cards.**

The entrance may look like a bicycle parking lot, but once you're inside, a warmly lit lounge space with comfortable couches awaits. The basement dancefloor boasts a good-quality sound system for its size. Simoon began with a reputation for hip hop and R&B, but has gradually broadened its scope to encompass reggae, house and more.

Vuenos Bar Tokyo

1F-B1F, 2-21 7 Dogenzaka, Shibuya-ku (5458 5963/ www.clubasia.co.jp). Shibuya station (Yamanote, Ginza lines), Hachiko exit; (Hanzomon line), exit 3A. **Open** 11pm-5am; days vary. **Admission** ¥2,500-¥3,000. **No credit cards. Map** p79.

Across from and owned by Club Asia (*see p209*), Vuenos opened in 1998 with a mission to spread the word about Latin, soul and dance music. At weekends, however, the line-up tends to be hip hop, R&B and reggae. It attracts a younger crowd and is very popular, so you may have to queue to get in.

Womb

2-16 Maruyamacho, Shibuya-ku (5459 0039/ www.womb.co.jp). Shibuya station (Yamanote, Ginza lines), Hachiko exit; (Hanzomon line), exit 3A. **Open** usually 10pm-5am Thur-Sat. **Admission** usually ¥2,000-¥4,000. **No credit cards. Map** p79.

In the middle of one of Tokyo's biggest love hotel districts, this gymnasium-like disco sits in a bare concrete building. The main floor is enormous (the ceiling is almost 9m/30ft high), and its huge mirror ball claims to be the biggest in Asia. Womb also boasts upstairs lounge areas and a super-bass sound system shipped all the way from New York. Each night varies, but there's always an impressive line-up of international DJs, with techno and deep house being the usual genres of choice.

Harajuku & Aoyama

Fai

Hachihonkan Bldg B1F-B2F, 5-10-1 Minami-Aoyama, Minato-ku (3486 4910/www.fai-aoyama.com). Omotesando station (Chiyoda, Ginza, Hanzomon lines), exit B1. **Open** 10pm-5am daily. **Admission** ¥2,000 (incl 1 drink) Mon-Thur; ¥2,500 (incl 2 drinks) Fri-Sun. **No credit cards.**

Arts & Entertainment

Only punk and techno are left off the musical menu at Fai, which specialises in sounds from the 1970s and '80s, notably disco, funk, soul and jazz. Fine drinks start at ¥700.

Maniac Love

B1F, 5-10-6 Minami-Aoyama, Minato-ku (3406 1166/www.maniaclove.com). Omotesando station (Chiyoda, Ginza, Hanzomon lines), exit B1. **Open** from 10pm Mon-Sat. **Admission** ¥2,000 Mon-Thur (incl 1 drink); ¥2,500 Fri, Sat (incl 1 drink); ¥1,000 from 5am Sun. **No credit cards.**

With its immense sound system and cool lighting effects, Maniac Love was designed as a mecca for dance fans. The after-hours party on Sunday mornings is legendary; it's not unusual to see the place full to bursting at 7am. Like many places in Tokyo, the venue can be tricky to find – it's in the basement of a plain-looking building. Drinks start at ¥700.

Mission Lounge

Aoyama Center Bldg B1, 3-8-40 Minami Aoyama, Minato-ku (3478 1107/www.missionlounge.com). Omotesando station (Chiyoda, Ginza, Hanzomon lines), exits A3, A4. **Open** from 8pm Mon-Thur, 8pm-4am Fri-Sun. **Admission** ¥2,000 (incl 2 drinks) Mon-Thur, Sun; ¥3,000 (incl 2 drinks) Fri, Sat. **No credit cards. Map** p85.

Originally called Mauve (though that name lasted a mere two months), this joint opened in autumn 2004. But the name was probably the least ill-conceived aspect of the venue. The music of the main floor drowns out the lounge DJ; the ceramic tile decor of one room evokes a cheap bathroom; and (at the time of writing, at least) the dancefloor is a rather lonely place. The business plan, it seems, is to lure people to the champagne room, where ¥2,000 will get you a sofa seat for two hours.

Mix

B1F, 3-6-19 Kita-Aoyama, Minato-ku (3797 1313/www.at-mix.com). Omotesando station (Chiyoda, Ginza, Hanzomon lines), exits A1, B4. **Open** 10pm-5am; days vary. **Admission** ¥2,000 (incl 2 drinks) Mon-Thur, Sun; ¥2,500 (incl 2 drinks) Fri, Sat. **No credit cards. Map** p85.

This tiny, narrow club makes full use of its limited space, somehow managing to fit a seating area between the dancefloor and bar, and get some interesting art up on the walls. It's usually rammed at the weekends and has been that way for over a decade. Expect a mixed, friendly crowd grooving to a range of sounds, tending towards reggae, dub, hip hop and dance hall. It was producer Adrian Sherwood's favourite Tokyo club when he visited Japan frequently in the 1990s.

The Orbient

Crystal Bldg B1F-B2F, 3-5-12 Kita-Aoyama, Minato-ku (5775 2555/www.orbient.jp). Omotesando station (Chiyoda, Ginza, Hanzomon lines), exits A2, A3. **Open** *Restaurant* 6pm-midnight daily. *Club* 7pm-1am daily. **Admission** ¥2,000-¥3,000 (incl 2 drinks). **No credit cards. Map** p85.

Café/club **Secobar**. *See p211.*

Looking smart is advisable if you want to fit in at this upmarket, golden-walled club. It has three bars, a reasonably sized dancefloor and an adequate sound system. Music varies nightly; it gets busy on Fridays with dance classics and disco, when the clientele is mainly teenyboppers and secretaries. Its reasonably priced Chinese restaurant is justifiably popular, though there's a table charge of ¥1,000 at weekends. Once you've finished dining, you can get into the club for free, though some of the cosiest seats require further outlay.

Ebisu & Daikanyama

The legendary **Liquid Room** (*see p240*), now in Ebisu, has shifted its focus to live acts, but still hosts clubbing events on occasion.

Air

Hikawa Bldg B1F-B2F, 2-11 Sarugakucho,
Shibuya-ku (5784 3386/www.air-tokyo.com).
Daikanyama station (Tokyu Toyoko line). **Open**
10pm-5am Mon, Thur-Sat. **Admission** from ¥2,500
(incl 1 drink). **No credit cards.**
Deep inside this rabbit's burrow near Daikanyama
station you'll find a comfortable DJ lounge. Go still
further and there's a cheap bar and spacious dancefloor. The international talent on offer is impressive.

Milk

Roob 6 Bldg B1F-B2F, 1-13-3 Ebisu-Nishi,
Shibuya-ku (5458 2826/www.milk-tokyo.com).
Ebisu station (Yamanote line), west exit; (Hibiya
line), exit 2. **Open** 10pm-5am; days vary.
Admission from ¥2,500. **No credit cards.**
Milk's mission when it opened in 1995 was to bring
the best of rock, punk and hardcore to Tokyo. These
days, even it has succumbed to the techno and house
sound that has swept Tokyo clubland, though occasional rock gigs still happen. It occupies the underground floors of the same building as the What the
Dickens pub (*see p162*). At the bottom is a lounge
area with a mysteriously lit, morgue-like 'kitchen'
where you can have a quiet chat while up above the
dancing continues on the cramped dancefloor.

Roppongi & Azabu-Juban

Alife

1-7-2 Nishi-Azabu, Minato-ku (5785 2531/
www.e-alife.net). Roppongi station (Hibiya, Oedo
lines), exit 2. **Open** *Lounge & restaurant* 11pm-5am
Mon-Sat. *Club* from 9pm Thur-Sat. **Admission**
Club ¥3,500 (incl 2 drinks) men; ¥2,500 (incl 2 drinks)
women. **No credit cards. Map** p109.
If you can stand the snotty attitude of the staff, this
big club is fairly well appointed, with a spacious
party lounge on the second floor, a stylish café on
the ground floor and a large dance area in the basement. It has a vibrant party atmosphere and is a
haven for hardcore clubbers, with guest DJs playing
trance or house on Sunday mornings.

Bar Matrix

Mizobuchi Bldg B1F, 3-13-6 Roppongi, Minato-ku
(3405 1066). Roppongi station (Hibiya, Oedo lines),
exit 3. **Open** 6pm-4am daily. **Admission** free.
Map p109.
Named after the Keanu Reeves movie, this Roppongi
bar/club has a futuristic, metallic interior and a
cyber feel – it could be considered emblematic of
Tokyo, or at least what travellers expect Tokyo to
be. The music is a mishmash of everything, but
tends towards hip hop and R&B, with trashy trance
making weekend appearances.

Bullet's

Kasumi Bldg B1F, 1-7-11 Nishi-Azabu, Minato-ku
(3401 4844/www.bul-lets.com). Roppongi station
(Hibiya, Oedo lines), exit 2. **Open** 10pm-5am Fri;
11pm-5am Sat. **Admission** ¥2,000 Fri; ¥1,500 Sat.
No credit cards. Map p109.

This friendly, cosy club has a front area with a bar
and tables, plus sofas and mattresses at the back for
ultimate chilling (leave your shoes at the edge of the
carpet). A good spot if you're into experimental DJs,
broken beats and breakbeats. The VJs and/or art on
display can be interesting too.

Club Jamaica

Nishi-Azabu Ishibashi Bldg B1F, 4-16-14 Nishi-
Azabu, Minato-ku (3407 8844/www.club-jamaica.
com). Roppongi station (Hibiya, Oedo lines), exit 1.
Open 10pm-5am Thur-Sat. **Admission** ¥1,000
(incl 1 drink) Thur; ¥2,500 (incl 2 drinks) Fri, Sat.
No credit cards.
Opened by a reggae fanatic in 1989, Club Jamaica
blasts out roots reggae on Thursday nights, then
pulls in a younger crowd at the weekend with dance
hall sounds. It's a small venue with a hard-to-find
entrance, but the atmosphere is friendly and the
sound system has some serious bass – the back wall
is piled high with speakers.

Core

TSK CCC Bldg B1F-B2F, 7-15-30 Roppongi,
Minato-ku (3470 5944/www.clubcore.net). Roppongi
station (Hibiya line), exit 4B; (Oedo line), exit 7.
Open from 10pm Wed-Sun. **Admission** usually
¥2,500 (incl 1 drink). **No credit cards. Map** p109.
Discretion is taken to new heights at Core, whose
owner claims he didn't put a sign outside because
he didn't want everyone to know it was there. It
features mostly house and techno, and has proved
popular with TV and sports personalities. Every
second Friday, it hosts a house and R&B event,
'Scene', where DJs Funakoshi and Yo-Gin spin the
tracks. The bar snacks are impressive (for a club)
and drinks start at ¥600.

Muse

4-1-1 Nishi-Azabu, Minato-ku (5467 1188/
www.muse-web.com). Roppongi station (Hibiya,
Oedo lines), exit 1. **Open** from 7pm Mon-Thur,
Sun; 7pm-5am Fri, Sat. **Admission** ¥2,000
(incl 2 drinks) Mon-Thur, Sun; ¥3,000 (incl 2 drinks)
Fri, Sat. **Dress code** not too casual. **No credit
cards. Map** p109.
This three-level club features a stellar bar and cave-
like areas, plus billiards and ping-pong tables in the
basement. So it's a shame that it's also a massive
meat market. It's located at the Nishi-Azabu crossing; walk past Hobson's ice-cream parlour towards
Hiroo on Gaien-Nishi Dori and look to your right.

La Scala – Roppongi

3-13-6 Roppongi, Minato-ku (3408 3910).
Roppongi station (Hibiya, Oedo lines), exit 3.
Open 7pm-1am Mon-Thur, Sun; 7pm-3am Fri, Sat.
Admission free. **Map** p109.
This welcoming, three-floor club almost redeems the
unfriendly, GI-filled, over-the-top party area of
Roppongi. There's a bar and restaurant on the first
floor, a dancefloor on the second and billiards and
karaoke lounges on the third. A great spot to chill
or dance – despite its location.

Space Lab Yellow

Cesaurus Nishi-Azabu Bldg B1F-B2F, 1-10-11 Nishi-Azabu, Minato-ku (3479 0690/www.club-yellow.com). Roppongi station (Hibiya, Oedo lines), exit 2. **Open** 10pm-5am; days vary. **Admission** usually ¥3,000. **No credit cards.** Map p109.

Better known as Yellow, this is the original hip venue in Japan; everyone from 808 State to Laurent Garnier and Timo Maas have played here. On Saturdays, guest appearances by hot foreign DJs still fill the place – definitely a sweaty experience. There's also a spacious (and totally white) lounge upstairs.

328 (San Ni Pa)

B1F, 3-24-20 Nishi-Azabu, Minato-ku (3401 4968/ www.02.246.ne.jp/~azabu328). Roppongi station (Hibiya, Oedo lines), exit 1. **Open** from 8pm daily. **Admission** ¥2,000 (incl 2 drinks) Mon-Thur, Sun; ¥2,500 (incl 2 drinks) Fri, Sat. **No credit cards.** Map p109.

You'll spot 328's large neon sign from the Nishi-Azabu crossing. A real veteran of the club scene, it opened way back in 1979. Expect a mix of genres, from soul to dance classics, and an older crowd. On Saturday there are more rare groove tunes and it gets packed (it's small), so arrive early. It usually stays open past midnight on weekends.

Vanilla

TSK Bldg, 7-15-30 Roppongi, Minato-ku (3401 6200/www.clubvanilla.com). Roppongi station (Hibiya, Oedo lines), exits 4A, 4B. **Open** 7pm-5am Thur-Sat. **Admission** usually ¥3,000/¥3,500 (incl 1 drink). **No credit cards.** Map p109.

Probably the most underused space in Tokyo. Vanilla is a vast club that can accommodate over 5,000 people, yet it never attracts a name big enough to lure such a crowd. When all the rooms are open, it's a fun place to party – with a variety of decors, from traditional Japanese style to carpeted playboy lounge – but the best rooms are usually closed, and punters are herded to the huge dancefloor to rub shoulders with the office worker crowd. It's also not a great place to get drunk in.

Velfarre

Velfarre Bldg, 7-14-22 Roppongi, Minato-ku (3402 8000/http://velfarre.avex.co.jp). Roppongi station (Hibiya, Oedo lines), exit 4. **Open** 7pm-1am Thur-Sun. **Admission** usually ¥3,000 (incl 2 drinks). **No credit cards.** Map p109.

This gigantic club and live venue, with a capacity of over 2,000, is a real throwback to the heady days of the 1980s. There's a vast dancefloor with an automated moveable stage and giant mirror ball, marble staircases, and more bars, restrooms and snack bars than you can count. Well known for the scantily clad girls dancing on platforms by the stage (and they're just patrons, not employees).

Warehouse

Fukuo Bldg B1F, 1-4-5 Azabu-Juban, Minato-ku (5775 2905). Azabu-Juban station (Nanboku, Oedo lines), exits 4, 7. **Open** 8pm-1am Mon-Thur, Sun; 8pm-3am Fri, Sat. **Admission** usually ¥2,500-¥4,000 (incl 1 drink). **No credit cards.**

A spacious venue that opened as this guide went to press. Its old incarnation – Luners – attracted good crowds and the occasional international DJ. Time will tell if Warehouse can match up.

Ikebukuro

Bed

Fukuri Bldg B1F, 3-29-9 Nishi-Ikebukuro, Toshima-ku (3981 5300/www.ikebukurobed.com). Ikebukuro station (Yamanote line), west exit; (Marunouchi, Yurakucho lines), exit 1A. **Open** 10pm-5am daily. **Admission** ¥2,000 (incl 2 drinks) Mon-Thur, Sun; ¥2,500 (incl 2 drinks) Fri, Sat. **No credit cards.** Map p119.

As you descend to Bed, you will be greeted by photo montages of previous, presumably satisfied customers. The clientele is on the young side, and the music mainly hip hop, with the occasional techno and warp house.

Further afield

Popular music venue **Club Que** (*see p242*) in Shimo-Kitazawa transforms itself into a rock-oriented club on weekend nights.

Ageha

2-2-10 Shinkiba, Koto-ku (5534 2525/ www.ageha.com). Shin-Kiba station (Rinkai, Yurakucho lines). **Open** 11pm-5am Thur-Sat. **Admission** usually ¥4,000 (incl 2 drinks). **No credit cards.**

The superclub in Tokyo. It host parties with internationally famous DJs, although well-known local spinners appear occasionally. With three dancefloors, a pool area and numerous bars/chill-out spaces, it's a huge if somewhat impersonal place, with a great sound system. Women should check out the cubicle nearest to the toilet entrance – it leads to a secret room. Ageha is far from downtown Tokyo, but the club provides a free bus from Shibuya every half hour throughout the night. Board at the start of Roppongi Dori, just across from Shibuya station; you'll need photo ID containing your birth date to be allowed on.

Bar Drop

2F-B1F, 1-29-6 Kichijoji-Honcho, Musashino-shi (0422 20 0737/www.drop.co.jp). Kichijoji station (Chuo, Sobu lines), central exit. **Open** from 9.30pm Mon-Thur; from 11pm Fri, Sat; varies Sun. **Admission** usually ¥1,500 (incl 1 drink) Mon-Thur; ¥2,000 (incl 1 or 2 drinks) Fri-Sun. **No credit cards.**

This Kichijoji club features a variety of 1990s US and UK pop music on its two dancefloors, with the downstairs floor offering a slightly more eclectic choice of sounds. Unusually for Tokyo, there's a large lounge space, with tables and chairs to cool off at once you've danced till you've dropped.

Film

There's more to Japanese cinema than *Seven Samurai*.

The Japanese film industry goes back a long way, having produced the documentary *Geisha No Teodori* in 1899. Mass Japanese cinema of the early 20th century started with foreign imports, however, and since the audience could not understand the foreign language inter-titles, a *benshi* or narrator was employed to explain the action and make it palatable to the Japanese. *Benshi* soon became valued artists who narrated both Japanese and foreign work – a tradition that has since died out. One early film of particular note is *A Page of Madness* (*Kurutta Ippeiji*, 1926) by Kinogasa Teinosuke, about a janitor in a mental asylum. Its images and techniques remain gripping today, testament to Kinogasa's vision, as well as to the sophistication of early Japanese film.

THE 'GOLDEN AGE'

The 1930s marked the dawn of the 'golden age' of Japanese cinema. Gifted directors such as Ozu Yasujiro, Mizoguchi Kenji, Naruse Mikio and the less-heralded Shimizu Hiroshi produced work that exhibited a remarkable mastery of the craft. Although Ozu is best known for his post-war films such as the famous *Tokyo Story* (*Tokyo Monogatari*, 1953), his pre-war work is edgier, more varied and equally accomplished. This period also saw the rise of the Japanese studio system. Much like their Hollywood counterparts, large studios such as Shochiku, Toho, Daiei and Nikkatsu started to put

directors under contract and control the content of their work. Filmmaking was a thriving and extremely profitable business, and the studios ruled it with an iron fist.

The hiccup of Word War II limited film production to mainly jingoistic drek, but the industry recovered its poise afterwards. General consensus holds that the golden age continued into the mid/late 1950s with Ozu, Mizoguchi and Naruse still active. In addition, new stars such as Kurosawa Akira – a man who would define Japanese cinema (especially abroad) for the next 40 years – were rising fast. This period saw the emergence of talented auteurs Ichikawa Kon, Masumura Yasuzo and Teshigahara Hiroshi.

'NUBERU BAGU'

In the late 1950s and early '60s the studio system thrived as never before, but it was challenged by youthful and radical directors of the 'Nuberu Bagu' (from the French term *Nouvelle Vague* or New Wave) movement, despite the fact that major studio Shochiku had launched this movement to attract younger fans. Oshima Nagisa, Imamura Shohei, Hani Susumu, Yoshida Yoshige and others made films exposing Japan's social problems, questioning the assumption of Western values and materialism, and addressing taboo subjects like sexuality. In addition, they broke the studios' grip on directors, eventually

Anime hit *Spirited Away*.

Directors

For the best in contemporary Japanese film, try the following directors. All have films available on DVD with English subtitles.

Aoyama Shinji (b 1964)

Aoyama has captured the urban alienation and lack of meaning in Japanese life in violent, starkly drawn movies like *Helpless* and *Two Punks* (both 1996). However, he also elegantly portrays heartbreak, memory and redemption in *Shady Grove* (1999) and *Eureka* (2000). The latter is long, at nearly four hours, but worth the effort.

Ichikawa Jun (b 1948)

A lyrical and subtle filmmaker, Ichikawa had a surge of creative juices in the 1990s, having mainly made commercials before that. He produced eight films in a decade; in particular, *Dying at a Hospital*, *Tokyo Siblings* and *Tokyo Marigold* were all superb. His films are firmly rooted in Japan's humanist tradition. His latest film, *Tony Takitani* (2004), is the only movie adaptation of a Murakami Haruki story.

Kore-eda Hirokazu (b 1962)

The brightest light in the explosion of Japanese cinema in the 1990s, Kore-eda's 1995 film *Mabarosi* was favourably compared to work by the master Ozu. He's made some difficult films (such as *Distance*, 2001), but in general his work is accessible and moving, such as *Nobody Knows*, whose 14-year-old star Yagira Yuya won a Best Actor prize at Cannes in 2004.

Kumai Kei (b 1930)

One of the lesser-known old guard of Japanese cinema, this insightful auteur has taken on such taboo topics as Japanese war crimes during World War II (*The Sea and Poison*, 1986) and the culpability of the Japanese police in the Aum Shinrikyo cult crimes (*Darkness in the Light*, 2001).

Kurosawa Kiyoshi (b 1955)

Kurosawa (no relation to Akira) endured working on trashy low-budget flicks before a meteoric rise to prominence at the end of the '90s. *Cure* (1997) was a brilliant, eerie horror/mystery, which Kurosawa followed with the coup of having films at the three major film festivals (Berlin, Cannes, Venice) in the same year (1999). Art-house yet affecting, Kurosawa is a premier director.

venturing out on their own and also forming the artistically noteworthy independent production company Art Theatre Guild (ATG).

The tapering-off of the Nuberu Bagu in the mid '70s triggered a crisis in Japanese cinema. Attendances had been falling for years and there were few new acclaimed directors appearing (although Kurosawa, Oshima and Imamura, among others, were still active). The situation continued in this vein for much of the 1980s. Although nearly half of Japanese box office receipts still derived from locally made fare (a claim that few countries could make), the studios continued to churn out formulaic, melodramatic pieces and were suffering financially – in 1972 Daiei went bankrupt and Nikkatsu turned to making softcore porn.

REBIRTH

Japanese cinema underwent an energetic rebirth in the 1990s with the arrival of young and/or fresh directors such as Kitano 'Beat' Takeshi – the most internationally successful of contemporary Japanese filmmakers – Iwai Shunji, Kurosawa Kiyoshi, Tsukamoto Shinya, Shinozaki Makoto and Ichikawa Jun. In addition, Japanese *anime* (animation), led by the genius of Miyazaki Hayao, started to conquer foreign markets and take huge profits at home – Miyazaki's *Spirited Away* (2001) is the highest grossing film of all time in Japan. Hollywood has also jumped on the bandwagon, winning box office success with remakes of a number of domestic hits, such as Nakata Hideo's horror mystery *Ringu* (1998) – remade as *The Ring* (2002). Nakata is currently working on the US version of his own 1999 sequel *Ringu 2*.

Nowadays Japanese cinema is once again a staple of important world film festivals, and the domestic box office for local product has stabilised at a very respectable 33 per cent.

TICKETS AND INFORMATION

Visiting a cinema in Tokyo is expensive, with most cinemas charging ¥1,800 for on-the-day admission (¥1,000-¥1,500 concessions). If you want to save money, you can buy advance tickets at convenience stores and ticket agencies for around ¥300-¥500 less (or go on the first day of the month, when admission is usually ¥1,000). The problem with this system is that tickets are sold for the film – not the cinema – so in theory any number of people can arrive to catch the latest blockbuster. Seats are not allocated, so people regularly arrive an hour in advance and then charge in as soon as the doors open to grab the best places. Seats can be reserved through agencies such as Pia (*see p237* **Tickets**), but this adds an extra ¥200-¥1,000 to the price. Some cinemas are cheaper; we've given ticket prices for those below. The cluster of Japanese cinemas in Shinjuku, Ginza, Shibuya and other busy areas all operate this ridiculous system. However, hope comes in the form of the new breed of multiplexes, which offer allocated seating at point of sale for no extra cost. Below are the best of the art-house and independent cinemas. Note that none accepts credit cards.

Most Hollywood or other foreign films are screened in their original version with Japanese subtitles. Cinemas occasionally screen a Japanese film with English subtitles (usually the last showing on a Sunday). If you visit in the autumn, you may catch one of the two international film festivals – the **Tokyo International Film Festival** (*see p199*) and **Tokyo Filmex** (www.filmex.net) – both of which show Japanese films with English subtitles. For film listings, check *Metropolis*, *Japan Times* and Tokyo Q (www.tokyoq.com).

Independent & repertory

Athénée Français Cultural Center
4F, 2-11 Kanda Surugadai, Chiyoda-ku (3291 4339/ www.athenee.net/culturalcenter). Suidobashi station (Chuo, Sobu lines), east exit; (Mita line), exit A1. **Tickets** vary. **Seats** 80.
Screens classics and discovers new filmmakers.

Ciné Amuse
CSF, 2-23 12 Dogenzaka, Shibuya-ku (3496 2888/ www.cineamuse.co.jp). Shibuya station (Yamanote, Ginza lines), Hachiko exit; (Hanzomon line), exit 3A. **Seats** *East Screen* 132. *West Screen* 129. **Map** p79.
Programming ranges from Japanese classics such as *Ai no Corrida* to new international films.

Le Cinema
Bunkamura 6F, 2-24-1 Dogenzaka, Shibuya-ku (3477 9264/www.bunkamura.co.jp). Shibuya station (Yamanote, Ginza lines), Hachiko exit; (Hanzomon line), exit 3A. **Seats** *Screen 1* 150. *Screen 2* 126. **Map** p79.
This two-screener in the giant Bunkamura arts complex offers mainly French fare. It's also the main venue for the annual Tokyo International Film Festival (*see p199*).

Cinema Artone Shimo-Kitazawa
Suzunari-Yokocho 2F, 1-45-15 Kitazawa, Setagaya-ku (5452 1400/www.cinekita.co.jp). Shimo-Kitazawa station (Keio Inokashira, Odakyu lines), south exit. **Tickets** ¥1,500, ¥1,000-¥1,300 concessions; ¥1,000 1st of mth (not Jan). **Seats** 50.
Independent films from around the world.

Cinema Rise
13-17 Udagawacho, Shibuya-ku (3464 0051/ www.cinemarise.com.). Shibuya station (Yamanote, Ginza lines), Hachiko exit; (Hanzomon line), exit 6. **Seats** *Screen 1* 220. *Screen 2* 303. **Map** p79.

A champion of independent cinema, Cinema Rise is where *Trainspotting* and *Buena Vista Social Club* first hit Tokyo. Foreign students (who must show ID) pay only ¥1,000.

Cinema Square Tokyu
Tokyu Milano Bldg 3F, 1-29-1 Kabuki-cho, Shinjuku-ku (3202 1189/www.tokyu-rec.co.jp/ table.html). Shinjuku station (Yamanote, Chuo lines), east exit; (Marunouchi line), exit B12; (Oedo, Shinjuku lines), exit 1. **Seats** 224.
The pioneer of art-house cinemas in Tokyo, showing mainly recent independent films.

Ciné Pathos
4-8-7 Ginza, Chuo-ku (3561 4660). Higashi-Ginza station (Asakusa, Hibiya lines), exit A2. **Seats** *Screen 1* 200. *Screen 2* 144. *Screen 3* 81. **Map** p60.
A three-screener with new films and classic revivals.

Ciné Quinto
Parco Part 3 8F, 14-5 Udagawa-cho, Shibuya-ku (3477 5905/www.parco-city.co.jp/cine_quinto). Shibuya station (Yamanote, Ginza lines), Hachiko exit; (Hanzomon line), exit 6. **Seats** 227. **Map** p79.
Quinto often screens new British films, and offers bizarre film-based discounts. For example, when Hong Kong film *The Eye* was on, anyone carrying a photo of a ghost got a discount of ¥800. Different rules are stipulated for each film. Keep your ticket stub to get ¥800 off your next visit.

Ciné Saison Shibuya
The Prime 6F, 2-29-5 Dogenzaka, Shibuya-ku (3770 1721/www.cinemabox.com). Shibuya station (Yamanote, Ginza lines), Hachiko exit; (Hanzomon line), exit 1. **Seats** 221. **Map** p79.
Revivals, mini festivals and independent productions are the lifeblood of this comfortable cinema.

Ciné Switch Ginza
Ginza-Hata Bldg B1F, 4-4-5 Ginza, Chuo-ku (3561 0707/www.cineswitch.com). Ginza station (Ginza, Hibiya, Marunouchi lines), exit B2. **Seats** *Screen 1* 273. *Screen 2* 182. **Map** p60.
Recent European and American films.

Ebisu Garden Cinema
Ebisu Garden Place, 4-20-2 Ebisu, Shibuya-ku (5420 6161/www.cineplex.co.jp). Ebisu station (Yamanote line), east exit; (Hibiya line), exit 1. **Seats** *Screen 1* 232. *Screen 2* 116.
A mix of American indies and foreign films. Film-goers are summoned in numbered batches, according to when they bought their tickets, so there's never any stampede for seats. Good system.

Euro Space
Tobu-Fuji Bldg 2F, 24-4 Sakuragaoka-cho, Shibuya-ku (3461 0211/www.eurospace.co.jp). Shibuya station (Yamanote, Ginza lines), south exit; (Hanzomon line), exit 5. **Seats** *Screen 1* 75. *Screen 2* 106. **Map** p79.
Independent films from Europe and Asia, as well as retrospectives of the likes of Eric Rohmer.

Arts & Entertainment

Ginza Théâtre Cinema

Ginza-Théâtre Bldg 5F, 1-11-2 Ginza, Chuo-ku (3535 6000/www.cinemabox.com). Kyobashi station (Ginza line), exit 2 or Ginza-Itchome station (Yurakucho line), exit 7. **Seats** 150. **Map** p60.
Late-night shows with interesting programmes.

Haiyu-za

4-9-2 Roppongi, Minato-ku (3470 2880/ www.haiyuzagekijou.co.jp/menu.html). Roppongi station (Oedo line), exit 6; (Hibiya line), exit 4A. **Tickets** vary. **Seats** 300. **Map** p60.
Roppongi's venerable old fleapit opens irregularly, but when it does its speciality is weird and avant-garde films from all continents. A Tokyo treasure that is worth a visit, if you can catch it open.

Hibiya Chanter Ciné

Chanter Bldg 2F, 1-2-2 Yurakucho, Chiyoda-ku (3591 1511/www.chantercine.com). Hibiya station (Chiyoda, Hibiya, Mita lines), exit A5. **Seats** *Screens 1 & 2* 226. *Screen 3* 192. **Map** p60.
Mainly recent European and American films.

Iidabashi Ginrei Hall

2-19 Kagurazaka, Shinjuku-ku (3269 3852/ www.cam.hi-ho.ne.jp/ginrei). Iidabashi station (Chuo, Sobu lines), west exit; (Oedo, Nanboku, Tozai, Yurakucho lines), exits B4A, B4B. **Tickets** ¥1,500; ¥1,000-¥1,200 concessions; ¥1,000 1st of mth. **Seats** 206.
Special double-features offer interesting combinations of second-run films. Pay ¥10,500 to join the Cinema Club and you can go as often as you like for a whole year without paying another yen.

Institut Franco-Japonais

15 Ichigaya-Funagawaramachi, Shinjuku-ku (5261 3933/www.ifjtokyo.or.jp/culture/cinema.html). Iidabashi station (Chuo, Sobu lines), west exit; (Oedo Nanboku, Tozai, Yurakucho lines), exits B3. **Tickets** ¥1,000. **Seats** 115. **Map** p66.
A pearl in the Japanese cinema scene, this French culture centre shows contemporary French films at the weekend, often with English subtitles.

Iwanami Hall

Iwanami Jinbocho Bldg 10F, 2-1 Kanda-Jinbocho, Chiyoda-ku (3262 5252/www.iwanami-hall.com). Jinbocho station (Hanzomon, Mita, Shinjuku lines), exit A6. **Seats** 220. **Map** p66.
This highbrow cinema has been screening international works of social realism since the 1970s. The focus is on female directors and political work.

Kichijoji Baus Theatre

1-11-23 Kichijoji-Honmachi, Musashino-shi (0422 22 3555/www.baustheater.com). Kichijoji station (Chuo line), north exit. **Seats** *Screen 1* 220. *Screen 2* 50. *Screen 3* 106.
Everything from Hollywood blockbusters to Japanese independent films, but with an emphasis on mainstream stuff these days. There are discounts for men on Mondays, women on Wednesdays and couples on Fridays.

Kineca Omori

Seiyu Omori 5F, 6-27-25 Minami-Oi, Shinagawa-ku (3762 6000/http://kineca.m78.com). Omori station (Keihin-Tohoku line), east exit. **Seats** *Screen 1* 134. *Screen 2* 69. *Screen 3* 40.
The late-night shows are often interesting, on themes such as the films of John Cassavetes. One screen shows only Asian films.

Laputa Asagaya

Laputa Bldg 2F, 2-12-21 Asagaya-Kita, Suginami-ku (3336 5440/www.laputa-jp.com). Asagaya station (Chuo, Sobu lines), north exit. **Tickets** ¥1,200; ¥1,000 concessions; ¥1,000 Wed. **Seats** 50.
A charming, tiny cinema that shows everything from Japanese indies to experimental fare – stuff that's usually not shown anywhere else in Tokyo.

National Film Centre

3-7-6 Kyobashi, Chuo-ku (5777 8600/ www.momat.go.jp). Kyobashi station (Ginza line), exit 1 or Takaracho station (Asakusa line), exit A4. **Tickets** ¥500. **Seats** *Screen 1* 310. *Screen 2* 151. **Map** p66.
Part of the National Museum of Modern Art, this venue has two cinemas, a gallery, a library and a café. It holds a collection of 19,000 films, and often revives Japanese classics.

Sanbyakunin Gekijo

2-29-10 Hon-Komagome, Bunkyo-ku (3944 5451/ www.bekkoame.ne.jp/~darts). Sengoku station (Mita line), exit A1. **Seats** 302.
Art-house specialist: classic features, revivals and cinema marathons. A place for serious cinephiles.

Sangenjaya Chuo Gekijo

2-14-5 Sangenjaya, Setagaya-ku (3421 4610). Sangenjaya station (Tokyu Denentoshi line), Setagaya Dori exit. **Tickets** ¥1,300, ¥800-¥1,100 concessions; ¥1,100 Fri; ¥1,000 1st of mth. **Seats** 262.
Second-run cinema with interesting double-features.

Shibuya Cinema Society

Fuji-Bldg 37 B1F, 1-18 Dogenzaka, Shibuya-ku (3496 3203). Shibuya station (Yamanote, Ginza lines), Hachiko exit; (Hanzomon line), exit 5. **Seats** 104. **Map** p79.
Recent European and American films, plus world cinema revivals. On Mondays, couples – gay or straight – pay ¥2,800.

Shimo-Takaido Cinema

3-27-26 Matsubara, Setagaya-ku (3328 1008/ www.ne.jp/asahi/kmr/ski/shimotakaido_cinema.html). Shimo-Takaido station (Keio line), east exit. **Tickets** ¥1,500; ¥1,000-¥1,300 concessions; ¥1,000 women Wed, 1st of mth. **Seats** 126.
A repertory cinema with a varied programming policy, from revivals to recent major films.

Shin-Bungeiza

Maruhan-Ikebukuro Bldg 3F, 1-43-5 Higashi-Ikebukuro, Toshima-ku (3971 9422/www.shin-bungeiza.com). Ikebukuro station (Yamanote,

Yurakucho lines), east exit; (Marunouchi line), exit 30. **Tickets** ¥1,300; ¥900-¥1,200 concessions. **Seats** 266. **Map** p119.

A legendary repertory house in Ikebukuro showing a wide range of films, from Japanese classics to Hollywood no-brainers.

Theatre Image Forum

2-10-2 Shibuya, Shibuya-ku (5766 0114/ www.imageforum.co.jp). Shibuya station (Yamanote, Ginza lines), east exit; (Hanzomon line), exit 12. **Tickets** vary. **Seats** *Screen 1* 64. *Screen 2* 108. **Map** p79.

Cutting-edge contemporary films, classics, avant-garde features and experimental work.

Tollywood

2F, 5-32-5 Daizawa, Setagaya-ku (3414 0433/ http://homepage1.nifty.com/tollywood). Shimo-Kitazawa station (Keio Inokashira, Odakyu lines), south exit. **Tickets** ¥600-¥1,500. **Seats** 46.

Art-house cinema specialising in shorts, famous directors' early works and new independent films.

Uplink Factory

Yokoyama Bldg 5F, 1-8-17 Jinnan, Shibuya-ku (5489 0750/www.uplink.co.jp). Shibuya station (Yamanote, Ginza lines), Hachiko exit; (Hanzomon line), exit 7. **Tickets** vary. **Seats** 50.

A fascinating mix, from Roman Polanski's early works to Eurotrash plus lots of experimental and short work. Uplink also holds film workshops and live performances.

Multiplexes

Cinema Mediage

Mediage, Aqua City 1F/2F, 1-7-1 Daiba, Minato-ku (5531 7878/www.cinema-mediage.com). Odaiba Kaihin-Koen station (Yurikamome line). **Seats** 13 screens seating 114-612. **Map** p113.

The home of the super premium love seat, designed for canoodling couples (¥6,000), Warners-owned Mediage provides a superior film-going experience, with all seats reserved at no extra charge.

Shinagawa Prince Cinema

Shinagawa Prince Hotel, Executive Tower 3F, 4-10-30 Takanawa, Minato-ku (5421 1113/ www.princehotels.co.jp/info1/shinagawa-executive/ cinema_imax/site/cinema/index.html). Shinagawa station (Yamanote line), Takanawa exit. **Seats** 10 screens seating 96-219.

All the latest hits appear at this ten-screen giant. Premium screens have wide, high-backed seats (¥2,500), and parents can leave kids in the hotel's day nursery (9am-6pm; call ahead to get a place).

Virgin Toho Cinemas Roppongi Hills

6-10-2 Roppongi, Minato-ku (5775 6090/ www.tohocinemas.co.jp/roppongi/index.html). Roppongi station (Hibiya line), exit 1C; (Oedo line), exit 3. **Seats** 9 screens seating 81-652. **Map** p109.

Virgin's nine-screen multiplex in Roppongi Hills offers all-night screenings on Thursday, Friday and Saturday. Very comfortable seats (¥1,800-¥3,000).

Indie hits top the bill at Shibuya's **Cinema Rise**. *See p217.*

Galleries

Tokyo's contemporary art spaces are many and thriving.

Art galleries move, close and new ones open with dizzying speed in Tokyo. At the latest count there were purportedly more than 1,000 galleries in Japan's capital. Although temples to tradition still line the streets of Ginza, the number of good, internationally minded contemporary art galleries seems to be increasing, and the rental and corporate spaces often bear surprises.

Conveniently, several premier galleries are located in two must-see complexes. A former paper warehouse in Shinkawa (Kayabacho station) houses **ShugoArts**, **Taka Ishii Gallery** and **Tomio Koyama Gallery**; it's spitting distance from the Sumida river and the Museum of Contemporary Art. About 20 minutes from Shinkawa on the Hibiya subway line, **Hiromi Yoshii**, **Ota Fine Arts**, **roentgenwerke** and **Taro Nasu Gallery** have joined forces in the Complex in Roppongi, near the new Mori Art Museum.

There are other high-density, centrally located art spots worth visiting. The **Okuno Building** in Ginza has five floors of closet-sized rental galleries inside one of the area's oldest tenements. Just a few blocks away, a large number of galleries cluster in the Kyobashi district. Across town in Omotesando, the white **Galeria Building** is home to Art-U Room, Promo-Arte and Gallery Gan, while other venues of interest nearby include **Gallery 360°** and **Spiral**.

INFORMATION

Despite such conglomerations, the city's galleries tend to be fairly spread out, so planning is essential. You'll find listings in *Metropolis*, the weekly art sections of newspapers – the *Japan Times* on Wednesday, the *Daily Yomiuri* on Thursday and the *International Herald Tribune* on Friday – and the quarterly *Tokyo Journal*.

Websites with arts listings and reviews include **Real Tokyo** (www.realtokyo.co.jp/english), **TAB** (www.tokyoartbeat.com) and the guide to what's cool in the city generally, **Tokyo Q** (www.tokyoq.com). Real Tokyo is also behind quarterly publication *Art-It* (www.artit.jp), Japan's first English-language magazine dedicated to the Japanese art world.

Note that many of the galleries below open only when they have an exhibition on, so it's wise to call in advance or check online.

Ginza

Galleria Grafica Tokyo

Ginza S2 Bldg 1 2F, 6-13-4 Ginza, Chuo-ku (5550 1335/www2.big.or.jp/~adel/grafica.html). Ginza station (Ginza, Hibiya, Marunouchi lines), exit A3. **Open** 11am-7pm Mon-Sat. **Map** p60.

Two distinct spaces are housed within Galleria Grafica. The ground floor is a rental space for up-and-coming artists, while the second floor is home to works by the likes of Picasso, Miró, Giacometti, Matisse and Man Ray, and concentrates mainly on lithographs and prints.

Gallery Koyanagi

1-7-5 Ginza, Chuo-ku (3561 1896). Ginza-Itchome station (Yurakucho Line), exit 7 or Ginza station (Ginza, Hibiya, Marunouchi lines), exit A13. **Open** 11am-7pm Tue-Sat. **Map** p60.

This long-standing gallery may have a reputation for photography, but that's been by chance rather than design. It still represents photographer Sugimoto Hiroshi as well as animation queen Tabaimo, and works with notable foreign artists such as Thomas Ruff and Sophie Calle.

Ginza Graphic Gallery

DNP Ginza Bldg 1F, 7-7-2 Ginza, Chuo-ku (3571 5206/www.dnp.co.jp/gallery). Ginza station (Ginza, Hibiya, Marunouchi lines), exit A2. **Open** 11am-7pm Mon-Fri; 11am-6pm Sat. **Map** p60.

Ginza Graphic Gallery.

One of Japan's largest printing companies presents contemporary design and graphics here. Although Japanese designers are prominent, recent shows included work by British typographer extraordinaire Jonathan Barnbrook.

INAX Gallery

INAX Ginza Showroom 9F, 3-6-18 Kyobashi, Chuo-ku (5250 6530/www.inax.co.jp/Culture/gallery/ 1_tokyo.html). Kyobashi station (Ginza line), exit 2 or Ginza-Itchome station (Yurakucho line), exit 7. **Open** 10am-6pm Mon-Sat. Closed 1wk Aug. **Map** p60.

Major ceramics maker INAX runs an architecture bookshop on the ground floor and two galleries upstairs at this premises. One gallery caters for emerging artists with a craft edge, while the other deals with exhibitions of traditional craft techniques from around the world.

Maison Hermès

Maison Hermès 8F Forum, 5-4-1 Ginza, Chuo-ku (3569 3611). Ginza station (Ginza, Hibiya, Marunouchi lines), exit B7. **Open** 11am-7pm Mon, Tue, Thur-Sun. **Map** p60.

The rounded glass-block walls of this beautiful, Renzo Piano-designed building both filter daylight and magnify neon at night. The gallery on the eighth floor holds shows of Japanese and international contemporary art and crafts, organised according to annual themes, such as 'the hand'.

Nishimura Gallery

Nishi Ginza Bldg B1F, 4-3-13 Ginza, Chuo-ku (3567 3906/www.nishimura-gallery.com). Ginza station (Ginza, Hibiya, Marunouchi lines), exit B4. **Open** 10.30am-6.30pm Tue-Sat. **Map** p60.

Yokoo Tadanori, Oshie Chieko, David Hockney and other Japanese and international artists appear here.

Okuno Building

1-9-8 Ginza, Chuo-ku (5250 8108). Ginza-Itchome station (Yurakucho line), exit 10 or Ginza station (Ginza, Hibiya, Marunouchi lines), exit A13. **Open** 11am-7pm Mon-Sat; hours can vary. **Map** p60.

One of Ginza's oldest buildings (built in the early 1930s), this tenement has plants hanging off its balconies and five floors crammed with miniscule rental galleries. Among these are Gallery Kobo (3567 8727, www.spinn-aker.co.jp), Gallery La Mer (5250 8108) and Ono Gallery II (3535 1185).

Shiseido Gallery

Tokyo Ginza Shiseido Bldg B1, 8-8-3 Ginza, Chuo-ku (3572 3901/www.shiseido.co.jp/gallery/ html). Shinbashi station (Yamanote line), Ginza exit; (Asakusa line), exit A3; (Ginza line), exit 1. **Open** 11am-7pm Tue-Sat; 11am-6pm Sun. Closed 1wk Dec. **Map** p60.

Like Maison Hermès (*see above*), this place – run by cosmetics giant Shiseido – is more of a *kunsthalle* than a commercial gallery. It hosts important group and solo shows by contemporary Japanese and international artists such as Nakamura Masato and Roman Signer, plus occasional retrospectives (Man Ray, for example) and fashion-related shows. The gallery is in the basement of the company's Ricardo Bofill-designed headquarters.

Tokyo Gallery

7F, 8-10-5 Ginza, Chuo-ku (3571 1808/ www.tokyo-gallery.com). Shinbashi station (Yamanote line), Ginza exit; (Asakusa line), exit A3; (Ginza line), exit 1. **Open** 11am-7pm Mon-Fri; 11am-5pm Sat. **Map** p60.

Tokyo Gallery shows modern and contemporary Japanese, Chinese and Korean artists. It opened a Beijing branch in 2003.

Arts & Entertainment

Wacoal Ginza Art Space

*Miyuki No.1 Bldg B1, 5-1-15 Ginza, Chuo-ku
(3573 3798/www.wacoal.co.jp/company/artspace).
Ginza station (Ginza, Hibiya, Marunouchi lines),
exit C2.* **Open** 11am-7pm Mon-Fri; 11am-5pm Sat.
Closed 1wk Aug, 2wks Dec-Jan. **Map** p60.
Underwear manufacturer Wacoal sponsors this
space for exhibitions of contemporary art in fabric
and other media, including ceramics.

Marunouchi

Base Gallery

*Koura Bldg 1 1F, 1-1-6 Nihonbashi-Kayabacho,
Chuo-ku (5623 6655/www.basegallery.com).
Kayabacho station (Hibiya, Tozai lines), exits 7, 8
or Nihonbashi station (Asakusa, Ginza, Tozai lines),
exit D2.* **Open** 11am-7pm Mon-Sat. **Map** p66.
This well-established space represents blue-chip
contemporary Japanese artists such as painter
Ohtake Shinro, and younger names including photographer Yokozawa Tsukasa.

Forum Art Shop

*B Block 1F, Tokyo International Forum, 3-5-1
Marunouchi, Chiyoda-ku (3286 6716/http://paper.
cup.com/forum). Yurakucho station (Yamanote line),
Tokyo International Forum exit; (Yurakucho line),
exit A4B.* **Open** 10am-8pm daily. **Map** p60.
Inside architect Rafael Vinoly's stunning landmark
convention and performance centre (*see also p235*),
this space exhibits contemporary Japanese *objets*,
arts and crafts.

Zeit-Foto Salon

*Matsumoto Bldg 4F, 1-10-5 Kyobashi, Chuo-ku
(3535 7188/www.zeit-foto.com/). Tokyo station
(Yamanote, Marunouchi lines), Yaesu exit or
Kyobashi station (Ginza line), exit B6.* **Open**
10.30am-6.30pm Tue-Fri; 10.30am-5.30pm Sat.
Closed 1wk Aug, 2wks Dec-Jan. **Map** p60.
This space behind the Bridgestone Museum of Art
claims to be the first photography gallery in Japan
(it opened in 1978). It's certainly one of the
strongest, with over 3,000 works in its possession.
Expect reliable and wide-ranging shows by
Japanese and international photographers.

Kayabacho-Shinkawa

ShugoArts

*2F, 1-31-6 Shinkawa, Chuo-ku (5542 3468/
www.shugoarts.com). Kayabacho station (Hibiya,
Tozai lines), exit 3.* **Open** 11am-7pm Tue-Sat.
One of three major galleries in the must-see
Shinkawa Gallery Complex is ShugoArts, showing
an eclectic range of contemporary Japanese and
international artists, such as Shimabuku and
Candice Breitz.

Taka Ishii Gallery

*1F, 1-31-6 Shinkawa, Chuo-ku (5542 3615/
www.takaishiigallery.com). Kayabacho station (Hibiya,
Tozai lines), exit 3.* **Open** 11am-7pm Tue-Sat.
Taka Ishii shows photography by major interna-
tional and Japanese artists (Araki Nobuyuki,
Hatakeyama Naoya, Thomas Demand).

Tomio Koyama Gallery

*1F, 1-31-6 Shinkawa, Chuo-ku (6222 1006).
Kayabacho station (Hibiya, Tozai lines), exit 3.*
Open 11am-7pm Tue-Sat.
One of Japan's most powerful contemporary gal-
leries represents major Japanese artists including
Murakami Takashi and Nara Yoshitomo, as well as

The aptly named **Spiral**.
See p224.

Art festivals

If you're keen to see work by young artists who don't win competitions and have no access to commercial galleries but still want to show and sell their work, then pay a visit to one of the twice-yearly festivals put on by **Design Festa** (*see p197*) or **Geisai** (*see p196*). Fashionistas, performers, designers, illustrators and artists pay a small amount to do their thing in booths measuring little more than three feet square. If design is your thing, aim to visit in October for three big events – **Tokyo Designer's Block**, **Designer's Week** and **Swedish Style** (*see p199*) – when Japanese designers are joined by their overseas counterparts in a week of shows, talks, symposiums and parties.

Big organisations are stirring things up at the grassroots level too. Major corporations such as Kirin and Philip Morris sponsor regular competitions for young artists. The arrival of the **Mori Art Museum** (*see p110*) in Roppongi Hills has also given the contemporary art scene a boost, and in April 2004 the Mori space held its first biennial of 50 artists currently living in Japan.

The inaugural **Yokohama Triennale** in 2001 gave the Tokyo area a much-needed high-profile international art event; the 2004 event had to be postponed due to financial trouble, but it is hoped that it will resurface at the end of 2005; for details, see www.jpf.go.jp/yt2005/e/.

Kenji Taki Gallery

3-18-2 Nishi-Shinjuku, Shinjuku-ku (3378 6051/ www2.odn.ne.jp/kenjitaki). Hatsudai station (Keio New Line), east exit. **Open** noon-7pm Tue-Sat.
Kenji Taki and Wako Works are neighbours in the shadow of Tokyo Opera City. Taki exhibits contemporary artists from home (Watanabe Eiji) and abroad (Wolfgang Laib).

Tokyo Opera City Art Gallery

3-20-2 Nishi-Shinjuku, Shinjuku-ku (5353 0756/ www.operacity.jp). Hatsudai station (Keio New line), east exit. **Open** noon-8pm Tue-Thur; noon-9pm Fri, Sat.
With money from Odakyu Railways, NTT and other giant corporations, Opera City is one of the city's largest and best-funded private contemporary art spaces. As well as its own exhibitions of Japanese and international artists, it brings in touring shows from around the world. Hori Motoaki, former curator at the Museum of Modern Art in Kamakura, has recently taken the helm.

Wako Works of Art

3-18-2-101 Nishi-Shinjuku, Shinjuku-ku (3373 2860). Hatsudai station (Keio New Line), east exit. **Open** 11am-7pm Tue-Sat.
Wako shows blue-chip and/or conceptual contemporary artists, both Japanese and foreign. Among the big names to appear are Gerhard Richter and Wolfgang Tillmans.

Shibuya

Gallerie Le Déco

Le Déco Bldg, 3-16-3 Shibuya, Shibuya-ku (5485 5188/http://home.att.ne.jp/gamma/ledeco). Shibuya station (Yamanote line), east exit; (Ginza line), Toyoko exit; (Hanzomon line), exit 9. **Open** 11am-7pm Tue-Sun. Closed 2wks Dec-Jan. **Map** p79.
Regular exhibitions of work by young Japanese artists of all kinds fill the six floors of this rental space. There's a café and lounge on the ground floor.

Harajuku & Aoyama

Canadian Embassy Gallery

B2, 7-3-38 Akasaka, Minato-ku (5412 6200/ www.canadanet.or.jp). Aoyama-Itchome station (Hanzomon, Ginza, Oedo lines), exit 4. **Open** 9am-5.30pm Mon-Fri; 1-5pm Sat.
Canada's best artists appear in the spacious, high-ceilinged granite basement of the distinctive, award-winning Canadian Embassy building, designed by Moriyama & Teshima Architects.

Las Chicas Café/D-Zone

5-47-6 Jingumae, Shibuya-ku (3407 6845/ www.vision.co.jp). Omotesando station (Chiyoda, Ginza, Hanzomon lines), exit B2. **Open** 11am-11pm daily. **Map** p79.
A fashion-conscious and cosmopolitan restaurant, bar and shop complex, located in a splendid al fresco

international figures such as American Dennis Hollingsworth. This is the third of the main spaces in the Shinkawa Complex.

Shinjuku

Public art is relatively scarce in Tokyo, but near the west exit of Shinjuku station is **Shinjuku I-Land**, a collection of outdoor pieces by such big names as Daniel Buren, Luciano Fabro and Roy Lichtenstein.

epSITE

Shinjuku Mitsui Bldg 1F, 2-1-1 Nishi-Shinjuku, Shinjuku-ku (3345 9881/http://epsite.epson.co.jp). Nishi-Shinjuku station (Marunouchi line), exit 1. **Open** 10.30am-6pm daily. Closed 1wk Aug, 1wk Dec-Jan. **Map** p73.
Epson uses its latest digital technology to create the enormous, impressively detailed photo prints displayed in its showcase gallery.

environment off the main drag. Frequent photography and painting shows by Tokyo resident artists (especially expats) are held in various bars and cafés, or in the main event space, Kyozon. English-friendly – most of the clientele are foreigners.

Galeria Building

5-51-3 Jingumae, Shibuya-ku. Omotesando station (Chiyoda, Ginza, Hanzomon lines), exit B2. **Open** 11am-7pm Tue-Sun; hours can vary. **Map** p79.
This building houses three galleries: Promo-Arte (3400 1995, www.promo-arte.com), Tokyo's main Latin American art space; Art-U Room (5467 3938, www.mmjp.or.jp/art-u/index.html), specialising in contemporary Asian art; and Gallery Gan (5468 6311, www.presskit.co.jp), which represents mainly Japanese artists.

Gallery 360°

2F, 5-1-27 Minami-Aoyama, Minato-ku (3406 5823/www.360.co.jp). Omotesando station (Chiyoda, Ginza, Hanzomon lines), exit B4. **Open** noon-7pm Tue-Sun. **Map** p85.
This well-located space emphasises works on paper and multiples by the likes of Lawrence Wiener and Homma Takashi, as well as examining the work of Fluxus, Buckminster Fuller and others.

MDS/G

36-18 Oyamacho, Shibuya-ku (3481 6711). Yoyogi-Uehara station (Chiyoda line), west exit. **Open** 1-7pm Tue-Sat.
Miyake Design Studio holds irregular contemporary art shows in a building designed by acclaimed Japanese architect Shigeru Ban.

Nadiff

Casa Real B1F, 4-9-8 Jingumae, Shibuya-ku (3403 8814/www.nadiff.com). Omotesando station (Chiyoda, Ginza, Hanzomon lines), exit A2. **Open** 11am-8pm daily. **Map** p85.
The city's best art and art-music bookstore (the flagship shop in a chain) has a small gallery showing hot young Japanese artists, often in order to promote their latest art book.

Sign

Yamazaki Bldg B1, 2-7-18 Kita-Aoyama, Minato-ku (5474 5040). Gaienmae station (Ginza line), exit 3. **Open** 10am-3am Mon-Fri; 11am-3am Sat, Sun.
This hip little café fills its awkwardly shaped basement gallery with photography and illustrations from up-and-coming young artists.

Spiral

Spiral Bldg 1F, 5-6-23 Minami-Aoyama, Minato-ku (3498 1171/www.spiral.co.jp). Omotesando station (Chiyoda, Ginza, Hanzomon lines), exit B1. **Open** 11am-8pm daily. Closed 1wk Aug, 1wk Dec-Jan. **Map** p85.
A ramp spirals around the circular open space at one end of the Maki Fumihiko-designed building, hence its name. A wide range of fashion, art and design shows appear here. There's also a café, bar, interior goods store and record/CD shop.

Ebisu & Daikanyama

A.R.T. Gallery

2-12-19 Ebisu Minami, Shibuya-ku (070 5465 1025). Ebisu station (Yamanote line), west exit; (Hibiya line), exit 1. **Open** 11am-7pm Tue-Sun.
Tokyo art scene fixture Johnny Walker holds regular exhibitions at his art space in Ebisu. The focus is on contemporary art by native Japanese and Japan-based foreign artists, although artists from overseas are shown too. Attracts a colourful, interesting and international crowd.

Gallery Speak For

Speak For Bldg B2, 28-2 Sarugakucho, Shibuya-ku (5459 6385/www.abahouse.co.jp). Daikanyama station (Tokyu Toyoko line). **Open** 11am-8pm Tue-Sun. Closed 1wk Dec-Jan.
Über-hip young designers and fashion photographers from Japan and abroad show at this fashion brand-owned gallery.

Roppongi

Gallery Ma

Toto Nogizaka Bldg 3F, 1-24-3 Minami-Aoyama, Minato-ku (3402 1010/www.toto.co.jp/gallerma). Nogizaka station (Chiyoda line), exit 3. **Open** 11am-6pm Tue-Thur, Sat; 11am-7pm Fri. Closed 3wks Dec-Jan. **Map** p109.
Sponsored by bathroom appliance maker Toto, Gallery Ma holds some of the city's best modern and contemporary architecture shows. Foreign architects featured recently include Angelo Mangiarotti (from Italy), Seung H-Sang (Korea) and Yung Ho Chang (China). There's a small bookshop too.

Hiromi Yoshii

Complex 1F, 6-8-14 Roppongi, Minato-ku (5786 3566). Roppongi station (Hibiya, Oedo lines), exits 3, 5. **Open** 11am-7pm Tue-Sat. **Map** p109.
This gallery used to be joined with the Gallery Koyanagi Viewing Room in Ginza and sold prints of artwork by Koyanagi's roster of artists. The two have since gone their separate ways, with Yoshii keeping the premises and now specialising in two areas: very young Japanese artists and new talent from art fairs abroad.

Ota Fine Arts

Complex 1F, 6-8-14 Roppongi, Minatoku (5786 2344/www.jade.dti.ne.jp/~aft/home.html). Roppongi station (Hibiya, Oedo lines), exits 3, 5. **Open** 11am-7pm Tue-Sat. **Map** p109.
Some of Japan's best-known contemporary artists – such as Kusama Yayoi, Ozawa Tsuyoshi and others who deal with the politics of identity – show at this well-established gallery.

roentgenwerke

Complex 3F, 6-8-14 Roppongi, Minato-ku (3475 0166/http://roentgenwerke.com). Roppongi station (Hibiya, Oedo lines), exits 3, 5. **Open** 11am-7pm Tue-Sat. **Map** p109.

Gallery Ma. *See p224.*

Roentgen (German for X-ray) was first the largest and then the smallest gallery in Tokyo. Now it's a happy medium-small, and holds exhibitions of conceptual work, mostly by Japanese artists, such as Yanobe Kenji.

Taro Nasu Gallery

Complex 2F, 6-8-14 Roppongi, Minato-ku (5411 7510/www.taronasugallery.com). Roppongi station (Hibiya, Oedo lines), exits 3, 5. **Open** 11am-7pm Tue-Sat. **Map** p109.

Young and emerging Japanese and international artists such as Matsue Taiji are displayed under Nasu's unusually thin fluorescent strip lighting.

Asakusa

Gallery ef

2-19-18 Kaminarimon, Taito-ku (3841 0442/ www.tctv.ne.jp/get2-ef). Asakusa station (Asakusa line), exit A5; (Ginza line), exit 2. **Open** noon-7pm Mon, Wed-Sun. **Map** p103.

The beamed ceilings and lacquer floors of this extremely rare example of a 19th-century earthen-walled warehouse are tough competition for the contemporary art that is shown here. The shows are mainly by lesser-known but interesting Japanese artists, with some international names joining in. There's a nice cafe too; *see p170.*

Yanaka

SCAI The Bathhouse

Kashiwayu-Ato, 6-1-23 Yanaka, Taito-ku (3821 1144/www.scaithebathhouse.com). Nippori station (Yamanote line), south exit. **Open** noon-7pm Tue-Sat. Closed 2wks Aug, 2wks Dec-Jan. **Map** p103.

Formerly a bathhouse (the building is 200 years old), this high-ceilinged space in a charming neighbourhood near Ueno Park features contemporary Japanese artists (Miyajima Tatsuo) and international practitioners (Lee Bul, Julian Opie).

Further afield

Depot

2-43-6 Kami-Maguro, Meguro-ku (5773 5502/ www.depotcrew.com). Naka-Meguro station (Hibiya line). **Open** 5-10pm Tue-Sun.

Tokyo's media and arts movers and shakers gather in this fashionable new café/gallery space in Naka-Meguro. Located beneath rumbling railway arches, Depot has a downtown New York feel, with shows focusing on graphics, illustration and street culture.

Mizuma Art Gallery

Fujiya Bldg 2F, 1-3-9 Kamimeguro, Meguro-ku (3793 7931/www.mizuma-art.co.jp). Naka-Meguro station (Hibiya, Tokyu Toyoko lines). **Open** 11am-7pm Tue-Sat. Closed 2wks Dec-Jan.

This Naka-Meguro gallery presents some of Japan's hottest contemporary artists, among them Aida Makoto and Ujino Muneteru.

Rice+

1-18-8 Kyojima, Sumida-ku (3617 3982/ www.riceplus.org). Hikifune station (Tobu Isesaki line) or Keisei-Hikifune station (Keisei Oshiage line). **Open** 6-11pm Tue-Fri; 1-11pm Sat, Sun. Closed 1wk Dec-Jan.

The concept of this 'alternative art space' is to link art to other aspects of everyday life, in particular food culture. As well as exhibitions, the space holds regular workshops (Saturday), talks and presentations (Thursday, Friday), often involving the serving of food. Rice+ also houses a café and runs an artist-in-residence programme for foreign artists.

Soh Gallery

2-14-35 Midori-cho, Koganei City (042 382 5338/ www.soh-gallery.com). Higashi-Koganei station (Chuo line), north exit; by appointment Wed, Thur. Closed 1wk Dec-Jan.

Soh has long-standing relationships with top Japanese artists such as Morimura Yasumasa, Suga Kishio and Yoshizawa Mika.

Arts & Entertainment

Gay & Lesbian

In the closet and on the pull.

Perhaps nowhere is the difference between Tokyo and other major first-world cities more apparent than around its gay scene. By day, there isn't one. At night, it's wild.

Of course, wild nights are not unknown in the gay West, but daytime invisibility is a throwback to the past. Tokyo doesn't even have any gay neighbourhoods, if a neighbourhood is a place where people actually live. It does have gay business districts full of bars and clubs, but even the biggest of them, **Shinjuku Ni-chome** – about halfway between Shinjuku-Sanchome and Shinjuku-Gyoenmae subway stations – is a ghost town until evening falls. Then the lights come on, the freaks come out and the fun begins. In many countries, such a divide might be ascribed to persecution, but in Japan, the issue is one of brutal social conformity.

While all societies recognise a difference between the way things really are and the way we see or present them, Japan has two important words that encapsulate the idea: *honne* (reality) and *tatemae* (agreed-upon appearance). Being homosexual is terribly nonconformist (*honne*), but as long as you do everyone the favour of staying in the closet, they will do you the favour of pretending to believe that you are straight (*tatemae*).

While this creates the illusion of harmony, it can cause severe stress. Many of the older men you see blowing off steam in Tokyo's gay haunts have wives and children at home. Some may not even hide this fact while visiting the gay world, because everyone there understands how it is.

The power of the Japanese closet means that gay political and social organisations are tiny and few, and related awareness is low. While virtually all Western gays and lesbians support gender and racial equality, it is not at all unusual for gay or lesbian establishments in Japan to exclude people on the grounds of race, gender or age.

But overt racism is not as widespread as some foreign gay visitors might think. The nature of the scene means that large, public bars are the exception rather than the rule. Most gay bars in Tokyo can't comfortably hold more than 20 people, which makes visiting one an intimate experience; it's akin to being in the living room of the *masutaa* (the Japanese pronunciation of 'master') who runs the place. The atmosphere and decor are very much a reflection of the master's personality, and every visitor will have to speak to him – or a member or his one- or two-person staff – personally.

In such an environment it's not foreigners who cause unease so much as people who don't speak Japanese. But if you know just enough for some rudimentary Q&A about your name, age, country and job, you should do fine. A polite if clueless smile will be the only communication skill you'll need for the rest of the evening.

When you walk into a gay bookshop, you'll see another result of the *honne/tatemae* closet. Since being gay in Japan is largely about getting laid, gay bookshops are devoted almost exclusively to pornography, with none of the novels or the books on history, politics, religion, art, fashion or health you'd find at such stores in the West. That said, modern Japanese erotica can be interesting, thanks to its manga influences. Try **Books Rose** in Ni-chome (2-14-11 Shinjuku, 3352 7023, www.books-rose.com), which also accepts overseas orders on its bilingual website.

One hopeful sign for gay culture in Tokyo is the annual **Tokyo International Lesbian & Gay Film Festival** (*see p197*). The festival lasts several days, showcasing films from both home and abroad, and usually squeezes in at least one big party.

INFORMATION

You can find more in *Otoko Machi Map* (*OMM*), an annual guide to gay bars and venues nationwide, with thousands of listings and numerous maps. Since the 1990s *OMM* has evolved from a staple-bound booklet into a large, glossy paperback of more than 300 pages. In 2004 it received the sincerest form of flattery when an imitator called *Gay Navi* appeared. Both are available at any gay bookshop, as is *Badi*, a brick-sized magazine whose pictures, display ads, comic strips and classified ads will give you some idea of the scene. These are worth picking up even if you don't know Japanese.

Bars & clubs

Advocates Bar

7th Tenka Bldg B1F, 2-18-1 Shinjuku, Shinjuku-ku (3358 8638/www.f-impression.com). Shinjuku-Sanchome station (Marunouchi, Shinjuku lines), exits C7, C8. **Open** 8pm-4am daily. **No credit cards. Map** p73.

This small, sometimes unbelievably smoky basement dance bar has a separate entrance around the corner from its sister, Advocates Café (*see below*). (Lingerie and porn shop Rainbow World is sandwiched between them.) Weekend DJ nights are hit and miss; follow the crowds from Advocates Café. There may be a cover charge.

Advocates Café

7th Tenka Bldg 1F, 2-18-1 Shinjuku, Shinjuku-ku (3358 3988/www.f-impression.com). Shinjuku-Sanchome station (Marunouchi, Shinjuku lines), exits C7, C8. **Open** 6pm-5am daily. **Credit** AmEx, DC, JCB, MC, V. **Map** p73.

With its zebra-striped walls and mirrored disco balls, this is not your average pavement café. But then Tokyo doesn't really do average pavement cafés: such places are still very rare and this is one of the few spots in the city where punters spill out on to the street, more than doubling the cafe's tiny size. Happy hour is 6-9pm Monday to Friday, and there's also a 'beer blast' on Sunday (6-9pm; all the beer you can drink for a set price). Open to all sexes and sexualities. A good place to find out where the crowds are heading.

Arty Farty

Dai 33 Kyutei Bldg 2F, 2-11-6 Shinjuku, Shinjuku-ku (3356 5388/www.arty-farty.net). Shinjuku-Sanchome station (Marunouchi, Shinjuku lines), exits C7, C8. **Open** 7pm-midnight Mon; 7pm-5am Tue-Fri; 5pm-5am Sat, Sun. **Admission** ¥800 Mon-Thur; ¥900-¥1,000 Fri-Sun. **Credit** AmEx, DC, JCB, MC, V. **Map** p73.

This bar with a dancefloor has a 'desert Southwest' look, with DJs on weekends and mint-flavoured beer any time. Gay Friends Tokyo (http://groups.yahoo.com/group/gayfriendstokyo), a new, English-speaking social group – which hopefully will fill the void left by the dissolution several years ago of the long-lived International Friends – meets here every Tuesday (8.30-11.30pm). Women are allowed 'with their gay friends' on Fridays and Sundays.

Backdraft

Tenka Bldg 6, B1F, 2-10-10 Shinjuku, Shinjuku-ku (5269 8131/www.bar-backdraft.com). Shinjuku-Sanchome station (Marunouchi, Shinjuku lines), exits C7, C8. **Open** 8pm-5am daily. **Admission** *Men* ¥1,500 (incl 1 drink). *Women* ¥3,000 (incl 3 drinks). **No credit cards**. **Map** p73.

The decor of this cosy, rock-walled den reflects the Japanese owner's past as a firefighter on a US military base. He and some of his all-bear staff speak English, and foreigners are welcome. A food menu of about 20 items is posted on the wall.

Chestnut & Squirrel

Minx 3F, 3-5-7 Shibuya, Shibuya-ku (090 9834 4842/http://2d-k.oops.jp/cs/cs.html). Shibuya station (Yamanote line), east exit; (Ginza line), Toyoko exit; (Hanzomon line), exit 9. **Open** 7pm-midnight Wed. **No credit cards. Map** p79.

The bright lights of **Shinjuku Ni-chome**.

Although open only one night a week, this small lesbian bar serves good food and draws a lively international crowd, including the occasional man. Mistress Chu speaks English and was one of the organisers of Team Japan at the 2002 Gay Games in Sydney. The name is a mischievous bilingual pun, as 'chestnut and squirrel' in Japanese is 'kuri to risu' – a homophone for 'clitoris'.

Club B Cool

Lions Mansion Nogeyama Koen Bldg 3F, 3-68 Miyagawa-cho, Naka-ku, Yokohama (045 231 9557/www.angel.ne.jp/~bcool). Sakuragicho station (Keihin line) or Hinodecho station (Keikyu line). **Open** 9pm-3am daily. **No credit cards**.

This bar is in Yokohama (*see pp262-7*), about an hour by train from Tokyo. The design is cold and austere – bare cement, brushed metal and Spawn figurines – but master Atsushi is a friendly guy who speaks some English. (If he's not in, be prepared to use Japanese.) The TV screens are likely to be playing tapes made at the various gay Yokohama events where he serves as impresario (see p230 **Dancing queens**). Gay men only.

Dragon

Accord Bldg B1F, 2-12-4 Shinjuku, Shinjuku-ku (3341 0606/www.bekkoame.ne.jp/ha/id25304/ dragon.html). Shinjuku-Sanchome station (Marunouchi, Shinjuku lines), exits C7, C8. **Open** 7pm-4am Mon-Thur, Sun; 8pm-5am Fri, Sat. **Admission** free Mon-Thur, Sun; ¥1,000 (incl 1 drink) Fri, Sat. **No credit cards**. **Map** p73.
Dragon is an aggressively male space in which women may not feel entirely welcome. On the other hand, its muscular, revealingly attired staff and always available dancefloor are major selling points. Be warned that it can get very crowded and sweaty if no other specifically gay event is happening in the city on a Friday or Saturday night. The dancefloor becomes a darkroom on Sunday afternoons and some weekday evenings.

Fellow

2-63-5 Ikebukuro, Toshima-ku (3971 5756). Ikebukuro station (Yamanote line), north exit; (Marunouchi, Yurakucho lines), exits 20A, 20B. **Open** 7pm-2am Mon-Wed, Fri, Sat. **No credit cards**. **Map** p119.

Drawing mainly middle-aged athletes, this is a good place for a cool-down drink after a workout at the Toshima Ward Sports Center, one block away across the tracks. Master Naka is a good cook, and walking through his door means you have ordered a plate of food that is likely to include quiche. Everyone is friendly, but you'll need to speak at least some Japanese.

Fuji

B1F, 2-12-16 Shinjuku, Shinjuku-ku (3354 2707/ www.14you.jp/fuji). Shinjuku-Sanchome station (Marunouchi, Shinjuku lines), exits C7, C8. **Open** 8pm-3am Mon-Thur; 8pm-5am Fri-Sun. **No credit cards**. **Map** p73.
After recent renovations this long-standing basement karaoke bar has begun to draw a younger, more international crowd than in the past.

GB

Shinjuku Plaza Bldg B1F, 2-12-3 Shinjuku, Shinjuku-ku (3352 8972/www.techtrans-japan.com/ GB/index.htm). Shinjuku-Sanchome station (Marunouchi, Shinjuku lines), exits C7, C8. **Open** 8pm-2am Mon-Thur, Sun; 8pm-3am Fri, Sat. **No credit cards**. **Map** p73.
Long the most famous bar in Tokyo for East/West encounters of the gay kind, and handily attached to a 'business hotel'. Large by Tokyo standards, GB has a less relaxed atmosphere than many places, but is always busy. It's located opposite Dragon (*see above*) and admits men only, except for one day in the year – Halloween.

Size does matter

Tokyo's gay bars tend to be tiny and intimate, and its sex clubs tend to be tiny and cramped. One astonishing exception is the 24 (Niju-Yon) Kaikan, a sexual 'theme park' so big it occupies three whole buildings in Asakusa, Ueno and Shinjuku. One foreign customer calls it 'Tokyo's best-kept secret'. Check the website – **www.juno.dti.ne.jp/~kazuo24/ index.htm** – for details (in Japanese, English and Korean) of the three venues.

The procedure is the same at each establishment. Put your shoes in a small locker out front, then hand in the key and the entrance fee (¥2,300 to ¥2,800 depending on the time and location) in exchange for a towel, bathrobe and key to a bigger locker for the rest of your clothes. Once inside, the first item on your agenda is a Japanese-style communal bath.

At the five-storey building in Asakusa, this means sitting between paintings on opposite walls by Tagame Gengoroh, the famous Japanese erotic artist. Both show fierce,

heavily muscled men in loincloths riding *mikoshi* portable shrines (a reference to the annual Sanja Festival in Asakusa). The hyper-masculine Tagame type is unlikely to be seen in person, though, as the Asakusa clientele tends towards grey-haired, older men and a few long-haired 'new halfs' (transsexuals). The bath area also includes two saunas (one dark) and a suffocatingly hot steam room, as well as several two-man shower stalls with latching doors.

Over at the ten-storey building in Ueno, the baths are bigger and so are the men, with lots of bodybuilders and robust blue-collar types. (In fact, most of the tenth floor is a large, well-equipped weights room.) The wall above the main tub is adorned with a Tagame mural of seven virile men in various states of traditional undress. It gives the place a slight Baths of Pompeii atmosphere in which you can imagine that burly fellow with the ripples lapping his nipples to be a horny centurion. The shower area has double-occupancy stalls.

Hug

2-15-8 Shinjuku, Shinjuku-ku (5379 5085).
Shinjuku-Sanchome station (Marunouchi, Shinjuku
lines), exits C7, C8. **Open** 9pm-6am Mon-Sat.
No credit cards. Map p73.
A women-only karaoke bar that tends to attract a
clientele aged 30 and above.

Kinsmen

2F, 2-18-5 Shinjuku, Shinjuku-ku (3354 4949).
Shinjuku-Sanchome station (Marunouchi, Shinjuku
lines), exits C7, C8. **Open** 8pm-3am Tue-Thur;
7pm-3am Fri, Sat; 7pm-1am Sun. **No credit cards.**
Map p73.
A fixture on the anglophone gay scene for more than
two decades, this spacious bar has been run since
Christmas 2002 by a jovial pair of guys who go by
the unlikely names of Nori and Ebi (Seaweed and
Shrimp). Beyond its famous, giant *ikebana* flower
arrangements, you'll find scented candles, tiny cacti,
antique-looking Western furniture and a piano that
sometimes actually gets played. Men, women and
foreigners are made to feel equally welcome at this
very laid-back place.

Kinswomyn

Daiichi Tenka Bldg 3F, 2-15-10 Shinjuku,
Shinjuku-ku (3354 8720). Shinjuku-Sanchome
station (Marunouchi, Shinjuku lines), exits C7, C8.
Open 8pm-3am Wed-Sun. **No credit cards.**
Map p73.
Kinswomyn (a sibling of the nearby men's bar; *see*
above) is Tokyo's most popular women-only bar.

Old-guard butch-femme types occasionally drop by,
but for the most part it's a cosy, relaxed crowd.

Monsoon

Shimazaki Bldg 6F, 2-14-9 Shinjuku, Shinjuku-ku
(3354 0470). Shinjuku-Sanchome station
(Marunouchi, Shinjuku lines), exits C7, C8. **Open**
3pm-6am daily. **Credit** AmEx, MC, V. **Map** p73.
A small, inexpensive, formerly men-only bar that
now admits everyone. Unusually long opening
hours make it one of the few places in Ni-chome
where you can get a drink before sunset. The artwork on the walls changes every few months.

New Sazae

Ishikawa Bldg 2F, 2-18-5 Shinjuku, Shinjuku-ku
(3354 1745/http://new_sazae.tripod.co.jp/open.htm).
Shinjuku-Sanchome station (Marunouchi, Shinjuku
lines), exits C7, C8. **Open** 9pm-6am Mon-Sat;
10pm-6am Sun. **Admission** ¥1,000 (incl 1 drink).
No credit cards. Map p73.
Despite the 'new' in its name, this is a blast from the
past – specifically the 1970s – in terms of both
music and decor. It gets going late and has an atti-
tude-free, anything-goes atmosphere. Fabulous, old,
seen-it-all drag queens can sometimes be found
propping up the bar.

Papi Chulos

M&T Bldg 8F, 2-12-15 Shinjuku, Shinjuku-ku
(3356 9833). Shinjuku-Sanchome station
(Marunouchi, Shinjuku lines), exits C7, C8.
Open 6pm-3am Mon-Fri; 6pm-5am Sat, Sun.
No credit cards. Map p73.

The seven-storey Shinjuku operation –
which opened in 2003 – has the largest bath
area of all, including more double shower
cubicles than the other two places combined,
some communicating with neighbouring stalls
via glory holes. There are two saunas, a
steam room, a mist room and a sling room
equipped with showerheads. No artwork,
but there's plenty to look at in terms of your
fellow customers. It's a younger crowd on
the whole, with the greatest variety in terms
of age, nationality and body type.

All three buildings have car parking at
street level, sunbathing on the roof and
a free condom at the front desk (plus
condom-vending machines). They also offer
bunkrooms and open, futon-floored rooms
where you may sleep, cuddle or 'play', as
well as hotel-style private rooms available
for an extra charge. Asakusa has a public
room set up like a peephole-riddled maze
and Shinjuku has a 'starlight room' where
ultraviolet light turns bodies into stark black

shapes against glowing white bedding.
You'll also find snack bars, tanning beds and
multiple TV lounges, and a large karaoke bar
at Asakusa. All three are open 24 hours a
day; credit cards are not accepted.

24 Kaikan Asakusa

2-29-16 Asakusa, Taito-ku (5827 2424).
Asakusa station (Asakusa line), exit A3;
(Ginza line) exits 7, 8. **Admission** ¥2,300
6am-8pm; ¥2,800 8pm-6am. **Map** p93.

24 Kaikan Ueno

1-8-7 Kita-Ueno, Taito-ku (3847 2424). Ueno
station (Yamanote line), Iriya exit; (Ginza,
Hibiya lines), exit 9. **Admission** ¥2,400
5am-9pm; ¥2,800 9pm-5am. **Map** p103.

24 Kaikan Shinjuku

2-13-1 Shinjuku, Shinjuku-ku (3354 2424).
Shinjuku-Sanchome station (Marunouchi,
Shinjuku lines), exits C7, C8. **Admission**
¥2,600 13hrs. **Map** p73.

Dancing queens

Advocates Café. *See p227*.

Most of Tokyo's major gay or gay-mixed club events happen outside Ni-chome. Nights bounce in and out of favour, so it's best to check where's hot and where's not with the pre-club crowds at Advocates Café (pictured; *see p227*). The music tends to be techno, although some places have secondary dancefloors with alternative sounds.

Red (www.joinac.com/red) at Unit (*see p244*) in Daikanyama has been a popular gay-mix party since 1998. It takes place on the second Saturday of the month and is renowned for its cute customers, not to mention a bevy of guest and resident drag queens and go-go boys.

Ni-chome venue Ace (Daini Hayakawa Bldg B1F, 2-14-6 Shinjuku, 3352 6297, www.akiplan.com/ace) hosts many of Tokyo's smaller gay dance parties. These include **Sanjudai de Naito**, held on the last Friday of odd-numbered months, which is designed specifically for 'businessmen in their 30s' and plays mainly 1980s dance tunes. This is a '*neruton* party' as well as a club, meaning that twice a night the organisers play matchmaker, pairing everyone off in the hope that some of the couples will click.

Live! (www.two-cowboys.com), held at Ace one Saturday every odd-numbered month, features some hot go-go boys, as does

Bang! (www.bang-z.com), a men-only party held about once a month at Ruins (5-11-2 Shinjuku, 3358-7141). **Dock** in Ni-chome (2-18-5 Shinjuku, 3226 4006) is a smallish cruising bar that hosts innumerable parties and events with DJs, generally of an overtly erotic nature – so wear your dancing shoes, if nothing else.

Women-only parties are a less common occurence than dances for the boys, but they do exist. **Goldfinger** (www.goldfinger-party.com) happens on the last Friday of the month at various venues – and men are strictly prohibited. The once-moribund **Diamond Cutter** women's event has made a comeback – it's held on the first Friday of every month at Ace.

Meanwhile, down in Yokohama there is a twice-yearly party (February and September) called **Get You!** Produced by Yokohama gay bar Club B Cool (*see p227*), it's basically a disco, fancied up with strippers and bondage demos, and usually held in a warehouse. The venue can change from one event to the next, so check the Club B Cool website in advance.

For the latest info, check out the *CIA* club guide or website (www.ciajapan.com), *Metropolis*, or look for flyers at Advocates Café and dance music shops such as Cisco (*see p194*) in Shibuya.

One of Ni-chome's newest bars (opened in summer 2004), Papi Chulos is a friendly place, welcoming all genders and nationalities. The agreeable, young, English-speaking master, Masa, enjoys experimenting with cocktail recipes; an early success is the lime-cranberry Haychini named after a regular customer. A small open-air balcony and a loft with fur-draped sofas make this an unusually comfortable bar, while the window-box installation art makes it a quirky one as well.

Snack 24

2-28-18 Asakusa, Taito-ku (3843 4424).
Asakusa station (Asakusa line), exit A3; (Ginza line), exits 7, 8. **Open** 6pm-2am daily. **Admission** ¥2,800 (incl 3 drinks). **No credit cards.** **Map** p93.

This bar, associated with the nearby branch of 24 Kaikan (*see p228* **Size does matter**), consists of two sections, with street clothes worn in one area and traditional Japanese loincloths in the other. Regular customers bring their own loincloths, but they can also be rented for ¥500, and first-timers will be taught how to tie one on. Occasional patrols by a flashlight-wielding barman ensure minimal hanky-panky in the main areas – but there is a back room. The crowd tends to be mostly middle-aged or older. Wednesday nights offer all-you-can-drink deals for ¥2,800.

Tac's Knot

3-11-12 Shinjuku, Shinjuku-ku (3341 9404/
www.asahi-net.or.jp/~Km5t-ootk/tacsknot.html).
Shinjuku-Sanchome station (Marunouchi, Shinjuku lines), exits C7, C8. **Open** 8pm-2am daily.
Admission ¥1,200 (incl 1 drink). **No credit cards.** **Map** p73.

Each month the walls of this tiny cocktail bar display the work of a different local gay artist. Master Tac is a local gay community leader and an artist of some note himself – his bejewelled reliquaries for pubic hair caused a stir back in the 1990s. You'll have to speak to him in Japanese.

Sex clubs

Dozens of Tokyo *hattenba* (sex clubs) are listed in *OMM*. They're usually small apartments or offices turned into 'cruising boxes', with flimsy partition walls, dim lighting and dodgy music. Some have themes (naked, swimwear, jockstraps and so on) on different nights – but the real theme is always the same. Those listed below accept foreign customers.

Pay close attention to the addresses as external signage is often minimal or nonexistent. Condoms are generally provided at the door, but it's wise to bring your own. When you arrive, a voice behind the counter may ask if you speak Japanese. Just say 'hai'.

For details about the 24 Kaikan mega sex clubs, *see p228* **Size does matter**.

HX

UI Bldg 1F, 5-9-6 Shinjuku, Shinjuku-ku (3226 4448/www.ruftuf-jp.com/hx). Shinjuku-Sanchome station (Marunouchi, Shinjuku lines), exits C7, C8. **Open** 24hrs daily; except 10am-3pm 2nd & 4th Thur of mth. **Admission** ¥1,700; ¥1,000 4-11am. **No credit cards.** **Map** p73.

You don't need to be a muscleboy to get into HX, once inside that's all you're likely to find. For that reason – and because there's a well but softly lit front area where you can eye prospective partners before leading them into the club's pitch-black recesses – this is arguably the hottest foreigner-friendly cruising box in Tokyo. It's located on the other side of Yasukuni Dori from Ni-chome, down the alley next to MosBurger.

Jinya

2-30-19 Ikebukuro, Toshima-ku (5951 0995). Ikebukuro station (Yamanote line), west exit; (Marunouchi, Yurakucho, lines), exit C1. **Open** 24hrs daily. **Admission** ¥2,200. **No credit cards.** **Map** p119.

This gay bathhouse may be smaller than the three 24 Kaikan (*see p228* **Size does matter**), but it certainly dwarfs ordinary *hattenba*. Facilities include a refreshment/television room, a communal bath, a sauna, private rooms with beds and locking doors, futon rooms with curtained doorways, and a large porn-viewing lounge with sofas and futons. You'll be issued with a towel and bathrobe upon entering the premises.

Spartacus

MK Bldg 4F, 2-14-3 Ikebukuro, Toshima-ku (5951 6556). Ikebukuro station (Yamanote line), west exit; (Marunouchi, Yurakucho, lines), exit C1. **Open** 24hrs daily. **Admission** ¥1,500; ¥1,000 5am-11am. **No credit cards.** **Map** p119.

The adverts for Spartacus say nobody 'over 40 or ill-mannered' will be admitted. As the club is on the fourth floor of a lift-less building, your physical state on arrival may reveal whether you are actually over 40. Then the cashier can reveal whether he is feeling ill-mannered. On weeknights the maze-like interior can be as dark and silent as a tomb, but it gets busier at weekends. Rikkyo University is nearby. Dress code: nude.

Treffpunkt

Fukutomi Bldg 4F, 2-13-14 Akasaka, Minato-ku (5563 0523). Akasaka station (Chiyoda line), exits 2, 5A, 5B. **Open** noon-11pm daily. **Admission** ¥1,700; ¥1,000 noon-3pm Mon-Fri. **No credit cards.**

A small club near Tokyo's business areas, laid out in such a way that it takes a while to explore all the nooks and crannies (including one alcove with a newly installed sling). Even on a Sunday evening, when the surrounding area is dead, Treffpunkt is likely to be busy, with many foreigners in the mix. Underwear is forbidden at weekends. Unlike most sex clubs, which are open 24 hours a day, Treffpunkt closes at 11pm.

Arts & Entertainment

Papi Chulos.
See p229.

Host clubs

'Host bar' is Japanese English for a place to hire rent boys. Japan's prostitution laws – at least as applied – pertain only to certain heterosexual acts, leaving gay bordellos free to operate openly. There are at least 14 such establishments in Ni-chome alone. At the two listed below, hosts will service foreigners. Step inside, have a drink at the bar, look over the assembled staff and take your pick.

Janny's

Tenka Bldg 3 2F, 2-14-8 Shinjuku (3341 3333/ www.jannys.net). Shinjuku-Sanchome station (Marunouchi, Shinjuku lines), exits C7, C8. **Open** 6pm-5am daily. **Admission** ¥1,300. **Credit** DC, JCB, MC, V. **Map** p73.

Easy to find, with a sign located just across the street from popular Advocates Café (*see p227*), Janny's boasts that all its hosts are aged 18 to 25; photos of the current crop can be seen on the sign outside or online. They cost ¥12,000 an hour, plus ¥2,500 for a room on the premises.

King of College

2-14-5 Shinjuku, Shinjuku-ku (3352 3930/www. kocnet.jp). Shinjuku-Sanchome station (Marunouchi, Shinjuku lines), exits C7, C8. **Open** 6pm-4am daily. **Credit** AmEx, DC, JCB, MC, V. **Map** p73.

Friendly, English-speaking staff make this place ideal. You can rent hosts (starting at ¥13,000 for 60 minutes on top of the ¥1,500 one-drink cover charge) in a free private room at the club or to take to your own home or hotel. The bilingual website has staff photos on the Japanese side.

Love hotels

Business Hotel S

2-12-3 Shinjuku, Shinjuku-ku (5367 2949). Shinjuku-Sanchome station (Marunouchi, Shinjuku lines), exits C7, C8. **Open** 24hrs daily. **Admission** ¥4,200 2hrs; ¥8,800 overnight. **No credit cards**. **Map** p73.

The word 'business' fools no one. Formerly known as Business Hotel T, this is a gay love hotel, pure and simple, conveniently located above GB (*see p228*). Rooms are small and spartan, but include a coin-operated minibar full of beer, and *yukata* bathrobes, presumably for modest post-coital lounging.

Hotel Le Monde

2-24-12 Asakusa, Taito-ku (3847 1921). Asakusa station (Asakusa line) exit A3; (Ginza line) exits 7, 8. **Open** 24hrs daily. **Admission** ¥4,000-¥5,500 2hrs; ¥7,000-¥9,000 overnight. **Credit** AmEx, DC, JCB, MC, V. **Map** p93.

Rooms are fairly uniform and not explosively campy – although nearly everything is white, and there are more mirrored surfaces than you'd find in an ordinary hotel. Foreigner-friendly and close to dozens of gay bars, including Snack 24 (*see p231*).

Hotel Nuts

1-16-5 Shinjuku, Shinjuku-ku (5379 1044). Shinjuku-Sanchome station (Marunouchi, Shinjuku lines), exit C8. **Open** 24hrs daily. **Admission** ¥5,800-¥7,400 2hrs. **Credit** AmEx, JCB, V.

The best known of Tokyo's smattering of gay love hotels, located just outside Shinjuku's main gay bar area. Basic rooms are pink, spotlessly clean and have decent bathrooms. The management has been known to refuse entry if neither customer is Japanese.

Music

From Bach to the blues, Tokyo awaits your listening pleasure.

The capital has a thriving live scene in all major musical genres, with venues running the gamut from tatty fleapit to state-of-the-art hall. Your only problem will be choosing what to hear.

Classical & opera

As befits the world's biggest metropolis, Tokyo has what is probably the world's largest number of venues devoted to classical music. Flush with Bubble-era cash, corporate titans and politicians hired brand-name architects and launched them on a building spree that has left 21st-century Tokyo with a number of gleaming entertainment venues including the **Tokyo Opera City** and **New National Theatre, Tokyo** complex (Tange Kenzo, 1996) and the **Tokyo International Forum** (Rafael Vinoly, 1996).

Perhaps less thought was given to how to fill all these new halls, but with dozens of amateur and professional orchestras in Tokyo, the city claims to offer more classical music events than any other city. Classical music has been popular in Japan since the country opened to the outside world in the 19th century, and has produced its own legitimate stars from conductor Seiji Ozawa and composer Toru Takamitsu to pianist Mitsuko Uchida and violinist Midori.

Tokyo has no fewer than five symphony orchestras; the most distinguished are the **NHK Symphony Orchestra** (founded in 1926 and based at NHK Hall, www.nhkso.or.jp) and the **Tokyo Symphony Orchestra** (founded in 1946, www.tokyosymphony.com). As is common elsewhere in Japan, most are led by star conductors from overseas, but native conductors like Ken Takaseki are beginning to make their mark.

Opera is represented by the venerable **Fujiwara Opera Company**, founded in 1934 and specialising in Western opera, and the **Nihon Opera Kyokai**, specialising in Japanese opera; both operate under the auspices of the Japan Opera Foundation (www.jof.or.jp). The government-run **New National Theatre, Tokyo** (NNTT) has its own chorus and presents operas in conjunction with the Tokyo Symphony Orchestra. The NNTT's high-profile artistic director, Austrian Thomas Novohradsky, recently ruffled feathers by abolishing the traditional double-cast system that paired foreign and domestic singers in lead roles. This has reduced opportunities for Japanese singers, but raised the overall quality of performances by importing top-class guest stars from abroad.

INFORMATION

Check out *Metropolis*, the *Daily Yomiuri*'s arts supplement on Thursday and the *International Herald Tribune/Asahi Shimbun*'s monthly music supplement. Most of the larger venues have detailed listings in English online.

Main venues

New National Theatre, Tokyo

1-1-1 Honmachi, Shibuya-ku (5352 9999/ www.nntt.jac.go.jp). Hatsudai station (Keio New line), central exit. **Capacity** *Opera House* 1,814. *Playhouse* 1,038. *The Pit* 468. **Box office** 10am-7pm daily. **Credit** AmEx, JCB, MC, V.
The National Theatre (*see p246*) focuses on traditional dance and theatre, while the New National Theatre (NNNT) caters to the modern generation. It calls its spaces the Opera House, the Playhouse and the Pit. The last two cater for mostly modern dance and drama, while the Opera House was purpose-built for opera, but sometimes hosts classical ballet performances. The complex that houses the spaces is worth a visit in its own right. Opera tickets cost from about ¥3,000 to ¥21,000.

NHK Hall

2-2-1 Jinnan, Shibuya-ku (3465 1751). Harajuku station (Yamanote line), Omotesando exit or Meiji-Jingumae station (Chiyoda line), exit 1. **Capacity** 3,677. **No credit cards**.
Located next to Yoyogi Park, the main auditorium of national broadcaster NHK is home to the NHK Orchestra, but also hosts a range of other productions from opera to ballet to pop concerts. Of simple, modernist design, the hall is serviceable, but it lacks the grandeur and audacity of Tokyo's newer performance spaces.

Orchard Hall

Bunkamura, 2-24-1 Dogenzaka, Shibuya-ku (3477 9999/www.bunkamura.co.jp). Shibuya station (Yamanote, Ginza, Hanzomon lines), Hachiko exit. **Capacity** 2,150. **Box office** 10am-5.30pm daily. **Credit** AmEx, JCB, MC, V. **Map** p79.
Located inside the Bunkamura arts complex in Shibuya, this is the largest shoebox-shaped hall in Japan, designed to produce the best possible

acoustics – though some complain it's rather echoey. Classical, opera and ballet are the norm, but works in other genres are also staged.

Sumida Triphony Hall

1-2-3 Kinshi, Sumida-ku (5608 1212/ www.triphony.com). Kinshicho station (Hanzomon, Sobu lines), north exit. **Capacity** *Large Hall* 1,801. *Small Hall* 252. **Box office** 10am-7pm daily. **No credit cards.**

This newish venue situated just across the Sumida river has a beautiful, old-fashioned lobby and a warm atmosphere. It's the home of the New Japan Philharmonic Orchestra, which makes regular appearances. You'll also find international artists, including jazz greats, gamelan orchestras and other world music events.

Trad sounds

Traditional Japanese music or *hogaku* has seen a resurgence of interest in recent years, as the Japanese shake off their inferiority complex toward the West and begin to reappraise their own culture. The **Yoshida Kyodai** (Yoshida Brothers) – who play the *shamisen*, a lute-like instrument with three strings – have achieved rock star status, while **Togi Hideki** has done much to popularise the rarified form known as *gagaku* (court music); he's a former member of the notoriously exclusive Imperial Palace Gagaku Orchestra. Artists such as **Yagi Michiyo**, mistress of the zither-like *koto*, and legendary *taiko* drum troupe **Kodo** are reinventing their traditions by experimenting with a range of contemporary musical contexts.

Good news for fans is that Tokyo now has a space devoted exclusively to traditional Japanese music – the recently opened Waon club.

Waon

6-60-9-5F Higashi-Nippori, Arakawa-ku (5850-8033/www.hogaku.com/waon/ index-e.html). Nippori station (Yamanote, Keisei lines), south exit. **Capacity** 100. **Box office** 3-6pm daily. **No credit cards.** Located in the older *shitamachi* district in northern Tokyo, this intimate, sparsely furnished and brightly lit venue hosts concerts of traditional Japanese music most nights of the week. It also provides information and introductions for those wishing to study an instrument, and sells teaching materials, videos and CDs. Tickets cost ¥2,500-¥3,500.

Suntory Hall

1-13-1 Akasaka, Minato-ku (3505 1001/ www.suntory.co.jp/suntoryhall/english). Roppongi-Itchome station (Nanboku line), exit 3. **Capacity** *Large Hall* 2,006. *Small Hall* 432. **Box office** 10am-7pm Mon-Sat; 10am-6pm Sun. **Credit** AmEx, JCB, MC, V. **Map** p109.

Run by local drinks company Suntory, this two-space venue is used mainly for orchestral concerts and recitals. The huge, Austrian-made pipe organ is the most striking visual feature of the Large Hall, giving it an almost church-like appearance. The acoustics are superb, with even legendary conductor Herbert von Karajan moved to describe the place as 'truly a jewel box of sound'. Soloists and chamber groups appear in the Small Hall.

Tokyo Bunka Kaikan

5-45 Ueno Koen, Taito-ku (3828 2111/ www.t-bunka.jp). Ueno station (Yamanote, Ginza, Hibiya lines), park exit. **Capacity** *Large Hall* 2,303. *Small Hall* 649. **Box office** 10am-7pm Mon-Sat; 10am-6pm Sun. **Credit** JCB, MC, V. **Map** p103.

Located in historic Ueno Park, also home to a number of important museums and Ueno Zoo, these halls were Tokyo's classical music mecca in the post-war period. Now more than 40 years old, they were refurbished at the end of the 1990s to make up for ground lost to newer, flashier venues, and currently present the gamut of classical music from orchestra to chamber music and opera to ballet. The main hall is one of the city's largest, and high enough to have four balconies. On the fourth floor of the building is Tokyo's main music library (open to the public), holding over 100,000 CDs, records, scores, music books and more.

Tokyo Opera City

3-20-2 Nishi-Shinjuku, Shinjuku-ku (5353 0770/ www.operacity.jp). Hatsudai station (Keio New line), east exit. **Capacity** *Main Hall* 1,632. *Recital Hall* 286. **Box office** 11am-7pm Tue-Sun. **Credit** AmEx, JCB, MC, V.

Part of the same huge complex as the NNTT (*see p233*), Tokyo Opera City presents all sorts of classical music events, but not – despite its name – much opera. The lobby's fusion of architectural styles is just a sign of what's to come in the Main Hall; the base of the hall is in the prevalent shoebox shape, but it rises into a soaring pyramid topped by a glass skylight. Built for the most advanced sound technology, the auditorium has a bright oak interior and a 3,826-pipe organ as its centrepiece. There's a space for solo performances too, which has also been designed to give the best acoustics.

Other venues

Casals Hall

1-6 Kanda-Surugadai, Chiyoda-ku (3294 1229). Ochanomizu station (Chuo, Sobu, Marunouchi lines), Ochanomizubashi exit. **Capacity** 511. **No credit cards.** **Map** p66.

Tokyo Opera City: for classical music, not opera. *See p234.*

This beautiful hall in the heart of Tokyo's university and bookshop district was designed exclusively for chamber music and small ensembles, and is recognised for its great acoustics.

Hakuju Hall

1-37-5 Tomigaya, Shibuya-ku (5478 8700/ www.hakujuhall.jp). Yoyogi-Koen station (Chiyoda line) or Yoyogi-Hachiman station (Odakyu line). **Capacity** 300; when reclined 162. **Box office** 10am-6pm Tue-Sat. **Credit** JCB, MC, V.
Opened in 2003 by health products company Hakuju, this small hall aims to provide an unrivalled musical experience. The acoustics are first rate, and every seat can be reclined (a world first!). You'll find mainly recitals, chamber groups and some world music. The open-air terrace on the ninth floor, open only to concert-goers, offers great views over Yoyogi Park and Shinjuku.

Kan'i Hoken Hall

8-4-13 Nishi-Gotanda, Shinagawa-ku (3490 5111/ www.u-port.kfj.go.jp). Gotanda station (Yamanote, Asakusa lines), west exit. **Capacity** 1,803.
A mainstay of the scene for more than 20 years, this acoustically impressive venue presents mainly classical music and ballet, but musicals, rock and jazz concerts, plus crooners both local and international, also make the bill.

Sogetsu Hall

7-2-21 Akasaka, Minato-ku (3408 1129/ www.sogetsu.or.jp/hall). Aoyama-Itchome station (Ginza, Hanzomon lines), exit A4. **Capacity** 530.
This smallish venue, which belongs to the *sogetsu-ryu* school of *ikebana* (flower arranging), stages classical music events as well as Japanese music recitals, poetry readings and even film previews. The funnel-shaped design can be frustrating for concert-goers with sharp ears, but it provides a much more intimate experience than other halls.

Tokyo International Forum

3-5-1 Marunouchi, Chiyoda-ku (5221 9000/ www.t-i-forum.co.jp/english). Yurakucho station (Yamanote, Yurakucho lines), Tokyo International Forum exit. **Capacity** A Hall 5,000. C Hall 1,500. **Map** p60.
This soaring, ship-like edifice of concrete and glass was opened in 1997 by the Tokyo Metropolitan Government, in the middle of the Marunouchi business district. Designed by award-winning architect Rafael Vinoly, it's a huge, multipurpose complex used for everything from conventions and trade fairs to exhibitions and pop concerts. Classical concerts are usually held in A and C Halls; the former is vast, with seating for 5,000, but still manages to offer superb acoustics and a warm atmosphere thanks to the lavish use of hardwoods.

Tokyo Metropolitan Art Space

1-8-1 Nishi-Ikebukuro, Toshima-ku (5391 2111/ www.geigeki.jp). Ikebukuro station (Yamanote line), west exit; (Marunouchi, Yurakucho lines), exit 2B. **Capacity** Main Hall 1,999. Medium Hall 841. Small Hall 1 300. Small Hall 2 300. **Box office** 10am-6pm daily. **Credit** JCB, MC, V. **Map** p117.
The first thing that strikes you about this building is the long escalator, travelling from the ground floor up to the fifth floor. Not to be outdone, the halls also have some unusual features – the Middle Hall's UFO-like shape is especially peculiar. Full-scale orchestras play in the Large Hall, while the Middle Hall is used for musicals, plays and ballets as well as classical music.

Jazz

The jazz scene in Tokyo is booming, with more than 30 large clubs and 20 smaller ones (most of them in the west of the city) crowded every night of the week. In a comprehensive and diverse scene, you'll find Latin, bop, free, big band, swing, experimental, fusion, jazz-funk and blues events, plus various open-air gigs during the summer. Japanese fans tend to be a friendly and welcoming bunch, and usually speak enough English to talk about their favourite musicians.

Unlike rock or classical music venues, where the admission price reflects the performer's pulling power, jazz clubs tend to have fixed entry charges (included below where available). Doors usually open at least 30 minutes before the music starts. Many clubs have two live sessions per evening, so check beforehand whether the entry fee covers you for both. Some of the bigger clubs accept credit cards, but in general expect to pay cash. In addition to the clubs, there are numerous jazz bars dotted around the city, with Shinjuku and Kichijoji boasting more than 25 such places between them. Many have extensive vinyl collections and bartenders who are happy to take requests.

Also look out for the weekend **Tokyo Jazz** festival (www.tokyo-jazz.com) in late August. Past headliners have included Herbie Hancock, Wayne Shorter and Dave Holland.

INFORMATION

Metropolis magazine and website Tokyo Q (www.tokyoq.com) tend to list only the bigger clubs. For wider coverage, the Shinjuku branch of record shop **Disk Union** (*see p194*) has an excellent jazz section, with flyers and jazz magazines advertising upcoming events. The haphazardly published *JazzNin* magazine is half-English, half-Japanese and worth seeking out, while Japanese-only magazines *Swing Journal* and *Jazzlife* are great sources if you've mastered the language.

Venues

Akai Karasu

Shirakaba Bldg 4F, 1-13-2 Kichijoji Honcho, Musashino-shi (0422 21 7594/www.akaikarasu. co.jp). Kichijoji station (Chuo line), north exit. **Shows** 7.30pm-midnight daily. **Admission** from ¥2,100.
The 'Red Crow' has been around more than 25 years and is a relaxing, unpretentious place with a good bar (drinks start at ¥730). The music is usually straight-ahead, with an emphasis on vocalists. It's best to book ahead (talk to the manager, Sugita-san) for seats at the front.

Aketa no Mise

Yoshino Bldg B101, 3-21-13 Nishi Ogi Kita, Suginami-ku (3395 9507/www.aketa.org). Nishi-Ogikubo station (Chuo, Marunouchi lines), north exit. **Shows** 7.30-11pm Mon-Fri; 7.30pm-1.30am Sat. **Admission** ¥2,500 (incl 1 drink).

The 30-year-old 'Open Shop' is one of the best jazz bars in Tokyo, if not the world. Old photos and posters line the dark walls of the basement space, creating an intimate atmosphere for some proper jazz listening. There is no set style for the acts; expect anything from free improv to Latin to piano trios. Shimada-san is the relaxed proprietor. Drinks start at a decent ¥400.

Alfie

Hama Roppongi Bldg 5F, 6-2-35 Roppongi, Minato-ku (3479 2037/http://homepage1.nifty.com/ live/alfie/index.html). Roppongi station (Hibiya, Oedo lines), exit 1. **Shows** 8pm-4am daily; jam sessions after midnight. **Admission** ¥3,500. **Map** p109.
A jazz oasis in drunken Roppongi, Alfie has a sleek interior and an upscale audience paying upscale prices to hear international musicians as well as top-flight local bands. The music (all genres) is always high-quality stuff.

B Flat

Akasaka Sakae Bldg B1F, 6-6-4 Akasaka, Minato-ku (5563 2563/www.bflat.jp). Akasaka station (Chiyoda line), exit 5A. **Shows** from 7.30pm daily. **Admission** ¥2,500-¥7,000. **Map** p109.
A large operation that serves decent food (sandwiches, pizza and Japanese dishes) to go with the good drinks. The groups are often the best in the city, and bands from the US and Europe perform a couple of times a month.

Blue Note Tokyo

Raika Bldg, 6-3-16 Minami Aoyama, Minato-ku, (5485 0088/www.bluenote.co.jp). Omotesando station (Chiyoda, Ginza, Hanzomon lines), exit B3. **Shows** from 7pm & 9.30pm Mon-Sat; from 6.30pm & 9pm Sun. **Admission** ¥6,000-¥10,000.
The largest, fanciest club in Tokyo – with prices to match – is part of the international Blue Note chain and well supported by the industry. Jazz, Latin, world and soul acts all appear. The one-set policy is aggravating and the short sets are not great value, but it's certainly an impressive club, and the musicians are first-rate.

Blues Alley Japan

Hotel Wing International Meguro B1F, 1-3-14 Meguro, Meguro-ku (5496 4381/www.bluesalley. co.jp). Meguro station (Yamanote, Mita, Namboku lines), west exit. **Shows** from 7.30pm daily. **Admission** ¥3,500-¥6,000.
Blues Alley showcases everything from jazz, big band, Latin, Brazilian, fusion and soul to pop and, yes, blues. The service is impeccable, the sound system crisp and the food tasty, but the atmosphere can be a bit on the sterile side.

Body & Soul

Anisu Minami Aoyama B1, 6-13-9 Minami Aoyama, Minato-ku (5466 3348/www.bodyandsoul.co.jp). Omotesando station (Chiyoda, Ginza, Hanzomon lines), exit B1. **Shows** from 8.30pm daily. **Admission** ¥3,500-¥6,000.

Jazz and jazz only at this great but pricey club, which has been in business since 1974. The best players in the city love to play to the savvy crowd here. Good food and wine too.

Buddy

Futaba Hall B2F, Asahigaoka 1-77-8, Nerima-ku, (3953 1152/www.buddy-tokyo.com). Ekoda station (Seibu Ikebukuro line), south exit. **Shows** from 7.30pm-midnight daily. **Admission** ¥1,500-¥4,000.

This largeish venue is a little out of the way, a few stops from Ikebukuro, but worth the trip. The main focus is jazz, but tango or prog-rock groups are almost as common.

Gate One

Maruishi Bldg B1F, 2-8-3 Takadanobaba, Shinjuku-ku (3200 1452/www.h3.dion.ne.jp/~gateone). Takadanobaba station (Yamanote, Tozai lines), Waseda exit. **Shows** from 7pm daily. **Admission** from ¥1,000.

Gate One is a small basement jazz bar owned by a husband-and-wife guitarist/vocalist duo. The decor is nothing out of the ordinary, but the music is great (with an emphasis on vocalists) and there are frequent jam sessions.

GH Nine

UNO Bldg 9F, 4-4-6 Ueno, Taito-ku (3837 2525/ http://homepage1.nifty.com/ghnine). Okachimachi station (Yamanote line), north exit or Ueno-Hirokoji station (Ginza line), exit 3. **Shows** from 8pm daily. **Admission** ¥3,000. **Map** p103.

A rare beast indeed – a jazz spot in east Tokyo – this futuristic space at the top of a postmodern building is always a little eerie in feel, but the music is of a consistently high quality.

Hot House

Liberal Takadanobaba B1F, 3-23-5 Takadanobaba, Shinjuku-ku (3367 1233/www2.vc-net.ne.jp/ ~winning/menu/hothouse/hothouse.html). Takadanobaba station (Yamanote, Tozai lines), Waseda exit. **Shows** from 8.30pm daily. **Admission** ¥3,500 (incl 1 drink).

This must be the world's smallest jazz club. An evening here is like listening to jazz in your living room, only with five or so other jazz lovers crammed on to the same sofa bench. Don't come late – the place is so tiny you can't get in when the pianist is seated. Expect duos and trios and (unsurprisingly) no amps.

Intro

NT Bldg B1F, 2-14-8 Takadanobaba, Shinjuku-ku (3200 4396/www.intro.co.jp). Takadanobaba station (Yamanote, Tozai lines), Waseda exit. **Shows** from 6.30pm daily. **Admission** varies; from ¥1,000.

Small, dark and with a great vinyl collection stacked above the bar, the Intro is one of the best jazz bars in the whole of Tokyo. It doesn't have scheduled performances every night, but the Saturday jam session (until 5am) is not to be missed, and is great value at only ¥1,000.

Tickets

Agencies throughout Tokyo sell tickets for rock gigs, classical concerts, theatre shows, films, sporting events – all kinds of things. The main agency is **Ticket Pia** (0570 029 111/http:/t.pia.co.jp), which has numerous outlets throughout the city, often in department stores, and publishes a weekly magazine listing thousands of events. Other agencies include **CN Playguide** (5802 9999/www.cnplayguide. com), **e-plus** (http://eee.eplus.co.jp) and convenience store chain **Lawson** (www2.lawsonticket.com), which has ticket vending machines in most stores. None of the websites is in English, but Pia operators can handle enquiries in English.

J

Royal Mansion B1, 5-1-1 Shinjuku, Shinjuku-ku (3354 0335/www.jazzspot-j.com). Shinjuku station (Yamanote, Marunouchi, Oedo, Shinjuku lines), east exit or Shinjuku-Sanchome station (Marunouchi, Shinjuku lines), exit C7. **Shows** from 7.15pm daily. **Admission** ¥1,500-¥2,000.

A 15-minute walk from central Shinjuku, this basement club is a classic Tokyo jazz spot. It specialises in up-and-coming talent, particularly vocalists.

Jirokichi

Koenji Bldg B1, 2-3-4 Koenji-kita, Suginami-ku (3339 2727/www.jirokichi.net). Koenji station (Chuo line), north exit. **Shows** from 7.30pm daily. **Admission** ¥2,100-¥4,000.

Jirokichi presents everything from klezmer to didgeridoo, jive blues or jazz piano trios. It's well run and fun, with a young, hip vibe. There's barely any room to dance, but people do anyway.

JZ Brat

Cerulean Tower Tokyu Hotel 2F, 26-1 Sakuragaoka-cho, Shibuya-ku (5728 0168/www.jzbrat.com). Shibuya station (Yamanote, Ginza, Hanzomon lines), south exit. **Shows** from 7.30pm daily. **Admission** from ¥4,200. **Map** p79.

The newest, smartest club in the city, housed inside the sprawling Cerulean Tower Tokyu hotel, is pricey but worth it. The booking policy is consistently good, with occasional overseas players. The space is large, so you can move and chat while the music plays. Plus point: the bar is open until 4am on Fridays and Saturdays.

Ko-Ko

2-26-5 Dogenzaka, Shibuya-ku (www7.plala.or.jp/ mic_t/koko.html). Shibuya station (Yamanote, Ginza, Hanzomon lines), Hachiko exit. **Shows** from 7pm daily. **Admission** from ¥2,200. **Map** p79.

Arts & Entertainment

This newish jazz bar in Shibuya is a cosy, smoky spot, with rowdy jam sessions every Wednesday and on the last Sunday of the month. Expect mostly bop and swing, with the occasional vocalist or fusion act. The whisky selection is great, but pricey.

Naru

Jujiya Bldg B1, 2-1 Kanda Surugadai, Chiyoda-ku (3291 2321/www.jazz-naru.com). Ochanomizu station (Chuo, Marunouchi, Sobu lines), Ochanomizubashi exit. **Shows** from 7.30pm daily. **Admission** from ¥2,500.

This medium-sized venue has a black lacquer interior and comfortable seating. Young, hot players predominate, but you'll find straight-ahead, satisfying old faves doing their stuff too. There's also a good selection of food and wine, making this a top spot for some serious jazz listening.

Rooster

Inoue Bldg B1, 5-16-15 Ogikubo, Suginami-ku (5347 7369/www.rooster.jp). Ogikubo station (Chuo, Marunouchi lines), west exit. **Shows** from 7pm daily. **Admission** ¥1,600-¥2,500.

A small, intimate spot, Rooster features the best blues (and bluesy jazz) from all over Tokyo, including acoustic, electric, New Orleans, East Side Chicago, slide and all points in between. Master Sato's collection of vintage posters lines the walls.

Shinjuku Pit Inn

Accord Shinjuku B1F, 2-12-4 Shinjuku, Shinjuku-ku (3354 2024/www.pit-inn.com). Shinjuku-Sanchome station (Marunouchi, Shinjuku lines), exit C5. **Shows** from 7.30pm daily. **Admission** ¥3,000-¥5,000. **Map** p73.

All chairs here face the stage, in reverence for the most respected jazz groups in town, who offer their latest to the adoring crowd. It's not a place for lingering or lounging– the atmosphere is too hallowed for that – but the music is always first class. An irregular afternoon slot at 2.30pm gives the stage to newly emerging bands.

Someday

1-20-9 Nishi Shinbashi, Minato-ku (3506 1777/ www.someday.net). Shinbashi station (Yamanote, Asakusa, Ginza lines), Karasumori exit. **Shows** from 7.45pm daily. **Admission** ¥2,500-¥3,700. **Map** p60.

Someday specialises in big band and Latin groups. The atmosphere is nothing special, though the crowd is always knowledgable and enthusiastic. There's an extensive (and expensive) selection of whisky, along with the usual Japanese snacks and small pizzas.

Sometime

1-11-31 Kichijoji Honcho, Musashino-shi (0422 21 6336/www.sometime.co.jp/sometime). Kichijoji station (Chuo line), north exit. **Shows** from 7.30pm daily. **Admission** from ¥1,600.

A Tokyo institution in jazz-filled Kichijoji. The stage sits in the centre of the club, so that you can see and hear up close. Don't arrive late and get stuck sitting below the band; it's cramped and the sound is not as good. Almost every top-notch player comes through Sometime sometime, and the management has kept the admission price reasonable for years. In the daytime (from 11am), it operates as a café.

STB139

6-7-11 Roppongi, Minato-ku (5474 1395/ http://stb139.co.jp). Roppongi station (Hibiya, Oedo lines), exit 3. **Shows** from 8pm Mon-Sat. **Admission** from ¥5,000. **Map** p109.

Liquid Room.
See p240.

Combine wining and dining with watching some world-class talent. The only competition to Blue Note Tokyo (*see p236*), STB139 does some things better: the layout is much friendlier and the atmosphere a bit more relaxed. There's more variety in the music too, which veers towards soul, Latin, R&B and classics rather than just plain jazz.

Strings

TN Clum Bldg B1F, 2-12-13 Kichijoji-Honcho, Musashino-shi (0422 28 5035). Kichijoji station (Chuo line), north exit. **Shows** from 8pm daily. **Admission** from ¥2,000.

A small venue with an emphasis on vocalists, plus Latin/bossa nova and some soul acts. If you're hungry, try the great, reasonably priced Italian food.

Tokyo TUC

Tokyo Uniform Center, Honsha Biru B1F, 2-16-5 Iwamotocho, Chiyoda-ku (3866 8393/ www.tokyouniform.com/tokyotuc). Kanda station (Yamanote, Ginza lines), north exit or Akihabara station (Yamanote, Hibiya lines), Showa Dori exit. **Shows** from 7.45pm Fri; from 7pm Sat. **Admission** ¥3,500-¥12,000. **Map** p66.

An excellent club, although it doesn't have jazz playing every night. When it does (and if you can find a place to sit or stand), expect to hear the best musicians from Japan and overseas.

Rock & pop

The rock scene in Tokyo is incredibly active. Venues run the whole gamut, from relaxed wine-and-dine seating to trashy underground pits, from tiny crammed spaces to enormous stadiums, with just about every shape, size and ambience in between.

The larger places will host a variety of music and bands as the size is more important than what's on. Smaller venues – termed 'live houses' – often tend to focus on a particular genre to build a following, making it possible to take a gamble on a gig by the venue alone. Medium-sized venues pick at everything in between and often offer the most interesting options.

Gigs often start at 7pm, even at weekends. At a few live houses, events kick off at 11pm or midnight, but more likely you'll be back on the streets by about 9.30pm. Smaller venues often host three to four bands a night. Expect to pay ¥2,000-¥4,000 for a local gig, somewhat more for established medium-sized bands, and at least twice as much for big overseas acts.

For information on the growing number of festivals, *see p241* **Feeling festive**.

INFORMATION

Metropolis provides pretty complete listings of upcoming events, while Tokyo Q (www.tokyoq.com) gives highlights and recommendations. *Tokyo Journal*, published

quarterly, does a good job with bigger events. Two big promoters also have useful gig guides, in English, on their websites: Creativeman (www.creativeman.co.jp/index.html) and Smash (http://smash-jpn.com/gig_guide.html).

Stadiums & large venues

Other venues sometimes used for rock and pop concerts include **NHK Hall** (*see p233*) and **Tokyo International Forum** (*see p235*).

Makuhari Messe

2-1 Nakase, Mihama-ku, Chiba-shi, Chiba-ken (043 296 0001/www.m-messe.co.jp/index_e.html). Kaihin Makuhari station (Keiyo line), south exit. **Capacity** approx 4,000.

The acoustics at this huge convention complex in Chiba City are generally bad, the place is impersonal and it's some distance from downtown Tokyo. Still, it's used for major festivals (*see p241* **Feeling festive**), and big bands such as the Prodigy and Limp Bizkit have entertained full houses here.

National Yoyogi Stadium

2-1-1 Jinnan, Shibuya-ku (3468 1171/ www.naash.go.jp/). Harajuku station (Yamanote line), Omotesando exit or Meiji-Jingumae station (Chiyoda line), exit 1. **Capacity** *Gymnasium 1* 13,600. *Gymnasium 2* 3,200.

Built for the 1964 Olympics, this place is used rarely and mainly for big-selling J-pop stars, though exhibitions and other events do occur. More interestingly, the adjacent public space near NHK has a live stage with irregular free gigs.

Nippon Budokan

2-3 Kitanomaru-koen, Chiyoda-ku (3216 5100/ www.nipponbudokan.or.jp). Kudanshita station (Hanzomon, Shinjuku, Tozai lines), exit 2. **Capacity** 14,950. **Map** p66.

The classic Tokyo live venue (think 'Dylan at the Budokan'). Unfortunately, this lasting reputation allows what is a horrible space to continue to host major rock shows. Built for martial arts competitions at the 1964 Olympics, it's still used for sports events. The acoustics are poor, the vibe sombre and the huge, ever-present Japanese flag hanging from the centre of the hall does not inspire a rock 'n' roll atmosphere. And if you're up in the balcony you might as well be outside.

Tokyo Bay NK Hall

1-8 Maihama, Urayasu-shi, Chiba-ken (047 355 7007/www.nkhall.co.jp). Maihama station (Keiyo line). **Capacity** 6,500.

This structure manages to combine the ambience of a Roman coliseum with state-of-the-art style. The oblong interior offers good sight lines and great acoustics while still being capacious. It is inconveniently situated in Chiba City, but lots of popular foreign acts appear here (Beck, Massive Attack, the Chemical Brothers and so on).

Arts & Entertainment

Tokyo Dome

1-3-61 Koraku, Bunkyo-ku (5800 9999/www.tokyo-dome.co.jp). Suidobashi station (Chuo line), west exit or Suidobashi station (Mita line), exits A3, A4, A5 or Korakuen station (Marunouchi, Namboku lines), exit 2 or Kasuga station (Mita, Oedo line), exit A1. **Capacity** 55,000-63,000.

Japan's first domed stadium opened in 1988, though it existed before that without the roof (it's the home of the Yomiuri Giants baseball team). The biggest music venue in the Tokyo area, it's used for the biggest bands (the Rolling Stones have played here numerous times), with tickets usually costing in excess of ¥10,000. The acoustics are atrocious. The huge complex also includes a spa, amusement centre and other attractions; *see p202.*

Yokohama Arena

3-10 Shin-Yokohama, Kohoku-ku, Kanagawa-ken (045 474 4000/www.yokohama-arena.co.jp/english). Shin-Yokohama station (Yokohama, Tokaido Shinkansen lines), north exit. **Capacity** 17,000.

An increasingly popular venue. In 2004 the first Rock Odyssey bash (*see p241* **Feeling festive**) was held here, and it's sure to be used by foreign rock acts in the future as the size and price are right. The acoustics aren't bad for the size.

Medium venues

Club Citta Kawasaki

1-26 Ogawacho, Kawasaki-ku, Kawasaki-shi, Kanagawa-ken (044 246 8888/http://clubcitta.co.jp). Kawasaki station (Tokaido line, Keihin Tohoku lines), east exit. **Capacity** 1,300.

Halfway to Yokohama, Club Citta Kawasaki is a great hive of activity, with a large hall for gigs. Thoroughly renovated in 2003, the lighting gear and stageside speaker stacks are put to good use, mainly by loud and proud rock acts. Club Citta is an aggressive promoter too; some foreign bands only play this venue. Sometimes it turns into a cinema with all-night festivals.

Hibiya Yagai Ongakudo

1-3 Hibiya Koen, Chiyoda-ku (3591 6388). Kasumigaseki station (Chiyoda, Hibiya, Marunouchi lines), exits B2, C4. **Capacity** 3,100. **Map** p60.

Used since 1923, this outdoor theatre in Hibiya Park puts enjoyment at the mercy of the weather. Umbrellas are not allowed, but turn up on a nice day and enjoy one of Tokyo's few open-air venues. Unfortunately, it is an ode to concrete, including the seats, even though it was rebuilt 20 years ago.

Koseinenkin Kaikan

5-3-1 Shinjuku, Shinjuku-ku (3356 1111/www.kjp.or.jp/hp_20/). Shinjuku-Sanchome station (Marunouchi, Shinjuku lines), exit C7. **Capacity** 2,000.

An early 1960s construction that went through major refurbishment a decade ago, this classical music-style hall is an enduring venue known for its great acoustics. The place where Bowie, Led Zep and many other '70s legends once played, it's still the venue of choice for many.

Liquid Room

3-16-6 Higashi, Shibuya-ku (5464 0800/www.liquidroom.net). Ebisu station (Yamanote, Hibiya lines), west exit. **Capacity** 1,100.

This live music and club venue is often described as 'legendary' in international publications. It recently moved from the rough and tumble of Shinjuku to upmarket Ebisu, so now there are fewer club nights and more straight-up live events. A long, rectangular room with a few seats in the back, it's a great place to catch a show. You can pick up a free monthly schedule from Tower or HMV.

Nakano Sun Plaza Hall

4-1-1 Nakano, Nakano-ku (3388 1151/www.sunplaza.or.jp/hall). Nakano station (Chuo, Tozai lines), north exit. **Capacity** 2,200.

An unassuming venue a few stops from Shinjuku, this hall has hosted top bands including the Clash, PiL and the Pogues, as well as many blues, folk rock (Suzanne Vega) and world music artists. The list of prohibitions recited before any concert is far more suited to a classical music hall, but it does still offer popular stuff. The acoustics are quite good.

Shibuya AX

2-1-1 Jinnan, Shibuya-ku (5738 2020/www.shibuya-ax.com). Harajuku station (Yamanote line), Omotesando exit or Meiji-Jingumae station (Chiyoda line), exit 1. **Capacity** 1,000.

This newish venue has grown in importance since the closing a few years ago of the similar-sized (and shaped) Akasaka Blitz. Many hot indie acts, both foreign and local, play here; the acoustics and sight lines are very good and the atmosphere intimate.

Shibuya Kokaido

1-1 Udagawacho, Shibuya-ku (3463 3022). Shibuya station (Yamanote, Ginza, Hanzomon lines), Hachiko exit. **Capacity** 2,300.

Another 1964 Olympics structure, this one survived the transition with the best reputation, thanks to its acoustics. Overseas mainstream rock groups and electric guitarists play here, plus Japanese artists.

Shibuya O-East

2-14-8 Dogenzaka, Shibuya-ku (5458 4681/www.shibuya-o.com). Shibuya station (Yamanote, Ginza, Hanzomon lines), Hachiko exit. **Capacity** 1,300. **Map** p79.

The O-East complex (opened mid 2004) houses a number of clubs and bars. The biggest venue is simply called Shibuya O-East and is where international rock bands and DJs play. The complex also houses a small bar, the Red Bar.

Zepp Tokyo

Palette Town 1F, 1 Aomi, Koto-ku (3599 0710/www.zepp.co.jp/tokyo). Aomi station (Yurikamome line) or Tokyo Teleport station (Rinkai line). **Capacity** 2,700. **Map** p113.

Feeling festive

Less than a decade ago Tokyo and its environs were devoid of any significant music festival – but times change. Japan's burgeoning music scene has exploded, and a plethora of international bashes now draws rock, dance, hip hop, reggae and world acts; some attract over 100,000 fans.

From the early 1970s common wisdom held that big festivals were too risky in Japan's expensive marketplace – viz the massive losses sustained by promoter Smash Corporation (www.smash-jpn.com, www.smash-uk.com) when the second day of its inaugural **Fuji Rock Festival** (www.fujirockfestival.com) was rained off in 1997. Yet Smash persevered, producing Fuji Rock again in '98 and today the festival is a gigantic musical and financial success.

Held in the mountain resort of Naeba (a two-and-a-half-hour drive from Tokyo), it's the biggest and most varied of the Japanese music fests. In 2004 the six-stage shindig welcomed such diverse acts as the Chemical Brothers, the White Stripes, Franz Ferdinand and Basement Jaxx. Held over the last weekend in July, it's all about dancing in the green mountains amid peace and partying; fights and other anti-social behaviour are unknown.

If Fuji Rock is the ultimate outdoor summer bash, **Summer Sonic** (www.summersonic.com), put on by Creativeman (www.creativeman.co.jp), has set itself up as Japan's premier city music festival. The four-stage rock/punk/hip hop knees-up is held at two adjacent venues – Makuhari Messe convention centre (*see p239*) and a baseball stadium – in Chiba city, a 40-minute train ride from downtown Tokyo. Spiky-haired punks mix with denim-clad rockers and saggy-panted hip hoppers to hear the likes of the Beastie Boys, N.E.R.D, Hoobastank and Green Day. Summer Sonic is essentially a youth festival – it's rare (unlike at Fuji Rock) to see a parent wheeling a pushchair – and is usually held on the first weekend in August.

The summer also sees **Rock Odyssey** (www.udo.co.jp/odyssey), which made its debut at Yokohama Arena (*see p240*) on the penultimate weekend of July 2004. Concentrating on huge-name rock acts – Aerosmith, Red Hot Chili Peppers, Lenny Kravitz – it's put together by the granddaddy of Japanese promoters, Udo. More like an

extended arena show, it has developed little character as yet – but these are early days.

The first weekend in September brings the underground, cutting-edge **True People's Celebration** (www.truepeoples.com), promoted by Phatleaf (www.organicgroove.com). In 2004 this dance- and jam-oriented jamboree was held at Chichibu Muse Park (about an hour from Tokyo) and brought acts as varied as Tabla Beat Science, DJ Spooky and Jimmy Cliff. It's a great place to experience alternative Japan.

World-music bash **Doo Bee Fes** is slated to start in October 2005. Organiser Pop Biz (www.popbiz.co.jp) is well established on the world music scene and suggests that the headliner will be *griot* superstar Salif Keita. At the end of November arrives the king of dance/electronic music festivities in Japan, **Electraglide** (www.electraglide.info). Pioneered by the resourceful Beat Ink (www.beatink.com), this bash has hosted Underworld, Fatboy Slim, Aphex Twin, Mouse on Mars and Squarepusher and is always a full-on party. It's held in the same convention centre as Summer Sonic.

Finally, check out Creativeman's **Sonicmania** (www.sonicmania.net), usually held on the first weekend in February. This rock, metal and hardcore event is aligned with the famed Australian music festival Big Day Out. As with Summer Sonic, the bash is held simultaneously in Tokyo and Osaka. Past acts have included Marilyn Manson, Good Charlotte and Kasabian.

Part of a chain with locations in four other cities, this large, rather sterile venue in Odaiba has become a well-used spot for more popular foreign rock and electronic acts, among them the Manic Street Preachers and George Clinton. Less convenient and definitely less characterful than similar venues, such as Shibuya AX (*see p240*).

Small venues

Club **Milk** (*see p213*) also hosts live gigs.

Antiknock

Ray Flat Shinjuku B1F, 4-3-15 Shinjuku, Shinjuku-ku (3350 5670/www.music.ne.jp/~antiknock). Shinjuku station (Yamanote, Marunouchi lines), new south exit; (Oedo, Shinjuku lines), exits 1, 2. Capacity 300. **Map** p73.

A small club near Takashimaya Times Square where Tokyo's colourful punks gather. It aims to present 'original' music, but, more importantly, the music has to rock. Need to vent your frustration with the Shinjuku station hordes? Pop down here.

Astro Hall

New Wave Harajuku Bldg B1F, 4-32-12 Jingumae, Shibuya-ku (3401 5352/www.astro-hall.com). Harajuku station (Yamanote line), Takeshita exit or Meiji-Jingumae station (Chiyoda line), exit 5. Capacity 400. **Map** p85.

When it opened in 2000 this was the venue of choice for many local indie bands, and it's been holding steady ever since. Some foreign acts trying to break in Japan also play here. Very intimate and generally well laid out, it's a good place to catch a show.

Ballroom

Za House Bldg, 1-34-17 Ebisu Nishi, Shibuya-ku (3484 1012/www.unit-tokyo.com). Daikanyama station (Tokyu Toyoko line). Capacity 400.

In the same building as Unit (*see p244*), Ballroom is smaller and slightly more intimate, but subscribes to the same wide-ranging booking policy. Keep an eye out for Organic Groove events by promoter Phatleaf, organiser of the True People's Celebration festival (*see p241* **Feeling festive**).

Cave-be

Kitazawa Plaza B1F, 2-14-16 Kitazawa, Setagaya-ku (3412 7373/www.cave-be.com). Shimo-Kitazawa station (Keio Inokashira, Odakyu lines), south exit. Capacity 150.

Opened in 2003 next to the Japanese indie music shop High Line Records, tiny Cave-be presents small local bands playing all sorts of rock styles. It gets busy on most nights.

Cay

Spiral Bldg B1F, 5-6-23 Minami-Aoyama, Minato-ku (3498 5790/www.spiral.co.jp/event). Omotesando station (Chiyoda, Ginza, Hanzomon lines), exit B1. Capacity 600. **Map** p85.

A restaurant that regularly turns into a live (sometimes all-night) venue. It's located in the Spiral

Building (*see p224*), a centre for contemporary arts and design, and the music matches the setting, with new electronica, world music-influenced and 'fusion' acts such as Karsh Kale or the homegrown Dakini Nights. There are two bars.

Club Quattro

Parco 4F, 32-13 Udagawa-cho, Shibuya-ku (3477 8750/www.net-flyer.com). Shibuya station (Yamanote, Ginza, Hanzomon lines), Hachiko exit. Capacity 750. **Map** p79.

On the top floor of the Parco 4 fashion store, Club Quattro is a superior venue with high-quality performers. It's not limited by genre, offering varied overseas acts plus some of the best local bands, even ones that would usually prefer to play at bigger venues. Despite some view-restricting architectural features, this is one of the most appealing music venues in town.

Club Que

Big Ben Bldg B2F, 2-5-2 Kitazawa, Setagaya-ku (3412 9979/www.ukproject.com/que). Shimo-Kitazawa station (Keio Inokashira, Odakyu lines), south exit. Capacity 250.

This place has built a strong reputation over the past decade and, despite its small size, some not-so-small local indie bands sometimes appear. Irregular, early-afternoon gigs are held on weekends and holidays, and it becomes a late-night DJ club on weekends.

Club 251

SY Bldg B1F, 5-29-15 Daizawa, Setagaya-ku (5481 4141/www.club251.co.jp). Shimo-Kitazawa station (Keio Inokashira, Odakyu lines), south exit. Capacity 350.

One of the main venues in Shimo-Kitazawa and a reliable place to drop in. There are no restrictions on musical styles, but gigs tend to be rock-oriented. It's a black, bare place showing its age, but that's a sign of popularity rather than neglect.

Crocodile

New Sekiguchi Bldg B1F, 6-18-8 Jingumae, Shibuya-ku (3499 5205/www.music.co.jp/~croco). Shibuya station (Yamanote, Ginza, Hanzomon lines), Miyamasuaka (east) exit or Harajuku station (Yamanote line), Omotesando exit or Meiji-Jingumae station (Chiyoda line), exit 4. Capacity 120-200. **Map** p85.

Although this venue bills itself as a modern music restaurant, it's best to skip the food and stick to the sounds. Crocodile presents anything from salsa to country, rock and jazz, plus combinations of any of these. The last people to arrive on a busy night won't get great seats.

DeSeO

Dai 2 Okazaki Bldg 1F, 3-3 Sakuragaoka-cho, Shibuya-ku (5457 0303/www.deseo.co.jp). Shibuya station (Yamanote, Ginza, Hanzomon lines), south exit. Capacity 250. **Map** p79.

This small live house along the JR tracks is another spot for bands warming up for bigger things. Some more established acts perform intermittently too.

Arts & Entertainment

Shinjuku Loft. *See p244.*

Eggman

1-6-8 Jinnan, Shibuya-ku (3496 1561/www.eggman.jp). Shibuya station (Yamanote, Ginza, Hanzomon lines), Hachiko exit. **Capacity** *350.* **Map** *p85.*
Eggman is close to the bigger Shibuya venues and is a bit of an institution too. Most nights you'll find local bands playing, particularly those with one eye on a record deal, so you should be able to catch some upcoming talent. A good venue for assorted, rock-oriented music styles.

440

SY Bldg 1F, 5-29-15 Daizawa, Setagaya-ku (3422 9440/www.club251.co.jp/440). Shimo-Kitazawa station (Keio Inokashira, Odakyu lines), south exit. **Capacity** *100-180.*
440 takes a softer approach to live music, and is one of very few café-style live houses outside the jazz circuit. It's part of the same group as Club 251 (*see p242*; only two minutes down the road) and is always booked weeks in advance. Open for food and drinks the rest of the time.

Gear

Tokyo Bldg B1F, 4-25-4 Koenji-Minami, Suginami-ku (3318 6948). Koenji station (Chuo line), south exit. **Capacity** *150.*
The place for bands that might not be allowed to play anywhere else, Gear serves up all sorts of 'core' offerings, with event names like 'Fangs Anal Satan'. A small venue with a big following.

Gig-antic

Sound Forum Bldg 2F, 3-20-15 Shibuya, Shibuya-ku (5466 9339/www.gig-antic.co.jp). Shibuya station (Yamanote, Ginza, Hanzomon lines), Miyamasuka (east) exit. **Capacity** *150.* **Map** *p79.*
Gig-antic is a small (despite the name) venue by the JR tracks, which presents bands from around

Japan. Expect a mix of hardcore and punk, with some events sold out in advance.

Heaven's Door

Keio Hallo Bldg B1F, 1-33-19 Sangenjaya, Setagaya-ku (3410 9581/www.geocities.jp/ xxxheavensdoorxxx). Sangenjaya station (Tokyu Denentoshi line), south exit. **Capacity** *300.*
Heaven's Door is another institution, in a rites-of-passage sense, for many loud Tokyo bands. Only a few established acts play here, yet everybody knows about it. There's not much decoration, but the speakers are huge and that's what matters.

La.mama Shibuya

Premier Dogenzaka B1F, 1-15-3 Dogenzaka, Shibuya-ku (3464 0801/www.lamama.net). Shibuya station (Yamanote, Ginza, Hanzomon lines), south exit. **Capacity** *120-250.* **Map** *p79.*
La.mama has been presenting bands at the start of (one hopes) successful careers for more than 20 years. It tends to host more J-pop and commercial rock than other venues in the area.

Live Inn Rosa

Rosa Kaikan B2F, 1-37-12 Nishi-Ikebukuro, Toshima-ku (5956 3463/www.live-inn-rosa.com). Ikebukuro station (Yamanote line), west exit; (Marunouchi, Yurakucho lines), exit 12. **Capacity** *100-300.* **Map** *p119.*
Proudly J-pop, this Ikebukuro venue also presents other types of music – including events combining live bands and DJs – and many artists on their first few appearances.

Live Spot 20000

Dai 8 Tokyo Bldg B2F, 4-25-4 Koenji-Minami, Suginami-ku (3316 6969/homepage2.nifty.com/ 20000volt/index.html). Koenji station (Chuo line), south exit. **Capacity** *180.*

Arts & Entertainment

Another institution, 'Niman Volt', as it's known, is the place for hard listening, with more than a nod to the experimental and noise set. Current local stars play here, as do big names in lesser known incarnations, such as Sonic Youth's Thurston Moore who appeared here as Diskaholics Anonymous Trio.

Mandala 2

2-8-6 Kichijoji Minami-cho, Musashino-shi (0422 42 1579/www.mandala.gr.jp/man2.html). Kichijoji station (Chuo line), south exit. **Capacity** 60.
More of a music venue than its sister in Minami-Aoyama, this branch of the mini Mandala empire specialises in experimental music. It's a hotbed of activity (one of the live CDs on John Zorn's Tzadik label was recorded here), where local stars sometimes show up unannounced for one-off gigs with friends. Check out Cicala Mvta, playing a mix of *chingdon* (Japanese marching music), klezmer and Eastern European folk.
Other locations: Mandala Minami-Aoyama MR Bldg B1F, 3-2-2 Minami-Aoyama, Minato-ku (5474 0411/www.mandala.gr.jp/aoyama.html).

Shelter Shimo-Kitazawa

Senda Bldg B1F, 2-6-10 Kitazawa, Setagaya-ku (3466 7430/www.loft-prj.co.jp). Shimo-Kitazawa station (Keio Inokashira, Odakyu lines), north exit. **Capacity** 250.
Part of the Loft group, this smallish venue is always booked with up-and-coming or even established local bands that might usually play bigger venues. Overseas acts perform on occasion. Shelter has been around for more than a decade and is exceedingly popular, so arrive early.

Shibuya O-West

2-3 Maruyama-cho, Shibuya-ku (5784 7088/ www.shibuya-o.com). Shibuya station (Yamanote, Ginza, Hanzomon lines), Hachiko exit. **Capacity** 500. **Map** p79.
Across the street from the Shibuya O-East complex (*see p240*), this space usually hosts better-known Japanese indie bands with a concentration on alt and mainstream rock. There are also two smaller venues in the same building: O-Nest (3462 4420, capacity 250) presents on-the-way-up Japanese bands and electronic music creators, and can tend towards the edgy or experimental; while intimate O-Crest (3770 1095, capacity 200) holds acoustic or low-key events.

Shinjuku Loft

Tatehana Bldg B2F, 1-12-9 Kabuki-cho, Shinjuku-ku (5272 0382/www.loft-prj.co.jp). Shinjuku station (Yamanote line), east exit; (Marunouchi line), exit B12; (Oedo, Shinjuku lines), exit 1. **Capacity** *Main stage* 550. *Sub-stage* 100.
Loft has been around for more than 25 years and is a dedicated promoter. Inside are two areas: one is for the main space for gigs, the other is a bar with a small stage. Expect loud music of any genre here. At times it offers more than just gigs, with all-night events that include DJs.

Shinjuku Loft Plus One

Hayashi Bldg B2F, 1-14-7 Kabuki-cho, Shinjuku-ku (3205 6864/www.loft-prj.co.jp). Shinjuku station (Yamanote line), east exit; (Marunouchi line), exit B12; (Oedo, Shinjuku lines), exit 1. **Capacity** 100-200. **Map** p73.
Another member of the Loft family, this is an unusual venue billing itself as a 'talk show live performance' space. No music, just people of all ages and walks of life talking about their passions.

Shinjuku Marz

Daiichi Tokiwa B1F, 2-45-1 Kabuki-cho, Shinjuku-ku (3202 8248/www.marz.jp). Shinjuku station (Yamanote line), east exit; (Marunouchi line), exit B13; (Oedo, Shinjuku lines), exit 1. **Capacity** 300.
Funk, rock and J-pop – what the bands here have in common is the ambition to set off on a musical career. Opened in 2001, Shinjuku Marz is doing well despite stiff local competition.

Star Pine's Café

1-20-16 Kichijoji-Honcho, Musashino-shi (0422 23 2251/www.mandala.gr.jp/spc.html). Kichijoji station (Chuo line), central exit. **Capacity** 350.
The biggest of the three Mandala venues (*see also above*), this one is a bit more bar-like. The artists are mostly experimental, and genres range from jazzy or progressive to avant-garde and dancey; most of the music is of high quality. It's also the venue du jour for obscure-ish overseas acts. All-night events follow weekend gigs.

Studio Jam

Central Bldg 1F, 2-3-23 Kabuki-cho, Shinjuku-ku (3232 8169/www.h4.dion.ne.jp/~studio/jam). Shinjuku station (Yamanote line), east exit; (Marunouchi line), exits B6, B7; (Oedo, Shinjuku lines), exit 1. **Capacity** 200.
In operation since 1980, Studio Jam, located in Shinjuku's red-light district, specialises in 1960s-70s music, with a bit of guitar pop thrown in.

Unit

Za House Bldg, 1-34-17 Ebisu-Nishi, Shibuya-ku (3484 1012/www.unit-tokyo.com). Daikanyama station (Tokyu Toyoko line). **Capacity** 600.
A newish medium-sized space that hosts all types of shows from Japanese indie rock bands such as Brahman to reggae greats like Horace Andy and even club nights such as a Ninja Tune event. It manged to nab the former booking manager of the old (Shinjuku) Liquid Room, so it's worth taking a look at its schedule.

Y2K

Aban Bldg B1F, 7-13-2 Roppongi, Minato-ku (5775 3676/www.explosionworks.net/y2k). Roppongi station (Hibiya line), exit 4A; (Oedo line), exit 7. **Capacity** 450. **Map** p107.
Opened in 1999 in the heart of Roppongi with a mission to bring live music to clubbers, this venue concentrates on smaller, local, rock-minded bands.

Performing Arts

A feast for all the senses.

You're spoilt for choice when it comes to the performing arts in Tokyo. Of most interest to visitors are probably the uniquely Japanese theatrical forms – whether traditional or more modern in style – but Western-inspired dramas and musicals are also very popular. English-language theatre is harder to come by, but there's an expat theatre scene and a smattering of comedy venues. Dance, both classical ballet and contemporary, is currently thriving too.

TICKETS AND INFORMATION

Performance listings are published in the English daily newspapers, as well as weekly magazine *Metropolis*. Theatre websites often feature show schedules, sometimes in English. You can buy tickets direct from the venue, or at convenience stores, department stores or by telephone from ticket agencies. It's a good idea to book ahead; tickets to touring Western shows, particularly those starring well-known actors, sell out especially quickly.

Traditional Japanese theatre

Fearsome masks, silken costumes, stylised dialogue, intricate choreography and the piquant tones of exotic instruments: these are only a few of the elements that beckon the curious into the mysterious world of traditional Japanese performing arts. Often impenetrable to the outsider, ancient forms such as *noh*, *bunraku* and *kabuki* employ archaic language and can even be difficult for locals to understand.

However, there is much to appreciate on an aesthetic basis alone, and many of the themes – clan battles, servant-master loyalty, revenge and justice, conflicts between duty and loyalty, unrequited love – are universal. Additionally, English programmes and simultaneous translations are increasingly available.

As with other traditional theatre forms throughout Asia, Japanese theatre integrates dance, music and lyrical narrative. In contrast to Western theatre's preoccupation with realism, the emphasis is on beauty, the mythic and the ritualistic. Another distinguishing feature is *ma*, perhaps best translated as a 'pregnant pause'. More than just silence, *ma* is the space that interrupts musical notes or words and is used to intensify the power of the dramatic moment.

The theatre-going experience is also markedly different from in the West. Cast aside all notions of hushed reverence and fur coats: a trip to the theatre is a social outing, and many people come for an afternoon at, say, Ginza's Kabuki-za, armed with flasks of hot drinks, packed meals and bags full of goodies, which are noisily chomped throughout the performance. Spectators often comment on the action as it happens, for example calling out the stage name of the performer at significant moments. A particularly fine tableau may well elicit a burst of spontaneous applause.

NOH AND KYOGEN

Japan's oldest professional theatre form, *noh*, dates back to 14th-century Shinto and Buddhist religious festivals and was used both to educate and entertain. The ritualistic nature of *noh* plays is emphasised by the masks worn by the principal character. Plays are grouped into categories, which can be likened to five courses of a formal meal, each with a different flavour. Invigorating celebratory dances about gods are followed by battle plays of warrior-ghosts; next are lyrical pieces about women, then themes of insanity, and finally demons. Presentation is mostly sombre, slow and deliberate. Plays explore the transience of this world, the sin of killing and the spiritual comfort to be found in Buddhism.

There are no group rehearsals: there is a pre-performance meeting, but the actors and musicians do not play together until the performance. This spontaneity is one of the appeals of this kind of theatre.

Kyogen are short, humorous interludes that show the foolishness of human nature through understated portrayal. They are interspersed for comic relief with *noh* pieces, but are intended to produce refined laughter, not boisterous humour.

BUNRAKU

While puppetry in Japan goes back at least to the 11th century, modern *bunraku* takes its name from the Bunraku-za organised in Osaka in the early 19th century, and was developed by city-dwelling commoners of the Edo period (1600-1868). The puppets used in *bunraku* are a half to two-thirds human size and require great skill and strength to operate. Each puppet is operated by two assistants and one chief puppeteer. Becoming a master puppeteer is a lengthy process, beginning with ten years' operating the legs, followed by another ten on the left arm before being permitted to manipulate the right arm, head and eyebrows.

Four main elements comprise a *bunraku* performance: the puppets themselves; the movements they make; the vocal delivery of the *tayu*, who chants the narrative and speaks the lines for every character, changing his voice to suit the role; and the solo accompaniment by the three-stringed, lute-like *shamisen*.

KABUKI

Kabuki is said to have originated with Okuni, a female attendant at the Izumo shrine in Kyoto, who first led her mostly female company in performances on the dry bed of the Kamogawa river in 1603. *Kabuki* means 'unusual' or 'shocking', and it quickly became the most popular form of theatre in 17th- and 18th-century Japan. However, concerns over the sexual antics of the entertainers, on and off stage, meant that women performers were banned in 1629 and now all *kabuki* actors are male. Women's parts are taken by *onnagata* (specialists in playing female roles), who portray a stylised feminine beauty. There is no pretence at realism, so the actor's real age is irrelevant – there is no incongruity in a 75-year-old man portraying an 18-year-old maiden.

Of all the traditional performing arts in Japan, *kabuki* is probably the most exciting. The actor is the most important element in *kabuki*, and everything that happens on stage is a vehicle for displaying his prowess. *Koken*, stage hands dressed in black, symbolising their supposed invisibility, hand the actor props, make running adjustments to his heavy costume and wig, and bring him a stool to perch on during long speeches or periods of inactivity.

Most *kabuki* programmes feature one *shosagoto* dance piece, one *jidaimono* and one *sewamono*. *Jidaimono* are dramas set in pre-Edo Japan. They feature gorgeous costumes and colourful make-up called *kumadori*, which is painted along the lines of the actor's face. The actor uses melodramatic elocution, but because *jidaimono* originated in the puppet theatre, the plays also feature accompaniment from a chanter who relates the storyline and emotions of the character while the actor expresses them in movement, facial expressions or poses. *Sewamono* are stories of everyday life during the Edo period and closer in style to Western drama.

Every *kabuki* theatre features a *hanamichi*, an elevated pathway for the performers that runs through the audience from the back of the theatre to the main stage. This is used for entrances and exits and contains a traplift through which supernatural characters emerge.

Cerulean Tower Noh Theatre

Cerulean Tower Tokyu Hotel B2F, 26-1 Sakuragaoka-cho, Shibuya-ku (5728 0168/ www.ceruleantower.com). Shibuya station (Yamanote, Ginza, Hanzomon lines), south exit. **Capacity** 185. **Box office** tickets sold at Cerulean Tower Tokyu Hotel (3476 3000). **Tickets** prices vary. **Credit** AmEx, DC, JCB, MC, V. **Map** p79.

Housed in the basement of the Cerulean Tower hotel, this is Tokyo's newest venue for Japanese theatre. It hosts professional and amateur *noh* and *kyogen* performances, without English translation.

Kabuki-za

4-12-15 Ginza, Chuo-ku (information 3541 3131/ box office 5565 6000/www.shochiku.co.jp/play/ kabukiza/theater). Higashi-Ginza station (Hibiya, Asakusa lines), exits A2, A3. **Capacity** 2,000. **Box office** 10am-6pm daily. **Tickets** ¥2,520-¥16,800. **Credit** AmEx, DC, JCB, MC, V. **Map** p60.

This traditional-looking theatre is a splendid place to see *kabuki*. The schedule changes monthly, with matinées starting around 11am and evening performances around 4.30pm. Shows can last up to five hours, including intervals. You can also buy tickets to watch just one act from the fourth floor; these go on sale from one hour beforehand and often sell out. An English-language programme (¥1,000) and earphone guide (¥400 plus a refundable deposit of ¥1,000) are invaluable. Note that the restaurants and souvenir shop inside the theatre are not accessible to fourth-floor visitors.

National Theatre

4-1 Hayabusa-cho, Chiyoda-ku (3230 3000/ www.ntj.jac.go.jp/english/index.html). Nagatacho station (Hanzomon, Nanboku, Yurakucho lines), exit 4. **Capacity** *Large Hall* 1,610. *Small Hall* 590. **Box office** 10am-6pm daily. **Tickets** *Large Hall* ¥1,500-¥12,000. *Small Hall* ¥1,500-¥6,000. **Credit** AmEx, DC, JCB, MC, V. **Map** p66.

Kabuki is staged seven months a year in the National Theatre's Large Hall, while *bunraku* is staged in the Small Hall four months a year. Programmes include the story in English, and English earphone guides are available (¥700 with a refundable ¥1,000 deposit).

National Noh Theatre

4-18-1 Sendagaya, Shibuya-ku (3230 3000/ www.ntj.jac.go.jp/english/index.html). Sendagaya station (Chuo, Sobu lines) or Kokuritsu-Kyogijo station (Oedo line), exit A4. **Capacity** 590. **Box office** 10am-6pm daily. **Tickets** ¥2,300-¥6,000; ¥1,700 concessions. **Credit** AmEx, DC, JCB, MC, V.

Noh performances are staged four or five times a month. A one-page explanation of the story in English is available.

The venerable **Kabuki-za** in Ginza, home of *kabuki. See p246.*

Modern dramas & musicals

Modern theatre productions often portray historical themes, such as *jidai geki* – samurai dramas set in the Edo period. Unlike in *kabuki*, female roles are played by women. No matter how tragic, *jidai geki* must end with a satisfactory resolution, whether it is the successful revenge of a murder or the ascent into heaven of the dead heroine aloft a podium. However, influenced by Western drama, plays with happy endings are on the increase.

Famous Western plays and musicals, translated into Japanese, are also common. The **New National Theatre, Tokyo** (*see p233*) provides a forum for the most respected Japanese directors, who take a contemporary approach to Western classics. Artistic director of both **Theatre Cocoon** (*see p251*) and the Saitama Arts Centre in suburban Tokyo, Ninogawa Yukio has made a notable splash with his trademark fusions of Japanese and Western aesthetics in productions such as *Hamlet*. **Gekidan Shiki** (Shiki Theatre Company), founded in 1953, currently has seven theatres around the country where it stages long-running Japanese versions of such well-known faves as *Cats, Beauty and the Beast* and *A Chorus Line*. At the time of writing, it had five separate productions on in Tokyo alone.

In a city as cosmopolitan as Tokyo, it may come as a surprise to learn that only a handful of productions in English are available each year, and some of these are because of touring troupes from Britain, such as the Royal Shakespeare Company, or the US. The city has been seeing more avant-garde productions from the likes of Robert Wilson, while the **Tokyo International Arts Festival** (www.anj.or.jp) showcases cutting-edge overseas and domestic work. It celebrates its 11th anniversary in 2005.

There is also a thriving avant-garde theatre subculture in the suburb of Shimo-Kitazawa, which has dozens of small venues.

TAKARAZUKA

Featuring an all-women, oft-moustachioed cast, the **Takarazuka Kagekidan** (Takarazuka Opera Company) is another uniquely Japanese creation. Created in 1913 by entertainment tycoon Kobayashi Ichizo to attract people to his Takarazuka resort near Osaka, *takarazuka* was to provide 'strictly wholesome entertainment suitable for women and children from good families'. It is another expression of the Japanese fixation with androgynous performers (*see p248* **Gender games**). Its famously disciplined stars perform campy revues combining elements of musicals, opera and Japanese classics in gaudy productions that drive its mostly female audience wild with pleasure. The recent rebuilding and reopening of the **Tokyo Takarazuka Theater** in Hibiya testifies to the continued vigour of this unusual art some 70 years after its launch.

Arts & Entertainment

Gender games

Nowadays it's hard to imagine that the venerable and grand spectacle of *kabuki* was once considered so raunchy that the Tokugawa shogunate was forced to act against it. Launched by the legendary Izumo shrine attendant Okuni at the dawn of the 17th century, *kabuki*'s alluring female entertainers were as notorious for their sexually provocative dances on stage as they were for selling sexual favours off it.

Some 30 years after its creation, the Tokugawa government banned women from performing, resulting in their replacement by attractive young men. They too were banned in 1652 for similar reasons, with a decree stating that all roles should be played by adult men. Since then *kabuki* has been an all-male preserve, renowned for its *onnagata*: male actors who specialise in playing the roles of female beauties.

Such gender-bending is not exclusive to *kabuki*, however. Less well known is that in other traditional performing arts such as *noh*, female roles are also played by male actors, and that Japanese women did not return to the stage for more than 250 years, until the 20th century.

When they did, however, they returned in force. The modern Takarazuka revue sports an all-female cast, with women playing highly idealised men. Gallant and dashingly romantic, these beautiful but strangely de-sexed figures may provide a substitute for the tired corporate drones that the mostly female audience actually comes home to in what is still a strongly patriarchal society. A similar theme can be seen in the recent proliferation of 'host clubs', where handsome young men cater to female patrons.

Spinning the coin yet again, transvestite shows are another popular form of gender-twisting in Japan. The king of the lot is the celebrated Kingyo nightclub in the middle of the Roppongi entertainment district (3-14-17 Roppongi, Minato-ku, 3478 3000, www.e-japannavi.com/enjoy/kingyo). In its thrice-nightly dinner show, muscular boys, petite lasses and *nyu hafu* ('new half' means surgically enhanced transsexuals) cavort about the stage in outlandish costumes. They enact skits, often surprisingly political and hard-hitting, such as one that deals with the rape of an Okinawan schoolgirl by US marines. When the show is over, the dancers transform into hostesses, emerging from backstage to chat up the delighted audience.

Renowned *onnagata* **Bando Tamasaburo** performing in *Umegoyomi*.

Dentsu Shiki Theatre Umi (SEA)

1-8-2 Higashi-Shinbashi, Minato-ku (0120 489 444/ www.shiki.gr.jp/siteinfo/english/). Shiodome station (Oedo line), exit A1; (Yurikamome line), Dentsu exit. **Capacity** 1,200. **Box office** 10am-8pm daily. **Tickets** ¥3,150-¥11,550. **Credit** DC, JCB, MC, V.
The newest Western-style theatre in Tokyo opened in December 2002 in advertising giant Dentsu's new headquarters in the Shiodome area of Tokyo. Part of the Shiki Theatre Company's empire, its remit is to provide Western musicals, sung in Japanese. *The Phantom of the Opera* opened in January 2005.

Koma Gekijo

1-19-1 Kabuki-cho, Shinjuku-ku (3200 2213/ www.koma-sta.co.jp). Shinjuku station, (Yamanote, Shinjuku lines), east exit; (Marunouchi, Oedo lines), exit B7. **Capacity** 2,100. **Box office** 9.30am-7pm daily. **Tickets** ¥3,000-¥8,500. **Credit** MC, JCB, V. **Map** p73.
This well-known theatre in the heart of Tokyo's red-light district has a revolving stage, and some great posters outside. Most performers are famous singers who appear in a period drama, then give a concert. No English translations.

Meiji-za

2-31-1 Nihonbashi-Hamacho, Chuo-ku (3660 3900/ www.meijiza.co.jp). Hamacho station (Shinjuku line), exit A2. **Capacity** 1,400. **Box office** 10am-5pm daily. **Tickets** ¥5,000-¥12,000. **Credit** DC, V.
Usually stages samurai dramas, often starring actors who play similar roles on TV. No English.

Shinbashi Embujo

6-18-2 Ginza, Chuo-ku (3541 2600/www.shochiku. co.jp/play/index.html). Higashi-Ginza station (Asakusa, Hibiya lines), exit A6. **Capacity** 1,400.
Box office 10am-6pm daily. **Tickets** ¥2,100-¥15,750. **Credit** AmEx, DC, JCB, MC, V. **Map** p60.
Ichikawa Ennosuke's 'Super-Kabuki', a jazzed-up, modernised version of the real thing, is staged here in April and May and at the Kabuki-za (*see p246*) in July. Samurai dramas are performed other months.

Tokyo Takarazuka Gekijo

1-1-3 Yurakucho, Chiyoda-ku (5251 2001/ http://kageki.hankyu.co.jp/english/index.html). Yurakucho station (Yamanote, Yurakucho lines), Hibiya exit or Hibiya station (Chiyoda, Hibiya, Mita lines), exit A13. **Capacity** 2,000. **Box office** 10am-6pm Mon, Tue, Thur-Sun. **Tickets** ¥3,500-¥10,000. **Credit** JCB, MC, V. **Map** p60.
Performances are in Japanese only.

Expat theatre

With the limited number of English-language performances by companies touring from abroad, Tokyo's expatriate community has stepped up to fill the gap. There are currently no fewer than four English-language theatre groups in Japan, three of them based in Tokyo.

The most venerable – with over a century of history – is the **Tokyo International Players**, while **Intrigue Theatre** (www.intriguetheatre.com) is a recent creation. Canadian director Robert Tsonos's **Sometimes Y Theatre** has recently relocated to Japan from Toronto and been staging challenging productions, such as Michael Healey's *The Drawer Boy* at the Canadian Embassy. Finally, Australian director Dwayne Lawler's **Rising Sun Theatre**, based in Nagoya, has shaken up the Tokyo theatre scene with a number of controversial shows. These include a cross-cultural re-envisioning of *Macbeth*, set to death metal music, at the New National Theatre.

Tokyo International Players

TIP information 090 6009 4171/www.tokyo players.org. Performances held at the Tokyo American Club, 2-1-2 Azabudai, Minato-ku (3224 3670/www.tokyoamericanclub.org). Kamiyacho station (Hibiya line), exit 2 or Azabu-Juban station (Nanboku, Oedo lines), exit 6. **Box office** 7.30am-11pm daily. **Tickets** ¥4,000; ¥2,500 concessions. **No credit cards. Map** p109.

A keen group of amateur and professional actors, TIP usually stages productions at the long-running Tokyo American Club near Roppongi. Productions for the 2005 season includes *Six Characters in Search of a Hamlet* and *A Chorus Line*.

Dance & performance art

Tokyo is currently experiencing an explosion of contemporary performing arts. Companies such as the butoh-influenced **Kim Itoh & the Glorious Future** (www.geocities.co.jp/Hollywood-Miyuki/3773/index_e.html), the comedic mime-based **Muzutoabura** (www.mizutoabura.com), and choreographers like **Yamada Un** (www1.ocn.ne.jp/~yaun/english.htm), who has transformed her joint disease into a source of inspiration, are integrating Eastern and Western aesthetics to create challenging and engaging spectacles.

Festivals, including the **Park Tower Next Dance Festival** (www.ozone.co.jp/parktowerhall/) in February, the **Tokyo Performing Arts Market** (www.tpam.co.jp) in August, and two biennial offerings, **Die Pratze Dance Festival** and **Dance Biennale Tokyo**, are increasingly ambitious, showcasing new works by provocative Japanese and foreign choreographers.

Classical ballet also possesses a devoted audience in Japan. The country has recently begun to churn out prima donnas noted for their technical proficiency, while visits by overseas groups such as the Leningrad State Ballet and the New York City Ballet occur regularly. Tokyo's own companies include the celebrated **Asami Maki Ballet** (www.ambt.jp), which stages productions ranging from *Swan Lake* to modern works such as the jazz-based *Duke Ellington Suite*, which grew out of the company's long-standing relationship with legendary French choreographer Roland Petit. Meanwhile, dancer and heart-throb **Kumakawa Tetsuya** – back from his position as soloist with the Royal Ballet in London – has been making waves with innovative productions from his **K-Ballet Company** (www.tbs.co.jp/kumakawa/).

Anything Western and extroverted is also the rage in Tokyo. Tap dancing seems to be the latest fashion, while Latin dance forms from tango to salsa are trendy; the **Asakusa Samba Carnival** (*see p198*) in late August regularly draws crowds close to half a million.

BUTOH

Japan's greatest contribution to performing arts in the 20th century was the inimitable and enigmatic avant-garde dance form known as butoh. Differing from both classical Japanese and Western modern dance, but utilising elements from both, butoh is immediately recognisable by the (mostly) shaved heads, white body paint and slow, often tortured movements of its performers.

Created by Hijikata Tatsumi and his fellow pioneers, butoh, originally termed by Hijikata *ankoku butoh* or 'dance of darkness', scandalised Japan in the late 1950s. It is inspired by Japanese folk dance, German Neue Tanz and is spiritually associated with *noh* – but looks like none of them. Dancers contort their bodies to express emotions ranging from pain and despair to absurdity and ecstasy. Sometimes they hardly move at all; a butoh spectacle can be simultaneously enthralling and exhausting.

Since the 1980s when butoh began to startle overseas audiences, companies such as **Dairakudakan** (www.dairakudakan.com) and **Sankai Juku** (www.sankaijuku.com) have toured abroad on a regular basis. The recent closure of Asbestoskan means Tokyo no longer has a specialist theatre for butoh, but it is still widely performed at venues such as the ambitious **Setagaya Public Theater** or the more intimate **Azabu Die Pratze**.

As well as the venues listed below, the **New National Theatre, Tokyo** (*see p233*) presents mainly modern dance and drama in its two smaller spaces, the Playhouse and the Pit.

Aoyama Round Theatre

5-53-1 Jingumae, Shibuya-ku (3797 5678/box office 3797 1400/www.aoyama.org). Omotesando station (Chiyoda, Ginza, Hanzomon lines), exit B2. **Capacity** 1,200. **Box office** 10am-6pm daily. **Tickets** prices vary. **No credit cards. Map** p79.

As its name suggests, this is a theatre that can be used in the round. It's one of very few in Tokyo, and attracts leading contemporary performers keen to make the most of the space.

Art Sphere

2-3-16 Higashi-Shinagawa, Shinagawa-ku (5460 9999/www.tennoz.co.jp/sphere/). Tennozu Isle station (Tokyo Monorail), Chuo exit; (Rinkai line), exits A, B. **Capacity** *Art Sphere* 750. *Sphere Mex* 200. **Box office** 10am-6pm daily. **Tickets** prices vary. **No credit cards.**

Art Sphere caters to the whims of well-off young fans of contemporary modern dance and is sure to book things that are considered 'in', but not too avant-garde or risqué. The venue's location, on Tennozu Isle, makes it one of the more interesting – and less accessible – of Tokyo's theatrical venues.

Azabu Die Pratze

1-26-6 Higashi-Azabu 2F, Minato-ku (5545 1385/ www.geocities.jp/azabubu). Akabanebashi station (Oedo line), Akabanebashi exit. **Capacity** 100. **Box office** 6-11pm daily. **Tickets** ¥3,000. **No credit cards.**

This cosy space is a locus for cutting-edge dance, performance and butoh, as well as the host of the annual Die Pratze Dance Festival.
Other locations: Kagurazaka Die Pratze 2-12 Nishi-Gokencho, Shinjuku-ku (3235 7990).

Session House

158 Yaraicho, Shinjuku-ku (3266 0461/www.session-house.net). Kagurazaka station (Tozai line), exit 1. **Capacity** 100. **Box office** 10am-7pm daily. **Tickets** ¥2,000-¥2,500. **No credit cards.**
Dancer Itoh Naoko started Session House in order to give solo dancers the opportunity to experiment. The aim is to showcase pure dance without extensive use of theatrical props and high-tech lighting.

Dancer/choreographer **Kuroda Ikuyo.**

Setagaya Public Theatre

4-1-1 Taishido, Setagaya-ku (5432 1526/ www.setagaya-ac.or.jp/sept/). Sangenjaya station (Tokyu Denentoshi line). **Capacity** *Public Theatre* 600. *Theatre Tram* 200. **Box office** 10am-7pm daily. **Tickets** prices vary. **No credit cards**.

Like the New National Theatre (*see p233*), this venue is a favourite with fans and performers. The main auditorium is modelled on a Greek open-air theatre, but can be changed to proscenium style. The smaller Theatre Tram is a popular venue for dance. The adopted home of the Sankai Juku butoh troupe, when it's in town.

Space Zero

2-12-10 Yoyogi, Shibuya-ku (3209 0222). Shinjuku station (Yamanote line), south exit; (Marunouchi, Oedo lines), exit A1; (Shinjuku line), exit 6. **Capacity** 550. **Box office** 10am-6pm Mon-Fri. **Tickets** prices vary. **No credit cards. Map** p73.

A middling-sized venue that stages mainly modern jazz dance performances.

Theatre Cocoon

Bunkamura, 2-24-1 Dogenzaka, Shibuya-ku (3477 9999/www.bunkamura.co.jp). Shibuya station (Yamanote, Ginza lines), Hachiko exit; (Hanzomon line), exit 3A. **Capacity** 750. **Box office** 10am-7pm daily. *Phone bookings* 10am-5.30pm daily. **Tickets** prices vary. **Credit** AmEx, DC, JCB, MC, V. **Map** p79.

The medium-sized venue of the giant Bunkamura arts centre in Shibuya is used mainly for musicals, ballet, concerts and opera.

Comedy

Japan has a tradition of humorous storytelling, called *rakugoh*, which can be seen at a few venues including **Asakusa Engei Hall** (1-43-12 Asakusa, Taito-ku, 3841 6545) and **National Engei Hall** (4-1 Hayabusa-cho, Chiyoda-ku, 3230 3000, www.ntj.jac.go.jp/english/index.html). However, you'll need to speak Japanese; nowhere in Tokyo offers English translations of such events.

Punchline Comedy Club

Shows at Pizza Express 3F, 4-30-3 Jingumae, Shibuya-ku (5775 3894/www.punchlinecomedy. com/tokyo). Harajuku station (Yamanote line), Meiji-Jingu exit or Meiji-Jingumae station (Chiyoda line), exit 5. **Shows** selected days Jan, Mar, June, Sept. **Tickets** ¥8,500 incl dinner & 2 drinks. **Credit** AmEx, DC, JCB, MC, V. **Map** p85.

John Moorhead started the Tokyo branch of this pan-Asian comedy club in 2001. Its mission is to bring top comedians from around the world, many from the UK, to perform before an expat crowd.

Suehiro-tei

3-6-12 Shinjuku, Shinjuku-ku (3351 2974/ www.suehirotei.com). Shinjuku-Sanchome station (Marunouchi, Shinjuku lines), exits B2, C4.

Butoh troupe **Torifune** in action.

Capacity 325. **Box office** noon-8.15pm daily. **Tickets** ¥2,200-¥2,700. **No credit cards. Map** p73.

A charming old theatre that looks alarmingly like a bathhouse, which hosts regular performances of *rakugoh*. No English translation.

Tokyo Comedy Store

Bar, Isn't It, MT Bldg 3F, 3-8-18 Roppongi, Minato-ku (3746 1598/www.tokyocomedy.com). Roppongi station (Hibiya line), exit 5. **Shows** 1st & 3rd Fri of mth. **Tickets** ¥2,000 incl 1 drink. **No credit cards. Map** p109.

Tokyo's best-organised English-language comedy group may have the same name as the celebrated venue in London, but there the similarity ends. Performers are keen amateurs ranging from the hilarious to the dire. New material is always sought, from both Japanese and foreign performers. The Comedy Store also holds improv classes and workshops in Japanese and English.

Tokyo Cynics

The Fiddler, Tajima Bldg B1F, 2-1-2 Takadanobaba, Shinjuku-ku (3204 2698/www.thefiddler.com). Takadanobaba station (Yamanote line), Waseda exit; (Tozai line), exit 3. **Shows** 2nd Tue of mth. **Admission** free.

A ramshackle bunch of English-speaking amateur comics and outright eccentrics who regularly enliven evenings at one of Tokyo's longest-established and most popular British-style pubs. They also perform in the Maple Leaf sports bar in Shibuya on the last Sunday of the month.

Sport & Fitness

Fighting, punching, wrestling – and that's just the Pride players.

Japan is no different from most other countries as regards its obsession with sport. It does, however, have certain idiosyncrasies – such as embracing team games from both sides of the Atlantic, while its own national sport consists of two wardrobe-sized men trying to push each other over. Japan has become internationalised in terms of both its adopted and indigenous games; you can find Japanese sports stars in US Major League baseball and European football, while sumo's current top star in 2004 was a Mongolian. In 2004 Japan even acquired its own cricket ground and hosted a series of World Cup qualifying matches. Was that the birth of a cricketing titan? Watch this space.

Martial arts is where the Japanese truly excel: they scooped up over half the judo gold medals at the Athens Olympics. The country is also the birthplace of karate and aikido, and many students travel to Japan to improve their skills. The nation is also obsessed with baseball, football, golf and – surprisingly enough – marathons, and has a fascination with the new breed of mixed martial art disciplines that travel under the banners K-1 and Pride.

Tickets for major events can be bought at ticket agencies and convenience stores and usually sell out very quickly. Ticket touts hang around many stadiums selling tickets at a premium – it's worth haggling, but be friendly and don't mess anybody around (local touts often control matters on behalf of gangsters).

Sports facilities abound within the capital, but are not always easy to use. Swimming pools, in particular, have strict, confusing and often amusing rules.

Spectator sports

American football

Gridiron in Japan has a surprisingly large presence considering its associations with big blokes sporting overdeveloped muscles. There is a strong university league and even a company league, known as the X-League (where firms import top players and give them 'jobs'), which finishes with the **X Bowl** in Kobe in mid December. The climax of the domestic season is the brilliantly named **Rice Bowl**, at the **Tokyo Dome** (*see p253*) in early January, when the college champions take on the

winners of the X-League. The same venue also hosts regular NFL pre-season tour matches in August under the American Bowl banner.

Athletics

The IAAF Japan Grand Prix is held every spring in Osaka, which will also host the 2007 World Championships. The International Super Track & Field event, the Tokyo area's main annual taste of top-class competition, usually takes place on 23 September (a national holiday) at the **International Stadium Yokohama** (*see p254*).

Japan's real athletics obsession has long been the marathon. The last two women's Olympic champions were Japanese and they quickly became household names. The **Tokyo International Marathon** is held in February, and the **Tokyo International Women's Marathon** (the world's first marathon for women) in November; both start and finish at the **National Stadium** (*see p254*). Both have strict entrance requirements (no fun-runs here) and attract some of the world's top runners.

Baseball

Introduced to Japan by Horace Wilson in 1873, baseball has long held a firm grip on local hearts and minds. The first pro side, the Yomiuri Giants, was founded in 1934, and by 1950 a professional competition had been set up. The league eventually split into two divisions (the Pacific League and the Central League) with six teams in each.

In 2004 declining attendances, combined with the weak economy, forced two teams to merge and there was even talk of a single ten-team league (two other teams were rumoured to be merging). This led to the first ever players' strike, and the game's administrators were forced to back down and allow a new team to form, the Rakuten Tohoku Eagles. Another demand from both players and fans was for interleague play, which means that the Pacific League sides will now be able to milk the cash cow known as the Yomiuri Giants – the New York Yankees of Japanese baseball. Each side plays 140 games a season (late March to October), with the winners of the Central and Pacific Leagues meeting in the Japan Series to decide the championship.

Uehara Koji, star pitcher for the **Yomiuri Giants**.

Two teams are based in central Tokyo: the **Yomiuri Giants** at **Tokyo Dome** (the salaryman's favourite, ergo somewhat dull) and the **Yakult Swallows** at **Jingu Stadium** (open-air, crazy fans and beer on tap – Jingu is the place to go). The **Hokkaido Nippon Ham Fighters** also play some games at Tokyo Dome, their former home. In the Tokyo area you can also see the **Yokohama BayStars**, **Chiba Lotte Marines** and the **Seibu Lions**.

More worrying for the future of the professional game in Japan has been the recent drain of local superstars to the US Major Leagues and the growing audiences for live broadcasts from across the Pacific. Matsui Hideki of the New York Yankees and Suzuki Ichiro of the Seattle Mariners are huge in Japan and most of their games are broadcast live.

Interest in amateur-level baseball is big as well. Every pitch of the spring and summer national high-school tournaments at Koshien Stadium near Osaka is televised live and brings much of the country to a virtual standstill as the fans watch teenage boys wilting in the heat.

Jingu Baseball Stadium

13 Kasumigaoka-machi, Shinjuku-ku (3404 8999). Kokuritsu-Kyogijo station (Oedo line), exit A4 or Sendagaya station (Chuo line) or Gaienmae station (Ginza line), exit 2. **Capacity** 46,000. **Tickets** ¥1,500-¥4,500.
This large open-air stadium is part of the complex that includes the National Stadium and was built for the 1964 Olympics.

Tokyo Dome

1-3-61 Koraku, Bunkyo-ku (5800 9999/www.tokyo-dome.co.jp). Suidobashi station (Chuo line), west exit or Suidobashi station (Mita line), exits A3, A4, A5 or Korakuen station (Marunouchi, Namboku lines), exit 2 or Kasuga station (Mita, Oedo line), exit A1.
The Dome or Big Egg is home to the Central League's Yomiuri Giants. In the past the Giants have claimed that every game was sold out, but the growing number of empty seats suggests that tickets are much easier to acquire than before.

Football

The 2002 World Cup saw the eyes of the football universe focused on Japan and co-hosts South Korea, although the closest Tokyo came in terms of venues was suburban Saitama and nearby Yokohama, which hosted the final. Tokyo was also left on the sidelines when the J.League was founded in 1993, but the capital now has two top-flight teams, **FC Tokyo** and **Tokyo Verdy 1969**, who share a ground in the west of the city. The **Urawa Reds** and **Omiya Ardija** in Saitama to the north, **JEF United Ichihara** to the east, and **Kawasaki Frontale** and the **Yokohama F Marinos** to the west are the other major local clubs. The J.League's official website (www.j-league.or.jp/eng) features English-language information on clubs, players and fixtures.

From 2005 the league expanded to 18 teams and has changed to a single-stage season. The

Arts & Entertainment

Emperor's Cup (Japan's FA Cup) takes place in December, with the final (*see p200*) on New Year's Day. The **Nabisco Cup** (the equivalent of the League Cup) runs throughout the season with the final in early November. International matches take place throughout the year and include Asian Cup and World Cup qualifiers, as well as the midsummer Kirin Cup. The **Japan Football Association**'s English website (www.jfa.or.jp/e/index.html) has information on forthcoming matches.

Ajinomoto Stadium

376-3 Nishimachi, Chofu (0424 40 0555/ www.ajinomotostadium.com). Tobitakyu station (Keio line). **Capacity** 50,000. **Tickets** J.League matches ¥1,200-¥6,000.
The large and impressive home of FC Tokyo and Tokyo Verdy 1969 opened in 2001.

International Stadium Yokohama

3300 Kozukue-cho, Kohoku-ku, Yokohama-shi (045 477 5000/www.hamaspo.com/stadium). Shin-Yokohama station (Tokaido Shinkansen, Yokohama lines), north exit then 15mins walk. **Capacity** 70,000.
Home of Nissan-sponsored Yokohama F Marinos, the J.League champions in 2003 and 2004. You can also take a World Cup tour; *see also p264*.

National Stadium

15 Kasumigaoka-machi, Shinjuku-ku (3403 4150). Kokuritsu-Kyogijo station (Oedo line), exit A4 or Sendagaya station (Chuo line) or Gaienmae station (Ginza line), exit 2. **Capacity** 60,000.
The 1964 Olympic Stadium still hosts many major events, including the start and finish of marathons, some international and J.League football matches, the Emperor's Cup final, the Nabisco Cup final and major rugby matches.

Saitama Stadium 2002

500 Nakanoda, Saitama (048 812 2002/ www.stadium2002.com). Urawa-Misono station (Nanboku, Saitama Railway lines). **Capacity** 63,700. **Tickets** J.League matches ¥2,000-¥4,500.
The country's largest soccer-only stadium. It's a 20-minute walk from Urawa-Misono station, which gets extremely crowded after major events.

Golf

Like much else in Japan, golf has suffered from the bursting of the economic bubble in the 1990s. At its peak, the Japan Golf Tour (JGTO) was the richest in the world; lucrative enough, in fact, to keep local golfers from playing abroad, so it developed into a major, if isolated, tour. But the Tiger factor, among others, has enabled America's PGA Tour to reclaim its pre-eminent position in world golf.

Reduced sponsorship has seen the Japanese tour contract slightly and a lack of charismatic stars has also hurt, but it retains very high standards. There are many professional events in the Tokyo area, and many foreign stars visit Japan after the end of the PGA and European tours. The biggest event in the Tokyo area is the **Sumitomo VISA Taiheiyo Masters** in Gotemba, an hour west of Tokyo – check out the JGTO website on www.jgto.org.

The women's tour has also produced its share of stars, notably Okamoto Ayako and Kobayashi Hiromi. In 2003 high-school student Miyazato Ai won a JLPGA tournament, turned pro and caught the imagination of the country, revitalising the waning women's tour. Yuri Fudo has also dominated, and British golfer Samantha Head has been a fixture.

Horse racing

The **Japan Racing Association** (JRA) manages the ten national tracks and stages the country's big races, while the **National Association of Racing** (NAR) oversees local courses. Racetracks are one of the few places in the country where gambling is legal. For details in English, visit the website of the **Japan Association for International Horse Racing** at www.jair.jrao.ne.jp.

Oi Racecourse

2-1-2 Katsushima, Shinagawa-ku (3763 2151). Oi Keibajomae station (Tokyo Monorail).
Run under the auspices of the NAR, with around 120 days' racing every year. Twinkle Races, evening events that Oi pioneered in the 1990s, have proved very popular with office workers.

Tokyo Racecourse

1-1 Hiyoshi-cho, Fuchu-shi (042 363 3141/ www.jra.go.jp/turf/tokyo/index.html). Fuchu-Honmachi station (Musashino line) or Fuchukeiba-Seimonmae station (Keio line).
Run by the JRA, Tokyo Racecourse hosts 40 days' racing a year, all at weekends. Many of the country's most famous races are held here, including November's Japan Cup (*see p199*) – an international invitational that attracts top riders and horses from around the world.

Hydroplane racing

After horse racing, *kyotei* is the second-most popular focus for betting in Japan (bets start at just ¥100). The race itself involves six motor-driven boats in what is essentially a very large swimming pool; they go round the 600-metre (1,970-foot) course three times, regularly reaching speeds of over 80kph (50mph). **Edogawa Kyotei** is the favourite Tokyo venue. The schedule is published in sports newspapers and at www.edogawa-kyotei.co.jp.

Edogawa Kyotei
3-1-1 Higashi-Komatsugawa, Edogawa-ku (3656 0641/www.edogawa-kyotei.co.jp). Funabori station (Shinjuku line), south exit. **Admission** ¥50.

Ice hockey

The economic recession has hit the Japan Ice Hockey League hard in recent years. It came close to folding, but fought back with a novel mode of expansion: importing teams from overseas. So there is now an Asian League (www.alhockey.com) consisting of the four remaining Japanese teams (Oji, Kokudo, Nikko Ice Bucks and Nippon Paper Cranes), two teams from China, and one each from Russia and South Korea.

Getting to see hockey in Tokyo is not always easy; **Kokudo** is the only team based nearby and they usually play at **Higashi Fushimi Ice Arena**, which is not exactly downtown. Other games are played at **Shin-Yokohama** and even at **Yoyogi Gymnasium** right in the middle of Tokyo. The season runs from October to March.

Higashi-Fushimi Ice Arena
3-1-25 Higashi-Fushimi, Hoya-shi (0424 67 7171). Higashi-Fushimi station (Seibu Shinjuku line).

National Yoyogi Stadium 1st Gymnasium
2-1-1 Jinnan, Shibuya-ku (3468 1171). Harajuku station (Yamanote line), Omotesando exit or Meiji-Jingumae station (Chiyoda line), exit 2. **Map** p85.

Shin-Yokohama Prince Hotel Skate Centre
2-11 Shin-Yokohama, Kohoku-ku, Yokohama-shi, Kanagawa (045 474 1112). Shin-Yokohama station (Tokaido Shinkansen, Yokohama lines), north exit then 10mins walk.

K-1

People are often surprised to learn that the record attendance (74,500) for a sports event at Tokyo Dome is held by K-1, a mishmash of martial arts. It's basically a combination of boxing and kick boxing, with bouts consisting of three three-minute rounds (if there are no knockouts). It has all the appearance of a real sport – bouts take place in a ring with a referee and three judges; doctors are in attendance; rules are enforced; it has a competitive structure – but is not taken completely seriously by some sports fans and writers.

Being a new sport, some of the participants have not been up to scratch, but it is growing and it is big. It is also exciting, with the climactic Grand Prix Final at Tokyo Dome broadcast in prime time on national TV.

Competitors have come from Muay Thai, sumo, American football, boxing, kick boxing and even Mongolian wrestling. There is also a lightweight division, where the fighters tend to be lighter, fitter and faster. Events are held most months at venues such as **Nippon Budokan** (*see below*), **Yoyogi Gymnasium** (*see above*) and **Tokyo Dome** (*see p253*).

Martial arts

Nippon Budokan
2-3 Kitanomaru-koen, Chiyoda-ku (3216 5100/ www.nipponbudokan.or.jp). Kudanshita station (Hanzomon, Shinjuku, Tozai lines), exit 2. **Map** p66.
The Budokan stages the All-Japan championships or equivalent-level demonstration events in all the martial arts except sumo. Advance tickets are not required, and in many cases admission is free. The stadium is also used for concerts; *see p239*.

Motor sports

Motor sports have a devoted following in Japan. The **Suzuka** circuit (0593 78 1111, www.suzukacircuit.co.jp/index.html), in Mie prefecture towards Nagoya, hosts the annual Formula 1 Japan Grand Prix. It's possible to make the return trip from Tokyo in a day. **Twin Ring Motegi** in Tochigi prefecture, a couple of hours north-east of the capital, boasts two types of circuit, including an oval course that's suitable for US-style motor sports. The permanent circuit hosts local Formula 3 and Formula Nippon races, the latter seen as a major stepping stone toward Formula 1.

Motorcycle racing is also a big draw in Japan and several top riders are home-grown. The Japanese Grand Prix is held in September at the Motegi circuit.

Twin Ring Motegi
120-1 Hiyama, Motegi-machi, Haga-gun, Tochigi-ken (0285 64 0001/www.twinring.jp/english/index.html). Motegi station (Moka line) then bus.

Pride

Pride competes for attention with K-1 in the mixed martial arts field, and is similar to the Ultimate Fighting Championships in the US. Pride's selling point is that it is 'as close as you can get to street fighting'; everything goes, almost – there's no biting or testicular activity. The sport contains elements of karate, boxing, judo, wrestling and kick boxing. Fights can include some sporty moments of punching and kicking, and other moments where one fighter sits on the other and beats him to a pulp. It's not for the faint-hearted.

Arts & Entertainment

The big boys

The sumo wrestler stands alongside Hello Kitty and Godzilla as one of Japan's great icons. Sumo is more than a sport; it's a symbol, reflecting cultural, spiritual and even religious aspects of Japan. Too bad then – at least for die-hard Japanese – that it's been dominated by foreigners in recent years. In the 1990s two Americans – both from Hawaii – made it to the prestigious rank of *yokozuna* (grand champion). Many of the old guard were aghast at this poisoning of Japanese culture, although for a while it made for some interesting battles against two Japanese superstars of the *dohyo*, brothers Takanohana and Wakanohana. However, Waka and then Taka retired, followed a couple of years ago by the Hawaiians (Akebono and Musashimaru).

Waddling into the breach came another foreigner, the Mongolian Asashoryu (pictured). This was too much for many Japanese and the 'Mad Mongolian' lived up (or down) to expectations with a series of controversial incidents, including kicking (a big no-no) fellow Mongolian Kyokushuzan after a match, refusing to attend his ex-stablemaster's funeral, arguing over money and rampaging drunkenly.

The reality is, of course, that Asashoryu is the best thing to hit sumo for years. He's a fantastic wrestler, he's young, he's got attitude and people either love him or hate

him. In 2004 he won five of the six Grand Tournaments, the sport's primary competitions. But what he really needs is a rival, preferably Japanese. However, to be promoted to *yokozuna* from *ozeki* (champion), you must have a dominating record over three tournaments and win a title or two. With Asashoryu dominating, that may not happen soon. In fact, with a Russian and several more Mongolians on the up, sumo could suffer its worst nightmare: foreign domination. The quality of wrestlers tends to move in cycles and the likelihood is that a challenger will emerge before too long.

Sumo bathed smugly in the glory of the Waka-Taka era – while at the same time discouraging the recruitment of foreign wrestlers – and is currently suffering an anti-climax. This means that seats are easier to get for the Grand Tournaments. Sumo will always be high on the list of tourist 'must-sees', so now is probably a good time to check it out.

To learn more about sumo's historical and religious aspects, check out one of the annual dedicatory ceremonies. Two are held at the **Meiji Shrine** (*see p87*), in early January and at the end of September; and one in April at the **Yasukuni Shrine** (*see p68* **Ghosts of war**), with 500 wrestlers, including *yokozuna*, taking part. Contact the tourist offices (*see p297*) for details.

Rugby

Japanese rugby underwent a major upheaval in 2003 with the introduction of a national professional league. Cynics would say Japan already had a professional operation for many years in the form of the corporate league; however, the game was amateurish and in dire need of reform. Now there is a national league, a national championship (which includes the top university teams) and a knockout trophy – and the Japan Rugby Football Union (JRFU) are keen to bring the 2011 World Cup to Japan.

Tokyo's Waseda University is one of the most popular sports 'franchises' in the country; matches are often held before 60,000 fans at the **National Stadium** (*see p254*). **Prince Chichibu Memorial Stadium** is the official 'home' of rugby and is slap bang in the centre of town, next to Jingu Baseball Stadium. Ticket information is available at the JRFU website: www.jrfu-members.com.

Prince Chichibu Memorial Stadium

2-8-35 Kita Aoyama, Minato-ku (3401 3881). Kokuritsu-Kyogijo station (Oedo line), exit A4 or Sendagaya station (Chuo line) or Gaienmae station (Ginza line), exit 2.
International and other big rugby matches not held at the National Stadium are played here.

Sumo

With a history dating back 2,000 years, Japan's national sport uniquely blends tradition, athleticism and religion. Its rules are simple: each combatant must try to force the other out of the ring (*dohyo*) or make him touch the floor with a part of his anatomy other than his feet. Tournaments take place over 15 days, with wrestlers fighting once a day. Those who achieve regular majorities (winning more than they lose) progress up through the rankings, the top of which is *yokozuna* (grand champion). Wrestlers failing to achieve a majority are demoted. *Yokozuna* must achieve a majority in every tournament or are expected to retire.

Three of the six annual tournaments take place in Tokyo (in January, May and September) at the **Ryogoku Kokugikan**, which also hosts one-day tournaments and retirement ceremonies. For ticket information, results and interviews, see the websites of the **Sumo Association** (www.sumo.or.jp/eng) and *Sumo World* magazine (www.sumoworld.com). *See also left* **The big boys**. For information on visiting a sumo stable, *see p97*.

Ryogoku Kokugikan

1-3-28 Yokoami, Sumida-ku (3623 5111/balcony seats booking 5237 9310). Ryogoku station (Sobu line), west exit; (Oedo line), exits A3, A4.
Tickets ¥3,600-¥14,300.
Advance tickets go on sale about a month before each tournament. They're not difficult to get hold of (apart from the most expensive box seats) – though weekends generally sell out. Some unreserved, back-row balcony seats (one per person) are always held back for sale from 8am on the day of the tournament. Many spectators watch bouts between younger fighters from downstairs box seats until the ticket holders arrive in the mid afternoon. There's also a small museum (closed on tournament days).

Tennis

In professional tennis, it's the women's game that gets the most attention in Japan. A number of women players have won Grand Slam doubles titles and Japan's most successful player of all time, Kimiko Date, made the semi-finals in the singles at Wimbledon. Recently, Sugiyama Ai has been rated the top doubles player in the world. The biggest event is the **Toray Pan Pacific Open** (*see p200*), a Tier I WTA tournament held in the week following the Australian Open at the end of January at **Tokyo Metropolitan Gymnasium**. The biggest men's event is the **Japan Open** (*see p199*) in October, which is held at **Ariake Tennis Forest** on Odaiba and also features a Tier III WTA event.

Ariake Tennis Forest/ Ariake Colosseum

2-2-22 Ariake, Koto-ku (3529 3301/www.tptc.or.jp/ park/ariake.htm). Ariake station (Yurikamome line) or Kokusai-Tenjijo station (Rinkai line). **Open** 9am-9pm daily. **Admission** ¥3,000 2hrs Mon-Fri; ¥3,600 2hrs Sat, Sun. **Map** p113.

Tokyo Metropolitan Gymnasium

1-17-1 Sendagaya, Shibuya-ku (5474 2111/www. tef.or.jp/tmg/index.html). Kokuritsu-Kyogijo station (Oedo line), exit A4 or Sendagaya station (Chuo line).

Active sports & fitness

Aussie Rules Football

The **Tokyo Goannas** (www.tokyogoannas.com) satisfy the Australian community's need for sport and drink.

Boxing

There are various gyms around Tokyo and boxercise fitness training is available at several sports clubs. Also try **Nitta Boxing Gym** (044 932 4639, www.nittagym.com).

Cricket

Decent cricket is available in Tokyo, notably among certain expat communities – check out the **Tokyo Wombats** (www.tokyowombats.com) and the **Indian Engineers** (www.iecc japan.com/kantocup.htm). The **Japan Cricket Association** site is at www.jca-cricket.ne.jp/index.php.

Football

There's quite a lot of soccer action in Tokyo with several competitions for all levels. Major organisations are the **Tokyo Metropolis League** (www.metropolis-league.com) and the **International Friendship Football League** (http://home.att.ne.jp/sun/iffl/).

Golf

With time and expense posing substantial obstacles to the capital's legion of would-be golfers, driving ranges line the city. The cost of membership at private golf clubs can easily run to millions of yen, while green fees run from ¥8,000 on weekdays to ¥30,000 at weekends. The least expensive courses are those along built-up riverbanks to the west and north of the capital. There are online reservation sites (try www.golfyoyaku.com), but only in Japanese. The **Tokyo Metropolitan Golf Course** (18 holes at par 63) is the cheapest of the city's public courses; booking essential at weekends.

Golf in Japan is usually a game of two halves, broken up by an hour-long lunch break. Courses are often crowded and play is slow, so 18 holes can take up to seven hours.

Tokyo Metropolitan Golf Course

1-15-1 Shinden, Adachi-ku (3919 0111). Oji-Kamiya station (Nanboku line). **Open** dawn-dusk daily. **Rates** ¥5,000-¥6,000 Mon-Fri; from ¥8,000 Sat, Sun.

Gyms

Membership of private gyms can be very expensive. Large hotels may have swimming pools or gyms, but sometimes charge extra for using them. If you are in need of some muscle-pumping action, head for one of the following – or, more cheaply, visit one of Tokyo's public sports centres (*see p260*).

Esforta

Shibuya Infoss Tower B1F, 20-1 Sakuragaokacho, Shibuya-ku (3780 5551/www.esforta.com). Shibuya station (Yamanote line), south exit; (Ginza, Hanzomon lines), Hachiko exit. **Open** 7am-10pm daily. Closed 1st Sun of mth. Joining fee ¥10,000 membership, then ¥15,000 per mth. **Map** p79.

Facilities typically include aerobics, sauna, weight machines and sunbeds. The Suidobashi and Akasaka branches have swimming pools.
Other locations: throughout the city.

Tipness

Kaleido Bldg 5F-7F, 7-1 Nishi-Shinjuku, Shinjuku-ku (3368 3531/freephone 0120 208 025/www.tipness.co.jp). Shinjuku station (Yamanote, Chuo, Sobu lines), east or west exit; (Marunouchi line), exit A18 or Shinjuku-Nishi station (Oedo line), exit D5. **Open** 7am-11.15pm Mon-Fri; 9.30am-10pm Sat; 9.30am-8pm Sun. **Membership** ¥3,150 membership, then plans up to ¥15,000/mth. **Credit** AmEx, MC, DC, JCB, V. **Map** p73.

Tipness has 25 branches within Tokyo. Most of them have a swimming pool, aerobics classes and weight gym.
Other locations: throughout the city.

Gold's Gym Harajuku

V28 Building 3F, 6-31-17 Jingumae, Shibuya-ku (5766 3131/www.goldsgym.jp). Harajuku station (Yamanote line), Omotesando exit or Meiji-Jingumae station (Chiyoda line), exit 6. **Open** 24hrs daily; closed 8pm Sun-7am Mon. **Membership** ¥5,250, then plans up to ¥8,400/mth. **Credit** AmEx, MC, DC, JCB, V. **Map** p85.

All the facilities you would expect from this world-wide gym chain.
Other locations: throughout the city.

Horse riding

Tokyo Horse Riding Club

4-8 Yoyogi Kamizono-cho, Shibuya-ku (3370 0984/www.tokyo-rc.jp/). Sangubashi station *(Odakyu line).* **Open** *Mar-Nov* 9am-5.45pm Tue-Sun. *Dec-Feb* 9am-4.45pm Tue-Sun. **Rates** ¥6,500 Tue-Fri; ¥7,500 Sat, Sun. **No credit cards.**

Japan's oldest riding club boasts 45 horses and seven instructors. Visitors don't, thankfully, have to pay the annual membership fee of ¥96,000 (to join the Tokyo Horse Riding Club you must be recommended by two members and pay a fee of ¥2 million). Booking is necessary.

Ice hockey

Contact the **Tokyo Canadians** (rough boys, be careful) at www.tokyocanadians.com.

Ice skating

Championship events are held at the **National Yoyogi Gymnasium** (*see p255*). Other ice hockey venues are also open to those who want to skate, as are the following rinks:

Meiji Jingu Ice Skating Rink

Gobanchi, Kasumigaoka, Shinjuku (3403 3458/www.meijijingugaien.jp/ice/). Kokuritsu-Kyogijo station (Oedo line), exit A2 or Sendagaya station (Chuo, Sobu lines). **Open** noon-6pm Mon-Fri;

Gold's Gym Harajuku. *See p258.*

10am-6pm Sat, Sun. **Admission** (last entry 5pm) ¥1,000-¥1,300; ¥500-¥900 children. *Skate rental* ¥500. **No credit cards**.

Takadanobaba Citizen Ice Skating Rink

4-29-27 Takadanobaba, Shinjuku-ku (3371 0910/ www.h2.dion.ne.jp/~c.i.s/). Takadanobaba station (Yamanote line), east exit; (Tozai line), exit 1. **Open** noon-7.45pm Mon-Sat; 10am-6.05pm Sun. **Admission** ¥1,000-¥1,300; ¥600-¥800 children. *Skate rental* ¥500. **No credit cards**.

Martial arts

Almost five million people practise martial arts in Japan. There are nine recognised modern forms – aikido, judo, *jukendo*, karate, kendo, *kyudo, naginata, shorinji kempo* and sumo – and a series of more traditional forms, known collectively as *kobudo*. The national associations of each discipline may have training facilities where spectators can view sessions. They may also know of *dojo* (gyms) that welcome visitors or potential students.

Aikido *Aikikai Federation, 17-18 Wakamatsucho, Shinjuku-ku (3203 9236/www.aikikai.or.jp).* Also check out the English website www.tokyo seidokan.com and American teacher Chris Koprowski.
Judo *All-Japan Judo Federation, 1-16-30 Kasuga, Bunkyo-ku (3818 4199/www.judo.or.jp/English www.kodokan.org).*

Jukendo *All-Japan Jukendo Federation, 2-3 Kitanomaru Koen, Chiyoda-ku (3201 1020/ www.jukendo.or.jp).*
Karate Be warned: there are three governing bodies for karate and they could be reproducing even as we speak. Try www.wpka-kobukan.org (which has a *dojo* in Nakano, Tokyo); www.karate-world.org (in Shinjuku); and the Japan Karatedo Federation (3503 6637, www.karatedo.co.jp) in Minato-ku .
Kendo *All-Japan Kendo Federation, Yasukuni Kudan Minami Bldg 2F, 2-3-14 Kudan-Minami, Chiyoda-ku (3234 6271/www.kendo.or.jp).* Wooden sword fighting, which is held, to some extent, in similar esteem to sumo. Favoured by rightists, politicians, gangsters and the police.
Kobudo *Nippon Kobudo Association, 2-3 Kitanomaru Koen, Chiyoda-ku (3216 5114).*
Kyudo *All-Japan Kyudo Federation, Kishi Kinen Taïukaikan, 1-1-1 Jinnan, Shibuya-ku (3481 2387/ www.kyudo.jp).*
Naginata *All-Japan Naginata Federation (Tokyo Office), Kishi Kinen Taïukaikan, 1-1-1 Jinnan, Shibuya-ku (3481 2411/http:// naginata.jp).*
Wooden spear fighting, popular with girls.
Shorinji Kempo *Shorinji Kempo Federation (Tokyo Office), 1-3-5 Uehara, Shibuya-ku (3481 5191/www.shorinjikempo.or.jp).*
Fascinating karate-type martial art created after the war 'with the aim of educating people with strong senses of compassion, courage and justice'.
Sumo (amateur) *Japan Sumo Federation, 1-15-20 Hyakunincho, Shinjyuku-ku (3368 2211/ English www.sumo.or.jp/eng).*

Running

The big events for hobby runners, held close to the date of the Tokyo Marathon, are the ten-kilometre and 30-kilometre road races in Ome in north-west Tokyo prefecture (information on 0428 24 6311). Those looking for a little gentle jogging might want to check out the five-kilometre route marked out at 100-metre intervals around the Imperial Palace. There is also a branch of the **Hash House Harriers** (http://tokyohash.org) for those runners in need of a serious drink at the end of their efforts.

Skiing & snowboarding

Just 90 minutes by train from Shinjuku lies a wide range of slopes that are snowy in winter. Between December and March, JR ticket windows offer all-in-one deals covering ski pass and day-return transport for the destination of your choice, with weekday prices starting from under ¥10,000. Also visit **Snodeck** (www.snodeck.net), an après-ski place run – and populated – by foreigners, which can fix up transport and/or accommodation and provide English-language snowboarding lessons. Closer at hand, there are year-round indoor slopes where you can ski when it's 30°C outside.

Snova Mizonokuchi-R246

1358-1 Shimo-Sakunobe, Takatsu-ku, Kawasaki-shi, Kanagazawa (044 844 1181/www.snova246. com). Tsudayama station (Nanbu line). **Open** 10am-11pm Mon-Fri; 9am-11.30pm Sat; 9am-11pm Sun. **Admission** ¥2,300 90mins, ¥3,500 4hrs Mon-Fri; ¥2,800 90mins, ¥4,000 4hrs Sat, Sun. ¥1,000 membership payable on 1st visit. **Credit** MC, JCB, V.
For both skiers and snowboarders, although lessons are for snowboarders only. Clothing, boots and board rental is available.

Sports centres

Each of Tokyo's 23 wards has sports facilities, with bargain prices for residents and commuters. Except for those in Shibuya-ku, sports centres are also open to non-residents and non-commuters, but at higher prices.

Chiyoda Kuritsu Sogo Taiikukan Pool

2-1-8 Uchi-Kanda, Chiyoda-ku (3256 8444/ www.city.chiyoda.tokyo.jp/sisetu/sports.htm#01). Kanda station (Yamanote line), west exit or Otemachi station (Chiyoda, Hanzomon, Marunouchi, Mita, Tozai lines), exit A2. **Open** *Pool* noon-9pm Mon, Tue, Thur, Sat; 5.30-9pm Wed, Fri; 9am-5pm Sun. *Gym* 9am-noon, 1-5pm, 6-9pm daily. Closed every 3rd Mon.

Admission *Pool* ¥600 2hrs. *Gym* ¥350. **No credit cards**. **Map** p66.
Swimming pool and gym within a weight's throw of Tokyo's business district.

Chuo-ku Sogo Sports Centre

Hamacho Koen Nai, 2-59-1 Nihonbashi-Hamacho, Chuo-ku (3666 1501). Hamacho station (Hibiya, Shinjuku lines), exit A2. **Open** *Pool* 9am-9.10pm daily. *Gym* 9am-8.30pm daily. Closed every 3rd Mon. **Admission** *Pool* ¥500. *Gym* ¥400. **No credit cards**.

Ikebukuro Sports Centre

Kenko Plaza Toshima Bldg 9F, 2-5-1 Kami-Ikebukuro, Toshima-ku (5974 7262). Ikebukuro station (Yamanote line), north exit; (Marunouchi, Yurakucho lines), exits C5, C6. **Open** 9am-9pm daily. Closed 2nd Mon of mth. **Admission** ¥600; ¥300 concessions. **No credit cards**. **Map** p119.
A 25m pool on the 11th floor and a well-equipped gym on the tenth floor. Both offer great views.

Minato-ku Sports Centre

3-1-19 Shibaura, Minato-ku (3452 4151/ www.anox.net/minato/sports/sp01.html). Tamachi station (Yamanote, Keihin Tohoku lines), Shibaura exit. **Open** 9am-9pm daily. Closed 1st & 3rd Mon of mth. **Admission** ¥700. **No credit cards**.
Pool, sauna, weight gym and aerobics classes.

Shinagawa Sogo Taiikukan Pool

5-6-11 Kita-Shinagawa, Shinagawa-ku (3449 4400/ www1.cts.ne.jp/~ssa/index.html). Osaki station (Yamanote line), east exit. **Open** varies.
Admission *Pool* ¥350 2hrs. **No credit cards**.
No-frills pool, as well as tennis and badminton.

Shinjuku-ku Sports Centre

3-5-1 Okubo, Shinjuku-ku (3232 0171). Shin-Okubo or Takadanobaba stations (Yamanote line), Waseda exit; (Tozai line), exit 3. **Open** 9am-9pm daily. Closed every 4th Mon. **Admission** *Pool* ¥400 2hrs. *Gym* ¥400 3hrs. **No credit cards**.

Tokyo Metropolitan Gymnasium Pool

1-17-1 Sendagaya, Shibuya-ku (5474 2111/ www.tef.or.jp/tmg/index.html). Kokuritsu-Kyogijo station (Oedo line), exit A4 or Sendagaya station (Chuo line). **Open** 9am-8pm daily. **Admission** *Pool* ¥600. *Gym* ¥450 2hrs. **No credit cards**.
Run by the Tokyo Metropolitan Government, this centre has both 25m and 50m swimming pools, a weight gym, arena and athletics field. The smaller pool is not open to the public every day and rarely before 1.30pm; phone to check before you go.

Tennis

Municipal courts exist for those who want a game, but applications are often by lottery and sometimes require a minimum of four players. Log on to www.tokyotennis.com for information in English. There's also the huge **Ariake Tennis Forest** (*see p257*).

Trips Out of Town

Yokohama

History and modernism collide in Japan's second city.

With a population of 3.6 million, Yokohama is Japan's second largest city and yet it's also one of the newest. Until 150 years ago it was a sleepy fishing village on Tokyo Bay, but that all changed after the US-Japanese Treaty of Amity of 1858. Designated one of the first ports open to foreign trade, the village expanded rapidly to become the country's biggest commercial port.

Thanks largely to its waterside location, Yokohama has a spacious feel – especially in the futuristic new landfill development area known as Minato Mirai (literally, 'Port Future'). It also has a cosmopolitan, outward-looking atmosphere and a more relaxed tempo than Tokyo. And although a modern city, it has some historic buildings, traditional gardens and museums to go with its bayside views. It's perfect for a day trip from the capital, being less than 30 minutes by train from Shibuya station, and relatively compact to boot.

ORIENTATION

There are five main areas of note in Yokohama, strung along the side of the bay. The commercial district around Yokohama station is worth skipping, unless you need to use the shopping malls, department stores or pick up an airport limousine bus at Yokohama City Air Terminal (YCAT). **Minato Mirai** offers entertainment and views, and also houses some major hotels. **Kannai** and **Bashamichi** form the city's administrative centre. The upmarket **Motomachi** shopping district lies next to **Chinatown**. And the historic **Yamate Bluff** area offers parks and views.

The city's two main stations, both easily reached from central Tokyo, are Yokohama and Shin-Yokohama (where the bullet trains stop; a 20-minute train ride from the city centre). The JR Keihin Tohoku line trains continue from Yokohama station to Sakuragi-cho station, which is convenient for Minato Mirai, while Tokyu Toyoko trains continue to Minato Mirai itself and on to Motomachi-Chukagai station (convenient for Chinatown) via the new Minato Mirai extension. Both Yokohama and Sakuragi-cho stations have tourist information booths.

You can get around the touristy part of the city by boat. **Sea Bass** (045 671 7719, www.yokohama-cruising.jp) has services linking Yokohama station east exit and Yamashita Pier via Minato Mirai every 20 to 30 minutes from 10am until 8.25pm daily. The full trip costs ¥600; ¥300 concessions.

For a more sedate view of the harbour, cruise ships depart from Yamashita Pier and tour the bay. Try **Marine Rouge**, **Marine Shuttle** (both with the same contact details as Sea Bass) or **Royal Wing** (045 662 6125,www.royal wing.co.jp). Short 40-minute cruises can cost as little as ¥900; 90-minute cruises start from around ¥2,000. More expensive dinner cruises are also available.

YOKOHAMA IN A DAY

Minato Mirai is a massive complex built on landfill reclaimed from old dockland and, five minutes north of Sakuragi-cho station, is a good place to begin exploring the city.

From the station, take the moving walkway outside the Minato Mirai exit and head towards the area's central feature, the aptly named **Landmark Tower** – the tallest building in Japan and home to the world's fastest lift. The lower floors house restaurants and designer boutiques, as does the adjoining **Queen's Square** shopping centre (045 682 1000, www.qsy.co.jp/english/index.htm, shops 11am-8pm, restaurants 11am-10pm daily), a giant shopping and dining complex consisting of several separate but linked tower blocks. (If you arrive by the Tokyu Toyoko/Minato Mirai line, the station is right under the shopping centre.)

This whole area is built on the port's old dry docks, one of which has been preserved for use as a public amphitheatre, adjacent to Queen's Square. Behind the Landmark Tower is the **Yokohama Museum of Art** with its collection of modern art and photography.

Retracing your steps past the *Nihon Maru*, a preserved pre-war sailing ship once known as the 'Swan of the Pacific', you reach the **Kisha-Michi Promenade** (almost directly in front of the tourist centre outside Sakuragi-cho station). Built along the route of an old freight railway track, this will take you towards the giant Ferris wheel in the **Yokohama Cosmoworld** amusement park.

Skirting around **Yokohama World Porters** (045 222 2000, www.yim.co.jp), another giant shopping centre, themed around the concept of international trade and housed in a former dockside warehouse, follow the signs for the **Red Brick Warehouses** (Aka Renga

Soko; www.yokohama-akarenga.jp). Yokohama landmarks, these two 100-year-old buildings lay empty from 1989 until they reopened, fully refurbished, in 2002. The smaller Warehouse One is home to an arts centre and exhibition space, and several crafts shops. Warehouse Two houses three floors of shops and restaurants, and top-notch jazz club **Motion Blue** (045 226 1919, www.motionblue.co.jp). The paved plaza between the two warehouses leads down to the water's edge, and is a pleasant place for an aimless stroll.

From a road bridge just behind Warehouse One, take a pedestrian walkway along an old elevated railway line to Yamashita Park. The red metal tower you can see in the distance is **Marine Tower**, once the highest structure in Yokohama and still the world's tallest inland lighthouse. Shortly before the walkway deposits you close to the park, you will see **Osanbashi Pier** on your left, jutting out into the sea. This is the terminal for international cruise ships and was extensively remodelled in 2002. The passenger terminal at the end of the pier has a platform with panoramic views of the harbour.

Yamashita Koen itself is a pleasant area of seaside greenery with 1930s cruise ship the *Hikawa Maru* moored alongside. Buildings overlooking the park include the **Silk Museum** (045 641 0841, www.silkmuseum.or.jp, open 9am-4.30pm Tue-Sun, admission ¥500), which examines the history of silk production and clothing. There's also the Kenmin Hall concert hall and the graceful old Hotel New Grand, whose main building maintains one room exactly as it was when used by General Douglas MacArthur, the commander of the US occupation forces after World War II. The nearby **Yokohama Archives of History** (045 201 2100, www.kaikou.city.yokohama.jp, open 9.30am-5pm Tue-Sun, ¥200) has an exhibition devoted to the history of the city.

From the far end of the park the walkway continues past the **Yokohama Doll Museum** in the direction of **Harbour View Park**, which lies at the top of a hill called Furansu (France) Yama. It's quite a steep climb, but worth it for the view of Yokohama Bay and its bridge. This park represents the boundary of one of the most historic areas of Yokohama.

Leave the park by the gates near British House, cross the road at the traffic lights to the right and continue straight on until you arrive at the **Foreign Cemetery**, which was established in 1854 to bury sailors who had accompanied Commodore Perry on his mission to open up Japan to foreign trade. It's the final resting place of 4,500 people from 40 countries who died in the city. Regrettably, the historic graves are off-limits, but you can stroll around the park area at the top and look at the small museum, which displays reproductions of documents, prints and photos.

Looking down the road from the cemetery, you will notice that this area of Yokohama bears a strong resemblance to an English village, complete with its own picture-postcard church. Well above the damp lowlands, this has been considered a desirable address ever since the first British started putting down their roots. An intriguing overview of the history of the area is provided at the **Yamate Museum**, located just before the church, while the young at heart might prefer the 3,000 tin toys from the 1890s to the 1960s on show at the lovely **Tin Toy Museum** (045 621 8710, www.toysclub.co.jp/muse/tintoy.html, 9.30am-7pm daily, ¥200) to the east of the church.

Dotted around the Bluff area are other houses built by early foreign settlers in Japan, although in many cases the houses have been moved here from elsewhere. A map is available from the museum, and most of the houses are open to visitors. Facing the museum is **Motomachi Koen**, at the top of which stands the Ehrismann Residence, built in 1925 by Antonin Raymond, a Czech assistant of American architect Frank Lloyd Wright. It was moved here in 1990 when its original site was turned into condominiums.

Cosmoworld/Landmark Tower. *See p262.*

Trips Out of Town

Chinatown: the largest in Japan.

You can skirt the park and continue south-west towards the Yamate hills and the **Diplomat's House,** one of the most fetching houses in the area. Alternatively, head downhill from the park and the road will eventually lead you to the pedestrianised **Motomachi** shopping street (www.motomachi.or.jp), the most upmarket stretch of shops and restaurants in Yokohama. Walk down towards the canal and make for the bridge on your left.

On the other side of the bridge stands the Suzaku-mon, one of the ceremonial gates to Yokohama's **Chinatown** (Chukagai in Japanese). The biggest such community in Japan, it is home to hundreds of restaurants and Chinese shops, some selling spectacular souvenirs. Needless to say you can eat well here after wandering the colourful streets. Leaving Chinatown by the Choyo-mon gate, near the Holiday Inn, turn right to find the entrance to

Motomachi-Chukagai station. From here you can take a train directly back to Shibuya, or to Yokohama if you want to change to the JR line. Alternatively, you can walk down to Yamashita Park and take the Sea Bass ferry across the harbour to Yokohama station (or Sakuragi-cho).

If you've got more time to explore, visit **Yokohama International Stadium**, venue for the 2002 World Cup final, which is a short walk from Shin-Yokohama station; or, further north, the **Kirin Yokohama Beer Village** near Namamugi station (1-17-1 Namamugi, Tsurumi-ku, 045 503 8250, www.kirin.co.jp/about/brewery/factory/yoko, open June-Sept 10am-8pm daily, Oct-May 10am-5pm Tue-Sun). There are free tours of the brewery every half hour. Near Negishi station to the south – about 40 minutes by bus from Yokohama station – Negishi holds the beautiful **Sankeien** garden and the **Negishi Memorial Racetrack** park.

Diplomat's House
16 Yamate-cho, Naka-ku (045 662 8819). Ishikawa-cho station (Negishi line), Motomachi (south) exit. **Open** *July, Aug* 9.30am-6pm daily. *Sept-June* 9.30am-5pm daily. Closed 4th Wed of mth. **Admission** free.
Part of the Italian Garden, a collection of period dwellings, this 1910 house was once the family home of Japanese diplomat Uchida Sadatsuchi.

Harbour View Park (Minato-no-Mieru Oka Koen)
114 Yamate-cho, Naka-ku (045 622 8244/British House 045 623 7812/Osaragi Jiro Memorial Museum 045 622 5002). Motomachi-Chukagai station (Minato Mirai line). **Open** *Park* 24hrs daily. *British House* 9.30am-5pm daily. Closed 4th Wed of mth. *Osaragi Jiro Memorial Museum* 10am-5.30pm daily. Closed 4th Mon of mth. **Admission** *Park & British House* free. *Osaragi Jiro Memorial Museum* ¥200; ¥100 concessions. **No credit cards**.
One of the city's first attempts at redevelopment, Harbour View Park opened in 1962. The building that housed the first British legation to Japan – now called British House Yokohama – still stands near the rose garden beside one of the park gates. The park also contains a museum dedicated to local novelist Osaragi Jiro (1897-1973).

International Stadium Yokohama: World Cup Stadium Tours
3300 Kozukue-cho, Kohoku-ku (045 477 5000/ www.hamaspo.com/stadium). Shin-Yokohama station, north exit then 15mins walk. **Tours** (except when stadium is in use) 10.30am, noon, 1.30pm, 3pm daily. **Admission** ¥500; ¥250 concessions. **No credit cards**.
The venue that hosted the Germany v Brazil final in 2002 has started to offer tours, taking in the dressing rooms, practice area and pitch. See the Brazilians' tactic-covered whiteboard, take a shot at a silhouette of famously fumbling German goalie Oliver Kahn and gaze in awe at the rubbish that the

teams left behind. There's also a chance to run out on to the pitch (well, as far as the running track) with the World Cup anthem blazing. The stadium hosts international matches and home games for J-League side Yokohama Marinos.

Landmark Tower

2-2-1-1 Minato Mirai, Nishi-ku (Sky Garden 045 222 5035/www.landmark.ne.jp). Minato Mirai station (Minato Mirai line), exit 5. **Open** *Sky Garden Mid July-Aug* 10am-10pm daily. *Sept-mid July* 10am-9pm Mon-Fri, Sun; 10am-10pm Sat.* **Admission** *Sky Garden* ¥900; ¥200-¥700 concessions. **No credit cards.**

Take the world's fastest lift (45kph/28mph) to the top of Japan's tallest building (296m/972ft) to feast on the spectacular views. On a clear day, you can easily make out Mt Fuji to the west, Tokyo to the north and the Boso Peninsula to the east. The rest of the building is devoted to offices and a hotel.

Marine Tower

15 Yamashita-cho, Naka-ku (045 641 7838/www.hmk.co.jp). Motomachi-Chukagai station (Minato Mirai line), exit 5. **Open** *Mar-Dec* 9.30am-9pm daily. *Jan, Feb* 9.30am-7pm daily. **Admission** ¥700; ¥250-¥500 concessions. **No credit cards.**

This lighthouse (106m/348ft) once towered above the whole of Yokohama, but now it's stranded inland, cut off from the waterfront and surrounded by taller buildings. The view from the top is no longer anything special, but it exudes a certain retro nostalgia, both inside and out. As well as the viewing platform, there is a rather sad amusement arcade, the highly kitsch Motion Display Museum – devoted to old American toys – and some rather tatty coffee and souvenir shops.

Negishi Memorial Racetrack & Equine Museum

1-3 Negishi-dai, Naka-ku (045 662 7581/www.bajibunka.jrao.ne.jp). Negishi station (Negishi line) or Sakuragi-cho station (Negishi line) then bus 21 to Takinoue. **Open** *Park* 9.30am-5pm daily. *Museum* 10am-4.30pm Tue-Sun. **Admission** *Park* free. *Museum* ¥100; ¥30 concessions. **No credit cards.**

A wonderful park built on the site of Japan's first Western-style racetrack – having served as a US naval base in the interim. (There is still some naval accommodation beside the park.) A derelict grandstand survives from its 19th-century glory days, and a museum examines horsey history and man's relationship with the creatures.

Sankeien

58-1 Honmoku-Sannotani, Naka-ku (045 621 0635/www.sankeien.or.jp). Yokohama station, east exit, then bus 8 or 125 from bus stop 2 to Honmoku Sankeien-mae. **Open** *Outer Garden* 9am-5pm daily. *Inner Garden* 9am-4.30pm daily. **Admission** ¥500; ¥200 concessions. **No credit cards.**

A beautiful traditional Japanese garden that was laid out by a silk merchant in 1906. The enormous grounds include a number of designated Japanese

historic monuments saved from the bulldozer elsewhere in Japan and moved here, including a three-storey pagoda. The park is open in the evening during cherry blossom season (April) and for Moon Viewing (September).

Yamashita Koen

Yamashita-cho, Naka-ku (Hikawa Maru 045 641 4362/www.hmk.co.jp). Motomachi-Chukagai station (Minato Mirai line), exit 5. **Open** *Park* 24hrs daily. *Hikawa Maru July, Aug* 9.30am-7.30pm daily. *Apr-June, Sept, Oct* 9.30am-7pm daily. *Jan-Mar, Nov, Dec* 9.30am-6.30pm daily. **Admission** *Park* free. *Hikawa Maru* ¥800; ¥300 concessions. **No credit cards.**

Verdant Yamashita Park has long been a favourite with courting couples. The statue in the middle depicts the *Little Girl in Red Shoes*, based on a Japanese song about the real-life story of Iwasaki Kimi. Born in 1902, she was adopted by American missionaries, and was thought destined for a life of luxury in the US. But, in fact, Kimi never left Japan: abandoned by her foster parents, she died alone, aged nine, of tuberculosis. Moored beside the park is the 1930s ocean liner *Hikawa Maru*, which has been preserved in its original state. Walk around it for a fascinating glimpse of the golden age of cruise liner life. The ship's most famous passenger was Charlie Chaplin, whose luxury cabin is still intact.

Yamate Museum

247 Yamate-cho, Naka-ku (045 622 1188). Motomachi-Chukagai station (Minato Mirai line), exit 5. **Open** 11am-4pm daily. **Admission** ¥200; ¥150 concessions. **No credit cards.**

Housed in the last Western-style wooden building still in its original setting, this museum provides a fascinating insight into the early days of Yokohama's development, and the thriving foreign community that soon grew here.

Yokohama Cosmoworld

2-8-1 Shinkou, Naka-ku (045 641 6591/www.senyo.co.jp/cosmo). Minato Mirai station (Minato Mirai line), exit 5. **Open** *Mid Mar-Nov* 11am-9pm Mon-Fri; 11am-10pm Sat, Sun. *Mid Nov-mid Mar* 11am-8pm Mon-Fri; 11am-9pm Sat, Sun. **Admission** free.

The Ferris wheel at the centre of this small amusement park, with its giant digital clock, is a true Yokohama landmark. At 112.5m (369ft) high and with room for 480 passengers, it's one of the largest in the world. The park has 27 rides in all, including a water rollercoaster.

Yokohama Doll Museum

18 Yamashita-cho, Naka-ku (045 671 9361/www.welcome.city.yokohama.jp/eng/doll). Motomachi-Chukagai station (Minato Mirai line), exit 5. **Open** 10am-6pm daily. Closed 3rd Mon of mth. **Admission** ¥300; ¥150 concessions. **No credit cards.**

Home to nearly 10,000 dolls from 140 countries, this museum appeals to children and serious collectors alike. It also holds occasional puppet shows.

Trips Out of Town

Yokohama Museum of Art

3-4-1 Minato Mirai, Nishi-ku (045 221 0300/
www.yma.city.yokohama.jp). Minato Mirai station
(Minato Mirai line), exit 5. **Open** 10am-6pm Mon-
Wed, Fri-Sun. **Admission** ¥500; ¥100-¥300
concessions; additional fee for special exhibitions.
No credit cards.

One of the region's major fine art museums, this
Tange Kenzo-designed building is set on a prime,
tree-lined plaza in Minato Mirai. Abundant light
pours in through a huge skylight above the courtyard in the centre of the entrance hall. To the right
of the court, temporary exhibitions range from
Leonardo da Vinci to contemporary artist Nara
Yoshitomo. To the left there are regularly changing
exhibitions drawn from the permanent collection of
European, American and Japanese modern art and
photography.

Where to eat & drink

Chinatown

Manchinro Honten

153 Yamashita-cho, Naka-ku (045 681 4004/
www.manchinro.co.jp). Ishikawa-cho station
(Negishi line), Chinatown (north) exit or Motomachi-
Chukagai station (Minato Mirai line), exit 2. **Open**
11am-10pm daily. **Average** ¥1,500 lunch; ¥3,000
dinner. **Credit** AmEx, DC, JCB, MC, V.

With a history dating back to 1892, this Cantonese
restaurant is one of the oldest in Chinatown. It
burned down in a fire but reopened in 2002 as the
grandest, most lavish restaurant in the area.

Peking Hanten (Beijing Fandian)

79-5 Yamashita-cho, Naka-ku (045 681 3535).
Motomachi-Chukagai station (Minato Mirai line),
exit 2. **Open** 11.30am-2am daily. **Average** ¥1,500
lunch; dinner set meals from ¥4,000. **Credit** AmEx,
DC, MC, JCB, V.

This charming restaurant, right by Choyo-mon,
Chinatown's main gate, claims to be the first in
Japan to have served Peking duck.

Tung Fat (Dohatsu Honkan)

148 Yamashita-cho, Naka-ku (045 681 7273/
www.douhatsu.co.jp). Ishikawa-cho station
(Negishi line), Chinatown (north) exit. **Open**
11.30am-9.30pm Mon, Wed-Sun. **Average** ¥5,000.
Credit DC, MC, V.

This place is popular for its Hong Kong-style
seafood dishes. So popular, in fact, that lunchtime is
a spectacle, with customers jostling for position
while the strict *mama-san* tries to keep everyone in
check. While waiting, look at the window display of
mouth-watering meats, whole chickens and ducks,
sausages and other less recognisable animal parts.

Yokohama Curry Museum

1-2-3 Isezaki-cho, Naka-ku (045 250 0833/
www.currymuseum.com). Kannai station (Negishi
line), north exit. **Open** 11am-9.40pm daily.
Admission free.

This small museum to the west of Chinatown traces
the history of curry in Japan since its arrival in the
19th century. The main reason to visit is the seven
curry restaurants.

Minato Mirai

Braustüberl Yokohama

World Porters Vivre 1F, 11 Shinkou, Naka-ku
(045 222 2108). Kannai station (Negishi line),
north exit or Bashamichi station (Minato Mirai line),
exit 6. **Open** 10.30am-11pm daily. **Average** ¥3,000.
Credit AmEx, DC, JCB, MC, V.

The menu at this brewpub features half a dozen
styles of German beer – all locally brewed, some in
the vats in the middle of the pub itself – backed up
by a good range of robust pub grub of German,
Italian and Spanish inspiration.

Kihachi Italian

Queen's East 2F, Minato Mirai 2-3-2, Nishi-ku
(045 222 2861/www.kihachi.co.jp/rest/yokohama_i/
rest007.html). Minato Mirai station (Minato Mirai
line), Queen's Square exit. **Open** Lunch 11.30am-
4pm, tea 2.30-5.30pm, dinner 6-11pm daily.
Average lunch from ¥2,625; dinner from ¥4,200.
Credit AmEx, DC, JCB, MC, V.

This bright, modern, casual restaurant looking out
towards the Museum of Art is one of the best places
to eat in the area. The Italian-light food, popular
with the mostly young, female clientele, is produced
with all the aplomb you would expect from the ever-
professional Kihachi group.

Motomachi

Aussie

1-12 Ishikawa-cho, Naka-ku (045 681 3671/
www.juno.dti.ne.jp/~aussie). Ishikawa-cho station
(Negishi line), Motomachi (south) exit. **Open** 5pm-
1am Mon, Wed-Sun. **Average** ¥3,500. **Credit**
AmEx, JCB, MC, V.

As the name suggests, this restaurant serves all
things Australian, the most popular dishes being
barbecued kangaroo and crocodile.

Mutekiro

2-96 Motomachi, Naka-ku (045 681 2926/
www.mutekiro.com). Motomachi-Chukagai station
(Minato Mirai line), exit 5. **Open** noon-3pm, 5-10pm
daily. **Average** ¥4,000 lunch; ¥15,000 dinner.
Credit AmEx, DC, JCB, MC, V.

Motomachi's most celebrated and upmarket French
restaurant has the motto 'Mode française, coeur
japonais'. This means that dishes often contain
typical Japanese ingredients, especially seafood, but
are prepared in a French way. Booking essential.

Pas à Pas

1-50 Motomachi, Naka-ku (045 651 5070).
Motomachi-Chukagai station (Minato Mirai line),
exit 5. **Open** 11am-9pm Tue-Sun. **Average** ¥1,000.
No credit cards.

Located appropriately near the France Yama end of the Motomachi shopping area, this French-style café serves lunchtime quiches and adventurous sarnies from noon to 2pm. The rest of the time it's cakes, coffee and, incongruously, Bass ale.

Shin-Yokohama

Shin-Yokohama Ramen Museum

2-14-21 Shin-Yokohama, Kohoku-ku (045 471 0503/ www.raumen.co.jp/home). Shin-Yokohama station, north exit. **Open** 11am-11pm Mon-Fri; 10.30am-11pm Sat, Sun. **Admission** ¥300; ¥100 concessions. **No credit cards**.

A couple of floors are devoted to the history of the variety of noodle that has become a national obsession in Japan, but the main attraction is the eight ramen shops in the basement. Each shop sells a different style of ramen, ranging from Sapporo ramen (miso-based soup) from the north, to Hakata ramen (pork- and chicken-based soup) from the south. Highly recommended is the miso ramen at Sumire – the shop with the longest queue.

Yokohama station

The Green Sheep

2-10-13 Minami-Saiwai, Nishi-ku (045 321 0950/ www.foodcom.jp). Yokohama station, west exit. **Open** 11am-2am Mon-Thur; 11am-4am Fri, Sat; 11am-midnight Sun. **Credit** AmEx, DC, JCB, MC, V.

Yokohama's newest Irish pub serves a predictable mix of beers and big-screen football. The food menu is better than most – especially the shepherd's pie and lamb burger – and staff are friendly.

Kinrinmon

Sky Building 29F, 2-19-12 Takashima, Nishi-ku (045 441 4888). Yokohama station, east exit (above YCAT). **Open** 11am-3pm, 5-9.30pm daily. **Average** ¥2,000 lunch; ¥7,000 dinner. **Credit** AmEx, DC, JCB, MC, V.

Besides offering good seafood dishes, this sophisticated Cantonese-style restaurant provides fantastic views over the city to the mountains in the west (often including Mt Fuji). The plentiful dim sum lunch menu (¥2,635) is always popular.

Thumbs Up

Sotetsu Movil 3F, 2-1-22 Minami-Saiwai, Nishi-ku (045 314 8705/www.terra.dti.ne.jp/ ~stoves/tup/ index.html). Yokohama station, west exit. **Open** 6pm-midnight Mon-Thur, Sun; 6pm-2am Fri, Sat. **Average** ¥3,000. **Credit** AmEx, JCB, MC, V.

A drab cinema complex in the heart of Yokohama is not the place you'd expect to find an American-style truck-stop diner. Food ranges from burgers, pizzas and ribs to more delicate Hawaiian and Asian-tinged offerings, with bourbon and Bud to wash it all down. Most nights there are live acts (anything from rockabilly to Hawaiian music), so there will be a cover charge.

Minato Mirai. *See p262.*

Getting there

By train

The opening of the Minato Mirai subway extension has made Yokohama even easier to get to from Tokyo. A super-express on the Tokyu Toyoko line from Shibuya station takes 27mins to reach Yokohama station (¥260 single) or 34mins to its terminus at Motomachi-Chukagai (¥460).

Those with JR rail passes may prefer to take the JR Keihin Tohoku line to Sakuragi-cho from Tokyo, Shinbashi or Shinagawa stations; or take the Shonan Shinjuku line from Shinjuku, Shibuya or Ebisu, then change at Yokohama on to the Negishi line for local stops. Bullet trains on the JR Tokaido Shinkansen line take about 15mins from Tokyo station to Shin-Yokohama station.

Tourist information

The **Yokohama Convention & Visitors Bureau** (YCVB) has four information booths, plus an excellent English-language website – www.welcome.city.yokohama.jp/eng/tourism – with downloadable maps and a hotel guide.

YCVB Sakuragi-cho station *1-1-62 Sakuragi-cho, Naka-ku (045 211 0111). Sakuragi-cho station (Negishi line).* **Open** 9am-7pm daily.
YCVB Sangyo Boeki Centre *2 Yamashita-cho, Naka-ku (045 641 4759). Kannai station (Negishi line) then 15mins walk.* **Open** 9am-5pm Mon-Fri.
YCVB Shin-Yokohama station *2937 Shinohara-cho, Kohoku-ku (045 473 2895). Shin-Yokohama station, Shinkansen exit.* **Open** 10am-1pm, 2-6pm daily.
YCVB Yokohama station *2-16-1 Takashima, Nishi-ku (045 441 7300). Yokohama station, on the east–west walkway.* **Open** 9am-7pm daily.

Hakone

Bubbling hot springs, mountain scenery and some world-class museums.

Hakone is where Tokyo comes to relax and get a taste of the countryside. Around one and a half hours from Shinjuku station by Odakyu line train, this mountainous area offers convenient transportation, beautiful scenery, a host of attractions and, best of all, a natural hot-spring bath, or *onsen*, around virtually every bend of the roads that twist through the mountains.

The best way to see Hakone is to buy the **Hakone Free Pass** (*see p271*), available at all Odakyu railway stations. The pass covers all public transport in Hakone – and what public transport it is. As well as a picturesque railway and a bus service, the Hakone area also has a funicular railway, a cable car and a boat that crosses Lake Ashinoko at its centre. All of these means of transport are interlinked, making it possible to 'do' the whole of the Hakone area in a day from Tokyo.

THE HAKONE CIRCUIT

Those in a hurry can make the most of their time by trying the 'Hakone circuit'. Get off the train at either Odawara or Hakone-Yumoto. From there, transfer to the Tozan mountain railway for the 50-minute ride to its terminus at Gora. At Gora, transfer on to the funicular railway up to the end of the line at Sounzan. Here, transfer to the cable car, which takes you down to the banks of Lake Ashinoko at Togendai station. To get across the lake, board one of the pleasure boats and stay on until Hakone-Machi or Moto-Hakone, from where you can take a bus back to where you started, at Hakone-Yumoto or Odawara. The round-trip should take about three hours, although in the busy summer months it may take longer.

THE FULL HAKONE

While the circuit will give you your fill of glorious scenery, you'll be missing out on a lot of what Hakone has to offer. If you decide to start your journey at Odawara, it's worth making a detour out of the east exit of the station to take the ten-minute walk to **Odawara Castle**, perched on a hill overlooking the town. First built in 1416, and rebuilt in 1960, this picturesque castle was for centuries an important strategic stronghold.

Back at the station, get on the old-fashioned Tozan railway for the next major stop (or the starting point for some), Hakone-Yumoto

station. 'Yumoto' means 'source of hot water', which should give you some clue as to what this small town is about. First mentioned in eighth-century poetry as a place to bathe, Hakone became a great favourite in the time of the Tokugawa shogunate (1600-1854), with bathers travelling two or three days on foot from Tokyo (then Edo) along the Tokaido Way, portions of which can still be seen over the other side of the river from the modern railway station. The station houses a small tourist office, but the main office is up the hill on the left-hand side. Here, you will find English-speaking assistants, who are happy to hand out maps and pamphlets. Restaurants and souvenir shops also line the same street; this is the place to buy the local speciality, small boxes and other objects made using *yosegi-zaiku*, a mosaic-style marquetry technique.

For dedicated modern bathers, the day may end in Hakone-Yumoto. Although the modern town is unremarkable, it is dotted with hot-spring baths: just about every building of any size is a hotel or *ryokan*, and many allow non-guests to use their facilities. One of the locals' favourites is located on the steep hillside on the other side of the tracks from the station. **Kappa Tengoku** has segregated open-air baths surrounded by dense woodland, and a steady army of bathers can be seen trooping up the steps to the baths well into the night. Bring your own towel and wash cloth if you want to save money.

Up the hill from the *onsen* is the delightful **Hakone Toy Museum**, crammed with old-fashioned Japanese and foreign tin toys from the 1890s to the 1960s. The souvenir shop sells wind-up robots and charmingly retro goods imported from China and elsewhere.

Back on the train from Hakone-Yumoto, take some time to enjoy the ride itself. It's claimed that this is the world's steepest train line and so sharp are the bends that at three points the train enters a switchback, going forward and then reversing out of a siding in order to continue its ascent. As you climb the mountain you will see water pouring out of the hillside and cascading under the tracks, some of it still hot.

The next station of any note is Miyanoshita. This is home to one of the highest concentrations of *onsen* baths in the area, and is where the first foreigners in Japan came to bathe in the

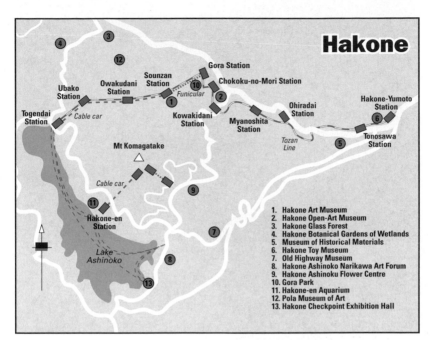

Hakone

Gora Station
Sounzan Station
Chokoku-no-Mori Station
Ubako Station
Owakudani Station
Funicular
Togendai Station
Cable car
Kowakidani Station
Myanoshita Station
Ohiradai Station
Hakone-Yumoto Station
Tozan Line
Tonosawa Station
Mt Komagatake
Cable car
Hakone-en Station
Lake Ashinoko

1. Hakone Art Museum
2. Hakone Open-Art Museum
3. Hakone Glass Forest
4. Hakone Botanical Gardens of Wetlands
5. Museum of Historical Materials
6. Hakone Toy Museum
7. Old Highway Museum
8. Hakone Ashinoko Narikawa Art Forum
9. Hakone Ashinoku Flower Centre
10. Gora Park
11. Hakone-en Aquarium
12. Pola Museum of Art
13. Hakone Checkpoint Exhibition Hall

19th century. To cater for them, the **Fujiya Hotel** was built in 1878. Miraculously, it's still standing today, a wooden mix of Japanese and Western styles. Non-residents are free to pop in for a coffee, a bite to eat or something stronger in the bar.

Two stops up the line, at Chokokuno-Mori station, is one of the great glories of Hakone. The **Hakone Open-Air Museum** must be one of the most spectacular in the world. Set on a mountainside overlooking a series of valleys leading to the sea, the museum is dedicated to modern sculpture from all over the globe. Exposed to the elements is a world-class collection of works by Moore, Rodin, Antony Gormley, Alexander Calder, Takamichi Ito and Niki de St Phalle. It's a great place for kids. There's also a display of ceramics by Picasso in a separate pavilion.

From here, it's a ten-minute walk to the next station, Gora, the terminus of the Tozan railway and the start of the funicular that climbs the mountainside. If you're changing from the train, there will be a carriage waiting for you. The first stop on the funicular, Koen Shita, provides a pleasant diversion in the shape of **Gora Park**, a landscaped hillside garden that makes great use of the natural hot water in its hot houses. A walk uphill through the park will bring you to the next stop on the funicular.

This is a good point to visit the **Pola Museum of Art**, deep in the surrounding forest. The museum houses 9,500 works by the likes of Renoir, Picasso and Monet. To avoid damaging the beauty of the countryside, the building is constructed three floors underground, and is only eight metres (27 feet) tall on the surface. To reach the museum, take a bus from Gora station bound for Shisseikaen.

The funicular terminates at Sounzan station, and it's here that many people's favourite part of the Hakone experience begins: the cable car, or Hakone Ropeway, as it's known. Riding over the peaks and valleys of Hakone, this 4.3-kilometre (2.7-mile) ride is Japan's longest cable car route. Around halfway along its length is **Owakudani** ('big boiling valley'), one of the most breathtaking sights in Hakone. The car passes over, at a height of around 60 metres (200 feet), a smoking hillside streaked with traces of sulphur from the volcanic activity below. The air simply reeks of rotten eggs.

On top of a mountain peak sits Owakudani station, the centre of a large tourist complex of restaurants and gift shops. On a clear day – though it's often too cloudy – you can see the peak of Mt Fuji looming over the mountain range in the distance. You can also walk to the source of some of the steam that rises out of the mountain, the ancient crater of Mt Kamiyama,

The smoking, bubbling hillside of **Owakudani**, with Mt Fuji in the distance.

the pathway passing over hot streams of bubbling water. The air is thick with hydrogen sulphide, and signs warn of the dangers of standing in one place for too long for fear of being overcome by fumes. If you feel like a snack, try a hard-boiled egg at the top of the path. Sold by the half-dozen for ¥500, the eggs have been cooked in the hot spring water, the sulphur turning their shells black.

From Owakudani, the Hakone Ropeway passes over several more valleys before descending to terminate at Togendai on the banks of Lake Ashinoko. The lake is believed to be in the crater of a volcano that blew its top 400,000 years ago. The volcanic activity that goes on beneath the waters to this day ensures that it never freezes over. From here, a pair of incredibly tacky pleasure boats, one done out as a Mississippi steamer, one as a Spanish galleon, cross the lake to Hakone-Machi and Moto-Hakone. Only 500 metres or so separate the two destinations, but for ease of walking, get off at Hakone-Machi and turn left (with the lake behind you) to head for Moto-Hakone.

On the way is the site of the **Old Hakone Checkpoint**, where travellers to and from Edo were stopped and often interrogated by border guards. Ruins of the original checkpoint still stand, while other buildings have been reconstructed and opened to the public as a museum. Set back a little from the modern road is what's left of a cedar avenue, planted along the Tokaido Way in the early 17th century. Paved sections of the Tokaido Way are still extant, and keen walkers can take a short hike from here along one such section, away from the lake towards Hatajuku.

On a promontory into the lake between the two boat stops is the **Hakone Detached Palace Garden**. The garden of an 1887 villa that once belonged to the imperial family but was destroyed in an earthquake, it has been open to the public since 1946. Further along, past Moto-Hakone and down the side of the lake, is **Hakone Shrine**, its history going back 1,200 years. The site is clearly marked by a red *torii* (gate) that stands in the lake.

Once you've walked your fill of the area – and there's lots more to see in the Hakone vicinity – head back to Moto-Hakone and take a bus back to Odawara. All buses to Odawara stop in Hakone-Yumoto too.

Gora Park

1300 Gora, Hakone-Machi, Shimogun (0460 22825/ www.hakone-tozan.co.jp/gorapark). **Open** 9am-5pm daily. **Admission** ¥500; free concessions. **No credit cards**.

Hakone Detached Palace Garden

171 Moto-Hakone, Hakone-Machi, Ashigara-Shimogun (0460 37484). **Open** *July, Aug* 9am-5pm daily. *Sept-June* 9am-5pm Mon, Wed-Sun. **Admission** free.

Hakone Open-Air Museum

1121 Ninotaira, Hakone-Machi, Ashigara-Shimogun (0460 21161/www.hakone-oam.or.jp). **Open** *Mar-Nov* 9am-5pm daily. *Dec-Feb* 9am-4pm daily. **Admission** ¥1,600; ¥800-¥1,100 concessions. **No credit cards**.

Hakone Toy Museum

740 Yumoto, Hakone-Machi, Ashigara-Shimogun (0460 64700/www.toymuseum.co.jp). **Open** 9am-5pm daily. **Admission** ¥800; ¥400 concessions. **Credit** AmEx, DC, JCB, MC, V.

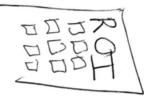

Tokyo National Museum (Ueno)

Photography Museum (Ebisu)

Ukiyo-e Ota Art (Harajuku)

Emoji-ji Tdl (Odaiba)

Kappa Tengoku
777 Yumoto, Hakone-Machi, Ashigara-Shimogun (0460 56121). **Open** 10am-10pm daily. **Admission** ¥750. *Towel* (to buy) ¥900. **No credit cards.**

Odawara Castle
6-1 Jonai,Odawara-shi (0465 231 373). **Open** 9am-4pm Tue-Sun. **Admission** *Park* free. *Castle* ¥400; ¥150 concessions. **No credit cards.**

Old Hakone Checkpoint
1 Hakone, Hakone-Machi, Ashigara-Shimogun (0460 36635). **Open** 9am-4pm daily. **Admission** ¥300; ¥150 concessions. **No credit cards.**

Pola Museum of Art
1285 Kozukayama, Sengokubara, Hakone-Machi, Ashigara-Shimogun (0460 42111/www.pola museum.or.jp). **Open** 9am-5pm daily. **Admission** ¥1,800; ¥700-¥1,300 concessions. **Credit** AmEx, DC, JCB, MC, V.

Where to eat & drink

Since most of the area's activity centres around the hotels, it's hardly surprising that there are remarkably few independent restaurants worth seeking out – though the village of Segokuhara has more options than most. For the truly hungry, there are snack bars serving curry, noodles and the like at Owakudani and Togendai stations, and on the lake at Hakone-Machi. The **Bella Foresta** restaurant in the Open-Air Museum serves a decent buffet lunch for around ¥1,500, while all the large hotels have at least four restaurants that are open to non-guests. At the **Pola Museum** there's a café serving snacks and drinks (10am-4.30pm daily) and an upmarket French-style restaurant (11am-4pm daily).

Where to stay

There are hundreds of places to stay in Hakone, ranging from cheap *ryokan* to top-class hotels. All have their own hot springs. Many have separate rates for weekdays and weekends, the former being cheaper. Expect top prices at peak periods such as New Year and Golden Week in May.

If you intend to use Hakone-Yumoto as a base, cheap options include **Kappa Tengoku** (*see above*), where a double room costs from around ¥7,000 per night on weekdays, although its proximity to the railway tracks might mean an earlier awakening than you'd bargained for.

Up in the mountains, the **Fujiya Hotel** (359 Miyanoshita, 0460 22211, www.fujiya hotel.co.jp) is peerless, with a range of rooms in five historic buildings; doubles start at ¥18,780 on weekdays, rising to ¥30,330 during peak season. In Segokuhara, the small

ryokan **Fuji-Hakone Guest House** (912 Segokuhara, 0460 4 6577, www.fujihakone.com, twin room ¥10,500-¥12,600) is a good budget choice. The friendly proprietor, Takahashi Masami, speaks English and is happy to offer sightseeing advice; ask him to direct you to local restaurant Daichi. You can get to the inn by bus direct from Odawara or Hakone-Yumoto stations; alight at the Senkyoro-mae bus stop. Sister outfit **Moto-Hakone Guest House** (0460 37880, same website, twin ¥10,000) is on the other side of Lake Ashinoko.

Overlooking the lake is the **Palace Hotel** (1245 Sengokuhara, Hakone-Machi, 0460 48501, www.hakone.palacehotel.co.jp), where doubles start at ¥18,900 during the low season. This luxury hotel often advertises special-stay plans in the Tokyo press, which can bring the price down further.

Getting there

By train
There are two types of **Hakone Free Pass**, available at all Odakyu stations and many travel agents. The weekday pass gives you unlimited journeys for two days and costs ¥4,700 from Shinjuku station. The weekend pass gives three days' unlimited transport and costs ¥5,500 from Shinjuku station. The ticket price also covers the basic fare on an Odakyu train from Shinjuku to Hakone. If you want to travel in comfort on the super express Romance Car, you will need to pay a supplement of ¥870.

If you hold a JR Pass, the most cost-effective way of reaching the area is to take a JR Tokaido *shinkansen* to Odawara station, then buy your Hakone Free Pass there. As this pass does not include transport to Tokyo, it costs ¥3,410 (weekdays) or ¥4,130 (weekends). The Free Pass also gives discounts at many local attractions. Look out for the Hakone Free Pass sticker.

Tourist information

Hakone-Yumoto Tourist Information
Kankou Bussankan, 698 Yumoto, Hakone-Machi, Ashigara-Shimogun (0460 58911). **Open** 9am-5pm daily.

Odakyu Sightseeing Service Centre
Ground-floor concourse near west exit, Odakyu Shinjuku station (5321 7887/www.odakyu-group. co.jp/english/center.html). **Open** 8am-6pm daily. The Odakyu train line's information counter inside the station is aimed at foreign visitors (staff speak English). You can buy the Hakone Free Pass here and make hotel reservations.

Odawara Tourist Information
1-1-9 Sakaemachi, Odawara-shi (0465 222 339). Odawara station, east exit. **Open** 9am-5pm daily.

Kamakura

For all your temple needs.

For 150 years, from the 12th to the 14th centuries, Kamakura was Japan's military and administrative capital, and the factors that made it a strategic location for the first military government – it has hills on three sides and Sagami Bay on the other – have also kept it separate from the encroaching sprawl of Yokohama. When you reach Kamakura, you feel that you have finally escaped the city, even though it's less than an hour by train from the heart of Tokyo.

The Minamoto family picked Kamakura for its new base after vanquishing the Taira clan in 1185 and setting up Japan's first military government – marking the start of 700 years of domination by shoguns. The new military rulers encouraged Zen Buddhism, which appealed for its strict self-discipline, and temples of various sects were established in the area. While traces of the government and military rule faded quickly after the Minamoto clan and their regents were defeated in 1333, the religious influence endures to this day.

There are still more than 70 temples and shrines dotted around Kamakura, from the large and eminent to the small and secluded. Still active today, they represent different Buddhist sects, among them Rinzai, Pure Land and Nichiren. Over the years the buildings and grounds of most temples have been lost through fires and earthquakes, the slow encroachment of housing or to make way for the railway line. Few buildings remain intact from the Kamakura period, but many temples and shrines appear unspoilt, giving visitors a rare opportunity to view authentic remnants of old Japan.

Kamakura is now a major tourist destination, and the temples and grounds are well looked after. Most temples require a small entry fee (¥100-¥300) – a contribution towards upkeep rather than an admission charge. The main attractions are scattered around, but most are within walking distance of Kamakura or Kita-Kamakura stations and can be covered in a day trip from Tokyo. Directions and distances to temples in each vicinity are marked in English at intervals around town. You can pick up a free map (partly in English) from the Tourist Information window at Kamakura station (just to the right of the station gates at the east exit). Most temples are open daily, from 9am until

4pm, but museums and treasure houses (and some shops) are usually closed on Mondays.

The town and the main sites are surprisingly busy at weekends and holidays. Festival days are especially crowded. The main ones are the Grand Festival (14-16 September) and the Kamakura Festival (from the second to the third Sunday in April). Both take place at Tsurugaoka Hachiman-gu – the town's main shrine and focal point – which is also immensely popular on the first few days of the New Year, when hordes of worshippers converge to make their auspicious, first shrine visit of the year. Each temple and shrine also holds its own festival, and the fireworks on the second Tuesday of August attract massive crowds to the beach area.

GETTING AROUND

Walking is the best way to see the city. Narrow streets take you through quiet residential areas with well-tended gardens, old wooden houses, coffee shops and teahouses. There are also some hiking routes along the ridges of the hills, linking different parts of town. After the initial ascent they are generally fairly easy walks, some leading to picnic areas and parks. The starting points are indicated on the road, as are destinations and estimated durations.

You can also explore by bicycle. Bikes can be rented from an office (0467 24 2319) behind the police box on the right as you leave the east exit of Kamakura station (open 8.30am to 6pm daily; ¥500 first hour, ¥250 extra hour, ¥1,500-¥1,600 full day; bring photo ID). Or you can rent a mountain bike for ¥3,250 a day from Grove (0467 23 6667), a specialist cycle shop on the left side of the main street (Wakamiya Oji) as you walk down towards the sea.

For a more leisurely mode of transport, take a rickshaw – look for the men in traditional garb outside the west exit of Kamakura station and on Wakamiya Oji, by the big *torii* (shrine gate). For half an hour, it costs ¥5,000 for one person, ¥8,000 for two (one hour ¥9,000/¥15,000).

Taxis can be caught from either side of the station. There are also regular bus services departing from the east exit. And no visit to Kamakura can be considered complete without a short trip on the venerable tram cars of the Enoden line (Enoshima Electric Railway), which winds from Kamakura station, past Hase station (the stop for Hase Kannon and

The famous **Daibutsu**.

Minamoto family. On the left (the west, the setting sun) is a smaller pond with four islands (the number representing death) symbolising the defeated Taira clan. Going straight on, you'll come to a dancing stage, then the steps to the main hall. The venerable gingko tree on the left is said to have stood here for 1,000 years (predating the shrine, which was moved to the site in 1180); it is famous for having concealed the murderer of the third Minamoto shogun, who was taken by surprise and killed as he was climbing the steps. The main shrine at the top is reached through a gate with two guardian figures (Yadaijin and Sadaijin). The steps descending to the right lead to other buildings and the treasure house, where historic, religious artworks from the area are displayed.

WEST OF TSURUGAOKA HACHIMAN-GU

Eisho-ji, the only active Buddhist nunnery in the area, allows access to parts of its grounds, as does nearby **Jufuku-ji**, reached by a long approach lined with maples. The ancient cemetery behind, reached by the path to the left of the gate, is a quiet place to explore and has many burial caves, some dating from the Kamakura period.

Walking for 20 minutes into the hills on this side of the city will bring you to **Zeniarai Benten**, the 'Money-Washing Shrine' dedicated to one of the seven lucky gods. A visit to this atmospheric site is highly recommended. A tunnel carved through the mountainside leads into a mysterious area with waterfalls, ponds and small shrines carved into the cliff face, the air filled with incense and ethereal music. Inside the main cave, place your money, notes and all, into bamboo baskets that you then dip in the water. The truly faithful will find it has doubled in value.

Slightly back towards the town, a turn-off to the right leads up through a tunnel of more than 100 small red *torii* to the **Sasuke Inari** shrine. There's not much to see up here apart from the semi-tame squirrels, but it is a marvellously peaceful glade.

From here, a 20-minute walk will bring you to Kotokuin temple, home of the **Daibutsu** statue, aka the Great Buddha – the best known of Kamakura's attractions. The temple dates from 741 and the bronze statue of Buddha from 1252. Over 11 metres (36 feet) high and weighing 125 tonnes, the figure appears ungainly and top-heavy from a distance, but from close up the proportions seem perfect. It was originally housed inside a hall, but fires and earthquakes destroyed the building several times before it was demolished for good by a tsunami in 1495. The Daibutsu was

the Great Buddha), down along the coast to Enoshima island and Fujisawa.

What follows is a list of highlights of the Kamakura area. For information on more sights or special events, check with the tourist office.

TSURUGAOKA HACHIMAN-GU

Kamakura's main shrine, **Tsurugaoka Hachiman-gu**, is ten minutes' walk from Kamakura station. Hachiman is seen today as the god of war, but in the past was regarded as the guardian of the whole nation. As one of the most important Shinto shrines in eastern Japan, it's an essential stop for all visitors.

To reach the shrine, head for the red *torii* in the left corner of the square outside the station's east exit. This leads into Komachi Dori, a narrow, pedestrian street lined with souvenir and craft shops, boutiques, food stalls and shops, and numerous restaurants. At the far end of this street, turn right to the shrine entrance. Alternatively, walk directly away from the station to Wakamiya Oji. This broad avenue forms a north–south axis from central Kamakura down to the sea. Turning left, make your way along the cherry-lined walkway up the centre of the street; the blossom here (early to mid April) is gorgeous.

The shrine and grounds of Tsurugaoka (Hill of Cranes) were built to subtle and strict specifications, the most striking example of which is found near the half-moon bridge at the entrance. On the right (the east, the rising sun) is a large lotus pond with three islands (a propitious number) symbolising the unscathed and has been in the open air ever since. For ¥20 you can go inside the statue.

Hase-dera (also known as **Hase Kannon**) temple is just down the road. The main feature here is the 11-faced statue of Kannon (goddess of mercy and compassion). Over nine metres (30 feet) tall, it was carved in 721 out of a single camphor tree. The temple is also famous for its thousands of small Jizo figurines offered in memory of deceased children and babies (including those who were never carried to full term). Hase-dera also has a revolving library containing Buddhist sutras – worshippers causing the library to rotate receive merit equivalent to reading the entire Buddhist canon – and a small network of caves with statues carved out of the rock. The treasure house contains objects and artefacts excavated from the temple during rebuilding. From Hase-dera there's a panoramic view of the town, the beach and Sagami Bay.

EAST OF TSURUGAOKA HACHIMAN-GU

Although none of the main sights is in this area, which thus attracts fewer crowds, there are still many smaller temples worth seeing. The first shrine as you come from Tsurugaoka Hachiman-gu is **Egara Tenjin**, founded in 1104. Tenjin is the patron deity of scholarship and literature, and every 25 January there is a ritualistic burning of writing brushes.

Nearby is **Kamakura-gu** shrine, founded by the Meiji Emperor in 1869. From here, turn left up a lane to **Kakuon-ji**. This small temple offers 45-minute tours by a priest (¥300) on the hour from 10am to 3pm (except noon on weekdays), although not if it is raining. The tour is in Japanese only, but the thatched buildings and old wooden statues do not need much explanation.

A 15-minute walk from Kamakura-gu takes you to **Zuisen-ji**, famous for its trees and flowers, especially the plum blossoms in February. A small temple, it has a Zen garden created in the 14th century by the celebrated priest and landscape gardener Muso Soseki.

From the intersection near Kamakura-gu, head along the main road to reach **Sugimoto-dera**, the oldest temple in Kamakura. It's a beautiful place, with white banners lining either side of the well-worn stone steps. Both the gate and temple have thatched roofs and were originally built in 734. Further along, on the other side of the road, is lovely **Hokoku-ji**, known as the bamboo temple for its extensive grove of giant bamboo, where you can sit and contemplate while sipping whisked green tea. From here it's a short walk to the **Shakado tunnel**, one of the original entrances to the ancient city cut through the hills. Only passable by pedestrians, this dark (and reputedly haunted) spot is very atmospheric.

Closer to the station is **Hongaku-ji**, a small temple whose ancient gate and guardian statues gaze out towards the entrance to **Myohon-ji**, the oldest and largest of the Nichiren sect temples in Kamakura. Founded in 1260, it nestles deep into a fold in the hills and is surprisingly quiet, given its proximity to the town centre. Another 15 minutes or so away is **Myoho-ji**, also known as the Moss Temple, where the priest Nichiren once resided. The ancient steps lead up to a hilltop vantage point that remains a favourite spot.

The only major temple close to the sea is **Komyo-ji**, established in 1243, which has a massive wooden *sanmon* gate and an attractive lotus pond with carp and terrapins. A path behind the main prayer hall (on the right next to the playground) leads up the hill, giving views on clear days right down the coast to Enoshima island and the Izu Peninsula, with Mount Fuji rising behind.

At this end of the bay are the remains of **Wakaejima**, the first artificial harbour in Japan. Built in 1232 to create a port for the city, it went into terminal decline after the capital reverted to Kyoto, and now the stones are only visible at low tide. **Zaimokuza Beach**, the eastern half of the bay, is favoured by dinghy sailors, windsurfers and ever-hopeful weekend surfers (the waves are usually minuscule).

A typical Shinto shrine in Kamakura.

The western section, **Yuigahama Beach**, is more popular with sunbathers. In summer, temporary huts are built along the sand to provide showers, changing facilities and deckchair rentals, as well as snacks and drinks.

KITA-KAMAKURA

This area, north of the town centre, is home to many Rinzai sect temples, among them the famous **Engaku-ji**, the largest Zen temple in Kamakura, situated bang in front of Kita-Kamakura station. The temple was founded in 1282, although the main gate was reconstructed in 1780. The precincts, which extend a long way up into the hills, house more than 15 smaller sub-temples. To the left of the main entrance you can often see people practising Zen archery. On the hill to the right is the famous temple bell – the biggest in Kamakura.

On the narrow road next to the railway tracks is the **Kamakura Old Pottery Museum** (10am-5pm Tue-Sun, admission ¥500), housed in a pleasant compound of old and reconstructed half-timbered buildings. Across the tracks is **Tokei-ji**, for a long time a nunnery that offered asylum to women seeking refuge from abusive husbands. It's worth a visit for its lovely garden and grounds, as well as the treasure house (entrance ¥300 extra), which keeps old sutras and scrolls.

Nearby is **Jochi-ji**, a Zen temple noted for the small, ancient bridge and steps at its entrance, its bell tower, the burial caves at the back and a tunnel between the cemeteries. A mountain path leading back to Kamakura station starts from the left of the entrance. On the other side of the main road is a pleasant street winding up to **Meigetsu-in**, a temple noted for its hydrangea gardens (in full bloom in June).

Heading towards Kamakura brings you to **Kencho-ji**, the oldest Zen temple in Japan. It's an imposing place with large buildings and grounds, although only ten of the 49 original sub-temples survive. Many of the halls have been rebuilt, but their arrangement hasn't changed for over 700 years. The second floor of the majestic *sanmon* gate houses 500 statues of *rakan* (Buddha's disciples), although they are not on view. Behind the last building there's a garden, from which a path leads to steps climbing to **Hanso-bo**, a shrine where statues of *tengu* (goblins) protect the temple. From here you can follow the Ten-en hiking path, which follows the hilltop ridge as far as Zuisen-ji temple in the east of Kamakura.

Back on the main road, a short flight of stairs near the tunnel marks the entrance to **Enno-ji**, a very small temple housing statues representing the ten judges of Hell.

Where to eat

Around Kamakura station, there are many restaurants along Komachi Dori, the narrow shopping street near the east exit. Friendly **T-Side** (Kotobuki Bldg 2F, 1-6-12 Komachi, 0467 24 9572, lunch sets ¥1,000-¥1,500) produces great Indian food. Around the corner is **Nakamura-an** (1-7-6 Komachi, 0467 25 3500, www.nakamura-an.com, closed Thur, from ¥800), a cosy noodle shop that serves hearty, hand-chopped *soba*.

In Kita-Kamakura, you can try a Japanese *kaiseki* meal at **Koko-tei** (605 Yamanouchi, 0467 46 5467, lunch from ¥3,150), a quiet, rustic restaurant hidden away in the hills. For a taste of Zen, **Hachinoki Honten** (7 Yamanouchi, 0467 22 8719, lunch from ¥2,310) serves elegant vegetarian meals of *shojin ryori* close to the main entrance of Kencho-ji temple. **Sasanoha** (499 Yamanouchi, 0467 23 2068, lunch from ¥1,300) offers delicious, additive-free (but not entirely vegetarian) meals with brown rice.

Facing the ocean in Inamuragasaki (on the Enoden line) is **Taverna Rondino** (2-6-11 Inamuragasaki, 0467 25 4355, set meals ¥1,800-¥5,250), an Italian restaurant as good as most in Tokyo. The bright yellow building also has a small outside terrace.

Getting there

By train

Kamakura is less than an hour by train from Tokyo. Both Kita-Kamakura and Kamakura stations are on the JR Yokosuka line from Tokyo (¥890 single), Shinbashi (¥780) or Shinagawa (¥690) stations; trains run every 10-15mins. There's a more limited service on the JR Shonan-Shinjuku line from Shinjuku (¥890), Shibuya (¥890) or Ebisu (¥780). A special one-day return, including unlimited rides on the Enoden line, is the Kamakura-Enoden Free Ticket (¥1,970 from any station inside the Yamanote line). A cheaper but rather longer (90mins) option is to take the Odakyu line from Shinjuku to Enoshima (¥610; ¥1,210 by express), then transfer on to the Enoden line (¥250 to Kamakura). Special price day-trip tickets (also with unlimited rides on the Enoden) are also available for ¥1,430.

If you don't have a ticket for the return journey to Tokyo, get one as soon as you arrive at Kamakura as there are always long queues later in the day.

Tourist information

Kamakura City Tourist Information Service

1-1-1 Komachi, Kamakura Eki Konai, Kanagawa-ken (0467 22 3350/www.city.kamakura.kanagawa.jp). **Open** 9am-5pm/5.30pm daily.
Also check out http://kamakuratoday.com/e/.

Trips Out of Town

Nikko

The lavish resting place of the shoguns.

If you haven't seen Nikko, then you can't say you've really lived – such is the gist of a Japanese saying that's been popular since the Edo period. For over 1,200 years this area of mountains, lakes, forests and hot springs has been considered a centre of great beauty and spiritual significance. But Nikko's main claim to fame is that it's where the first Tokugawa shogun, Ieyasu, is enshrined and buried. The impressive scale and lavish ornamentation of his mausoleum make Nikko one of the most fascinating sites in the country.

In Japanese, Nikko means 'sun light', but the name also derives from that of the sacred mountain behind the city, Futara, which is now known as Mt Nantai. It was here that the priest Shodo Shonin established a centre for Esoteric Buddhism in 782, and it remains a centre of pilgrimage for religious ascetics.

Ieyasu's mausoleum, the Toshogu, is surrounded by numerous temples and shrines, including the equally ornate Taiyu-in, the mausoleum of his grandson, Iemitsu, the third Tokugawa shogun. The entire complex, a UNESCO World Heritage Site, can be seen in half a day. Most visitors, though, stay overnight so they can also see the area above Nikko, including Lake Chuzenji, the dramatic Kegon Falls, Yumoto Onsen and the vast Oku-Nikko national park, with its *onsen* (hot springs), hiking, camping, boating, skiing and skating.

Nikko lies at the foot of the mountains on the edge of the Kanto plain, about two hours by train due north of Tokyo. It is a small city (population circa 20,000), with souvenir shops, antique dealers and restaurants lining the main street that runs from the two train stations up to Shinkyo, the sacred bridge that marks the entrance to the shrines and temples.

This handsome, red-lacquered bridge spanning the Daiyagawa gorge marks the spot where legend says Shodo Shonin was carried across by two huge serpents. The first bridge was built here in 1636, as the main approach to Toshogu. Destroyed by floods in 1902 and rebuilt five years later, the second bridge carried such vast numbers of tourists that it had to be rebuilt again, its third incarnation opening in April 2005.

Cross the road in front of the bridge and follow the steps into the forested national park to reach the Toshogu complex, ten minutes away. The road to the left leads to Lake Chuzenji, via the sprawling newer part of Nikko with its unsightly hotels and souvenir shops.

The cluster of religious buildings on the far side of Shinkyo bridge includes Rinno-ji temple, Toshogu, Futarasan Shrine and the Taiyu-in Mausoleum. Entrance fees are ¥900, ¥1,300, ¥200 and ¥550 respectively, but if you want to see them all it's much cheaper to buy the combined ticket for ¥1,000 (this can be bought as you enter Rinno-ji or at the Tobu bus counter in the station on arrival). This also allows entry to Yakushido (inside Toshogu), though not to the Sleeping Cat (a well-known carving), Oku-sha (Ieyasu's tomb) or the shrines inside the grounds of Futarasan Jinja.

Places are generally open daily from 8am to 5pm (4pm from December to March).

RINNO-JI

Rinno-ji, founded in 766, is the largest of the Buddhist temples in the area. Its main hall is called the Sanbutsu-do, after the trinity of Buddhas that are the main attraction. Over five metres (16 feet) high, these gilt-covered wooden statues depict Amida Nyorai, the Thousand-Armed Kannon and the Horse-Headed Kannon – a Buddhist representation of the gods of Nikko's three sacred mountains. Off to one side is a tall pillar, Sorinto, built in 1643 to repel evil.

In front of the Sanbutsu-do is the temple's treasure house and the **Shoyo-en**, a beautiful Edo-style strolling garden (admission ¥300), with a 200-year-old cherry tree that has been declared a national monument. To the left of the Sanbutsu-do stands a black gate, the Kuremon, and the path that leads to Toshogu.

TOSHOGU

Even if you forego the other buildings in the complex, the **Toshogu** is a must-see. Because of its popularity, it is advisable to arrive first thing in the morning, before the tour buses converge, or late in the afternoon. It's also very busy during its three annual festivals. On 17 May horseback archery in medieval hunting attire takes place in front of the shrine, while on 18 May the Sennin Gyoretsu procession recreates the transfer of the remains of Ieyasu. The 1,000 participants dress as samurai, priests and others in the style of the days of the shogun. A festival on 17 October combines both, but on a smaller scale.

The **Yomeimon**, one of the most spectacular sights at Toshogu.

Toshogu was completed in 1636, during the reign of the third shogun, Iemitsu, according to instructions left by Ieyasu, who had died in 1616. The finest craftsmen were brought in and it's said that as many as 15,000 people were involved. Unusually, it blends both Shinto and Buddhist elements, and its flamboyant decorations owe more to Chinese and Korean influences than to native Japanese design. Nearly all the surfaces are brightly painted, with extremely ornate and intricate carvings.

Inside the first gate (*torii*) is a five-storey pagoda built in 1818, and the ticket office. A short flight of stairs leads you through the **Otemon**, also known as the Deva Gate after its fearsome statues, said to scare away evil spirits. The building on the left after the gate is **Shinkyusha** (the Sacred Stable), where a sacred white horse is housed most of the year. This unpainted building is famous for its monkey carvings, including the renowned San-saru (Three Monkeys) representing the ideal way of life ('hear no evil, see no evil, speak no evil'). The three buildings on the right of the Otemon are repositories for costumes and other festival items. Keep an eye out for the carving of the phantasmagorical elephants.

Another flight of stairs takes you up to the spectacular **Yomeimon** (Twilight Gate). With its 500 Chinese-style carvings of sages, dragons, giraffes and other imaginary creatures, it is the most elaborate edifice of its kind in Japan. Off to the left before this gate is the Yakushi-do, famous for the large painting of a dragon on the ceiling and for the roaring echo, which the priest regularly demonstrates. There are also 12 ancient statues inside, representing the years of the Chinese zodiac.

Just above the Yomeimon is the similarly ornate **Karamon**, leading to the Oratory and Main Hall. The dragon motif continues in the oratory, with more carvings at the entrance, and another 100 on the ceiling. To the right of Karamon is the entrance to the **Oku-sha**, the

shogun's tomb (an extra ¥520 if you hold the combined ticket). Over the door by the ticket booth is the carving of the **Nemuri-neko** (Sleeping Cat). The stairs lead up the mountain to a quiet and secluded area with two small buildings simply painted in blue and gold, and behind these is the tomb.

The path leading to the left before the entrance *torii* goes to the **Toshogu Treasure Museum** (¥500), where a small selection of the treasures is exhibited on rotation.

The second path to the left (between the pagoda and the Otemon) leads to **Futarasan Jinja**. This shrine has three other sites: the summit of Mt Nantai; the shore of Lake Chuzenji; and the bank of the Daiyagawa river. There is little to see inside the shrine, but the sacred spring and other buildings at the back (admission ¥200) are quite atmospheric.

TAIYU-IN MAUSOLEUM

Further into the hills is the **Taiyu-in Mausoleum**, where the third shogun, Iemitsu, is buried. Built in 1652, the gates and buildings are rather more restrained in scale and style than Toshogu and definitely worth visiting. Many people prefer the black and gold colour scheme and relatively quiet atmosphere.

The first gate has Nio (heavenly kings) guardian figures; soon after comes the Nitenmon, with statues of Komokuten and Jikokuten, two Buddhist guardians. The next gate is the Yashamon, with statues of four demons known as Yashan, and the last is the Karamon, before the main hall of worship. A few artefacts and old treasures are displayed inside. A walk around the main hall leads to the Kokamon gate and towards the shogun's actual burial site, though this is locked at all times.

Back near the Shinkyo bridge, there's a trail leading upstream along the Daiyagawa river to the Ganmangafuchi Abyss, famous for a series of old mossy statues along a stretch of the river filled with large volcanic rocks.

LAKE CHUZENJI AND MT NANTAI

To see the area's famed natural beauty, be sure to visit **Lake Chuzenji**, situated high above Nikko. The road zigzags up the Iroha-zaka road to an altitude of 1,300 metres (4,265 feet) – watch out for the aggressive monkeys alongside the road. The lake offers swimming, fishing and boating, and the surrounding area has many campsites and hiking trails.

Most tourists come to view the **Kegon Falls**, where the lake's waters plunge 100 metres (328 feet) into the Daiyagawa river. The waterfalls, which include 12 minor cascades, are some of the finest in all Japan – and are especially photogenic in midwinter when they occasionally freeze over. A lift (¥520) takes you down to an observation platform level with the bottom of the falls. The nearby Chanoki-daira ropeway gives views of the lake, Kegon Falls and Mt Nantai. There's also a botanical garden with alpine plants.

North of the lake, **Mt Nantai** rises to almost 2,400 metres (7,877 feet). There is a crater at the top, but most climbers making the five-hour ascent (May to October only) do so for religious reasons, to visit Okumiya Shrine. The side of the mountain gets crowded with worshippers during its festival (31 July-8 August).

Further north from Chuzenji is **Yumoto Onsen**, a hot spring resort by Lake Yumoto with a good range of accommodation. The road passes through gorgeous sub-alpine meadows and has great views of the mountains.

Where to stay & eat

Although it's possible to see Nikko in a day, there are several good hotels. Prices below are for double rooms.

One of the oldest hotels in Japan, the **Nikko Kanaya Hotel** (1300 Kami-Hatsuishi, 0288 54 0001, www.kanayahotel. co.jp, ¥11,550-¥46,200) opened for business in 1873. It's a five-minute ride from either station on a Tobu bus (¥190) heading for Nishisando, Kiyotaki, Okuhosoo, Chuzenji or Yumoto Onsen; get off at the Shinkyo stop. Another option is the **Nikko Tamozawa Hotel** (2010 Hanaishimachi, 0288 54 1152, www.tobu.co.jp/kogyo/tamozawa/, from ¥12,000), a 12-minute ride on the same buses. Alight at Rengeseki Tamozawa.

There's also the **Turtle Inn Nikko**, a small inn by the river near Shinkyo (2-16 Takumi-cho, 0288 53 3168, www.turtle-nikko. com, ¥9,000-¥11,200). It also has an annex called **Hotori-an** (8-28 Takumi-cho, 0288 53 3663, ¥12,400) a few minutes away. Get off at the Sogo Kaikanmae bus stop for either. Staff speak English.

There are plenty of hotels and pensions in the Lake Chuzenji area, and many of these have natural hot-spring baths (*onsen*). Cream of the crop is the **Chuzenji Kanaya Hotel** (2482 Chugushi, 0288 51 0001, www.kanaya hotel.co.jp, from ¥23,100). The bus to Yumoto Onsen stops right in front of the hotel.

It would be a definite shame to leave Nikko without trying the local speciality, *yuba* (soya milk skin). **Gyoushin-Tei** (2339-1 Yama-uchi, 0288 53 3751, closed Thur) is set in a 12th-century garden and serves *yuba* in *shojin ryori* (¥3,500) or *kaiseki ryori* (¥5,000) courses. There are also numerous noodle shops serving soba (including *yuba* soba) along Nikko's main street, and up at Lake Chuzenji. **Enya** (443 Ishiyamachi, 0288 53 5605, www.nikko-enya.co.jp, closed Mon) offers a selection of Japanese and Western meat dishes and over 80 different world beers.

Getting there

By train

Both Tobu and JR trains go to Nikko, terminating at different but nearby stations in the centre of town. The Tobu trains are faster and cheaper, and their bus service to the sights is more regular.
By Tobu: From Tobu Asakusa station, limited express trains go direct to Tobu Nikko station (¥2,740 single; journey 1hr 50mins). Regular (*kaisoku*) trains cost ¥1,320 and take 20mins longer. *Kaisoku* tickets are always available from ticket machines, but seats on limited express trains must be reserved; book in good time, especially at weekends and holidays. Check with Tobu in Tokyo (3623 1171).
By JR: Take the *shinkansen* (bullet train) from Tokyo station (1hr) or regular train from Ueno (90-110mins) to Utsunomiya; from there it's 45mins on a local train to JR Nikko station. Single fare ¥2,520 regular; ¥4,920 by bullet train. There are also some trains from Shinjuku (¥2,520, 2hrs 25mins).

From both stations it's a few minutes by bus (¥190) to Shinkyo bridge and the entrance to Toshogu, or a 25mins walk. Tobu runs buses to Lake Chuzenji (30mins, ¥1,100; a two-day ticket allowing unlimited use of the buses is ¥2,000). There are also occasional buses to Yumoto Onsen.

Tourist information

Nikko Tourist Information Centre

591 Gokomachi, Nikko-shi, Tochigi-ken (0288 54 2496/www.nikko-jp.org/english/index.html). **Open** 9am-5pm daily.
The office is located just off Nikko's main street. The website has a detailed guide to all the sights.

Sightseeing Inquiry Office

Inside Tobu Nikko station, 4-3 Matsubara-cho, Nikko-shi, Tochigi-ken (0288 53 4511). **Open** 8.30am-5pm daily.

Other Trips

Get a taste of village life, plus Japan's most famous mountain.

Here are some more obscure options for day trips from Tokyo. The first offers a glimpse of Edo-era Japan; the second takes you on a pleasant walk to an ancient hilltop temple; the third to a stone-quarrying region. In midsummer, you can also join the hordes climbing Mt Fuji.

Kawagoe

With inner-city rice paddies, wide streets and an overall slower pace of life, Kawagoe – less than an hour by train west from central Tokyo – is, in many ways, typical of the suburbs that encompass the city. But the place also has a distinctive side, as hinted at in its nickname, 'Little Edo'. Kawagoe boasts one of Japan's most extensive collections of intact merchants' houses dating from the 19th century.

The collection isn't huge – fewer than 30 buildings – and they owe their survival (ironically) to the Great Kawagoe Fire of 1893, which destroyed more than a third of the city. As Kawagoe was rebuilt, merchants chose fire-resistant mortar walls and elaborately tiled *onigawara* roofs in the style of the *kura* (the traditional Japanese warehouse) as a safeguard against future disaster. The surviving structures, known as *kurazukuri*, offer a rare glimpse of a Japan long disappeared.

Conveniently for the visitor, most of the remaining *kurazukuri* are situated along one street, Ichiban-gai, a ten-minute walk from Hon-Kawagoe train station. Impressively designed, with elaborately carved shutters and supports, some of the buildings are now shops, which are worth entering as much for their interiors as for the goods on sale. Original furnishings and decorations remain, and shopkeepers won't mind if you choose not to come away with a bamboo flute or a kimono.

In between are some stately Western-style buildings erected at the beginning of the 20th century, as well as *kurazukuri* reproductions. The latter are not as crass as they sound, and offer a viable alternative to the 'concrete box' school of modern Japanese architecture.

Beyond Ichiban-gai is a maze of narrow, winding streets where a clutch of traditional sweet shops vies for attention with ten or so temples. The generations-old method of preparing the hard candies is on show for all who are curious to see a near-extinct craft.

Back towards the station is **Kita-in** temple (0492 22 0859, open 9am-4pm daily, admission ¥400), built in 830 and rebuilt in the 17th century using structures from the original Edo Castle. A side yard contains around 540 *rakan*, stone statues of Buddha's 500 mythical disciples. They're quite a sight; each face is different, representing a host of emotions, from joy to serenity to grief to madness.

Looming majestically above all this is the symbol of Kawagoe, the three-storey **Tokino Kane Tower**. Originally constructed in 1624, and rebuilt after the Great Fire, the wooden tower houses a bell that still chimes four times a day, serving to remind all of Kawagoe's place of importance in historical Japan.

Where to eat

Kotobukian (0492 25 1184, open 11.30am-5pm, until 8pm Sat, Sun, closed Wed), near Kita-in temple, specialises in *wariko-soba*, a concoction of green tea buckwheat noodles with five different toppings, served in a five-tiered box. For snacks, try **Kurazukuri Chaya** (0492 25 5252, open 9am-7pm daily) on Ichiban-gai. **Oni** (0492 25 4179, open 6-11.30pm Mon-Sat), also located in a *kurazukuri*, near Kawagoe station, offers locally brewed beer and good food. Don't miss the sunken fireplace.

Getting there

By train

The Seibu Shinjuku express leaves every 15mins from Seibu Shinjuku station to Hon-Kawagoe station (journey 46mins, ¥480 single). Kawagoe station, slightly further from the city's sights, is on the Tobu Toju line from Ikebukuro (the fastest route: 30mins, ¥450); an express departs every 15mins. Kawagoe is also on the JR Saikyo line from Shinjuku station (57mins, ¥740); trains run every 20mins. The 'Co Edo Loop Bus', a vintage-style shuttle bus, connects Kawagoe and Hon-Kawagoe stations with the main sights. Single trips cost ¥180, a day pass is ¥500.

Tourist information

Kawagoe City Tourist Information Bureau

Inside Kawagoe station, 39-19 Wakita Honcho, Kawagoe-shi (0492 22 5556/www.city.kawagoe. saitama.jp). **Open** 9am-4.30pm daily.

Climbing Mt Fuji

Japan's most famous and highest mountain (at 3,776 metres/12,388 feet), is renowned for its beauty and spiritual significance. For centuries pilgrims have made their way to the summit, with shrines on the way up doubling as inns; pilgrims would pray and rest at each stage before reaching the summit in time for sunrise. For years this was a men-only affair; women were only allowed to join in a few years after the Meiji Restoration of 1868.

Religious travellers are few and far between these days, but climbing Fuji remains very popular. People still go up to see the sunrise, but most use transport to the fifth stage, where the road stops. Since the mountain is covered in snow most of the year, the official climbing season is limited to July and August, although there is transport to the fifth stage from April until November (out of season the trails are open, but facilities are closed). The best time is the middle four weeks of the climbing season; the most crowded time is Obon Week in mid August. The climb is worthwhile but not easy: a saying goes that there are two kinds of fools, those who never climb Fuji and those who climb it twice.

Choosing from which side to tackle Mt Fuji affects how easy the climb is. Most people follow the Yoshidaguchi Trail from the Kawaguchiko side (north), which offers a 7.5-kilometre (4.7-mile) climb that takes five hours, plus three for the descent. You can also head from the south-west side, starting at one of two new fifth stages, one near Gotemba (six and a half hours up and three down) or another further west (five hours up and three and a half down).

There are two ways to tackle the volcano. One is to set off at nightfall, timing the ascent to arrive in time for sunrise. More sensible souls climb in daylight and rest in one of the lodges near the peak. With up to 600 people crammed into the huts, arriving and departing constantly, you won't get a sound sleep but you will appreciate the break. Lodges at the

eighth stage on the Kawaguchiko side include **Hakuunsou** (0555 24 6514, ¥5,250-¥8,400 per person) and **Honhachigo Tomoekan** (0555 24 6511, ¥7,350-¥8,400). At the seventh stage on the Gotemba side, try **Hinodekan** (0550 89 2867, ¥5,500).

The temperature at the summit can be 20°C lower than at the base; the average in July is 4.8°C (40.5°F) and in August 5.8°C (42.5°F). It's often below zero before sunrise. Essential items include good shoes, rainwear, a torch, water and food (available at huts, but overpriced). Don't forget toilet paper and some bags for your rubbish.

Once you reach the peak, you might be slightly disappointed to find it is no longer a place of solitude and contemplation. Restaurants, souvenir shops, vending machines, portaloos, a shrine and several hundred people will be waiting for you; and the spectacle of the sunrise is not necessarily enhanced by loudspeakers blasting dramatic music. But it is still an amazing feeling to be standing atop Japan's most iconic peak.

Getting there

Details below are for July and August; in other months transport connections are fewer.

By bus

The fastest and cheapest way to Kawaguchiko is by bus from Nishi-Shinjuku's Keio Shinjuku Expressway Bus Terminal (1hr 45mins, ¥1,700 single). From the Keio bus terminal at Kawaguchiko station to the fifth stage it takes 50mins (¥1,700 single, ¥2,000 return); there are five buses a day. There are also six daily buses from Shinjuku direct to the fifth stage (2hrs 25mins, ¥2,600).

By train

Take the JR Chuo line from Shinjuku to Otsuki station (1hr 20mins, ¥1,280). From there, take the Fuji-Kyuko line to Kawaguchiko (50mins, ¥1,110) – timetables can be

Trips Out of Town

Jiko-ji Temple

The oldest temple in the Kanto region outside Tokyo sits on a hilltop in the middle of a green landscape about 70 kilometres (44 miles) north of the capital. Infrequent transport connections mean it takes pretty much all day to get there

and back – but the slow journey, followed by a peaceful hour-long walk to the temple itself, is a perfect antidote to the chaos of the capital.

From Ikebukuro station, the Tobu Tojo line maps a course through sprawling suburbia to its terminal at **Ogawamachi**, just over an hour away. Surrounded by rolling hills, the town was

checked with JR in Otsuki (0554 22 0125) or Fuji-Kyuko in Kawaguchiko (0555 72 2911). From Kawaguchiko station to the fifth stage by bus takes another hour.

If you want to start the climb from Gotemba, there are four direct trains (express Asagiri) daily from Shinjuku on the Odakyu line (¥2,720, 2hrs). From Gotemba there are three to four buses to the new fifth stage (¥1,500 single, ¥2,000 return; 1hr).

Tourist information

Kawaguchiko Tourist Information

In front of Kawaguchiko station, 3631-5 Funatsu, Kawaguchiko-Machi (0555 72 6700). **Open** 8.30am-6pm daily.

once noted as a centre for *washi* (Japanese paper) manufacturing, and today families still carry on the gruelling task of turning pulped wood into the uniquely textured material.

From Ogawamachi, the JR Hachiko line has little diesel trains on the hour to the next station, **Myokaku**. From there it's a ten-minute

bus ride to the sleepy hamlet of **Nishi-Daira**, where old houses with their adjoining *kura* (warehouses) are the norm, and hens appear to outnumber people. From the bus stop, a two-minute walk into Nishi-Daira will bring you to a crossroads. Here, turn right on to the steep road that disappears into the forested hills above. Where the village ends there is a small temple called **Nyonindo** that is worth a look if only for its historical significance. During the Kamakura era (1185-1333), this was the final stop for women pilgrims. Beyond, as far as Jiko-ji at the top, it was a men-only affair.

The climb is spectacular, with breathtaking views of the opposing hills as they emerge in hazy layers. But the walk is far from exhausting and offers an absorbing hour of peace before the tiled roofs of Jiko-ji come into view.

Like temples throughout Asia, **Jiko-ji** commands a stunning location. Half-hidden between groves of thick blue bamboo, the various temple buildings are connected by a maze of stone steps. At the entrance stands an old wooden tower supporting a huge bell (dating from 1245) that is rung twice a day. Above are the main structures, many displaying intricately carved designs.

Pre-dating the Late Nara period (710-94), Jiko-ji is believed to have been established in 673 by a priest called Jiko (hence its name). The advent of the Kamakura era saw the temple's rise in prominence, and it quickly became the religious centre for 75 satellite temples that mushroomed across the adjoining hills.

The modern treasure house (open 9am-4pm daily, ¥300) contains a number of valuable items, including the Lotus Sutra, a scroll-like masterpiece of calligraphy painstakingly transcribed by Emperor Gotoba (1183-98), and now a National Treasure. Kannondo, which stands at the highest point in the compound, also guards a collection of treasures, the principal one being an image of Senju Kannon, the main deity of the area. The image is only open to public viewing on 17 April, the day of the temple's annual festival.

From Jiko-ji, the walk back to Nishi-Daira takes less than half an hour. If time allows, retrace your steps into the village and drop by **Tategu Kaikan** (0493 67 0014, open 9am-4.30pm Tue-Sun), a souvenir shop that stocks an array of locally made food and woodcraft.

Where to eat

There's nowhere to eat near Jiko-ji. Best to bring a packed lunch or try Myokaku or Ogawamachi, where there are lots of *unagi* (freshwater eel) restaurants. **Futaba Honten** (0493 72 0038, www.futaba.to, open 11am-

2.30pm, 4-8pm Tue-Sun), five minutes along the shopping street from Ogawamachi station, has belonged to the same family for 250 years and specialises in *chushichi-meshi*, a soup of rice in green tea, and the ubiquitous *unagi*.

Getting there

From Ikebukuro station take the Tobu Tojo special express to Ogawamachi station (journey 1hr, ¥780 single), then the JR Hachioji line to Myokaku (10mins, ¥200), then the Tokikawa Son'ei bus to Nishi-Daira (10mins). Services are infrequent – this is rural Japan – so best to check timings in advance.

Oya-machi

It is no coincidence that the small town of Oya-machi, lying about 110 kilometres (68 miles) north of Tokyo, in Tochigi prefecture, has at its heart a 27-metre (89-foot) statue carved from a sheer rock face. The town sits on a mountain of volcanic stone and has been a mining centre for centuries.

Oya-machi is reached by a dusty road that leads to an expansive stone atrium. Huge doorways have been cut into the surrounding cliffs with staggering precision. Within this area is the deceptively small **Oya Stone Museum** (028 652 1232, open 9am-4.30pm Mon-Wed, Fri-Sun, admission ¥600). On display are a number of miners' tools, early photos of the quarrying process, and an exhibit

about Frank Lloyd Wright's Imperial Hotel in Tokyo (demolished in 1968), for which he insisted on using Oya stone. Then things get really interesting: you descend a stairwell into a vast underground ex-quarry 60 metres (197 feet) deep and large enough to swallow Tokyo Dome. The quarry has been used as an aircraft factory in World War II, a mushroom farm and, more recently, a concert hall.

From the museum, it is a short walk back to the bus stop and into Oya-machi proper. There are a handful of shops and houses, many made entirely of stone. At the top of the slope that leads off to the left of the main street are the red gates of **Oya-ji** temple (0286 52 0128, open usually 8.30am-5pm daily, closed 2wks Dec and some Thur, ¥300), a small, ornate structure wedged tightly beneath a bulging cliff.

Founded in 810, the temple has been a tourist destination ever since, largely because of its remarkable reliefs. The first you encounter is the 42-armed Senju Kannon. Carved directly into the rock wall, it dates to the early part of the Heian era (794-1185), and is believed to have originally been lacquered and painted with gold leaf. On the adjoining wall are another nine reliefs of varying sizes and quality, created between 600 and 1,000 years ago. A small museum contains little of interest except the remains of an 11,000-year-old skeleton, discovered in the grounds during restoration.

Across the street, flanked by souvenir shops, stands a massive rectangular entrance cut through the hill. Head through here and you reach the towering 17-metre (56-foot) **Heiwa Kannon** (Goddess of Peace) statue. Completed in 1954, she hangs from the cliff, gazing benevolently out over the town.

Where to eat

Oya's tourist cafeterias are uninspiring, so better to bring a packed lunch or eat near Utsunomiya station before boarding the bus. Just before the Heiwa Kannon bus stop is **Drive-in Kannon Oya** (0286 52 0111, open 8.30am-5.30pm daily), which offers a set menu with various *kampyo* dishes (dried sliced gourd) – a Tochigi prefecture speciality.

Getting there

From Ueno station take the JR Tohoku line to Utsunomiya station; journey times and prices vary from 45mins/¥4,600 by bullet train to 1hr 40mins/ ¥1,890 single by regular train. Take the west exit at Utsunomiya and catch bus 45 from bus stop 8 to Oya Shiryokan (also called Shimin no Ie, 30mins) – pay as you get off. When you leave, it's best to use the Heiwa Kannon bus stop. Oya-machi is a tiny place, so it's hard to get lost.

Heiwa Kannon statue.

Trips Out of Town

Directory

Features

Directory

Getting Around

To & from the airport

Two airports serve Tokyo. Most overseas flights arrive at **Narita International Airport**, which is nearly 70 kilometres (45 miles) from Tokyo and well served by rail and bus links to the city. It's less likely that you'll arrive at **Haneda International Airport**, closer to the city and to the south, which handles mainly internal flights.

Narita International Airport

Flight information 0476 34 5000/ English-language enquiries 0476 32 2802/www.narita-airport.or.jp.
The **Narita Express train** (3423 0111, www.jreast.co.jp/e/nex), run by Japan Railways (JR), is the fastest way to get into Tokyo from Narita, but it's also the most expensive. Seats must be reserved and there's limited standing room, so during particularly busy times you may have to wait around. All trains go to Tokyo station (¥2,940), with some also serving Shinjuku (¥3,110), Ikebukuro (¥3,110), Omiya (¥3,740) and Yokohama (¥4,180). Trains depart every 30 to 40 minutes.

The **Keisei Skyliner** (Narita 0476 32 8505, Ueno 3831 0131, www.keisei.co.jp), operated by a private rail company, is a cheaper option. Trains on this line will take you into Ueno or Nippori station (¥1,920) in around an hour. Cheaper still is a Keisei limited express (*tokkyu*), a regular train that makes a few stops on its 75-minute route to Ueno station (¥1,000).

Limousine buses (3665 7220, www.limousinebus.co.jp) also run regularly to various key points and certain hotels in the city. There are ticket counters inside the arrivals halls near the exits of both terminals 1 and 2; the buses depart from just outside. Fares are ¥3,000.

Taxis are recommended only for those with bottomless wallets: they cost from ¥30,000 and are often slower than the train.

Haneda International Airport

Flight information 5757 8111/ www.tokyo-airport-bldg.co.jp.
Haneda is served by the **Tokyo Monorail** (www.tokyo-monorail.co.jp), which leaves every five to ten minutes from 5.10am to 11.50pm, linking up to Hamamatsucho station (¥470) on the Yamanote line in a little over 20 minutes. The **Keikyu line** (045 441 0999, www.keikyu.co.jp) can take you to Shinagawa, also on the Yamanote line, in 19 minutes (¥400). From here you can link up with major JR lines.

Limousine buses to central Tokyo cost in the region of ¥1,000, depending on which part of the city you want to go to. A **taxi** will cost a minimum of ¥6,000.

By train

Most of Japan's vast and efficient rail network is run by **Japan Railways** (JR). One of the fastest but most expensive ways to travel Japan's elongated countryside is by *shinkansen* (bullet train), which travels at speeds up to 270 kilometres (168 miles) per hour. Tickets can be purchased at JR reservation 'Green Window' areas or travel agents, or online at www.world.eki-net.com. Call the **JR East Infoline** (*see p285*) for information in English.

Trains depart from different stations depending on destination; most leave from Tokyo or Ueno stations. Slower, cheaper trains go to many destinations. Marks on the train platforms show where the numbered carriages will stop. Most carriages have reserved seats only (reservations cost extra), but some carriages are set aside for unreserved seating on each train. Arrive early if you want to sit down.

By coach

Long-distance buses provide one of the cheapest ways to travel through Japan, although anyone over 5ft 6in (1m 68cm) may find the seats small. Most of these buses leave at midnight and arrive early the next morning; all are air-conditioned and have ample space for luggage. Seats can be reserved through a travel agent. Long-distance buses are run by the railway companies; for information, *see p285* **JR trains** and **Private train lines**.

Trains & subway

Tokyo has one of the most efficient train and subway systems in the world: in the rare event of delays in the morning rush, staff give out apology slips for workers to show their bosses. Services are fast, clean, safe, reliable and – with a little thought and the right map – remarkably easy to use. Almost all stations have signs in English, and signs telling you which exit to take. Subways and train lines are colour-coded.

Subways and trains operate from 5am to around midnight (JR lines slightly later). Rush hours are 7.30-9.30am and 5-7pm, and the last train of the day can be a nightmare.

Tokyo's rail network is run by several different companies, and changing trains between competing systems can mean paying for two tickets. Transfer tickets are usually available to take you from one line to another, but cost the same as buying two separate tickets and can be tricky to figure out. Since there are no refunds for mistakenly purchased tickets, it's generally a good idea to get a prepaid travel pass. Armed with a **Suica** and a **Passnet** (*see below* **Tickets & passes**), you can ride on any regular train in Tokyo.

The user-friendly **Jorudan** website (www.jorudan.co.jp) is in English and allows you to type in your starting point and destination to learn routes, times and prices. For a map showing the (huge) rail and subway network across Greater Tokyo, *see pp316-7*.

JR trains

Overland trains in Tokyo are operated by **Japan Railways East** (www.jreast.co.jp/e), part of the main JR group. It's impossible to stay in Tokyo for more than a few hours without using JR's **Yamanote line**, the loop that defines the city centre – and with which all Tokyo's subway and rail lines link at some point (for connections at each station on the loop, *see p320*). The main stations on the Yamanote line (colour-coded green) are Tokyo, Ueno, Ikebukuro, Shinjuku, Shibuya and Shinagawa. It's very foreigner-friendly, with an infoline in English (*see below*) and information centres at major stations (look for the question mark symbol) that offer help in English.

JR's other major lines in Tokyo are: **Chuo** (orange), **Sobu** (yellow), **Saikyo** (turquoise) and **Keihin Tohoku** (blue). Because of its notoriety for perverts (*chikan*), the insanely crowded Saikyo line offers women-only cars during peak hours.

JR East Infoline
3423 0111. **Open** 10am-6pm Mon-Fri.

Subways

There are 12 subway lines in Tokyo. Most are run by **Tokyo Metro** (www.tokyometro.jp/e), formerly the Teito Rapid Transit Authority (Eidan). Its eight colour-coded lines are: **Chiyoda** (dark green), **Ginza** (orange), **Hanzomon** (purple), **Hibiya** (grey), **Marunouchi** (red), **Nanboku** (light green), **Tozai** (turquoise) and **Yurakucho** (yellow), which includes **New Yurakucho** (brown), called Shin-Sen in Japanese.

Four – slightly pricier – subway lines are run by the metropolitan government, **Toei** (5322 0400, www.kotsu. metro.tokyo.jp). They are: **Asakusa** (pale pink), **Mita** (blue), **Oedo** (bright pink) and **Shinjuku** (green). If transferring from Tokyo Metro to Toei trains, buying a transfer ticket is ¥70 cheaper than buying separate tickets.

Subway maps posted in stations are in Japanese. For a subway map in English, *see pp318-9*; you can also get one at tourist offices (*see p297*).

Private train lines

Tokyo's private railway lines mainly ferry commuters to the outlying districts of the city. Because most were founded by companies that also run department stores, they usually terminate inside, or next to, one of their branches.

The major private lines are run by **Keio** (www.keio.co.jp), **Odakyu** (www.odakyu-group. co.jp), **Seibu** (www.seibu-group.co.jp/railways), **Tobu** (www.tobuland.com), **Tokyu** (www.tokyu.co.jp), **Keisei** (www.keisei.co.jp) and **Keikyu** (www.keikyu.co.jp).

You can pick up a full map showing all lines and subways from the airport information counter on arrival. Keio lines offer women-only cars during peak hours.

Tickets & passes

Standard tickets

Standard single tickets for adults (under-12s pay half-price, under-6s travel free) can be bought at automatic ticket machines at any station. Many machines feature a symbol saying which notes they accept. Touch-screen ticket machines can display information in English, but should you be unsure of your destination (or unable to read it from the Japanese map), buy a ticket for the minimum fare (¥160) and settle up in a fare adjustment machine (or window) at your destination. All stations have them, just before the exit barriers. Travellers with incorrect tickets do not have to pay punitive fines.

Transferring from one line to another, provided it is run by the same operator, will be covered by the price of your ticket. If your journey involves transferring from one network to another, you will have to buy a transfer ticket (if available) or buy another ticket at the transfer point.

Buying individual tickets is time-consuming, so if you're in town for any length of time you're better off buying a travel pass of some kind.

Suica

Suica is a prepaid travel pass issued by JR, distinctive for its bright green colour and penguin logo. It can be used on all JR lines. It contains an integrated circuit detected at ticket gates when the pass is swiped over the right point. The minimum fare is automatically deducted from your balance on entry to the station, with the balance being picked up on exit at your destination. Suica cards can be purchased at JR 'Green Window' areas or at JR ticket machines. A card costs ¥2,000, including a ¥500 returnable deposit. Credit on the card can be topped up at ticket machines (up to ¥10,000).

With a Suica card you don't have to queue, nor do you have to try to find your destination station on a map in order to work out the required fare – you just walk up to the gates and go through.

Passnet

This prepaid travel pass covers all of Tokyo's railway lines (subway and overland) – *except* for JR. Available in denominations of ¥1,000, ¥3,000 or ¥5,000, it allows you to transfer from one operator's line to another without buying new tickets. The fare is automatically deducted from your remaining credit at the computerised ticket barriers. Unlike the Suica, this card must be inserted into the ticket gate. It only saves a small amount of cash, but it does save you time fiddling for change and trying to figure out the maps.

Frequent-travel tickets

There's a huge variety of frequent-travel tickets available, from prepaid cards to 11-for-the-price-of-ten trip tickets. There are also combination tickets and one-day passes for one, two or three networks. For more details in English, call the **JR East Infoline** (*see p285*).

JR passes

The **Japan Rail Pass** (www.japanrailpass.net) provides for virtually unlimited travel on the entire national JR network, including *shinkansen* and all JR lines in Tokyo, including the Yamanote line. It cannot, however, be used on the new 'Nozomi' super-express *shinkansen*. It costs from ¥28,300 for seven days, about the same price as a middle-distance *shinkansen* return ticket. It's essential if you're planning to travel much around Japan.

The JR Pass is available only to visitors from abroad travelling under the entry status of 'temporary visitor', and must be purchased *before* coming to Japan. You buy an Exchange Order abroad, which is then changed into a pass on arrival in Japan at an exchange office (you'll need to show your passport).

JR East, which runs trains in and around Tokyo, has its own version of the pass (www.jreast.co.jp/e/eastpass), which costs from ¥20,000 for five days. If you are not intending to travel beyond the JR East area (Tokyo and the area to the north and east), this makes a sensible choice. The same conditions apply.

Exchange Orders can be bought at overseas offices of the Japan Travel Bureau International, Nippon Travel Agency, Kinki Nippon Tourist, Tokyu Tourist Corporation and other associated local travel agents, or at an overseas Japan Airlines office if you're travelling by Japan Airlines. Check the Japan Rail Pass website for overseas locations.

Buses

Like the trains, buses in Tokyo are run by several companies. Travelling by bus can be confusing if you're new to Japan, as signs are rarely in English. Toei and Keio bus fares cost ¥200, other buses are ¥210 – no matter what the distance (half-price for kids). Get on the bus at the front and off at the back. Drop the exact fare into the slot in front of the driver. If you don't have it, use the change machine, usually to the right, which will deduct your fare from the money. Fare machines accept ¥50, ¥100 and ¥500 coins and ¥1,000 notes. Stops are usually announced by a pre-recorded voice. A Toei bus route guide in English is available at Toei subway stations and hotels.

Tokyo Bus Association

5360 7111/www.tokyobus.or.jp.
The website and phone line provide information on all bus routes within and leaving Tokyo, in Japanese only.

Cycling

The bicycle remains the most common form of local transport in Tokyo, and thefts are rare, although unattended bikes should always be locked. Areas in and around stations are usually no-parking zones for bikes, a rule that locals gleefully ignore, but which can result in your bike being impounded. Some hotels will loan bicycles to guests.

Driving

Rental costs for garages are equivalent to those for small apartments in Tokyo, so if you rent a car you will have to pay astronomical parking fees (usually around ¥100 for 30 minutes, more in the centre). If you do decide to hire a car, you'll need an international driving licence backed up by at least six months' driving experience. English-speaking rental assistance is available at many of the large hotels as well as at the airport.

The **Japan Automobile Federation** (www.jaf.or.jp) publishes a 'Rules of the Road' guide (¥1,000) in English. Call or visit one of these branch offices to request one: 3-11-6 Otsuka, Bunkyo-ku (5976 9716) or 2-4-5 Azabudai, Minato-ku (3578 1471).

A Metropolitan Expressway map in English is available from the **Metropolitan Expressway Public Corporation**, Isomura Bldg 5F, 1-1-3 Toranomon, Minato-ku (3580 1881); Toranomon station (Ginza line), exit 7.

If you want to drive outside the capital (a much safer option), JR offers rail and car rental packages. Call the **JR East Infoline** (*see p285*) for details.

Toyota Rent-a-lease

Narita International Airport Terminals 1 & 2 (0476 32 1020/ fax 0476 32 1088/http://rent.toyota. co.jp). **Open** 7am-10pm daily. **Other locations**: throughout the city.

Walking

Tokyo is great for walking. There are no no-go areas, and the whole place is 99.9 per cent safe 24 hours a day. Walking is the best way to discover the hidden nooks and crannies that exist in nearly every district. The **Tokyo TIC** (*see p297*) offers info on free walking tours of parts of Tokyo.

The worst thing about walking in Tokyo is the crowds. Because it's so safe and so crowded, Japanese people have a different sense of personal space and are often unaware of what's going on behind them. This results in colossal 'people jams'. People also tend to walk at speeds associated with village fêtes rather than capital cities, sometimes while sending mail from their mobiles; be prepared to experience some frustration.

When crossing the road, always do so at marked crossings and always wait for the green man. If you cross on red, urban legend says that you could be held responsible for the death of those behind you, who may blindly follow you into the traffic.

Taxis

Taxi fares begin at ¥660 for the first two kilometres and then it's about ¥100 for every 350 metres. Prices rise at weekends and between 11pm and 5am. Taxi stands are located near stations, most hotels, department stores and major intersections. The rear doors open automatically, so look out. Tipping is not expected. Virtually all taxis are the same model, Toyota Crown.

Hinomaru Limousine

Ark Hills Mori Bldg, 1-12-32 Akasaka, Minato-ku (3505 1717/ www.hinomaru.co.jp). Roppongi-Itchome station (Chiyoda line), exit 3. Stretch limos and the like, with English-speaking chauffeurs.

Guided tours

Bus tours

Hato Bus

3435 6081/www.hatobus.co.jp/english. **Bookings** 9am-7pm daily. **Credit** AmEx, DC, MC, V.
A variety of tours, including half-day, full-day and night tours with English-speaking guides. Only the Edo Tokyo tour requires advance booking, with seats subject to availability on the others. Prices start at around ¥4,000; the Dynamic Tokyo Tour is the priciest, at ¥12,000. Buses depart from Tokyo station.

Japan Gray Line Company

3433 5745/www.jgl.co.jp. **Bookings** 7am-5.45pm daily. **Credit** AmEx, DC, MC, V.
A selection of morning, afternoon and evening tours of the biggest sights the city has to offer, in English. Prices range from ¥4,000 to ¥15,000. Conveniently, buses pick up at many hotels.

Sky Bus Tokyo

3215 0008/www.skybus.jp. **Bookings** 10am-6pm daily. **Credit** AmEx, DC, MC, V.
Launched in autumn 2004, this open-top red double-decker takes 45mins to tour the Marunouchi and Imperial Palace area. The ticket office is on the ground floor of the Mitsubishi Building, next to the Marunouchi

Building. Tours run on the hour and cost ¥1,200 (¥600 under-12s).

Sunrise Tours

5796 5454/www.jtb.co.jp/sunrisetour. **Bookings** 9am-6pm Mon-Fri. **Credit** AmEx, DC, MC, V.
Run by leading travel agent Japan Travel Bureau, Sunrise provides the widest range of English-language tours in Tokyo, and also offers trips out of town to Mt Fuji (*see p280*), Tokyo Disney Resort (*see p128*) and the hot springs of Hakone (*see pp268-71*), plus full-day, half-day or night-time tours of the city. Phone enquiries for Tokyo tours can be made at any time of day or night.

On foot

Mr Oka's Walking Tours of Tokyo

0422 51 7673/www.homestead.com/mroka. **Bookings** 7-10pm daily. **No credit cards**.
Retired historian Oka-san offers a variety of introductory walking tours of Tokyo in English, ranging from ¥2,000 to ¥4,000. Private tours can be arranged for parties of up to ten people. The fee does not include any transport costs. No matter how much you think you know, you're bound to pick up some informative snippet, as Mr Oka's passion for Tokyo is matched only by his detailed knowledge.

Directory

Resources A-Z

Age restrictions

There is no age of consent in Japan, and the legal age for smoking and drinking is 20; the ubiquity of vending machines, however, makes the law virtually impossible to enforce. The minimum voting age is also 20.

Attitude & etiquette

Japanese people are generally forgiving of visitors' clumsy attempts at correct behaviour, but there are certain rules that must be followed to avoid offending your hosts. For general etiquette tips, *see p91* **Etiquette**. For how to behave in a bathhouse, *see p114* **Getting into hot water**. For business etiquette, *see below*.

Business

Etiquette

Doing business in Japan is a very different proposition from doing it in the West. The Japanese place great emphasis on personal relationships between business partners, and socialising before and after the deal is done is de rigueur. Here are some basic business tips:

● Carry plenty of business cards. You will be spraying them around like confetti.
● Always pass business cards with two hands. Do not write on another person's business card, fold it or put it in your back pocket. When in meetings, read the cards that you have just received carefully and leave them face up on the table throughout.
● If you need an interpreter, hire one of your own and ask them to interpret body language for you.
● Crossing your legs at the knee or the ankle indicates disrespect.
● When out eating with a group, wait for your comrades to indicate your seat.
● Never offer to split a restaurant bill. Just say thank you (*'Gochisosama'*) if someone else pays.
● If you receive a gift from your host, do not open it in front of them. If you give a gift, make sure it is professionally wrapped.
● Be prepared to give details of your personal life in a way that would be inappropriate elsewhere.

Conventions & conferences

Japan hosts more conventions and exhibitions than any other Asian country. Many larger hotels have conference and business rooms for hire. For Tokyo's major annual trade fairs, *see pp196-201*.

Makuhari Messe

Nippon Convention Center, Nakase 2-1 Nakase, Mihama-ku, Chiba-shi (043 296 0001/www.m-messe.co.jp). Kaihin-Makuhari station (Keiyo line), south exit.

Tokyo Big Sight

Tokyo International Exhibition Center, 3-21-2 Ariake, Koto-ku (5530 1111/www.bigsight.jp/ english/). Kokusai-Tenjijo Seimon station (Yurikamome line) or Kokusai-Tenjijo station (Rinkai line) or Ariake terminal (Suijo water bus). **Map** p113.

Tokyo International Forum

3-5-1 Marunouchi, Chiyoda-ku (5221 9000/www.t-i-forum.co.jp/ english). Yurakucho station (Yamanote, Yurakucho lines), Tokyo International Forum exit. **Map** p60.

Chambers of commerce

American Chamber of Commerce *3433 5381/fax 3433 8454/www.accj.or.jp.*
Australian & New Zealand Chamber of Commerce *5157 5615/fax 5157 5616/www.anzccj.jp.*
British Chamber of Commerce *3267 1901/fax 3267 1903/ www.bccjapan.com.*
Canadian Chamber of Commerce *3556 9566/fax 3556 9567/www.cccj.or.jp.*

Copy shops

Kinko's *0120 001 966/ www.kinkos.co.jp.*
A complete range of print services, and internet access. Check the website for details of 24-hour locations.

Couriers

Federal Express *0120 003 200/www.fedex.com.*
Hubnet *0120 881 084/www.hub-net.co.jp.*
UPS Yamato Express *0120 271 040/www.ups.com.*

Office space

Servcorp *5288 5100/ www.servcorp.net.*
Has several locations in Tokyo with executive service starting from ¥250,000 per month plus deposit.

Travel advice

For up-to-date information on travel to a specific country – including the latest news on safety and security, health issues, local laws and customs – contact your home country government's department of foreign affairs. Most have websites packed with useful advice for would-be travellers.

Australia
www.smartraveller.gov.au
Canada
www.voyage.gc.ca
New Zealand
www.mft.govt.nz/travel

Republic of Ireland
http://foreignaffairs.gov.ie
UK
www.fco.gov.uk/travel
USA
www.state.gov/travel

Public relations

IRI *Hatchobori Bldg 7F, 2-19-8 Hatchobori, Chuo-ku (5543 1221/ www.iri-japan.co.jp). Hatchobori station (Hibiya, Keiyo lines), exit A5.*
Kyodo PR *Dowa Bldg 7F, 7-2-22 Ginza, Chuo-ku (3571 5171/ www.kyodo-pr.co.jp). Ginza station (Ginza, Hibiya, Marunouchi lines), exit C3.*

Secretarial service

Telephone Secretary Centre
5413 7320/gh6m-situ@asahi-net.or.jp.
An answering service starting at ¥10,000 a month, including bilingual secretaries, word processing and typing. Japanese lessons for new customers are thrown in for free.

Telephone answering service

Bell24 System *3590 4646/ www.tas.bell24.co.jp.*
Services start from ¥15,000, but bilingual service is provided at a slightly higher cost.

Translators

Simul International
Toranomon 34 MT Bldg 1F, 1-25-5 Toranomon, Minato-ku (3539 3900/www.simul.co.jp). Toranomon station (Ginza line), exits 1, 4.
Transpacific Enterprises
Asunaro T Bldg 3F, 2-2-5 Shibasaki, Tachikawa-shi (042 528 8282/ www.transpacific.jp). Tachikawa station (Chuo line), south exit.

Useful organisations

JETRO (Japan External Trade Organisation)
3582 5511/www.jetro.go.jp.
Japanese-only automated phone menu.

Customs

The duty-free allowances for non-residents coming into Japan are: 400 cigarettes or 100 cigars or 250g of tobacco; three 750ml bottles of spirits; 57g (20oz) of perfume; gifts or souvenirs up to a value of ¥200,000. There is no limit on the amount of Japanese or foreign currency that can be brought into the country.

Penalties are severe for drug importation: deportation is the lenient option. Pornography laws are very strict too: anything showing pubic hair may be confiscated.

For more information, visit **Japan Customs** at: www.customs.go.jp.

Disabled

Tokyo is not easy for those with disabilities, particularly when it comes to public transport. Stations, especially the bigger ones, have long corridors and many staircases, and only some have escalators, lifts or wheelchair-moving facilities, though train workers will assist those in need. More common are raised dots on the ground, to guide the visually impaired, and pedestrian crossings that make a variety of noises. Trains have 'silver seats' near carriage exits for use by the disabled, elderly or pregnant.

The best resource in English for travellers with disabilities is an online service, **Accessible Tokyo**: http://accessible.jp.org.

Club Tourism Division Barrier-free Travel *Centre Kinki Nippon Tourist Co, Shinjuku Island Wing 10F, 6-3-1 Nishi-Shinjuku, Shinjuku-ku (5323 6915/www.club-t.com). Nishi-Shinjuku station (Marunouchi line), Island Wing exit.*
Open 9.30am-5.30pm daily.
Organises tours that take into account the special needs of disabled travellers. Make an appointment to guarantee you speak with an English-speaking staff member.

Drinking

In Japan, you can legally drink – and smoke – when you reach 20. Tokyo's licensing laws are virtually non-existent, and many bars in livelier areas stay open all night, with customers staggering home on the first train. Public drunkenness is common, and late Friday-night trains can be unpleasant.

Intoxication is considered a valid excuse for behaviour, particularly sexual harassment, that would be cause for a lawsuit in the West – the next day, all is forgotten, or at least avoided. Beware: foreigners are expected to have a higher alcohol tolerance than their Japanese drinking pals.

Drugs

Drugs can be found in Tokyo, but penalties for possession are severe. Expect deportation or imprisonment.

Electricity & gas

Electric current in Japan runs like the USA's, at 100V AC, rather than the 220-240V European standard. Plugs have two flat-sided prongs. If bringing electrical appliances from Europe, you need to purchase an adapter.

Electricity in Tokyo is provided by **Tokyo Electric Power Company** (TEPCO, 3501 8111); gas by **Tokyo Gas** (3433 2111).

Embassies

Embassies are usually open 9am to 5pm Monday to Friday; opening times for visa sections may vary.

Australian Embassy
2-1-14 Mita, Minato-ku (5232 4111/www.australia.or.jp). Azabu-Juban station (Nanboku, Oedo lines), exit 2.
British Embassy
1 Ichibansho, Chiyoda-ku (5211 1100/www.uknow.or.jp). Hanzomon station (Hanzomon line), exit 4.
Canadian Embassy
7-3-38 Akasaka, Minato-ku (5412 6200/www.canadanet.or.jp). Aoyama-Itchome station (Ginza, Hanzomon, Oedo lines), exit 4.
Irish Embassy
2-10-7 Kojimachi, Chiyoda-ku (3263 0695/www.embassy-avenue.jp/ ireland). Hanzomon station (Hanzomon line), exit 4.
New Zealand Embassy
20-40 Kamiyamacho, Shibuya-ku (3467 2271/www.nzembassy.com/ japan). Yoyogi-Koen station (Chiyoda line), exit 2.

Directory

Understanding addresses

In a city with no street names, how do you find your way around? The answer, even for Japanese people, is 'with difficulty'. The Japanese system of writing addresses is based on numbers, rather than street names. Central Tokyo is divided into 23 wards, or *ku*. Within each *ku*, there are many smaller districts, or *cho*, which also have their own names. Most *cho* are further subdivided into numbered areas, or *chome*, then into blocks, and finally into individual buildings, which sometimes have names of their own. Japan uses the continental system of floor numbering. The abbreviation 1F is the ground floor, English style; 2F means the second floor, or first floor English style.

Thus, the address of the Office bar – **Yamazaki Bldg 5F, 2-7-18 Kita-Aoyama, Minato-ku** – means that it's on the fifth floor of the Yamazaki Building, which is the 18th building of the seventh block of the second area of Kita-Aoyama, in Minato ward.

To track down an address, first invest in a detailed bilingual atlas, such as the *Tokyo City Atlas* (Kodansha), which contains numbered *cho* and *chome*. Then follow your progress towards your destination by monitoring the metal plaques affixed to lamp-posts or the front of some buildings. Alternatively, ask a policeman. It's what the locals do, and it's one of the main functions of the local *koban* (police box), all of which have detailed maps of their area.

In addition, most station exits in the Tokyo metropolitan area have detailed street plans of the vicinity posted, and maps can often be found on the streets themselves (though these are usually only in Japanese).

If you have access to a fax machine, it's common practice to phone your destination and ask them to fax you a map of how to get there. Most hotels allow guests to receive faxes for this purpose. Alternatively, if you have internet access, type the destination's website (if it has one), and look for the map of how to get there. Japanese websites always have such maps. How else would their customers ever find them?

South Africa Embassy *Zenkyoren Bldg 4F, 2-7-9 Hirakawacho, Chiyoda-ku (3265 3366/ www.rsatk.com). Nagatacho station (Hanzomon, Nanboku, Yurakucho lines), exit 4.*
US Embassy *1-10-5 Akasaka, Minato-ku (3224 5000/ http://tokyo.usembassy.gov). Tameike-Sanno station (Ginza, Nanboku lines), exit 13.*

Emergencies

To contact the police (*keisatsu*) in an emergency, call **110**; to call an ambulance (*kyukyu-sha*) or fire department (*kaji*), call **119**. From a public phone, press the red button first. The person answering should, in theory, speak English, but if you are with a Japanese speaker, get them to call.

Japan Help Line (*see p291*) offers 24-hour, English-language support, but is not equipped to deal with time-sensitive emergencies.

For emergency rooms at hospitals, *see below* **Accident & emergency**.

Health

For the Japanese, medical insurance provided by employers or the state covers 70 per cent of the cost of medical treatment; those aged over 70 pay only ten per cent. Visitors will be expected to pay the full amount for any treatment received, so should take out medical insurance before leaving their own country. Calls to hospitals (except those to **Tokyo Medical Clinic**; *see p291*) are answered in Japanese, but say '*Eigo de hanashite yoroshi dess ka?*' ('May I speak English?') and you'll be transferred to an English-speaker. No vaccinations are required to enter Japan.

Tokyo Metropolitan Health & Medical Information Centre
5285 8181 9am-5pm Mon-Fri/ 5285 8185 5-8pm Mon-Fri; 9am-8pm Sat, Sun/www.himawari. metro.tokyo.jp.

The *himawari* service provides medical and health information in English, Chinese, Korean, Thai and Spanish and can direct you to the most suitable clinic. The out-of-hours number provides interpretation to help foreign nationals get emergency care. If you get to the hospital and can't communicate with the doctor, call them. But if you're at home bleeding, call 119.

Accident & emergency

The following offer regular appointments, deal with 24-hour emergencies and have English-speaking staff.

Japan Red Cross Medical Centre
4-1-22 Hiroo, Shibuya-ku (3400 1311/www.med.jrc.or.jp). Hiroo station (Hibiya line), exit 3. **Open** 8.30-11am Mon-Fri.

St Luke's International Hospital
9-1 Akashicho, Chuo-ku (3541 5151/ www.luke.or.jp). Tsukiji station (Hibiya line), exits 3, 4. **Open** 8.30-11am Mon-Fri; appointments only from noon.

Directory

Seibo International Catholic Hospital

2-5-1 Naka-Ochiai, Shinjuku-ku (3951 1111/www.seibokai.or.jp). Shimo-Ochiai station (Seibu Shinjuku line), north exit. **Open** 8-11am Mon-Sat; appointments only from 12.30pm. Closed 3rd Sat of mth.

Tokyo Medical Clinic & Surgical Clinic

Mori Bldg 32 2F, 3-4-30 Shiba-koen, Minato-ku (3436 3028/www.tmsc.jp). Shiba-Koen station (Mita line), exit A2. **Open** 8.30am-5.30pm Mon-Fri; 8.30am-noon Sat.
Doctors hail from the UK, America, Germany or Japan and all speak English. The clinic also has a pharmacy on the first floor.

Contraception & abortion

Condoms reign supreme in terms of contraception in Japan, largely because until 1999 the pill was available only to women with menstrual problems, and taking it is still generally considered risky. Condoms are sold in most convenience stores, and in vending machines, often near pharmacies. Abortion is legal, and is generally seen as a sad necessity, not a morally controversial issue. The signature of the 'father' is required. Clinics have different rules regarding how far into the pregnancy they will perform abortions. Medical abortions are not available.

Dentists

Both of the following have English-speaking staff.

Dr JS Wong

1-22-3 Kami-Osaki, Shinagawa-ku (3473 2901). Meguro station (Yamanote, Mita, Nanboku lines), east exit. **Open** by appointment only Mon-Wed, Fri, Sat.

Tokyo Clinic Dental Office

Mori Bldg 32 2F, 3-4-30 Shiba-Koen, Minato-ku (3431 4225). Kamiyacho station (Hibiya line), exit 1 or Akabanebashi station (Oedo line), Tokyo Tower exit. **Open** by appointment only Mon-Sat. Japanese insurance accepted.

Doctors

Both have English-speaking staff. Also consider the **Tokyo Medical Clinic & Surgical Clinic** (*see above*).

Tokyo Adventist Hospital

3-17-3 Amanuma, Suginami-ku (3392 6151/www.tokyoeisei.com). Ogikubo station (Chuo, Marunouchi lines), north exit. **Open** 8.30-11am Mon-Fri; by appointment afternoons Mon-Thur. No emergencies.

Tokyo British Clinic

Daikanyama Y Bldg 2F, 2-13-7 Ebisu-Nishi, Shibuya-ku (5458 6099). Ebisu station (Yamanote, Hibiya lines), west exit. **Open** 9am-5.30pm Mon-Fri; 9am-12.30pm Sat. Run by a British doctor, this clinic caters for most aspects of general practice including paediatrics. Round-the-clock cover is provided.

Opticians

See p183.

Pharmacies

See p191.

Helplines

The following helplines offer advice or information in English.

AIDS Hotline
0570 000 911. **Open** 24hrs daily.
Alcoholics Anonymous
3971 1471 (taped message)/ www.aatokyo.org.
HELP Asian Women's Shelter
3368 8855. **Open** 10am-4pm Mon-Fri; in Japanese and English.
Immigration Information Centre
5796 7112. **Open** 9am-5pm Mon-Fri.
Japan Help Line
0120 46 1997/http://jhelp.com.
Open 24hrs daily.
A non-profit-making worldwide assistance service. Among other services, it produces the Japan Help Line Card, which contains useful telephone numbers and essential information for non-Japanese speakers, as well as a numbered phrase list in English and Japanese for use in emergencies.
Tokyo English Life Line (TELL)
5774 0992/www.telljp.com.
Open 9am-11pm daily.
Counselling and assistance service run by trained volunteers.

Tokyo Foreign Residents' Advisory Centre
5320 7744. **Open** 9.30am-noon, 1-4pm Mon-Fri.
Run by the Tokyo Metropolitan Government, this will help newcomers to adjust to Japanese life.

ID

It's most unlikely, but foreign visitors can, in theory, be arrested for not carrying ID (a passport) at all times. Long-term residents should carry their Alien Registration Card.

Internet & email

Many of Tokyo's venerable 24-hour manga (comic-book) coffee shops also offer cheap internet services, and are usually clustered around train stations; for the GeraGera chain, *see p169*.

The chain of cafés run by Yahoo! Japan in collaboration with Starbucks has been whittled down to a mere four branches, including one each at Narita and Haneda airports. For all locations, see http://café.yahoo.co.jp.

Internet cafés seem to open and close in the blink of an eye, so your best bet is to try a Kinkos, which has 24-hour locations all around the city. (www.kinkos.co.jp). For a list of internet cafés ordered by station, check out www.tcvb.or.jp/en/guide/09cafe.html.

Personal computers fitted with wireless LAN cards that meet the 802.11b wifi standard (such as Apple's Airport card) can access the internet in many locations around Tokyo. An up-to-date list of wireless hotspots in the city can be found at www.hotspot-locations.com.

Café de Pres

5-1-27 Minami-Azabu, Minato-ku (3488 0039/www.hiramitsu.co.jp). Hiroo station (Hibiya line), exit 3. **Open** 9.30am-midnight daily.
Order anything at this internet café in foreigner-friendly Hiroo to get an hour's free internet access.

Directory

Language

For information on Japanese language and pronunciation, and a list of useful words and phrases, *see p302*.

There are hundreds of schools in Tokyo running courses in Japanese. Most of these offer intensive studies for those who want to learn as quickly as possible or who need Japanese for work or school. They may offer longer courses too. Private schools tend to be expensive, so check out lessons run by your ward office. Ward lessons cost from ¥100 a month to ¥500 every two months – a bargain compared to ¥3,000 an hour for group lessons.

Arc Academy *1-9-1 Shibuya, Shibuya-ku (3409 0391/www.arc-academy.net/nihongo/Eindex.asp). Shibuya station (Yamanote, Ginza, Hanzomon lines), east exit.*
Offers a wide variety of courses.
Meguro Language Centre *NT Bldg 3F, 1-4-11 Meguro, Meguro-ku (3493 3727/www.mlcjapanese.co.jp). Meguro station (Yamanote, Mita, Nanboku lines), west exit.*
A wide range of courses, from private lessons to group lessons.
Temple University *2-8-12 Minami-Azabu, Minato-ku (0120 861 026/www.tuj.ac.jp). Shirokane-Takanawa station (Mita, Nanboku lines), exit 2; Azabu-Juban station (Nanboku, Oedo lines), exit 1.*
Temple University offers fairly cheap evening classes as part of its continuing education programme.

Legal advice

Legal Counselling Centre *Bar Association Bldg, 1-1-3 Kasumigaseki, Chiyoda-ku (3581 2255/www.niben.jp). Kasumigaseki station (Chiyoda line), exit C1; (Hibiya line), exit A1; (Marunouchi line), exit B1.* **Open** by appointment only 1-4pm.
Consultations in English (¥5,000 for first half hour, ¥2,500 for subsequent half hours). Free for the impoverished on Thursday afternoon. Topics cover a range of issues including crime, immigration and labour problems. Appointments are on a first come, first served basis.
Tokyo Human Rights Counselling Centre *Iidabashi Joint Government Bldg 6F, 1-9-20 Koraku, Bunkyo-ku*

(5689 0518). Iidabashi station (Chuo, Mita, Nanboku, Yurakucho lines), exit C2; (Oedo line), Suidobashi exit. **Open** 1.30-3.30pm Tue, Thur.
Free counselling in English by phone.

Libraries

Each ward has a central lending library with a limited number of English-language titles; you need an Alien Registration Card to borrow books. The following reference libraries have a healthy number of books in English. All close on national holidays.

British Council Library & Information Centre *1-2 Kagurazaka, Shinjuku-ku (3235 8031/www.uknow.or.jp). Iidabashi station (Chuo, Mita, Nanboku, Yurakucho lines), exits B2A, B3; (Oedo line), west exit.* **Open** 9am-9pm Mon-Fri; 9.30am-5.30pm Sat.
Information on the UK, plus internet access, and BBC World is always on. For ¥500 a day you can use all the facilities. Library loans for members only. Under-18s not admitted.
Japan Foundation Library *Ark Mori Bldg, West Wing 20F, 1-12-32 Akasaka, Minato-ku (5562 3527/www.jpf.go.jp/e/learn/library/libindex.html). Roppongi-Itchome station (Nanboku line), exit 3.* **Open** 10am-5pm Mon-Fri. Closed last Mon of mth.
Books, mags, reference material and doctoral works on all aspects of Japan. Specialises in humanities and social sciences, and also has translations of Japanese novels. Houses about 25,000 books and 300 magazine titles. Lending as well as reference. Under-18s not admitted.
JETRO Library *Ark Mori Bldg 6F, 1-12-32 Akasaka, Minato-ku (3582 1775/www.jetro.go.jp). Tameike-Sanno station (Ginza, Nanboku lines), exit 13.* **Open** 9am-5pm Mon-Fri. Closed 3rd Tue of mth.
Houses information about trade, the economy and investment for just about any country in the world. Lots of statistics as well as basic business directories. Under-18s not admitted.
National Diet Library *1-10-1 Nagatacho, Chiyoda-ku (3581 2331/www.ndl.go.jp). Nagatacho station (Hanzomon, Nanboku, Yurakucho lines), exits 2, 3.* **Open** 9.30am-5pm Mon-Fri. Closed occasional Mon.
Japan's main library, which has the largest number of foreign-language books and materials. Over two million books, 50,000 mags and 1,500 newspapers and periodicals. Under-20s not admitted.

Tokyo Metropolitan Central Library *5-7-13 Minami-Azabu, Minato-ku (3442 8451/www.library.metro.tokyo.jp). Hiroo station (Hibiya line), exit 1.* **Open** 1-8pm Mon; 9.30am-8pm Tue-Fri; 9.30am-5pm Sat, Sun.
This is the main library for the Tokyo government, with the largest collection of books about Tokyo. Over 150,000 titles in foreign languages. Under-16s not admitted.

Litter

Foreign visitors are often impressed by how clean Tokyo is in comparison to their home cities.

After the subway sarin gas attack in March 1995, most litter bins were removed from subway stations. JR stations, however, have bins near the exits. They are divided into three sections: cans, magazines and newspapers, and other rubbish. If you can't find a bin, take your rubbish home.

Domestic rubbish should be divided into four categories: burnable, unburnable, recyclable and large items. For more information, contact your local ward office.

Lost property

If you leave a bag or package somewhere, just go back: it will probably still be there. If you left it in a train station or other public area, go to the stationmaster's office or nearest *koban* (police box) and ask for English-language assistance. Items handed in at the station are logged in a book. You will have to sign in and show ID in order to receive your item. Alternatively, ring the general JR/police information numbers below. If you leave something in a taxi on the way to or from a hotel, try the hotel reception – taxi drivers often bring the lost item straight back.

JR (Yamanote line) *3423 0111*
English-speaking service.
Metropolitan Police *3501 0110*
English-speaking service.

Eidan subway *3834 5577*
Japanese only.
Narita Airport *0476 322 802*
Japanese only.
Toei subway & buses *3812 2011*
Japanese only.
Taxi *3648 0300.*
Japanese only.

Media

Newspapers

The Japanese are among the keenest newspaper readers in the world, with daily sales of over 70 million copies. *Yomiuri Shimbun* is the world's largest circulation newspaper, with a daily circulation of 16 million. For English readers the choice is limited to three newspapers: the *Daily Yomiuri*, the *Japan Times* and the *International Herald Tribune*, which incorporates the English version of the *Asahi Shimbun*. All cost ¥120-¥150 and are available at most central Tokyo station kiosks.

Daily Yomiuri
www.yomiuri.co.jp/index-e.htm.
Produces supplements together with other world newspapers including the *Independent* (Sunday) and the *Washington Post* (Friday). There's a what's-on supplement on Thursdays.
International Herald Tribune/Asahi Shimbun
www.asahi.com/english.
Launched in April 2001 as a joint venture between the *International Herald Tribune* and the *Asahi Shimbun*, and the only English-language paper in Tokyo to read like English is its first language.
Japan Times
www.japantimes.co.jp.
The longest-established English-language newspaper in Japan. Consists mainly of agency reports. Heavy on business. Motto 'All the news without fear or favour' could read 'All the news without fear or flavour'.
Nikkei Weekly
www.nni.nikkei.co.jp.
The Japanese *Financial Times* equivalent produces this weekly digest from the world of finance.

Free reads

EL Magazine
www.elmagazine.com.
'Entertainment and lifestyle' just means movie and music reviews.

Metropolis
www.metropolis.japantoday.com.
Formerly known as *Tokyo Classified*, this is Tokyo's biggest and best free weekly magazine, with listings and adverts galore. It's distributed at foreigner-friendly bars, clubs, shops and hotels every Friday.
Tokyo Notice Board
www.tokyonoticeboard.co.jp.
The most visible rival to *Metropolis*, but smaller and less slick.
Tokyo Weekender
www.weekender.co.jp.
Can be tricky to find. Contains bland, expat community gossip and news.
Japanzine
www.japan-zine.com.
This humorous magazine takes an irreverent look at some of the quirkier aspects of Japan life. It includes both Tokyo and Kansai listings, and is home to the popular cartoon 'Charisma Man'.

Magazines

If you read Japanese, there's a wealth of what's-on details in weekly publications such as *Pia* and *Tokyo Walker* (both ¥320). If not, there's Tokyo's only paid-for English-language listings monthly, *Tokyo Journal* (www.tokyo.to).

Radio

InterFM
www.interfm.co.jp.
Broadcasting on 76.1MHz, this is Tokyo's main bilingual station. Plays rock and pop.
NHK Radio Japan
www.nhk.or.jp/rj.
News on the internet.

Television

Japanese state broadcaster NHK runs two commercial-free terrestrial channels – NHK General (channel 1) and NHK Educational (channel 3) – and two satellite channels, BS1 and BS2. Tokyo's five other terrestrial channels – Nihon TV (channel 4), Tokyo Broadcasting System (channel 6), Fuji Television (channel 8), Television Asahi (channel 10) and TV Tokyo (channel 12) – show a constant stream of unimaginative pap, relieved occasionally by a worthwhile documentary or drama series.

NHK General news at 7pm and 9pm daily is broadcast simultaneously in both English and Japanese: to access the English version you'll need a bilingual TV set (most big hotels have them). Many non-Japanese TV series and films are also broadcast bilingually.

Japan's main satellite broadcaster is Rupert Murdoch's SkyPerfect! TV, which offers a host of familiar channels, including CNN, BBC World and Sky Sports.

Money

The yen is not divided into smaller units and comes in denominations of ¥1, ¥5, ¥10, ¥50, ¥100 and ¥500 (coins) and ¥1,000, ¥2,000, ¥5,000 and ¥10,000 (notes). The ¥2,000 note is rarely seen. New ¥1,000, ¥5,000 and ¥10,000 notes were issued in November 2004; the old notes will remain in circulation for about two years.

Prices on display must include five per cent sales tax.

ATMs & credit cards

Japan is still a cash-based society, and restaurants and bars may refuse credit cards. Larger shops, restaurants and hotels accept major cards, but you should always keep some cash on you.

ATMs are rarely open after 7pm and often close at 5pm on Saturdays. Many banks charge for withdrawals made after 6pm, and on Sundays and public holidays. Still, there is a growing number of 24-hour ATMs in Tokyo, mostly round major train stations. All ATMs have logos showing which cards are accepted, but most will not take foreign-issued cards. Among the banks, **Citibank** is the most useful, with 24-hour ATMs all over Tokyo (information 0120 50 4189). However, as we went to press there were rumours that a bank takeover might force the closure of its ATMs. **Mitsui-Sumitomo Bank** (head office 3282 5111) has a good reputation for dealing with foreigners.

This means that the numerous **post offices** (*see p295*) are probably your best bet: their ATMs allow you to withdraw cash by foreign Visa, Plus, MasterCard, Eurocard, Maestro, Cirrus, American Express, Diners and JCB cards, and have instructions in English. But they may not be open 24 hours a day.

The ATMs at Narita Airport only work during banking hours. Ensure you have some Japanese cash if arriving early in the morning or late at night.

To report lost or stolen credit cards, dial one of these 24-hour freephone numbers:

American Express *0120 020 120* English message follows Japanese. **Diners Club** *0120 074 024* **MasterCard** *00531 11 3886* **Visa** *00531 44 0022*

Banks

Banks are open 9am to 3pm Monday to Friday. Do not go to a bank if you're in a hurry – queues are long, especially on Fridays, and you have to take a number and wait.

Opening a bank account is quite easy if you have an Alien Registration Card. For savings accounts you will be issued a book and card. Getting a card can take up to two weeks; it's usually delivered to your home and you must be there to sign for it. Or ask the bank to tell you when it arrives, and pick it up. You can also open an account at a post office and withdraw money from any other post office branch.

Changing money

You can cash travellers' cheques or change foreign currency at any authorised foreign exchange bank (look for the signs). If you want to exchange money outside regular banking hours, some large hotels change travellers' cheques and currency, as do large department stores, which are open until about 8pm. Narita Airport has several bureaux de change staffed by English-speakers, open daily from 7am to 10pm.

Natural hazards

The Great Kanto Earthquake of 1923 destroyed much of Tokyo, and the chances of a future disaster remain high. Despite precautions, the 'Big One' could cause terrible damage. The Kobe earthquake of 1995 left over 6,000 dead and the tremor in Niigata in October 2004 killed 30 and left many thousands homeless.

Every year on 1 September, the anniversary of the 1923 quake, Tokyo practises how to cope with a major earthquake. Residents are advised to keep a small bag handy, containing essentials such as a bottle of water, preserved foodstuffs, some cash and a torch. If you are caught up, try to shut off any stoves and gas mains, secure an exit, and look for a table or similar to protect you.

Opening hours

Department stores and larger shops in Tokyo are open daily from 10am (sometimes earlier, sometimes later) to around 8pm or 9pm. Smaller shops are open the same hours six days a week. Monday and Wednesday are the commonest closing days; Sunday is a normal shopping day. Convenience stores offer 24-hour shopping at slightly higher prices than supermarkets, and are found all over the city. The major chains are 7-Eleven, AM-PM, Family Mart and Lawson's.

Most restaurants open at around 11am and close around 11pm, though some bars and *izakaya* are open till 5am. Some of them don't close until the last customer has gone.

Banks are open 9am to 3pm Monday to Friday. Main post offices are open 9am to 7pm weekdays, and often on Saturdays (usually 9am-3pm) or even Sundays; smaller post offices close at 5pm Monday to Friday and at weekends.

Office hours are 9am to 5pm. On national holidays, many places keep Sunday hours (closing earlier), but most are closed on 1 and 2 January.

Police

For a foreign visitor or resident, the most frequent contact with the police is usually through the *koban* – the police boxes dotted around every neighbourhood (marked by two red lights with a gold seal in-between), from which officers patrol the area by car and bicycle. Each major *koban* has four officers on duty at any one time to deal with enquiries and complaints from the public. It's estimated that the *koban* outside Shibuya station's Hachiko exit receives around 3,000 visitors a day.

Common causes of friction between Japanese police and foreign nationals are being drunk and aggressive, having noisy parties at home, traffic violations and bicycle theft (if you buy a bike, take careful note of the registration number – you'll need it).

If you are stopped by police officers in Tokyo, present your passport or Alien Registration Card (you're legally required to carry it with you at all times). If detained at a police station, ask to speak to someone from your embassy. Claim you speak no Japanese, even if you do, and don't sign anything you can't read.

To contact the Tokyo police in non-emergencies, call **3501 0110** (English service). For emergencies, *see p290*.

Postal services

The postal system is run by **Japan Post** (www.post. japanpost.jp). Sending a postcard overseas costs ¥70; aerograms cost ¥90; letters under 25g cost ¥90 (Asian countries), ¥110 (Europe, North America, Oceania) or ¥130 (Africa, South America). Post boxes are red; the slot on the left is for domestic mail, the one on the right is for other mail. When writing addresses, English script is acceptable, as long as it's clearly written. Larger department stores can arrange postage if you buy major items. You can purchase stamps at convenience stores. For couriers, *see p288*.

Postal Services Information Line

3560 1139. **Open** 9.30am-4.30pm Mon-Fri. Information in English.

Post offices

Post offices (*yubin-kyoku*) – indicated by a red and white sign like a letter 'T' with a line over it – are plentiful. Local post offices open from 9am to 5pm Monday to Friday, and are closed at weekends and on public holidays. Larger post offices close at 7pm on weekdays, and may open on Saturdays (usually 9am-3pm) or even Sundays. Post office ATMs accept foreign bank and credit cards.

Poste restante

Poste restante is available at the following post offices; mail is held for up to 30 days. You'll need to show your passport to collect mail.

International Post Office

2-3-3 Otemachi, Chiyoda-ku, Tokyo 100-0004 (3241 4891/ www.yuubinkyoku.com). Otemachi station (Chiyoda, Hanzomon, Mita, Marunouchi, Tozai lines), exit A2. **Open** 9am-7pm Mon-Fri; 9am-5pm Sat; 9am-noon Sun.

A 24-hour service is available at a counter to the rear of the main building.

Tokyo Central Post Office

2-7-2 Marunouchi, Chiyoda-ku, Tokyo 100 (3284 9540/ www.yuubinkyoku.com). Tokyo station (Yamanote, Marunouchi lines), South Marunouchi exit. **Open** 8am-8pm Mon-Fri; 8am-5pm Sat; 9am-12.30pm Sun.

Religion

The *Religion Yearbook* issued by the Agency for Cultural Affairs suggests that 208 million Japanese are members of religious organisations – and that's almost twice the population of the country. It's not unusual for a family to celebrate birth with Shinto rites, tie the knot with a Christian marriage, and pay last respects at a Buddhist ceremony. Freedom of worship is a constitutional right.

For more information on Japan's two major religions, Shinto and Buddhism, and on visiting religious sites, *see p86* **Points of faith**.

Safety

Japan is one of the safest countries for foreign visitors. Theft is still amazingly rare, so it's not unusual to wander around with the equivalent of hundreds of pounds on you without giving it a second thought. Of course, crime does occur from time to time and it's best to take the usual precautions to keep money and valuables safe.

There are certain areas, such as Roppongi or Shinjuku's Kabuki-cho, as well as airports and crowded trains, where you should be particularly wary.

Smoking

Around 40 per cent of the adult population in Japan smoke, more than in any other similarly industrialised nation,

and cigarettes are relatively cheap, at around ¥280 per packet, and readily available from vending machines and convenience stores. Smoking is common in restaurants and cafés, although a growing number of venues have started to offer no-smoking areas; very few restaurants are entirely smoke-free. In October 2002 central Tokyo's Chiyoda-ku became the first area in Japan to ban smoking on the streets, because cigarettes posed a danger to clothes and babies' heads in the area. Smoking is banned on the platforms of all private train lines in Tokyo, although JR station platforms still have smoking areas.

Telephones

The virtual monopoly enjoyed by **NTT** (Nippon Telegraph & Telephone) on domestic telephone services was broken in 2001 with the introduction of the Myline system, which allows customers to choose phone service providers for local and long-distance calls. If you have your own phone line in Tokyo, call the **Myline Information Centre** (0120 000 406, www.myline.org) to register your choice of provider (English-speaking operators are available).

Repair Service *113.*
Moving & Relocating *116.*

Dialling & codes

The country code for Japan is 81. The area code for Tokyo is 03. Throughout this guide, we have omitted the 03 from the beginning of Tokyo telephone numbers, as you don't need to dial it when calling from within the city. If you're phoning from outside the city, you need to use the area code. If you're phoning from outside Japan, dial the international access code plus 81 plus 3, followed by the main eight-digit number.

Numbers that start with 0120 are **freephone** (receiver-paid or toll-free).

International calls

Different companies provide international call services, and charge roughly the same rates. Dial 001 (KDDI), 0041 (Japan Telecom), 0033 (NTT Communications) or 0061 (Cable & Wireless IDC), followed by your country's international code, area code (minus any initial zero) and the phone number. The cheapest time to call is between 11pm and 8am, when an off-peak discount of 40 per cent applies.

To use a public phone you need to buy a prepaid card or have a lot of change (some old phones refuse all prepaid cards). Find a booth with 'ISDN' or 'International' on the side – usually a green or grey phone. Blue 'credit phones' allow you to make calls using your credit card. Instructions should be given in English as well as Japanese.

If you set up the 'home country direct' service before leaving home, you can dial from most public phones and charge it to your home bill.

The international code for the UK is 44; 1 for the US and Canada; 353 for the Irish Republic; 61 for Australia; 64 for New Zealand; and 27 for South Africa.

Public phones

NTT still controls nearly all public phones in Tokyo. These are widely available, found in all stations, department stores and on the street, but different varieties will keep most visitors concentrating.

Green phones take flexible phone cards and ¥10 and ¥100 coins, but don't always allow international calls; grey phones are the same, but usually allow international calls; grey and orange phones only take

IC cards (snap off the corner before use) and coins, but you can always make international calls; the blue credit phones require a credit card to make international calls and are hard to find. The old pink phones, sometimes the only option even in touristy towns, only take ¥10 coins and cannot make international calls.

Domestic calls cost ¥10 for the first three minutes, ¥10 for every subsequent minute.

Prepaid phone cards

Before the advent of mobile phones, everyone used these in the ubiquitous green phones, and they are still useful if you're not getting a mobile. Several kinds of international phone card can be bought in Tokyo, and you can often find promotions like *Metropolis*.

KDDI (0077 7 111 – no English, www.kddi.com/english) produces a 'Super World' prepaid card for international phone calls, sold at most major convenience stores. They come in four values (¥1,000, ¥3,000, ¥5,000 and ¥7,000) and can be used with any push-button phone.

NTT East (0120 364 463 – no English, www.ntt-east.co.jp/ptd_e/index.html) produces two cards, one mainly for the domestic market, the other – an IC card – for both national and international calls. Both cards cost ¥1,000 and are available from vending machines in some phoneboxes and convenience stores.

Mobile phones

Mobile phones (*keitai denwa*) are a way of life in Tokyo. Japanese mobiles can be used to take photos, surf the net, send email, photos and movies. And you can talk on them too.

While it's possible to take a Japanese mobile phone abroad and use it, it's not as simple

the other way around. There are three major mobile phone networks in Japan – the biggest, **DoCoMo** (0120 005 250, www.nttdocomo.com; from NTT), plus **J-Phone** (0088 21 2000, ww.vodafone.jp; owned by Vodafone) and **Au** (from Tu-Ka; Tu-Ka Cellular Tokai Customer Centre 0077 788 151). They all use technologies incompatible with each other and with phones from overseas. Information and maintenance is covered by the store selling the phone.

Residents can buy a phone on a long-term contract, but visitors will have to either buy a prepaid phone or rent one. For both you'll need to produce your address while staying in Japan (a hotel will be fine). Check in advance whether your phone has bilingual menus and voicemail.

Buying a contract phone

Go to one of the outlets operated by the mobile phone companies or an electronics store. You will have to show your Alien Registration Card and passport. Applications will not be accepted if your visa is due to expire within 90 days.

Buying a prepaid phone

You can purchase a phone for ¥5,000 to ¥10,000 and a prepaid card for ¥3,000 or ¥5,000 from any phone or electronics store. You will need to bring your passport.

Renting a phone

Smart hotels will often rent phones to guests, or you can do it yourself at a rental outlet or at Narita Airport.

DoCoMo Mova Rental Centre
Shin-Otemachi Bldg 1F, 2-2-21 Otemachi (freephone 0120 680 100/ 3243 6801/www.docomosentu.co.jp/ Web/english). Tokyo station (Yamanote, Marunouchi lines), North exit. **Open** 10am-7pm Mon-Fri; 10am-5pm Sat. Rates start at ¥10,500/wk plus ¥60/min domestic calls.

Vodafone Global Rental *5114 8420/www.vodafone-rental.jp.* Has counters in the departure and arrival halls of terminals 1 and 2 at Narita, open 7am-9pm daily. Rates start at ¥535/day plus ¥105/min for domestic calls plus insurance.

Telephone directories

Unless you're fluent, using a Japanese phonebook is out of the question. NTT publishes an English-language version, 'Town Page', available free from **English Townpage Centre** (0120 460 815) or at http://english.itp.ne.jp.

Useful numbers

Domestic operator **100**; domestic directory enquiries **104**; international directory enquiries **0051**. These numbers are non-English-speaking. The following numbers are for information and maintenance for land lines:

KDDI Information service
0057.
Japan Telecom
0088 41/www.japan-telecom.co.jp/ english.
NTT Communications
0120 506 506/www.ntt.com.
English information follows the Japanese.

Telegrams

Domestic telegrams – 115 (in Japanese). International telegrams – 005 3519 or freephone 0120 445 124.

Time

Japan is nine hours ahead of Greenwich Mean Time (GMT). Daylight Saving Time is not used, but is a recurring topic.

Tipping

Tipping is not expected in Japan and people will often be embarrassed if you try. If you leave money at a restaurant, for example, a member of staff may try to return it. At smart establishments, a service charge is often included.

Toilets

Public toilets can be found in and around most stations, often near the entrance or just outside the exit. Station toilets usually offer Japanese-style commodes where you squat facing the back wall.

Many public toilets have no toilet paper. Buy it from machines or take it (for free) from the workers handing out tissues on the street. The packets are ads for local companies and services.

Western-style toilets are the norm in large shops. In some women's toilets there may be a small box with a button: pushing it produces the sound of flushing. Many Japanese women flush the toilet to cover the sounds they make, and the fake flush was designed to save water.

If you're staying in a Japanese home or good hotel, you may find that your toilet looks like the command seat on the Starship Enterprise. Controls to the right of the seat operate its heating and in-built bidet. Don't push the buttons unless you like surprises – and if surprised, do *not* jump up!

Tourist information

The **Japan National Tourist Organisation (JNTO)** is the national English-language tourist service for visitors coming to Japan. It has various offices abroad, plus three **Tourist Information Centres** (TIC) in Tokyo – two at Narita Airport and one next to Yurakucho station. Its website, **www.jnto.go.jp**, is packed with useful info.

There's also the **Tokyo Convention & Visitors Bureau (TCVB)**, which has lots of handy area guides at its office near the Imperial Palace, and an informative website, **www.tcvb.or.jp**. The **Tokyo Tourist Information Centre** is run by the Tokyo Metropolitan Government in its HQ building in Shinjuku.

Tokyo TIC

Tokyo Kotsu Kaikan 10F, 2-10-1 Yurakucho, Chiyoda-ku (3201 3331). Yurakucho station (Yamanote line), Kyobashi exit; (Yurakucho line), exit A8. **Open** 9am-5pm daily. **Map** p60. Friendly, multilingual staff and a wealth of information: there are maps, event booklets, books on Japanese customs, even NTT English phonebooks, plus a useful budget hotel booking service via the Welcome Inn Reservation Centre (*see p35*). There's nothing on the outside of the building to indicate the tourist office is here – just take the lift to the tenth floor, where there is a sign. **Other locations:** *Arrival floor, Terminal 1, Narita Airport (0476 30 3383); Arrival floor, Terminal 2, Narita Airport (0476 34 6251).* **Open** 8am-8pm daily.

TCVB Information Centre

Tokyo Chamber of Commerce & Industry Bldg 1F, 3-2-2 Marunouchi, Chiyoda-ku (3287 7024). **Open** 10am-5pm Mon-Fri; 10am-4pm Sat, Sun. **Map** p66.

Tokyo Tourist Information Centre

Tokyo Metropolitan Government Bldg No.1 1F, 2-8-1 Nishi-Shinjuku, Shinjuku-ku (5321 3077/www.kanko. metro.tokyo.jp/public/center.html). Tochomae station (Oedo line), exit 4. **Open** 9.30am-6.30pm daily. **Map** p73.
If you're visiting the observation deck in the Tokyo Metropolitan Government Building, pop into this ground-floor office. **Other locations:** 1-60 Ueno-Koen, Taito-ku (3836 3471). In front of the Keisei Ueno station ticket gate 60.

JNTO (UK)

Heathcoat House, 20 Savile Row, London W1S 3PR (020 7734 9638/fax 020 7734 4290/ www.seejapan.co.uk). **Open** 9.30am-5.30pm daily.
Contact for free maps, guides and brochures – but not hotel booking. Check the website for details of other overseas offices.

Odakyu Sightseeing Service Centre

Ground-floor concourse, Shinjuku station (5321 7887). **Open** 8am-6pm daily. **Map** p73.
Staff speak English, Chinese and Korean.

Japan Travel Phone

3201 3331. **Open** 9am-5pm daily.
A free nationwide service for those in need of English-language assistance and travel information on places outside Tokyo and Kyoto.

Directory

Visas

Japan has general visa-exemption arrangements with the UK, the USA, Canada and the Republic of Ireland, and their citizens may stay in Japan for up to 90 days. Japan also has working holiday visa arrangements with Australia, Canada, New Zealand and the UK for people aged 18 to 30. For information, go to the **Ministry of Foreign Affairs** (www.mofa.go.jp/ j_info/visit).

The following types of visa are available:

Tourist visa
A 'short-term-stay' visa, good for those not intending to work in Japan.
Working visa
It's illegal to work in Japan without a visa. If you arrive as a tourist and work, your company has to sponsor you for a work visa. You generally must then go abroad to make the application (South Korea is the cheapest option). If you plan to stay in Japan for more than 90 days, you need an Alien Registration Card. For this, you need to provide two passport-sized photographs, a passport, an address and a signature.

Immigration Information Centre

Tokyo Regional Immigration Bureau, 5-5-30 Konan, Minato-ku (5796 7112/www.moj.go.jp/ENGLISH/IB/ib-18.html). Shinagawa station (Yamanote line), east exit then bus (follow signs). **Open** 9am-noon, 1-4pm Mon-Fri.

Weights & measures

Japan uses the metric system – although some room sizes are measured by how many tatami (straw mats) they can hold.

When to go

Spring begins with winds and cherry blossom viewing. The rainy season for Honshu (the main island) begins in June. This is followed by the hot, humid days of summer. Autumn sees the changing of the leaves, while winter brings clear skies, cold days and the occasional snowstorm. Temperatures range from around 3°C (37°F) in January to 35°C (95°F) in July/August.

Summer in Tokyo can be unbearable for those not used to humidity. Carry a fan, some water and a wet cotton cloth with you. Fans are often handed out in the street for advertising campaigns. Spring (March to May) and autumn (September to November) are the nicest times to visit Tokyo.

The two big holiday periods, when much of Tokyo shuts down, are **Golden Week** (29 April-5 May) and the **New Year** (28 Dec-4 Jan). For annual festivals, *see pp196-201*.

Public holidays

Japan has 14 public holidays: New Year's Day (Ganjitsu) **1 January**; Coming of Age Day (Seijin no Hi) **second Monday in January**; National Foundation Day (Kenkoku Kinen no Hi) **11 February**; Vernal Equinox Day (Shumbun no Hi) **around 21 March**; Greenery Day (Midori no Hi) **29 April**; Constitution Day (Kempo Kinenbi) **3 May**; Children's Day (Kodomo no Hi) **5 May**; Marine Day (Umi no Hi) **20 July**; Respect for the Aged Day (Keiro no Hi) **15 September**; Autumnal Equinox Day (Shubun no Hi) **around 23 September**; Sports Day (Taiiku no Hi) **second Monday in October**; Culture Day (Bunka no Hi) **3 November**; Labour Thanksgiving Day (Kinro Kansha no Hi) **23 November**; Emperor's Birthday (Tenno Tanjobi) **23 December**.

Saturday remains an official workday, but holidays falling on a Sunday shift to Monday. If both 3 May and 5 May fall on weekdays, then 4 May also becomes a holiday.

Women travellers

The crime rate in Japan is very low compared to that in many countries. Women should exercise standard precautions, but the risk of rape or assault is not high, and women can ride the subways at night or wander the streets with little concern. A woman alone might be harassed by staggering, drunken salarymen, but they are rarely serious; ignoring them generally does the trick.

This said, Tokyo is not immune from urban dangers. You should not let fear spoil your holiday, but do exercise caution at night, particularly in areas such as Roppongi and Shinjuku's Kabuki-cho.

A less serious type of assault occurs every day on packed rush-hour trains, where women are sometimes groped (or worse). Many Japanese women ignore the offence, hesitant to draw attention to themselves, but shouting in English can be effective. For issues affecting Western women, see *p24* **Girl talk**.

Average climate

	Temp (˚C/˚F)	Rainfall (mm/in)	Sunshine (hrs per day)
Jan	6/42.8	50/2	6
Feb	7/44.6	60/2.4	5.7
Mar	9/48.2	100/3.9	5.1
Apr	14/57.2	130/5.1	5.5
May	18/64.4	135/5.3	5.8
June	21/69.8	165/6.5	4.0
July	26/78.8	160/6.3	4.7
Aug	28/82.4	155/6.1	5.7
Sept	23/73.4	200/7.9	3.8
Oct	18/64.4	165/6.5	4.2
Nov	13/55.4	90/3.5	4.7
Dec	7/44.6	40/1.6	5.5

Directory

Further Reference

Books

Fiction

Abe, Kobe *The Woman in the Dunes*
Weird classic about a lost village of sand.
Birnbaum, Alfred (ed) *Monkey Brain Sushi*
Decent selection of 'younger' Japanese writers.
Erickson, Steve *The Sea Came in at Midnight*
American novel set partly in a Tokyo 'memory hotel'.
Howell, Brian *Head of a Girl & others*
Elegantly weird short story by expat English writer based close to Tokyo.
Kawabata, Yasuwari *Snow Country*
Japan's first Nobel prize-winner for literature.
Mishima, Yukio *Confessions of a Mask & others*
Japan's most famous novelist, 20 years after his suicide.
Mitchell, David *Ghostwritten & Number9Dream*
Ambitious novels by expat UK writer teaching English in Hiroshima.
Murakami, Haruki *Norwegian Wood & others*
Most of Murakami's many books are set in Tokyo.
Murakami, Ryu *Coin Locker Babies & others*
Hip modern novelist, unrelated to Haruki.
Oe, Kenzoburo *A Personal Matter & others*
Japan's second winner of the Nobel prize.
Yoshimoto, Banana *Kitchen & others*
Modern writer who's made a splash in the west.

Non-fiction

Birchall, Jonathan *Ultra Nippon*
British journo follows Japanese soccer team and fans, for a year.
Bird, Isabella *Unbeaten Tracks in Japan*
Amazing memoirs of intrepid Victorian explorer.
Bix, Herbert P *Hirohito and the Making of Modern Japan*
Post-war Japan under the wartime Emperor.
Bornoff, Nicholas *Pink Samurai: Love, Marriage and Sex in Contemporary Japan*
All you ever wanted to know about the subjects, but were perhaps too confused to ask.

Cavaye, Ronald, Griffith, Paul & Senda, Akihiko *The World of the Japanese Stage*
All you need to know about traditional Japanese performing arts.
Chang, Iris *The Rape of Nanking: The Forgotten Holocaust of World War II*
The Japanese Imperial Army's atrocities in all their horror.
Dower, John W *Embracing Defeat: Japan in the Wake of World War II*
Award-winning account of the American-led post-war reconstruction of Japan.
Ferguson, Will *Hokkaido Highway Blues*
One man's manic mission to hitchhike through Japan following the progress of the cherry blossom.
Galbraith, Stuart *Giant Monsters Are Attacking Tokyo: Incredible World of Japanese Fantasy Films*
The ultimate guide to the weird and wacky world of the city-stomping giants of Japanese cinema.
Gravett, Paul *Manga: Sixty Years of Japanese Comics*
Beautifully illustrated, large-format survey of the history of the art form that's taking over the world.
Harper, Philip *The Insider's Guide to Sake*
Readable introduction to Japan's national libation.
Kaplan, David & Marshall, Andrew *The Cult At The End of The World*
Terrifying story of Aum and the subway gas attacks.
Kaplan, David & Dubro, Alec *Yakuza: Japan's Criminal Underworld*
Inside look at the gangs who control Japan's underworld.
Kawakami, Kenji & Don Papia *101 Unuseless Japanese Inventions: The Art of Chindogu*
Everything you never knew you needed.
Kennedy, Rick *Little Adventures in Tokyo*
Entertaining trips through the off-beat side of the city.
Martin, John H & Phyllis G *Tokyo: A Cultural Guide to Japan's Capital City*
Enjoyable ramble through Tokyo with two amiable authors.
Okakura, Kazuko *The Book of Tea*
Tea as the answer to life, the universe and everything. Which, as every Japanese knows, it is.
Ototake, Hirotada *No One's Perfect*
True story of a boy who overcame handicaps and prejudice. A record-breaking bestseller.

Pompian, Susan *Tokyo For Free*
Good but dated guide to help out the skinflints.
Richie, Donald *Public People, Private People and Tokyo: A View of the City*
Acclaimed writer and long-time Japan resident on the Japanese and their capital.
Richie, Donald *Tokyo*
That man again, with a beautifully produced work from Reaktion Books.
Satterwhite, Robb *What's What in Japanese Restaurants*
An invaluable guide to navigating the menu maze.
Schilling, Mark *Encyclopedia of Japanese Pop Culture*
From karaoke to Hello Kitty, ramen to Doraemon.
Schilling, Mark *The Yakuza Movie Book : A Guide to Japanese Gangster Films*
A testament to the enduring appeal of the gangster in Japanese movies.
Schlesinger, Jacob M *Shadow Shoguns: The Rise and Fall of Japan's Postwar Political Machine*
Pretty good, non-academic read.
Schodt, Fredrick L *Dreamland Japan: Writings on Modern Manga*
Leading Western authority on Japan's publishing phenomenon.
Schreiber, Mark *Tokyo Confidential: Titillating Tales from Japan's Wild Weeklies*
Japan laid bare through translated magazine stories.
Seidensticker, Edward *Tokyo Rising & Low City, High City*
Eminently readable histories of the city.
Sharnoff, Lora *Grand Sumo*
Exhaustive account, if a little on the dry side.
Tajima, Noriyuki *Tokyo: Guide to Recent Architecture*
Pocket-sized guide with outstanding pictures.
Tajima, Noriyuki & Powell, Catherine *Tokyo: Labyrinth City*
LP-sized guide to more recent projects.
Takemoto, Tadao & Ohara, Yasuo *The Alleged 'Nanking Massacre': Japan's Rebuttal to China's Forged Claims*
The right-wing Japanese take on the Imperial Army's actions in China.
Twigger, Robert *Angry White Pyjamas*
Scrawny Oxford poet trains with Japanese riot police.
Walters, Gary *Day Walks Near Tokyo & More Day Walks Near Tokyo*
No surprises here: detailed routes for walkers wanting to escape the city's crowds.

Whiting, Robert *You Gotta Have Wa*
US baseball stars + Japan = culture clash. The template for many sports books written since.
Whiting, Robert *Tokyo Underworld: The Fast Life and Times of an American Gangster in Japan*
An enthralling story of underworld life in the bowels of modern Japan.

Language

Three A Network/Minna no Nihongo Shokyuu
Book 1 for beginners, 2 for pre-intermediate.
Integrated Approach to Intermediate Japanese
Well balanced in grammar, reading and conversation.
A Dictionary of Basic Japanese Grammar
Standard book from the *Japan Times*.
The Modern Reader's Japanese-English Dictionary
Known affectionately as Nelson, this is the definitive tool for students of the written language.

Maps & guides

Shobunsha Tokyo Metropolitan Atlas
Negotiate those tricky addresses with confidence.
Japan As It Is
Eccentric explanations of all things Japanese.
Asahi Shinbun's Japan Almanac
The ultimate book of lists, published annually.

Films

Akira
(Otomo Katsuhiro, 1988)
The film that started the West's anime craze. Freewheeling youth gangs try to stay alive in Neo-Tokyo.
Audition
(Takashi Miike, 1999)
A lonely widower, a beautiful actress: another Japanese shocker.
Diary of a Shinjuku Thief
(Oshima Nagisa, 1968)
A picaresque trip through 1960s Tokyo with a master director.
The Eel
(Imamura Shohei, 1996)
Yakusho Koji in a bizarre tale of love in the aftermath of murder.
Gamera 3
(Shusuke Kaneko, 1999)
Countless Tokyo dwellers' dreams are realised when a turbo-powered turtle demolishes Shibuya.
Ghost in the Shell
(Mamoru Oshii, 1995)
Complex, animated look at a future society where computers house human minds – and vice versa.

Godzilla, King of the Monsters
(Honda Inoshiro, 1954)
The big green guy makes his debut following an atomic accident, and smashes up Ginza. Subtext: Japan recovers from the blast of Hiroshima.
Hana-Bi
(Kitano Takeshi, 1997)
Kitano's best film won him a Venice prize, but in his native country he is still better known as a TV comedian.
House of Bamboo
(Samuel Fuller, 1955)
A gang led by an American pulls off raids in Tokyo and Yokohama.
Lost in Translation
(Sofia Coppola, 2003)
Bill Murray and Scarlett Johansson reach across the generations to form an unusual bond. Shot in and around Shinjuku and Shibuya.
Mononoke Hime (Princess Mononoke)
(Miyazaki Hiyao, 1997)
Record-breaking animated fable of man's butchery of the environment.
Rashomon
(Kurosawa Akira, 1951)
Influential tale of robbery from Japan's most famous film-maker.
The Ring
(Nakata Hideo, 1998)
Chilling urban ghost story, which has spawned a seemingly endless boom of psycho-horror movies.
Spirited Away
(Miyazaki Hayao, 2001)
Oscar-winning animated feature from the same studio as *Princess Mononoke*.
Tampopo
(Itami Juzo, 1986)
The idiosyncratic and sadly missed director's trawl through the Japanese obsession for food, with particular reference to ramen noodles.
Tokyo Pop
(Fran Rubel Kazui, 1988)
Aspiring artiste can't make it in New York, so heads off to Tokyo.
Tokyo Story
(Ozu Yasujiro, 1953)
Life in the metropolis and the generation gap it produces are explored in Ozu's masterpiece.
Une avenue à Tokyo
(Tsunekichi Shibata, 1898)
One of the earliest short films showing Meiji-era life in Japan.
Until the End of the World
(Wim Wenders, 1991)
William Hurt and Sam Neill lurk briefly around Shinjuku in Wenders's worthy but dull SF epic.
The Yakuza
(Sydney Pollack, 1974)
Robert Mitchum stars in writer Paul Schrader's tribute to the Japanese gangster movie.
You Only Live Twice
(Lewis Gilbert, 1967)
Connery's 007 comes to Tokyo. The New Otani Hotel doubles as the HQ of the malevolent Osato Corporation.

Music

Denki Groove *A*
A multi-faceted band that does pop, dance music and techno. One member, Takkyu Ishino, has toured in Europe as a DJ.
Dragon Ash *Morrow*
One of the most popular rap groups in Japan.
Hajime Chitose *Konomachi*
Born on Amami Oshima island. She sings poppy versions of traditional local songs in a unique warble.
Hamasaki Ayumi *A Ballads*
Top-selling female vocalist in Japan.
Misia *Misia Greatest Hits*
The Japanese queen of ballads.
Quruli *The World is Mine*
One of Japan's most talented bands.
Rovo *Flage*
Heavy, progressive rock, with pronounced jazz influence. Great live.
Sheena Ringo *Karuki Zamen Kuri no Hana*
Top female rocker.
SMAP *Sekaini Hitotsudake no Hana*
Only in Japan would a group of pop stars host their own cookery show.
Tokyo SKA Paradise Orchestra *A Quick Drunkard*
The name says it all: innovative music bases on SKA beats.
Yoshida Brothers *Soulful*
Two young *shamisen* players play traditional music to modern backing tracks.
Utada Hikaru *Colors*
Japan's answer to Sade.

Websites

Getting around

Hyperdia
www.hyperdia.com
Very useful interactive route planner. Enter Japanese cities or Tokyo stations and you will be given recommended routes between them.
Japan Travel Updates
www.jnto.go.jp
Site of the Japan National Tourist Organisation (JNTO), featuring a selection of useful travel information, tips, an online booking service and several sketchy reference city maps.
Japanese Guest Houses
www.japaneseguesthouses.com
Guide to traditional *ryokan* accommodation in Tokyo, Kyoto and other cities, with online booking.
NTT Townpage
http://english.itp.ne.jp
NTT's English-language phonebook.
Japan Guide
www.japan-guide.com
User-friendly online guide to travelling and living in Japan. Practical information covering the whole of the country.

Subway Navigator
www.subwaynavigator.com
Interactive subway route planner.
Enter your departure and destination
stations and it'll provide the route
as well as how much time to allow
for your journey.
Tokyo Life Navigator
www.ima-chan.co.jp/guide/index.htm
The place to start if you know
nothing about Tokyo and want
to swot up before you go get here.
Tokyo Subway Maps
www.tokyometro.jp/e
Up-to-date maps of the sometimes
baffling subway system.

Lesbian & gay

Cruising
*www.cruisingforsex.com/elsewhere
listings.html*
Long list of recommendations plus
good information on saunas.
Film Festival
www.tokyo-lgff.org
Home page of the queer film festival
staged annually in July.
Gay Net Japan
www.gnj.or.jp
English and Japanese forums,
classifieds and support groups.
Especially good for making short-
term friendships.
Utopia
www.utopia-asia.com/tipsjapn.htm
Useful, fun and informative page of
listings, links and more from this
Asian gay portal site.

Media

Daily Yomiuri
www.yomiuri.co.jp/index-e.htm
Tokyo's second English-language
newspaper's site (after the *Japan
Times*) is smaller but prettier.
Debito's Home Page
www.debito.org
Amusing and informative home
page of one Arudou Debito, a former
US citizen called David Aldwinkle
(Debito is David in Japanese), now
a Japanese national, crusader for
foreigners' rights and chronicler
of the curiosities of life in Japan.
i-mode
www.nttdocomo.com
Company home page linking to
information on the successful
Japanese mobile internet system.
Japan Inc
www.japaninc.com
Online version of the monthly
magazine tracking Japan's progress
in the so-called 'New Economy'.
Japan Times
www.japantimes.com
The most comprehensive news
about Japan available on the web.
The events section of the site is
only sporadically updated.

Japan Today
www.japantoday.com
Tabloid news about Japan.
Mainichi Daily News
http://mdn.mainichi.co.jp
Formerly a printed English-language
newspaper, now internet only. Great
for quirky stories.
Radio On
www.radioonactive.com
One of Tokyo's best alternative
radio stations, on the net.

Music & clubs

CIA (Club Information Agency)
www.ciajapan.com
Online version of this monthly
guide to club events in Tokyo has
listings and party pictures.
CyberJapan
www.cyberjapan.tv
Stylish youth-culture site has fashion
reports, news and streaming videos
from Tokyo clubland.
Smash
www.smash-jpn.com
Home page in Japanese and English
of one of Tokyo's biggest concert
promoters.
Tokyo Record Stores
www.bento.com/rekodoya.html
Where to get your hands on the
vinyl you've been hunting for, be
it techno, bebop, hip hop, ambient
house, Latin jazz, rockabilly, easy
listening, jungle or any other genre.

Offbeat

Engrish
www.engrish.com
Hundreds of prime examples of
the Japanese mutilation of the
English language. And surprisingly
amusing.
Quirky Japan
www.quirkyjapan.or.tv
Off-beat home page 'dedicated to
digression, kitsch, eccentricity and
originality' with alternative things
to do in Tokyo when you're 'tired
of shrines and temples'.
Ramen
www.worldramen.net
All the best ramen noodle
restaurants in the world, rated and
reviewed in English. Particularly
good Tokyo section.
Sake World
www.sake-world.com
Everything you ever wanted to
know about Japan's national tipple,
put together by sake columnist
John Gauntner.
Tokyo DV
www.tokyodv.com
One for broadband users, with full-
length films to download. Check
out the penis-worshipping festival.
Also features gossip from the world
of Japanese showbiz.

Portal sites

Insite
www.insite-tokyo.com
An upper-end portal that carries
lots of interesting articles on
controversial topics.
Japan Reference
www.jref.com
Extensive database with over 10,000
Japan-related links, plus tourism
and culture guides, and forums.
Tokyodoko
www.tokyodoko.com
Portal with an easy-to-use and
relatively in-depth reference
search facility.
Tokyo Pop
www.tokyopop.com
Cute site covering Japanese
pop culture from every angle.
Yahoo Japan
www.yahoo.co.jp
Yahoo is a big success in Japan:
the nation's most popular search
engine and information provider.
Zigzag Asia
www.zigzagasia.com
Has some original sections and
also includes an impressive list
of Japan-related sites.

What's on

Cool Girls Japan
www.coolgirlsjapan.biz
Fun page revealing the finer
details of fashion and fads
among Tokyo's hippest chicks.
Metropolis
www.metropolis.co.jp
Metropolis is the most reliably
updated English-language source
for what's-on listings for clubs,
concerts and art galleries, as
well as feature articles and
classified ads.
Ski Japan
www.skijapanguide.com
During the winter, it's more
than possible to head off to the
mountains for a day's skiing and
be back in Tokyo by nightfall.
This page tells you exactly how
to go about it.
Superfuture
www.superfuture.com
Hyper-stylish site mapping out
all the coolest shops and bars,
and the best restaurants.
Tokyo Food Page
www.bento.com
An awe-inspiring restaurant
guide to the city searchable by
cuisine, location or both. Also
has recipes, beer news and so
much more.
Tokyo Q
www.tokyoq.com
Tokyo's best-known online mag,
it's crammed with details on
restaurants, hotels, clubs, what's
on in Tokyo and more.

Directory

Getting by in Japanese

Pronunciation

Japanese pronunciation presents few problems for native English speakers, the most difficult trick to master being the doubling of vowels or consonants.

Vowels

a as in bad
e as in bed
i as in feet
o as in long
u as in look

Long vowels

aa as in father
ee as in fair
ii as in feet, but longer
oo as in fought
uu as in chute

Consonants

Consonants in Japanese are pronounced the same as in English, but are always hard ('g' as in 'girl', rather than 'gyrate', for example). The only exceptions are the 'l/r' sound, which is one sound in Japanese, and falls halfway between the English pronunciation of the two letters, and 'v', which is pronounced as a 'b'. When consonants are doubled, they are pronounced as such: a 'tt' as in 'matte' (wait) is pronounced more like the 't' sound in 'get to' than in 'getting'.

Reading the phrases

When reading the phrases below, remember to separate the syllables. Despite the funny way it looks in English, the common name Takeshita is pronounced Ta-ke-shit-ta. Similarly, made (until) is 'ma-de', not the English 'made', and shite (doing) is 'shi-te, rather than anything else. When a 'u' falls at the end of the word, it is barely spoken: 'desu' is closer to 'dess' than to 'de-su'.

Reading and writing

The Japanese writing system is fiendishly complicated and is the main deterrent to learning the language. Japanese uses two syllabaries (not alphabets, because the letters represent complete sounds), *hiragana* and *katakana*, in conjunction with *kanji*, characters imported from China many centuries ago. The average Japanese person will be able to read over 6,000 *kanji*. For all but the most determined visitor, learning to read before you go is out of the question. However, learning *katakana* is relatively simple and will yield quick results, since it is used mainly to spell out foreign words (many imported from English). For books on learning Japanese, *see page 299*.

USEFUL WORDS AND PHRASES

Numbers

1 *ichi*	9 *kyuu*
2 *ni*	10 *juu*
3 *san*	11 *juu-ichi*
4 *yon*	12 *juu-ni*
5 *go*	100 *hyaku*
6 *roku*	1,000 *sen*
7 *nana*	10,000 *man*
8 *hachi*	100,000 *juu-man*

Days

Monday *getsu-yoobi*
Tuesday *ka-yoobi*
Wednesday *sui-yoobi*
Thursday *moku-yoobi*
Friday *kin-yoobi*
Saturday *do-yoobi*
Sunday *nichi-yoobi*

Time

It's at ...o'clock ...*ji desu*
Excuse me, do you have the time?
sumimasen, ima nan-ji desu ka
noon/midnight *shougo/mayonaka*

Months

January *ichi-gatsu*
February *ni-gatsu*
March *san-gatsu*
April *shi-gatsu*
May *go-gatsu*
June *roku-gatsu*
July *shichi-gatsu*
August *hachi-gatsu*
September *ku-gatsu*
October *juu-gatsu*
November *juu-ichi-gatsu*
December *juu-ni-gatsu*

Dates

this morning/this afternoon/this evening
kesa/kyoo no gogo/konban
yesterday/today/tomorrow
kinoo/kyoo/ashita
last week/this week/next week
sen-shuu/kon-shuu/rai-shuu
the weekend *shuumatsu*

Basic expressions

Yes/no *hai/iie*
Okay *ookee*
Please (asking for a favour) *onegai shimasu*
Please (offering a favour) *doozo*
Thank you (very much) *(doomo) arigatoo*
Thank you (for having me) *osewa ni*
narimashita
Hello/hi *kon nichiwa*
Good morning *ohayoo gozaimasu*
Good afternoon *kon nichi wa*
Good evening *kon ban wa*
Goodnight *oyasumi nasai*
Goodbye *sayonara*
How are you? *ogenki desu ka*
Excuse me (getting attention) *sumimasen*
Excuse me (may I get past?)
shitsurei shimasu
Excuse me/sorry *gomen nasai*
Don't mention it/never mind
ki ni shinai de kudasai
It's okay *daiyoobu desu*
My name is…
(watashi no namae wa)… desu
What's your name?
o namae wa nan desu ka
Pleased to meet you *doozo yoroshiku*
Cheers! *kampai*

Communication

Do you speak English?
eigo o hanashi masu ka
I don't speak (much) Japanese
nihongo o (amari) hanashi masen
Could you speak more slowly?
yukkuri itte kudasai
Could you repeat that?
moo ichido itte kudasai
I understand *wakari mashita*
I don't understand *wakari masen*
Do you understand? *wakari masu ka?*
Where is it? *doko desu ka*
When is it? *itsu desu ka*
What is it? *nan desu ka*

Eating out

See also p155 **Menu Reader**.
bar *izakaya/nomiya*
canteen *shokudo*
coffee shop *kissaten*
noodle stall *ramen-ya*
restaurant (smart) *ryotei*

May I see the menu?
Menyuu onegai shimasu
Do you have an English menu?
eigo no menyuu wa arimasu ka
I'm a vegetarian
watashi wa bejitarian desu
Please can we have the bill?
okanjoo onegai shimasu

Hotels

Do you have a room? *heya wa arimasu ka?*
I'd like a single/double room *shinguru/*
daburu no heya o onegai shimasu
I'd like a room with…
…tsuki no heya o onegai shimasu
a bath/shower *furo/shawa*

Reception

I have a reservation
yoyaku shite arimasu
Is there… in the room?
heya ni… wa arimasu ka
air-conditioning *eakon*
TV/telephone *terebi/denwa*
We'll be staying… *…tomari masu*
one night only *ippaku dake*
a week *isshuu-kan*
I don't know yet *mada wakari masen*
I'd like to stay an extra night
moo ippaku sasete kudasai
How much is…? *…ikura desu ka?*
including/excluding breakfast
chooshoku komi/nuki de
Does the price include…?
kono nedan wa… komi desu ka
sales tax (VAT) *shoohi zee*
breakfast/meal *chooshoku/shokuji*
Is there a reduction for children?
kodomo no waribiki wa arimasu ka
What time is breakfast served?
chooshoku wa nan-ji desu ka
Is there room service?
ruumu saabisu wa arimasu ka
The key to room…, please
…goo-shitsu no kagi o kudasai
I've lost my key *kagi o nakushi mashita*
Could you wake me up at…?
…ji ni okoshite kudasai
bathtowel/blanket/pillow
basu taoru/moofu/makura
Are there any messages for me?
messeeji wa arimasu ka
What time do we have to check out by?
chekkuauto wa nan-ji made desu ka
Could I have my bill, please?
kaikei o onegai shimasu
Could I have a receipt, please?
reshiito o onegai shimasu
Could you order me a taxi, please?
takushii o yonde kudasai

Shops & services

pharmacy *yakkyoku/doraggu sutoaa*
off-licence/liquor store *saka-ya*
newsstand *kiosuku*
department store *depaato*
bookshop *hon-ya*
supermarket *supaa*
camera store *kamera-ya*
I'd like… *…o kudasai*
Do you have…? *…wa arimasu ka*
How much is that? *ikura desu ka*
Could you help me? *onegai shimasu*
Can I try this on? *kite mite mo ii desu ka?*
I'm looking for… *…o sagashite imasu*
larger/smaller motto *ookii/mottoo chiisai*
I'll take it *sore ni shimasu*
That's all, thank you *sore de zenbu desu*

Bank/currency exchange

dollars *doru*
pounds *pondo*
yen *en*
currency exchange *ryoogae-jo*
I'd like to change some pounds into yen
pondo o en ni kaetain desu ga
Could I have some small change, please?
kozeni o kudasai

Health

Where can I find a hospital/dental surgery?
byooin/hai-sha wa doko desu ka
I need a doctor *isha ga hitsuyoo desu*
Is there a doctor/dentist who speaks English?
*eego ga dekiru isha/ha-isha wa
imasu ka*
What are the surgery hours?
shinryoo jikan wa nan-zi desu ka
Could the doctor come to see me here?
ooshin shite kuremasu ka
Could I make an appointment for…?
…yoyaku shitain desu ga
as soon as possible *dekirudake hayaku*
It's urgent *shikyuu onegai shimasu*
I'm diabetic *watashi wa toonyoobyoo desu*
I'm asthmatic *watashi wa zensoku desu*
I'm allergic to… *…arerugi desu*
contraceptive *hinin yoo piru*

Symptons

I feel faint *memai ga shimasu*
I have a fever *netsu ga arimasu*
I've been vomiting *modoshi mashita*
I've got diarrhoea *geri shitemasu*
It hurts here *koko ga itai desu*
I have a headache *zutsu ga shimasu*
I have a sore throat *nodo ga itai desu*
I have a stomach ache *onaka ga itai*
I have a toothache *ha ga itai desu*
I've lost a filling/tooth
tsumemono/ha ga toremashita
I don't want it extracted *nukanaide kudasai*

Sightseeing

Where's the tourist office?
kankoo annai-jo wa doko desu ka
Do you have any information on…?
…no annai wa arimasu ka
sightseeing tour *kankoo tsuaa*
Are there any trips to…?
…e no tsuaa wa arimasu ka
gallery *bijutsukan*
hot springs *onsen*
mountain *san*
museum *hakubutsukan*
palace *kyuden*
park *kooen*
shrine *jinja*
temple *ji/tera*

On tour

We'd like to have a look at the…
…o mitain desu ga
to take photographs
shasin o toritain desu ga
to buy souvenirs
omiyage o kaitain desu ga
to use the toilets *toire ni ikitain desu ga*
Can we stop here? *koko de tomare masu ka*
Could you take a photo of us, please?
shasin o totte kudasai
Are we allowed to take photos? *shashin o
totte mo ii desu ka*

Travel

Where's the nearest underground station?
chikatetsu no eki wa doko desu ka
Could I have a map of the underground?
chikatetsu no rosenzu o kudasai
To…, please *…made onegai shimasu*
Single/return tickets
katamichi/oofuku kippu
Where can I buy a ticket?
kippu wa doko de kaemasu ka
I'm going to… *…ni ikimasu*
on my own *hitori*
with my family *kazoku to issho*
I'm with a group *guruupu de kimashita*
I'm here on holiday/business
kankoo/shigoto de kimashita
How much…? *…wa ikura desu ka?*
When does the train for… leave?
…iki no densha wa nan-ji ni demasu ka
Can you tell me when we get to…?
…ni tsuitara oshiete kudasai
ticket office *kippu-uriba*
ticket gate *kaisatsu-guchi*
ticket vending *machines kenbai-ki*
bus *basu*
train *densha*
bullet train *shinkansen*
subway *chikatetsu*
taxi *takushii*

SIGNS

General

左 *hidari* left

右 *migi* right

入口 *iriguchi* entrance

出口 *deguchi* exit

トイレ/お手洗い *toire/o-tearai* toilets

男/男性 *otoko/dansei* men

女/女性 *onna/jyosei* women

禁煙 *kin-en* no smoking

危険 *kiken* danger

立ち入り禁止 *tachiiri kinshi* no entry

引く/押す *hiku/osu* pull/push

遺失物取扱所 *ishitsu butsu toriatsukai jo* lost property

水泳禁止 *suiei kinshi* no swimming

飲料水 *inryoosui* drinking water

関係者以外立ち入り禁止 *kankeisha igai tachiiri kinshi* private

地下道 *chikadoo* underpass (subway)

足元注意 *ashimoto chuui* mind the step

ペンキ塗り立て *penki nuritate* wet paint

頭上注意 *zujoo chuui* mind your head

Road signs

止まれ *tomare* stop

徐行 *jokoo* slow

一方通行 *ippoo tsuukoo* one way

駐車禁止 *chuusha kinshi* no parking

高速道路 *koosoku dooro* motorway

料金 *ryookin* toll

信号 *shingoo* traffic lights

交差点 *koosaten* junction

Airport/station

案内 *an-nai* information

免税 *menzee* duty free

入国管理 *nyuukoku kanri* immigration

到着 *touchaku* arrivals

出発 *shuppatsu* departures

コインロッカー *koin rokkaa* luggage lockers

荷物引き渡し所 *nimotsu hikiwatashi jo* luggage reclaim

手荷物カート *tenimotsu kaato* trolleys

バス/鉄道 *basu/tetsudoo* bus/train

レンタカー *rentakaa* car rental

地下鉄 *chikatetsu* underground

Hotels/restaurants

フロント *furonto* reception

予約 *yoyaku* reservation

非常口 *hijyooguchi* emergency/fire exit

湯 *yu* hot (water)

冷 *ree* cold (water)

バー *baa* bar

Shops

営業中 *eegyoo chuu* open

閉店 *heeten* closed

階 *kai* floor

地下 *chika* basement

エレベーター *erebeetaa* lift

エスカレーター *esukareetaa* escalator

会計 *kaikee* cashier

Sightseeing

入場無料 *nyuujoo muryoo* free admission

大人/子供 小人 *otona/kodomo* adults/children

割引 (学生/高齢者) *waribiki (gakusei/koureisha)* reduction (students/senior citizens)

お土産 *o-miyage* souvenirs

手を触れないでください *te o furenai de kudasai* do not touch

撮影禁止 *satsuei kinshi* no photography

Public buildings

病院 *byooin* hospital

交番 *kouban* police box

銀行 *ginkoo* bank

郵便局 *yuubin kyoku* post office

プール *puuru* swimming pool

博物館 *hakubutsu-kan* museum

Directory

Index

Numbers in **bold** indicate
the key entry for the topic;
numbers in *italics* indicate
photographs.

a

abortion 291
accident & emergency
services 290
accommodation 34-52
by price:
budget 38, 40, 43, 44, 47,
49, 51
deluxe 35-36, 37, 38, 40,
41, 45-47, 49, 50
expensive 36, 37, 40-41,
43, 47, 49-50, 51
moderate 36-37, 37-38,
40, 41, 43, 43-44, 47, 51
the best 36
booking agencies 35
capsule hotels 34, **51-52**
minshuku 34, **51**
long-term accommodation
52
love hotels 30-31
gay 232
Adams, Will 12
addresses 290
ADMT Advertising Museum
Tokyo 61
age restrictions 288
airports 284
Akasaka
restaurants 140, 141, 146,
147
where to stay 45-47
Akasaka Detached Palace
26, **72**
Akasaka Prince Hotel 28
Akihabara 65, 174, **181**
Akihito, Emperor 18, 22
Ako Gishi-sai *see* 47 Ronin
Memorial Service
Ako, Lord **14**, 128
America & Japan **14-15**, 19
Ameyoko 101, **177**
Ameyoko Market *99*, 101
Ameyoko Plaza Food &
Clothes Market 177
Amlux Toyota Auto Salon
120
amusement parks 202-230
Ancient Orient Museum
118, **121**
Ando Tadao 28, 83
Anglo-Japanese alliance 19
Annex Katsutaro Ryokan 105
Anniversaire 83
Aoyama Cemetery 84
Aoyama Complex 175
Aoyama *see* Harajuku &
Aoyama
Aoyama Shinji 216
Aoyama Technical College
25, 27
Aqua City 112
aquariums 95, 121, **203**
Arakawa Streetcar Line
97, **120**
architecture 25-28

the best 27
Ariake 95
arriving & leaving Tokyo 284
Art-Link Ueno-Yanaka 198
art
festivals 223
galleries, contemporary
220-225
see also museums &
galleries in Tokyo
arts, performing 245-251
arts & entertainment 195-260
Asagaya 126
Asahi Building 92
Asaka Hirohito, Prince 91
Asakura Choso Museum
105, *105*, **106**
Asakura Funio 105, **106**
Asakusa 55, **92-98**, 165
coffee shops 170
galleries 225
restaurants 150
where to stay 41-43
Asakusa Culture &
Sightseeing Centre 94
Asakusa Engei Hall 94
Asakusa Jinja 92
Asakusa Kannon (Senso-ji)
Temple 10, 26, 55, 87, 92,
95, *96*, **97**
Asakusa Samba Carnival
92, **198**, 249
Asakuyama Park 120
Asami Maki Ballet 249
Asashoryu 23, **256**, *256*
Ashikaga Takauji 11
Ashinoko, Lake 268, 270
athletics 252
ATMs 293
atomic bomb attacks on
Hiroshima and Nagasaki
17, 19
attitudes 288
Aum Shinrikyo 18, 126
Aussie Rules football 257
Autumn Leaves (Koyo) 199
Awa Odori 198
Azubu-Juban 110
clubs 213-214

b

babysitting 206
Bae Yong Joon 23
ballet 249
Bank of Japan 15, 26, **65**
banks 294
bars 156-166
the best 157
gay & lesbian 226-231
in Golden Gai 163
baseball 197, **252**
Basho Matsuo 12
bathhouses, public 114-115
baths, hot-spring **114-115**,
268, 271
Battledore Market
(Hagoita Ichi) 199
Bayside Shakedown 2 112
beaches 274, 275
beauty salons 190-191
beer 158

Beer Museum Yebisu 89
Bentendo 100
'black ships' **14**, 19
boat trips 95
books 299
shops 177-179
Bourgeois, Louise 107
boxing 257
Bridgestone Museum of Art
64, **65**
'Bubble economy' **18**, 19, 22
Buddhism, introduction of
10, 19
bullet trains 18, 19
Bunka Gakuen Costume
Museum 72, **74**
Bunka-Bunsei period 19
Bunkamura 78
Bunkamura The Museum 80
bunraku 245
buses
long-distance 284
within Tokyo 286
tours 287
bushido 11
business services 288-289
butoh 249

c

camera shops 179
capsule hotels 34
Caretta Shiodome 61, **176**
car rental 286
Casals Hall 234
CD shops 194
CEATEC Japan 198
Center Gai 77, *77*
Century Tower 28
chambers of commerce 288
Chanel building **28**, 183
cherry blossom viewing
(Hanami) 196, *198*
children 202-206
clothes shops 182
'children's halls' 204
China & Japan 23
Chinatown, Yokohama
262, **264**, *264*
Choan-ji 104
Christmas Eve & Christmas
Day 200
Chrysanthemum Festival 199
Chuo Dori 58
Chuo line 55, 122, **124-125**
Chuzenji, Lake 276, **278**
cinemas 216-219
classical music *see* music
climate 298
clothes shops 180-183
clubs 80, 107, **207-214**
the best 210
gay & lesbian 226-231
host clubs 232
sex clubs 231
coffee shops 167-171
comedy 251
Coming of Age Day
(Seijin no Hi) 200
Communications Museum
64, **67**
Complex 108

Conder, Joseph 15, **26**, 65, 101
confectionery shops 186
contemporary theatre 247-249
contraception 291
conventions & conferences
288
copy shops 288
cosmetics shops 191
couriers 288
craft shops 188-190
Crafts Gallery 26
credit cards 293
cricket 258
cuisine, Japanese 134-135
Currency Museum 65, **67**
customs allowances 289
cycling 286

d

Daibutsu 273, *273*
Daien-ji 105
Daiichi Insurance Building 28
Daikanyama *see* Ebisu &
Daikanyama
Daimaru 172
Daimyo Clock Museum
105, **106**
dance 249-251
festivals 249
Dance Biennale Tokyo 249
Danjuro IX 12
Daruma Fair 201
Decks 112
Dejima 12
Denryoku-kan *see* TEPCO
Electric Energy Museum
dentists 291
department stores 172-175
depato 172
Design Festa **197**, 223
designer fashion shops
182-183
Designer's Week 199, **223**
Dezome-shiki *see* Tokyo
Metropolitan Fire
Brigade Parade
Die Pratze Dance Festival 249
Diet Building 27
Diplomat's House, Yokohama
264
directors, the best
contemporary Japanese
film 216
directory 284-305
disabled visitors 289
doctors 291
Dojunkai Aoyama tenement
buildings 27
Doo Bee Fes 241
drinking 289
driving 286
drugs 289
Drum Museum (Taiko-kan)
94, **97**
duty-free goods 174

e

earthquake of 1855 **14**, 19
earthquakes 14, 16, 18, 19,
21, 98

Place of interest	
Park	
Hospital/university	
Post office	✉
Temple	卍
Shrine	卅
Railway station	
Subway station	**S**
District	GINZA
Ward	**SHIBUYA-KU**
Hotel/guesthouse	
Sightseeing venue	●
Eating/drinking venue	
Shop	○
Arts/entertainment venue	○

Maps

Mainland Japan

Nikko
See p276
Imaichi

Kanuma
Utsunomiya
See p282
Moko

Shibukawa
Kiryu
Tochigi
Mito

Takasaki
Maebashi
Ashikaga
Oyama
Shimodate
Mito

Fujioka
Isesaki
Ota
Tatebayashi
Kago
Ishioka

Kumagaya
Tsukuba
Lake
Kasumigaura

Chichibu
Ageo
Kasukabe
Nado
Sarawa

Kawagoe
See p279
Omiya
Saitama
Abiko
Sakura

Sayama
Tachikawa
Kawaguchi
Funabashi
Narita
Airport

Ome
Hachioji
TOKYO
Yotsukaido

Kofu
Mt Takao
Tokyo Bay
Chiba

Otsuki
Sagamihara
Kawasaki
Ichihara

Atsugi
Yokohama
See p262
Mobara

Mt Fuji
See p280
Hadano
Chigasaki
Fujisawa
Kisarazu

Gotemba
Odawara
Kamakura
See p272
Yokosuka
Boso
Peninsula

Fujinomiya
Hakone
See p268

Fuji
Mishima
Numazu

Ito
Sagami Bay
Tateyama

Izu
Peninsula

Oshima
Island
PACIFIC OCEAN

Shimoda
Izu
Islands

0   40 km
0   20 miles
© Copyright Time Out Group 2005

Trips Out of Town

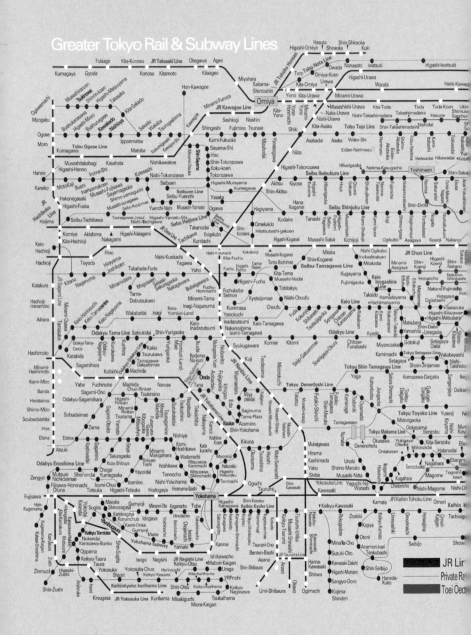

Greater Tokyo Rail & Subway Lines

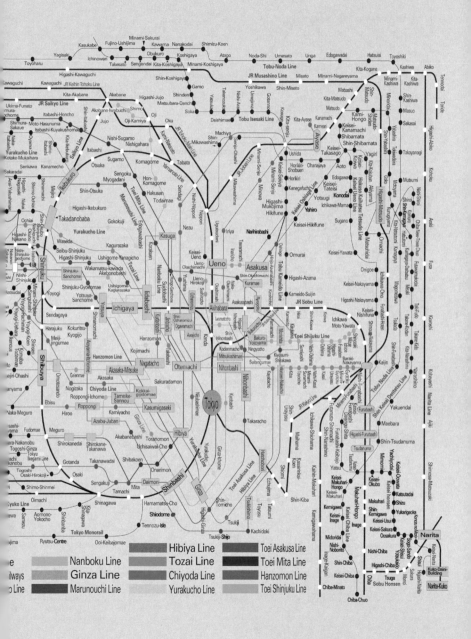

Nanboku Line
Ginza Line
Marunouchi Line
Hibiya Line
Tozai Line
Chiyoda Line
Yurakucho Line
Toei Asakusa Line
Toei Mita Line
Hanzomon Line
Toei Shinjuku Line

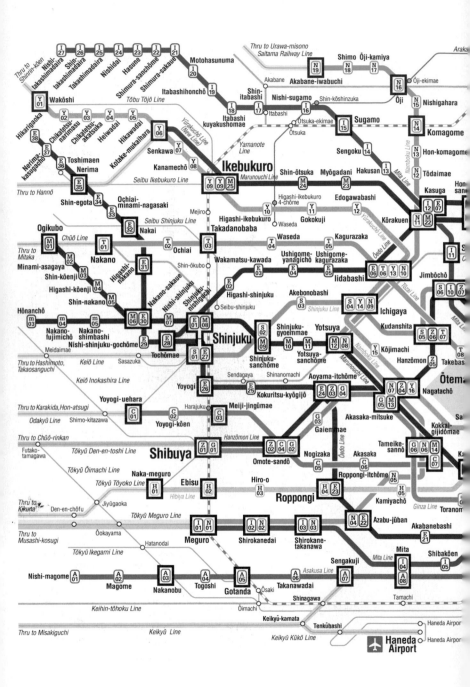

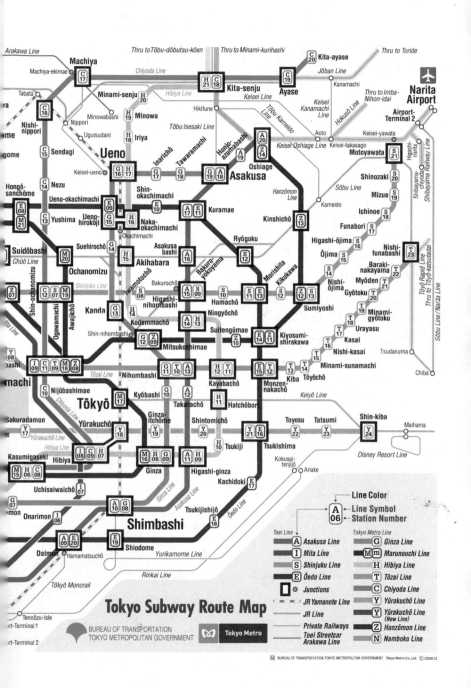

Tokyo Subway Route Map

BUREAU OF TRANSPORTATION
TOKYO METROPOLITAN GOVERNMENT

Tokyo Metro

Line Color

A — Line Symbol
06 — Station Number

Toei Line		Tokyo Metro Line	
A	Asakusa Line	G	Ginza Line
I	Mita Line	m	Marunouchi Line
S	Shinjuku Line	H	Hibiya Line
E	Ōedo Line	T	Tōzai Line
	Junctions	C	Chiyoda Line
	JR Yamanote Line	Y	Yūrakuchō Line
	JR Line	Y	Yūrakuchō Line (New Line)
	Private Railways	Z	Hanzōmon Line
	Toei Streetcar Arakawa Line	N	Namboku Line

BUREAU OF TRANSPORTATION TOKYO METROPOLITAN GOVERNMENT   Tokyo Metro Co., Ltd. © 2004.12

Yamanote Line Connections

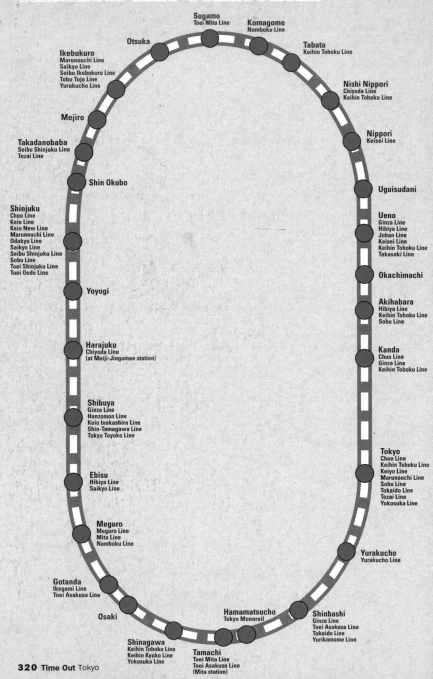

Sugamo
Toei Mita Line

Komagome
Namboku Line

Otsuka

Tabata
Keihin Tohoku Line

Ikebukuro
Marunouchi Line
Saikyo Line
Seibu Ikebukuro Line
Tobu Tojo Line
Yurakucho Line

Nishi Nippori
Chiyoda Line
Keihin Tohoku Line

Mejiro

Nippori
Keisei Line

Takadanobaba
Seibu Shinjuku Line
Tozai Line

Shin Okubo

Uguisudani

Shinjuku
Chuo Line
Keio Line
Keio New Line
Marunouchi Line
Odakyu Line
Saikyo Line
Seibu Shinjuku Line
Sobu Line
Toei Shinjuku Line
Toei Oedo Line

Ueno
Ginza Line
Hibiya Line
Joban Line
Keisei Line
Keihin Tohoku Line
Takasaki Line

Okachimachi

Yoyogi

Akihabara
Hibiya Line
Keihin Tohoku Line
Sobu Line

Harajuku
Chiyoda Line
(at Meiji-Jingumae station)

Kanda
Chuo Line
Ginza Line
Keihin Tohoku Line

Shibuya
Ginza Line
Hanzomon Line
Keio Inokashira Line
Shin-Tamagawa Line
Tokyu Toyoko Line

Ebisu
Hibiya Line
Saikyo Line

Tokyo
Chuo Line
Keihin Tohoku Line
Keiyo Line
Marunouchi Line
Sobu Line
Tokaido Line
Tozai Line
Yokosuka Line

Meguro
Meguro Line
Mita Line
Namboku Line

Yurakucho
Yurakucho Line

Gotanda
Ikegami Line
Toei Asakusa Line

Osaki

Hamamatsucho
Tokyo Monorail

Shinbashi
Ginza Line
Toei Asakusa Line
Tokaido Line
Yurikamome Line

Shinagawa
Keihin Tohoku Line
Keihin Kyuko Line
Yokosuka Line

Tamachi
Toei Mita Line
Toei Asakusa Line
(Mita station)